moving history / dancing cultures

moving history / dancing cultures

A DANCE HISTORY READER

Edited by
ANN DILS &
ANN COOPER
ALBRIGHT

Wesleyan University Press / *Middletown, Connecticut*

Wesleyan University Press
© 2001 Wesleyan University Press

ISBN 0-8195-6412-5 cloth
ISBN 0-8195-6413-3 paper

Printed in the United States of America
Design & composition by Chris Crochetière,
B. Williams & Associates, Durham, North Carolina

Title page photo: Ruth St. Denis in *Radha* (1906). Reprinted
courtesy of the Dance Division, The New York Public Library
for the Performing Arts, Astor, Lenox and Tilden Foundations.

5   4

CIP data and permissions appear at the end of the book

acknowledgments

Picture this: as the summer wanes, dance teachers across the nation are bent over the photocopier frantically trying to assemble packets for their dance history classes. In an effort to avoid the perennial question of whether to photocopy or not to photocopy (or at least to reduce the quantity of copying), the editors of this reader have tried to assemble a collection of articles and essays that will serve a variety of undergraduate dance history courses. Our goal was to make something useful—to make a book that stimulated teachers and students alike. We wanted to make a reader that would show students that dance too was an intellectual discipline (see, it's available in the textbook section), one that would guide them into new ways of thinking creatively about what they were engaged in practicing.

Obviously, any project this extensive required the support, help, and advice of many people. The beginnings of this collection lie in the countless conversations we have had with dance teachers over the past six years about the need for an undergraduate reader. We appreciate the generous advice and shared syllabi of the many scholars who helped shape this project. Thanks to the participants of the 1998 Congress on Research in Dance conference who filled out our questionnaire and responded with enthusiasm to the idea of this reader. Thanks also go to members of the Dance History Teachers Discussion Group and e-mail discussion list, marvelously facilitated by Tricia Henry Young and sponsored by the Florida State University Department of Dance, and to scholars who shared their ideas at CORD and Society of Dance History Scholars conferences. Their kindness helped us face the daunting task of selecting the readings.

This project, however, would have remained in the realm of the theoretical if we had not had the support of Suzanna Tamminen, editor-in-chief of Wesleyan University Press. Over the years that she has been at Wesleyan, Suzanna has worked tirelessly to create a dance series that is both intellectually stimulating and accessible to readers throughout the dance field. Her enthusiasm for this project reflects her commitment to expanding dance literacy within all levels of higher education. In addition to our editor's support, we wish to acknowledge the importance of Rachel Wheeler's contribution. As an editorial assistant, Rachel worked many hours paving the way for this project to go to press by researching and obtaining the various permissions needed.

Thanks to the Dean's Office at Oberlin College and the Ohio Arts Council for supporting this reader in various ways. Thanks also to faculty of the Department of Dance, School of Health and Human Performance, University of North Carolina at Greensboro (Susan W. Stinson, chair, and Robert Christina, dean); and to the Research Grants Committee and the Office of Research Services, University of North Carolina at Greensboro (Beverly Maddox-Britt, director), for their support of this project. Ann Dils thanks students in the Department of Dance, University of North Carolina at Greensboro, for their many contributions. Stephanie Barkley, Julie Boulton, Amanda Kinzer, Julie Mayo, Karen Mozingo, Jennifer Oldham, Douglas Risner, Melissa J. Saint Amour, Amy Jo Smith, and Lauren Tepper were especially helpful in preparing this volume. Ann Cooper Albright would like to acknowledge the assistance of Carolyn Husted, Jason Miller, and Abby Rasminsky, as well as the intellectual contributions of students in her dance history classes at Oberlin College.

Finally, the editors want to thank their families for putting up with crazy schedules and absent moms. Jahan, Mitra, and Cully Salehi were especially patient with the process, as were Cyrus Cooper Newlin and Isabel Albright Newlin. A very special acknowledgment goes to Thomas Newlin, whose intellectual and emotional support has reached out to catch the pieces in so many different areas. These people are the ground for our various flights of plain and fancy.

contents

PART III—*America Dancing*

PART IV—*Contemporary Dance: Global Contexts*

illustrations

1. Mark Dendy as "Martha, the Priestess" in *Dream Analysis*. Photo by Phyllis Graber Jensen.

First Steps: Moving into the Study of Dance History

Choreographer Mark Dendy makes dance historians smile. A seriously tongue-in-cheek dance history buff, his dances mine the riches of early modern and social dance forms. Sometimes these works are personal histories, sometimes they are parodies, but always they relay the importance of moving history from the books to the stage. One of his most recent works, *I'm Going to My Room to Be Cool Now, and I Don't Want to Be Disturbed,* is a pop-inspired, semiautobiographical dance suite about coming of age in the 1970s. Set to songs by artists such as Jimi Hendrix, Janis Joplin, Ike and Tina Turner, and Patti Smith, the dance presents social dancing as a safe way to experiment with different identities. It is a place to play with the expression of sexuality, to act out frustrations and feelings, and to try out new (hipper?) ways of being. Dendy also presents dancing as transformative. Dancing can give you hope in a hopeless situation, it can help you find community, it can be fun, doing it well can make you—as it has made Dendy and his dancers—a star.

Dendy's *I'm Going to My Room* . . . combines historical revisioning with a remarkable eye for intriguing movement and fashion detail. If this dance and other Dendy dances (such as *Dream Analysis,* featuring dual drag Martha Grahams and dual Vaslav Nijinskys, and his recent remake of *Swan Lake* for a German ballet company) weren't enough to demonstrate his commitment to history, he is also engaging and articulate about his affection for and artistic debt to dance history. In a talk after the June 28, 2000 performance of *I'm Going to My Room* . . . at the American Dance Festival, Dendy remarked that his most important choreographic inspiration arrived via Graham's film, *A Dancer's World,* shown in a dance history class at the North Carolina School for the Arts. As a teenager, he loved Graham's divadom. She was a woman in female drag, and her unflinching stare, combined with her overblown, deadly serious discussion about dancers as chosen people—as acrobats of God—inspired both his spiritual reverence and his sweet yet campy impersonation of her grandiose style. For Dendy, dancing is a kind of contemporary ritual. It is a spiritual opportunity to share energy, join in a sense of *communitas,* and to connect to one's movement ancestors. He is also acutely aware of critical issues surrounding the display of dancing bodies and the ways in which meaning gets constructed on the stage. Thus, Dendy's dances rarely simply repeat history; rather, they recast figures from dance history in order to speak to a contemporary sensibility.

As an example of (re)embodying history, Dendy's recent work is remarkable—indeed, memorable—for its demonstration of how history reverberates, how it can be artistically and intellectually engaging to dancers now. Dendy personalizes his dance legacies, making them a vital part of his current performance life. In addition to validating and celebrating the use of the past as a source of inspiration and movement material, Dendy makes clear to his audience how these events sit with him, live with him, provide a way of knowing himself. Any historian would recognize this interconnectedness of past and present.

Although their style and chosen media may differ from Dendy's, the writers in this volume share with Mark Dendy a personal commitment to the subject of dance history and a fervent belief that studying dances from other times and cultures can enrich and enliven our own dance practices and artistic visions. As we researched, edited, and prepared the contents of this book, we looked to shape a dance history reader that would demonstrate how the study of dance can be both intellectually and physically inspiring for today's students. Like Dendy, we are enthusiastic about the creative potential embedded in historical inquiry. While we come to dance from different intellectual and physical perspectives, each of us has had deeply significant and transformative experiences researching, writing, and living other movement histories. To be caught up in a desire to learn more about a particular dancing culture or historical period is one of the most satisfying physical sensations available to dancers. Yes, physical—for dance, even as a historical study, is always first a physical activity. For this reason, we have endeavored to create a text that speaks to both the bodies and the minds of undergraduate dancers.

Mark Dendy may dance at the most energized edge of dance history thought and practice, but his work underscores several points important to this volume:

1. Dance historians are a diverse group of artists, journalists, and academics involved in the study of dance as a cultural as well as an aesthetic practice. This means that we have enlarged our interpretation of historical discourse to encompass studies that approach dance from a variety of disciplines, including anthropology, ethnography, the study of art and architecture, literary and cultural studies, feminist theory, and performance studies.

2. Dance history is not a historical record set in stone or even in print, but an evolving discussion about the past that can take on many shapes (performed,

written, personal testimony, or public manifesto) and can happen as memoir, biography, dance criticism, ethnography, and research compilation, as well as cultural or critical histories.

3. The study of the past, whether that means studying a dance form from a thousand years ago, a choreographer working a hundred years ago, or a dance concert seen last week, is simultaneously of and about past and present. We encourage a passionate approach to the production of knowledge, for the strength of our understanding of the past relies upon the commitment with which we engage the present. Our sense of dance history as a field of inquiry changes as scholars bring new aspects of dance history to our attention and as current issues in the dance world create an interest in different aspects of the past.

4. The ultimate reward of dance history is that it is useful. This does not mean that we "use" the past, unfairly plundering or misinterpreting past lives and events and misrepresenting history in order to validate our own agendas. Dance historians study the past to illuminate people's lives, explicate past dance practices, and understand the complex interconnections between bodies, movement, and other social practices that are a result of specific cultural beliefs and epistemological frameworks. Dancing is a way of knowing the world. History helps us recognize that fact.

For dancers, the usefulness of the past is that it provides us with inspiring legacies, helps us to clarify our own choreographic visions, gives us a sense of continuity and belonging, and allows us to see our field with a tempered, critical eye. Indeed, the study of dance history can help us see how movement both reflects and shapes important questions within many cultures about identity, the making of community, aesthetic beauty, the physical training of bodies, economic productivity, and the distribution of power within social groups.

In what follows, we discuss further the evolving shape of the discipline and the issues crucial to our understanding of the field. As we pursue these points, we envision dance history as a landscape that can be observed and analyzed from varying perspectives, one that changes as the quality of light cast on its surface varies. We also discuss the people who populate this landscape, as well as those who are trying to map out its contours.

The Dance History Landscape

Moving History/Dancing Cultures provides a broad introduction to the study of dance history for American college students. The essays in this volume, like the survey courses in which this volume will most likely be used, establish an entry into a much larger body of practice, theory, and writing. The entryway and subsequent pathways and points of interest established here are both the result of our interests and teaching practices and an attempt to respond to the needs of other dancers and scholars teaching history and dance appreciation courses. We focus on dance in America but include articles on dance traditions in Africa, Asia, the Middle East, and Europe. We place a priority on information about modern dance and its more contemporary offspring but include articles on social dance and ballet. Articles that can be read against one another to provoke critical thinking concerning issues of representation and dance within different cultural contexts are an important feature of the volume. We conclude each section with brief (and necessarily incomplete) selections of readings for the curious student or for further research assignments.

It is important to be clear right from the beginning that these readings map out only certain topographical details within the total dance history landscape. Because of space and copyright constraints, the volume is not encyclopedic. We have largely eschewed the methods of organization that traditionally make sense of historical information. There is no one overall chronology. We have not traced the history of the great "geniuses" of American modern dance. We don't explain the "isms" important to much Western art history: romanticism, classicism, expressionism, neoclassicism, modernism, postmodernism.

Instead, we balance articles on a variety of dance cultures with essays that explore similar dance traditions, but from different methodological or historical perspectives. The articles are grouped into four parts: (1) "Thinking about Dance History: Theories and Practices," (2) "World Dance Traditions," (3) "America Dancing," and (4) "Contemporary Dance: Global Contexts." We have chosen the articles such that intellectual concepts are built upon and developed across the sections. Often, specific dance traditions are explored through small clusters of articles. We call these clusters "constellations of strategic thoroughness," because they include not only essays documenting the same genre but also essays that highlight similar issues (changes in the representation of the female body, for instance) within other dance traditions. These clusters may not be found directly next to each other. Drawing lines between the various pieces, however, provides a theoretical or historical constellation. Thus, for instance, we pair a longer essay by a scholar-choreographer with a written dialogue between two practitioners on the classical Indian dance form *bharata natyam*. Yet these writings appear in different parts of the volume ("World Dance Traditions" and "Contemporary Dance: Global Contexts") for they trace a dance form from its mythic origins through to its contemporary manifestations. Some of these interconnections we chart in this introduction, and some you will find for yourself as you explore their movement across the landscape of this reader.

Our organizational strategy is intentionally improvisational, a response, in part, to the pressures of the field to produce a reader that expands the traditional canon of modern dance history. By the 1980s, dance historians began to realize that, like their counterparts in other fields of the humanities, they were representing dance history in surveys limited to the history of Western theatrical dance, setting apart "ethnic" or folk dance forms into sections labeled, not as history, but as anthropology. Most of us who went to college in the seventies and early eighties were taught a great deal about the all-white "big four" of modern dance (Martha Graham, Doris Humphrey, Charles Weidman, and Hanya Holm) and very little about dancers such as Helmsley Winfield, Pearl Primus, Katherine Dunham, and Michio Ito, whose work complicated the aesthetic terms validated by modern theatrical dancing.

This is not to suggest that Martha Graham and Doris Humphrey were not important—quite the contrary. But their repeated, exclusive presence gave dance history an odd shape. Often we were encouraged to think about modern dance in terms of its refusal of ballet, but not about its connections to American social dancing or, except in studying Ruth St. Denis, to the dance forms of Asia, Africa, and the Middle East. Presenting some dance forms as history and others as anthropology created a sense that some dances were art, and perhaps of higher complexity or status, and some dances simply expressions of social behavior or religious belief. Twenty years into a critical rethinking of canons, dance historians and dance history teachers are still debating the political implications of what and how they teach. Members of the Dance History Teachers Discussion Group, for example, discussed strategies for including dances of the African diaspora in dance history courses at a 1999 luncheon meeting held at the annual meeting of the Congress on Research in Dance and continued this discussion through an e-mail discussion list. *Moving History/Dancing Cultures* responds to these debates through a conscious framing of dance traditions across categories (such as American versus world dance) that have historically signaled racist distinctions between "ethnic," folk, and theatrical dancing. Sometimes this means that we leave out important aspects of dance history that we feel have been amply represented elsewhere in order to include articles and essays that document less visible histories.

Populating the Dance History Landscape

You, students slumped in chairs or sitting alert at desks, with highlighters, pens, and notepads ready, will be (along with, perhaps, the shadowy form of Mark Dendy) the first inhabitants of this landscape. You are probably a varied bunch. Many of you are dancers, people who spend much of your time in studios, moving through the cycles of inner contemplation and physical exertion that mark a technique class, creating dances for choreography classes, and engaging in endless hours of rehearsals. Others have dropped in on the dance world from English, nursing, or chemistry departments to fulfill some personal interest or liberal arts requirement.

You enter this landscape with your everyday experiences and education, religious and political beliefs, and the social attitudes and ideas you gained from family and community. Your physical experience is especially important to the study of dance history, as dance is made from, imbued with, and influences the physicality of everyone's daily life. What distinguishes your experience of body and motion? Do you navigate on legs or wheels? Do you sit or stand? What gestures and postures are part of your social life and religious expression? The articles collected in *Moving History/Dancing Cultures* will expand your knowledge of dance, enhance your sensitivity to movement and the meanings of your own body, and hone your observation and writing skills. More importantly, you will encounter ideas about dancing bodies and cultural movements that clarify or challenge your own beliefs and understandings. Are there, for example, acceptable movement behaviors for men and women? Do these vary with context, including in performance?

Next, populate your dance history landscape with the editors of this collection and the dance writers in it. Most of us have been working in the field for over twenty years. Many of us, although not all, are women. Professionally, we work as academics, journalists, or dance artists, or in combinations of these roles. Our fields of study and the interests and approaches that shape our writing include dance, art history, architecture, anthropology, journalism, performance studies, women's studies, African studies, and American studies. The authors in this collection, perhaps a representative sample of the scholars whose work is readily available in America, are mostly Americans, but we also come from Korea, India, Canada, and England. Others have spent significant time studying in the Philippines, Korea, Brazil, India, Egypt, and Zaire. Few people writing about dance identify themselves solely as historians, but more often in some hybrid way: dance critic and historian, feminist scholar and performer, critic and cultural theorist. These multiple identities shape the research and writing presented here.

The scholarly resources current dance writers use include written documentation; images; interviews with choreographers, dancers, and audience members; personal experience within the form; and a witnessing of the dancing (seen live or on videotape). Generally speaking, a particular focus or question frames these resources, or raw materials. This scholarly methodology can serve as a kind of lens through which the researcher looks at certain issues about the dance and the historical moment in which it thrived. For instance, certain writers might examine a particular dance as a microcosm of political structure, seeing the spatial arrangement of couples on the floor as a reflection of social hierarchy. Others might see aspects of the movement style as embodying a particular cultural trait or attitude toward space, rhythm, the natural world, religious devotion, or emotional experience—and these are only a few possibilities. Indeed, many of the writers included in this reader see dance as a rich and interesting expressive form through which to view cultural perceptions about the human body.

Drawing on theoretical frameworks in feminist theory and gender studies, several authors discuss how men or women are represented through dancing. Ramsay Burt (part I) explores nineteenth-century perceptions of male ballet dancers and Thomas DeFrantz (part III) discusses twentieth-century perceptions of African American male modern dancers. Ann Cooper Albright (part I) discusses perceptions of disabled and nondisabled women dancers in the United States, and Avanthi Meduri and Karin van Nieuwkerk consider perceptions of women dancers in India and Egypt. Many authors investigate the meaning of dance forms as tools of cultural survival, emblems of group identity, or the visible signs of intercultural tensions. Sally Ann Ness (part I) and Kathleen Foreman (part IV) discuss dance in the Philippines. Lisa Doolittle and Heather Elton (part II) and Sharyn Udall (part III) investigate Native American performance in Canada and the United States. Marian Hannah Winter, Brenda Dixon Gottschild, and Thomas DeFrantz (part III) discuss the importance of African dance traditions to American dance and perceptions of African American dancers by white Americans. Other writers build bridges between dance and ethnography, literary, and feminist theory, and cultural history (see Ramsay Burt, Ann Cooper Albright, and Sally Ann Ness, part I).

Also embedded in these articles are various histories. One history that is especially intriguing, yet often underdeveloped, is the history of writing dance histories. Most of the articles included here were first published in the 1990s, but a few were published earlier, and some refer to earlier publications. Marian Hannah Winter's "Juba and American Minstrelsy" (part III) was first published in 1947, and although her language may seem dated, her essay continues to be an important historical resource. Erika Bourgignon's "Trance and Ecstatic Dance" (part II) was first published in 1968 by *Dance Perspectives*, a journal very important to the development of dance history. In what remains a formative work of dance ethnology, Joann Kealiinohomoku (part I) deconstructs the ideological biases of early twentieth-century dance historians. So too, the writings by Deborah Jowitt and Marcia B. Siegel, two important dance critics, were instrumental in shaping much of the intellectual discourse surrounding American modern and postmodern dance. Seen as part of a larger constellation, these essays give us a sense of the historical landscape of dance studies.

It's important to think about the diverse perspectives and interests of authors because reading should be a critical enterprise, performed with attention to the information and ideas included in the writing and to the critical stance of the writer. The author is an interpreter of ideas and experience and creator of texts. She's not writing all there is to know about a subject, but rather her particular take on that subject. It's useful to keep an eye on the kinds of experiences and interpretive and critical perspectives that shape the writings. This helps you understand the information presented, think about what other perspectives might be valuable to your understanding of a subject, and to make connections between these articles and reading you might be doing in other fields.

Dancers theorize about dancing as a way of knowing, a way of perceiving the world around us. As an expressive bodily discourse, dance can be analyzed not only in terms of the characters or images portrayed within the performance or choreography, but also in terms of how we approach the act of seeing. What is it about dancing bodies that encourages certain ways of looking? How do those ways of seeing change across time and different cultures? In addition to the material experience of dancers (which includes the physical conditions of working and performing, economic situations, etc.), dance is a form of cultural representation. This means that many of the articles presented here also engage with theories of visual appreciation derived for the most part from art, film, and media studies. Yet as a moving, most often live, performing art, dance refuses and confuses many of these theories of representation imported from other disciplines. This reader reflects efforts among scholars to create specifically dance theory, stretching cross-disciplinary discussions through a focus on dance's unique role in most cultures. For many authors, the practice of writing history is seen not only as the production of knowledge but also as an opportunity for self-reflection.

Finally, populate your dance history landscape with the dancers, choreographers, audience members, patrons, and impresarios we represent through our writings. They come from all over the globe and from vastly varied time periods. You will, through your reading, form different kinds of relationships with and understandings of these people, envisioning some of them in good detail while others are partially or dimly present. At times, dancer and author are one and the same, and you will be treated to the dancer's thinking, as well as a description of her dancing. At other times, you may see the dancer only as a nameless representative of a dance form or as an illustration or example for some argument made by an author. You may also notice (and mentally fill in) absent dancers. These may be the dancers closest to your heart: Irish step dancers; Flamenco dancers; cloggers; swing dancers; breakers; the stars of MTV, BET, and VH1; jazz dancers; Chinese opera performers; and the stars of movie musicals such as Fred Astaire and Gene Kelly.

Because many of you are heirs to a Western concert dance tradition, we hope that you will enjoy learning about the histories of the choreographers and performers who have worked and continue to work in this genre. Given both the global influences on American dance and the usefulness of cross-cultural comparisons, we have also included many writings about dance in different traditions. For some dancers, studying history is a way of finding a historical legacy, giving them a feeling of being brought into the fold—a way of building a spiritual home and identity within the dance world. For others, like Mark Dendy, it opens a fascinating world of choreographic inspiration. Among the dancers who populate these historical landscapes, you will find fierce individualists, believers in community and group process, those attracted to the spiritual nature of dance, and others struggling with perceptions of their skin colors, fitness, gender, or sexuality. We hope that their movement experiences, as well as the intellectual methodologies that frame the discussions of those experiences, will inspire you to continue your studies of dance.

PART ONE

Thinking about Dance History: Theories and Practices

The Pleasures of Studying Dance History

After seeing Mark Dendy's concert, you're restless with the images and ideas set dancing in your head and body by his *I'm Going to My Room.* . . . You want to share what the dance means to you, that special insight you have about the work. How do you get that down on paper in a way that enlivens and enriches the dance, rather than trapping its energy in lines of type?

You open an envelope from a family friend containing treasures he found in cleaning out his grandparents' home. The envelope contains some old, hand-tinted images of Ruth St. Denis, and a letter from "Harry" postmarked April 12, 1914. In the letter, Harry told your friend's grandmother about his new job managing Ruth St. Denis, a "remarkable dancer," and detailing her performances in Paducah, Kentucky. The image of this sari-clad beauty, lifting her tray of incense, stepping out on stage in 1914 in what must have been a very Christian, very conservative town is intriguing. How might you capture that moment and uncover how St. Denis's audience experienced her dancing?

Issues related to your latest computer-mediated dance keep playing in your mind. The work includes a video of you dancing, but you've digitally altered the image: sometimes you're ten feet tall, sometimes only the outer contours of your body are apparent, and sometimes you float upward, undisturbed by gravity. There's something very playful and yet very sad about this virtual self. Even though you get to see yourself

moving in new ways, the image strikes you as curiously lifeless, limited by your editing and animation skills and subject to the uncertainties of power outages and equipment failure. What, you wonder, is lost between the physical desire to move and the virtual traces of movement? There is a generational gap in people's reactions to your work, and you realize how much dance is related to the way people learn to see movement and digital images. How might you use your own experiences with this dance to critique your daily reliance on and embrace of technology?

Experiences like these are launching points for dance history, for asking questions about the role of dance within our culture. They are questions that push the process of historical, cultural, aesthetic, and philosophical inquiry forward, keeping historians visiting libraries and writing books, and students engrossed in dance history classes. Curiosity is but one of the very real pleasures of intellectual study. Authors in this part, "Thinking about Dance History: Theories and Practices," explore or illustrate many of these pleasures, including the joy of witnessing a dance as it unfolds and the rewards of reconstructing dance from historical evidence. Implicit in all the pleasures of dance study are the various meanings of the title of this volume—*Moving History/Dancing Cultures.* In studying moving bodies, we are ourselves moved and, potentially, as the conceptual body accommodates our actions and takes on the imprints of our dancing, we can move history.

You will notice in this introduction and throughout the volume that we broadly define dance scholarship as the physical and intellectual investigation of dance. We see it as both a cultural product (written descriptions of dancing) and a practice (the act of learning to see, learning to move). This hybrid field of inquiry is often called dance history, but may also include writings that could be labeled ethnography, anthropology, or arts criticism. In reflecting the blurring of these boundaries within dance studies, we hope to emphasize—as the authors whose works are collected in this volume richly illustrate—the interconnectedness of history in all its social, cultural, aesthetic, and intellectual dimensions.

Writers engage with culture as they explore the questions sparked by their piqued curiosities, examining the relationships between various images of the female dancer, say, or discussing the relationships between dancing and the representation of race or class. Other writers might critique their own practice, investigating how writing dance history relates to the colonialist legacy of Western epistemology (cataloguing the "other") or global economics. Theories are the fruits of thinking deeply about movement cultures. A theory is an explanation of how some cultural force or process operates and often involves exposing the constructed (nonnatural) character of our attitudes, habits of thought, or perceptions. Sometimes we dancers can get caught up in a dualistic mindset that sees analysis as opposed to creativity and separates theory from practice. Beginning to understand the myriad ways in which female dancers have been positioned historically as objects of the (presumably male) gaze can help young women dancers make strategic decisions about how they choose to represent themselves choreographically. Because theories and examples from other cultures allow us to pay attention to aspects of the moving world that we might have previously ignored, they help us become better dancers.

To witness a dance is to attend to it in a special way. To witness dancing is to make a commitment to meet the action with our senses sharpened—the stored, embodied fruits of our daily lives and academic studies at the ready. It also suggests a willingness to respond with our own personality and insights. The authors of the first two articles in this section, Deborah Jowitt in "Beyond Description" and Joan Acocella in "Imagining Dance," articulate this process of witnessing and inspire us to observe and to write about dancing more vividly. Jowitt conceptualizes movement description as a way of documenting the embodied, sensual nature of dance, as well as a mode of intellectual analysis. Good description preserves the lived motional sensation of dance. This is particularly important because most dances don't have the same permanence as literature or visual art. Yet, she argues, good description can also convey very pointed ideas: what the dance means, how it operates artistically, and how it refers to the world. Through a selection of examples, Jowitt illuminates how description can both pull apart and preserve the layered ways in which dance communicates. In her description of Graham's *Night Journey*, for example, she unpacks how a single moment of the dance is made rich with multiple meanings through Graham's use of a timing device. Because we know that the central character, Jocasta, is remembering past events, we simultaneously see the terror of living through a horrific event and the distanced quality of remembered action.

Joan Acocella thinks we understand dance through a special kind of intelligence, one different from the intelligences we use to dream or to understand math, poetry, or music. Part of the way we understand dance has to do with a "biochemical" affinity with patterns and relationships formed in space and time. We respond innately, she argues, to the steady flow of dancers moving rapidly down a diagonal path or to a small shape shooting through a larger, slower mass. Although Acocella says some aspects of dancing appeal to us in an immediate, visceral (what she describes as a "premoral") manner, her writing underscores the reciprocal relationships between our facility with language and our facility with apprehending (seeing/feeling) movement. Creating beautiful, nuanced descriptions both sharpens and depends upon our capacities to feel and to see movement.

Walking into the past, in search of some long-ago

dancer or lost dance event, is another pleasure of studying dance history. Studying history is always a current enterprise and dependent on the availability of resources, the needs of particular projects, and the lenses of current scholarship. Still, the possibility of finding yourself—however speculatively—in a different age, becoming familiar with dancers from another historical moment, or beginning to understand the experiences of movement in another culture, is a powerful lure. Part of this fascination lies in being exposed to differences, and part of it is the synthetic process that history necessitates, the act of building a world out of bits and pieces of the past using the force of your own imagination.

In "Searching for Nijinsky's *Sacre*," Millicent Hodson shares part of the research journey that led to her celebrated reconstruction of Vaslav Nijinsky's 1913 *Le Sacre du Printemps* for the Joffrey Ballet. Hodson lets us peek over her shoulder as she accumulates information from Nijinsky's diaries, sketchbooks, and costumes housed in London archives, and from the insights of scholars in various fields. She allows us to sit in on her conversations with Nijinsky's relatives and with dancers and musicians who had some connection with the ballet. She also lets us experience her thinking and, through her words and her sketches, the beginnings of the imaginative enterprise that was her reconstruction of Nijinsky's work. Hodson's sketches are especially evocative. As Hodson draws bodies with angled heads and turned in feet, and sketches dancers moving in taut lines or huddled in groups, we see her weave bits of evidence into the tapestry of the total dance event.

The pleasure of reenvisioning the present by placing the moving body at the center of historical study is the same pleasure a child experiences in running through a flock of pigeons, then watching them resettle, or that teachers experience when a previously quiet student comes up with something brilliant. The established order is interrupted, new patterns and relationships become apparent, and these cause us to adjust our perceptions and reassess our assumptions. The authors of the next two articles, Deidre Sklar and Joann Kealiinohomoku, launch convincing and cogent arguments for body-centered cultural inquiry. Sklar, in her "Five Premises for a Culturally Sensitive Approach to Dance," points out that movement is its own experience, a kind of knowledge not replicated by other life experiences. She believes that because moving calls up emotions and memories, it commits us to our ideals on a visceral level: "The concrete and sensory, in other words bodily, aspects of social life provide the glue that holds world views and cosmologies, values and political convictions, together."

Joann Kealiinohomoku's "An Anthropologist Looks at Ballet as a Form of Ethnic Dance," first published in 1970, is a seminal piece of dance ethnology. In her detailed critique of the Western categorization of non-Western dance, Kealiinohomoku attempts to reverse our assumptions about differences between the dance forms of ballet and modern dance and ethnic dance forms, by making the familiar strange—by thinking of ballet as "ethnic" dance. She accomplishes this, in part, by carefully analyzing her experience of Hopi dances in the face of the often inadequate, generalized discussions of the nature of "primitive" dance. She counters a 1939 statement by John Martin, in which he says "in simpler cultures than ours we find a mass of art actually treated and practiced by the people as a whole" with her experience of the Hopi Bean Dances. These dances vary from village to village, both in an expected stylistic way and as a result of individual innovation. Hopi dancers recognize and critique these innovations, with "their 'own' [changes] usually (but not always) coming out as being aesthetically more satisfying."

The authors of the final articles in this section are all engaged in cultural critique. In "The Trouble with the Male Dancer," Ramsay Burt investigates past and current attitudes about men in dance. Burt analyzes the gender dynamic implicit in looking at dancers' bodies and argues that as the nineteenth century progressed, men became increasingly uncomfortable with looking at other men onstage. Class-consciousness was a critical element in this discomfort, as middle-class men increasingly came to disdain both the aristocratic foppishness of dance costuming and gesture, and what was perceived as crude (and therefore lower-class) displays of muscular strength. Burt shows how the solidification of bourgeois culture in Europe came at the expense of male dancing. *Real* men no longer made spectacles of themselves.

In "Strategic Abilities: Negotiating the Disabled Body in Dance," Ann Cooper Albright brings together her own temporary experience of disability, insights into the dance works and press materials of the company Cleveland Ballet Dancing Wheels, and her experiences in contact improvisation workshops for mixed-ability dancers. Through these, she theorizes that we see disability as binary—one is either disabled or nondisabled—and that our definition of who is a dancer follows this split. She deconstructs the exclusionary ideology of our culture which allows only tall, thin, beautiful, and able-bodied young women to be seen as dancers, reconceptualizing ways of watching movement that resist this ablist gaze. For Albright, "ability" can be reframed so that it is no longer simply an issue of defining standards of fitness, technical accomplishment, or beauty, but one of recognizing a variety of gifts and facilities—learning to reinvent dance to suit personal needs and to realize pleasure in many kinds of movement.

In "Dancing in the Field: Notes from Memory," Sally Ann Ness discusses dance lessons she took in Bali and the Philippines. Ness provides us with an analysis of what she learned, discussing movement as embodying cultural patterns of partnering, hand contact, energy usage, balance, and stepping. She theorizes that because dancing is physically exposing, allowing others to see both our talents and our nervousness, it creates an immediate rapport with relative strangers. She also critiques the nature of the ethnographic text by calling into question its refinement, its distance from the field experience, and the safety of its academic anonymity.

Her fieldnotes (her written-downs) appear without being written up into a polished text; this she contrasts with the sophisticated "performed" quality of the rest of her writing. Ness produces a sense of restlessness and flux in the text by describing her movement from home office to field site to home office, and finally through the streets of Davao City, Philippines.

Albright's and Ness's approaches to scholarship are persuasive because of the generosity—the self exposure—involved in their writing. The pleasures of cultural critique and of theorizing come, increasingly, with a responsibility to position oneself inside the research. Albright and Ness are so clear in doing this that their writings sit somewhere between memoir, ethnography, and dance history. This is not just a matter of inserting a personal story, but of continually making clear one's negotiation of the intellectual and personal material throughout the text. Albright exposes her changing relationship to issues of disability by interweaving her life experiences throughout a critical discussion of cultural representation. Ness positions herself in her text as a cultural outsider who looks to expert dancers within the culture for "authentic" insights. Yet at the same time, she also critiques this outsider position, recognizing the complexities and lived realities of a colonial legacy. The ending of her essay is especially moving, letting us understand her misgivings about the "war" of anthropological contact and her personal, physical sensations of intrusion and aggression.

Making your relationship to your research clear is especially important in a world where questions of positionality are increasingly complex. Writers have the same kinds of complicated personal and educational histories that mark, and enrich, the work of contemporary choreographers. We need to both take advantage of and explicate the issues involved in hybridity. What, for example, are the ramifications of studying a Nigerian dance form using a Western analysis system such as Laban-based movement analysis? Or those of using French or American feminist theory to talk about the work of a Korean choreographer? What "gaze" do we use to evaluate Goth club dancing or the works of gay choreographers? When you position yourself within your writing rather than presenting yourself as an authority on the subject at hand, you create an opening for the use of a broad number of scholarly tools. You also invite others to think along with you, allowing them to experience some of the pleasures of historical study.

Beyond Description: Writing beneath the Surface

DEBORAH JOWITT

In a 1990 review of Susan Marshall's *Articles of Faith*, Joan Acocella noted the references one might draw from the dance—tall Eileen Thomas as a shaman or priest, Jews pushing through the desert, a community struggling to fight the ugliness within, and so on. However, she went on to say that the power of the piece does not lie in our ability to connect Marshall's work with social meanings or to deduce "archetypal dramatic" action: "It is the qualities that belong specifically to the movement—its shape in the air, its weight, speed, attack—that speak to us secretly. That is why a would-be profound dance may seem frivolous, a happy dance seem sad, or vice versa; because the movement has told us the secret truth behind the narrative."

And that is one reason why it has always seemed so important to me that we who write about the famously evanescent art of dance ground our responses in the work itself, providing enough of a sense of what happened to support formal analogies, considerations of meaning, style, social significance, historical connections, opinionated response—whatever criticism can legitimately take up. The point is, in searching for what a dance may mean, not to lose sight of what it is, or appears to be. The other reason that description figures more importantly in criticism of dance than in criticism of any other art form is dance's (let us not forget it for a minute) ephemerality. It doesn't hang about on walls to be revisited or wait by your bed with a bookmark in it or spill out of your glove compartment ready to be popped into a car's cassette deck.

Descriptive writing—a certain kind of it—is the best way I know to assert the interdependence of content and form, of narration and movement's "secret truths." Suzanne Langer, or perhaps one of her exegetes (from whom I once took a course at the New School), offered the example of the whirlpool made by water flowing down a drain. We can explain the phenomenon in terms of impetus, gravity, and the shape of the basin, but the whirlpool itself is a created thing and vanishes when the faucet is turned off. We can attempt to dissect the mutual wizardry that form and content in art exercise upon each other, but the impact of the whole may slip away in the process. It is that created illusion that I yearn to evoke through words.

Martha Graham's *Night Journey* can't be reduced to a synopsis claiming it as the tragedy of Oedipus told from Jocasta's point of view, any more than it can be explained only by an analysis of the huge, angular, percussive moves that wrench the dancers' bodies and psyches around the stage. Ceremonious processions give it immense formality; like a Noh actor, the protagonist moves from remembering action to re-entering it. So her hobbled advance—hands lifting to frame silent calls for help, while Oedipus reaches from behind to touch her breasts, her belly—affects us in a complex way: we see a woman fleeing impending rape *and* a woman in the act of remembering that moment, her gestures polished and restrained by the passage of time (in itself an artistic illusion). *And* we see a creature stalked by an intruder (we feel the disruption in our own senses), her every step forward blocked by a new impediment hooking around her, invisible until it touches her. In recent years, there has been grumbling about the attention some American dance critics (me certainly among them) give to descriptive writing. Complaints link it to now suspect "formalism." In 1993, an article by Roger Copeland entitled "Dance Criticism and the Descriptive Bias" appeared in Britain's *Dance Theatre Journal.* Copeland laments dance's failure to produce a Clement Greenberg, a Charles Rosen, a Lionel Trilling. True, he praises dance writers' ability to capture in words the quality of dancing. Nor is he pushing for theorizing unmoored to the art in question ("I for one am not anxious to see the sensuous surface of the dancer's body vaporized beneath the blowtorch of deconstruction").

However, Copeland sets up a (to me) disturbing polarity between "description" and "ideas," which he finds descriptive writing essentially devoid of (although he fails to clarify what he means by "ideas" and how they differ from "theory"). He blames the supposed "bias for description" on a semi-conscious collusion among choreographers, spectators, and writers to preserve the ineffableness of dance—a desire he considers a kind of willful primitivism, related to dance's power to induce kinaesthesia, and to the allure its ritual roots and its semblance of wholeness have for a fractured contemporary society. It's as if the anti-intellectual stance legendarily attributed to dancers and choreographers is now presumed to have infected critics as well, and that the "describer's" responses are too intuitive, too close to the work, or demand too little brain power to count as intellectual. In other words, we dive in and come up dripping.

Interestingly, judging by their remarks, some choreographers agree with Copeland. They want their work dignified by the intellectual display and distanced tone they see in some film criticism and art criticism. They want to be linked to trends in art and popular culture and *fin de siècle* malaise (as indeed I'm eager to do—if not on a weekly basis).

The casting of description in an adversarial role to

"ideas" troubles me—as if the more description a review contains, the lighter it becomes. This is a new wrinkle in the mind-body split. Before I attempt to argue further, or to analyze "description," I'd like to examine it as an aspect of critical theories that stress focusing on the work itself. The "new" literary criticism that emerged in America in the 1920s and became prominent in the 1940s and 1950s concerned itself less with what a text meant than with how it revealed that meaning. To T. S. Eliot, reducing a poem to its "prose core" indeed reduced it; instead, the task of the critic was to exhibit the "differential, residue, or tissue which keeps the object poetical or entire." Such a view was certainly once shared by artists (Picasso dismissed some art critics with "People who try to *explain* pictures are usually barking up the wrong tree").

It was a critical bias toward content (narrative, artistic biography, social ramifications, etc.) that Susan Sontag reacted to in her influential 1960s essays in *Against Interpretation.* She was not, remember, against interpretation in its broadest sense; brilliant analysis, as in her examination of Alain Resnais's film *Muriel,* gave the lie to that. I for one gladly latched on to Sontag's ideas as vindication of my goals. She put it enticingly: "The best criticism dissolves considerations of content into those of form." And: "Equally valuable would be acts of criticism which would supply a really accurate, sharp, loving description of the appearance of a work of art." I believed that for many years, and, to some extent, still believe it.

If I have slightly altered my view of critical writing, it is in part because dance has changed; so have the contexts in which we can view it. Although dance videos are not as common or as numerous as CDs on store shelves, the critic of the nineties has access to enough of them (and affordable home equipment to play them on) to make comparing and tracing bloodlines a process you can fall right into, entranced. (Coincidence handed me, juxtaposed on one tape, Shirley Clarke's 1957 film of Anna Sokolow's solo *Bullfight* and Madonna's recent video *Say Goodbye.* Guess which woman ends up on satin sheets with the matador.)

Also, much of the art that we were writing about in the 1960s and early 1970s seemed designed to thwart attempts to psychoanalyze it. Choreographers like Trisha Brown and Twyla Tharp shunned fiction and drew our attention to structure and process (and profoundly luscious movement). For some time, Merce Cunningham and George Balanchine had been telling us in maddeningly, charmingly elliptical statements that the movement was the meaning. The "sensuous surfaces" Sontag referred to had almost nothing to do with superficiality, and writing about them—describing them—could be an intoxicatingly deep experience.

Since the mid-eighties, however, dance has fallen in love with narrative, drama, text, social and political commentary, and the heady postmodern welter of eclecticism, historical reference, and deconstruction of previous works of art. Art critic Suzy Gablik writes, "In the multi-dimensional and slippery world of postmodern art, anything goes with anything, like a game without rules. Floating images such as those we see in the painting of David Salle maintain no relationship with anything at all, and meaning becomes detachable like keys on a keyring."

If this is true, today's art and structuralist critique are made for one another. Digging into the work to extract allusions and archetypal elements can become a seductive brain game.

I resist this to a degree. Certainly the dance of today and my own studies in history have made me more aware that, individual creativity notwithstanding, art is indeed a cultural artifact, and as anthropologist Clifford Geertz points out, so are our responses to it. But because of that we need to keep grounding speculation in the created worlds before us. Performance artist Diane Torr disguises herself as a man to perform wildly stereotypical male "numbers." She gives cross-dressing workshops. Amid the critical discourse on empowerment of women and how a woman feels in drag, surely it is important to confront (although I didn't until the act of writing this) the conflicts within the image itself: an "imperfect" or ersatz male masquerading as a self-defined quintessential male. Surely the contrast between round, smooth cheeks and assertive moustache, the loud, depthless voice, and the big, gruff gestures that make us laugh—*because* we know that this is a woman—need to be attended to, to be "described." In them reside truths about contemporary gender styles and essential gender differences.

Description at its best is not simply about surface. It hints at what lurks within a work. It links images through imaginative wordplay. The patterns of language can echo the rhythms and the impetus of dancing, as well as the responses of the spectator. I am not plumping for reportage or for reviews that are 80 percent description. Certainly facts are useful, as in Edwin Denby's squaring off, early in his great review of Balanchine's *Agon* in 1957, "The curtain rises on a stage bare and silent. Upstage four boys are seen with their backs to the public and motionless. They wear the company's dance uniform. Lightly they stand in an intent stillness. They whirl, four at once, to face you. The soundless whirl is a downbeat that starts the action."

This is an elegant and necessary laying of the framework within which other less linear forms of description will bloom. But blow-by-blow accounts of physical actions are useful only in small, skilled doses. To say, "She slowly extends her right arm diagonally forward, at the some time stretching one leg to the rear. Then she bends the leg on which she is standing and inclines her ribcage slightly toward her hipbone . . . " is not only singularly unentrancing to read, its pacing may actually violate the truth of an image that the eye and mind have grasped in a second or two as a fluid entity. Denby could get away with following a vivid, forthright image of Tamara Toumanova ("the force with which she rams her squared-off toe shoe into the floor") with a questionably fancy one ("her free leg deploys its mass from the leg she stands on"). A leg deploying its mass is hard enough to countenance in Denby. Those influenced by Denby (as indeed we all were) can flounder quite dreadfully attempting similar exercises.

Criticism can't provide a print analogue for a dance. Why should it? For one thing, criticism is irrevocably subjective, however fair-minded it may be; description can only offer some accurate facts, a pinpointing of style, and an evocation of a work's essential nature—a vision filtered through particular eyes and a particular sensibility.

In descriptive passages I admire, the self-reflection that Copeland misses in dance criticism has sometimes occurred (perhaps even half-consciously) *before* the description is written, and is embedded in it. Back in 1981, I followed a not especially memorable description of a Senegalese dance troupe (the polyrhythmic display of softly thudding feet, the nodding heads, rolling shoulders, and churning hips) by this sentence: "I imagine the dancers take their bodies apart at night before sleeping and put a pat of butter in every joint." I was startled then to see this sentence appear, typed, apparently, by my fingers. It surprises me now. Where did it come from? It says something, it seems to me, about the secret aura that surrounds ritual, about my own awe in the face of admired "otherness," about the bedrock of African tradition still informing this modern theatrical company, and about my (and by implication, possibly other spectators') connection to the whole thing on some intuitive level. Perhaps I'm making one frail sentence bear too much weight. The burden may not be theories, but I *think* they are ideas.

Years ago, Laura Shapiro produced a dead-on image of Murray Louis showing off his impishly flexible body "like a housewife with a new kitchen, every dial and switch activating something sudden and impressive. Quick shifts of weight, spontaneous rebounds from one extremity to the next, the twitch of a shoulder or a knee, these charge him with a recurrent flow of power."

Not only do I find this a supremely accurate picture of Louis's personal style, but the simile situates him in a playful, possibly lightweight world in which the body is separated from its controlling agent—a gadget for its owner's endlessly delighted manipulating. Puppet and puppeteer rolled into one. Shapiro *could* have gone on to discuss the relation between Louis and his mentor Alwin Nikolais, who was once a puppeteer, to lay out Nikolais's reaction against the ego-centered dramas of modern

dance, and theories about the puppet by Heinrich Kleist and Gordon Craig. But the ideas gleaming in her description are provocative in themselves.

Marcia Siegel's account of Douglas Dunn in Graz in 1976 creates print structures that evoke Dunn's casualness, bluntness, and eccentricity: "Later, arriving downstage in a corner, he found some stairs and a door in a wall. There he did a set of variations on whether to continue or make his escape. He'd lunge determinedly at the stairs, panic, whirl down them again, put a hand out the door, reconsider—till he was weaving and feinting in an ecstasy of indecision."

How telling that "he found some stairs . . . "

When we write about something as informal as Douglas Dunn moseying around in Graz, our choice of words and the length and shape of sentences may—with luck—differ from those used to evoke Balanchine's ripe, dreamily romantic *Liebeslieder Waltzes* or Molissa Fenley's amazonian solo *Rite of Spring*. Often, in great criticism, the prose style mirrors something of the dance style.

Joan Acocella fixes her eye and heart on Mark Morris's *Strict Songs:* "Five couples (the full cast) are onstage. In each couple, one person lies down on the floor on his back, and the other person, placing the first person's feet against his stomach, launches himself into the air, where he levitates, balanced atop the first person's legs, as the curtain comes down.

This is a hellishly difficult maneuver. For the second person—the 'flier'—not to fall, the feet must be placed exactly right on the abdomen, and the takeoff into the air must be done with exactly the right thrust. We watch the dancers going through all this with immense care and deliberation. But then once fliers are launched, we are shown an amazing sight: five people floating in the air. They have died and gone to heaven. At the same time, in the effort they have gone through—some of them are still trembling as they float there—we see how hard it is to die, how hard to get to heaven. Or rather, we feel it, in the body, because it is the body's struggle that we have witnessed."

As in Morris's dance, the meticulous, factual setting

up of the situation not only anchors the last burst of poetry, it engenders it, just as the actions of the dancers produce an image that goes beyond the placement of foot and the girding of muscles.

Sometimes the insights that emerge through the descriptive mode can literally bring tears to my eyes. When Arlene Croce says of Balanchine's *Ivesiana,* "[It] is about that American distance, that equalizing yet comfortless space that separates Americans from Americans under the neutral American sky. It is about the lack of perimeters and journeys pressing onward despite that lack. It is about situations, not destinations, and in it the stage is a box with no sides. Dancers come and go and seem to fall off the edges into eternity."

Analogy is rooted in observation—as fluid as the transactions between pond water and fish. In such an ecosystem, everything nourishes everything else. And ideas spring like water lilies.

Imagining Dance

JOAN ACOCELLA

Periodically, one or another dance organization, to promote mutual understanding, will stage a choreographers-meet-the-critics symposium, and at such gatherings someone always asks the critics whether, when they set out to review something, they bother to find out what the artist is trying to do, what his or her intention is. I take this to be a very naive question, and very demeaning to choreographers, as if their work were so obscure and incomplete that it needed to carry a statement of intent. Worse, it implies that the truth of a dance lies somewhere other than in the dance, that the dance is a sort of side-effect, whereas the real event is the intellectual process that supposedly underlies it.

To all appearances, intellect does not *under*lie the kinetic imagination, but instead is hooked up to it in an oblique, sidelong manner, perhaps something like the hookup between the eye and the ear. There is no question that the eye and the ear are connected, and affect each other's functioning, yet each lives its own life, has its own neurology, its own range of sensations, and if one dies, the other cannot make it live again. Likewise, Balanchine might have said to himself, "I think I'll make a *Midsummer Night's Dream* ballet." He might also have said, "I think I'll end it with a pas de deux that, after all those lovers' quarrels, will show love's harmony restored."[1] But then the kinetic imagination would have taken over, with its own logic, its own world of gesture and meaning.

Consider that pas de deux, for example, the Act II pas de deux from *A Midsummer Night's Dream,* created in 1962 for Violette Verdy and Conrad Ludlow. There are things in it—little bows, entwinings of the arms, an ecstatic backbend at the end—of which, if they were described to you in words, you might say, "Ah yes, love's harmony restored," for they are related to the mimodrama of real life. But there are hundreds of other things in here that have no clear relation to life. What does it mean, for instance, when the woman stands in front of the man in second position on point, and he lifts her, turns her 180 degrees—while in the air, she performs one soft beat with her feet—and then places her down again in second position on point? What are we to make of this fastidious little action? I could say a lot of things—about the intimacy of so small an adjustment, about how the little entrechat seems tucked in like a secret, about how the man, moving the woman this way twice, turns her 360 degrees, thus drawing a perfect circle around them, which seems to shut them off and enclose them. In other words, I could try to make connections between the ballet and the facts of our normal life, and that is what I would do if I were reviewing it. But do we fool ourselves that because we can make these connections, the ballet is really like life and moves with a parallel, translatable logic? If so, what are we to make of the fact that the woman has those peculiar shoes on, and the man is wearing tights instead of trousers, and they are doing all this in a lighted box while we sit in the dark and watch it, and pay money to do so?

No, dance is not a portrayal of the way we live, and

to think that it is seems to me to betray an excessive attachment to the way we live, or the way we explain our lives to ourselves, in the language of reason and morals. As everyone knows, the mind can operate in completely different languages—dream, music, higher mathematics—and dance is one of those languages. Its logic is not discursive but lyric. Like music, it is a force field, an orchestration of lines of force, lines of energy, and that is the only way to start understanding it. Dance is not a story; it is a song.

By this I don't mean that dance is devoid of psychology. As Merce Cunningham has repeatedly protested, anything done by the human body is "expressive." I would guess that anything originating in the human brain is probably expressive—that is, marked by intention and emotion—and if it weren't, we wouldn't bother with it. Even a dance that aims to be emotionless is filled with emotion. When I watch Yvonne Rainer's *Trio A,* which Rainer created with the intent of making a dance devoid of all hierarchy, repetition, accent, or any other form of emphasis that might create a human drama, what holds my attention is the human drama of that intent: its sheer futility and the touching, upright, girls-college seriousness with which it is pursued. I like Rainer for trying to do this; the world needs these anti-sentimental campaigns. She fails nobly, and this makes an interesting dance.

But when we look at dance not as moral fable but as an orchestration of energies, I think we reach a psychology that lies entirely apart from morality—something deep in our experience, something that may correspond to actual biochemical processes. Who knows? I am talking about very basic facts of dance, patterns of energy flow that we see repeatedly, such as:

- somebody suddenly hopping in out of nowhere
- a lateral line of dancers moving downstage simultaneously, in a ground sweep
- a line of dancers (often a line of couples) flowing out of an upstage wing and moving downstage on the diagonal, as in a polonaise
- displacement, where something small (a solo dancer or a couple) is replaced by something large (a mass of dancers), or vice versa
- cutting through, where something small and sharp (such as one dancer, moving fast) flies through something large and "soft" (a mass of dancers)

These are only a few. They are the choreographer's stock in trade, the things dance drama is made of. But I think they are also reflections of deep habits of human consciousness. Take displacement. In Mark Morris's *L'Allegro, il Penseroso ed il Moderato* there is a moment when a dancer representing the lark hops around the stage all alone, in a picky, birdlike little way. Then, as he exits, a great mass of dancers flies onto the stage behind him—the whole flock. This is a thrilling moment, just in theatrical terms. It is also a pretty exact representation of what is happening in the score (vocal solo followed by big sweep of orchestral forces). But it is more than this. I think it reflects all experience that our brains know and love, the experience of being overwhelmed by a huge rush of something. The sudden constriction or dilation of the blood vessels, the neurotransmitters flooding the synapses of the neural pathways, terror, wonder, illness: many things happen to us not evenly, but in a big flood, and dangerous though this is, we love it, like the hero of Poe's "A Descent into the Maelstrom," who stares down into the screaming vortex and then, with something like joy, descends. When Morris's little bird is replaced by the huge, cascading flock, our very bones answer, "Yes, we know."

Now take an example of cutting through. In Balanchine's *Square Dance* there is a moment when the ballerina, having been off the stage for a minute or so, suddenly comes tearing back in an arc of coupés jetés, cutting a path through the mass of dancers on the stage. This is approximately the opposite of the bird maneuver. There, something big and massy followed something small and sharp. Here, something small and sharp slices through something masslike. Again, it is very thrilling, in a psychological but premoral sense. Like shot through a goose, I always think when I see it.

2. Merrill Ashley dancing *Square Dance*. Choreography by George Balanchine, copyright © The George Balanchine Trust, photograph by Steven Caras, copyright © Steven Caras.

And it has all the innocently brutal pleasure that we get from that phrase, before we remember that the goose dies from the shot. (This is what I mean by premoral. These pleasures have nothing to do with the way we feel the world should be.) We love to see small things cut through big things: the bicyclist cut through the tangle of traffic, a sharp argument cut through a lot of nonsense. Again, I would bet there is a biochemical basis for this pattern. In any case, it is a pattern that repeats and repeats itself in our thoughts and our art. And it is full of psychological meaning, from the most elementary (the pleasure of being small and fast as opposed to big and slow) to the most advanced (love of ingenuity, respect for the "little guy," pride in hearing a different drummer). These are the chimes that ring in us when Merrill Ashley flies onstage in those coupés jetés.

I will take one more example, though this one is more complicated and not premoral. Again and again in nineteenth-century ballets there is a moment when the hero walks onstage, finds a large number of women who look alike and are dressed alike (the corps de ballet), and seeks among them for the one woman who is his. (The trope is repeated in the Astaire-Rogers movie *Shall We Dance?* and in a rather surreal fashion, for the women not only all look like Ginger Rogers, they are all wearing Ginger Rogers masks, including Ginger Rogers. Fred Astaire has a hard job here.) The psychoanalysts would say this is an extrapolation from the childhood experience of separation from the mother. Siegfried seeking Odette among the swan maidens is only our third-grade self, coming out of school, scanning the group of mothers for the one who is *our* mother. But I would say that that too is only one facet of a more comprehensive and generalized experience, that of matching.

In Plato's *Symposium* Aristophanes tells the story that once upon a time all human creatures were spherical, and they were so powerful and happy, rolling around, that the gods, in order to protect themselves, split the humans in half. So that is what we are—halves of former wholes—and we spend our lives seeking our lost half. For Plato, as for psychoanalysts, this is a theory of love, but I would guess there is a vast range of mental and biological experience that is governed by the same effort: to make things fit together, to have part answer part. From the duplication of our cells, with the DNA strands separating and then manufacturing new partners for themselves, to the most complex intellectual action, such as understanding a difficult argument or making one's own argument understood, this matching process occupies our lives. In fact, one could say that with its dialectical opposite, the process of forging into the unknown, it *is* our lives. In any case, our whole selves recognize it onstage, and not just when Siegfried finds Odette, but in much more elementary pairings: spatial, dynamic, rhythmic. When the circle of dancers at stage right matches the one at stage left, when the ballerina's staccato phrasing matches that of the violin accompanying her—whenever something calls and something answers—we rejoice. (And sometimes when things don't match we rejoice. Indeed, we feel a thrill of vicarious disobedience. And then we wait for things to match in the end.)

Going back now to the Act II pas de deux of Balanchine's *Midsummer Night's Dream,* where is the meaning in that dance? Not in the backbend, but again, in an elementary pattern of energies: here, the deployment of huge forces in small gestures. Nothing could be fuller, more round and rich and brimming, than the flow of dance energy in this piece. It never quickens, it never halts; it flows and flows, like honey from the vine. Yet it is dispensed, for the most part, in small, polite, fastidious gestures. We have already looked at one of them. Another, its match, is the supported cabriole,

which occurs again and again in the piece. The man lifts the woman; she taps her feet together; he puts her down. Rhythmically, it is like the beating of a heart in a body at rest. Pictorially, it is like a beautiful confinement: she is running, he is catching her. Dynamically, it is gentle and precise, like an action they both know how to do, have done a hundred times. So this is the feeling of great power in a quiet state, the calm of having plenty and not having to use it up. There are many things that fit such a pattern—a full stomach, a trust fund—but one of the most obvious things is married love, and that, of course, is why this dance is the way it is: because it is being given at a wedding, the wedding of the lovers from Act 1, and it is intended to show the peaceful ways of a *lived* love after the storms of love's discovery. Nothing in the dance actually represents married love; nothing in the dance represents anything. What is happening is that the dance is drawing on patterns of energy that we associate with certain habits—habits that, in turn, further down the road, we associate with marriage. The dance wasn't caused by, can't be explained by, didn't grow out of the idea of marriage. Rather, marriage and this dance are two branches growing out of the same trunk, both equally real.

As I have said, I think the imaginative process by which this dance is made may have a strong biological basis. And that may be the thing that has enabled dance, unlike almost every other modern art form in the West, to be passed down by memory. We remember it easily (and also adapt it easily) because it so deeply belongs to us. I don't mean by this that dance is more natural than language, or more true. I see dance that is untrue every day of the week: dance that is full of clichés and ballast and nonsense. As for language, I think it is a heroic endeavor. No, each is as true and false as the other. People who say that movement does not lie generally assume that language is a doctored or at least indirect version of truths that dance expresses directly. This is the reverse of the position of those who want us, before we review a dance, to determine the choreographer's intent: they think that dance is an indirect version of truths that language can speak directly. Neither view is correct. And this should come as a comfort, at least to dance-watchers. So much of life is spent in the difficult task of trying to understand things, to see *through* them to what's on the other side. But the truths of dance are not on the other side. They are in the very bones of the dance, which our bones know how to read, if we let them.

Note

1. I offer this only for the sake of argument. The truth is certainly that Balanchine's kinetic imagination was set in motion, by love of Mendelssohn's music, long before he framed the intention of making the ballet.

Searching for Nijinsky's *Sacre*

MILLICENT HODSON

When Seiji Ozawa recently conducted the Boston Symphony Orchestra in *Le Sacre du Printemps* (Carnegie Hall, December 13, 1979), the audience saw something of the legendary premiere of 1913. Ozawa looked like a Nijinsky dancer—knees bent, toes turned in, his body leaning into the ostinati that shape the music, his arms swinging out from the core of the rhythm until they seemed to touch the tympani. He was conducting, of course, not dancing; but for some members of the audience his movements suddenly evoked photographs, sketches, and written accounts that survive from the original production.

Nijinsky's *Sacre du Printemps* is a mystery. The few remaining documents connected with the ballet are considered relics of a lost masterpiece. *Le Sacre* is celebrated as the harbinger of modern dance, the work that broke the ground of twentieth-century choreography. The ballet released tremendous energy; then it disappeared. Five performances at the Champs-Elysées in Paris beginning May 29, 1913, three at the Drury Lane in London beginning July 11 in the same year, and that was all. For decades dancers and scholars have assumed that reconstruction of the ballet was impossible. A year ago I realized that the last possible moment to recover it had come. Participants from the original production still survive. While crucial documents may surface in the future, nothing can bring back the experience of the artists who lived the event.

Le Sacre climaxed the pre-war period of Diaghilev's Ballets Russes. It was an innovation the company itself could hardly bear. Stravinsky's polyrhythmic music with constant time changes and dissonant chords was difficult enough. But Nijinsky's choreography caused mutiny in the corps. The dancers did not abandon their ballet technique for Nijinsky's "primitive" steps without a struggle. Such verbal descriptions of the dance as do exist reveal in Nijinsky a remarkable sense of design. He seems to have liberated the energy inherent in rhythm, color, and line. Imagine, for example, the end of Part I—women in scarlet dresses, their dark braids flying, "run wildly round the stage in a great circle," racing "to the notes of the main theme."[1] Inside and against their fiery circle run men in white robes "ceaselessly splitting up into tiny groups," their smaller circles swinging "in threefold counterpoint."[2] "The people dance passionately on the earth," the libretto says, "sanctifying it and becoming one with it."[3] To see these swirling circles of red and white against the vibrant green décor, and the dancers pulling at the polyrhythms to release their force—an audience today would *still* be astonished.

The premiere of the ballet was a *succès de scandale*. Parisians were incited to riot by the strange tension of the dancing and the stark contrasts of the décor and music. Stravinsky's score came as a shock, and even still it has power to excite, amaze, and break old habits of hearing. *Le Sacre du Printemps* brought people to their feet, hissing or hushing, fighting for or against the event on the stage. One elegant lady, armed with a hat pin, went straight for the throat of Jean Cocteau, avant-garde poet and partisan, soon to be a collaborator with the Ballets Russes. Diaghilev, so the story goes, pleaded for order and got pelted with fruit. Nijinsky backstage kept shouting counts in Russian while Pierre Monteaux—"nerveless as a crocodile" according to Stravinsky—never faltered for an instant as he led the musicians through the melée.[4]

The *Sacre* premiere literally became a legend overnight. Succeeding performances in Paris and London were relatively calm so that talk of the first night became part of the experience of the ballet itself. In an interview after the London premiere, Nijinsky was quoted as thanking the English public for its serious interest. The immediate mythologizing of his ballet did not seem to affect the choreographer, except that the Paris premiere became, even for him, the criterion of response:

> There was no ridicule of the ballet on Friday and there was great applause. People who say that the piece was hissed cannot know what real hissing is. But the newspapers seem to have been much less sympathetic than the audience. I am accused of a "crime against grace," among other things.[5]

Le Sacre du Printemps was also a mystery in the ritual sense. It originated in a dream of Stravinsky's about an ancient Slavic rite.[6] He saw a young woman, encircled by wise old men, dancing herself to death to awaken the spring. Stravinsky recounted the dream to Nicholas Roerich, a painter and archeologist who had traveled throughout Russia collecting artifacts, deciphering signs, seeking out the ancestral gods. Roerich made a number of expeditions with his friend Princess Tenisheva whose estate, Talashkino, became the center of the Slavic arts movement in the first decade of the century.[7] Stravinsky and Roerich met there in 1911 to conceive the ballet based on his dream. They created a scenario with a ritual structure. It opens with an old witch who divines the action of the ballet, predicting its games and ceremonies. An elderly sage consecrates these actions with a solemn kiss of the earth. During the mystic dances of the young women, one among

them falls into trance. A game of fate confirms her as the Chosen Virgin. In a convulsive dance of possession she sacrifices herself to the god of spring, Yarilo, ancient spirit of light and creativity.[8]

Nicholas Roerich is remembered as the designer of the brilliantly colored costumes and sets of *Le Sacre*. But his more fundamental role was as the archivist, scenarist, and spiritual advisor of the project. Stravinsky acknowledged his debt to Roerich by dedicating the score to him. Recent conversations with Nijinsky's relatives have clarified Roerich's profound influence on the choreographer.[9] What Nijinsky absorbed from Roerich must be explored if the spirit of the original *Sacre* is to be preserved. In a public address twenty years later, Roerich suggested that the audience of the ballet premiere had undergone a ritual experience:

> I remember how during the first performance in Paris, in 1913, the entire audience whistled and roared so that nothing could even be heard. Who knows, perhaps at this very moment they were enjoying themselves with the same emotions of primitive people. But this savage primitiveness had nothing in common with the refined primitiveness of our ancestors, for whom rhythm . . . symbol, and refinement of gesture were great and sacred concepts.[10]

The statement indicates something of his respect for archaic culture and the authenticity he must have urged upon his collaborators. Whether Roerich discussed ritual sources of dance with Nijinsky—and whether these ideas were integrated into the choreography—may never be known. But it is possible to know what Roerich studied in the period prior to his work on *Le Sacre du Printemps*. Research into his knowledge of Slavic ritual may disclose ground patterns, gestures, and even steps that ultimately turn up in Nijinsky's dance.

The year after Nijinsky's *Sacre* performances Europe was at war; civilization was reduced to its raw elements. Young men who had defended the ballet at the Champs-Elysées—young men throughout Europe—

lay dead in the trenches. Nijinsky's last public appearance (in St. Moritz in 1919) would be an elegy which he improvised for them.[11] During the war, the dancer and his recent bride, the Hungarian Romola de Pulsky, were interned as prisoners of war in Budapest. On a journey to Russia they had stopped in Budapest to visit Romola's family; the war broke out and they were detained. Isolated from the theater and a company of dancers, Nijinsky experimented with his choreography. He began developing a system of movement notation which, through a curious twist of fate, brought about his release from Hungary. Officials grew suspicious of his work, thinking that the symbols on his movement charts were code for military secrets. After days of investigation, however, they recognized the truth and the chief of police, impressed by the genius of Nijinsky's system, befriended him. By the fall of 1915 this man arranged to get Nijinsky and his wife transferred out of Budapest, with a stopover in Vienna which served as an escape route. From there, with the intervention of the Austrian emperor, the king of Spain, and eventually the Pope, the Nijinskys left for New York to lead the first American tour (1916) of Diaghilev's Ballets Russes.[12]

After the war Diaghilev decided to revive *Le Sacre du Printemps*. Nijinsky's marriage to Romola in the meantime led to a personal and finally a professional split with Diaghilev. What had probably been a nervous breakdown in 1914 evolved into a chronic condition diagnosed by 1919 as schizophrenia. Within seven years of its creation in 1913, Nijinsky's choreography for *Le Sacre* was given up for lost. No one seemed to remember the steps, although members of the original cast were still performing with the Ballets Russes. Perhaps the initial difficulty of learning the dance made them want to forget it; they had resisted Nijinsky and his assistant, Marie Rambert, every step of the way. So for the 1920 season Diaghilev commissioned a new version of the choreography from Nijinsky's successor, Leonide Massine (premiered at Champs-Elysées, December 15). Thus began a new controversy—the question of "les deux Sacres," the two *Sacres*. The early rejection by the press

had put Nijinsky's version out of the repertoire. A second version by the Ballets Russes doomed the first to oblivion. Stravinsky's shifting allegiances between the two versions is a fascinating story in itself, chronicled by Robert Craft in his review of Lincoln Kirstein's *Nijinsky Dancing*.[13] Kirstein championed Nijinsky as choreographer, and Craft, taking up the challenge, called for a reconstruction of *Le Sacre*, based on promptbook scores by Stravinsky and Rambert.

From my work thus far I am convinced that the task of reconstruction can and must be accomplished. Book after book retells the fabulous tale of the Paris premiere, proclaiming Nijinsky's *Sacre* the seminal work of the century. If it really is the parent of contemporary dance, then the relics must not only be preserved but seen in the theatrical context to which they belong. The choreography is still a mystery, to be solved like an intricate puzzle, piece by piece. This challenge has led me on many adventures. The results of my search I am organizing into a book of drawings which transpose all movement clues into figures and groups (see figure 3). The book collates information from interviews, scores, and newly discovered as well as familiar verbal and visual sources. Ultimately I hope to use it as a production handbook, working with dancers to restage the ballet. With a certain amount of the reconstruction in rough draft, I went last spring to the Stravinsky-Diaghilev Foundation. The director, Parmenia Migel Ekstrom, encouraged my efforts and provided letters of reference for the first of my adventures searching for Nijinsky's *Sacre*.

I. Marie Rambert: The Revelation of Nijinsky's Postures (London, April 1979)

My journey to London to see Rambert was a return to the source. London is the city where the early rehearsals of the ballet took place. The only surviving interviews with Nijinsky about *Le Sacre* are from the English press during that time and after the London premiere. Marie Rambert, an expert on Dalcroze Eurythmics, had been hired by Diaghilev to help Nijinsky

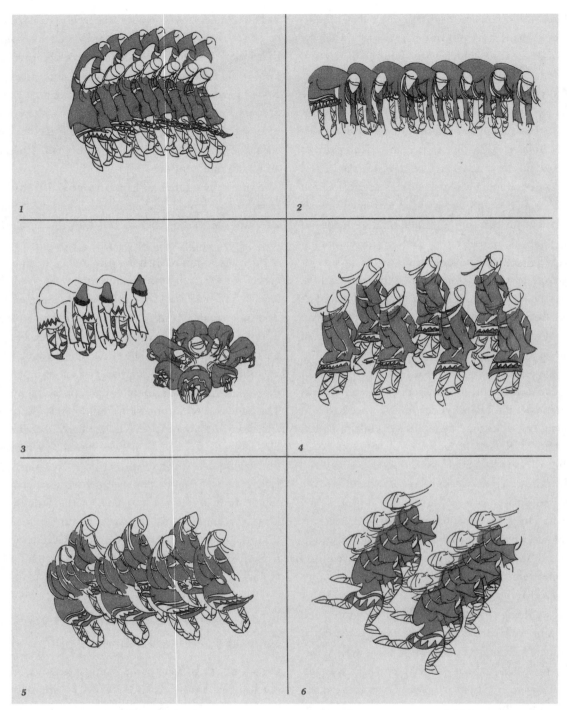

3. Reconstruction drawings by Millicent Hodson of the following dances from *Le Sacre du Printemps:* transition from "Ritual of Abduction" to "Spring Rounds," "Spring Rounds," "Spring Rounds," "Games of the Rival Tribes," "Dance of the Earth," "Dance of the Earth." Based on information from the Valentine Gross materials (Theatre Collection, Victoria and Albert Museum), *The Rite of Spring Sketches, 1911–1913* (London: Boosey and Hawkes, 1969), and a synthesis of accounts from the time of the Paris premiere. Copyright © Millicent Hodson.

break down the complicated counts of the score as they set the work on the dancers. A performer as well in the original production, Rambert survived an ordeal unprecedented in ballet history. Rambert was midwife to the production, Nijinsky's friend, confidante, and his first line of defense against the infuriated ballet-trained corps. Rambert, of course, went on to create her own company and to shape, quite literally, the future of ballet in Britain. A dancer influenced by Isadora Duncan, she persevered in her loyalty to Nijinsky's *Sacre,* honoring it still as her somewhat contradictory initiation into the ballet world and praising it always as the best of many versions of the dance.

During the interview, Rambert and I saw together a film of the Massine version which I had brought with me to refresh her memory and to stimulate thoughts about the differences in "les deux Sacres." While watching the film, which was silent, she shook her head and stood up. With the delicate grandeur of her ninety years, she began to demonstrate Nijinsky's grounded posture, *singing* Stravinsky for bars on end—an extraordinary accomplishment in itself. More emphatically than indicated in her biography *Quicksilver,*[14] Rambert stressed to me the discipline of the distinctive posture in Nijinsky's *Sacre:*

The foundation of the choreography was the turned-in position. And bent. A questioning. And fists—not strong, not showing strength, just not opened yet. . . . That's what he called "kuluchiki." It is a diminutive—fistikins. That was one of the poses, and you had to *dance* in that pose. When you had to jump with the feet like this [demonstrating], turning in, the position was difficult to keep, and it came from terribly difficult rhythms which you had to remember. It was a torture. Why do you make me remember it all?

She continued, nonetheless, showing how this focus on posture characterized Nijinsky as a choreographer:

You see, Nijinsky tied one *hand and foot* by giving a very difficult basic position for a ballet . . . for

Faune . . . the body was like this. [She moved in the hieratic, two-dimensional posture of the dance.] You had to learn to walk with your feet straight, the body sideways and the head turned. The arms had to move from that position. For *Sacre* we had a hundred rehearsals, not less. And for *Faune,* each time we did it we had to have extra rehearsals.[15]

Watching Rambert I began to understand—the *Sacre* posture concentrated energy earthward, literally gathering force from its low center of gravity as do postures in Kung Fu and other martial arts. The experience of changing mood through posture is a classic technique in acting, and altering consciousness through posture is a yogic concept. Nijinsky's posture for *Le Sacre,* which had so agonized the dancers, was no mere stylization but a means of channeling physical and psychic energy. This revelation put into another dimension what I knew of his method of composing—postural meditations, like Isadora Duncan's standing positions, as a way to generate movement.

Rambert suggested that the integrity of design in Nijinsky's choreography derived from body posture, extending first through the arm, hand, and head gestures, and then through the groupings of dancers and patterns in space. While Rambert described his choreography in terms of form, Nijinsky described it, during early rehearsal, in terms of energy forces:

Le Sacre . . . will prove a strangely interesting work. It is really the soul of nature expressed by movement to music. It is really the life of the stones and the trees. There are no human beings in it. It will be danced only by the corps de ballet, for it is a thing of concrete masses, not of individual effects.[16]

In addition to the scores that Rambert and Stravinsky marked with entrance cues and actions, plus the verified existence of other marked scores, there are rumored to be notations of the dance in Nijinsky's own system.[17] A conversation on this subject, just prior to

Nijinsky's final appearance in 1919, has been recorded by Maurice Sondoz:

> What I want to do is write down the dance, gesture by gesture. I have invented symbols to represent the dancers. The note on the stave represents their head, their gestures are indicated by stylized attitudes. I have transcribed the *Sacre* and intend to transcribe all of the. . . . And in ten, twenty, a hundred years, they will be able to dance these ballets as they dance them today.[18]

Nijinsky made a movement score for his *L'Après-midi d'un Faune* (Théâtre du Châtelet, May 29, 1912), which he notated in Budapest from August to September 1915, and dedicated to his wife. Madame Nijinsky subsequently gave it to the Manuscript Division of the British Museum, where it is available for study. A movement score for *Le Sacre* may one day emerge, but apart from that miracle, it is possible that letters or journals from lesser-known members of the Ballets Russes may contain clues to the choreography. Rambert recalled that in the corps "everybody was going about with a little notebook trying to learn the timing." The difficulty of the dance makes it all the more likely that participants kept notes for themselves, complained to their families, or, one hopes, confided to someone how beautiful it was.

II. Le Sacre Hieroglyphs: Unpublished Sketches by Valentine Gross (London, April 1979)

While in London my adventures continued as I tried to locate documents reputedly housed in the London Theatre Museum. After repeated proof that no such place existed, I prevailed again upon Rambert's assistant, John Webley, who had already set up the interview, rewired plugs for the occasion, and posed questions to Rambert that did not occur to me. Through Webley's hunches I found myself in the closed Theatre Collection of the Victoria and Albert Museum. "Some-

time in the '80s," I was assured by Jennifer Aylmer, the assistant curator, "a Theatre Museum *will* open at Covent Garden." The primary object of my search was a notebook of crayon sketches made by the French artist Valentine Gross during the last night (June 3, 1913) of *Le Sacre* in Paris.[19] More than sketches, they are really notations and provide a kind of hieroglyphic record of various sections of the dance. Quick, abbreviated renderings of movement, they have an internal consistency that makes it possible to read from one to the next.[20] According to Rambert, they are accurate in their groupings, direction, and line. The hieroglyphs gave me raw material for drawing major blocks of choreography. (See figure 4.)

As I traced the hieroglyphs, Jennifer Aylmer appeared at the door, half-hidden by an enormous bundle of garments. "The costumes," she announced, hanging them around the room. I stood up in amazement, realizing that, even though I knew better, I had always thought of *Le Sacre* in the black-and-white of photographs from a 1913 issue of *Comoedia*. Hundreds of colors were painted on the women's silk dresses and the men's white flannel robes—magenta, ochre, turquoise, golds, and greens. The staff kept piling up treasures, bringing them up from the basement, or down from the mezzanine; clipping files, letters, the journal of Valentine Gross, her pastels and pencil drawings. (See figures 4 and 5.) Jennifer Aylmer was gracious to open the closed doors of a collection in storage, but she went beyond the call of both duty and courtesy with her help and interest. The Victoria and Albert treasures multiplied the possibilities of my reconstruction work.

III. Choreographics: Work-in-Progress (New York, Summer 1979)

Back in New York I synthesized some of the new information into the first set of *Sacre* drawings for the handbook. Dame Marie Rambert—was it impossible to thank her for the interview, to acknowledge her revelation?—had agreed to look over my drawings when they were ready, to correct them. "Oh yes, yes," she

4. "Augurs of Spring—Dance of the Maidens." (1) An example of the hieroglyphic sketches Valentine Gross made while watching *Le Sacre* in 1913; (2) and (3) more finished drawings of the same movements, which is the first entrance of the maidens in the ballet; (4) a published version of the drawing identifying it with the music cue for the entrance—two measures before 27. A series of such drawings with music cues appeared in *Montjoie!* in May 1913. The drawing is reprinted in *Rannie Balety Stravinskogo/Stravinsky's Early Ballets*, by I. Ya. Vershinina (Moscow, 1967), 135.

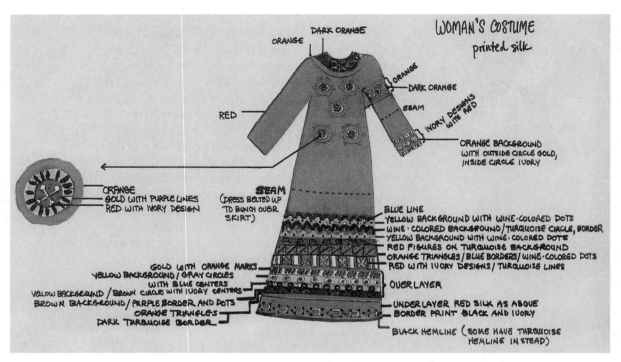

The labels within the sketch read:

DARK ORANGE
ORANGE
WOMAN'S COSTUME
printed silk

RED

ORANGE
DARK ORANGE
SEAM
IVORY DESIGNS WITH RED

ORANGE BACKGROUND WITH OUTSIDE CIRCLE GOLD, INSIDE CIRCLE IVORY

ORANGE
GOLD WITH PURPLE LINES
RED WITH IVORY DESIGN

SEAM
(DRESS BELTED UP TO BUNCH OVER SKIRT)

BLUE LINE
YELLOW BACKGROUND WITH WINE·COLORED DOTS
WINE·COLORED BACKGROUND/TURQUOISE CIRCLE, BORDER
YELLOW BACKGROUND WITH WINE·COLORED DOTS
RED FIGURES ON TURQUOISE BACKGROUND
ORANGE TRIANGLES/BLUE BORDERS/WINE·COLORED DOTS
RED WITH IVORY DESIGNS/TURQUOISE LINES

OVER LAYER

UNDER LAYER RED SILK AS ABOVE
BORDER PRINT BLACK AND IVORY

BLACK HEMLINE (SOME HAVE TURQUOISE HEMLINE INSTEAD)

GOLD WITH ORANGE MARKS
YELLOW BACKGROUND/GRAY CIRCLES WITH BLUE CENTERS
YELLOW BACKGROUND/BROWN CIRCLES WITH IVORY CENTERS
BROWN BACKGROUND/PURPLE BORDER AND DOTS
ORANGE TRIANGLES
DARK TURQUOISE BORDER

5. Sketch of one of Roerich's costumes for the original production, copied by Millicent Hodson, Theatre Collection, Victoria and Albert Museum. Copyright © Millicent Hodson.

exclaimed, balancing a plié with the back of a chair, "I will correct." At an exhibit entitled "Choreographics" I showed the *Sacre* series among other of my dance drawings in the loft of the Taller Latino-americano. From the exhibit and a lecture the same month at the College of New Rochelle came a number of leads, among them the names of musicians from the Paris premiere.

IV. The Unexpected (New York, Summer and Fall, 1979)

On a summer Sunday I was walking peacefully in the theater district when a *Variety* headline stopped me short:

LONDON SOTHEBY TO AUCTION
UNABRIDGED NIJINSKY DIARY;
PROMO ANGLES FOR TWO PICS

"The unabridged diary," I raced through the text, "will go to the highest bidder . . . remarkable document,

written in Russian. . . . Included are 15 pages of dance notation with 10 pages of diagrams."[21] When Colin Franklin, a book collector from Oxfordshire, bought the *Diary*, he soon received a letter from the Stravinsky-Diaghilev Foundation inquiring about future publication of the manuscript and describing the *Sacre* reconstruction project. By return mail, in a generous and unforgettable gesture, Mr. Franklin sent xerographed copies of excerpts from the *Diary*. Given the mention in the material of all the other Nijinsky ballets, *Le Sacre du Printemps* was conspicuous by its absence, suggesting that if documentation does exist, it must be in a notebook of its own. In the introduction to the excerpts sent by Mr. Franklin there is reference to another notebook, one that was not included in the three Romola Nijinsky gave to her literary agents shortly before her death in 1978:

The fourth, discovered in 1934, was filled with (Nijinsky's) notes toward a system of choreography;

it is said to exist in an institution but nobody quite knows its whereabouts.[22]

Beyond this notebook, the *Diary*, and the score of *Faune*, all of which were done in the period after the marriage, it is intriguing to remember Cocteau's description of Nijinsky at work during his residence with Diaghilev: "At the Hotel Crillon . . . he would put on a bath wrap, pull the hood over his head and make notes for his choreographies."[23] If such notes as these were left with Diaghilev during the 1913 South American tour that became Nijinsky's ill-fated honeymoon, they may yet turn up, perhaps in Paris.

V. Louis Speyer: *Le Sacre* from the Orchestra (Boston, November 1979)

"An oboist from the Paris premiere is alive and living in Boston," announced a friend on the phone. "But what can he tell you," she asked cautiously, her daughter being a concert oboist, "wasn't his back to the stage?" I immediately took a train to Boston's Back Bay and soon was climbing the steps to Louis Speyer's home. "I played for Isadora Duncan and Nijinsky," he told me, "and never saw a step." We discussed the wisdom of gamelon orchestras in Bali, flanking the *sides* of the performance space. Nevertheless, Louis Speyer told animated stories, with especially vivid portraits of Monteux. Since he had recently written down his "Reminiscences" in a short manuscript of that title, he shared them with me, in such cameos as follow:

> Stravinsky and Monteux in contrast made an interesting pair, Igor nervous, Pierre calm and master of the situation. . . . When Monteaux asked a question, the composer explained using his cane to beat out the difficult rhythms. No matter how complicated these became, Monteux smiled and accepted the explanation. For the bassoonist, at the beginning of the ballet, there was a surprise—the register was so high that the player had to devise radi-

cally new fingerings . . . the instrument sounded more like a "saxophone."[24]

Mr. Speyer thoughtfully, rather gallantly, gave me the manuscript and told me to sleep with it under my pillow, on the hope, I suppose, that a dream would recover the *Sacre* that neither of us saw.

VI. Treasures from the Russian (New York, November 1979)

Research at the Dance Collection and other branches of The New York Public Library enabled me, by this point, to account for most of the known documents about *Le Sacre* in English and French. The time had come to recover the Russian accounts. Susan Cook Summer of the Stravinsky-Diaghilev Foundation guided me through materials there and at the Slavic Division of the NYPL. She translated not only from periodicals and dance books—such as the major history of Krassovskaya—but also from ethnological texts [see figure 6]. Among the discoveries was an account of divination procedures which led me back to English, back to Roerich, to learn that he and Stravinsky had inscribed beams of the house at Talashkino with their first ideas for *Le Sacre*.[25] In addition to wondering whether documents were preserved in the Soviet Union, I needed to know whether any mention was made of ritual sources of choreography. In a coincidence of perfect timing, we located a recent paper by Richard Taruskin, professor of musicology at Columbia University, entitled "Russian Folk Melodies in the *Rite of Spring*." The paper demonstrates how certain parts of Stravinsky's score can be identified with music from Slavic rituals. Specific melodies in the sections called "Spring Rounds," "Dance of the Earth," and "Ritual Action of the Ancestors" are recognizable as ancient chants, some of which were performed with movement. Dance chants of this sort had the purpose of collective conjuring, "to facilitate," for example, "the quick awakening of nature."[26] Discoveries of ceremonial movements associated with

B

[KRASOUSKAYA DOCUMENTATION]

SACRE DU PRINTEMPS   SCENE I   AUGURS OF SPRING

The curtain, rising, revealed scattered members of the male corps de ballet
prayerfully spread over the stage. One group raised itself up, stamping their
feet, rhythmically twitching and almost not moving from place. Each participant,
touching the next with the elbow of his bent arm, was invisibly tied to his
neighbor - a tiny unit of a breathing, moving, flinching organism.

Amidst the
dancing figures scurried the "300 year old witch" - the dancer Gluck - urging
on the other groups with spasmodic leaps, and they gradually fell into the dance.

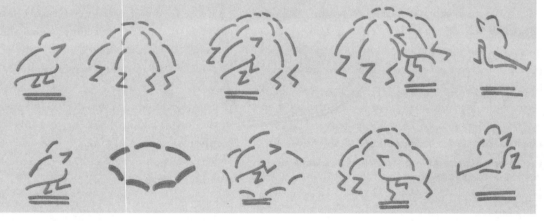

6. "Augurs of Spring—Dance of the Maidens." Notation of floor patterns from an extensive reconstruction notebook by Millicent Hodson, based in part on documentation by Vera Krassovskaya, *Russkii Baletnyi Teatr Nachalaxx Veka/The Russian Ballet Theatre at the Beginning of the Twentieth Century* (Leningrad, 1971), 426, from passages translated by Susan Cook Summer, Stravinsky-Diaghilev Foundation, New York. The double line signifies the witch in motion. During composition of *Le Sacre du Printemps*, Stravinsky wrote in a letter to Roerich: "The picture of the old woman in a squirrel fur sticks in my mind. She is constantly before my eyes as I compose the 'Divination with Twigs': I see her running in front of the group, stopping them sometimes, and interrupting the rhythmic flow. I am convinced that the action must be danced and not pantomimed, which is why I have connected—a smooth jointure with which I am very pleased—the 'Dance of the Maidens' and the 'Divination with Twigs.'" (September 26, 1911, published in the appendix, *The Rite of Spring Sketches, 1911–1913*), 30.

Stravinsky's score may be the synapse to what Roerich gave Nijinsky.

VII. Nijinsky's Relatives (Los Angeles and San Francisco, December 1979)

During a conversation last spring with John Webley at the Ballet Rambert, I stated my interest, among the current versions of *Le Sacre du Printemps*, in the choreography by Glen Tetley. "Well then, why don't you tell him yourself?" Webley said, opening the door to the next room. As if by magic, Glen Tetley began to tell me his own engrossing adventures with *Le Sacre* (American Ballet Theatre; the actual premiere, however, was with the Bavarian State Opera Ballet, Munich, April 1974). He also spoke of history, modern dance, and Nijinsky's work with his sister Bronislava. "They called what they did New Dance," he explained. "You must go to Los Angeles and talk with Bronislava's daughter." Irina Nijinska traveled and taught with her mother for years. She has preserved the rare journals and choreography notebooks that Bronislava wrote throughout her long life. These writings comprise much of the text in the biography that Irina Nijinska is now completing about her mother.[27] When I went to Los Angeles, we spoke at length about Bronislava's school in Kiev where she developed ideas discovered in Nijinsky's *Sacre* and other dances. Bronislava worked in secret with Nijinsky on his first experiments for *Le Sacre*, especially on the Dance of the Chosen Virgin. As Bronislava told the story, Nijinsky would sit or stand for a time, meditating on the movement. Then he would go to the center of the floor, take a posture, and begin to dance. Bronislava watched him silently, then as soon as he stopped, she repeated everything so that none of his steps would get lost. As they progressed, developing the trance-like movements of the solo, he had her visualize the skies in Roerich's paintings while she danced. It would be a disservice in a short space to summarize the knowledge Irina Nijinska communicates with such ardent passion and factual detail. Suffice it to say that I came to understand the reconstruction of *Le Sacre* to be one step in the rediscovery of Nijinsky's technique. It is not so much a dance technique as a technique of making dances, a creative method that generates from posture a unique vocabulary of movement for every new dance.

My adventures to date concluded appropriately with Nijinsky's daughter, Kyra—dancer, musician, painter, poet, and mystic. She was kind enough to see me at her home in San Francisco, even though it was Christmas afternoon. She makes you feel Nijinsky's spirit and hear the creative plea of his *Diary*. "I want to dance, to draw, to play the piano, to write verses, I want to love everybody. That is the object of my life."[28] Kyra Nijinsky sends out waves of artistic energy. She sang and danced and brought out her favorite paintings—madonnas, mystical roses, Nijinsky as the god of the dance. Her blues and greens, solid and intense, catch light like icons from touches of gold and silver leaf. Standing in her kitchen, looking at her work, I remembered a letter Stravinsky kept. Nijinsky wrote him, ecstatic with creativity:

> I know what *Le Sacre du Printemps* will be when everything is as we both want it. For some it will open new horizons, huge horizons flooded with different rays of sun. People will see new and different colors and different lines, all different, unexpected, and beautiful. . . .[29]

Notes

1. The description combines accounts by a London critic, *The Times*, July 27, 1913, and W. A. Propert, *The Russian Ballet in Western Europe, 1909–1920* (London: John Lane, Bodley Head, 1921), 81. The *Times* review is conveniently reprinted in Nesta MacDonald, *Diaghilev Observed* (New York: Dance Horizons; London: Dance Books), 103.

2. Ibid.

3. From Stravinsky's translation of the libretto, repro-

duced in Vera Stravinsky and Robert Craft, *Stravinsky in Pictures and Documents* (New York: Simon & Schuster, 1978), 75.

4. Richard Buckle provides a wonderful composite of many different accounts in his definitive biography, *Nijinsky* (New York: Simon & Schuster, 1971, now an Avon paperback), 299–302.

5. From a review in the *Daily Mail*, London, July 12, 1913, quoted in MacDonald, *Diaghilev Observed*, 100.

6. The dream is described in the context of Stravinsky's working process on *Le Sacre* in Robert Craft, "*The Rite of Spring*: Genesis of a Masterpiece," a lecture from 1966 which was later published in *The Rite of Spring Sketches 1911–1913* (London: Boosey & Hawkes, 1969), xvi.

7. John E. Bowlt, "Two Russian Maecanases, Savva Mamontov and Princess Tenisheva," *Apollo* (London, December 1973), 444–453. More needs to be known about the work Roerich and Tenisheva did together. Roerich himself began the documentation in *Talachkino, L'Art Décoratif des ateliers de la princesse Tenichef* (St. Petersburg, 1906).

8. From Stravinsky's translation of the libretto and two versions of the scenario by Roerich in Stravinsky and Craft, *Stravinsky in Pictures and Documents*, 75–76; my synthesis of the scenario also reflects reports by contemporary critics.

9. Conversations with Irina Nijinska and family, Los Angeles, December 17–18, 1979.

10. Nicholas Roerich, "Sacre," address at the Wannamaker Auditorium, under the auspices of the League of Composers, 1930, an event surely given in conjunction with the League's sponsorship of the American premiere of *Le Sacre* as a ballet. Roerich once again did the décor as he had in 1920 when Diaghilev revived the work, commissioning new choreography by Leonide Massine, who presented his version again for the 1930 production, with Martha Graham in the solo role of the Chosen Virgin (New York, Metropolitan Opera House, April 23). The address is published in Nicholas Roerich, *The Realm of Light* (New York: New Era Library, 1931), 185–191.

11. The Suvretta House concert (January 19, 1919, St. Moritz, Switzerland) is documented by Buckle, *Nijinsky*, 406–408, from the points of view of Nijinsky, his wife Romola, and a stranger, Maurice Sandoz, who later wote an essay about it. The event, with its opening confrontation of the audience and its improvised but ritualistic protest against war, is the prototype of a whole genre of anti-war performances in the United States and Europe during the Vietnam war, which is not to say that Nijinsky's elegy was sufficiently known about to serve as a model. The account by Sandoz, useful for its detail on gesture, is published in

his *Diaghilev-Nijinsky and Other Vignettes* (New York: Kamin, 1956), 41–47.

12. Buckle, *Nijinsky*, 348–349, and Romola Nijinsky's own version in her *Nijinsky* (London: Gollancz, 1933), 226–239.

13. Robert Craft, "Nijinsky and 'Le Sacre,'" *New York Review of Books*, April 15, 1976, 39. Kirstin's book was published in New York by Alfred A. Knopf in 1975.

14. The interview with Dame Marie Rambert took place at her home in London on April 20, 1979. Her recollections in *Quicksilver* (London and New York: Macmillan, 1972), include a number of references to *Le Sacre*.

15. *L'Après-midi d'un Faune*, music by Claude Debussy, décor by Leon Bakst, Paris, Théâtre du Châtelet, May 29, 1912.

16. From an interview in the *Pall Mall Gazette*, February 15, 1915, quoted in MacDonald, *Diaghilev Observed*, 90.

17. Some of the rumors about the existence of Nijinsky notations derive from a project by Madame Legat, the wife of Nicolas Legat, one of Nijinsky's teachers. Mme. Legat wanted to make Nijinsky's system available to the public. Her lecture on the subject was reviewed by *Dance and Dancers* (London, August 1956, 35 and 37): "Although Madame Legat has Madame Romola Nijinsky's permission to consult the original manuscripts, her knowledge is not based on these but on a poor French translation." The reviewer seems not to have doubted the existence of all the reputed manuscripts; "it is interesting to learn that Nijinsky wrote down all his own ballets by this system as well as *Les Sylphides* and *Petrushka*."

18. Maurice Sandoz, *Diaghilev-Nijinsky and Other Vignettes*, 39.

19. Valentine Gross dated the sketches and reflected on them in her handwritten *Journal* (Theatre Collection, Victoria and Albert Museum); "La seconde fois que j'assistai au *Sacre du Printemps*, le 3 juin, j'emportai come d'habitude avec moi un petit carnet et des bouts de crayons bleus. Dans la demi obscurité de la salle je pris de notes filiformes, sténographiées à ma manière de la danse et de la musique. Quelques unes sont devenues indéchiffrables dans ces centames de lignes en mouvement sue les poussières des sous. Pour moi, les unes évoquant les autres, les dances de ce ballet y sont vivantes et je ne peux extendre la musique sans voir presque malgré moi ce que j'ai vu." Translation: "The second time that I saw *Le Sacre du Printemps*, June 3 [1913], I took with me, as usual, a little sketchbook and stubs of blue crayon. In the semi-darkness of the theater, I took rough, stenographic notes, in my style, of the dance and music. Some of them became indecipherable among the

hundreds of lines in motion on top of the debris of those underneath. For me, each one evoking the others, the dances of this ballet are alive among them, and I cannot hear the music without seeing, almost in spite of myself, what I saw then."

20. The pages of the notebook are loose, so the original sequence is not intact. Some of the sketches reappear as more finished pencil drawings which Gross identified with bars of music (see figure 4). The rest of the sketches can, through cross-referencing with verbal accounts and other sources, be identified by sections of the ballet.

21. *Variety*, New York, July 4, 1979.

22. Introduction to *Diary* excerpts, no author cited, 6.

23. Jean Cocteau, "On Diaghilev and Nijinsky," *The Difficulty of Being* (Monaco: Editions du Rocher, 1957; first American edition, trans. Elizabeth Sprigge, New York: Corward-McCass, 1967), 45.

24. Louis Speyer, "Reminiscences," unpublished manuscript, written April 1979, in Brookline, Mass.; the manuscript is on file at the Stravinsky-Diaghilev Foundation, New York.

25. Nicholas Roerich, "Sacre," 186.

26. Quoted by Taruskin from *Melodika kalendarnyx peser* (Leningrad, 1975), 78–81, on page 22 of his paper, "(various accounts) bear witness to the magic function of the movements, the incessant movements of the springtime songs, whose purpose was to facilitate the quick awakening of nature—the growth of grass, the opening up of the rivers, the flight of birds, and so on. . . . These descriptions make clear *the connection between the performance of the spring invocations and some form of action*" [italics original to Taruskin's source].

27. Madame Nijinska's memoir is *Bronislava Nijinska, Early Memoirs,* trans. and ed. Irina Nijinska and Jean Rawlinson, with intro. by and in consultation with Anna Kisselgoff (New York: Holt, Rinehart & Winston, 1981).

28. *The Diary of Vaslav Nijinsky*, ed. Romola Nijinsky (New York: Simon & Schuster, 1936; paperback edition, Berkeley: University of California Press, 1968), 186.

29. Quoted in Craft, "Nijinsky and 'Le Sacre.'" In conclusion I wish to acknowledge Prof. VèVè Clark for documents sent from the University of California, Berkeley.

Five Premises for a Culturally Sensitive Approach to Dance

DEIDRE SKLAR

In the course of preparing the oral defense for my doctoral dissertation—a "movement ethnography" of a religious fiesta performed annually in Las Cruces, New Mexico—I elaborated a list of working premises for an ethnographic approach to movement analysis.[1] These premises, I argued, are the essential theoretical parameters for considering movement or dance in cultural context. I offer these working premises here to encourage an examination and widening of the frames through which we look at and conceptualize dance and movement.

1. Movement knowledge is a kind of cultural knowledge.

To speak of movement as a way of knowing implies that the way people move is as much a clue to who they are as the way they speak. (It was Allegra Fuller Snyder who first conceptualized the idea of dance as a "way of knowing.")[2] The postures and movements of people in an Episcopalian church congregation, for example, are not only different from the postures and movements of people at a Pentecostal meeting, they embody different social and religious realities. Likewise, someone performing the body postures and movements of ballet embodies a piece of "cultural knowledge" that is different from the knowledge embodied by a performer of the hula. If I move in an Episcopalian church the way I would in a Pentecostal, or if I dance in a ballet with the movements and aes-

thetic appropriate to a hula, I would immediately be recognized as "not belonging."

The way people move is more than biology, more than art, and more than entertainment. All movement must be considered as an *embodiment* of cultural knowledge, a kinesthetic equivalent, that is not quite equivalent, to using the local language. Movement is an essential aspect of culture that has been undervalued and underexamined, even trivialized. It is time to deal with movement in a culturally sensitive way and to give movement a more central place in the study of culture and culture a more central place in the study of movement.

2. Movement knowledge is conceptual and emotional as well as kinesthetic.

Especially in the codified and stylized movement of dance and ritual, movement embodies ideas about life's "large questions": Where do I belong in the world? How do human beings behave? Where do I come from and with whom do I go through life? What do I value? Embedded in the kneeling, sitting, and standing scenario of an Episcopalian church ritual is cognizance and acceptance of Christian doctrine. Embedded in the forms and aesthetics of ballet, as Joann Kealiino-homoku points out, are the concepts and values of European chivalry, in which are embedded, in turn, powerful conventions about idealized man-ness and woman-ness.[3] The moves of church and stage literally *embody* culture-specific ideas about nature, society, and the cosmos.

Further, the postures and movements of church and stage don't only embody people's *ideas* of order and meaning, they trigger emotions about these as well. For, beneath concepts, movement inevitably involves feeling. Simply to move is to feel something as the body changes. More important, habitual patterns of movement are colored with associated emotions. For a person who has gone to an Episcopalian church every week of her life, the sensory triggers of church performance, including the required uncrossed legs and straight spine, the smell of incense, and the proximity of other bodies, call up emotions. So, too, does the sight, sound, and vicarious kinesthetic sensation of watching a ballet for someone accustomed to ballet. However, although a virtuoso ballet duet might bring tears of joy to an audience weaned on ballet, it would be unlikely to have the same effect on a Hawaiian weaned on hula. The concrete and sensory, in other words *bodily*, aspects of social life provide the glue that holds world views and cosmologies, values and political convictions, together. From this follow two related premises:

3. Movement knowledge is intertwined with other kinds of cultural knowledge.

4. One has to look beyond movement to get at its meaning.

When a man in church slips into a kneel, he is not just doing something with his body; he is honoring a divine being. As a researcher, I need to know something about that being to understand the man's experience of kneeling. I might be able to identify a quality of humility in his kneeling posture, but I couldn't know that both the kneeling and the humility have to do with the complex relationships between living human beings and a divinity called Jesus Christ. Unless I asked somebody. Likewise, I couldn't know that the moves of ballet refer to codes of chivalry and medieval court rituals,

unless someone told me or unless I opened some books. The concepts embodied in movement are not necessarily evident in the movement itself. To understand movement as cultural behavior, one has to move into words. Nonetheless, and this is my final premise:

5. Movement is always an immediate corporeal experience.

Although one must resort to words to understand the symbolic meaning of movement, talking cannot reveal what is known through the *media* of movement. The cultural knowledge that is embodied in movement can only be known via movement. This is why I am uncomfortable with the currently popular semiotic metaphor which treats everything as "texts" to be "read." The metaphor is certainly useful, but it overvalues the visual while ignoring the kinesthetic. What I know through kneeling in church is different from what I know through reading the Bible, even though the two are connected. Putting my body through the motions of kneeling, getting down on my knees, provides me with a unique bodily experience that cannot be duplicated in words. In order to understand the knowledge embodied in movement, one must approach movement as immediate corporeal experience.

In my own research, I tried to understand the movement experience of people whose cultural assumptions were entirely different from my own. How, then, could I come to understand, or even appreciate, their movement experience? My answer was threefold. I observed and analyzed movement in detail and qualitatively, for it is the "how," rather than the "what" of moving that gives clues beyond visual effect toward the sensations and feelings of moving. Second, I immersed myself in the actions and concepts of people's everyday lives for almost two years, talking with people, not just about dance, but about virtually everything. Finally, and most important for approaching the lived-through experience of dancing, I relied heavily on a process that I call "empathic kinesthetic perception."

Empathic kinesthetic perception suggests a combination of mimesis and empathy. Paradoxically, it implies that one has to close one's eyes to look at movement, ignoring its visual effects and concentrating instead on feeling oneself to be in the other's body, moving.[4] Whereas visual perception implies an "object" to be perceived from a distance with the eyes alone, empathic kinesthetic perception implies a bridging between subjectivities. This kind of "connected knowing" produces a very intimate kind of knowledge, a taste of those ineffable movement experiences that can't be easily put into words. Paradoxically, as feminist psychologist Judith Jordan points out, the kind of temporary joining that occurs in empathy produces not a blurry merger but an articulated perception of differences.

At the same time that I perceived empathically and kinesthetically, however, I also relied on words. I asked dancers what their experience had been and also how they interpreted their experiences. Talking served as a check against the dangers of projection. My research went back and forth between mimesis, observation, and conceptualization, combining the empathic kinesthetic techniques I'd developed with more traditional research methods.

In summary, based on the premise that movement embodies cultural knowledge, I am advocating an approach that considers movement performance not just as visual spectacle but as kinesthetic, conceptual, and emotional experience that depends upon cultural learning. Since we all inevitably embody our own very particular cultural perspectives, we must do more than look at movement when we write about dance.

Notes

1. Deidre Sklar, "Enacting Religious Belief: A Movement Ethnography of the Annual Fiesta of Tortugas, New Mexico" (Ph.D. diss., New York University, 1991).

2. Allegra Fuller Snyder, "The Dance Symbol," in *CORD Research Annual VI: New Dimensions in Dance Research: Anthropology and Dance–The American Indian,* ed. Tamara Comstock (New York: CORD, 1974), 213–224.

3. Joann Kealiinohomoku, "An Anthropologist Looks at Ballet as a Form of Ethnic Dance," *Impulse* (1970): 24–33.

4. Judith Jordan, "Empathy and Self Boundaries," *Work in Progress* 16. (Wellesley, Mass.: Stone Center for Developmental Services and Studies, 1984).

An Anthropologist Looks at Ballet as a Form of Ethnic Dance

JOANN KEALIINOHOMOKU

It is good anthropology to think of ballet as a form of ethnic dance. Currently, that idea is unacceptable to most Western dance scholars. This lack of agreement shows clearly that something is amiss in the communication of ideas between the scholars of dance and those of anthropology, and this paper is an attempt to bridge that communication gap.

The faults and errors of anthropologists in their approach to dance are many, but they are largely due to their hesitation to deal with something which seems esoteric and out of their field of competence. However, a handful of dance anthropologists are trying to rectify this by publishing in the social science journals and by participating in formal and informal meetings with other anthropologists.

By ethnic dance, anthropologists mean to convey the idea that all forms of dance reflect the cultural traditions within which they developed. Dancers and dance scholars, as this paper will show, use this term, and the related terms *ethnologic, primitive,* and *folk dance,* differently and, in fact, in a way which reveals their limited knowledge of non-Western dance forms.

In preparing to formulate this paper, I reread in an intense period pertinent writings by DeMille, Haskell, Holt, the Kinneys, Kirstein, La Meri, Martin, Sachs, Sorell, and Terry. In addition I carefully reread the definitions pertaining to dance in *Webster's New International Dictionary,* the second edition definitions which were written by Humphrey, and the third edition definitions which were written by Kurath. Although these

and other sources are listed in the endnotes, I name these scholars here to focus my frame of reference.[1]

The experience of this intense rereading as an anthropologist rather than as a dancer, was both instructive and disturbing. The readings are rife with unsubstantiated deductive reasoning, poorly documented "proofs," a plethora of half-truths, many out-and-out errors, and a pervasive ethnocentric bias. Where the writers championed non-Western dance they were either apologists or patronistic. Most discouraging of all, these authors saw fit to change only the pictures and not the text when they reissued their books after as many as seventeen years later; they only updated the Euro-American dance scene.

This survey of the literature reveals an amazing divergence of opinions. We are able to read that the origin of dance was in play and that it was not in play, that it was for magical and religious purposes, and that it was not for those things; that it was for courtship and that it was not for courtship; that it was the first form of communication and that communication did not enter into dance until it became an "art." In addition we can read that it was serious and purposeful and that at the same time it was an outgrowth of exuberance, was totally spontaneous, and originated in the spirit of fun. Moreover, we can read that it was only a group activity for tribal solidarity and that it was strictly for the pleasure and self-expression of the one dancing. We can learn also, that animals danced before man did, and yet that dance is a human activity!

It has been a long time since anthropologists concerned themselves with unknowable origins, and I will not add another origin theory for dance, because I don't know anyone who was there. Our dance writers, however, suggest evidence for origins from archeological finds, and from models exemplified by contemporary primitive groups. For the first, one must remember that man had been on this earth for a long time before he made cave paintings and statuary, so that archeological finds can hardly tell us about the beginnings of dance. For the second set of evidence, that of using models from contemporary primitives, one must not confuse the word "primitive" with "primeval," even though one author actually does equate these two terms.[2] About the dance of primeval man we really know nothing. About primitive dance, on the other hand, we know a great deal. The first thing that we know is that there is no such thing as *a* primitive dance. There *are* dances performed by primitives, and they are too varied to fit any stereotype.

It is a gross error to think of groups of peoples or their dances as being monolithic wholes. "The African dance" never existed; there are, however, Dahomean dances, Hausa dances, Masai dances, and so forth. "The American Indian" is a fiction and so is a prototype of "Indian dance." There are, however, Iroquois, Kwakiutl, and Hopis, to name a few, and they have dances.

Despite all anthropological evidence to the contrary, however, Western dance scholars set themselves up as authorities on the characteristics of primitive dance. Sorell combines most of these so-called characteristics of the primitive stereotype. He tells us that primitive dancers have no technique, and no artistry, but that they are "unfailing masters of their bodies"! He states that their dances are disorganized and frenzied, but that they are able to translate all their feelings and emotions into movement! He claims the dances are spontaneous but also purposeful! Primitive dances, he tells us, are serious but social! He claims that they have "complete freedom" but that men and women can't dance together. He qualifies that last statement by

saying that men and women dance together after the dance degenerates into an orgy! Sorell also asserts that primitives cannot distinguish between the concrete and the symbolic, that they dance for every occasion, and that they stamp around a lot! Further, Sorell asserts that dance in primitive societies is a special prerogative of males, especially chieftains, shamans, and witch doctors.[3] Kirstein also characterizes the dances of "natural, unfettered societies" (whatever that means). Although the whole body participates according to Kirstein, he claims that the emphasis of movement is with the lower half of the torso. He concludes that primitive dance is repetitious, limited, unconscious, and with "retardative and closed expression"! Still, though it may be unconscious, Kirstein tells his readers that dance is useful to the tribe and that it is based on the seasons. Primitive dance, or as he phrases it, "earlier manifestations of human activity," is everywhere found to be "almost identically formulated." He never really tells us what these formulations are except that they have little to offer in methodology or structure, and that they are examples of "instinctive exuberance."[4]

Terry describes the functions of primitive dance, and he uses American Indians as his model. In his book *The Dance in America* he writes sympathetically towards American Indians and "his primitive brothers." However, his paternalistic feelings on the one hand, and his sense of ethnocentricity on the other, prompt him to set aside any thought that people with whom he identifies could share contemporarily those same dance characteristics, because he states "the white man's dance heritage, except for the most ancient of days, was wholly different."[5]

With the rejection of the so-called primitive characteristics for the white man, it is common to ascribe these characteristics to groups existing among African tribes, Indians of North and South America, and Pacific peoples. These are the same peoples who are labeled by these authors as "ethnic." No wonder that balletomanes reject the idea that ballet is a form of ethnic dance! But Africans, North and South Amerindians, and Pacific peoples would be just as horrified to be called ethnic under the terms of the stereotype. Those so-called characteristics-as-a-group do not prevail anywhere!

Another significant obstacle to the identification of Western dancers with non-Western dance forms, be they primitive or "ethnologic" in the sense that Sorell uses the latter term as "the art expression of a race" which is "executed for the enjoyment and edification of the audience" is the double myth that the dance grew out of some spontaneous mob action and that once formed, became frozen.[6] American anthropologists and many folklorists have been most distressed about the popularity of these widespread misconceptions. Apparently it satisfies our own ethnocentric needs to believe in the uniqueness of our dance forms, and it is much more convenient to believe that primitive dances, like Topsy, just "growed," and that "ethnological" dances are part of an unchanging tradition. Even books and articles which purport to be about the dances of the *world* devote three-quarters of the text and photos to Western dance. We explicate our historic eras, our royal patrons, dancing masters, choreographers, and performers. The rest of the world is condensed diachronically and synchronically to the remaining quarter of the book. This smaller portion, which must cover all the rest of the world, is usually divided up so that the portions at the beginning imply that the ethnic forms fit on some kind of an evolutionary continuum, and the remaining portions at the end of the book for, say, American Negro dance, give the appearance of a post-script, as if they too "also ran." In short we treat Western dance, ballet particularly, as if it was the one great divinely ordained apogee of the performing arts. This notion is exemplified, and reinforced, by the way dance photos are published. Unless the non-Western performer has made a "hit" on our stages, we seldom bother to give him a name in the captions, even though he might be considered a fine artist among his peers (Martin is the exception). For example, see Claire Holt's article "Two Dance Worlds."[7] The captions under the photos of Javanese dancers list no names, but you may be sure that we are always told when Martha Graham appears in a photo. A scholar friend of mine was looking over the books by our dance historians, and he observed that they were not interested in the whole world of dance; they were really only interested in *their* world of dance. Can anyone deny this allegation?

Let it be noted, once and for all, that within the various "ethnologic" dance worlds there are also patrons, dancing masters, choreographers, and performers with names woven into a very real historical fabric. The bias which those dancers have toward their own dance and artists is just as strong as ours. The difference is that they usually don't pretend to be scholars of other dance forms, nor even very much interested in them. It is instructive, however, to remind ourselves that all dances are subject to change and development no matter how convenient we may find it to dismiss some form as practically unchanged for 2,000 years.[8] It is convenient to us, of course, because once having said that, we feel that our job is finished.

As for the presumed lack of creators of dance among primitive and folk groups, let us reconsider that assumption after reading Martin's statement:

> In simpler cultures than ours we find a mass of art actually treated and practiced by the people as a whole.[9]

The first question which such a statement raises is what is a "mass of art"? Martin never really defines art, but if he means art as a refined aesthetic expression, then it can be asked how such could ever be a collective product. Does he mean that it appeared spontaneously? Does he really think there can be art without artists? And if he believes that there must be artists, does he mean to imply that a "people as a whole" are artists? If so, what a wonderful group of people they must be. Let us learn from them!

Doubtless, Martin probably will say that I have taken his statement to an absurd extension of his meaning, but I believe that such thoughtless statements deserve to be pushed to their extreme.

It is true that some cultures do not place the same

value on preserving the names of their innovators as we do. That is a matter of tradition also. But we must not be deceived into believing that a few hundred people all got together and with one unanimous surge created a dance tradition which, having once been created, never changed from that day forward.

Among the Hopi Indians of Northern Arizona, for example, there is no tradition of naming a choreographer. Nevertheless they definitely know who, within a Kiva group or a society, made certain innovations and why. A dramatic example of the variety permitted in what is otherwise considered to be a static dance tradition is to see, as I have, the "same" dance ceremonies performed in several different villages at several different times. To illustrate, I observed the important Hopi "bean dances" which are held every February, in five different villages during the winters of 1965 and 1968. There were the distinguishing differences between villages which are predictable differences, once one becomes familiar with a village "style." But, in addition, there were creative and not necessarily predictable differences which occurred from one time to the next. The Hopis know clearly what the predictable differences are, and they also know who and what circumstances led to the timely innovations. Not only do they know these things, but they are quite free in their evaluation of the merits and demerits of those differences, with their "own" usually (but not always) coming out as being aesthetically more satisfying.

In Martin's *Introduction to the Dance* (1939) the first plate contains two reproductions of drawings of Hopi kachinas. Judging from its position among the plates, this must be Martin's single example of dances from a primitive group. DeMille also shows Hopis as examples of primitive dancers.[10] Let us see how well the Hopis compare to the generalities attributed to primitive dancers.

Paradigm

Hopi dances are immaculately organized, are never frenzied (not even, in fact especially, in their famous snake dance), nor is there a desire to translate feelings and emotions into movement. The dances are indeed serious, if this is synonymous with purposeful, but many dances are not serious if that word negates the fact that many dances are humorous, use clowns as personnel, and contain both derision and satire. Hopi dance is also social if one is speaking as a sociologist, but they have only one prescribed genre of dance which the Hopis themselves consider "social" in the sense that they can be performed by uninitiated members of the society. Hopis would find the idea of "complete freedom" in their dance to be an alien idea, because much of the form and behavior is rigidly prescribed. Certainly they would never lapse into an orgy! Nor do they "hurl themselves on the ground and roll in the mud" after the rains begin.[11]

Hopis would be offended if you told them that they could not distinguish between the concrete and the symbolic. They are not children, after all. They certainly understand natural causes. But does it make them primitive, by definition, if they ask their gods to help their crops grow by bringing rain? Don't farmers within the mainstream of America and Europe frequently pray to a Judeo-Christian God for the same thing? Are the Hopis more illogical than we are when they dance their prayers instead of attending religious services with responsive readings, and a variety of motor activities such as rising, sitting, folding hands, and the like?

Once again assessing the Hopis in the light of the characteristics presumably found for primitive dancers, we find that Hopis don't dance for the three specific life events which supposedly are "always" recognized in dance. That is, Hopis don't dance at births, marriages, or deaths.

Obviously, it cannot be said that they dance on "every" occasion. Furthermore, the Hopi stamping would surely be a disappointment to Sorell if he expected the Hopis to "make the earth tremble under his feet."[12] DeMille might also be surprised that there is no "state of exaltation" or "ecstasy" in Hopi dance.[13]

It is true that more Hopi dances are performed by

males than by females, but females also dance under certain circumstances and for certain rituals which are the sole prerogative of females. What is more important is that women participate a great deal if one thinks of them as non-dancer participants, and one must, because it is the entire dance *event* which is important to the Hopis rather than just the actual rhythmic movement.

For the Hopis, it is meaningless to say that the primary dancers are the chieftains, witch doctors, and shamans. Traditionally they have no real "government" as such, and every clan has its own rituals and societies which are further divided according to the village in which they live. Thus everyone will participate to some degree or another in a variety of roles. There is no shaman as such, so of course there cannot be shamanistic dances. As for witch doctors, they do not dance in that role although they dance to fulfill some of their other roles in their clan and residence groups.

I do not know what is meant by a "natural, unfettered society," but whatever it is I am sure that description does not fit the Hopis. In their dance movements the whole body does not participate, and there is no pelvic movement as such. The dances are indeed repetitious, but that does not interfere in the least with the real dramatic impact of the performance. Within the "limitations" of the dance culture, Hopi dance still has an enormous range of variations, and this is especially true because the dance "event" is so richly orchestrated.

Far from being an "unconscious" dance form, Hopi dancing is a very conscious activity. And I cannot believe that it is any more "retardative" or closed within its own framework than any other dance form, bar none. Finally, I find nothing in Hopi dance that can be called "instinctively exuberant," but perhaps that is because I don't know what "instinctive exuberance" is. If it is what I think it is, such a description is inappropriate for Hopi dances.

Lest someone say that perhaps the Hopis are the exception to prove the rule, or, perhaps, that they are not really "primitive," let me make two points. First, if they are not "primitive" they do not fit into any other category offered by the dance scholars discussed in this article.

Their dances are not "folk dance" as described, nor do they have "ethnologic dances," nor "art dances," nor "theatre dance" as these terms are used in the writings under consideration. Clearly, in the light of these writers' descriptions, they are a "primitive," "ethnic" group with dances in kind. Secondly, I know of no group anywhere which fits the descriptions for primitive dance such as given by DeMille, Sorell, Terry, and Martin. Certainly I know of no justification for Haskell's statement that "many dances of primitive tribes still living are said to be identical with those of birds and apes."[14] Unfortunately, Haskell does not document any of his statements and we cannot trace the source of such a blatant piece of misinformation.

It is necessary to hammer home the idea that there is no such thing as a "primitive dance" form. Those who teach courses called "primitive dance" are perpetuating a dangerous myth. As a corollary to this let it be noted that no living primitive group will reveal to us the way our European ancestors behaved. Every group has had its own unique history and has been subject to both internal and external modifications. Contemporary primitives are not children in fact, nor can they be pigeonholed into some convenient slot on an evolutionary scale.

I suggest that one cause for so much inaccurate and shocking misunderstanding on the subject of primitive groups is due to an overdependence on the words of Sir James Frazer and Curt Sachs whose works have been outdated as source material for better than three decades.[15] In their stead I would suggest that they read some of the works of Gertrude P. Kurath, whose bibliography appeared in the January, 1970 issue of *Ethnomusicology.* This and other suggested readings are given at the end of this article.

Definitions

It is disconcerting to discover that writers tend to use key words without attempting real definitions which are neither too exclusive nor too inclusive. Even the word *dance,* itself, is never adequately defined to apply cross-culturally through time and space. Instead of definitions we are given descriptions, which are a different matter altogether. I have been closely questioned as to the need for definitions "as long as we all mean the same thing anyway," and I have even been asked what difference it makes what we call something as long as we all understand how some term is being used. The answers are twofold: without the discipline of attempting to define specific terms we are not sure we do all mean the same thing or that we understand how a term is being used. On the other hand, the tacit agreement about frames of reference can distort the focus of emphasis rather than giving the broadly based objectivity which comes from using a term denotatively.

For seven years I pondered over a definition of dance, and in 1965 I tentatively set out the following definition which has since undergone some slight modifications. In its current form it reads:

> Dance is a transient mode of expression, performed in a given form and style by the human body moving in space. Dance occurs through purposefully selected and controlled rhythmic movements; the resulting phenomenon is recognized as dance both by the performer and the observing members of a given group.[16]

The two crucial points which distinguish this definition from others are the limiting of dance to that of human behavior since there is no reason to believe that birds or apes perform with the *intent* to dance. Intent to dance and acknowledgment of the activity as dance by a given group is the second distinguishing feature of my definition. This is the crucial point for applying the definition cross-culturally as well as setting dance apart from other activities which might appear to be dance to the outsider but which are considered, say, sports or ritual to the participants. *Webster's International Dictionary* shows much contrast in the definitions of dance between the second and third editions. The reason for the contrasts is clear when it is understood that a performer-choreographer of Western dance wrote the dance entries for the second edition (Doris Humphrey), while an ethnochoreologist (Gertrude P. Kurath) wrote the entries for the third edition.

We cannot accept Kirstein's contention that "it is apparent . . . that the idea of tension, from the very beginning, has been foremost in people's minds when they have thought about dancing seriously enough to invent or adapt word-sounds for it."[17] Alber (Charles J. Alber 1970, personal communication) assures me that both Japanese and Mandarin Chinese have time-honored words for dance and related activities and that the idea of tension does not occur at all in these words. Clearly Kirstein's statement indicates that he has not looked beyond the models set out in Indo-European languages. Can we really believe that only white Europeans are "advanced" enough to speak about dance?

The notion of tension through the etymology of European words for dance does reveal something about the Western aesthetic of dance which is apparent from the Western dance ideals of pull-up, body lift, and bodily extensions. Elsewhere these things are not highly valued. Indeed my "good" Western-trained body alignment and resultant tension is a handicap in performing dances from other cultures. Martin seems to have the greatest insight in the relativity of dance aesthetics when he describes dance as a universal urge but without a universal form.[18] Further he states:

> It is impossible to say that any of these approaches is exclusively right or wrong, better or worse than any other. . . . They are all absolutely right, therefore, for the specific circumstances under which they have been created.[19]

Indeed Martin comes the closest to the kind of relativity which most American anthropologists feel is necessary for observing and analyzing any aspect of culture and human behavior.[20] It is true that Sorell and others speak of differences caused by environment and other pertinent circumstances, but Sorell also ascribes much of the difference to "race," to "racial memory," and to "innate" differences which are "in the blood."[21] These ideas are so outdated in current anthropology, that I might believe his book was written at the end of the nineteenth century rather than in 1967.

It is true that many cross-cultural differences in dance style and dance aesthetics are due to both genetically determined physical differences and learned cultural patterns. In some cases the differences are clear. For example, a heavy Mohave Indian woman could not, and would not perform the jumps of the Masai people of East Africa. Other differences are not clear because they are part of a chicken/egg argument until further research is done and until more of the right questions are asked. We do not know, for example, whether people who squat easily with both feet flat on the ground do so because their leg tendons are genetically different from non-squatters, or if anyone could have the same tendon configuration if they habitually assumed such postures.[22] As for "innate" qualities, we have almost no real evidence. There is nothing to support claims such as "barefoot savages have an ear for rhythms most Europeans lack."[23] There is much we do not know about bodies and genetics and cultural dynamics, and in addition, we are especially ignorant about systems of aesthetics. It would be wiser for Western dance scholars to leave qualifying remarks and openendedness in their discussions of these things, or else these scholars may have a lot of recanting to do.

Two terms which now require discussion are "primitive dance" and "folk dance." These comments are to be understood against the framework of my definition of dance which I have already given.

British, and especially American, folklorists are concerned with defining the "folk" in order to know what "folk dances" are. Our dance scholars, on the other hand, usually use "folk dance" as a kind of catch-all term. For example, DeMille lists Azuma Kabuki under her chapter on folk dance companies.[24] To call this highly refined theatrical form "folk dance" doesn't agree with Sorell's argument that folk dance is dance that has not gone "through a process of refinement"; that has not been "tamed."[25] Perhaps such discrepancies help to show why definitions are so important and

what a state of confusion can exist when we presume we all "mean the same thing."

Rather than following Sachs's contention that the "folk" or the "peasant" is an evolutionary stage between primitive and civilized man, I shall follow the more anthropologically sophisticated distinctions which are discussed by the anthropologist Redfield in his book *Peasant Society and Culture*.[26] In brief, a primitive society is an autonomous and self-contained system with its own set of customs and institutions. It may be isolated or it may have more or less contact with other systems. It is usually economically independent and the people are often, if not always, nonliterate. (Notice that the term nonliterate refers to a group which has never had a written language of their own devising. This is quite different from the term illiterate which means that there is a written language, but an illiterate is not sufficiently educated to know the written form. Thus DeMille's statement that the primitives are illiterate is a contradiction of terms.)[27] In contrast, peasant or folk societies are not autonomous. Economically and culturally such a community is in a symbiotic relationship with a larger society with which it constantly interacts. It is the "little tradition of the largely unreflective many" which is incomplete without the "great tradition of the reflective few." Often the people in peasant societies are more or less illiterate. If one adds the word dance to the above descriptions of primitive and folk (or peasant) there might be a more objective agreement on what is meant by "primitive dance" and by "folk dance."

Another troublesome term is that of "ethnic dance," as I have already indicated. In the generally accepted anthropological view, ethnic means a group which holds in common genetic, linguistic, and cultural ties, with special emphasis on cultural tradition. By definition, therefore, every dance form must be an ethnic form. Although claims have been made for universal dance forms (such as Wisnoe Wardhana has been attempting to develop in Java: personal communication 1960), or international forms (such has been claimed for ballet by Terry), in actuality neither a universal form nor a truly international form of dance is in existence and it is doubtful whether any such dance form can ever exist except in theory.[28] DeMille says this, in effect, when she writes that "theatre always reflects the culture that produces it."[29] However, others insist on some special properties for ballet. La Meri insists that "the ballet is not an ethnic dance because it is the product of the social customs and artistic reflections of several widely-differing national cultures."[30] Nevertheless, ballet is a product of the Western world, and it is a dance form developed by Caucasians who speak Indo-European languages and who share a common European tradition. Granted that ballet is international in that it "belongs" to European countries plus groups of European descendants in the Americas. But, when ballet appears in such countries as Japan or Korea it becomes a borrowed and alien form. Granted also that ballet has had a complex history of influences, this does not undermine its effectiveness as an ethnic form. Martin tells us this, although he probably could not guess that his statement would be used for such a proof:

> The great spectacular dance form of the Western world is, of course, the ballet. . . . Properly, the term ballet refers to a particular form of theater dance, which came into being in the Renaissance and which has a tradition, technic and an aesthetic basis all its own.[31]

Further quotations could be made to show the ethnicity of ballet, such as Kirstein's opening remarks in his 1935 book, *Dance*.

Ethnicity of Ballet

I have made listings of the themes and other characteristics of ballet and ballet performances, and these lists show over and over again just how "ethnic" ballet is. Consider, for example, how Western is the tradition of the proscenium stage, the usual three part performance which lasts for about two hours, our star system, our use of curtain calls and applause, and our usage of French terminology. Think how culturally revealing it is to see the stylized Western customs enacted on the stage, such as the mannerisms from the age of chivalry, courting, weddings, christenings, burial, and mourning customs. Think how our world view is revealed in the oft recurring themes of unrequited love, sorcery, self-sacrifice through long suffering, mistaken identity, and misunderstandings which have tragic consequences. Think how our religious heritage is revealed through pre-Christian customs such as Walpurgisnacht, through the use of biblical themes, Christian holidays such as Christmas, and the beliefs in life after death. Our cultural heritage is revealed also in the roles which appear repeatedly in our ballets such as humans transformed into animals, fairies, witches, gnomes, performers of evil magic, villains and seductresses in black, evil stepparents, royalty and peasants, and especially, beautiful pure young women and their consorts.

Our aesthetic values are shown in the long line of lifted, extended bodies, in the total revealing of legs, of small heads and tiny feet for women, in slender bodies for both sexes, and in the coveted airy quality which is best shown in the lifts and carryings of the female. To us this is tremendously pleasing aesthetically, but there are societies whose members would be shocked at the public display of the male touching the female's thighs! So distinctive is the "look" of ballet, that it is probably safe to say that ballet dances graphically rendered by silhouettes would never be mistaken for anything else. An interesting proof of this is the ballet *Koshare* which was based on a Hopi Indian story. In silhouettes of even still photos, the dance looked like ballet and not like a Hopi dance.

The ethnicity of ballet is revealed also in the kinds of flora and fauna which appear regularly. Horses and swans are esteemed fauna. In contrast we have no tradition of esteeming for theatrical purposes pigs, sharks, eagles, buffalo, or crocodiles even though these are indeed highly esteemed animals used in dance themes elsewhere in the world. In ballet, grains, roses, and lilies are suitable flora, but we would not likely find much call for taro, yams, coconuts, acorns, or squash blossoms.

Many economic pursuits are reflected in the roles played in ballet such as spinners, foresters, soldiers, even factory workers, sailors, and filling station attendants. However, we would not expect to find pottery makers, canoe builders, grain pounders, llama herders, giraffe stalkers, or slash and burn agriculturists!

The question is not whether ballet reflects its own heritage. The question is why we seem to need to believe that ballet has somehow become acultural. Why are we afraid to call it an ethnic form?

The answer, I believe, is that Western dance scholars have not used the word *ethnic* in its objective sense; they have used it as a euphemism for such old-fashioned terms as "heathen," "pagan," "savage," or the more recent term "exotic." When the term ethnic began to be used widely in the thirties, there apparently arose a problem in trying to refer to dance forms which came from "high" cultures such as India and Japan, and the term "ethnologic" gained its current meaning for dance scholars such as Sorell, Terry, and La Meri.[32] (An interesting article by Bunzell on the "Sociology of Dance" in the 1949 edition of *Dance Encyclopedia* rejects the use of the word "art" for these dance forms, however. In the context of his criticism, his point is well taken.)[33] I do not know why La Meri chose to discard this usage and substituted the word "ethnic" for "ethnologic" in her 1967 version of the *Dance Encyclopedia* article. She did not otherwise change her article, and since it was originally written with the above mentioned dichotomy implicit in her discussion, her 1967 version becomes illogical. (For a critical review of the *Dance Encyclopedia* and especially of La Meri's entries see Renouf.)[34]

It is not clear to me who first created the dichotomy between "ethnic dance" and "ethnologic dance." Certainly this dichotomy is meaningless to anthropologists. As a matter of fact, European cultural anthropologists often prefer to call themselves ethnologists, and for them the term "ethnologic" refers to the objects of their study.[35] The term "ethnological" does not have much currency among American cultural anthropologists although they understand the term to mean "of or

relating to ethnology," and "ethnology" deals with the comparative and analytical study of cultures (see entries in *Webster's New International Dictionary,* third edition). Because "culture," in a simplified anthropological sense, includes all of the learned behavior and customs of any given group of people, there is no such thing as a cultureless people. Therefore, "ethnologic dances" should refer to a variety of dance cultures subject to comparison and analysis. Ethnic dance should mean a dance form of a given group of people who share common genetic, linguistic, and cultural ties, as mentioned before. In the most precise usage it is a redundancy to speak of "an ethnic dance," since any dance could fit that description. The term is most valid when used in a collective and contrastive way.[36]

Apparently one pan-human trait is to divide the world into "we" and "they." The Greeks did this when "they" were called *barbarians.* Similarly, the Romans called the "they" *pagans,* Hawaiians call "they" *kanaka'e,* and Hopis call the "they" *bahana.* All of these terms imply not only foreign, but creatures who are uncouth, unnatural, ignorant and, in short, less than human. The yardstick for measuring humanity, of course, is the "we." "We" are always good, civilized, superior; in short, "we" are the only creatures worthy of being considered fully human. This phenomenon reveals the world view of the speakers in every language, so far as I know. Often the phenomenon is very dramatic. According to a scholar of Mandarin and Japanese languages, in Mandarin the "they" are truly "foreign devils," and in Japanese the "they" are "outsiders" (Charles Alber, personal communication, 1970).

I suggest that, due to the social climate which rejects the connotations with which our former words for "they" were invested, and because of a certain sophistication assumed by the apologists for the "they," English-speaking scholars were hard pressed to find designators for the kinds of non-Western dance which they wished to discuss. Hence the euphemistic terms "ethnic" and "ethnologic" seemed to serve that purpose.

It is perfectly legitimate to use "ethnic" and "ethnologic" as long as we don't let those terms become connotative of the very things which caused us to abandon the other terms. We should indeed speak of ethnic dance forms, and we should not believe that this term is derisive when it includes ballet since ballet reflects the cultural traditions from which it developed.

I must make it clear that I am critical of our foremost Western dance scholars only where they have stepped outside their fields of authority. Within their fields they command my great respect, and I would not want to argue their relative merits. Scholars that they are, they will agree with me, I feel confident, that whatever are the rewards of scholarship, comfortable complacency cannot be one of them.

Notes

1. References not cited in other notes include Doris Humphrey, "Dance," and related entries, *Webster's New International Dictionary,* 2d ed., unabridged (Springfield, Mass.: Merriam, 1950); Troy and Margaret West Kinney, *The Dance,* New York: Frederick A. Stokes, 1924); Gertrude Prokosch Kurath, "Dance" and related entries, *Webster's New International Dictionary,* 3d ed., unabridged (Springfield, Mass.: Merriam, 1966); La Meri, "Ethnic Dance," in *The Dance Encyclopedia,* comp. and ed. Anatole Chujoy (New York: A. S. Barnes, 1949), 177–178; John Martin (*John Martin's Book of*) *The Dance* (New York: Tudor Publishing, 1963); Walter Terry, "Dance, History of," in *The Dance Encyclopedia,* comp. and ed. Anatole Chujoy and P. W. Manchester (New York: Simon & Schuster, 1967), 255–259; Walter Terry, "History of Dance," in *The Dance Encyclopedia,* comp. and ed. Anatole Chujoy (New York: A. S. Barnes, 1949), 238–243.

2. Walter Sorell, *The Dance through the Ages* (New York: Grosset & Dunlap, 1967), 14.

3. Ibid., 10–11.

4. Lincoln Kirstein, *The Book of Dance* (Garden City, N.Y.: Garden City Publishing, 1942), 3–5.

5. Walter Terry, *The Dance in America* (New York: Harper, 1956), 3–4, 195–198.

6. Sorell, *The Dance through the Ages,* 76.

7. Claire Holt, "Two Dance Worlds," in *Anthology of Impulse,* ed. Marian Van Tuyl (New York: Dance Horizons, 1969), 116–131.

8. Agnes DeMille, *The Book of the Dance* (New York: Golden Press, 1963), 48.

9. John Martin, *Introduction to the Dance* (New York: Norton, 1939), 15.

10. DeMille, *The Book of the Dance,* 33, 35.

11. Ibid., 35.

12. Sorell, *The Dance through the Ages,* 15.

13. DeMille, *The Book of the Dance,* 34, 67.

14. Arnold Haskell, *The Wonderful World of Dance* (New York: Garden City Books, 1960), 9.

15. Sir James Frazer, *The Golden Bough* (New York: Macmillan, 1947); Curt Sachs, *World History of the Dance,* trans. Bessie Schönberg (New York: Bonanza Books, 1937).

16. Joann Wheeler Kealiinohomoku, "A Comparative Study of Dance as a Constellation of Motor Behaviors among African and United States Negroes" (master's thesis, Northwestern University, 1965), 6 (revised 1970).

17. Lincoln Kirstein, *Dance* (New York: Putnam's Sons, 1935), 1.

18. John Martin, *The Dance* (New York: Tudor Publishing, 1946), 12.

19. Ibid., 17.

20. Martin, *Introduction to the Dance,* 92–93, 108.

21. Sorell, *The Dance through the Ages,* 75–76, 275, 282, 283.

22. See Martin, *Introduction to the Dance,* 97.

23. DeMille, *The Book of the Dance,* 48.

24. Ibid., 74.

25. Sorell, *The Dance through the Ages,* 73.

26. Sachs, *World History of the Dance,* 216; Robert Redfield, *The Little Community* and *Peasant Society and Culture* (Chicago: University of Chicago Press, 1969), 23, 40–41.

27. DeMille, *The Book of the Dance,* 23.

28. Terry, *The Dance in America,* 187.

29. DeMille, *The Book of the Dance,* 74.

30. La Meri, "Ethnic Dance," in *The Dance Encyclopedia,* ed. Anatole Chujoy and P. W. Manchester (New York: Simon & Schuster, 1967), 339.

31. Martin, *Introduction to the Dance,* 173.

32. Sorell, *The Dance through the Ages,* 72; Terry, *The*

Dance in America, 87, 196; and La Meri, "Ethnic Dance," 177–178.

33. Joseph Bunzel, "Sociology of the Dance," in *The Dance Encyclopedia* (New York: Simon & Schuster, 1967), 437.

34. Renée Renouf, "Review of *The Dance Encyclopedia*," *Ethnomusicology* 13, no. 2 (May 1969): 383–384.

35. See Herta Haselberger, "Method of Studying Ethnological Art," *Current Anthropology* 2, no. 4 (October 1961): 341.

36. Peggy Harper, "Dance in a Changing Society," *African Arts/Arts d'Afrique* 1, no. 1 (autumn 1967): 10–13, 76–77, 78–80. Harper (10) distinguishes between ethnic and theatrical dance on the basis of "integral function of a society" and dance which is "deliberately organized" to be performed for a general, impersonal audience. This dichotomy, which is based on genre rather than the society, provides a good working classification. However, the distinction fails when the terms are tested. Thus one can have ethnic dances of an ethnic society, but not theatrical dance of a theatrical society. It seems clear that "ethnic" is a more embracing category under which "traditional" and "theatrical" might be convenient subdivisions. In any case, Harper's discussion is thought-provoking.

To further investigate anthropological approaches and issues in dance research, see Adriann G. H. Claerhout, "The Concept of Primitive Applied to Art," *Current Anthropology* 6, no. 4 (October 1965); Adrienne L. Kaeppler, "Folklore as Expressed in the Dance in Tonga," *Journal of American Folklore* 80 (April –June 1967): 316; Adrienne L. Kaeppler, "The Structure of Tongan Dance" (Ph.D. diss., University of Hawaii, 1967); Joann W. Kealiinohomoku and Frank J. Gillis, "Special Bibliography: Gertrude Prokosch Kurath," *Ethnomusicology* 14, no. 1 (January 1970); Gertrude Prokosch Kurath, "Panorama of Dance Ethnology," *Current Anthropology,* 1, no. 3 (May 1960); Armistead P. Rood, "Bete Masked Dance: A View from Within," *African Arts/Arts d'Afrique* 2, no. 3 (spring 1969).

The Trouble with the Male Dancer . . .

RAMSAY BURT

"The unpleasant thing about a danseuse is that she sometimes brings along a male dancer." This is the title of one of Edouard de Beaumont's lithographs of scenes at the Paris Opera in the nineteenth century.[1] It shows a male figure dancing, while behind him slightly to one side is a ballerina with little sylph wings who turns her head deferentially towards him. He wears tights, has an ugly face, solid thighs and big hands. The artist, however, has not made him look grotesque, just less attractive than the ballerina. The implication is that the viewer would rather look at her, but the male dancer wants you to look at him, and anyway he is in the way. The title appeals to a shared prejudice about these "unpleasant things." At the end of the twentieth century, one is tempted to read into the scene more recent prejudices against the male dancer. Nevertheless the print captures a particular historical moment with its associated attitudes towards class, gender and aesthetics, all of which have had a strong influence on the development of later attitudes. Up until the nineteenth century in Europe, prejudices against the male dancer did not exist. By the end of the twentieth century these have developed and changed in response to a variety of social and historical factors. The print takes for granted that everyone knows what is wrong with the male dancer, but more or less leaves it unstated. That which is unstated, and by implication should not be stated in polite company, can be a powerful incitement to prejudice. So what then is the trouble with the male dancer?

Today one might answer this question in a number of ways, depending upon point of view and the sort of dance with which one is familiar. One might feel distaste at macho displays of male energy on the dance stage—what are they trying to prove, etc.? Or one might feel that male dancers are generally a disappointment—they just don't look very masculine. Or again one might feel that the ways in which one has seen masculinity represented in dance do not seem very relevant to one's own experience of class, race, gender, sexuality, etc. Then there are those who do enjoy watching male dance, and wish there were more male dancers around to watch. In the area of modern and experimental dance during the twentieth century, a large number of male dancers did not actually discover dance until their late teens or early twenties. This is undoubtedly largely the result of prejudices against the male dancer.

For much of the twentieth century, the dance world has tended to appear to be predominantly a feminine realm in terms of audiences, dancers, and teachers. The fact that, for example, in Britain and the United States ballet and modern dance teachers have been predominantly women has been cited as one reason for male dancers' "effeminacy."[2] But for many people, a key source of contemporary prejudice is the association between male dancers and homosexuality. It is certainly true that there are a lot of gay men involved in the dance world. Although by no means all male dancers are gay, this is what prejudice suggests. One explanation of

7. "The unpleasant thing about a danseuse is that she sometimes brings along a male dancer." Lithograph by Edouard de Beaumont from his series *L'Opéra au XIX siècle* (British Museum).

macho male display dance is sometimes surely that dancers are trying to show that they are not effeminate, where "effeminate" is a code word for homosexual.

There is a profound silence in the dance world on the subject of male dance and homosexuality. Commenting on the fact that the early American modern dancer Ted Shawn was gay, Judith Lynn Hanna in her book *Dance, Sex and Gender* points to the irony in the time and effort he and his company of male dancers "spent trying to prove that they were not what Shawn and many of the company were."[3] What she doesn't seem to realize is that for gay men at that time "coming out" was not an option. With the trial of Oscar Wilde as a terrible example, and with fear of blackmail, it is not surprising that so many in the dance world have, in order to protect individuals, taken the line of denying any knowledge of homosexuality among dancers.

By no means all male dancers are gay, and the belief that they are is not in itself an entirely satisfactory explanation of the prejudice. If one takes a historical perspective, there is as yet no firm evidence of gay involvement in ballet before the time of Diaghilev and Nijinsky at the beginning of the twentieth century, whereas the prejudice against the male dancer developed during the flowering of the Romantic ballet, in the second quarter of the nineteenth century when de Beaumont drew the lithograph discussed above. Examination of attitudes towards the male dancer during this earlier period (considered below) suggests that what is at stake is the development of modern, middle-class attitudes towards the male body and the expressive aspects of male social behaviour. Gender representations in cultural forms, including theatre dance, do not merely reflect changing social definitions of femininity and masculinity but are actively involved in the processes through which gender is constructed. What concerns us here is the way that the socially produced parameters of and limits on male behaviour are expressed in representations of masculinity in theatre dance. At stake is the appearance of the dancing male body as spectacle.

What Rosalind Coward has commented on, in relation to contemporary film, in many ways sums up a modern attitude to the gendered body:

> Under the sheer weight of attention to women's bodies we seem to have become blind to something. Nobody seems to have noticed that men's bodies have quietly absented themselves. Somewhere along the line, men have managed to keep out of the glare, escaping from the relentless activity of sexual definitions.[4]

Over the last two centuries, however, it is not that male dancers have quietly absented themselves, but that they have been nervously dismissed. When the male dancer gradually disappeared from the stages of western European theatres during the period of the Romantic ballet, his place in some cases was taken by the female dancer dressed *en travestie*.[5] There is a similar disappearance of the male nude as a subject for painting and sculpture, and male forms of dress underwent what J. C. Flugel has brilliantly characterized as "the great male renunciation"—the adoption of the plain, black, bourgeois suit.[6] What became conflictual and consequently repressed was anything that might draw attention to the spectacle of the male body. That it was the spectacle and not the activity of dancing which underlay the prejudice against the male dancer becomes clear when one compares ballet and social dance at this time. There was no evident decline in the number of men participating in and enjoying social dance. What one should therefore be looking for to explain this prejudice is the development during this period of modern attitudes to the body and gender. It was these attitudes which brought about a situation in which it seemed "natural" not to look at the male body, and therefore problematic and conflictual for men to enjoy looking at men dancing.

Research into the historical development of gender ideologies suggests that masculinity as a socially constructed identity was rarely a stable identity. Rather than enjoying a secure autonomy, men have continually needed to adjust and redefine the meanings attributed to sexual difference in order to maintain dominance in the face of changing social circumstances. This [essay] aims to reveal some of the conflictual and contradictory aspects of the construction of modern masculine identities, and the way these determine and are determined by images of men in cultural forms. Dance is an area in which some of the holes in the construction of male identity can sometimes be revealed. It is argued that the unease that sometimes accompanies the idea of the male dancer is produced by structures which defend dominant male norms.

The Modern Body

The development of modern ideas about the body, and about the biology of gender difference, developed as a result of the breakdown of older notions of the body in Greek thought and its assimilation within medieval and Renaissance Christian thought. The older Christian model of the sinful flesh became recast with new, scientific features by the rational French bourgeoisie and their evangelical protestant English counterparts. By the nineteenth century, the idea that the body as an entity is execrable not only persisted but became increasingly important in new and more anxious forms. The body itself was no longer admired, and lost its status as an unproblematic symbol of society. The male nude, as Margaret Walters has shown, gradually during the early years of the nineteenth century began to seem irrelevant in modern society, and faded out as a subject for painting and sculpture.[7] Thomas Malthus (1766–1834) pointed out that the healthy body is a body that has the potential to procreate and thus, as he saw it, to threaten the demise of society through overpopulation—his argument being that population grows at a faster rate than food production.[8] The body, with everything it implied, became a problem and a threat. These new social attitudes and ideas were initially developed in eighteenth-century scientific and rational thought; but, despite the fact that new discoveries discredited them, they survived as signifiers of class. Thus the new anxieties about the body related to the world-view of the new middle classes within complex hierarchies of relations within society.[9]

The anthropologist Mary Douglas's purity rule is useful for understanding these ideas of purity and impurity in relation to the body. She proposes that when the physical body is under strong social pressure, the social system seeks progressively to disembody or etherealize the forms of expression, and social intercourse increasingly "pretends to take place between disembodied spirits."[10] Thus, "physical events, defecation, urination, vomiting and their products uniformly carry a pejorative sign for formal discourse. . . . Front is more dignified and respect-worthy than back. Greater space means more formality, nearness means intimacy."[11] New anxieties about the body resulted, during the nineteenth century, in changes in attitudes towards bodily display including display in theatre dance. Ballet is, within Douglas's terms, a pre-eminently dignified form. In the ballet ideal, dancers aspire to the condition of disembodied spirits. It was female dancers rather than males who represented in the nineteenth century these disembodied spirits. To understand why, it is necessary to examine the way nineteenth-century ideas about the body underpinned new ideologies of gender.

It is with the increasing acceptance of a rational and scientific approach to the body that Aristotelian ideas of the metaphysical inferiority of women gradually became untenable. The idea that men and women have the same potential to be free, reasoning subjects implicitly threatened male power. Christine Battersby has shown the conflicting nature of the arguments which were put forward by philosophers at that time to maintain male dominance.[12] Scientists and commentators sought to prove that women were physically and tem-

peramentally unsuited to serious thinking, while at the same time they appropriated for male genius aspects that had previously been ascribed to the feminine temperament. This justification of the subordination of women was, as Thomas Lacqueur has shown, based on supposedly scientific evidence of the unsuitability of the female body (in comparison with the male body) for involvement in public life.[13] Lacqueur has shown how, for much of the nineteenth century, female menses were thought to be equivalent to animals being on heat. The womb thus became the centre of the female psychological system with all women's nervous energy going into controlling and transcending their animal nature during menses. This transcendence of their animal natures was the grounds for claiming women's moral superiority; but the fact that it used up all their mental or physical energy was supposed to make them unfit for any "serious" employment (hence the "female" disease hysteria). If there was any comparable attempt to limit male behaviour by referring to anatomically grounded definitions of the male temperament, this is to be found in the notion of the healthy mind in a healthy body and its development in competitive male sports.[14] The male body was, of course, the norm against which female anatomical and temperamental traits were judged. Men, by default and by implication, were considered to be less capable of transcending their natural lusts and desires and thus morally inferior. Thus women had some grounds for claiming to be purer and more disembodied than men. It was more appropriate therefore for female dancers to evoke the ballet ideal than for male dancers.[15]

Emotionality, Dance and Artistic Genius

This definition of gendered difference is part of the larger separation of the middle-class (male) public world of work and politics from the (female) private world of the home and family.[16] Artistic expression itself became gendered so that, as Paul Hoch has suggested, "Art, as an emotional (and therefore feminine) representation of the inner life became even further estranged from science, the representative mode of thought in the cruel, emotionless masculine world 'outside.'"[17] The Romantic notion of the artist as inspired genius is the obvious exception to the rule that men should appear unemotional and inexpressive. Christine Battersby points out that the (male) Romantic artist was excepted from gendered divisions of social behaviour through being allowed to have "feminine" qualities such as sensitivity, passivity, emotionality and introspective self-consciousness. Battersby argues that artists could appropriate these "feminine" characteristics by evoking the notion of genius, and thus without suffering the lower social status of being female. When the Romantic artist expresses the underlying forces of sublime nature, this is a male creative energy responding to the male energy of nature: according to Edmund Burke (1729–97), the grandeur of an avalanche in the Alps is sublime, as are also "kings and commanders discharging their terrible strength and destroying all obstacles in their path."[18] The new notion of male artistic self-expression was linked to the body and physicality. A sublime muscular dynamism was identified in Michelangelo's art. On another level creativity was linked to virility and male sexuality: Battersby calls this the Virility School of creativity, and one aim of her book is to reveal the misogynistic way these ideas have been used to create a climate within which women were excluded from being considered geniuses or great artists.

The Romantic idea of male artistic self-expression clearly underlies much of the hype that has surrounded the recent popularity of the male dancer. It is paradoxical, however, that these notions should initially have been developed at the time when the male dancer was disappearing in western Europe as a result of strong social disapproval. The Romantic genius was allowed a wide range of self-expression that would have been considered unacceptable in men not considered to be gifted. The way in which the Romantic composer might pound his piano while performing his own work, or the emotionalism of the Romantic poet, or the way the brush strokes betray the painter's emo-

tions:[19] the implicit or explicit physicality of all these seems to have been acceptable for male artists in the nineteenth century. As far as theatre dance is concerned, during the nineteenth century the dancing of ballet movements was not recognized as a reputable means of artistic self-expression, let alone a means through which male genius manifests itself. The general low status of the performing arts, and of dance as a non-verbal form within them, contributed to the exclusion of the male dancer from the realm of genius. To a certain extent denunciations of the male dancer could draw on diatribes against the immorality of actors as a whole. There is also the fact that the male dancer displayed himself, and thus was in danger of infringing the conventions which circumscribed the way men could be looked at.

Homophobia and the Male Dancer

Increasingly since the nineteenth century, it has been considered appropriate for men not to appear soft and not to appear emotionally expressive. An individual who does not conform to these behavioural norms, and cannot claim to be a genius, has been in danger of being considered "not to be a proper man," a euphemistic phrase that generally means homosexual. The cluster of fears associated with homosexuality is sometimes called homophobia. Homophobia is the social mechanism which prohibits or makes fearful the idea of intimate contact or communication with members of the same sex. It is generally argued that homophobia is a mechanism for regulating the behaviour of all men rather than just self-identified homosexuals. It has been proposed that homophobia is an essential characteristic of patriarchal society. Joseph Bristow puts it thus: "homophobia comes into operation so that men can be as close as possible—to work powerfully together in the interests of men—without ever being too (sexually) close to one another . . . homophobia actually brings men into a close homosocial relation."[20] The mechanisms which limit the subversive potential of some representations of masculinity (which include disapproval of male dance) can be seen to serve the purpose of keeping out of sight anything which might disrupt the relations within which men work powerfully together in the interests of men.

Eve Kosofsky Sedgwick proposes that homophobia in western society is directly related to the way men relate to one another homosocially. She argues that a fundamental triangular structure in our male-dominated society is one in which a woman is situated in a subordinate and intermediary position between two men. Men use women in order to impress other men as part of a "traffic in women."[21] In this structure, women are the intermediaries of what Sedgwick calls male homosocial desire.

Her argument is that, in men's relationships with other men in contemporary western society, emotional and sexual expression is necessarily suppressed in the interests of maintaining male power. In a broader historical and anthropological perspective, she argues, this sort of male bonding is atypical: a similar break does not occur in female bonding in modern western society, nor did it exist, for example, for Greek men at the time of Socrates. In the latter examples, there is a continuum between social, political and sexual expression. Sedgwick argues that male homosocial relationships in our society are characterized by intense homophobia, fear and hatred of homosexuality. This repressed homosexual component of male sexuality accounts for "correspondences and similarities between the most sanctioned forms of male homosocial bonding and the most reprobate expressions of male homosexuality."[22] Men are in a double bind in that they are drawn to other men, but this acceptable attraction is not clearly distinguishable from forbidden homosexual interest. "For a man to be a man's man is separated only by an invisible, carefully blurred, always-already crossed line from being 'interested in men.'"[23] The main objection to the concept of homophobia is that it doesn't actually offer an explanation of why modern western society is prejudiced against and discriminates against homosexuals. Homosexual men were subject to sometimes violent discrimination prior to the nineteenth century, at times when performances by leading male ballet dancers were greeted with considerable approval. There is no simple linkage between homosexuality, homophobia and uneasiness at professional male dancers. The usefulness of the concept of homophobia is perhaps strategic, in that to give a name to the way social restrictions function to maintain certain norms of male behaviour is to make visible aspects of male experience that are otherwise hidden. It then also becomes possible to discuss the way male-male social relationships have been represented in theatre dance in terms of homophobia.

It is surely these social strictures which, since the mid-nineteenth century, have caused the display of male dancing to be a source of anxiety. Male appearance signifies power and success: as John Berger has put it, a man's appearance tells you what he can do to you or for you.[24] If, however, his appearance is also desirable, he is, from the point of view of a male spectator, drawing attention to the always-already crossed line between homosocial bonding and homosexual sexuality. His appearance therefore carries with it for the male spectator the threat of revealing the suppressed homosexual component within the links he has with other men and through which he maintains his power and status in patriarchal society.

It is the inability of the male ballet dancer to represent the power and status of men in bourgeois society which was proposed by one nineteenth-century writer as being the trouble with the male dancer.

The Male Ballet Dancer During the Nineteenth Century: Green Box Trees

As has already been stated, the male ballet dancer became an object of distaste in London, Paris and many other European cities during the first half of the nineteenth century. With ballet coming to be defined as an idealized feminine world, there was, on a material level, a decline in demand for male dancers. The fashion for the all-white female *corps de ballet* must have contributed to the disappearance of men from the *corps de ballet* in most of Europe. There were still male dancers around who were valued for their technical ability as dancers. Peter Brinson has suggested:

> The more the employment, and so the technical standards of male dancers as regular members of ballet companies declined throughout the second half of the nineteenth century, the more the practice grew of employing for particular occasions the few who could display any sort of technical brilliance. These men moved from company to company like a circus act.[25]

One example of professional male dancers in Italy were the Fighting Dancers or Tramagnini who performed speciality danced combats as part of theatrical spectacles in Florence during the second half of the nineteenth century.[26] This, however, seems to have been an isolated phenomenon. Elsewhere, male dancers increasingly performed roles that demanded acting skills and mime, such as Drosselmeyer in *The Nutcracker* (1892 Petipa/Ivanov) or Dr. Coppélius in *Coppélia* (1870 Saint-Léon), parts that could be performed by dancers past their prime. Overall one must conclude that the career structure for male dancers collapsed in ballet under bourgeois patronage at this time.

When, with Nijinsky and the male dancers of the Ballets Russes, the male dancer made his comeback, critics and audiences realized that the female dancer looked better when supported by a good male dancer. Nineteenth-century ballet critics, however, seemed to find the male dancer a conflictual figure. He appeared so either through association with the degenerate style of the old aristocracy or by his resembling the rude prowess of the working classes. It is these associations which stopped male dancers representing middle-class male values. Ivor Guest in *The Romantic Ballet in Paris* quotes at length from a tirade against the male dancer written by Jules Janin in 1840. For Janin, the ballet is a feminine spectacle: "Speak to us of a pretty dancing girl who displays the grace of her features and the elegance of her figure, who reveals so fleetingly all the treasures of her beauty. Thank God, I understand that perfectly."[27] What he can't understand is of course the male dancer. In giving reasons why men do not look right on the ballet stage, he refers to the social position of middle-class men:

> That this bewhiskered individual who is a pillar of the community, an elector, a municipal councilor, a man whose business is to make and above all unmake laws, should come before us in a tunic of sky-blue satin, his head covered with a hat with a waving plume amorously caressing his cheek . . . —this was surely impossible and we have done well to remove such great artists from our pleasures.[28]

The male dancer dressed in sky blue satin and wearing a feathered hat has little in common with the picture of middle-class male public life which Janin evokes. In 1840, the on-stage style and manner of male ballet dancers may have been too reminiscent of the male *danseur noble* of the pre-Romantic ballet and thus with the aristocrats who had been its patrons. These aristocratic associations surely prevented the male dancer presenting a role that mediated male middle-class values.

Alain Corbin argues, in a history of smells and odours, that the mid-nineteenth century middle classes regarded the use of strong-smelling animal-based perfumes by the older aristocracy as a sign of their decadence, degeneracy and lack of hygiene.[29] Prudish attitudes towards ballet and the male dancer in particular were surely another area in which middle-class distaste for what they perceived as aristocratic degeneracy was expressed. It was in countries like Britain and France where the ballet was under bourgeois rather than royal and aristocratic patronage that the decline of the male ballet dancer mainly occurred, while it was at the courts in Copenhagen and St. Petersburg that the career structure of male ballet dancing survived.[30]

Janin is also perhaps suggesting that the male dancer is effeminate, as he goes on to object to woman as queen of the ballet being "forced to cut off half her silk petticoat to dress her partner with it."[31] He seems to have felt that the ballet dancer didn't look sufficiently manly—the mid-nineteenth century being a period, as Sedgwick has suggested, in which personal style was increasingly stressed, absolute and politically significant for bourgeois men; or Janin may have associated cross-dressing with homosexuality: although the word "homosexual" did not yet exist, the behaviour and practices associated with it were taboo.[32] For Janin, ballet was a feminine sphere within which men either did not appear manly or, if they looked too manly, did not appear ideal. "Today the dancing man is no longer tolerated except as a useful accessory. He is the shading of the picture, the green box trees surrounding the garden flowers, the necessary foil."[33]

While on the one hand middle-class sensibilities were disgusted by the spectre of a degenerate and decadent aristocracy, they also feared and were disgusted by the vigour and fecundity of the working classes. Catherine Gallagher has suggested that for the Victorian middle classes the social body, far from representing a perfectible ideal, was imagined to be

> a chronically and incurably ill organism that could only be kept alive by constant flushing, draining, and excising of various deleterious elements. These dangerous elements, moreover, were often not themselves unhealthy but rather were overly vigorous and fecund individuals.[34]

These overly vigorous and fecund individuals were of course members of the working classes. For the bourgeoisie, the body with everything it implied became a problem and a threat. J. S. Bratton, discussing the hornpipe within the context of nineteenth-century British working-class entertainment, suggests that it was the sort of act through which a performer could exhibit admired qualities of dexterity, physical prowess, inventiveness and pluck, within dances which would be familiar as "working or holiday accomplishments of the audience, carried to a pitch they had not the leisure to attain."[35] Bratton suggests that underlying middle-class distaste for this sort of performance was a real or imagined

fear of the mass of working-class people going out in the street, getting together, and being induced to drunken disorder by the physical excitement of singing and dancing, and, ultimately, incited to riot by shows and plays which might have radical tendencies.[36]

For the mid-nineteenth-century bourgeois ballet critic, vigorous and manly displays of dancing might sometimes have carried negative connotations of working-class entertainment. One of the better known denunciations of the male ballet dancer was written in May 1838 by Théophile Gautier: "Nothing is more distasteful than a man who shows his red neck, his big muscular arms, his legs with the calves of a parish beadle, and all his strong massive frame shaken by leaps and pirouettes."[37] What Gautier appears to find offensive is the spectacle of the male dancer's strength and virtuosity. The rude strength and vigour Gautier describes seems more appropriate to a description of a male performer in a working-class entertainment rather than of a ballet dancer. The social and ideological meanings underlying Gautier's expressed distaste for vigorous male dance are surely the same as those described by Bratton and Gallagher.

The context in which Gautier above likened the male dancer's legs to those of a parish beadle was a review of *La Volière* (1838) choreographed by Thérèse Elssler in which, dressed *en travestie,* she partnered her sister Fanny. In another review of Fanny Elssler, Gautier announced that "an actress is a statue or a picture which is exhibited to you and can be freely criticized."[38] This is a rather ambiguous statement. Gautier is remembered for advancing the idea that watching ballet is a purely aesthetic experience. Pictures and statues are works of art but, like many female dancers of the time, could also be bought and possessed. This is an example of double standards typically used by men of his class and time: it suited them to be able to claim to be involved in a disinterested evaluation of formal, aesthetic qualities and thus avoid having to admit the erotic motivation behind looking in an objectifying way at women.

The male dancer must undoubtedly have got in the way of erotic appreciation of feminine display. Lynn Garafola has pointed out that men were freer to enjoy this erotic spectacle when male dancers were eliminated and their roles performed by women dancers *en travestie*.[39] Not only did the male dancer become out of place on the newly feminine ballet stage but, because male appreciation of the spectacle of the ballerina took on sexual aspects, the ways that male dancers appeared on stage became a source of anxiety to bourgeois male spectators. To enjoy the spectacle of men dancing is to be interested in men. Because there was no acknowledged distinction between ballet as aesthetic experience and ballet as erotic spectacle, let alone any understanding of the way art expresses social and political meanings, the pleasures of watching men dancing became, in the mid-nineteenth century, marred by anxieties about masculine identity. The male ballet dancer came too close for comfort to the blurred and problematic line that separates, or as Sedgwick implies fails to separate, necessary and approved homosocial male bonding from forbidden homosexual sexuality.

The contradiction which led to the decline of the male ballet dancer under bourgeois patronage during the nineteenth century was that on the one hand the male dancer was required as a necessary foil to dance with the ballerina, but on the other hand his presence provoked anxiety not only in relation to class position but also in relation to the difference between homosocial and homosexual relations. The prejudice did not therefore arise because of any actual belief that male dancers were homosexual. When, however, gay men did become involved in dance and ballet, with Shawn and Nijinsky, the homophobic structures were already there to police any infringement of heterosexual norms.

Homosexuality and the Male Dancer

There is a widespread reluctance to talk about dance and homosexuality, surely making it the dance that does not speak its name. The reference here is to Oscar Wilde who, during his trial in 1895 for homosexual offences, made a celebrated speech in defence of the love that dared not speak its name in his century. Over the years since then, a homosexual culture or subcultures have developed with diverse, shifting memberships and significant inputs from artists and intellectuals. In recent years, partly as a result of the gay rights movement, theoretical work has been done on the way homosexuality has been and is represented in the arts and mass media, and research has been done into the work of gay and lesbian artists. While Melanie Weeks and Christy Adair have written about lesbianism and dance, surprisingly little attention has been given to gay men and dance.[40] One recent book that has considered homosexuality and dance is Judith Lynne Hanna's *Dance, Sex and Gender*. Although the sections on gay men reflect the large amount of material Hanna has researched for the book, they show little sympathy or understanding of the situation in which gay people live in our society and Hanna seems to be unaware of the underlying sexual politics. She sees homosexuality as a problem for gay people, which of course it may be, but she doesn't consider what sort of a problem. There is a difference between thinking of homosexuality as a psychopathology, and seeing any neurosis suffered by a homosexual as a result of internalizing society's negative image of homosexuality. The latter way of defining the problem opens up a fruitful avenue for examining gay art, but one which Hanna does not explore. Instead her concern is with "why male homosexuals are disproportionally attracted to dance," and she suggests ways in which for gay people an involvement in the dance world can alleviate or be an escape from their "problem."[41] The problem, however, is not just the result of internalizing society's negative image of homosexuality but the fact that western society is and has for hundreds of years been profoundly homophobic.

The source of much of Hanna's material on gay men in ballet is the essay "Toeing the Line: In Search of the Gay Male Image in Classical Ballet," written in 1976 by the Canadian writer Graham Jackson.[42] This considers the institutional structures and pressures that influence and limit the production of ballets that deal with gay themes or subject matter and some of the ways in which a gay sensibility is expressed or can be read into ballet. This essay stands out as one of the very few pieces to consider this subject. Written in the mid-1970s the essay has a very optimistic tone—coming out seems, for Jackson, the solution for all gay men's problems. Thus his central concern is with the fact that although a large proportion of dancers, choreographers or those holding administrative positions in the dance world are gay men, and there is a large gay audience for dance, ballet (as opposed to modern dance) companies rarely if ever produce work that directly addresses the experiences and sensibilities of gay people. They don't rock the boat.

There are obvious reasons why there has been a silence on the subject of gay male dancers and choreographers. Arnold Haskell writing in 1934 is doubtless protecting individuals when he states: "of the outstanding male dancers that I know, and I know them all, not one is effeminate in manner, and very few indeed are not thoroughly normal."[43] But he is surely also protecting the institution of ballet itself. With the liberalization of laws about homosexuality and substantial changes in social attitudes, the continuation of the taboo on discussions of dance and homosexuality is surely both unnecessary and unhelpful.

One possible reason why the taboo still persists is the need for dance and ballet companies to raise funding and attract sponsorship from private individuals and businesses. If this is the case, it is not a very good one, whereas the arguments for greater openness are surely compelling. Not talking about something doesn't make it go away, and may insidiously make it take on greater significance than it really deserves. All male dancers are placed under suspicion with the result that, as is widely recognized, far fewer boys and men are involved in the dance world than girls and women. Moreover homophobic prejudice can, as Jackson observes, "paralyze talented dancers from developing a personal dancing style reflective of their characters [and] limit the range of male dancing severely."[44]

This holds true for gay and heterosexual dancers. The initial reasons for keeping quiet about gay male dancers are surely no longer valid, and silences now do more harm than good. Perhaps there are now more choreographers dealing with homosexual themes than there were when Jackson wrote "Toeing the Line," but only in the marginalized, underfunded, experimental fringes. In the mainstream, fear, prejudice and the old boy network still ensure the status quo. It is a commonplace that fear and prejudice breed on ignorance. Homophobic mechanisms channel and block our understanding and appreciation of representations of masculinity that are made by both gay and straight dance artists. It is through understanding the ways in which these mechanisms work that their effectiveness is undermined, and the possibility of positive change is brought about.

Notes

1. Illustrated in Ivor Guest, *Romantic Ballet in Paris* (London: Dance Books, 1966), plate 12.

2. P. W. Manchester, "English Male Dancers: A Cautious Prophecy," *Ballet Annual* 4 (1950): 98–99.

3. Judith Lynn Hanna, *Dance, Sex and Gender* (Austin: University of Texas Press, 1988), 141.

4. Rosalind Coward, *Female Desire* (London: Paladin, 1984), 227.

5. Lynn Garafola, "The Travesty Dancer in the Nineteenth-Century Ballet." See part II of this reader.

6. See J. C. Fugel, *The Psychology of Clothes* (London: Hogarth Press, 1930); and Margaret Walters, *The Male Nude* (Harmondsworth: Penguin, 1979).

7. Walters, *The Male Nude*.

8. Catherine Gallagher, "The Body versus the Social Body in the Works of Thomas Malthus and Henry Mayhew," in *The Making of the Modern Body*, ed. Catherine Gallagher and Thomas Lacquer (Berkeley: University of Berkeley Press, 1987).

9. Gallagher and Lacquer, *The Making of the Modern Body*.

10. Mary Douglas, *Natural Symbols* (London: Barrie and Jenkins, 1970), 100.

11. Ibid.

12. Christine Battersby, *Gender and Genius* (London: Women's Press, 1989).

13. Thomas Lacquer, "Orgasm, Generation and the Politics of Reproductive Biology," in Gallagher and Lacquer *The Making of the Modern Body.*

14. J. A. Mangan, *Athleticism in the Victorian and Edwardian Public School* (Cambridge: Cambridge University Press, 1981).

15. But Victorian women were stuck within this notion of purity, so that if they didn't conform absolutely to it they were in danger of becoming fallen women. This dichotomy of virgin/whore allowed female ballet dancers to be considered to be sexually available.

16. See J. Wolff and J. Sneed, eds., *The Culture of Capital* (Manchester: Manchester University Press, 1987); and L. Davidoff and C. Hall, *Family Fortunes: Men and Women of the English Middle Class, 1780–1859* (London: Hutchinson, 1987).

17. P. Hoch, *White Hero, Black Beast* (London: Pluto, 1979).

18. Battersby, *Gender and Genius,* 74.

19. For example the brush strokes of Romantic painters like Delacroix, Constable or Géricault might be seen as expressive of emotional struggle, while the touch of impressionist painters like Manet, Monet and Renoir could be seen as a sign of their extreme sensitivity. Were they not considered "great artists," such expressiveness would have been considered inappropriate behaviour for men.

20. Joseph Bristow, "How Men Are," *New Formations* 6 (winter 1988): 128.

21. Sedgwick refers to work on structures of kinship by Lévi-Strauss and Gayle Rubin's critique of the former's work on kinship systems (1978). Rubin argues that women have been used as an object of exchange which she characterizes as traffic in women.

22. Eve K. Sedgwick, *Between Men: English Literature and Male Homosocial Desire* (New York: Columbia University Press, 1985), 89.

23. Ibid.

24. John Berger, *Ways of Seeing* (Harmondsworth: Penguin, 1972).

25. P. Brinson, *Background to European Ballet* (Leyden: A. W. Sithoff, 1966), 72.

26. G. Poesio, "The Story of the Fighting Dancers," *Dance Research* 8, no. 1 (spring 1990): 25–36.

27. Guest, *Romantic Ballet in Paris,* 21.

28. Ibid.

29. Alain Corbin, *The Fragment and the Foul: Odour and the French Social Imagination* (Cambridge, Mass.: Harvard University Press, 1986).

30. A different view could be taken of the male dancer in Bournonville's work. One could argue that Bournonville's ballets—particularly his later ones like *Life Guards on Amager* (1871)—kept apace with new ideas and developments in the theatre in a way that ballet did not do elsewhere during the nineteenth century. It is surely more than a coincidence for example that when Ibsen's *A Doll's House* was premièred at The Royal Danish Theatre in 1879, the lead role of Nora was played by Betty Hennings (née Schnell), an ex-ballerina who had danced roles in several Bournonville ballets including Hilde in *A Folk Tale* and Sigyn in *The Lay of Thrym.* Despite Royal patronage, Bournonville's ballets might therefore be said to have created a contemporary bourgeois world-view. See E. Aschengreen, "Bournonville and Male Dancing," *Danish Journal,* special issue, "The Royal Danish Ballet and Bournonville" (1979): 24–27; and M. Hallar and A. Scavenius, *Bournonvilleana* (London: Dance Books, 1992).

31. Guest, *Romantic Ballet in Paris,* 21.

32. Sedgwick, *Between Men,* 206; M. Meyer, "Unveiling the Word: Science and Narration in Transsexual Striptease," in *Gender in Performance,* ed. L. Senelick (Hanover, N.H.: Tufts University Press, 1992), 69.

33. Guest, *Romantic Ballet in Paris,* 21.

34. Gallagher, "The Body versus the Social Body in the works of Thomas Malthus and Henry Mayhew," 90.

35. J. S. Bratton, "Dancing a Hornpipe in Fetters," *Folk Music Journal* 6, no. 1 (1990): 68.

36. Ibid., 74.

37. Théophile Gautier, *The Romantic Ballet* (London: C. W. Beaumont, 1947), 24.

38. Ibid., 20.

39. Lynn Garafola, "The Travesty Dancer in the Nineteenth-Century Ballet." See part II in this reader.

40. Christy Adair, *Women and Dance: Sylphs and Sirens*

(London: Macmillan, 1992); and Melanie Weeks, "Breaking the Conspiracy of Silence! Lesbianism and Dance," *New Dance* 41 (July 1987).

41. Hanna, *Dance, Sex and Gender,* 130.

42. Graham Jackson, *Dance as Dance* (Toronto: Catalyst, 1978).

43. Arnold Haskell, *Balletomania* (London: Victor Gollancz, 1934).

44. Graham Jackson, *Dance as Dance,* 41.

Strategic Abilities: Negotiating the Disabled Body in Dance

ANN COOPER ALBRIGHT

The dance's opening image haunted me long before I ever choreographed the piece. Indeed, it was the power of this image—its visual and physical effect on me—that gave me the courage both to create a performance about the undoing of my life as I knew it and to stage it in the middle of a dance concert. Through this process of performing the unperformable, of telling the untold story, of staging the antithesis of my identity as a dance professional, I began to reclaim the expressive power of my body.

What do you see? A back? A backless wheelchair? A woman? A nude? Do you see pain or pleasure? Are you in pain or pleasure? How do you see me?

Most likely you don't see a dancer, for the combined discourses of idealized femininity and aesthetic virtuosity which serve to regulate theatrical dancing throughout much of the Western world refuse the very possibility of this opening moment. As a dancer, I am a body on display. As a body on display, I am expected to reside within a certain continuum of fitness and bodily control, not to mention sexuality and beauty. But as a woman in a wheelchair, I am neither expected to be a dancer nor to position myself in front of an audience's gaze. In doing this performance, I confronted a whole host of contradictions both within myself and within the audience. The work was a conscious attempt to both deconstruct the representational codes of dance production and communicate an "other" bodily reality. It was also one of the hardest pieces I've ever performed.

I take my place in total darkness, carefully situating myself in the backless wheelchair set center stage. Gradually a square frame of light comes up around me to reveal the glint of metal and the softness of my naked flesh. I am still for a long time, allowing the audience time to absorb this image, and giving myself time to experience the physical and emotional vulnerability that is central to this performance. I focus on my breathing, allowing it to expand through my back. Soon, I can feel the audience beginning to notice the small motions of the constant expansion and contraction of my breathing. This moment is interrupted by a recorded voice which tells the mythic story of another woman many centuries ago, whose parents carved the names of their enemies onto her back. The first image fades into blackness as my voice continues:

> Two years ago, when I was severely, albeit temporarily, disabled, this scene from Maxine Hong Kingston's *The Woman Warrior* kept reappearing in my dreams. I see now that disability is like those knives that cut and marked her skin. Sometimes it leaves physical scars, but mostly it marks one's psyche, preying upon one's sense of well-being with a deep recognition of the frailty of life.

What followed when the lights came up again was a performance about disability—both cultural constructions of disability and the textures of my own experiences with disability. The spoken text was structured around stories, stories about my son's frantic first days

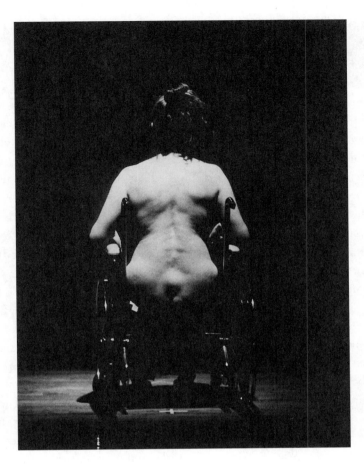

8. Ann Cooper Albright performing a dance about disability. Photo by John Seyfried.

of life in intensive care, about my grandfather's life with multiple sclerosis and the recent diagnosis of MS in one of my students, as well as the story of my own spinal degeneration and episodes of partial paralysis. These bodily histories interlaced with my dancing to provide a genealogy of gestures, emotional states, and physical experiences surrounding many of our personal and social reactions to disability.

Because my performance was staged on a body at once marked by the physical and psychic scars of disability and yet unmarked by any specifically visible physical limitation, I was consciously challenging the usual representational codes of theatrical dance. Indeed, I wanted the audience to be put off balance, not knowing whether this was an enactment of disability or the real thing. Was this artistic expression or autobiographical confession? Did I choose not to do more technical dancing (artistic interpretation), or was this all that I could accomplish (aesthetic limitation)? And why would I, a dance professor, want to expose myself (including my ample buttocks and disfigured spine) like that anyway? Given that Western theatrical dance has traditionally been structured by an exclusionary mindset that projects a very narrow vision of a dancer as white, female, thin, long-limbed, flexible, heterosexual, and able-bodied, my desire to stage the cultural antithesis of the fit, healthy body disrupted the conventional voyeuristic pleasures inherent in watching most dancers. Traditionally, when dancers take their place in front of the spotlight, they are displayed in ways that accentuate the double role of technical prowess and sexual desirability (the latter being implicit in the very fact of a body's visual availability). In contrast, the disabled body is supposed to be covered up or hidden from view, to be compensated for or overcome (either literally or metaphorically) in an attempt to live as "normal" a life as possible. When a disabled dancer takes the stage, he or she stakes claim to a radical space, an unruly location where disparate assumptions about representation, subjectivity, and visual pleasure collide with one another.

This is an essay about dance and disability. It is an essay which, on the one hand, will detail how American culture constructs these realms of experience oppositionally in terms of either fit or frail, beautiful or ugly, and, on the other hand, will discuss the growing desire among various dance communities and professional companies to challenge this binary paradigm by reenvisioning just what kind of movements can constitute a dance and, by extension, what kind of body can constitute a dancer. It is an essay about a cultural movement (in both the political and physical senses of the word) that radically revises the aesthetic structures of dance performances and just as radically extends the theoretical space of disability studies into the realm of live performing bodies. This intersection of dance and disability is an extraordinarily rich site at which to explore the overlapping constructions of the body's physical ability, subjectivity, and cultural visibility that are implicated within many of our dominant cultural paradigms of health and self-determination. Excavating the social meanings of these constructions is like an archaeological dig into the deep psychic fears that disability creates within the field of professional dance. In order to examine ablist preconceptions in the dance world, one must confront both the ideological and symbolic meanings that the disabled body holds in our culture, as well as the practical conditions of disability. Watching disabled bodies dancing forces us to see with a double vision, and helps us to recognize that while a dance performance is grounded in the physical capacities of a dancer, it is not limited by them.

Over the last seven years, I have followed the evolution of various dance groups which are working to integrate visibly disabled and visibly nondisabled dancers. (I use the term "visibly" to shift the currency of the term disability from an either/or paradigm to a continuum which might include not only the most easily identifiable disabilities, such as some mobility impairments, but also less visible disabilities, including ones such as eating disorders and histories of severe abuse. It seems to me that all of these disabilities profoundly affect one's physical position in the world, although they certainly don't all affect the accessibility of the world in the same way.) Each year, the list grows longer as groups such as Mobility Junction (NYC), Danceability (Eugene), Diverse Dance (Vachon Island), Cleveland Ballet Dancing Wheels (Cleveland), Light Motion (Seattle), and Can*do*co (England) inspire other dance communities to engage with this work. In addition, there are several dance companies such as Liz Lerman's Dancers of the Third Age, which work with older performers, as well as various contemporary choreographers who consistently work with nontraditional performers from diverse backgrounds and experiences. These include dance artists such as Johanna Boyce, Ann Carlson, David Dorfman, and Jennifer Monson, to mention only a few. Unfortunately, the radical work of these groups is often tokenized in the dance press in terms of "special" human interest profiles rather than choreographic rigor. Of course this critical marginalization implicitly suggests that this new work, while important, won't really disrupt the existing aesthetic structures of cultural institutions. For instance, when Dancing Wheels, a group dedicated to promoting "the diversity of dance and the abilities of artists with physical challenges," joined up with the Cleveland Ballet in 1990 (to become Cleveland Ballet Dancing Wheels), it was as an educational and outreach extension of the mainstream arts organization. The Dancing Wheels dancers rarely perform in the company's regular repertoire, and certainly never in classical works such as Balanchine's *Serenade*. Even in the less mainstream examples of integrated dancing, the financial reality of grassroots arts organizations often means that nondisabled dancers receive much more touring and teaching work than even the most highly renowned disabled dancers. It is still prohibitively expensive to travel as a disabled person, especially if one needs to bring an aide along.

Even though many of us are familiar with the work of disabled writers, artists, and musicians, physically disabled dancers are still seen as a contradiction in terms. This is because dance, unlike other forms of cultural production such as books or painting, makes the body visible within the representation itself. Thus when we look at dance with disabled dancers, we are looking at both the choreography and the disability. Cracking the porcelain image of the dancer as graceful sylph, disabled dancers force the viewer to confront the cultural opposite of the classical body—the grotesque body. I am using the term "grotesque" as Bakhtin invokes it in his analysis of representation within Rabelais. In her discussion of carnival, spectacle, and Bakhtinian theory, Mary Russo identifies these two bodily tropes in the following manner:

> The grotesque body is the open, protruding, extended, secreting body, the body of becoming, process, and change. The grotesque body is opposed to the classical body, which is monumental, static, closed and sleek, corresponding to the aspirations of bourgeois individualism; the grotesque body is connected to the rest of the world.[1]

It is not my intention to invoke old stereotypes of disabled bodies as grotesque bodies. I employ these terms not to describe specific bodies, but rather to call upon cultural constructs that deeply influence our attitudes toward bodies, particularly dancing bodies. Over the past few years, I have felt this opposition of classical and grotesque bodies profoundly as I have fought my way back to the stage. Look again at the opening image of my performance and then at any other image of a dancer in *Dancemagazine,* or another popular dance journal. The difference is striking, and I believe that it has much to do with the cultural separation between these bodies.[2]

In the rest of this essay, I would like to explore the transgressive nature of the "grotesque" body in order to see if and how the disabled body could deconstruct and radically reform the representational structures of dance performances. But just as all disabilities are not created equal, dances made with disabled dancers are not completely alike. Many of these dances recreate the representational frames of traditional proscenium performances, emphasizing the elements of virtuosity and technical expertise to reaffirm a classical body in spite of its limitations. In contrast, some dances, particularly those influenced by the dance practice of contact improvisation, work to break down the distinctions between the classical and the grotesque body, radically restructuring traditional ways of seeing dancers. While all dance created on disabled bodies must negotiate the palpable contradictions between the discourses of ideal and deviant bodies, each piece meets this challenge in a different way.

At the start of *Gypsy,* tall and elegant Todd Goodman enters pulling the ends of a long scarf wrapped around the shoulders of his partner, Mary Verdi-Fletcher, gliding behind him. To the Gypsy Kings, he winds her in and out with the scarf. Her bare shoulders tingle with the ecstasy of performing. She flings back her head with trusting abandon as he dips her deeply backward. Holding the fabric she glides like a skater, alternately releasing and regaining control. At the climax he swoops her up in her chair and whirls her around. Did I mention that Verdi-Fletcher dances in her wheelchair?[3]

Gus Solomons's account of a romantic duet describes one of the first choreographic ventures of Cleveland Ballet Dancing Wheels, a professional dance company comprised of dancers on legs and dancers in wheelchairs. Essentially a pas de deux for legs and wheels, *Gypsy* extends the aesthetic heritage of nineteenth-century Romantic ballet into several intriguing new directions. Like a traditional balletic duet, *Gypsy* is built on an illusion of grace provided by the fluid movements and physics of partnering. The use of the fabric in conjunction with the wheels gives the movement a continuous quality that is difficult to achieve on legs. When Solomons describes Verdi-

Fletcher's dancing as "gliding," he is describing more than a metaphor; rather, he is transcribing the physical reality of her movement. Whether they are physically touching or connected only by their silken umbilical cord, the dancers in this pas de deux partner one another with a combination of the delicacy of ballet and the mystery of tango.

Solomons is an African American dance critic and independent choreographer who has been involved in the contemporary dance scene since his days dancing for Merce Cunningham in the 1970s. An active member of the Dance Critics Association, he has spoken eloquently about the need to include diverse communities within our definitions of mainstream dance. And yet Solomons, like many other liberal cultural critics and arts reviewers, sets up in the above passage a peculiar rhetoric which tries to deny difference. His remark, "Did I mention that Verdi-Fletcher dances in her wheelchair?" suggests that the presence of a dancer in a wheelchair is merely an incidental detail that hardly interrupts the seamless flow of the romantic pas de deux. In assuming that disability does *not* make a (big) difference, this writer is, in fact, limiting the (real) difference that disability can make in radically refiguring how we look at, conceive of, and organize bodies in the twenty-first century. Why, for instance, does Solomons begin with a description of Goodman's able body as "tall and elegant," and then fail to describe Verdi-Fletcher's body at all? Why do most articles on Verdi-Fletcher's seminal dance company spend so much time celebrating how she has "overcome" her disability to "become" a dancer rather than inquiring how her bodily presence might radically refigure the very category of dancer itself?

The answers to these questions lie not only in an examination of the critical reception of *Gypsy* and other choreographic ventures by Cleveland Ballet Dancing Wheels, but also in an analysis of the ways in which this company paradoxically acknowledges and then covers over the difference that disability makes. There are contradictions embedded within this company's differing aesthetic and social priorities; while their outreach work has laid an important groundwork for the structural inclusion of people with disabilities in dance training programs and performance venues, the conservative aesthetic which guides much of Cleveland Ballet Dancing Wheels' performance work paradoxically reinforces, rather than disrupts, the negative connotations of disability.

The early 1980s genesis of Cleveland Ballet Dancing Wheels is anecdotally related by Cleveland Ballet's artistic director Dennis Nahat, who recalls meeting Verdi-Fletcher at a reception when she introduced herself as a dancer and told him that she was interested in dancing with the Cleveland Ballet. In the annotated biography of Verdi-Fletcher's dance career which was commissioned for Dancing Wheels' fifteenth anniversary gala, Nahat is quoted as saying: "When I first saw Mary perform, I said 'That is a dancer.' There was no mistake about it. She had the spark, the spirit that makes a dancer."[4] I am interested in pursuing this notion of "spirit" a bit, especially as it is used frequently within the company's own press literature. For instance, in the elaborate press packet assembled for a media event to celebrate the collaboration with Invacare Corporation's "Action Technology" (a line of wheelchairs that are designed for extra ease and mobility), there is a picture of the company with the caption "A Victory of Spirit over Body" underneath.

I find this notion of a dancing "spirit" that transcends the limitations of a disabled body rather troubling. Although it seems to signal liberatory language—one should not be "confined" by social definitions of identity based on bodily attributes (of race, gender, ability, etc.)—this rhetoric is actually based on ablist notions of overcoming physical handicaps (the "supercrip" theory) in order to become a "real" dancer, one whose "spirit" doesn't let the limitations of her body get in the way. Given that dancers' bodies are generally on display in a performance, this commitment to "spirit over body" risks covering over or erasing disabled bodies altogether. Just how do we represent spirit? Smiling faces, joyful lifts into the air? The publicity photograph of the company on the same page gives us one example of the visual downplaying of disabled bodies.

In this studio shot, the three dancers in wheelchairs are artistically surrounded by the able-bodied dancers such that we can barely see the wheelchairs at all; in fact, Verdi-Fletcher is raised up and closely flanked by four men such that she looks as if she is standing in the third row. But most striking is the way in which the ballerina sitting on the right has her long, slender legs extended across the bottom of the picture. The effect, oddly enough, is to fetishize these working legs while at the same time making the "other" mobility—the wheels—invisible. I am not suggesting that this photo was deliberately set up to minimize the visual representation of disability. But this example shows us that unless we consciously construct new images and ways of imaging the disabled body, we will inevitably end up reproducing an ablist aesthetic. Although the text jubilantly claims its identity, "Greetings from Cleveland Ballet Dancing Wheels," the picture normalizes the "difference" in bodies, reassuring prospective presenters and the press that they won't see anything too discomfiting.

In a short but potent essay reflecting on the interconnected issues of difference, disability, and identity politics entitled "The Other Body," Ynestra King describes a disabled woman in a wheelchair whom she sees on her way to work each day. "She can barely move. She has a pretty face, and tiny legs she could not possibly walk on. Yet she wears black lace stockings and spike high heels. [. . .] That she could flaunt her sexual being violates the code of acceptable appearance for a disabled woman."[5] What appeals to King about this woman's sartorial display is the way that she at once refuses her cultural position as an asexual being and deconstructs the icons of feminine sexuality (who can really walk in those spike heels anyway?) Watching Verdi-Fletcher perform brings us face to face with the contradictions involved in being positioned as both a classical dancer (at once sexualized and objectified), and a disabled woman (an asexual child who needs help). Yet instead of one position bringing tension to or fracturing the other (as in King's example of the disabled woman with high heels and black lace stockings),

Verdi-Fletcher seems here to be embracing a position which is doubly disempowering.

Mary Verdi-Fletcher is a dancer, and like many other dancers, both disabled and nondisabled, she has internalized an aesthetic of beauty, grace, and line which, if not centered on a completely mobile body, is nonetheless beholden to an idealized body image. There are very few professions where the struggle to maintain a "perfect" (or at least near-perfect) body has taken up as much psychic and physical energy as in the dance field. With few exceptions, this is true whether one's preferred technique is classical ballet, American modern dance, bharata natyam, or a form of African American dance. Although the styles and looks of bodies favored by different dance cultures may allow for some degree of variation (for instance, the director of Urban Bush Women, Jawole Willa Jo Zollar, talks about the freedom to have and move one's butt in African dance as wonderfully liberating after years of being told to tuck it in in modern dance classes), most professional dance is still inundated by body image and weight issues, particularly for women. Even companies, such as the Bill T. Jones and Arnie Zane Dance Company, who pride themselves on the physical diversity of their dancers, rarely have much variation among the women dancers (all of whom are quite slim). Any time a dancer's body is not completely svelte, the press usually mentions it. In fact, the discourse of weight and dieting in dance is so pervasive (especially, but certainly not exclusively for women) that we often don't even register it anymore. I am constantly amazed at dancers who have consciously deconstructed traditional images of female dancers in their choreographic work, and yet still complain of their extra weight, wrinkles, gray hair, or sagging whatevers. As a body on display, the female dancer is subject to the regulating gaze of the choreographer and the public, but neither of these gazes is usually quite as debilitating or oppressive as the gaze which meets its own image in the mirror.

I find it ironic that just as disability is finally beginning to enter the public consciousness and the independent living movement is beginning to gain momentum, American culture is emphasizing with a passion heretofore unfathomed the need for physical and bodily control.[6] As King makes clear in her essay, this fetishization of control marks the disabled body as the antithesis of the ideal body:

> It is no longer enough to be thin; one must have ubiquitous muscle definition, nothing loose, flabby, or ill defined, no fuzzy boundaries. And of course, there's the importance of control. Control over aging, bodily processes, weight, fertility, muscle tone, skin quality, and movement. Disabled women, regardless of how thin, are without full bodily control. (74)

This issue of control is, I am convinced, key to understanding not only the specific issues of prejudice against the disabled, but also the larger symbolic place that disability holds in our culture's psychic imagination. In dance, the contrast between the classical and grotesque bodies is often framed in terms of physical control and technical virtuosity. Although the dancing body is moving and, in this sense, is always changing and in flux, the choreography or movement style can emphasize images resonant of the classical body. For instance, the statuesque poses of ballet are clear icons of the classical body. So too, however, are the dancers in some modern and contemporary companies which privilege an abstract body, for example those coolly elegant bodies performing with the Merce Cunningham Dance Company these days. Based as it is in the live body, dance contains the cultural anxiety that the grotesque body will erupt (unexpectedly) through the image of the classical body, shattering the illusion of ease and grace by the disruptive presence of fleshy experience—heavy breathing, sweat, technical mistakes, physical injury, even evidence of a dancer's age or mortality.

Although companies such as Cleveland Ballet Dancing Wheels are producing work that stretches the categories of dance and dancing bodies, I feel that much of their work is still informed by an ethos that reinstates classical conceptions of grace, speed, agility,

and control within the disabled body. These groups have surely broadened the cultural imagination about who can become a dancer. However, they have not, to my mind, fully deconstructed the privileging of a certain kind of ability within dance. That more radical cultural work is currently taking place within the contact improvisation community.

Giving a coherent description of contact improvisation is a tricky business, for the form has grown exponentially over time and has traveled through many countries and dance communities. Although it was developed in the seventies, contact improvisation has recognizable roots in the social and aesthetic revolutions of the sixties. Contact at once embraces the casual, individualistic, improvisatory ethos of social dancing in addition to the experimentation with pedestrian and task-like movement favored by early postmodern dance groups such as the Judson Dance Theater. Resisting both the idealized body of ballet as well as the dramatically expressive body of modern dance, contact seeks to create what Cynthia Jean Cohen Bull calls a "responsive" body, one based in the physical exchange of weight.[7] Unlike many genres of dance which stress the need to control one's movement (with admonitions to pull up, tighten, and place the body), the physical training of contact emphasizes the release of the body's weight into the floor or into a partner's body. In contact, the experience of internal sensations and flow of the movement between two bodies is more important than specific shapes or formal positions. Dancers learn to move with a consciousness of the physical communication implicit within the dancing. Curt Siddall, an early exponent of contact improvisation, describes the form as a combination of kinesthetic forces: "Contact Improvisation is a movement form, improvisational in nature, involving the two bodies in contact. Impulses, weight, and momentum are communicated through a point of physical contact that continually rolls across and around the bodies of the dancers."[8]

But human bodies, especially bodies in physical contact with one another, are difficult to see only in terms of physical counterbalance, weight, and momentum. By interpreting the body as both literal (the physics of weight) and metaphoric (evoking the community body, for example), contact exposes the interconnectedness of social, physical, and aesthetic concerns. Indeed, an important part of contact improvisation today is a willingness to allow the physical metaphors and narratives of love, power, and competition to evolve from an original emphasis on the workings of a physical interaction. On first seeing contact, people often wonder whether this is, in fact, professional dancing or rather a recreational or therapeutic form. Gone are the formal lines of much classical dance. Gone are the traditional approaches to choreography and the conventions of the proscenium stage. In their place is an improvisational movement form based on the expressive communication involved when two people begin to share their weight and physical support. Instead of privileging an ideal type of body or movement style, contact improvisation privileges a willingness to take physical and emotional risks, producing a certain psychic disorientation in which the seemingly stable categories of able and disable become dislodged.

Disability in professional dance has often been a code for one type of disability—namely the paralysis of the lower body. Yet in contact-based gatherings such as the annual DanceAbility workshop and the Breitenbush Jam, the dancers have a much wider range of disabilities, including vision impairments, deafness, and neurological conditions such as cerebral palsy. Steve Paxton, one of the originators of the form, creates an apt metaphor for this mélange of talents when he writes:

> A group including various disabilities is like a United Nations of the senses. Instructions must be translated into specifics appropriate for those on legs, wheels, crutches, and must be signed for the deaf. Demonstrations must be verbalized for those who can't see, which is in itself a translating skill, because English is not a very flexible language in terms of the body.[9]

My first physical experience with this work occurred in the spring of 1992 when I went to the annual Breitenbush dance jam. Held in a hot springs retreat in Oregon, the Breitenbush Jam is not designed specifically for people with physical disabilities as are the DanceAbility workshops, so I take it to be a measure of the success of true integration within the contact community that people with various movement styles and physical abilities come to participate as dancers. At the beginning of the jam, while we were introducing ourselves to the group, Bruce Curtis, who was facilitating this particular exercise, suggested that we go around in the circle to give each dancer an opportunity to talk about his or her own physical needs and desires for the week of non-stop dancing. Curtis was speaking from the point of view that lots of people have special needs—not just the most obviously "disabled" ones. This awareness of ability as a continuum and not as an either/or situation allowed everyone present to speak without the stigma of necessarily categorizing oneself as abled or disabled solely on the basis of physical capacity.

Since that jam, I have had many more experiences dancing with people (including children) who are physically disabled. Yet it would be disingenuous to suggest that my first dancing with Curtis was just like doing contact with anybody else. It wasn't—a fact that had more to do with my preconceptions than his physicality. At first, I was scared of crushing his body. After seeing him dance with other people more familiar with him, I recognized that he was up for some pretty feisty dancing, and gradually I began to trust our physical communication enough to be able to release the internal alarm in my head that kept reminding me I was dancing with someone with a disability (i.e., a fragile body). My ability to move into a different dancing relationship with Curtis was a result not only of contact improvisation's open acceptance of any body, but also of its training (both physical and psychic), which gave me the willingness to feel intensely awkward and uncomfortable. The issue was not whether I was dancing with a classical body or not, but rather whether I could release the classical expectations of my own body. Fortunately, the training in disorientation that is fundamental to contact helped me recreate my body in response to his. As I move from dancer to critic, the question which remains for me is: does contact improvisation reorganize our viewing priorities in the same way that it reorganized my physical priorities?

Emery Blackwell and Alito Alessi both live in Eugene, Oregon, a city specifically designed to be wheelchair accessible. Blackwell was the president of OIL (Oregonians for Independent Living) until he resigned in order to devote himself to dance. Alessi, a veteran contacter who has had various experiences with physical disabilities (including an accident which severed the tendons on one ankle), has been coordinating the DanceAbility workshops in Eugene for the last five years. In addition to their participation in this kind of forum, Blackwell and Alessi have been dancing together for the past eight years, creating both choreographic works, such as their duet *Wheels of Fortune,* and improvisational duets like the one I saw during a performance at Breitenbush Jam.

Blackwell and Alessi's duet begins with Alessi rolling around on the floor and Blackwell rolling around the periphery of the performance space in a wheelchair. Their eyes are focused on one another, creating a connection that gives their separate rolling motions a certain synchrony of purpose. After several circles of the space, Blackwell stops his wheelchair, all the while looking at his partner. The intensity of his gaze is reflected in the constant vibrations of movement impulses in his head and hands, and his stare draws Alessi closer to him. Blackwell offers Alessi a hand and initiates a series of weight exchanges which begins with Alessi gently leaning away from Blackwell's center of weight and ends with him riding upside down on Blackwell's lap. Later, Blackwell half slides, half wriggles out of his chair and walks on his knees over to Alessi. Arms outstretched, the two men mirror one another until an erratic impulse brings Blackwell and Alessi to the floor. They are rolling in tandem across the floor when suddenly Blackwell's movement frequency fires up and his body literally begins to bounce

with excess energy. Alessi responds in kind, and the two men briefly engage in a good-natured rough and tumble wrestling match. After a while they become exhausted and begin to settle down, slowly rolling side by side out of the performance space.

Earlier I argued that, precisely because the disabled body is culturally coded as "grotesque," many integrated dance groups emphasize the classical dimensions of the disabled body's movements—the grace of a wheelchair's gliding, the strength and agility of people's upper bodies, etc. What intrigues me about Blackwell's dancing in this duet is the fact that his movement at once evokes images of the grotesque and then leads our eyes through the spectacle of his body into the experience of his particular physicality. Paxton once wrote a detailed description of Blackwell's dancing which reveals just how much the viewer becomes aware of the internal motivations as well as the external consequences of Blackwell's dancing.

> Emery has said that to get his arm raised above his head requires about 20 seconds of imaging to accomplish. Extension and contraction impulses in his muscles fire frequently and unpredictably, and he must somehow select the right impulses consciously, or produce for himself a movement image of the correct quality to get the arm to respond as he wants. We observers can get entranced with what he is doing with his mind. More objectively, we can see that as he tries he excites his motor impulses and the random firing happens with more vigor. His dancing has a built-in Catch-22. And we feel the quandary and see that he is pitched against his nervous system and wins, with effort and a kind of mechanism in his mind we able-bodied have not had to learn. His facility with them allows us to feel them subtly in our own minds.[10]

Steve Paxton is considered by many people to be the father of contact improvisation, for it was his workshop and performance at Oberlin College in 1972 that first sparked the experimentations that later became this dance form. Given Paxton's engagement with contact for twenty-five years, it makes sense that he would be an expert witness to Blackwell's dancing. Paxton's description of Blackwell's movement captures the way in which contact improvisation focuses on the becoming—the improvisational process of evolving which never really reaches an endpoint. Contact improvisation can represent the disabled body differently precisely because it doesn't try to recreate the aesthetic frames of the classical body or traditional dance contexts. Despite their good intentions, these situations tend to marginalize anything but the most virtuosic movements. Contact, on the other hand, by concentrating on the becoming of a particular dance, refuses a static representation of disability, pulling the audience in as witness to the ongoing negotiations of that physical experience. It is important to realize that Alessi's dancing, by being responsive but not precious, helps to provide the context for this kind of witnessing engagement as well. In their duet, Alessi and Blackwell are engaged in an improvisational movement dialogue in which each partner is moving and being moved by the other. I find this duet compelling because it demonstrates the extraordinary potential of bringing two people with very different physical abilities together to share in one another's motion. In this space between social dancing, combat, and physical intimacy, lies a dance form whose open aesthetic and attentiveness to the flexibility of movement identities can inform and be informed by any body's movement.

Needless to say, my involvement with contact improvisation—training, teaching, and researching the form—during the last fifteen years has primed me to see these liberatory possibilities in this work. That training has also allowed me to reimagine my own physicality in the midst of a disability. Although I would not want to minimize the excruciatingly painful process of dealing with a sudden and severe mobility impairment—the exhaustion, the intense and unrelenting pain, not to mention the aggravating bureaucracy of American medical institutions—I was grateful

that I never once thought of giving up dancing. Contact helped me imagine other ways of moving, other ways to be fully present in my body. Although I still struggled with my own preconceptions about how to dance, and although I still found it difficult to accept the limitations and boundaries of my changed physical possibilities, I was deeply grateful for the model that the DanceAbility work gave me. Yet perhaps more important than helping me to imagine how to dance with my disability, contact helped me continue to reconceive dancing even as I began to regain my range of motion and strength in my back. Suddenly I wasn't interested in getting, as one self-help book put it, "back into shape," for I didn't want simply to return to dancing as I had experienced it before. Rather, I wanted to acknowledge this powerful legacy of disability, to keep it marked on my body.

Many of our ideas about autonomy, health, and self-determination in this late-twentieth-century culture are based on a model of the body as an efficient machine over which we should have total control. This is particularly true of the current medical establishment, which is based upon an arrogant belief that doctors should be able to "fix" whatever goes wrong, returning us all as quickly as possible to that classical ideal. Talking over with doctors all the possible interventions into my condition made me realize that I wasn't sure I wanted to take part in such a system. Indeed, these medical personnel never seemed to notice the irony in their contradictory advice, suggesting, on the one hand, that I should retire from dancing (at the ripe old age of thirty-four), and on the other hand claiming that they could fix me up "as good as new" with the latest technological advances in surgery. What they could never envision is that the experience of disability was tremendously important to me—through it I began to really understand my own body and recognize that no matter how limited, mine were strategic abilities.

I refused the surgery and made a dance.

Notes

1. Mary Russo, "Female Grotesques: Carnival and Theory," in *Feminist Studies/Critical Studies*, ed. Teresa de Lauretis (Bloomington: Indiana University Press, 1986), 219.

2. Of course, it is important to recognize that almost every category of cultural identity predicated on the body (gender, class, race, sexuality, age, as well as ability) fits into this classical/grotesque divide.

3. Gus Solomons Jr., "Seven Men," *Village Voice*, March 17, 1992.

4. Melinda Ule-Grohol, *Dance Movements in Time* (Cleveland: Professional Flair, 1995), 1.

5. Ynestra King, "The Other Body," *Ms.*, March/April 1993, 74.

6. One might argue that this is no mere historical coincidence, but rather a very specific social backlash against proactive groups working on disability issues. For further discussions of how society molds bodies into its own ideological images, see Susan Bordo, *Unbearable Weight: Feminism, Western Culture, and the Body* (Berkeley: University of California Press, 1993), and Emily Martin, *Flexible Bodies: The Role of Immunity in American Culture from the Days of Polio to the Age of AIDS* (Boston: Beacon Press, 1997).

7. Cynthia Jean Cohen Bull [Cynthia Novack], *Sharing the Dance: Contact Improvisation and American Culture* (Madison: University of Wisconsin Press, 1990), 186. For references to Judson Dance Theater, see Sally Banes's work on the era, especially *Terpsichore in Sneakers* and *Democracy's Body: Judson Dance Theater, 1962–1964*.

8. Curt Siddall, "Contact Improvisation," *East Bay Review*, September 1976, cited in John Gamble, "On Contact Improvisation," *Painted Bride Quarterly* 4, no.1 (spring 1977): 36.

9. Steve Paxton, "3 Days," *Contact Quarterly* 17, no. 1 (winter 1992): 13.

10. Ibid., 16.

Dancing in the Field: Notes from Memory

SALLY ANN NESS

12 April 1993 · *UC Irvine, Humanities Research Institute*[1]

You are looking at work still in motion, actually just coming into motion or entering a "performative mode."[2]

I am "drafting a new form of text."[3] This text fails to shine as a polished product. It says "no" to the document.[4] It will open up a space for new perceptions of the writing work of ethnography as it connects human beings to each other—subjects, readers, others, writers, objects, selves, etc. It [produces] a failure of completion, capable of representing ethnographic events as ongoing occurrences, happening now, currently transforming.[5]

These notes are involved in several temporally concentric ethnographic processes: they are part of the initiation of what will become a five-to-seven-year study of tourism and performance in insular Southeast Asia, a project now in its infancy with only a few months of fieldwork accomplished; they also follow up a previous eight-year effort to come to terms with an earlier experience of living in this part of the world.[6] These texts are my "written-downs":[7] subjective, spontaneous, private, unpublishable narratives of some incidents that occurred in Indonesia and the Philippines, during a summer of fieldwork in 1992. They include failures of objectivity, states of confusion, excessive pleasures that are traditionally excluded from published accounts,[8] exposing the difference between "what one feels oneself

to be and what one would claim in public."[9] They are first encounters or arrival stories, moments when the subjectivity of the ethnographer has traditionally been allowed to be incorporated into the "writing up." They focus on establishing rapport through dance, on embodied knowledge as a means of transcending other identity categories.

They are not my memories intact. They are keeping my memories from dying. "They" are also worth keeping alive and intact as *corpora*, as "bodies of text," not as a replacement for [the] monograph form of writing, but to show, as Kirsten Hastrup suggests, "there need be no 'loss' from fieldwork to writing."[10]

I don't want my [published] writing to deny, mask, sacrifice, or replace notework, but to enliven it, to represent that temporal boundary[11] when you move from being still "in the writing": to the moment when you decide to allow something to "stand as writing," the moment when you find you are now willing to "only tell what you know."[12]

That moment—that decision about when to let writing stand as credible publishable ethnographic work—is governed by the ethnographic corporation.[13] It is one of its most strictly governed movements. My task:

- A text that breaks with the logic of the ethnographic corporation, in this case by *telling* something "way too soon."
- A text that writes against the separation of the

ethnography and the memoir,[14] a text written between author and fieldnote-maker, the fallible,
multivocal, inconsistent, imaginative individual
who existed when the notes were written down,
who has since outgrown herself, but who is also
an outgrowth of the earlier figure, who maintains
a limited substantive continuity as an organism
and as a form of memory.

All ethnographic work is inherently in motion, unfinishable, partially true, in James Clifford's terms committed
and incomplete.[15] These excerpts are merely "written
up"—transfigured into a piece of ethnography—in a
form that foregrounds vividly that vital unfinishable
condition.[16]

Episode 1: A Tourist's Dance Lesson in Ubud, Bali, Indonesia

12 May 1992: Finding a Teacher   Ubud, Bali[17]

I'd gone to the tourist information center earlier. The
arrows directed me into a not-yet-finished room, but
on a second try I found the counter. When I asked
about a lesson, the woman behind first said Wednesday
afternoon to go to the Puri;[18] I said I had less time. She
then said this afternoon at 3:00. I wasn't sure she understood, but could get no further with her.

At 3pm, I appeared at the Puri. Three or so guys
outside sold me a ticket first;[19] then got it that I wanted
to find a teacher. One said "his friend" could do it, another said there were four or five ladies coming who
could do it and to wait. I went into the Puri and sat on
the pavillion where the *gamelan*[20] was set up. Little
girls were playing on the others; soon they started to
put on sarongs. I waited about half an hour. Another
tourist, in long pants and printed *barong* shirt was
waiting also. He didn't speak to me. After a while the
little girls started to disappear into the inner courtyard.
The guy waved me to follow them if I wanted to watch
the rehearsal. . . .

At around 4:30 a woman came over to me. . . . The
woman gave me her card and we made a 7:30 date for

Thursday. She described her location. Her rate was
10,000 [rupiah] an hour—what I'd heard was the going rate. She seemed surprised I wanted only one lesson, but she was willing. Her English was as good as
the tourist workers' in general. Rina was her name.

I left elated, having acomplished my mission.
Clearly, no set pattern for one-time dance lessons was
yet standard tourist fare. Also, there were not yet
tourist-oriented specialists—Rina was clearly also a local in-house teacher—the "real thing." Laura [a Balinese dance expert and longtime Ubud resident] looked
at her card later and said she was an ASTI[21] graduate,
but she didn't know her personally. The dance network
is large enough for some anonymity.

14 May 1992: Lesson Day   Ubud, Bali

I was up at 6:30am for my lesson. No one at the main
desk knew of Jalan Suweta[22] so they told me to go
down to the main street and ask. I was surprised to find
that the street was right there at the Puri and #7 was only
100 meters off. I stopped for coffee and got *nasi*[23] as
well (1500 rupiah), and got to the house at 7:35am.

Rina said hello, and that she thought I'd decided
not to come since I was five minutes late. So much for
Balinese time.[24] She asked where my sarong was—I
apologized (even though she had said nothing about
bringing one).

I took off my shoes and we started. The lesson went
for almost an hour including a break. She gave me
eight or so exercises and then we stopped. Then we got
up and started through them again. She was very com-
plimentary and wanted me to come back. She had had
several students from the West and Japan. They usually
came for one or two months. I was the only one-timer
so far. She used English to count and knew some body
part words. Most of her corrections were non-verbal—
I felt like a tree with branches that she arranged.

Experiences with the technique:

• My triceps (just the shoulder cuff area) hurt intensely from elevating the arms.

- The *celedet* ("eyes looking") was completely foreign; I couldn't even monitor my own blinking. It seemed deeply unjust, giving up the freedom of the eyes.
- The joint relations of the arm were too complex to mirror or remember; mainly I grasped the principle of rising [symbol used] in the elbows [symbol used].
- The top of my hand and lower arm hurt from the hyperextending; I realize what a project it was to keep sending energy out of the palms in these moves; mine kept buckling into flexion.
- The lower body seemed not so foreign; the plié with hyperextension at least felt like a learnable technique and my legs didn't tire as quickly as my arms had.
- The hand postures were completely beyond me; I was able only to begin to master the thumb patterning of contract and stretch [symbols used] and see that the index fingers led the wrist flips. The amount of Bound/Quick[25] needed for these actions was extraordinary.
- In the arm pattern "*ngalut*" which is like a figure 8, I couldn't follow the trace form of the hands; it seemed odd to me that I couldn't; there was something about the hand situation that made the rotation unreadable to me.
- Walking with head, weight center, hand/rising in counter balance felt good; the strength of the step, the sway of the weight felt very feminine and centered; there is something serene and joyful about this step style—and humorous.

Ben[26] was saying that he liked Wayan's[27] technique at Swastika[28] of getting the tourists to dance. Then, Ben said, it was the tourists who looked ridiculous. I must have looked ridiculous also, but Rina was more understanding than Ben. I think Wayan is onto something. The complexity of the technique was made much more accessible to me as a student. I gained enormous respect in that hour, and some concrete awareness of my own specific limitations. Every tourist should be put

through a lesson. . . . The local economy is resistant to short-term exchange, however. It is not the tourists who have cut themselves off. . . .

Episode 2: A Tourist Dance Lesson in Davao City, Philippines

20 June 1992: The Lesson
                                    Davao City, Philippines[29]

[This dance lesson occurred during the "audience participation" finale of a tourist dance performance I attended at the restaurant of Davao City's most ostentatious tourist hotel. I had been told by local acquaintances about regular dance shows at the Inn and had contacted the company director, Karen, a few days prior to this performance. Karen agreed to be interviewed by me on this occasion.]

The [hotel] was a disappointment from the start. . . . At the desk they were uncertain if there would be a [tourist/cultural dance] show, but called back and sent me on around. I passed the Vinta Lounge, Bagobo and T'boli meeting rooms,[30] none of which looked at all distinctive, and headed for a large open-air pavilion showing a buffet and a dance stage. It was empty, surrounded by an enormous lawn scattered with tables on a large beach. Since night was falling I couldn't see much of the grounds or take pictures.

The restaurant was empty. The waiter recognized my reservation and showed me to a corner table marked "reserved," which seemed absurd under the circumstances. They put on a Sousa-like march that somebody mocked in the background and took my order for some calamansi juice, suggesting I go to the appetizer section. I tried the *kinilaw*[31] and seaweed and some German potato salad, some macaroni salad, and a chicken marinade (?)—everything just as it should be. While eating, one of the waiters I questioned (they had nothing to do) said there were only forty-five guests (185 keys in the hotel).

I ate in an hour, wanting to be done by 7 PM in case Karen[32] arrived on time. . . .

Guests began to trickle in around 6:30 PM. Some

English-speaking men sat near me, one making a comment directly to me about the light and my reading. I smiled, half hoping to be drawn in and half hoping Karen would show and change their image of me abruptly. Karen did show, not until 7:45, but she did show. It had been raining thru dinner so my hopes weren't that high about seeing the show and I expected to find out from the desk that they'd cancelled. But I was in luck.

She arrived quietly, wearing a silk print outfit of the standard elite style. Her hair hung simply in a slight wave just past her chin. Her face was serious, she smoked and ordered brandy (I joined her). She seemed unamused by me and unhappy though not hostile. I decided almost immediately not to try to win her over, but to just speak directly from my heart. She struck me as a sober, engaged person of character, an interesting person, an individual who'd faced some dark hours independently. I decided she could judge me for herself and we'd know sooner than later if something might work out.

I started complaining about the lack of good floor space and she connected, understanding my need and sympathizing, saying I'd have to build one if I wanted something good and that it was too bad I hadn't come when she'd had her studio downtown. She later asked me if I might be interested in giving a seminar on interpretive dance, and I knew I was in by the enthusiasm in her voice and face. . . .

She told me a little about her dance company:

- Started in 1976 (4?) and continued thru the present, even while [Karen and her husband] had lived in Cebu (1982–1990: NPA[33] threats and strikes forced them to flee and start over from zero).
- One mother/daughter pair was dancing, also a mother and son.
- The performers ranged from thirteen to thirty-eight years of age.
- The dancers live all around the area, making it difficult driving them all home.

- One just finished his nursing credential (all proud).
- They get fed two times each performance and rehearsal.
- They rehearse two times a week.

The Inn pays 2500 pesos for each performance because it is a regular deal.

- The hotel is now managed by . . . a Swiss/German couple who recently replaced the long-time manager who died.
- The [managers] will be leaving in July when Intercontinental pulls out of the hotel, leaving it entirely in local hands.
- Karen believes the new management won't renew her agreement, since they have less appreciation for Philippine culture than the foreigners did (a fact she found ironic).

Other performances ran for 4000 pesos:

- City Hall for VIP occasions.
- Family occasions.
- Christmas celebrations.

(Pearl Farm Beach Resort[34] has a tentative invitation for July for 4000 pesos.)

The choreography for the performance was based on Karen's own work and research (no Bayanihan[35] borrowing). She encouraged her dancers to be "natural" in their performance, showing the audience their own enjoyment—the effect was genuine; the Effort life[36] of the smiles of these dancers was Drive level and posturally supportive. The audience was won over by it, me included. Bali seemed very far away. . . .

- The performance was a series of three suites:
    Muslim tribes[37]
    Maria Clara[38]
    Rural dances[39] (*tinikling*).
- Bayanihan "suite" format identical.

- Some costumes were original Bogobo.
- Length of dances was less than three minutes each.
- Visual appeal successful—no lag in scenes.
- Accompaniment: *kulintang*[40] and combo on guitars.

At the end, audience members were invited to learn the *tinikling*[41] and I was first. They didn't stop until I'd missed, which took a long time. I was a hit—one of the men at the next table wanted to shake my hand and [another] said, "you really mastered it." Karen said to my partner "*dancer siya*"[42] by way of explanation, which was enough to make the whole trip worthwhile. I felt I'd passed a rite of initiation and had a rapport with the company that was an excellent start for the future.

27–29 May 1993   *Riverside, California*

These notes speak in different ways about two different lived interactions, two participatory arrival experiences, two varied instances of embodying knowledge upon a first encounter. The contrasting records provide an opportunity to theorize more fully the significance of embodied knowledge in the production of ethnographic relations, as well as in relation to the writing of ethnographic literature (the construction of monographs, the "writing-up"). As Judith Okley has observed, the latter activity is more than "pure cerebration" as it has sometimes been depicted.[43] Writing-up—and these episodes are [particularly exemplary] cases in point—necessarily involves some sort of recounting of bodily memory.[44]

Obviously, everything written since the entry from Davao [is now] a recounting of my body, triggered by the notes but not fully expressed in them. In making this piece of ethnography, I express [and will forget] even more of my lived experience of the episodes. [I thus proceed with] making the "written-up" [incurring] a loss of life. [This entry takes more out of my body than any other, being nothing other than remem-bered expression of the now absent field sites. My body is little more at present than a writing memory.]

To further clarify the episode recorded:

(1) As regards the knowledge embodied:

In both Bali and Davao episodes, what was given for practice were patterns of bodily conduct that had transgenerational histories of regular articulation, patterns that had been made sense of in ways regarded as common by untold numbers of dancers in that culture. Yet, despite the common fact of their being body-oriented, the knowledge imparted in these patterns was of different sorts. In the Balinese case, the patterns were designed for an individual body preparing to dance in a highly codified movement technique, heroic character roles from epic sacred narratives; in the Davao case, the *tinikling* step pattern was designed to coordinate the unison locomotive action of relatively unmarked bodies dancing in partnership amongst a field of moving objects. What one needed to learn to achieve performative adequacy and understanding of each of these dance forms revealed very different aspects of self-awareness and lived experience.

In the Balinese case, the knowledge imparted and embodied was of several kinds. There were recipes for counterbalancing the dance of multiple exertions at play with one another throughout the dancer in performance.[45] The recipes in performance assumed the character of systemic proprioceptive feelings of pressure. They might be verbalized as "*Whiles*," "pushing (myself) up here" *while* "pressing (myself) back there," *while* "lifting this (area of myself)," *while* "flexing that (area of myself)," *while* "bending this," *while* "spreading that," *while* "tilting this," *while* "holding that," etc. These instructive impulses stabilized within the standing being the routing of intense pressing energy investments throughout the body. The effect was a stabilization that enabled the most extreme intensification of those investments sent simultaneously into different areas of the dancer.

The density of the bodily areas energized in this

dance of "whiling" altered continually, necessitating a continuous reassessment of the exertions themselves. And, so, there were also maps of checkpoints where assessing and reminding oneself of one's investments and their effects could most easily ensure steady traffic among the forces travelling throughout the regions of the dancing figure. Many joints were marked for relational checking and rechecking in such a way, elbows *vis-à-vis* shoulders, knees *vis-à-vis* hip joints, but also other kinds of areas, such as palms, the inner surfaces of the fingers, and thumbs.

In addition to the proprioceptive systemic monitoring, there were also trail routes given for dancing actions. These paths traced ways through a microcosm delimited by the physical reach limits of the body. Tracking devices, ephemeral cairns-in-memory delineated intricately twisted journeys for the upper limbs and more straightforward passages for the lower limbs. The imaginary cairns of this invisible territory were more viscerally than visually locatable, learned in danced duplications of another dancer's travels, the imitative act reproducing in one's own movement-sphere both the map and the territory of the teacher.

To dance the steps of the *tinikling*—at least the single-step pattern that I was given to learn on the hotel's stage that rainy night—I needed knowledge about more than how to conduct myself inside some reachable imaginary microcosm. There was a partner to deal with less than an arm's length away, a man confronting me face to face, holding both of my hands, a body whose steps, grasp, smile, and gaze, were to be considered at my every step. The knowledge embodied in my dance was in part a knowledge of his dancing, his buoyancy, his timing, his agility, his finely measured touch. It was a knowledge that became embodied through my hands, which "listened" avidly to his in order to move with him, reading the energy patterning manifest there and following it, absorbing it, reflecting it as movement dispersed throughout myself, up my forearms and down into my feet, seeping from the distal ends towards my center of gravity. We had only a very small area of contact. We were not even joined

with our whole hands, our thumbs were not intertwining, only our palms and fingers loosely rested inside one another, making this monitoring a fragile activity, requiring a sustained, though not powerful and not critical, attention. Yet, enhanced by visual readings of the movement, the hold was more than enough of a lifeline to produce a rhythmic merger in our steps. It was evident we both knew in our dancing how to read a partner's grasp for these sorts of messages. We went on together matching each other's stride and spring and hold under more and more stressful conditions when the dance progressed to faster and faster tempos. Innumerable minute adjustments of pressure, speed, and direction, were registered, "heard" and understood performatively through the linking of our hands. The knowledge embodied was of both a very general and a very individual sort.

Unlike the Balinese dancing lesson, I was not solely in command of my balance in this *tinikling* balancing act. In addition to my human partner guiding me manually through the steps, there were poles in motion under my feet, whose rhythmic meeting and parting continually undermined my stance, threatening my uprightness, now one way, now another, perpetually dislocating me, causing me to spring from foot to foot, now putting me alongside, now in between, now in between [other foot], now along another side of the poles. I was always changing feet, but not always changing pole sides, encountering in this way rapidly changing, though mesmerizingly repetitious, circumstances designed to catch me off-balance.

The *tinikling* is a dance made for learning about temptations, entrapments, and diversions, and about understanding cumulative disorientation. There is the temptation to keep worrying about the meeting of the poles, about their parting, to track them with one's eyes, and to decide upon where to step on the basis of this tracking, using a logic of relative placement destined to fail as the dance's tempo quickens. The knowledge embodied in the dancing is in some sense a knowledge of what *not* to do, how *not* to use the hands (to try to find a supportive base for one's own weight in one's partner's grasp—the hands must learn to join delicately in part to avoid throwing one's partner off-balance), how *not* to use the eyes (to watch the moving poles beneath; one's eyes are more helpful fixed on one's partner—having/being a partner is helpful in establishing a relatively safe haven for one's gaze), how *not* to use one's legs (as seekers of unoccupied territory; the legs must learn to ignore the dance of the poles, trusting the regularity of that movement the legs need know only their own springing rhythm and when to step in place, when to step side—a knowledge unrelated to their orientation to the poles, they need to be thought through *less* than a naive observer might think), how *not* to use one's feet (to find solid ground; the feet must accustom themselves to exploring the air, striking the ground so as to become airborne).

With respect to all of the elements involved in the dance, knowledge of the *tinikling* step consisted of strategies of other-oriented tuning, tuning in and tuning out information arriving from sources beyond my own body. The conditions of the dance necessitated planning for the monitoring of and adjusting to other animate beings' behaviors.

To say simply that one has "embodied knowledge" doesn't take a reader very far in comprehending a specific lived experience of embodiment. These episodes of dancing produced radically different kinds of movement knowledge, about the self as an individual and as a partner, about stability and mobility in relation to balance. The skills developed vary, their acquisition exposing different aspects of lived experience and personality. The embodiments themselves put the relationships developing on two different footings.

(2) As regards the learning processes of embodiment:

A basic difference in these episodes as recorded appears in the context of embodiment—in the markedly different learning situations themselves, which would seem to have determined to a great extent not only the patterns of instruction and the relationships that evolved out

of them, but also the production of the notes as well. In Bali, my desire for instruction was overt and premeditated, and the dance event recorded was constructed at my request with a teacher who labeled herself as a professional conducting herself in a "lesson" situation. It took well over an hour. The notes reflect a rank novice's attempt to glean as much information as possible from the learning technique, articulating the limits of my initial attempts to make bodily sense of the largely inaccessible forms.[46] In Davao, in contrast, I had had no intention of learning anything myself on the occasion recorded. I was persuaded to participate by a performer who himself had next to no stake in the teaching *persona* he briefly adopted for the sole purpose of getting me into the company's closing act. The "lesson" was an impromptu, momentary, extremely task-specific occurrence, geared towards "embodiment" as the former episode had been towards "knowledge." The notes made, and particularly those unmade in words but kept in memory,[47] reflect less a novice's first encounter than a more deeply felt relation of familiarity to the process of embodiment that went on in the brief *tinikling* partnership, to its status as a subjectively unforgettable act of embodiment primarily because it entailed prior experience to such an extent that the knowledge acquired felt as if it had already been learned, before it had ever been encountered.

Yet, different as the two learning events may have been in these contextual respects, they nonetheless produced relationships that were remarkably similar in one aspect, an aspect that itself served to unfound, although only for brief instants, the contextual differences. I am referring here to the effects of the dancers' embodiment of "instructivity," their seemingly total engagement in that knowledge-imparting mode, and the temporary relationship of identity that this instructivity produced. In both cases, in Bali and in Davao, teaching/learning the dance required a number of acts of forgetting, momentary, but in their moments, all-encompassing.

These momentary relations may have been magnified by the fact that in both episodes linguistic instruction played a very limited role in the learning process, with only a few aspects of the dance translated into speech terms and exchanged along linguistic lines. Rina used language mainly for counting, to keep the exercises moving along at an even tempo and to mark the routes of the arm and hand gestures at given temporal intervals. She would say "one, *two*, three, *four*," as she performed some action and would look at me on the stressed numbers so as to cue me to look at her and where she was as she paused in her dancing to say these numbers. Or, she would count as she guided me through a movement phrase, stopping my limbs on a certain count so I could feel the relationships before progressing. It was by means of these rearranging actions that I began to sense the recipes and checkpoints noted above. Unlike my partner in the *tinikling*, there was no fragility in Rina's handwork. Her adjustments were firmly determined, sculpted with a couturier's precision around the bony landmarks she was manipulating. The power I felt contained within her hands was greater than that which lay within my arms, or within my entire ribcage. It was an easy matter to yield to her replacements and find a wealth of explanatory information embodied in them. The verbal counts became like proper names for moments in the dancing that were primarily tactually defined, so that a certain pose would "be" *the* "one" of an eight-count progression. This crude accounting function was the main purpose served by language in the lesson, except for the announcement of body parts in English that served as the titles of the exercises themselves. The rest of the time, I imitated, observed contrasting demonstrations, and took tactile corrections.

Rina's relation with me was produced mainly in terms of what she could feel and see about my imitativeness, and my adjustability once informed of a modification. Her knowledge of me was largely focused on observing how consistently I re-incorporated corrections after her instruction, how capable I was of taking one of her suggestions "to heart" and making a habit of it in my practicing for the remainder of the lesson. The pace of our exchange of knowledge was not lost on her. She told me in a definitive tone near the close of the lesson that I needed "one month" of practice and would then be dancing on a par with advanced performers. By the break in the lesson, she had me demonstrating spine stretches from "modern dance technique," and she was following along, commenting in movement (demonstrating the contrasts) on the absence of hyperextension in the lower spine, which was itself essential in the Balinese style of dance.[48] The time allotted for the lesson cut short this exchange, but the exercises traded back and forth, however cursorily, began to develop a shared activity sphere for Rina and me, a basis for relating to one another marked mainly by body parts and their articulations, unidentified, at least performatively, as anything save anatomically specific.

My *tinikling* partner in Davao, likewise, used next to no language in our "lesson." He first positioned me between the not yet moving poles, and then demonstrated the three weight-shifting moves of the step pattern (one side, two in place, always alternating feet). If this procedure was accompanied by some sort of spoken elaboration, it was lost on me in my fixation on the stepping demonstration that was occurring in relation to the poles. As I was being led reluctantly up to the performance space, I had reasoned to myself that, if I were to get through this surprise exhibition gracefully at all, I would have to imitate my partner's dancing carefully and stay in synchrony with him. As the poles began to move and we began to dance, I followed my partner without mishap. All I heard him say after the dance began, as we were springing in and out amongst the poles, me gradually loosening what I soon realized was an inappropriately firm grip on his hands, and spending my energy rising spinally up "off of" my legs, were the words, "higher," and "faster." He said them repeatedly, more and more breathlessly, as the pace of the poles' movements accelerated. I didn't understand the reason for these utterances at all initially, didn't even register them as being directed at me, until they had been repeated more than once, I was so completely absorbed by what I was learning about the game implicit in the *tinikling* form, intrigued to find it was ultimately more about staying light in one's weight center than about aiming accurately into the ground with one's feet, and that the lightness of the grasp seemed the final test of one's mastery. Everything seemed to be going along fine; I had slipped out of "learning mode." With a feeling of mild shock at the recognition that I was being addressed and advised by these terms, I eventually took the verbal cues to mean that I should lift my feet "higher" off the ground as I danced, which made the stepping all the more staccato in its phrasing, closer to *petit jeté* than to minimal jogging, and that I should expect to feel a "faster" tempo along with him. He must have repeated the words a dozen times each, his tone becoming more insistent each time, which puzzled me because I could feel his tempo wasn't changing. Aside from these ambiguous commands, however, all of his contributions to the exchange were made through movement. In movement, he was not ambiguous, setting himself up as a behavioral example cuing me both through his hands and by exaggerating the initiations of his steps for me to see. The clarity of this gesturing only increased as the dance progressed, so that he continuously re-enabled me to follow him as long as I was managing to hold up my end of the performance. By its end, the performance had produced an understanding between us, a very limited understanding, tested in co-action, that referred to a few isolated facts about body parts and articulations, how eyes and feet might be connected, how handshakes and jumps coordinated, how temporal stress could be mediated, how the poles could be avoided.

There may have been little ability to resort to verbal translation in each case, since my instructor spoke only limited English, and I more limited Indonesian and Filipino, but, more to the point, there was even less motivation. We dealt with "how to go on," how to keep effecting embodiment, through observation, movement, and touch. What these expert dancers shared, in my experience, despite their different investments in the instructive scenarios, was an immediate responsiveness in the act of registering my apprehen-

sion of their dance. When I was performing their material, they produced physical affirmations by *returning to the dance.*

(3) As regards the consequences of the embodiment:

> "Doing fieldwork exposes you to the judgments of others." Jean Jackson (1990).[49]

The consequences of these episodes of embodiment have yet to fully manifest. Rina, after our lesson, simply invited me to study further, expressing regret that my stay was so short. I have practiced her exercises regularly since the lesson and wonder what progress she will note upon my return. Karen, after the show, invited me back to her home, where we spoke for a while as her company ate supper. A few days later, I was invited to be a guest at a resort she owned and operated. When I left Davao for Manila, she put me in touch with her friends there in the dance world, some of the leading figures in the country. It would be impossible to say what the precise contribution of the episode may have been in establishing the beginning of a rapport that crossed cultural boundaries in such a significant way for my research. My having made a public spectacle of myself may be viewed as merely a fortuitous start in a chain of events that provided only an initial opening for a conversation that quickly acquired a momentum of its own. It may have been the magnification produced by the spectacle context more than the successful act of embodiment in and of itself that influenced the connection and identified me simply as a "dancer" for Karen. In any case, however, the dancing produced a relationship that included a highly specific common experience.

Learning how to embody new forms of movement in cross-cultural encounters exposes in a highly specific way some of one's most personal judgments to others, and in this respect can accelerate a certain kind of body-based intimacy in the production of ethnographic relationships. Rina witnessed how I knew to tilt my pelvis, how unused I was to shifting my gaze without blinking, how difficult it was for me to keep my shoulders lifted up around my ears and to keep my knees bent to their maximum flexion. My partner in Davao learned how well acquainted I seemed to be with the kind of footwork he performed, how my breathing patterns changed when fatigued, how my hands shook and perspired under stress. Regardless of the differences in the knowledge embodied in both episodes, the work done established a personal connection whose immediacy and mutuality was less open to question than any I managed to establish in other situations. The episode stands out in my experience in this regard. A professed interest in embodying knowledge, regardless of the success or failure of the attempt, is more likely to expose one's self in an engaging way in cross-cultural encounters than perhaps any other form of interaction.

I am afield. Note: (Dancerly writing
   dancing.   "down")
I am afield note-dancing.   (Writerly writing
                       "down")
I am a field notedancing.   (Dance experience)
I am a fieldnote dancing.   (Writing "up")

14–24 August 1993   *Davao City, Philippines*[50]

Once again in Davao, I give the last word to a site of embodiment. It is a word that has taken more than one year's time and more than thirty thousand miles travelled to produce. The production of ethnographic literature typically (or at least in classic examples) relies upon such transcontinental, temporally extended "choreography." These notes have overscored that corporeal patterning by registering the necessary movements and placements (sites) of the text's composition. Solo (or pseudo-soloist) moves, global pathways, landings among diverse cultural sites, acts of embodiment, recollection, and text-making, all form vital elements of an ethnographer's corporeal score, an existential dance of fancy leaps, exotic gestures, and bizarre positionings.

In Riverside, I planned to devote this final "made in Southeast Asia" section to "theory," theorizing about the making of ethnographic literature and the composing of the "written-up," about the geopolitics of the "mono" in monographic writing.[51] This privileged "final" writing, which drives the ethnographic enterprise, entails a loss of life (gained at field sites), the choreography of which can be better understood once it is recognized as precisely that, as a "corpo-reality" in which lived experience is transformed into expression written out through acts of disembodiment. Supported, influenced, galvanized and disciplined by field notes, recollected experience is dismembered as it is articulated linguistically in the construction of the work of literature.[52] It was to this ultimate phase of text production that I meant to turn, to question the classical corporeal score of ethnography and its use of recollection in conjunction with the removal of the ethnographer's body from the field site. The present composition has gone literally to great lengths in this final entry to deviate from the classical score, to release memory from all but its most vital role in writing up, to produce itself from a different existential patterning, the theoretical benefits of which I discuss below.

Being in Davao, however, I realize that this plan for theory-making was a more site-specific plan than I had realized in Riverside. Such a theoretical discussion would have been inconceivable here. The tropical climate alone would have pre-empted it, as Nietzsche might have expected.[53] I still attempt to execute the plan, but I could never have envisioned it. It is by virtue of memory alone that I make here what I should in theory make nowhere else. It is theory here that must now be simply recollected, all associated disadvantages included. It is the field site that has the benefit of being at hand. That was the plan. And the plan has been affected by the experience I am now living, inevitably, predictably affected. Davao will have a last word, of mine, of its own.

Concerning the "choreography" of ethnographic production, this writing has been composed so as to de-simplify what I have termed the classical ethnographic score. The score designates a largely myth-ical practice, but is still ideologically and pedagogi-cally influential within the discipline.[54] The classical production involves the close integration of two move-ment patterns: (1) a reversible move of the ethnogra-pher's body of the greatest imaginable/feasibly con-structible magnitude:

home office — field site — home office.

This trans-cultural re-positioning is synchronized with (2) the action sequence of:

research conceptualization — participant/observation (embodiment/notework) — writing-up.

The dual movement processes create an arrangement in which acts of embodying cultural knowledge (gath-ering culturally novel forms of lived experience) are po-sitioned in complementary geographic and historical distribution with reading and writing-"up"—literary activity. "Writing-up" in particular occurs at a site where only memory work (not ongoing lived experi-ence) regarding the field site makes a bodily contribu-tion to the most literary phase of text-making."[55] The ethnographer's memory and otherwise physical figure are thus dissociated in the classical score as these two aspects of the self are sequenced in the process of text-making. As Kirsten Hastrup has noted, fieldwork expe-rience becomes memory before it becomes text.[56]

The bodily dissociation of the ethnographer paral-lels a similar site-related process of dissociation as well, as the field site becomes opposed to the home office with respect to the relative absence and presence of an-alytic work and writing of a literary calibre. The alter-ity of the field site can thus be inaccurately enhanced, the "Field" inappropriately reified as a non-literary place where embodied knowledge of other sorts is pre-dominant. Writing-"up" at a designated "field" site can thus-act also as a writing "against," against the splitting of the writer's person sequentially into simply memory and simply body, and against the "de-literacizing" of the written site.

The imposed dichotomy of home/field is an arbi-trary projection, a by-product inherent in the composi-tion of the classical score. The effect is akin to the by-product inherent in the monographic format resisted by this polygraphic notework. The "*mono*-graph" cre-ates an effect of *authorial* (versus personal) omnipres-ence (or unipresence), an author whose *writerly* faculty is independent of the site it writes about, and, in fact, in some cases insistent on being dissociated from it.[57] This effect is countered in the monograph genre only via the relatively weak strategy of adopting an "ethno-graphic past" tense and/or providing notes on the re-search process in supplementary material. The mono-graphic style denies the significance of the processual development of authorial consciousness and assigns the home office the exclusive role of authorial residence. Monographic texts thus relinquish or repress what Derrida has termed the "spacing" of the text,[58] the tex-tual presentation (the literary representation) of the gaps and movements involved in the writing experi-ence itself, which in ethnographic work are geographi-cally and geopolitically marked (and thus salient). A monographic text does not expose inherent displace-ment(s) that affect and delimit its realm(s) of analytic presence. Unlike the present entries, which are the sub-stance of an abbreviated monograph stripped of its rhetorical omnipresence, monographic writing pre-tends to be a homogeneous text, the performative writerly element acknowledging no voids, no spacing, no contradictions, no alternation of positions with re-gard to the making of the narrative.

Such are the distortions inherent in the classical style of ethnographic production. It designates none of its own distance to the *writing* body no longer living in the field. Note forms, in contrast, privilege heterogeneity—both of the sites of production and of the authorial self ("I am afield note-dancing").

In loosening the coordination of traveling and writing-up, I insert a dislodgement in the classical ethnographic patterning. By writing in the space of that dislodgement I am making room for questions about how relationships between the speech acts of cultural anthropology (now dominated by its ethnographic literature) and episodes of cross-cultural meaning-making congeal, crystallize, and develop.

The alterations in this corporeal score have been designed so the field sites in this composition are not restricted to non-literary episodes of embodying knowledge and intermediate, substandard acts of inscription/denotation. What has been vital to the production of this text, rather than any standardized corporeal patterning or movement sequence, has been its insistence on a certain kind of writerly body in motion, a body that participates and is affected by other bodies,[59] that learns, remembers and forgets others, a body that decorporates its memory on the move. Ethnographic work requires such a traveling body, always shifting its sites of lived experience, visiting diverse cultural locations, carefully aiming and timing its displacements and replacements so as to draw connections in between them.[60]

Which brings me to what is other than my memory, to what interferes with my recollection, to what insists on being written today.

[*Readers be advised: the spacing here is particularly disjunctive.*]

In Davao, I go out daily walking the streets alone. Such is the behavior of an orphan who can't afford even *jeepney* fare, but it is an unchangeable habit nonetheless. I pass by San Pedro Street, Legaspi Street, and Bonifacio Street on my way to and from Magallenes, the street where I live. Spanish is well represented on the city plan. Even though official maps have been revised to make use of postcolonial heroes, force of spoken habit still works in the first conqueror's favor.

Since my return to Davao, I have been haunted on these streets. This is not a surprising occurrence for someone odd enough to go around alone. The local *spiritu* are sometimes called "white ladies"—very tall female supernatural figures who wear long flowing white gowns and have long flowing hair. They look like me. I have even been taken for such ghosts on occasion. They are souls not yet at rest who require the further prayers of the living, who may invade the spaces of

the living unpredictably, appearing inside cars or gardens or homes or in unlit places out in the open after dark (they *are* like me). They terrify their witnesses. They discourage solitary activity.

My ghost, however, is no white lady, no human figure at all. It appears in the form of a concept. It is the brainchild of Arjun Appadurai's overly sanitary model of global cultural flow and disjuncture,[61] of Kirsten Hastrup's concept of violent cultural intrusion[62] and of Gayatri Spivak's concept of the postcolonial wound.[63] I am haunted here in Davao by a certain notion of "aperture" or, rather, of "aperture-ing" that I observe manifesting on a cultural scale. Like a ghost, it seems invisible to others. It pursues me relentlessly, at every step and every turn. It has pursued me all the way from Irvine, California.

I go out onto the street and I see on the glass doors of businesses signs that read, "OPEN" (not the Visayan "bukas"). I feel depressed. I look along the street and I see the English signs: "Kerosene Sold Here," "Dormitory Facilities Available," "Hairdresser: Aesthetic and Facial Care," "New Victory Dental Supply." I fight a growing panic edged with anger. The swimming pool at the Apo View Hotel[64] has a sign: "Rules and Regulations"; all nine are listed in English. Disappointment deepens as I read easily down the list. When I look among the newspapers pinned up for sale on the wooden cabinets that line the uneven sidewalks of the city's main avenues, I read a labyrinth of headlines: "Drug pusher gunned down," "Dureza implicated in Palo murder-rape case?" "Massacre kills 3, hurts one person," "Flashflood leaves 4 dead, scores homeless, 3 bridges down." Only a few newspapers are not in English.

Each word of English stings me. I see each as an aperture, a minute tear in the local symbolic fabric. Every "Sorry," every "Welcome," every "Entrance," every "Free Delivery," every "Please Come In," sets off a transnational alarm. Another unguarded neo-colonial opening awaiting English-speaking abuse, another symbolic mistake. Each sign hurts, becoming more cause for regret. Every English word I see appears injurious, and there are millions of them, all dangerous invitations for foreign consumption in foreigners' terms. The streets I walk bleed uncontrollably from the millions of grams of English there inscribed. The city has become like one of its own miraculous *santos*; its stigmata cover every surface. They even hang in the air, spoken signs gushing their cultural blood. Innumerable wounds are rendered daily, hourly, by the second. I am covered in blood. I do not want to make any more of these signs.

When the children on the street call out to me, "Good afternoon," "Hello," "Where are you going?" I choke on my English replies they call forth, unable to prevent this visceral response. I gag at the thought of being an unwitting aperturist. I smile, saying nothing, closing off the verbal exchange, passing out of earshot with just a facial gesture of goodwill and gratitude instead. I do not want to abandon Davao consumed by some unearned guilt. I do not want to leave the city to multinational forces of "development" and their in-house collaborators, or to all those who capitalize on limiting international interactions to such easily denigrated encounters, where the foreigners are always "ugly" foreigners with always all of the same flaws. But witnessing the bleeding hurts me also now.

Claude Lévi-Strauss once characterized anthropological fieldwork as a kind of war, as essentially war-like in its opening of virginal lines of communication between peoples and cultures, even when that communication was not practiced under the banner of colonial or missionary oppression.[65] The definition seems somewhat self-imposing when applied to Davao, where most of the residents encountered by an incoming First World professional are themselves members of transnational families, one or more in the immediate family residing abroad. Davao is already millions of *grams* away from any kind of "first contact" scenario, any essential opening of communication. The traces of such events are antique artifacts, family heirlooms—material for archaeologists and historians.

The situation of Davao pre-empts any Lévi-Straussian confrontation or opening of anything that might be construed as "virginal." How could such apertures be made at a site already so overloaded with leaking figures, a site where it is possible to choreograph an ethnographic practice situated entirely within the openings of others, where the field is less an unopened land than an open market, a honeycomb of long-established apertures. How does one wage the "anthropological war" with the wife of the Commissioner of the San Francisco Airport (also the daughter of the city's "Grand Hotel" owner)? or with the mother of a Chicago psychiatrist (also a founding member of several of the city's most active women's organizations)? or a former AFS exchange student to Pasadena (also a kidnapping victim of local Islamic separatist terrorists)? or the father of a "neo-ethnic" choreographer who holds an MFA from Ohio State University (also a resident of Davao since the era of pre–World War II Japanese-run abaca plantations)?

The scenario of ethnography as primary aperture-ing leaves unconsidered the contemporary predicament of sites where trans-cultural communicative openings are highly unoriginal, well-practiced, and generally gilded in layers of polysemic ambiguity. "English" typically works as a cloaking device, serving to confuse while it lures a foreign speaker into an apparent aperture—but that discussion is for another essay. I am still covered in cultural blood. It precludes text-making enterprises that achieve anything other than the creation of novel openings, or perhaps the enlargement of existing opened wounds—no possibility of a writing that might work to seal-off or plug existing openings, no writing of closure or limited access. It denies writing that reveals its own inevitable half-telling-ness,[66] its own "spacing."

These note entries seek to ensure the visibility of their own unfoldings and foreclosures, reflecting the further possibilities for interpretation and invention still available in subsequent site-specific compositions. The gaps in between the dates of writing make openings—voids that are not apertures but closures to the flow of information, closures of the writer's presence, announcing the limits of the view, the turnings of the gaze. They make the steps of composition clearer as well as the no-man's land between the steps.

They make the ruptures in the ethnographic process literary realities.

Davao was and is my field site. I remember it, but don't *simply* remember it. Since I live in it now, it remembers me as well. It is not simply a *position* in a process of writing for some theoretical interest, assumed to be of universal relevance or origin. And, it is I who adopt positions here, theoretical and otherwise.

It is I who will have to leave them when I leave this place, and discontinue the stories following from them, theoretical and otherwise, that I might, otherwise, have told.

[Readers are invited to return to the opening Irvine entry to conclude their reading.]

Notes

1. The notes in this chapter have not been written at the date of the entry. They have been added subsequently in multiple writings. The first entry, "12 April 1993," which represents an oral presentation made at the Humanities Research Institute from detailed notes, has been edited by means of both omission and recombination. Subsequent entries, with the exception of the final entry (see note 50), have been edited only by means of omission. Brackets are used in the text to indicate information added to the entry after its writing date.

2. "Work" on this occasion, referred to my body as well as to the fieldnotes that had been distributed to the group. The "performative mode" is defined by Peggy Phelan as "a writerly present that corresponds with the present invigorated by the performative now" (Phelan, *Unmarked: The Politics of Performance* [New York: Routledge, 1993]). In the performative mode, as I employ the term, the process of the writing experience remains vital to the reading of the text, including both reader and writing author in the text's foundational discursive development.

3. Anthropologist Dan Rose in "Ethnography as a Form of Life: The Written Word and the Work of the World," in *Anthropology and Literature*, ed. Paul Benson (Chicago: University of Illinois Press, 1993), 216, argues that the standard methodological scenario asserted in anthropological training—which constrains the relations developed in the field—depicts a radically fractured ethnographic activity sequence in which the reading and "serious" (publishing-oriented) writing are (falsely) separated out from the field-working phase, denying the fact that fieldworkers actually do inhabit a writerly present while on site. Research projects that challenge this mythic sequence of reading, field-working, and ("real") writing, generate a greater awareness

of cross-cultural inquiry as lived experience by what James Clifford, in "Introduction: Partial Truths," in *Writing Culture: The Poetics and Politics of Ethnography*, ed. James E. Clifford and George E. Marcus (Berkeley: University of California Press, 1986), 13, has termed a *specification* of its discourse. Research representing in relatively graphic detail its own immediate relations of production exposes the initial rendering of the symbolic aperture out of which information from the site is flowing, as well as the boundaries across which it is moving (field/home; other/West; private/public; personal/professional; individual/institutional, etc.).

4. Michel de Certeau, in *The Writing of History*, trans. Tom Conley (New York: Columbia University Press, 1988), 72–77, argues that the creation of a "document" is both a founding gesture for the discipline of history and a means of exiling whatever it is that becomes "the documented" from the sphere of practice, in order to secure its status as an object of knowledge. The production, study, and reproduction of "documents" involves an inherently hegemonic operation by which state-level power structures reify, institutionalize, and make knowable through acts of (mis)representation objects of intellectual inquiry. Saying "no" to the document in this case involves retreating from the production of a text that would reduce the people involved to mere objects of anthropological inquiry, either by making comprehensive knowledge claims about their practices or by formulating conclusive arguments about their cultural predicament.

5. On the capacity of failure to establish aperture, see Heidi Gilpin, "Failure, Repetition, Amputation, and Disappearance: Issues of Composition in Contemporary European Movement Performance" (Ph.D. diss., Harvard Uni-

versity, 1993), and "Static and Uncertain Bodies: Invisibility and Instability in Movement Performance," *Assaph: Studies in the Theatre* 8 (1993): 99–121. On the processual nature of ethnography, see Judith Okley and Helen Calloway, eds., *Anthropology and Autobiography: Participatory Experience and Embodied Knowledge* (London: Routledge, 1993), 1–28; see also Simon Ottenberg's discussion of fieldnotes as reflections of the growth process of ethnography in "Thirty Years of Fieldnotes: Changing Relationships to the Text," in *Fieldnotes: The Makings of Anthropology*, ed. Roger Sanjek (Ithaca: Cornell University Press, 1990), 139–160.

6. See Sally Ann Ness, *Body, Movement and Culture: Kinesthetic and Visual Symbolism in a Philippine Country* (Philadelphia: University of Pennsylvania Press, 1992).

7. The phrase was coined by J. Fabian to distinguish the work of site-specific note-taking from the construction of published monographs (see Fabian as cited in Okley and Calloway, *Anthropology and Autobiography*, 3). Notework is generally viewed as a relatively "low" form of writing, considered more chaotic, less reliable, more transparent, less analytical, more subjective, less thoughtfully conceived, overly rigorous, confined to descriptive detail, impulsive, compulsive, conceptually incomplete. The contradictory characteristics attributed to notework indicate the intimacy of its role in ethnographic research, which may cause it to vary greatly from project to project, from site to site, and from researcher to researcher. In this regard, notework is a particularly salient index of the heterogeneity of ethnographic research.

8. See Clifford ("Introduction: Partial Truths," 13). Clifford argues that this exclusionary tactic was employed in pre-1960s classical ethnographies in order to preclude too close a connection between "authorial style and the reality represented." The omission of the author's subjectivity served to establish other referents in the text as objectively representable.

9. A difference noted by Mary Russo, remarks made in discussion session, Irvine, 5 April 1993.

10. See Kirsten Hastrup, "Writing Ethnography; State of the Art," in Okley and Calloway, *Anthropology and Autobiography*, 117. What is not lost in the presentation of the note material per se, Hastrup argues, is its influence on a fieldworker's "form of life," its contribution to the performance of cross-cultural interactions while on site, what Jean-Paul Dumont, in *Visayan Vignettes: Ethnographic Traces of a Philippine Island* (Chicago: Chicago University Press, 1992), 5, refers to as "the living texture of social life." What is saved and made into print is the specificity of the fieldworkers' author function that continually intervenes in the field research. Departing from Hastrup, however, what is saved in this particular instance of writing as well is something saved from linguistic representation altogether, something saved from becoming a part of the writing-up. What is not lost is an array of memories of lived experience that will remain partially embodied precisely because they will never be completely written-up and/or down. They will not be fully expressed as words on a page, the complete expression of which would require a disembodiment of the lived experience, an absolute forgetting. Rather, some memory will remain as known by heart still inhabiting and affecting my body, still potentially dynamically corporeal. Most, however, will be given to the text.

11. Remarks made by Mary Russo in discussion session, Irvine, 5 April 1993. Jean Jackson in "'I am a Fieldnote': Fieldnotes as a Symbol of Professional Identity," in Sanjek, *Fieldnotes*, 14, has also characterized fieldnotes as being threshold-like or liminal, situating them between memory and publication, still *en route* from an internal and other-cultural state. As regards the potential masking effects of published writing Jean-Paul Dumont (*Visayan Vignettes*, 2–3), has also noted the tendency of anthropologists to mask the emergent aspects of their own writing process for the sake of a "fallacious coherence" in their published work, arguing that "the apparent coherence of an ethnographic situation is always the result of a writing, not to say rhetorical, effort, achieved at the cost *of doing violence to the evidence*" (my emphasis).

12. James Clifford ("Introduction: Partial Truths," 9), quoting a Cree hunter in Montreal describing his frame of mind when deciding to testify in court concerning the fate of his hunting lands in the new James Bay hydroelectric scheme.

13. "Corporation," as used here, refers to the institutionally sanctioned and sponsored frameworks—legal-rational cultural formations—that support and contain ethnographic inquiry in the U.S.; see Dan Rose, "Ethnography as a Form of Life," for an extended discussion of the ethnographic corporation.

14. As Edward Bruner has recently argued in "Introduction: The Ethographic Self and Personal Self," in Benson,

Anthropology and Literature, the separation of the memoir from the ethnography creates a false dichotomy that distorts the lived experience of fieldwork when it is rendered into textual form. Uniting the memoir and the ethnography in published accounts restores a lost degree of accuracy to the memory work generating cross-cultural representation. It also serves as a critique of the still powerful realist manner of ethnographic discourse that requires a sharp separation between subject and object in order to retain an authoritative narrative voice. As Okley and Calloway (in *Anthropology and Autobiography*) have suggested, strategies that insert personal narrative or employ other autobiographical techniques in the "writing-up" phase of ethnographic work can assist persuasively in this critique insofar as they serve to insist on a critical scrutiny of the ethnographer's position with respect to its admission of marginalized individuality (its construction of an authorial "I" that will not make a claim to generalizations within a dominant discourse, but will say "in my experience"; an I that is open to a critique of being non-representative), and on the given narrative as being one of many possible renditions of the represented collective lived experience engaged in by the fieldworker. Such effects encourage anthropological readerships to acknowledge their involvement in an enterprise that works to create or maintain apertures through which information flows out of "other" cultures into the West.

15. See Clifford ("Introduction: Partial Truths," 7). See also Jean-Paul Dumont (*Visayan Vignettes*, 2), who has characterized anthropological writings as evoking realities that are always localized, partial, and ephemeral.

16. "Writing-up"—the making of ethnographic literature—can produce various transformations. Among those mentioned in essays on the subject are: articulating a general validity beyond the moment of recorded events, cultivating an engaged clarity, allowing the reality that begins to emerge during fieldwork to take shape in writing, recounting specific ways in which the ethnographer learned about the culture experienced, recognizing openly writing's own overdeterminedness by forces ultimately beyond the control of either an author or an interpretive community, making the familiar strange and the exotic quotidian, recognizing writing's own marginal situation between powerful systems of meaning.

17. Ubud, located inland about an hour's drive from the tourist beaches near Bali's capital city, Densapar, is the principal site of Balinese art tourism, particularly for the performing arts. Tourists seeking a cultural/ethnic experience are attracted to Ubud and its surrounding *desa* (village-level communities) to attend dance and music performances, and to visit the galleries and studios of expert painters, sculptors, and carvers. Ubud has been a tourist destination for decades. It can currently accommodate a range of tourist clientele, from student travelers to international celebrities.

18. *Puri* means palace. The *puri* grounds in Ubud included a large courtyard surrounded by several pavilions where nightly dance performances were staged. During the afternoons, several days a week, schoolchildren learned Balinese dances there as well.

19. The ticket sold was for that evening's tourist performance of traditional Balinese dance.

20. A *gamelan* is a traditional Balinese gong orchestra. Classical Balinese dance is typically accompanied by *gamelan* music.

21. ASTI (Akademi Seni Tari Indonesia—Academy of Indonesian Dance Art), renamed STSI (Sekolah Tinggi Seni Indonesia—School of Indonesian Fine Art) in 1992, is Bali's state academy of the performing arts. The school has acquired a reputation for excellence in technical training of performing artists over the course of the last few decades under the leadership of I Made Bandem, a senior scholar of Balinese performance studies and a world-class master of Balinese dance theater. While it is still possible for students of Balinese classical dance to study with local masters at a variety of *desa* who have no connection with the academy, STSI is currently the predominant site of native dance training at the expert level in Bali. The success of the academy is having a significant impact on the dance arts of Bali, since the style of dance employed there is taught to students coming from all over the island, who learn it and bring it back to their *desa,* where it supplants the local style. Rina's ASTI certification indicated that she belonged to an accredited circle of Balinese dance experts.

22. Jalan Suweta or "Suweta Street" was Rina's address.

23. *Nasi goreng* is a typical breakfast dish of fried rice and vegetables.

24. My acquaintances in Bali jokingly used the phrase "Balinese time" to refer to what was assumed to be a standard practice of announcing that a given future event was going to begin at a certain time and then expecting that

the event would actually begin much later than the time indicated.

25. These terms are taken from the technical vocabulary of the Effort model of Laban Movement Analysis (see Cecily Dell, *A Primer for Movement Description* [New York: Dance Notation Bureau, 1970]); Rudolf Laban and F. C. Lawrence, *Effort* [Estover, England: MacDonald & Evans, 1974]); and Irmgrad Bartenieff with Dori Lewis, *Body Movement: Coping with the Environment* [New York: Gordon & Breach, 1980]). "Bound" refers to the apparent quality of controlling the flow of movement through the body (as opposed to a visible intent to release that movement to flow out and beyond the body's limits). "Quick" refers to the apparent quality of acceleration of the movement impulse, a condensation of the dynamic of duration.

26. Ben was a U.S. scholar in Bali researching a book on performance.

27. Wayan was a renowned master of classical Balinese dance and former teacher of Ben.

28. A tourist establishment in Bali staging regular shows of Balinese dance.

29. Davao City, the principal port of Mindanao Island, is currently in the formative stages of developing a tourism industry. The province was targeted by the nation's Department of Tourism as a top priority development site shortly after the Aquino administration came to power. While the site has no history of tourism, it has been compared to Bali by tourism officials in terms of its potential as a destination, given its ethnic diversity and scenic beauty. The advent of a tourist economy is apparent in Davao in several respects: the appearance of professionally designed postcards portraying newly opened natural reserves and cultural sites, the construction of a number of pensions, hotels, and resorts, the improvement of the provincial airport (planned to become an international port of entry), and the employment by the larger resorts and civic organizations of dance companies who perform an array of traditional dances from the region on a fairly regular basis. The tourist dance economy of Davao is at an early stage of development, and its dance forms are drawn from a wide array of cultural communities and practices. Dances are taught and practiced at private homes, family-operated studios/schools, and in physical education programs from primary grades through college.

30. *Vinta* is a sailing vessel traditionally used by Islamic peoples inhabiting the coastal areas of the southern Philip-

pines. Bagobo and T'boli are two of the most well-known non-Islamic, non-Christian cultural communities of Mindanao, whose textile work is widely admired throughout the nation.

31. White fish marinated in coconut milk, vinegar, garlic, and onion.

32. The company choreographer and artistic director.

33. The New People's Army is the armed wing of the Communist Party of the Philippines.

34. Located on nearby Samal Island, Pearl Farm Beach Resort is the area's most luxurious resort destination. Originally an actual pearl farm and marine biology station, the resort recently re-opened in 1992 after having been completely remodeled to accommodate first-class European tourists.

35. The Bayanihan dance company is one of the Philippines' most famous internationally touring ensembles, presenting stylized renditions of the traditional dances of the Philippines to audiences all over the world. Karen had worked extensively with the company's artistic directors and was fully capable of creating duplicates of the Bayanihan performances.

36. "Effort" is used here as a technical term from the Effort model of Laban Movement Analysis (see Dell, *A Primer for Movement Description*; Laban and Lawrence, *Effort*; and Bartenieff, *Body Movement: Coping with the Environment*). Defined as, "a mover's attitude toward investing their energy in movement," Effort qualities are theorized as being the visible manifestations of four general dynamic factors (Time, Space, Weight, and Flow) that comprise all movement events, but only become apparent as qualities when a movement process engages a modification of one or more of them. When three factors are simultaneously engaged in a movement process, a "Drive" level of Effort investment is observable.

37. "Muslim" is a shorthand classifier for choreography modeled on the dance practices of the Islamic ethnic groups of the southern Philippines. The costumes, musical accompaniment, and choreography of these dances is markedly different from those of non-Islamic Philippine groups. Dances may include the use of ornamental fans, *malong* textiles, and bamboo poles, over and amongst which the dancers process.

38. "Maria Clara" is a shorthand term referring to the relatively formal, Hispanic social dance practices of lowland

communities, associated with elite Christian culture. "Maria Clara" refers to a specific woman's costume of Hispanic design.

39. "Rural dances" refers to choreography modeled on the relatively informal dance practices of lowland Philippine communities, associated with laborer and peasant classes. Dances include fiesta-oriented game events and social partner dances.

40. The *kulintang* is a gong ensemble found throughout the southern Philippines. It generally consists of one or several large hanging gongs, a drum, and an array of eight smaller gongs set horizontally in a single line on a wooden frame.

41. The *tinikling* is a widely practiced, well-known, social game/dance performed by rural lowland Christian Visayan communities at fiesta time and on other special occasions. See Reynaldo Alejandro, *Sayaw Silingan: The Dance in the Philippines* (New York: Dance Perspectives Foundation, 1972); Libertad Fajardo, *Visayan Folk Dances* (Manila: n.p., 1979); and Fransisca Reyes Aquino, *Philippine Folk Dances* (Manila: n.p., 1983). The *tinikling* involves a dancer stepping into and out of mildly treacherous temporary spaces created and collapsed by two other players' continuously moving a pair of parallel bamboo poles towards and away from one another in a rhythmic sequence. The effect is vaguely similar to jumping double ropes. See Gregoria Baty-Smith, "Tinikling in Laban Notation: A Search for Transcribing a Non-Western Dance," paper presented at the Fifth International Dance Conference, Hong Kong, 1990, for a detailed analysis of the dance form.

42. "She [or he] is a dancer."

43. Okley and Calloway (*Anthropology and Autobiography*, 16) cite Richard Fardon, ed., "General Introduction," in *Localizing Strategies* (Edinburgh: Scottish Academic Press, 1990), 3, in this regard.

44. Okley and Calloway (*Anthropology and Autobiography*, 16), argue that the immersion of the anthropologist for an extended period of time in another culture results in a life experience that involves the whole being, and which subsequently requires the whole being's participation in making sense of recorded material. In semiotic terms, the symbolic reality of the fieldwork ensures that the iconic capacity of the record—its descriptive effectiveness—however detailed, will never exhaust completely its dicent indexical aspect. Given that the notes represent symbols, there will always be more to recollect.

45. This aspect of Balinese classical dance technique has been theorized in terms of its epistemological salience by Gregory Bateson ("Bali: The Value System of a Steady State," *Steps to an Ecology of Mind* [New York: Ballantine Books, 1972]) in his analysis of what he termed the Balinese "steady-state" cultural temperament in the essay "Form and Function of the Dance in Bali." While Bateson's theory is untenable, given its extremely reductive character, as well as being empirically insubstantial, his attempt is nonetheless one of the few in the literature of cultural anthropology of his period to suggest that the body may be a site for the production of knowledge that is generalizable to all other domains of cultural life and action.

46. I am indebted to Randy Martin and his remarks in discussion, 12 April 1993, for leading me to this observation. Another basic difference reflected in this record, which influenced the writing more strongly than I was aware of at the time, concerns the degree of mastery achieved in these learning experiences. The Balinese dance lesson was largely a failure in this respect. The lesson ended with very few actions accurately or fully embodied. The notes are mainly a record of the limits of learning with respect to specific body areas. The degree of detail and description given corresponds to the specificity of the failure experienced. The notes sketch out the magnitude of the still unlearned and possibly unlearnable realms of knowledge embodied in the technique. The length of the entry is an inverse measure of the sense of mastery of the technique.

The same follows in the Davao episode as well, although in this case the opposite result was achieved. Against the odds, having been selected out of the audience to perform inexpertly, to prove by contrast the virtuosity of the company members, I was set up to fail by my partner when he directed me to achieve "higher" and "faster" movements. As we finished and the warmth of the applause struck me, I realized that my performance to all watching was something out of the ordinary. The feeling of being such a public success was a profound relief. Perfect strangers had reconfirmed the expertise that would serve as the basis of mutual respect in my future dealings with this company. The memorableness of the occasion warranted little recording. Indeed, I remember as I wrote the entry that I felt certain I could remember the evening in detail without the aid of fieldnotes. In this episode again, the volume of the notes is an inverse measure of the sense of mastery of the technique.

47. What Ottenberg has referred to as "headnotes" ("Thirty Years of Fieldnotes," 5), remembered observations, unwritten knowledge incorporating a concept of ethnographic salience.

48. Another feature Gregory Bateson and Claire Holt remarked upon as well in "Form and Function of the Dance in Bali," in *Traditional Balinese Culture*, ed. Jane Belo (New York: Columbia University Press, 1970), 322–330.

49. From Jackson's essay "'I Am a Fieldnote,'" 18.

50. This entry, unlike the preceding ones, has been subject to some editing, done in Riverside, California, as it was entered into a word-processing format. It was first written up entirely by hand without a laptop or other computer support in Davao. Ironically, it approaches most closely the monographic style it claims to resist.

51. The "monograph," defined technically as a treatise that provides detailed factual information on a particular subject, is one of the basic documentary formats of ethnographic literature. Modeled historically on writing in the natural sciences, monographs are typically considered to be the first form of publication an ethnographer "writes up" after completing fieldwork, and which is most specifically written for other practicing anthropologists. Ethnographic monographs originally were essentially descriptive accounts, that reported as comprehensively as possible on every aspect of the specific culture observed. However, in contemporary cultural anthropological work, "monographic" writing (writing which concentrates on a single research interest, ethnic situation, or fieldwork site) has overtaken comparative and more generalizing forms of ethnological writing as these alternative forms have become stigmatized as neo-colonial master narratives that mask without relinquishing chauvinistically ethnocentric perspectives.

52. As Okley and Calloway (*Anthropology and Autobiography,* 16), have argued, and as the Riverside entry of this chapter exemplifies, fieldnotes are inherently incomplete records, often no more than a trigger for the embodied knowledge—lived experience held in memory—that once expressed constitutes the actual subject of written-up ethnography. Memory, Bourdieu has noted in *Outline of a Theory of Practice* (Cambridge: Cambridge University Press, 1977), 94, can be nothing other than bodily habitus. In this regard, writing-up can rely at least as much upon divestitures of memory/bodily dismemberings, as it does upon re-presentations and enhancements of field writings. The divesting of lived experience in the rendering of the text, the physical aspects of retrieval, recollection, and expression in memory work are what I am referring to as "corporealities." Their influence on the text-making process is literally formative. See also note 10.

53. Nietzsche in *Ecce Homo* argues, "The influence of climate on our metabolism, its retardation, its acceleration, goes so far that a mistaken choice of place and climate, can not only estrange a man from his task but can actually keep it from him: he never gets to see it" (cited in Rudolphe Gasché, "*Ecce Homo* or the Written Body," *Oxford Literary Review* 7, nos. 1 and 2 [1985]: 12). Keeping me from having seen the theoretical task at hand in Davao, for example, were a series of fungal skin rashes, brought on by the polluted tropical climate, that took forty days to cure, during which time I was under doctor's orders to "avoid perspiring" and to follow a daily regimen involving multiple washings, and time-consuming applications of medicinal lotion. The treatment interfered with every aspect of life and work, and, if ever it was abandoned, the resulting discomfort made analytical writing impossible.

54. See, for example, Dan Rose's account of the model of the standard logic of ethnographic inquiry ("Ethnography as a Form of Life," 194) he learned from graduate anthropological methodological training and from reading the products of ethnographic research. Rose's progression also isolates acts of reading and writing from the experiences of fieldwork. See note 3. See also remarks about writing-up "from afar" in Dumont, *Visayan Vignettes*, 4, 6.

55. See note 52 on the corporeality of memory.

56. See Kirsten Hastrup, "Writing as Ethnography: State of the Art," in Okley and Calloway, *Anthropology and Autobiography*, 125.

57. Some anthropologists argue that being off-site is critical to the activity of writing-up, although the issue is a subject of debate. See Ottenberg, "Thirty Years of Fieldnotes," 146–148.

58. See remarks in *Positions,* 80-96. See also Dumont's remarks on false narrative coherence in ethnographic writing-up (*Visayan Vignettes,* 2–8).

59. In Spinoza's terms a "dynamic body" (versus a kinetic body): one defined by the effects that constitute it and of which it is capable. See Gilles Deleuze, "Ethology: Spinoza and Us," in *Zone 6: Incorporations,* ed. Jonathan Crary and Sanford Kwinter (New York: Urzone, 1992), 625.

60. The interest in moving from a here/there perspective on diverse cultural sites towards the intersubjective creation of a world of "betweenness" is one of the primary motivations for interpretive ethnographic writing. See Hastrup ("Writing as Ethnography," 118) and Dennis Tedlock's remarks in *The Spoken Word and the Work of Interpretation* (Philadelphia: University of Pennsylvania Press, 1983), 323–324.

61. See Arjun Appadurai, "Disjuncture and Difference in the Global Cultural Economy," *Public Culture* 2, no. 2 (1990): 1–24. The model depicts a postgeographically determined global situation in which shifting "scapes" of media-generated, financial, technical, ethnic, and ideological materials form cultural disjunctures and transcultural interrelationships as a result of their heterogeneously fluid states. I characterize the model as "overly sanitary" in the sense that it is written-up in a neutral voice, reified without affect or particular emphasis given to the human suffering incurred by the conditions it objectifies. I would not argue that Appadurai's strategy is flawed or inappropriate. I simply note that from the field position I was in, it appeared "overly" sanitary. See also Robert Martins, "World Music and the Global Cultural Economy," *Diaspora* 2, no. 2 (1992): 240–241, for a critical assessment of the model.

62. See Hastrup, "Writing as Ethnography," 123.

63. See Gayatri Chakrovorty Spivak, "Acting Bits; Identity Talk," *Critical Inquiry* 18 (1992): 770.

64. Named for the nearby Mount Apo, a spectacular volcanic peak that has become a dominant symbol for the city's tourism industry.

65. See Michael Jackson, *Paths toward a Clearing* (Bloomington: University of Indiana Press, 1989), 107.

66. What Dumont (*Visayan Vignettes,* 7) refers to as "displacing the responsibility for interpretive closure." See Jackson, *Paths toward a Clearing,* 109.

Thinking about Dance History: Further Readings

Acocella, Joan. "Imagining Dance." *Dance Ink* 1, no. 2 (December 1990).

———. "Virtual Critics and Critical Values." *Drama Review* 41, no. 1 (spring 1997).

Adshead, Janet, and June Layson, eds. *Dance History: A Methodology for Study.* London: Dance Books, 1983.

———. *Dance History: An Introduction.* London and New York: Routledge, 1994.

Albright, Ann Cooper. "Mining the Dancefield: Spectacle, Moving Subjects, and Feminist Theory." *Contact Quarterly* 15, no. 2 (spring/summer 1990).

———. "Strategic Abilities: Negotiating the Disabled Body in Dance." *Michigan Quarterly Review* 38, no. 3 (summer 1998).

Awkward, Michael. *Negotiating Difference: Race, Gender, and the Politics of Positionality.* Chicago: University of Chicago Press, 1995.

Banes, Sally. "Criticism as Ethnography." In *Dance Critics Association Conference Proceedings.* New York: Dance Critics Association, 1990.

———. *Dancing Women: Female Bodies on Stage.* New York: Routledge, 1998.

———. "Terpsichore Combat Continued." *Drama Review* 33, no. 4 (winter 1989).

———. "Terpsichore in Combat Boots." *Drama Review* 33, no. 1 (spring 1989).

Birringer, Johannes. *Media and Performance: Along the Border.* Baltimore: Johns Hopkins University Press, 1998.

Bloomer, Kent C., and Charles W. Moore. *Body, Memory, and Architecture.* New Haven: Yale University Press, 1977.

Bordo, Susan. *Unbearable Weight: Feminism, Western Culture, and the Body.* Berkeley: University of California Press, 1993.

Bull, Cynthia Jean Cohen. "Ethnography and History: A Case Study of Dance Improvisers." In *Society of Dance History Scholars Conference Proceedings.* Townsend, Md.: Scholars, 1984.

Burke, Peter, ed. *New Perspectives on Historical Writing.* University Park: Pennsylvania State University Press, 1991.

Burt, Ramsay. *Alien Bodies: Representations of Modernity, Race, and Nation in Early Modern Dance.* London: Routledge, 1998.

———. *The Male Dancer: Bodies, Spectacle, Sexualities.* London: Routledge, 1995.

Carter, Alexandra, ed. *The Routledge Dance Studies Reader.* London: Routledge, 1998.

Case, Sue Ellen, Philip Brett, and Susan Leigh Foster, eds. *Cruising the Performative: Interventions into the Representation of Ethnicity, Nationality, and Sexuality.* Bloomington: Indiana University Press, 1995.

Chapple, Eliot D., and Martha Davis. "Expressive Movement and Performance: Toward a Unifying Theory." *Drama Review* 32, no. 4 (winter 1988).

Clifford, James. *The Predicament of Culture: Twentieth-Century Ethnography, Literature, and Art.* Cambridge, Mass.: Harvard University Press, 1988.

Cohen, Selma Jean. *Next Week, Swan Lake: Reflections on Dance and Dances.* Middletown, Conn.: Wesleyan University Press, 1982.

Copeland, Roger. "Between Description and Deconstruction." *Routledge Dance Studies Reader.* London: Routledge, 1998.

Copeland, Roger, and Marshall Cohen, eds. *What Is Dance?* New York: Oxford University Press, 1983.

Croce, Arlene. "Discussing the Undiscussable." *New Yorker* 70, no. 43 (December 26, 1994).

Daly, Ann. "The Balanchine Woman: Of Hummingbirds and Channel Swimmers." *Drama Review* 31, no. 1 (spring 1987).

———. "Dance History and Feminist Theory: Reconsidering Isadora Duncan and the Male Gaze." In *Gender in Performance*, ed. Laurence Senelick. Hanover, N.H.: University Press of New England, 1992.

———. "Movement Analysis: Piecing Together the Puzzle." *Drama Review* 32, no. 4 (winter 1988).

———. "Unlimited Partnership: Dance and Feminist Analysis." *Dance Research Journal* 23, no. 1 (spring 1991).

———. "What Revolution? The New Dance Scholarship in America." *Tanz International* 2, no. 1 (January 1991).

———. "'Woman,' Women, and Subversion: Some Nagging Questions from a Dance Historian." *Choreography and Dance* 5, pt. 1 (1998).

Dell, Cecily. *A Primer for Movement Description Using Effort-Shape and Supplementary Concepts.* New York: Dance Notation Bureau, Center for Movement Research and Analysis, 1977.

Dils, Ann. "*Choreographing History* and Dance Historiography." *Dance Research Journal* 29, no. 2 (fall 1997).

Elton, Heather. "The Archaeology of Dance." *Dance Connection* 10, no. 3 (September/October 1992).

Foster, Susan Leigh, ed. *Choreographing History.* Bloomington: University of Indiana Press, 1995.

———, ed. *Corporealities: Dancing Knowledge, Culture and Power.* New York: Routledge, 1996.

Goellner, Ellen W., and Jacqueline Shea Murphy, eds. *Bodies of the Text: Dance as Theory, Literature as Dance.* New Brunswick, N.J.: Rutgers University Press, 1995.

Goldberg, Marianne. "Ballerinas and Ball Passing." *Women and Performance* 3, no. 2, (1987–88).

———. "Be to Want I: A Performance Piece for Print." *Women and Performance* 10, nos. 1–2 (1999).

Gottschild, Brenda Dixon. *Digging the Africanist Presence in American Performance: Dance and Other Contexts.* Westport, Conn.: Greenwood Press, 1996.

Hodson, Millicent. "Searching for Nijinsky's *Sacre*." *Dance Magazine* (June 1980).

hooks, bell. *Black Looks: Race and Representation.* Boston: South End Press, 1989.

Jablonko, Allison, and Elizabeth Kagan. "An Experiment in Looking: Reexamining the Process of Observation." *Drama Review* 32, no. 4 (winter 1988).

Jackson, Naomi M. "Dance Analysis in the Publications of Janet Adshead and Susan Foster." *Dance Research* 12, no. 1 (spring 1994).

———. "Founding the 92nd Street YM–YWHA Dance Center, 1934–1936." *Dance Chronicle* 21, no. 2 (1998).

Jowitt, Deborah. "Beyond Description: Writing beneath the Surface." *Writings on Dance*, no. 16 (winter 1997).

Kealiinohomoku, Joann. "An Anthropologist Looks at Ballet as a Form of Ethnic Dance." In *What Is Dance?* ed. Roger Copeland and Marshall Cohen. New York: Oxford University Press, 1983.

Layson, June. "Dance History Methodology: Dynamic Models for Teaching, Learning and Research." In *Hong Kong International Dance Conference Papers* 2. Hong Kong: Hong Kong Academy of Performing Arts, 1990.

Manning, Susan. "Cultural Theft or Love?" *Dance Theatre Journal* 13, no. 4 (autumn 1997).

———. "Modernist Dogma and Post-modern Rhetoric." *Drama Review* 32, no. 4 (winter 1988).

Martin, Randy. *Performance as Political Act: The Embodied Self.* New York: Bergin & Garvey, 1990.

McCarren, Felicia M. *Dance Pathologies: Performance, Poetics, Medicine.* Stanford, Calif.: Stanford University Press, 1998.

McCullagh, C. Behan. *The Truth of History.* New York: Routledge, 1998.

Minh-ha, Trinh T. *Woman, Native, Other: Writing Postcoloniality and Feminism.* Bloomington: Indiana University Press, 1989.

Morrison, Toni. "The Site of Memory." In *Out There: Marginalization and Contemporary Cultures*, ed. Russell Ferguson. New York: Museum of Contemporary Art; Cambridge, Mass.: MIT Press, 1990.

Ness, Sally Ann. *Body, Movement, and Culture: Kinesthetic and Visual Symbolism in a Philippine Community.* Philadelphia: University of Pennsylvania Press, 1992.

———. "Dancing in the Field: Notes from Memory." In *Corporealities: Dancing Knowledge, Culture and Power*, ed. Susan Leigh Foster. New York: Routledge, 1996.

———. "Understanding Cultural Performance: Trobriand Cricket." *Drama Review* 32, no. 4 (winter 1988).

Ralph, Richard. "On the Light Fantastic Toe: Dance Scholarship and Academic Fashion." *Dance Chronicle* 18, no. 2 (1995).

Sheets-Johnson, Maxine. *The Phenomenology of Dance.* Madison: University of Wisconsin Press, 1966.

Siegel, Marcia B. "Education of a Dance Critic: The Bonsai and the Lumberjack." *Dance Scope* 15, no. 1 (1981).

———. "History Today." *DCA News* (summer 1992).

———. "The Truth about Apples and Oranges." *Drama Review* 32, no. 4 (winter 1988).

———. "Virtual Criticism and the Dance of Death." *Drama Review* 40, no. 2 (summer 1996).

Sklar, Deidre. "All the Dances Have Meaning to That Apparition: Felt Knowledge and the Danzantes of Tortugas, in Las Cruces, New Mexico." *Dance Research Journal* 31, no. 2 (fall 1999).

———. "Five Premises for a Culturally Sensitive Approach to Dance." *DCA News* (summer 1991).

———. "On Dance Ethnography." *Dance Research Journal* 23, no. 1 (spring 1991).

Thomas, Helen. *Dance, Modernity and Culture: Explorations in the Sociology of Dance.* London: Routledge, 1995.

Van Zile, Judy. "What Is Dance? Implications for Dance Notation." *Dance Research Journal* 17, no. 2 & 18, no. 1 (fall 1985/spring 1986).

Washabaugh, William, ed. *The Passion of Music and Dance: Body, Gender and Sexuality.* Oxford: Berg, 1998.

Zinsser, William, ed. *Inventing the Truth: The Art and Craft of Memoir.* Boston: Houghton Mifflin, 1987.

PART TWO

World Dance Traditions

Looking at World Dance

The twenty-first century began for many Americans with televised snippets of New Year celebrations from around the world. Many of these events featured some sort of traditional folk dance or collective movement ritual in which people joined hands, coming together to mark the entrance of a new millennium. Most of the celebrations took place out-of-doors, either in a town square, on a city street, on the side of a mountain, or by the sea. Even though these events were, for the most part, clearly staged for the camera, they still evoked a sense of the spontaneous gathering of human and natural energies at the dawn of a new millennium.

In the midst of these pastoral rituals was the live action from New York City's Times Square. Here, thousands upon thousands of people were packed into the streets, waiting for the traditional New Year's ball to descend. The commentators kept highlighting how many visitors from other countries were in the crowd. In addition to the prerecorded celebratory moments from across the ocean, and the live action in Times Square, most networks had their own in-house party going which included popular singers and performers as well as their happily receptive live audiences—all dancing, of course. The mini performances presented a smorgasbord of dance which included such African diasporic forms as hip-hop, house, samba, and capoeira, an Afro-Brazilian martial dance. During this extraordinary televised global moment, dance—people dancing together—was staged both to signal a distinctive national, ethnic, or generational identity, and to suggest a commonality across these cultural differences. The millennium began with dancing presented as a universal experience. Cutting from celebration to celebration, the media was able to collapse time (the world is celebrating at once) and space (we can see all those worlds from the comfort of our living rooms) to give its viewing audience a sense that the whole world was dancing *now*.

The question that arises in the face of such a wonderfully eclectic array of movement forms is "What is world dance?" Is it the smiling, multiracial line of casually dressed Israelis holding hands and weaving in and out of the traditional hora? Is it the Israeli national dance troupe performing abstract modern dance movements on a dance floor constructed on the side of a mountain? Is it the crowd of twenty-somethings on dance floors in New York or Brazil moving in synch to the rhythms of a global youth culture? Is world dance local or transnational? "Native" or cosmopolitan? Rural or urban? Traditional or contemporary? Does the term "world" in the title of this section function as a code for non-Western or "ethnic" dance? What is ethnic dance? Folk or professional? Functional or aesthetic? Radical or conservative? Feminist or patriarchal?

What looking carefully at world dance teaches us is the very misguided nature of those oppositional questions. The essays which follow at once refuse and confuse any static notion of a "traditional" dance form. While all the writings here highlight the importance of distinctive cultural traditions, foregrounding the embodied aspects of regional, national, or ethnic identities, they also reveal the contested nature of any historical legacy. Most of the dance forms represented in this section can trace a history back several hundred (sometimes several thousand) years. Yet that journey across time is rarely smooth or uninterrupted. The dances presented in this section are wonderful examples of how specific traditions have been and continue to be negotiated by the expressive needs and artistic imaginations of the individuals who reembody these forms. While Western dance history has often juxtaposed traditional dance with contemporary work that consciously attempts to distance itself from any previously articulated techniques, world dance history shows us how traditions are always being at once reconstructed and reinvented.

This part of the book, "World Dance Traditions," is meant to mark the importance of a wide variety of dancing that has become increasingly visible and often accessible to the average student of dance. Aside from the enormous variety of dance styles available in any urban center, most dance departments offer at least one course in an African or an African diasporic dance form, be it West African, blues styles, hip-hop, or capoeira. Frequently, students are able to take additional workshops in belly dancing, flamenco, or even a classical Indian dance form such as bharatha natyam. For instance, over the past two decades, without leaving American soil, we have seen a wide range of dances from around the world and have taken intensive workshops in classical Indian dance, Korean dance, and West African dance, as well as master classes in capoeira, butoh, and the hula. The fact that many important master teachers of these forms have immigrated to or have grown up in the United States disturbs any simplistic distinctions between Western and non-Western dance. Many dance students today, regardless of their ethnic or racial backgrounds, have more physical affinities with African diasporic dance than with European ballet. But most have never explored the implications of that kind of cultural hybridity. The essays in this section help create a broader intellectual context for this kind of physical exchange. By foregrounding the critical issues at stake in a range of dance forms, these essays help us to look at familiar ways of dancing with fresh eyes.

How Are We Looking?

The world dance forms discussed here encompass a wide variety of movement styles, and each form is marked by different priorities. Learning how to "see" the dances in the midst of written language—how to read movement between the lines, so to speak, requires an active visual and kinesthetic imagination. This means that we have to allow our own embodied experience to guide and enrich our perceptions about the dance we are studying. Focusing on the very basic grammar of a particular dance style—looking, for instance, at where the movement is initiated, the quality of energy or physical attack, the phrasing of the movement, use of weight as well as the various relationships between the head, limbs, and torso—can help us get a sense of the immediate corporeal experience. Yet this microscopic lens takes in only what is happening within the frame of the individual dancer's kinesphere. As Deidre Sklar makes abundantly clear in "Five Premises for a Culturally Sensitive Approach to Dance," "One has to look beyond movement to get at its meaning."[1]

Every dance reveals its own aesthetic and cultural moorings within both its basic movement vocabulary and the stylistic or compositional elements that serve to frame the movement. Looking carefully, for instance, we can begin to distinguish between the use of hands to signify specific gestural images (such as the hand mudras in bharatha natyam) or as extensions of the spatial line of the arm (such as in ballet or some contemporary American styles). We can begin to understand the process through which dance communicates meaning by asking questions such as: Is the facial expressivity critical to the dance's power to communicate, or is the face intentionally masked? Which parts of the dancers' bodies are specifically articulated? Is a sense of rhythmic unity important, or are spatial formations a stronger priority?

Very often, when dealing with dance across a variety of cultures, we need to open our vision of what constitutes the "dance" itself to include not only the immediate performance arena (including the dancers, musicians, and spectators), but also issues of when and where the dancing takes place. We need to ask questions such as: Is it a special occasion, a specific time of the year (harvest festivals, for instance)? How does the event begin and end? What are the aesthetic and social criteria that people use to talk about what they are seeing or participating in? In addition, there are broader concerns about who dances and who doesn't (women, men, children, elders, the initiated), whether participation changes one's social or political status in the community, and whether any transformation occurs and, if so, how that change is marked. In order to fully understand the levels of symbolic exchange within dance, it is critical to know enough of the broader cultural context to understand the layers of meaning embodied within the movement.

What Are We Looking At?

Because it engages with attitudes about the body as well as aesthetic concerns about movement, music, and the organization of space, dance is a wonderfully rich lens through which to look at a wide range of cultures. The essays selected for this section highlight these layered histories. Erika Bourgignon's classic 1968 study, "Trance and Ecstatic Dance," provides an important cross-cultural comparison of trance and possession dances across the world. She distinguishes between masked dancing in which the identity of the wearer is hidden, and possession trance in which the dancer's identity changes only when a spirit becomes incorporated within her or his body.

World dance tells many stories, including those of power and resistance, sexuality and the physical ideologies of gender, tradition, and innovation. Avanthi

Meduri begins her essay with an imperative: "Let me tell you a story." Yet her story, rather than being a simple child's folktale or a linear narrative of her dance training in the Indian form of bharatha natyam, folds itself into many other stories, including, the story of women's social and economic position in South India, the story of an Indian nationalistic agenda which strove to recuperate temple dancing by reconstructing dance as a "classical" tradition, the story of the development of middle-class moral sensibilities in postcolonial India, the story of dance's role within Indian religious traditions, and the gendered story of men's artistic patronage of women in dance. While Meduri embraces the physically expressive essence of bharatha natyam, she critiques the static representation of women within many traditional narratives. Because she is a dancer/scholar who performs and writes in appreciation of and resistance to these various stories, Meduri weaves her own saga back and forth across history and geography, continuing a tradition—but with important differences.

These issues of tradition, authenticity, and innovation are particularly complex with African and African-diasporic dance forms. Given the persistent and global persecution of African peoples over the past centuries, it is a testament to the enduring power of African dance that it has had such a vital influence on dance throughout the world. Kariamu Welsh Asante's classic "Commonalties in African Dance" takes an Africanist position in highlighting the crucial connectedness within the enormous variety of African and African-diasporic dances. She argues that, regardless of whether the dance is located in Africa, the Caribbean, or the Americas, there is an important sharing of aesthetic foundations among these different forms. In her essay "Invention and Reinvention in the Traditional Arts," Z. S. Strother documents an intriguing example of how the masking tradition in the Central Pende region of Zaire is deployed by a young male dancer to comment on the age hierarchy within his community. By remaking a masquerading tradition so that it becomes playfully relevant to his life, this performer literally re-animates a tradition that had begun to die out.

This sense of a specifically embodied cultural identity which is nonetheless open to contemporary influences also shapes Judy Van Zile's survey of Korean dance from the more traditional court forms to the contemporary hybrids. In "The Many Faces of Korean Dance," Van Zile articulates the specific cultural characteristics that animate many of the folk dances, distinguishing these forms from court dances that reveal the enduring influence of Confucianism. The companion piece by Lee Kyong-hee describes the dancing of Lee Ae-ju, a famous sungmu performer. In this short piece, we get to glimpse a dancer's own understanding of the interconnectedness of the spiritual and the physical aspects of this traditional nun's dance.

Mark Franko's essay "Writing Dancing, 1573" traces how bodies became physical metaphors for the carefully arranged distribution of state power in Renaissance Europe. It was as if the neat, often symmetrical, patterns of dancers suggested the obedience of loyal subjects. As state power writ large, the choreography carried symbolic messages that the audience could decipher or "read." The irony, of course, is that in order to create new images of this figured orderliness, the dancers needed to dissolve one pattern in order to create its sequel, thus at once preserving and undoing the spatial symbols of political control. Catherine Turocy's article on French eighteenth-century choreographic conventions provides another wonderful illustration of how sophisticated dance literacy had become in a culture in which one's social status was measured by one's physical comportment.

Perhaps one of the most vivid examples of political resistance is the Afro-Brazilian martial dance form capoeira. Barbara Browning's evocatively titled "Headspin: Capoeira's Ironic Inversions" shows how capoeira was used as a form of improvised resistance, not only in terms of the colonial institution of slavery, but also within other, more local, dynamics of racialized power. What is really fascinating is the way that this "resistance" is not simply a question of how capoeira was deployed within Brazilian history, but, as Browning makes clear, how resistance is actually embedded

within the physical experience of being upside-down—the inversion of self and society. Sometimes dances operate as a form of resistance and as a form which builds a strong consciousness of communal identity. Lisa Doolittle and Heather Elton's article "Medicine of the Brave" documents the ways in which Native American dance has functioned to consolidate spiritual energies within tribes (the Sun Dance) as well as to bring First Peoples together to resist outside oppressors (the infamous nineteenth-century Ghost Dance). Twentieth-century powwows are the most recent example of dancing which crosses over tribal and regional differences in order to create a communal sense of "Native" identity. In looking at Native American dance, we also see the importance of ritual dance events that can last many days and produce altered states of perception, including visionary trances.

Throughout the world, dance has often come to be associated with the female body and women's experiences. It is, therefore, not simply coincidental that many of the essays in this section foreground feminist issues concerning the physical display and symbolic sexualization of women's bodies within dance. From Avanthi Meduri's stories of the temple dancers in India to evocations of sylphs, innocent girls, and gypsies within nineteenth-century European ballet and to the "new" woman image championed by early German and American modern dance, these essays chart how women dancers have negotiated various historical and representational frames.

One of the most complex examples of how women have been empowered, disempowered, and re-empowered is that of belly dancing. Shawna Helland's article "The Belly Dance: Ancient Ritual to Cabaret Performance" is paired with Karin van Nieuwkerk's "Changing Images and Shifting Identities: Female Performers in Egypt" to present a layered case study of a dance whose origins may be traced back to the beginning of human culture. Read together, these essays document the contradictions that arise out of a dance form that both consolidates the physical and emotional power of a women's community (dancing together in birthing rites or celebrating within an all-women's space such as the harem or contemporary private studios), and yet often reduces that tradition to a bawdy and disreputable entertainment (belly dancing in Middle Eastern restaurants). The issue at stake here concerns who is dancing (almost exclusively women) and who is watching (mostly men), and the unequal power dynamic within this sexualized gaze. Lynn Garafola takes up this theme within a very different genre of dance in her essay on the travesty dancer in European ballet. The travesty dancer, Garafola asserts, "symbolized in her complex persona the many shades of lust projected by the audience on the nineteenth-century dancer."

Susan Allene Manning and Melissa Benson's discussion of modern dance in Germany demonstrates how early twentieth-century women dancers drew on modern paradigms of physical culture and art making to create a new space in which they could experiment with forcefully expressive movements and visionary choreographic forms. As their brief survey shows, however, these new models of dancing were rarely able to retain their utopian visions in the face of increasing political coercion. Once again, we can see how world dance, whether from Africa, Asia, or Europe, is constantly negotiating the intersecting realms of political, spiritual, social, and artistic influence.

Why Are We Looking?

One of the most amazing aspects of studying world dance is recognizing the incredible power that dance has in some cultures to literally transform reality. Any study of world dance allows us to bring out the layers of cultural meaning in ways that often remain invisible within one's own experience until one begins to engage in comparative analyses. Reading about the selected examples of dance forms in this section helps us to expand our notion of what dancing can be. In certain circumstances, this means that we need to confront our ethnocentric biases about what kind of movements constitute dancing, or at least which ones we immediately call "beautiful" or "awesome." At other times, we may need to revise our ideas about when we think dancing is appropriate. (Is it OK to dance in church, or at a funeral, for instance?) Looking at dance across cultures can bring us face to face with the hidden ideologies in our own dance techniques, forcing us to ask: why and for what purpose do we dance? For the editors of this volume who were trained in modern and contemporary American dance—with its emphasis on the individual expressive voice—the study of world dance helps us to realize the myriad ways in which dancing can be communally as well as personally transformative.

Note

1. See part I, "Thinking about Dance History: Theories and Practices," for the full article.

Trance and Ecstatic Dance

ERIKA BOURGIGNON

The Italian physician S. Brambilla, writing in a psychiatric journal in 1939,[1] reported a curious illness he had observed among the peoples of Eritrea and Amhara (Ethiopia). The illness was called *cherbé* or "devil's illness." Attacked by it, the patient executes movements and gestures in time to the rhythm of the singing and playing of music provided by a circle of men and women gesticulating frantically. The patient is believed to be possessed by a devil or "cherbé," and the rhythmical dancing constitutes not only an expression of his illness but also an attempt to cure him of it. While possessed by the evil spirit he is in a state of trance or dissociation, only dimly aware of what goes on around him. Afterwards he may remember none of the events. His illness consists of periodic attacks of such possession trance states which may be provoked by the music of the cure, and the cure consists precisely in inducing the attack through the music and dancing. During the performance, an attempt is made to exorcise or drive out the "devil."

In Apulia in Southern Italy, a team of anthropologists under the direction of the late Professor Ernesto de Martino studied a similar phenomenon in 1959.[2] This is an illness known as *tarantismo*. In related older forms are found the origins of the most famous of all Italian dances, the tarantella. In Apulia, persons who believe that they were bitten by the tarantula, and who suffer from various emotional and psychosomatic disturbances, undergo a special cure every year on the days of St. Peter and St. Paul (the 28th and 29th of June). At home, in the circle of his relatives and friends, to music specially provided for the occasion, the patient is made to dance to exhaustion. Later, in a public ceremony, all those in the region who are afflicted by the disease of *tarantismo* gather at the Chapel of St. Paul in the town of Salento. Here a sizeable number of persons experience states of dissociation that are frequently of considerable violence and which terminate in a loss of consciousness. These ceremonial cures are repeated every year. Similar practices have been reported from Sicily, from Sardinia and from Spain. In former times they occurred in the South of France as well.

Mass dance epidemics spread through Europe periodically during the later Middle Ages and extended over a period of several hundred years. Writers who have described these phenomena[3] tell us that there were sects of "dancers" who believed in dancing as a form of ritual and worship. Some could not help themselves and felt forced to dance compulsively. Certain members of the clergy viewed these activities as manifestations of demoniac possession and as a result they proceeded to drive out the devils and exorcise the dancers. In spite of this negative view by some of the priests, remnants of dance as ritual—healing and protective ritual—have come down to the present. In some towns in Belgium and Luxemburg such dancing processions are still held annually. In a suburb of the city of Charleroi in the Belgian coal mining region of the Borinage (where the young Vincent Van Gogh spent some months as an evangelist), one of the most impressive of these processions is to be seen. The priest, carrying the Host, follows the procession. As they step on to *l'terre al danse* (the place where legend says the dancing mania manifested itself) the entire group, and the priest with it, begin to dance, moving forward across the open space. It is as if the ground on which they step irresistibly forces this dancing motion on them, as if they were seized by it. In contrast to the dancing procession at Echternach in the Grand Duchy of Luxemburg, which is perhaps more famous, they do not move two steps forward and one step back, and the dancing is limited to the special area reserved for it. Today these are ritualized, formalized performances that attract numerous onlookers and curious visitors. Still they serve to remind us of the compulsive, dissociated nature of the dances of the great epidemics, even though the processions today are not only a reminder but are themselves a part of ritual and worship.

These examples are chosen almost at random from several hundred known to us. In them we find dance and worship, belief in spirits who may possess people, and the experience of trance or dissociation; we find ritual and illness and therapy. Religion, medicine and art are all intermingled here, and the dance is seen in its multiple forms as expressive of ecstasy and of illness, and at the same time as having the power to heal and undo illness.

The belief in possession by spirits—whether evil or helpful spirits—that may take control of the human body is widespread. It occurs in all parts of the world but is most prevalent in Africa, in Europe and in Asia. Spirit possession may manifest itself in a variety of ways: in physical illness, in the acquisition of supernatural or superhuman powers for good or for evil, in mental illness or deviant behavior, or in states of dissociation or trance that form a part of ritual practices rather than of illness. States of dissociation, whether ritual or pathological, are of course not necessarily interpreted by the people among whom they occur as due to such possession. Other explanations occur with equal frequency. They may be interpreted as due to be-

ing bewitched, to having lost one's soul, to supernatural inspiration, or to a variety of other causes.

From the point of view of the scientific observer rather than that of the participant and believer, we may speak of trance in somewhat different terms. We may define it as a state of altered consciousness; that is, a state in which one or several psychological and physiological changes occur: a change in the perception of time and form, of colors and brightness, of sound and movement, of tastes and odors, a change in the feel of one's own body, in sensations of pain, of heat or cold, of touch; a change in memory or in notions of one's own identity. Such changes may last for shorter or longer periods, may be of greater or lesser intensity, may be frequent or rare or even a single event in the life of the individual. They may be fleeting experiences given little or no cultural interpretation or value, they may be terrifying events of major proportions. Or they may be prized and cultivated, intentionally induced, as a means toward a supreme experience of the self or of the powers of the universe.

The reader will recognize in these comments some of the effects attributed to hallucinogenic drugs. The whole field of altered states of consciousness has in recent years acquired a popular fascination and an aura of familiarity. But drugs are only one of many ways to achieve such states. They have been sought, or feared and avoided, given cultural explanations and treated ritually in many hundreds of societies for thousands of years. The "psychedelic movement" and the "psychedelic experience" in contemporary America represent only a special, local variant of a major theme in human cultural history.

While trance states can be—and often are—induced by drugs, in the ritual context these methods are especially typical of South American Indians and of some North Asiatic peoples. Where drugs are used the aim will be to have visions, to communicate with spirits, to gain special powers, to send one's soul on errands to find lost objects or to bring back the abducted souls of sick persons. Indeed, the Siberian or South American shaman sends his soul "on a journey"—and we are not very far from the hippy term, "to take a trip." Elsewhere, particularly in Africa and among descendants of Africans in the Americas, drugs are rarely used for this purpose. Nor are dissociational states generally utilized to attain visions or insights. Instead, they are part of public ceremonial occasions in which dissociated individuals are believed to be possessed by certain spirits and act out the behavior of these spirits. Typically, musical rhythms associated with a given spirit or group of spirits are played, and the trancers dance the characteristic steps and movements of the spirits. They may be dressed to fit the part, often in elaborate costumes, but significantly, while impersonating the spirits they generally do not wear masks. Masks, representing other groups of spirits, involve a different type of impersonation and are associated with other occasions, other dances and other dancers.

Possession trance and the wearing of masks have much in common: their wide distribution, their frequent association with the dance and—most particularly—the fact that both involve the impersonation of spiritual entities by human beings. Yet they rarely occur together. Despite the similarities between masks and possession trance, there is an important difference: the mask hides the true identity of the wearer. In some cases, in fact, masks are used primarily for this purpose rather than to impersonate another being. But even where they are used for impersonation, the matter of disguise and hiding is still important. This is not true generally in the case of possession trance. It may therefore be suggested that masks and possession trance involve *alternate* ways of achieving convincing impersonation. Where the mask is used the identity of the wearer is generally unknown, or at least it seems desirable that it be unknown. Thus masks are frequently used by secret societies that attempt to use police powers: the Poro in Liberia or the Ku Klux Klan in the United States are no exceptions to this. Masks also appear in the context of tribal initiations where the young—and the women—are supposed to believe that the spirits, in the form of the maskers, have really come to the village. Part of the initiation into manhood con-

sists in finding out the truth. Women, incidentally, very rarely wear masks; this is generally the privilege of adult men.

In the case of possession trance, however, the identity of the impersonator is known to all. Instead of covering the face and body with a mask or disguise, the body itself, so to speak, becomes the "mask" that clothes the identity of the spirit who now inhabits the body. While the actor manipulates the mask, the "possessed" person is, as it were, manipulated by the spirits that are temporarily incarnated in him. The transformation of the trancer then is much more fundamental than that of the masker. As this radical and dramatic transformation is visible to all through the physical and psychological signs and symptoms of the trance state, the discontinuity in the personal identity of the trancer may be emphasized and heightened (as in Vietnam or Korea) by placing a cloth over the person's face at the moment of the spirit's supposed entry into the body of his human medium.

Through spirit possession public proof and demonstration of the reality of the spirits and of their intervention in human affairs is given. Thus no mask is needed. The mask, then, represents an *external* transformation, a change in the appearance of the actor. Possession trance, on the other hand, represents an *inner* transformation, a change in the impersonator's essence.

Some people use both masks and possession trance to impersonate spirits on different occasions. This is the case, for example, among the Alaskan Eskimos where the difference is strongly emphasized. Thus, Margaret Lantis[4] tells us that among these people, as among many others who use masks for such purposes, it is believed that the spirit resides in the mask itself, not in the masker. Indeed it is considered important that the spirit stay in the mask which is therefore so constructed that the wearer can look only downward. This is done to prevent the spirit of the mask from entering the wearer, which it would do otherwise.

Like the mask, the possession trance phenomenon is intimately related to the dance. Indeed this is the kind of trance state (or dissociational state) most frequently linked to the dance. Non-possession trance, particularly the drug-induced variety, is essentially a passive, subjective and private experience, even when it occurs to several persons at the same time or to one person in the presence of others. The effect of the drug is likely to alter the perception of sound, of music and rhythm, and to limit more or less severely the controlled, co-ordinated and disciplined execution of patterns of motion. This in itself would tend to make dance performance unlikely. Possession trance, with its emphasis on impersonation, is an objectively demonstrated, active, public phenomenon. It requires an audience not only to validate the experience but, in most cases, to bring it about in the first place. Furthermore, possession trance may at times be more significant for the group that observes it than for the individual who experiences it; this is particularly true when, as is frequently the case, the experience is not remembered by the subject. The dance and the accompanying music may be used to initiate dissociation, or, in the language of the believers, to "invite" the spirits, or the dance may be the characteristic motion of the spirit. Or again—where the spirits are to be dispatched, forcing the trancer to dance to exhaustion, to unconsciousness—the dance may be the preferred method of exorcising or removing the possessing, interfering, alien spirit.

Dance, music, handclapping, singing, costuming, the presence of an expectant and participating audience, a ritual setting at an appropriate place and time—all these are ideally suited to produce both induction of dissociation and the therapeutic results of the ritual. Expectation and suggestion are obviously of great importance in bringing these about. The music, with its increasing frequency and intensity, facilitates rhythmical movement and itself has a clear psychological effect: it may help to release the dancer of part of his responsibility for his movements and actions. But it may have a physiological effect on the brain as well, helping to induce dissociation. The dance itself will contribute to an alteration of breathing patterns; it may bring about hyperventilation and—if prolonged—partial exhaustion, both of which again facilitate disso-

ciation. Another significant factor, however, is to be found in the frequent whirl-ing and turning, of circular and rotational movements. These tend to affect the sense of balance and equilibrium, thus leading to dizziness. Disturbances of balance are likely to be experienced, involving a loss of control over the body and thus over the self. They may indicate the impending loss of consciousness. If, furthermore, a disturbance in the sense of balance is believed to be a preliminary to possession, to being "mounted" by a spirit as it is so frequently phrased, this in itself will contribute to the likelihood of the occurrence of trance.

Thus there are many types of ritualized, patterned forms of trance; there are many types of beliefs in possession by spirits. In fact, several such types of trance and spirit-possession belief may co-exist in the same society or in different segments of the same society. When trance is interpreted as due to spirit possession and when spirit possession finds its expression in states of trance, then we are also likely to find a linkage between trance and dance. Non-possession trance more rarely uses the dance as its vehicle of expression and it is least likely to do so when hallucinogenic drugs are employed. Where spirit possession trance occurs, the trancer impersonates the spirit, but he is unlikely to utilize masks among his accessories.

Ritualized, formalized dissociational states are found worldwide, are given a great variety of cultural interpretations and are embedded into many different institutions, customs, traditions and practices, most of which are religious in nature. The very wide distribution of these states among the peoples of the world would suggest that they are very ancient.

Our own Western tradition has its deepest roots in the Mediterranean world of Jew and Greek, and we find what we are looking for in both of these traditions. For example, we are told in the Bible (I Samuel 10) that Saul travelled with a company of ecstatic prophets. "And David danced before the Lord with all his might" (II Samuel 6). He leaped and danced ecstatically before the Ark while he and his men played on such instruments as harps and psaltries, timbrels, cornets and cymbals, as the King James Version lists them. Ecstatic and dissociated behavior, visions and voices, appear throughout the Bible, both in the Old and New Testaments. The dancing sects and dancing epidemics of the Middle Ages, and the dancing processions of present-day Belgium and Luxemburg, are all reminders of these Biblical traditions and practices. So were the ecstatic dances of the Hasidim among the Jews of Eastern Europe which inspired the choreography of *Fiddler on the Roof.* In all these dances there is a heightened sense of participation in the mystic powers of the Divine. All of our examples refer to group dances, to forms of collective mysticism. There is no acting out here of the characters of diverse specific spirits, of impersonation or role playing, for there is only one Spirit and all share in His power.

The impersonating, acting-out type of possession trance, however, appears to have played a significant part in the other ancestral cultural stream: the religious life of ancient Greece. The cults of Dionysos and of the Corybantes are only sketchily known to us from a few fragmentary references in the remnants of Greek literature and iconography. However, we know that the cult of Dionysos, which gave rise to the theater in its classic form, also involved periodic trances of the god's followers. There is every reason to believe that Euripides' play *The Bacchae* contains a strong element of historic truth in its representation of the frenzied, dissociated states of the Maenads. Greek painting and sculpture offer examples of the movements and faces of the Maenads in no uncertain terms. The few references we have to Corybantic rituals tell us about dances and music specific for each spirit that is invoked and of the use of these spirit rituals in the treatment of "mania" or madness. The French classical philologist H. Jeanmaire[5] has suggested that these practices bear strong resemblances to those of the *zar* cult in modern Ethiopia and that a study of the *zar* cult may help us to understand the small number of tantalizingly brief references to these ritual practices by ancient Greek authors.

There are, however, at least two kinds of ecstatic, dissociational dances and dance rituals in the culture area of classical Greece that have survived to modern times and that are likely to reveal at least an element of direct continuity with the past. First of all, we find in Northern Greece and in neighboring Bulgaria as well, rituals of fire dancing. Fire dancing (or walking) has a wide but spotty distribution in many parts of the world and we may safely assume that its origins go back into the distant past. However, the form and significance of these practices and of the psychological experiences associated with them vary widely from region to region and from culture to culture. In modern Greece fire dancing is celebrated on the day of St. Helena in memory of her recovery of the True Cross. Today the dance is a major tourist attraction. Indeed, the development from religion to performance, from ritual to theater, is one that has taken place over and over again. Still, it is not without interest that modern fire walking occurs in Thrace, a region that is one of the purported homelands of Dionysos.

A second ecstatic practice of ritual of this area, which has also been turned into an annual performance, is the striking dance of the whirling Mevlevi dervishes of Konya in central Anatolia. This town is unique in Turkey in that it originated and still maintains this somewhat deviant form of Muslim brotherhood. Trance dancing appears to be absent elsewhere in Turkey and the Konya dervishes, together with other Muslim practitioners and practices, had been outlawed by the government in the 1920s. Today, the annual public performance of the whirling ecstatic dance is preserved and permitted as an attraction and a museum piece. But in the local folk practices of Konya the whirling dervishes still play a role in the religious and religio-medical life of the people. Konya, too, is one of the ancestral homes of the Phrygian Dionysos.

We do not know with any certainty whether the ancient Greek cults have any connection with diverse other ecstatic dancing practices in the Mediterranean basin in later times: tarantism and related patterns in Apulia, Sardinia, Spain and Provence; the *zar* cult of North East Africa; the *stambuli* or *bori* cults of Tunisia, Algeria and Morocco and several others. Still, the occasions for contact for groups of diverse cultural backgrounds throughout this region were many. Christianity is known to have incorporated various Greek and other pagan elements and thus to have helped in their diffusion. Nevertheless, however fascinating such speculations about possible contacts might be, we risk being led to unfounded and hence useless conclusions by this sort of guesswork. We can learn more by looking at the concrete examples of contemporary peoples whom we can study at firsthand, observing their activities and finding out from their own statements what these activities represent to them.

We can say with some assurance that the ecstatic dance, the dance connected in some way with the phenomena of trance, is very widespread and undoubtedly a very ancient element of ritual. It appears in many forms and takes on many cultural styles, including a variety of styles of dance. It is also linked to a great variety of beliefs and of social and ritual practices. However, to put some order into our materials, we may distinguish two basic types of ecstatic dance: that used as a vehicle for achieving mystic states and that used in the ritual enactment of a role.

Notes

1. Silvio Brambilla, "Contributo allo studio delle manifestazioni psicopatologiche delle popolazioni dell' Imperio," *Revista di Patologia Nervosa e Mentale* 53 (1939): 187–206.

2. Ernesto de Martino, *La Terra del Rimorso* (Milan, 1961).

3. J. F. C. Hecker, *The Dancing Mania* (New York: Fitzgerald, 1885). Alfred Martin, "Geschichte der Tanzkrankheit in Deutschland," *Zeitschrift des Vereins für Volkskunde* 24 (1914): 113–134, 225–239.

4. Margaret Lantis, *Alaskan Eskimo Ceremonialism* (New York: Augustin, 1947).

5. H. Jeanmaire, *Dionysos, histoire du culte de Bacchus* (Paris: Payot, 1951).

Bharatha Natyam—What Are You?

AVANTHI MEDURI

Let me tell you a story. I grew up in the cultural city of Madras, where I learned *bharatha natyam,* a form of South Indian classical dance, from a very young age. My dance teachers told me a story, a story they were never tired of repeating. They told me that *bharatha natyam* traces its origins to the *Natyashastra,* a detailed, ancient text on dramaturgy authored by the sage Bharatha (Bharatha-Muni), ca. 300 B.C. Sitting at their feet, I listened in wide-eyed awe. They told me that this dance was once called *sadir* and that it was performed in the sacred precincts of the temple. They said that the *devadasi* (temple dancers) who practiced this art form lived and danced happily in the temple environments. I nodded my head in agreement. But then the *devadasi* turned "corrupt" and profaned the art form, they said suddenly, and rather angrily. Frightened by their anger, I asked rather hesitantly about how they had profaned the art. They looked around them to see if anybody was eavesdropping, and whispered into my ear: they said that dancing became associated with *nautch* girls because of the corrupt ways of the *devadasi.* Their personal life, reflected in the art form, expressed itself in the crude and literal language of the *nautch* girl. I did not understand anything they said. I was too young and frightened. A highly complex system rooted in religion had become "corrupted" till the "respectable" people of the south initiated a campaign in the late 1920s to abolish the ill-reputed *devadasi* system. What about the dance then, I interjected? They smiled benevolently at my anxiety and said that important cultural institutions, such as the Music Academy in Madras, and eminent individuals, like E. Krishna Iyer, saved the dance from extinction. I asked them how it happened, instead of asking them why it happened. I was too young to know the difference.

When I repeated this story to my grandmother—for this had now become my own story—she told me that my great-grandfather, T. Prakasam, had as chief minister of the composite Madras and Andhra Pradesh states of India publicly urged the people, especially the respectable women, to take to dancing and thus lend something of the purity of their own lives to the art form. I was perplexed. Is this why I was taught dancing, for someone's idea of respectability? I remember feeling disappointed.

But to go on with the other story . . . My teachers reiterated proudly and with stern faces the three propitious happenings that revolutionized the history of *bharatha natyam:* (1) the name of the dance form was changed from *sadir* to *bharatha natyam* in 1932; (2) Rukmini Devi, an upper-class Brahmin, learned the dance form, thereby investing it with dignity, and established a dance school called Kalakshetra (Academy for Fine Arts) for the transmission of traditional knowledge; and (3) the great dancer Balasaraswati, whose artistry depended to a large extent on her ancestral connection to the *devadasi* tradition, spread the fame of *bharatha natyam* to the far corners of the globe. They said that *sadir,* by force of these three circumstances, was firmly launched on its transformational journey under the new name *bharatha natyam.* In time, this story became my own, until it was no longer a "story" to me.

Today I wish to look at this integral narrative of my life in subjective reflexiveness. My Indian teachers, I remember, exhorted me even as a child to quiet the restless agitation of my questioning mind. They extolled the virtues of transcendental knowledge *(alaukika gnana),* which is characterized by intellectual detachment. This view of reality terrified me then as it does today, for it undercuts plurality and forces one to consciously efface or transcend Self. So, I shall articulate my questions about Indian dance today self-consciously and without the desire to be neutral. These unasked questions were the dark shadows of my adolescent years, and they still possess the power to rock the adult foundation of my rationalized peace.

I shall begin by describing briefly some of the salient features of Indian dance, if only to create a context in which to frame my questions. *Bharatha natyam* in theory and practice refers to Bharatha's *Natyashastra* (Rules of drama), probably compiled in the second to third centuries A.D.[1] But the *Natyashastra* is not exclusively a text on dance technique. Rather, it is a comprehensive treatise on Indian dramaturgy that includes dance. Dance is conceived as being a part of drama in Bharatha's theatre, just as color is perceived as being intimately connected to music, which in turn influences emotional representation. The rules that govern Indian dramaturgy are also the principles that define classical dance. Bharatha's vision, then, enunciates a total theatre that links all the minutest units of dramatic representation. Each unit, such as dance, can be analyzed and described separately, and yet assumes theatrical significance only in the context of the whole dramatic representation. If a minute aspect of the whole is disturbed or exaggerated, the theatre loses its characteristic, significant coherence. Bharatha's attention to theatrical unity and aesthetic wholeness evokes in the meditative mind a philosophic, cosmic vision of unity. This might explain the theatre's abiding popularity in Indian aesthetics and its compelling centrality in religious discourse.

Dance, a part of drama, is divided into three distinct categories: *natya, nrithya,* and *nrtta. Natya* corresponds to drama, *nrithya* to mime performed to song and music, and *nrtta* to pure dance that employs sculpturesque poses and body movements that do not refer back to narrative. The performer has four means of communication, or *abhinaya* (expression): *vacika* (speech), *aharya* (costume), *angika* (body), and *sattvika* (psychological states). Bharatha, as Ghosh points out in his English translation of the *Natyashastra,* does not espouse the *lokadharmi* mode of explicit or realistic representation of emotion.[2] He values the *natyadharmi* mode of communication, which evokes emotion in an artistic and subtle manner. The latter technique is valued because it helps maintain the illusion of art, the necessary difference between realism and representation. The illusion of art is further reinforced by the religious themes of dance and drama, stories which are usually extracts from legend and Vedic scriptures. The ideal spectator *(sahrydaya),* absorbed in the religious stories evoked in the conventionalized mode of representation, experiences *rasa,* or aesthetic delight—a state of joy characterized by emotional plenitude. Endowed with superior artistic and intellectual capabilities, Bharatha's sympathetic spectator harmonizes differences into unities by the power of his own mind. He, like the performer, perceives the sublime in the erotic, the divine in the human.

Indian dance thus encapsulates both in structure and in content the philosophic aspirations of the Indian mind. It appears as a sublime synthesis of philosophy, sculpture, music, and literature. It gathers all these strands and sets them in motion before the eye. Yet, because it weaves together so many artistic streams and evokes a compelling vision of aesthetic immensity and philosophic magnitude, it resists clear description as an artifact having its own unique temporality. When one begins to speak about Indian dance, one is entering a philosophical discourse on ethics, aesthetics, and social reality, all at once. This process resembles the sinuous dance of the elusive snake which dances always with its tail in its mouth. Mesmerizing no doubt, but very difficult to evaluate in terms of art appreciation.

Moved as I am by Bharatha's aesthetic theatre of complex unity, it presents some immediate problems in translations to the contemporary world. First, this theatre is an expression of one religious world view, one very different from the plural reality of contemporary India. Rent asunder by colonialism, regionalism, and political strife, India today is psychologically restless and far removed from Bharatha's religious state of mind characterized by *visrati* (expansive quiet). Bharatha's theatre, in accordance with its world view, unfolds in a slow process of cumulative classical elaboration that is the opposite of the fractured, hurried reality of the twentieth century—it represents at its best the aesthetic and philosophic ideal of Indian art. Indian dance today, however, functions in a secular reality—in the gap between philosophic vision and everyday reality. Today's *bharatha natyam*, with its danced stories of God evoked in a secular world, is analogous to a human being walking forward with his face turned backwards. I hasten to add that this peculiar analogy is true only of contemporary Indian dance. *Sadir*, practiced by *devadaisi* and housed in the physical context of the temple, its immediate theatre, fused ritual-form and religious fervor into one nondualistic whole. The temple was the natural home for Bharatha's ancient theatre, itself articulated in religious inspirations. So it fused physical context with ideology, form with content. And the *devadasi* symbolized this fusion till she and the dance were ousted from the temple in the first half of the twentieth century by civil laws that prohibited temple dancing. Let us now dwell briefly on the *devadasi* story.

The *devadasi*, literally "servant of God," danced and sang the stories of God before temple deities to propitiate and entertain them. She also performed the ritual oblations in the temple. For this reason, she was dedicated to the temple even before she attained puberty. Some time thereafter, she was formally married to the temple deity in a sacred thread ceremony *(tali kettu).*

The sacred thread tied around her neck solemnized her marriage to the deity and precluded her from marrying a mortal man, although she could have discreet sexual relations with priest or king. The *devadasi,* at the height of her glory under the rulership of the Chola kings in the ninth through twelfth centuries A.D., linked temple to court and balanced patronage with personal independence. Well-versed in the arts, she was considered a jewel of both court and temple alike. Both these institutions mutually cared for her rather lavish economic needs. Even in her marginalized social position, she was unique in that she epitomized the freedom of the plural woman outside of caste and not defined in the biological role of a madonna. The *devadasi* tradition continued into the eighteenth and nineteenth centuries, but without the robust commitment of the preceding generations. Kapila Vatsyayan sums this up rather neatly:

> the generation that went to colleges founded by the British in the early nineteenth century was isolated from the art traditions of the country. Apparently the art had died by the twentieth century and what could be seen of it was only a diluted, almost degenerated form of what was known as *Sadir* in the South. It was like a shadow of a bygone reality.[3]

Muthulakshmi Reddi, speaking at the Madras legislature in 1901, sharply pointed to this degeneracy when she said: "Now the appellation of the *devadasi* as every one of us here knows, whatever the original meaning may have been, stands for prostitute."[4] This anti-*devadasi* feeling was reinforced again in the Madras Census Report of 1911, which on page 2601 described the *devadasi* system thus: "In South India, a girl may marry an arrow, a tree, perhaps to escape the reproach of attaining puberty unmarried. She may marry an idol which generally implies she has become a prostitute."[5] Public disapproval, as we can see in the above statement, was directed at both the *devadasi* and the tradition she represented. The issue was complex because exploitation, child marriage, and child traffic had become incorporated into the system. It was, however, the *devadasi's* availability to all who visited the temple, patrons and commoners alike, that enraged the South Indian sense of decorum. It was inconceivable to them that she, who danced the stories of God by day, could actually indulge in the mortal delights of humans at night. They believed that "inner purity" (whatever that term means) had to synchronize with outer action. Thus, they promulgated the laws that abolished temple dancing once and for all. The "respectable" women of the south had entered the arena, wrested the dance from these traditional custodians, and mastered it. The *devadasi* were thus rudely dismissed, while the dance itself, like the mythical phoenix, rose from the ashes.

I believe the anti-*devadasi* sentiment failed to distinguish between cause and effect. If the *devadasi* had turned "corrupt," as the traditionalists argue (though I would prefer the word "indiscriminate"), it was not from moral depravity. Benevolent monarchy was being replaced by Muslim and foreign invasions, culminating finally in the twentieth-century independence movement. Caught in this changing, uneasy political atmosphere, with her former generous patronage vanishing, the *devadasi* had been forced to choose between economic necessity and man-made rules of decorum. She chose the former. Can I cast the proverbial stone at her who wished to live on her own moral terms? How does one begin to apportion blame, on whom, and based on what ethical values? But we did just that. We pronounced her alone guilty. Having polluted the sacred precincts of the temple, almost as reparation she was forbidden to dance there. What about the psychological reality of her ceremonial marriage to the idol? Hundreds of *devadasi* were forced from the temple in ignominy and shame, not knowing where to go or what to do next. The laws that had no heart had clever solutions. Almost as an afterthought they offered the *devadasi* a secular stage as a new home. Did the *devadasi* want this new home? Would the dance survive on this platform, cut off from the ritual roots of the temple? I will attempt to answer this by posing other questions.

The *devadasi,* expelled from the temple, arrived helplessly on the secular stage. The bright cunning stage lights, that focused on her sharply and penetratingly, mercilessly exposed the dying flame of her life. But the history of contemporary *bharatha natyam* actually begins earlier, in India's recent political history. India in the nineteenth century was beginning to cast off the foreign yoke. My grandfather, I believe, set fire to his Western clothes, as did millions in every hamlet of India, reverting to *khadhi,* the cotton cloth spun in the seed and toil of the Indian earth. India was rediscovering its beaten-down authenticity. Ordinary men were transformed into little gods, and they strutted about the earth in proud dignity. Indian dance, imaged in the silence of the temple, fell into this noisy rhetoric. In 1931 the South Indian *devadasi* dancers were featured on the Music Academy platform in Madras, and the academy continued this tradition despite strong public opposition. Balasaraswati, who later became the legendary figure of *bharatha natyam,* herself belonging to the *devadasi* tradition, was featured on this platform in 1934, when barely in her teens. Krishna Iyer, V. Raghavan, and other liberal-minded scholars eulogized the transcendental glories of the two-thousand-year-old tradition in their lectures, even as the dancers danced out their social shame in public. In this political atmosphere the *devadasi* was transformed almost completely into an object, valued only as the repository of the ancient tradition she had mastered—as its symbol. In this we see the first signs of the split that society initiated and then seemed to sanction, the division between inner and outer, self and culture, which is also the special schizophrenia of the contemporary dancer. The questions that haunt me are these: why was the nineteenth-century *devadasi* in the temple condemned for not fusing her inner life with the outer? And why, on the twentieth-century secular stage, because respectable people sanctioned it, was the disjunction deemed acceptable and even worthwhile? How could this be? Dance in the early twentieth century, both in the temple and outside it, was being defined, it seems to me, in the shabby clothes of "respectability," but not in its autonomy, and definitely not for its own sake.

How did Balasaraswati, alone among *devadasi,*

9. Avanthi Meduri performs "Woman looking at herself in a mirror." Photo by Danna Byron.

achieve status and prestige under the new system? I wish for sanity's sake that I could answer this question unreflexively, by admitting simply to her extraordinary talent, a talent that could offer almost effortlessly a momentary experience of *rasa*. The issue, however, is far more complex and unassuring. "Some aver," says Gowri Ramnarayan, "that Rukmini Devi [the respected upper-middle-class Brahmin dancer and scholar] was indirectly responsible for Bala's shining as an unchal-

lenged star."[6] Whatever Balasaraswati was or was not, it is clear that middle-class notions of respectability had now become tied up with dance. Class had certainly become an issue, had raised its ugly head in a purportedly autonomous medium such as art. How we are going to untangle all these interwoven issues is a challenge for posterity.

Add to these complicating issues yet another theoretical issue. Nineteenth- and early twentieth-century aestheticians and scholars involved in formulating the history of Indian dance, in attempting to compensate for its progressive "degradation," elevated dance to a new high. They did two things: they extolled the technical virtues of Bharatha's *Natyashastra,* and they incorporated Abhinavagupta's eleventh-century reinterpretation of the *Natyashastra* into their new propaganda, while continuing to speak of dance in terms of the *Natyashastra* itself.[7] Abhinavagupta commented on the *Natyashastra* in the sophisticated language of psychology and ontology, being and awareness. His language, springing from a certain specific world view, was given to abstraction and phenomenology, to art as a state of mind. And it was accessible to the nineteenth-century rational consciousness, separated from the dualisms and superstitions of uncivilized man (if civilization means growth of rationality). So Bharatha's *Natyashastra,* probably written in the second to third century A.D., was reinterpreted in the eleventh-century language of Abhinavagupta, and the historical differences between the two were considered inconsequential by nineteenth- and early twentieth-century scholars. Theory, I believe, begins to operate in a vacuum unconnected with reality when it misses these differences. The *devadasi* practicing her art form in the temple might have been better able to harmonize these shifting world views than the scholars, as hers was an inherited oral tradition open to change and sensitive to difference. However unreflexive her tradition might have been, it was a living tradition that fused belief with practice. The aesthetic experience after Abhinavagupta, says Vatsyayan, "was considered second only to the supreme experience and was thus termed its twin brother *(brahmanandasahodara).*"[8] Bharatha himself, however, did not address the metaphysical nature of his aesthetic theatre. It was the later scholars who inquired into the psychology and ontology of the art experience, who elevated dance and drama to the status of a high religion *(vedanta),*[9] perceiving it as an experience that embodied transcendental knowledge, cosmic oneness, and religious concentration.

Aestheticians and scholars of the nineteenth and early twentieth centuries unwittingly opened up a new kind of void for the contemporary performing artist when they cogently verbalized and made explicit the implicit philosophic rules that underlie and govern Indian art. The twentieth-century performing artist, living in a secular reality, struggles to embrace, emotionally and intellectually, the theoretical ideal that has been set up. If she cannot personally achieve the ideal, she repeats the theory. So theoretician and artist trace the same circle, the figure eight, in which both are held mutually captive. This figure eight excludes the secular practice of *bharatha natyam* and the important contemporary reality of the performing artist. In the words of Kapila Vatsyayan, "Matter and style, the idea and the manifestation of it in form, go on merging into one another, and the one cannot be separated from the other."[10] This merging, I believe, chokes the vital breath of *bharatha natyam* by not accounting for its secularization. As a first step, the dance now needs to be described on its own terms, as if it were a separate phenomenon existing outside of time. In this first step would be total freedom, the autonomy that all art aspires towards, but seldom achieves. If I could thus freeze *bharatha natyam,* I would then ask it a hypothetical question:

> *Bharatha natyam*—Are you
> The vision urging me on,
> The memory holding me back,
> Or are you the dance at the heart
> That does not move?

Asking this reflexive question might imply the latent possibility of rediscovering the past in the constantly changing present, of articulating a theory that can account for the practice of *bharatha natyam.*

Aestheticians and scholars tried to reclaim *sadir,* which they renamed *bharatha natyam.* But in the process they invested the new creation with their own notions of respectability. Rukmini Devi and others of her high social class saw the existing dance form as being too crude and literal. They felt it would not satisfy the aesthetic taste of sophisticated society in which it must of necessity now function. Rukmini Devi believed that the love (shringara) portrayed by devadasi was "very ordinary, low shringara."[11] Love was not sensuality for her, but rather devotion (bhakti), and she therefore began to exalt devotion in her presentations. In contrast to this, Balasaraswati, a direct descendant of the devadasi community, felt that love was preeminent in the dance tradition because it emphasized both the self and the other, inner and outer—in short, life itself. She said:

> The shringara we experience in bharatha natyam is never carnal—never, never. For those who have yielded themselves to this discipline with total dedication, dance like music is the practice of presence, it cannot merely be the body's rapture.[12]

When Balasaraswati performed, one felt blessed and revitalized. Anna Kisselgoff said in the New York Times: "In one flash, the sacred origins of classical dance became clear. Perfectly modern sophisticates who know nothing about Indian dance begin to use such words as epiphany, spiritual, sublime as they leave the theatre."[13] Balasaraswati herself never tired of saying: "There is nothing in Bharatha Natyam which can be purified afresh; it is divine and is innately so."[14] Yet Rukmini Devi and many educated Brahmins thought differently. Whose gaze was it then that differentiated the vulgar from the sublime? And on what criteria? Who is to say what love is or what it is not? It seems as if the Brahmins were bringing their own philosophical and ideological biases to bear upon bharatha natyam. By doing this, they were radically altering an ancient art form of the temple and shaping its future destiny. By surrounding it with social ritual and philosophical dogma, they invested the new dance with awe and respect, the only means by which they could assure its continuance in a social environment. It is common knowledge that Balasaraswati lashed out at this cleaned-up, "Brahminized" dance, calling it in her turn "vulgar."

So we see the beginning of a dialectic in the styles propagated by these two women. If Balasaraswati focused on inner feeling, on surrender to the medium that led effortlessly to the concentration of the Yogic mind, Rukmini Devi approached the same goal through body control, mind and awareness. In a typical Brahminical manner, she focused on ritual, style, and form, and saw form as revealing content. And Rukmini Devi had a reason for focusing on form—she was anticipating the secularization that is the most singular feature of Indian dance today. By anticipating it, she was able to conceive of her academy (Kalakshetra) as an institution for the preservation and transmission of dance traditions that would become the boon and buffer for all of us who have learned dance after her. And by merely anticipating it, she actually began the secularization she so strongly abhorred. The academy's aim, to "educate public opinion and develop good taste through concerts, public lectures, demonstrations, exhibitions and publications," actually launched dance into a new era of intellectual awareness.[15] The notes and the extensive explanations that accompany a dance recital today are a direct offshoot of the academy's intellectual inheritance. Without the intellectual awareness, we might have lost forever a meaningful cultural experience. Yet because of it we have lost something of the spirit of Balasaraswati, that inner spiritual exuberance or fullness.

It may be useful to point out that Rukmini Devi and the other scholars who helped mobilize support for bharatha natyam did not "rediscover" India as many claimed; rather, they reinterpreted it in a respectable language for the modern masses. A number of factors—urbanization, diversity of languages, and a political history which has interrupted the continuity of Indian art—prevent any authentic rediscovery. Neither did the Madras Music Academy, an institution involved in the political reformulation of bharatha natyam, actually help make the dance more respectable. The 1937 resolution of the academy said that "in order to make dancing respectable, it is necessary to encourage public performances thereof before respectable people."[16] The resolution proposed, in other words, to rectify the closed system of exploitation which had victimized the *devadasi* by opening up the dance to the public. But the question that bothered me even as an adolescent was: What makes dancing really "respectable"? Did dance performed on platforms before the educated and respected classes of society—and thus in an "open system"—acquire respectability by virtue of being presented before this public? That would mean that the dance itself was not any more respectable than before. To whom did the resolution's phrase "respectable people" refer? The politicians and the educated elite class, or the connoisseurs? What happened to Bharatha's ideal spectator, who is not clothed in society's garments of respectability but is tuned into the art experience for its own sake? Why was this person conspicuously left out? It seems to me that this "open system" was not so open after all. It excluded some segments of society, and by doing so did not, as purported, let art permeate the social infrastructure. On the contrary, dance became the exclusive entertainment of the "respectable"—the elite and middle class. Nor has the "open system" of public performances lent any new dignity or status to the contemporary performer. She is still dependent on a male system, even more so in fact than in the days of *sadir*. If the *devadasi* was protected at least marginally by the temple or the patron, the contemporary dancer is completely at the mercy of a new urban system represented not by one male but by many. This is a harsher reality than the *devadasi* ever faced. Ironically, the academy was reversing a process it intended to push forward, and today the dancer is forced to play fully the dual roles of traditional and modern woman: onstage she dances the stories of the gods, while offstage in a ruthlessly competitive secular world she must be both intelligent and ambitious. These two opposing world views are her historical inheritance, and only she knows what this inner tension does to her.

The contemporary traditional dancer knows that her social reality is different from the social context in which Balasaraswati and Rukmini Devi danced. She admires and remembers them both in deep reverence, but she knows that she cannot emulate them. Yamini Krishnamurthi, an exponent of *bharatha natyam* in the city of New Delhi, says "Bala [Balasaraswati] was like a fabulous flower. Her talent depressed me because I realized it would be impossible to be like her."[17] In this poignant statement I perceive a robust honesty, an awareness that the dancer's life can never be the way it once was. Heraclitus said that you can never put your hand in the same water twice. Dancers today more than at any other point in time are aware of this agonizing yet joyful truth. Intellectually tough, often educated, belonging to respectable upper-middle-class society, the young dancers of India are ambitious, independent, and articulate. If they have the economic means, they buy the best instruction available. If they do not, but have the talent, then they struggle. The path to fame is not easy. The students with economic power shop around for the best teachers and test them out. It used to be the other way around. Mothers more often than not enter the battlefield along with their daughters, canvass for them, and undertake the promotional work. At all times money is needed.

I am not suggesting that there was a "blessed time" in history when material power was not connected with the arts. I am rather pointing out that when the arts and material power interweave and make a mutual pact to nurture each other, two things happen: a certain kind of political propaganda is generated (e.g., *sadir* is renamed *bharatha natyam)*; and a hierarchical power structure is created in which a certain kind of transaction occurs, one which forces a parasitical relationship of mutual interdependence. Rukmini Devi perceived this dynamic and called it the secularization of the *devadasi* dance. In her idealistic manner, however, she saw secularization as synonymous with decay:

> The deterioration set in when dances began to be organized in the houses of the rich as entertainment during weddings and other family festivities.[18]

It seems to me that Rukmini Devi was pointing not just to a power transaction but also to an unhealthy relationship between money and the arts—a relationship which exists today. Well-meaning, educated, influential industrialists have risen to the occasion, as in the instance of S. Viswanathan, who set up the Kala Mandir (Temple for Fine Arts) Trust in Madras to offer financial assistance to the talented needy. I am amazed at the repetitive nature of this pattern. When the *devadasi* dance became "corrupted," as the story goes, powerful people invested it with respectability, thus ensuring its continuance. Today, dance does not need this intellectual reinforcement—it is now considered "respectable" to be a dancer. Dance now needs money, which trusts and various arts associations are providing to ensure its continuity.

The question I am now leading up to is very simple: Who has the money in the present system? In a traditional patriarchal society such as India, men have always been invested with power and they have always made the rules. The female dancer then, by returning to this system, is actually returning to man. She has no other recourse. What is she making herself into? Not only does she look to him for nurture, she is also judged and evaluated by him. She has to court and pander to the often-egotistical wishes of male critics. I remember articulating this dilemma in Madras, in a press forum held at the Krishna Gana Sabha, a cultural association for the promotion of dance/music. I said, "I feel demeaned seeking the patronage of critics, which I must do if I want to survive in this system. Is there a way out of this for me?" The press and dancers chose to ignore my indignant plea. They thought I was simply foolish and young. The contemporary dancer must be intelligent, educated, strong, and articulate to succeed today, yet she is still in a servile position.

Alone in her dressing room, in the silence of her soul, she peels off layer after layer of thick makeup, rich costumes, and jewelry, and recognizes briefly but unforgettably, in the nakedness of her face, the pale imitation that she has become. She cannot forget her ideal, her history, and asks her reflection: Am I any different from my *devadasi* mother, forced to leave the precincts of the temple? Has history repeated itself? Has the pattern come full circle? Am I now like my *devadasi* mother, becoming essentially expendable, valueless? She pauses, but briefly. It is time for the next performance. She swings back into action from that center of nullity, of joyless negation, with vengeance. Her dance seems militant and aggressive, and her leaps and bounds across the stage often seem pointless. Balasaraswati lashed out, bemoaned this "vulgarity," this exaggerated display of empty rhythm and unproductive energy. Rukmini Devi quietly turned her face away: she went to her illusory tower, her Kalakshetra, and said in self-justification:

You can take a horse to the water but you can't make it drink. I have given the students of Kalakshetra all the opportunities. But supposing it doesn't work, don't you think that, if you have worked all your life, you have sown the seeds?[19]

What seeds, I ask? Can those seeds even sprout in the earth today? What about the external circumstances, the weeds that stifle this energy? All that one can really do is to understand, if at all possible, the inner pain of this dancer. Isn't that all that tradition is anyway, a birth and a death? Why not pause on this death, this moment in time, in quiet contemplation, without hope for a future, without mourning.

But the wheel spins on and dancers spin on it. Some seek traditional answers to the present-day dilemma. Padma Subramanyam says, "I completely agree that my dancing is different from the prevalent style of *bharatha natyam*. I would like to clarify that this deviation from the norm is only a return to the roots of tradition."[20] Which tradition? Indian dancers wish to connect, at least theoretically, to a unity, a stability, which they like to call tradition. In practice, however, they see tradition as a dynamic process. This search for a single theoretical unity is the characteristic mythical search of the Indian mind, a search which reiterates circularity and sameness. This is understandable; a dancer is as much a product of her past as she is a reflection of her times. Some other dancers, like Sonal Mansingh, say quite simply, they wish to create "little pools of delight." Chandralekha, a radical idealist, gave up the life of a traditional performer. She urges dancers to stop this repetitive practice of spectacle performances, of nostalgic return to traditional narrative, and to focus on form. In form, she believes, is embedded the unity of Indian life. My own response was to flee the country at twenty-two. Having lived all my life under the protection of men in a patriarchal society, I wished to discover my separateness from them. Men had defined so much of my life and thought: Bharatha's historical presence loomed large in my earlier life; then it was my teacher, who came to occupy a position next to God; and finally there was my father, without whose protection I could not have honorably survived in India. I fled to America in an effort to free myself from the shackles of being an attractive talented woman, a performer, an object, who could be independent only on the basis of these criteria. I wished to assert the power of my mind over my sex. I knew even then that I was exchanging one prison for another, but I had no other choice. Yeats in his poem "Choice" sums up my own predicament: "The intellect of man is forced to choose / Perfection of the life or of the work." Perfection of the work was not possible for me without the discovery of my self. So I left India. In exile, I wished to give birth to my tradition in body, thought, and action. Most traditional dancers don't experience this choice. They see life as separate from art, art being a representation of ideal time as opposed to temporal time.

Reflexive awareness for today's educated dancers has come at a great price. It has disillusioned some, forced others into a tighter illusory embrace with tradition, and propelled still others, like myself, out of the country. It is not a tranquil situation. Each is trying to discover a tradition, an authentic expression. But as long as Shiva's theoretical dancing snake continues to frame Indian dance,[21] its mesmerizing power, which resides in the Indian heart, will, I believe, overpower and negate the contemporary performance phenomena. The practice of *bharatha natyam* has for a variety of secular reasons broken the bounds of ancient theory. I think we need a post-colonial aesthetic, a theory that can describe and evaluate the secular reality of dance in all its marvelous multiplicity.[22] I articulate today, many thousands of miles away from home, some of the questions of my childhood, in the belief that serious questioning must have some meaning, however small, in human activity.

Notes

1. Bharata-Muni, *The Natyashastra,* trans. Manomohan Ghosh (vol. 1, 2d ed., Calcutta: Granthalaya, 1967; vol. 2, Calcutta: Asiatic Society, 1961).

2. Ibid.

3. Kapila Vatsyayan, *Indian Classical Dance* (New Delhi: Ministry of Information and Broadcasting, 1974), 4.

4. Anne-Marie Gaston, *Siva in Dance, Myth, and Iconography* (Bombay: Delhi University Press, 1982), 7.

5. Ibid., 8.

6. Gowri Ramnarayan, "Dancer and Reformer," *Sruti* (July 1984): 25.

7. Abhinavagupta, *Abhinava Bharati,* ed. Ramakrishna Kavi (Baroda: Gaekward Oriental Press, 1926).

8. Kapila Vatsyayan, *Indian Classical Dance in Literature and the Arts* (New Delhi: Ministry of Information and Broadcasting, 1968), 5.

9. *Vedanta* is a complex branch of Indian philosophy that articulates the theory of the *atman* (soul).

10. Vatsyayan, *Indian Classical Dance in Literature and the Arts,* 167.

11. Gowri Ramnarayan, "A Quest for Beauty," *Sruti* (June 1984): 23.

12. Pattabhi Raman and Anandhi Ramachandran, "The Whole World in Her Hands," *Sruti* (March 1984): 28.

13. Ibid., 27.

14. Ibid.

15. Gowri Ramnarayan, "Dancer and Reformer," *Sruti* (July 1984): 22.

16. Arudra, "The Transfiguration of a Traditional Dance" *Sruti* (December–January 1986–87): 20.

17. Leela Samson, "Yamini Krishnamurthis: A Capital Dancer in Twilight," *Sruti* (October 1984): 28.

18. Gowri Ramnarayan, "A Quest for Beauty," *Sruti* (June 1984): 22.

19. Gowri Ramnarayan, "Rukmini Devi: Restoration and Creation," *Sruti* (August 1984): 38.

20. Gowri Ramnarayan, "Interview: Padma Subramanyam," *Sruti* (December 1984): 37.

21. Shiva is the Preceptor God of Indian dance. The snake adorns his neck.

22. As a practitioner of the art, I have choreographed a dance drama that includes Bharatha's four modes of expression: *vacika* (speech), *aharya* (costume), *angika* (movement), and *sattvika* (psychological states). But the resemblance ends there. In content, my dance drama does not seek to produce a sense of oneness, but rather consciously juxtaposes the platonic and the existential world views, a tension I have experienced both in life and in art.

Medicine of the Brave: A Look at the Changing Role of Dance in Native Culture from the Buffalo Days to the Modern Powwow

LISA DOOLITTLE AND HEATHER ELTON

Dance played a surprisingly important role in the everyday life of Plains Indian culture. Hardly an event went by without cause for a ceremonial act involving dance. Life on the plains appears to have provided sufficient leisure time to fully appreciate and worship the land they loved. Dance became an integral part of native religion. The Indians believed that the Great Spirit taught them to dance so that they could express thoughts and feelings to him. No other form of communication with the spirit world was as adequate or complete. Because Plains culture was so deeply rooted in a sense of place, animals, weather patterns—like the dramatic prairie lightning storms—and other manifestations in nature profoundly influenced their world view. Dance became a means to understand these fantastic natural occurrences, and was possibly an attempt to exert some control over them. Tribes sharing a physical landscape developed a similar belief system and, consequently, had similar dances. There were dance rituals acknowledging changes in the human life cycle—birth, puberty, marriage and death—as well as seasonal change in nature. There were dances to welcome strangers, to create ceremonial friendship, to bring good luck in times of war and hunting, to cure illness and to make peace. Dances of sacrifice, appeals for future blessing and thanksgiving were usually associated with war, hunting and crops. There were medicine dances of magic and healing. Dream cults existed where individuals shared dreams of a particular animal and through dance they enacted their dream experi-

ence. Other dances were entirely social, for pleasure, amusement and humour.

Because dance was so inseparable from daily life, it was only reasonable that when high Plains culture came to an abrupt end in the late 1880s the dances changed accordingly. Disease, death, isolation and outright suppression affected the survival of tradition. With the buffalo destroyed and life confined to the reservation, there was obviously no longer any need to dance to ensure the success of a good buffalo hunt. The dancing which had been a part of their culture for as long as 9,000 years was no longer relevant. Plains society was thrown into a cultural crisis.

As the old warriors passed away, the once distinct dances intermingled making new forms. One of the first signs of Pan-Indianism was the rise of the Grass Dance. Originating in the early reservation period among warrior societies, it spread from tribe to tribe through formal exchange of warrior regalia, dance steps and songs. The Grass Dance is a clear predecessor of modern powwow dances with its exciting singing and dancing, feasting and gift exchange, and celebration of deeds of bravery. The Grass Dance also marked the first signs of a switch from sacred to secular and was among the first to be performed out of context for the titillation of white audiences who believed they were watching a "war dance."

Conditions on reservations continued to worsen as white settlement increased. In the midst of despair, a new religion emerged in the form of the Ghost Dance.

The Indians passionately threw themselves into its performance believing that the dance would bring about the return of the buffalo days. At the time, white authorities felt threatened by any native gathering believing it to be a sign of uprising. The Ghost Dance was brutally suppressed and the practise of native culture became increasingly prohibited.

In Canada the Indian Act of 1885 outlawed performance of the Sun Dance, forcing it underground where it was practised in private, until the suppression was lifted in 1951. Today it is the only traditional dance practised where the old symbolism is still relevant in contemporary society.

It is amazing that any traditions survived at all. Though we may mourn the passing of traditional Indian society, the end of an era whose destruction we so calculatingly orchestrated, and which we so romantically mythologize in our industrialized hindsight, we certainly cannot announce the death of Indian cultural traditions. Native dance is very much alive.

Dancing will be at the centre of powwows throughout Alberta and across the continent, as the year-round circuit of competitive dancing heats up for the summer season. The word *powwow* comes from an Algonquin term meaning "rekindle," and the modern version of the powwow is truly a rekindling of the spirit of traditional celebrations. In fact, throughout the transitions in native society, dance continued to play a prominent role in the preservation of traditional culture. In the thirties and forties, Indians performed fragments of traditionally sacred Grass Dances at rodeos, fairs and even at non-Indian events, side by side with European waltzes and jigs. But it wasn't until the general economic improvement following World War II that intertribal contacts revived, and formerly outlawed large gatherings, including dances, began to take place. Liberalized governments and human rights legislation contributed to the establishment of annual Indian Days celebrations, which were popular in the fifties and sixties and were the forerunner of the modern powwow. In the seventies, traditional dance and song joined with radical politics at native gatherings like the Wounded Knee occupation of 1973; the theme song of the highly political American Indian Movement was composed in traditional Grass Dance style. In the eighties, powwows integrate ceremonial events, artistic exchanges, casual socializing and intense competitions. They are sites for both politicking and partying and are a vital expression of native culture.

The format of powwows varies from region to region and from year to year, but generally includes a selection of ceremonial dances (Honor dances, Grand Entry Dance, Victory Dance), social dances (intertribal dances, Friendship or Round Dances), and competition dances (Men's and Ladies' Traditional and Fancy Dances). Unlike the atmosphere associated with "white" dance performances, powwows are casual and sometimes chaotic with drums blaring over the public address system and hordes of small children incessantly swooping in and out of the dance grounds. Powwow dancing can last all day long and go into late evening, sometimes for four days in a row. Different too is the intense dance performance style. The stone-faced calm of the dancers is startling to non-Indian observers. In the European-based theatrical dance traditions, displays of emotional and physical extremes are applauded. The pronounced emotional restraint of native performers, apparent in their facial expression, their contained gestures, the controlled steps and patterns, all reflect specific cultural values of strength, dignity and bravery. The dancers move every muscle of their body in precise coordination with the drum beat. Some dances are strictly choreographed, others more improvised. In competition, traditions can be mixed and matched in a bewildering potpourri of steps, their origins often less important than their impact. Each dancer develops their own unique style. All competition dances are solo dances, done en masse to the beat of a drum. Drumming groups are essential to the powwow, and their songs, as varied and vital as the dances, have their own "top forty" style popularity among natives young and old. The astonishing costumes, which take months to produce and can be very costly, are sometimes faithful reproductions of traditional ritual dress, sometimes fantastic modern variations on traditional themes.

Some regret the commercialization and the apparent lack of spirituality in powwows these days. The show business and competition are evidence of the separation of dance from everyday life, a sharp contrast to the traditional integration of dance into all aspects of society. Yet even the most casual observer can sense the underlying values of these festivals. First of all the dances themselves are remarkable demonstrations of the resilience of ancient traditions. Dances from as far away as Oklahoma and New Mexico find their way into, and out of, Alberta over a span of years and miles without sacrificing stylistic integrity, demonstrating a wonderful capacity for flexibility in the midst of a powerful determination to preserve cultural identity. Whether the purpose of attending a powwow is social, artistic, economic or political the participant asserts membership in a tribe, and in the great Pan-Indian community, playing a part in preserving tradition, creatively adapted to current circumstances. The dancers move in synchrony with ancestral patterns and yet are in step with modern times.[1]

Notes

We are grateful for the assistance of Murdoch Burnett, Lisa Churchill, Hugh Dempsey and Eldon Yellowhorn.

1. For further information on dances of the Native peoples of North America, see Black Elk, *The Sacred Pipe: Black Elk's Account of the Seven Rites of the Oglala Sioux*, ed. Joseph Epes Brown (Norman: University of Oklahoma Press, 1953); George Catlin, *North American Indians: Letters and Notes on the Manners, Costumes and Conditions* (London, 1884); Samuel W. Corrigan, "The Plains Indian Powwow: Cultural Integration in Manitoba and Saskatchewan." *Anthropologica* 12, no. 2 (1970): 253–280; Edward S. Curtis, *The Sacred Manner in Which We Live* (New York: Weathervane Press, 1967); Orin T. Hatton, "In the Tradition: Grass Dance Musical Style and Female Powwow Singers." *Ethnomusicology* 30, no. 3 (1986): 197–222; Adolph Hungry Wolf and Beverley Hungry Wolf, *Powwow* (Calgary: Northwest Printing and Lithographing, 1983), vol. 1; Alice B. Kehoe, "The Give-Away Ceremony of Blackfoot and Plains Cree," *Plains Anthropologist* 25, no. 87 (1980): 17–26; Gladys Laubin and Reginald Laubin, *Indian Dances of North America: Their Importance to Indian Life* (Norman: University of Oklahoma Press, 1977); Terry Lusty, "The Drum Sounds . . . and We Dance." *Windspeaker Powwow Country*, May 13, 1988; Thomas Mails, *Sundancing at Rosebud and Pine Ridge* (Sioux Falls, S.D.: University of Nebraska Press, 1978); James Mooney, *Ghost Dance Religion* (Chicago: University of Chicago Press, 1965); Anne Marie Shea and Citron Atay, "The Powwow of the Thunderbird American Indian Dancers," *Drama Review* 26, no. 2 (T94) (1982): 73–88.

The Ghost Dance

In 1881, when Sitting Bull and the Sioux nation reluctantly surrendered to the U.S. authorities, the buffalo days were over and a chapter ended in the history of Plains Indian culture. By this time all the tribes had been moved onto reservations which consisted mostly of parched, worthless land that would have defeated an expert agriculturalist. Their treaties had been violated and their rations cut to the point of starvation; they were virtually prisoners of war. For the proud Sioux, who had never been defeated in battle, the 1880s were a time of suffering, misery and despondency. In the midst of their despair came word of a new religion, the Ghost Dance.

In 1886, on a Nevada reservation, a Paiute prophet named Wovoka had a vision promising the "revival of the old Indian ways, the return of the buffalo, and the annihilation of the race responsible for all their troubles." Naturally such a doctrine would interest the Indians. Wovoka's religious theory was a mixture of Indian and Christian beliefs that he had acquired from his childhood. His talents as a magician helped to convince people that he was a real prophet. When he discovered that an eclipse of the sun was scheduled for January 1, 1889, he decided to die and coincide his return with the eclipse. He was reborn as an "Indian Messiah" who promised the Indians that if they danced "a new world would be ushered in with a great earthquake, followed by a flood, which would wash away and destroy all unbelievers. The new world would be covered with green grass and herds of deer, elk, antelope and buffalo, and the Indians would live in a paradise, untroubled by war, disease or famine."[1]

When a delegation of Indian leaders, including Sitting Bull and Kicking Bear, stole off the reserve and silently crossed several hundred miles of emerging white settlements to visit him in Nevada, Wovoka made every effort to impress them. Using his shamanistic and magic skills he appeared mysteriously from clouds of smoke and in bizarre locations. Showing them his scars as proof, he told them he was Christ, saying that because the white man had persecuted him he had come back to save the Indian people from their oppressors. These were the stories that Sitting Bull took back to his people.

Wovoka's preachings spread like wildfire among the disheartened Indians. Soon rumours crept into the white settlements that the Sioux were doing "some kind of war dance." Paranoia led them to believe that the Indians were preparing for a great uprising. According to the Ghost Dance moral code, "there was to be no fighting; all good people must live together; trouble-makers of both races were to be wiped out." Wovoka told them that they were to live in peace. But the Sioux, as a warring nation who for good reason distrusted the whites, militarized the dance. Perhaps as protection, they created a sacred costume which they believed would make bullets harmless. In preparation they bathed, purified themselves in a sweat lodge and dried their bodies with sweet grass. They painted their faces red, with a black crescent on their forehead or cheek. Ghost Shirts were made of muslin and colorful designs were applied using a sacred paint. They wore bright leggings painted in red stripes. No one wore jewelry or carried guns. The hundreds of men, women and children dressed in this attire must have made a striking impression.

The dancing started around noon on Sundays. No instruments were heard. As a display of patronage and a gesture of peace, the dancers tied an American flag to the top of a small pine tree and erected it in the centre of the circle. A mournful chant was sung and everyone joined in, dancing fast with "hands moving from side to side, their bodies swaying, their arms, with hands gripped tightly to their neighbour's, swung back and forth with all their might." They thought only of God and that they would soon be reunited with their families, and wept until tears fell to the ground. Circles with as many as four hundred dancers were seen by some observers. The actual dance step was similar to the social Round or Circle dance, "with the left foot leading, lifting higher than the right, but at the same time there was a plunge forward. The right foot then dragged to position. It was a grapevine step." Those who fell into exhausted trances were believed to be visiting the Spirit World. One spectator reported seeing a hundred people lying on the ground, unconscious. They told their stories to the head priest who shouted them to the dancers.

Sitting Bull was interested in the Ghost Dance but was also skeptical. White authorities wanted Sitting Bull to order the dancing stopped. He refused, saying that if his people wanted to dance, they had a right to do so. Consequently, in the predawn of December 15, 1890, Indian police descended upon Sitting Bull's cabin and arrested him. As the old chief tried to resist, a gun went off and in the ensuing confusion Sitting Bull, his son Crowfoot, and fourteen others were killed. With the death of the old warrior and medicine man, panic overtook the people on the Standing Rock reservation. Hundreds fled and 3,000 troops were sent in by the U.S. army, many of whom had fought under General Custer, to return them to their reservations. What ensued was the ultimate tragedy at Wounded Knee.

For many, the Ghost Dance brings back bitter memories, and the horrible massacre will forever haunt the Sioux. Close to fifty tribes participated in the Ghost Dance, totalling about 60,000 dancers. Some 26,000 were Sioux. Had the Indians been granted the same privilege as the Seventh Day Adventists, or other white religious organizations, it might have continued to be a dream for a better world.

Note

1. All Ghost Dance quotes taken from *Indian Dances of North America* by Reginald Laubin and Gladys Laubin (Norman: University of Oklahoma Press, 1977).

The Sun Dance

The Sun Dance is a great religious drama in which individuals pledge vows to the Great Spirit in return for his help. The Sun Dance contains all of the Plains Indian ceremonies practised during the year, integrating their entire belief system in a ceremony full of significance, power, and drama. According to the Sioux, it has been performed by over twenty Plains tribes since 1685 A.D. Because so many tribes had their own version of the Sun Dance, it is impossible to describe a "typical" performance. The following description is composed from reading largely Sioux material. The reader should keep in mind that between any significant action, hours of detailed prayer and ritual took place. Thus the description is, at best, skeletal.

The Sun Dance is customarily held outside and performed in a large circle called the Mystery Circle or Hoop. It takes place over a duration of four days and nights, during the Moon of Fattening (June) or the Moon of Ripening Cherries (July). The participants have absolute faith that the ceremony will ensure the well-being of the entire tribe and answer the prayers of those dancers taking part in the most physically painful aspects.

During the first part of the ceremony, friends and relatives from surrounding bands come together to participate in the festival. Sacred objects are found, sacred symbols made, medicinal roots gathered, and preparations for the tepee, sun dance lodge and sweat lodge commence. Those who have pledged to dance receive instructions from a shaman on the meaning of the rituals and symbolism. One of the pledgers is chosen to find a tall cottonwood tree, with a forked top, which will be placed in the centre of the Mystery Circle. The cottonwood tree is the most sacred object because its leaf is believed to have inspired the shape of the original tepee. The trunk of the tree is painted white, yellow, green and black; the colors of the four cardinal directions. A small bundle of cherry branches and the symbols of a male buffalo and male human are tied below the fork. A bag of fat is placed under the base of the sacred tree in a special hole at the centre of the Mystery Circle. When the tree is properly positioned, rituals of celebration and purification take place. Smoke from the sacred pipe is seen to represent their prayers by physically tracing the spiritual pathway from earth to heaven.

The surrounding lodge is constructed by standing twenty-eight forked trees upright around the Mystery Circle. From the fork of each tree, a pole is placed which reaches the sacred tree at the centre. The sun dance lodge is a symbolic reflection of the universe. The circular shape emphasizes the belief that life is a process of continual change. The outside trees are singular acts of creation, the circle is the entire creation, and the one tree at the centre, upon which the twenty-eight trees rest, is the Great Spirit, the centre of everything. All life comes from him, and sooner or later returns to him. Four is the prime sacred number. There are four cardinal directions, four seasons, four elements, four life stages. There are seven sacred rituals of the Sioux, of which the Sun Dance is one. Four times seven equals twenty-eight. The moon lives for twenty-eight days, each of which is sacred, and the buffalo has twenty-eight ribs. This philosophy is vividly symbolized in the Sun Dance.

After the sun lodge has been prepared a sacred song is sung. After the chanting of the song the people cry, and then, for the rest of the day and night, they dance. This dance represents the people in their "darkness and ignorance; not yet worthy to meet the Light of the Great Spirit which will shine upon them with the coming of the next day; first they must suffer and purify themselves."[1] The pledgers are painted with colors and symbols representing their vows and the degree of pain they have pledged to suffer.

By going to the centre of the Mystery Circle the pledgers "go to the centre of the world and take upon themselves the suffering of all people." Each pledger declares the sacrifices he will undergo and either agrees to attach his body to the thongs of the Great Spirit which comes down to Earth, or pledges "flesh offerings," or fasts and dances until exhausted. Singers and drummers chant, steadily increasing their rhythm. The leader of the dancers lies down on a buffalo robe and the medicine man or intercessor pulls up the skin of his left breast and thrusts a skewer through the loose skin. The skewers are attached to the thongs hanging from the sacred tree. He is helped to his feet and then leans back, with his weight against the rope, and continues to dance in this manner, trying to rip his flesh free from the thongs. Symbolically, flesh represents ignorance. When they break loose from the thong, they are being freed from the bonds of the flesh.

Some people have witnessed pledgers suffering for days, but usually the ritual is over quickly, depending on how deeply the pledger is pierced. Some dancers are pierced on their shoulders and breasts, and hang suspended by four thongs, making it more difficult for the skin to break. Others hang buffalo skulls onto the thongs to further apply pressure on the skewers. The pain experienced from piercing proves the man's sincerity to his vows. Those who faint are revered because it is believed that visions are received in this unconscious state. At the end of the ritual the door of the lodge is opened four times, between sips of water and pipe smoking. The men return to the sacred tepee where much food is brought to them and they rejoice.

Note

1. All Sun Dance quotes taken from *The Sacred Pipe: Black Elk's Account of the Seven Rites of the Oglala Sioux* (Norman: University of Oklahoma Press, 1953).

Dance in Native Culture: Contemporary Dialogues

ELDON YELLOWHORN

Originally from the Peigan Reserve, Yellowhorn currently resides in Calgary. A graduate of the University of Calgary with a B.A. in archeology, he is currently working as an ethnologist and archeological field worker for the Smithsonian Institute.

How would you describe the role of native dance in Plains traditional culture?

It was about as close as they ever came to developing the art of theatre. Dance enacted a lot of the legends and reaffirmed their world view. For example, when any human culture develops a close predatory relationship with animals, and especially when that animal is their staff of life, it has a certain mystique about it. So the dance ritual, before a hunt, was not just a token effort to get the animal or to make them feel less guilty about killing the animal. There were even resurrection dances where the buffalo were reborn into the herd. You can see it worked because the buffalo population on the Plains was very stable.

When you speak of a world view, do you mean a Plains Indian world view?

Yes. It is a variation on the theme that is cross-cultural, practically universal. If you look at what was happening at the time, you find parallels in all the tribes. They all celebrated a variation of the Sun Dance and had a buffalo hunting complex very closely tied to their mythology. The Plains Cree were originally a woodlands tribe of central and northern Saskatchewan who moved with the fur trade. As soon as they got onto the plains they abandoned a lot of their former life ways and changed their ideologies to suit their new environment. Sun dancing was not typical of the Cree, yet within a generation it was part of their mythology and social roles. Similarly, with the Plains Ojibwa, when they were living in the forest they had a story about a spirit called Wehtiko who preyed on humans. When they came onto the plains they no longer had this association of fear with Wehtiko so he became a comical figure. They let go of the myth or cultural baggage when it was no longer applicable to their environment.

Is there any reason to keep traditional dances?

It's a hold-over, something that should have gone extinct with the buffalo days, but for some reason it still endures. The same reason that there are still Indians around. The same reason that they have powwows every year. There was so much cultural baggage and not everything survived the transition. Some dances are lost from this generation and some have survived, but in a very diluted form.

Which traditional dances have survived?

The Sun Dance is about the only one, probably because it was at the heart of the culture. Whether you live on the reserve or in the city, there is still a demand for cultural retention. The Sun Dance is one way of remaining unique in a society that has become so standardized. It is associated with religious ideas, but in very real terms it serves a concrete purpose and consequently relates to modern life.

Is the powwow specific to Plains culture?

It used to be. Now it has become Pan-Indian. Powwows have become synonymous with being Indian. It would take a lot to destroy the powwow movement now.

Is it growing quite substantially?

Oh yes. But on the Peigan reserve powwows are not going to last much longer because only the wealthy reserves can put the lure of prize money up for the dancers.

One of the things I noticed last summer when I attended a powwow were children dressed and moving like animals. Is their affinity with a particular animal a result of a vision quest?

No, these days it's much more pedestrian than that. It is just a costume. There might still be peripheral or residual powers, through legends or stories, but the concept and execution of design no longer has any religious or magical connotations. Someone probably had an extra headdress made from a fox skin, that sort of thing.

But some of these people spend eight months working on their costume, beading it by hand.

Nobody will look at you if you have a shabby costume.

Is there no longer any symbolism in the design?

No. Designs are no longer associated with dreams. That is a part of the past.

So, the role of dance has changed in modern powwows from what it was in more traditional times?

10. Indian boy at Kainai Indian Days, 1987. Photo by Heather Elton.

The powwow itself is where the culture lies. The dances are just subcategories of the powwow.

LLOYD EWENIN

A Cree Indian originally from Saskatchewan, Ewenin resides in Calgary, where he is a counsellor and teacher of tradition and spirituality at the Plains Indian Cultural Survival School. He is also a Traditional Dancer on the powwow circuit.

How would you describe a powwow?

Powwow today is a little bit commercialized because we now dance for money, we're competing; but there is still a lot of spirituality and respect for traditions. Powwows have always been celebrations. In traditional times a single tribe celebrated a successful hunt, a successful war party, or overcoming a sickness. Today it is still the same idea but now it is all tribes together and there is dance competition for cash. The money helps, because many now go to powwows throughout Canada and the United States, every weekend, just like cowboys on the rodeo circuit, only they do the powwow circuit. In Alberta alone there might be two or three powwows on the same weekend. At one in Bismarck, North Dakota, in Men's Traditional Dancing there were over a hundred dancers. There were three categories for men and three categories for women. Within those categories there were different age groups, even for children. There must have been 1,500 dancers, not counting the drummers. There were twenty-five drums. That was one of the biggest; around here if you get about thirty dancers in one category you are doing well.

What kind of prize money are we talking about?

You compete for anything from a hundred dollars to place, up to as much as fifteen hundred dollars for a win at a big powwow.

Can you describe some traditions still honored in the powwow dancing we see today?

Modern-day Traditional Dancers wear bustles made out of eagle feathers. The eagle is still a bird that is highly respected, and a feather from an eagle is a symbol of bravery and honesty. If you see an eagle feather drop from a costume in a powwow, it is like a warrior that is wounded, and there is a special ritual to pick it up. Members of warrior societies wore the eagle feathers. With the eagle feather, you don't go backwards because that shows fear, and a warrior is not supposed to show fear, so in dances, they always go forward. You will notice we dance in a circle, always moving in the same direction. The sun travels in one direction and that's the way the Indian people go, clockwise. When I say powwow today still has some of the spirituality, that is the kind of thing I mean.

What about the music? Do the drummers compete?

The drummers and singers are not competing. Most of the time the drums are paid. You can't have a powwow without the drummers and singers.

What is their relationship to the dancing?

The drumming is meant to be the beat of mother earth. The function of the dance is to keep time to that beat. It is easy to see the spirituality in that. We don't use recorded music.

I guess, because any of the different drumming groups might play, you have to be ready to dance to whatever they choose.

They announce which drum is going to play which beat. Every song has four push-ups, each song repeats four times. Four is an important number in Indian culture: the four stages of man (baby, adolescence, adulthood, elder), the four seasons, the four cardinal directions. Dancers repeat the sequence four times. At the end you get ready to stop on the drum beat, you don't over step.

What kinds of dances do the competitors perform?

Basically, they do either Traditional or Fancy dancing. In Men's Traditional you see the *sneak up* and the *shake*. I've heard this is an imitation of looking for a wounded warrior, or tracking an animal. The dancer will go down on one knee when the beat gets faster and make a shaking sound. There is also the *crowhop*. The Sioux say the *crowhop* beat sounds like the galloping horses of warriors returning to camp. The Crow people's version is that it imitates the jumping around of the crow. Most dances are done to a straight beat, but the Owl Dance and the Round Dance have a double beat. For the women there is the Jingle Dress dance. It originated with the Ojibways. The dresses are made out of tin Copenhagen snuff lids, sewn on close together, so when you jump, they make noise.

Are there songs and dances not for competition?

The Grand Entry song begins the powwow of the day. The dancers come in single file. In traditional times they gave this song when warriors or hunters returned to camp. In powwow they do that for the dancers. The song's words refer to war, to veterans. Then, there is a Flag song, sort of like singing "Oh Canada" at the beginning of a hockey game. Then, dancers dance to the Victory song. The Honor song is also not a competition song. When you are initiated into the powwow circuit, if it is the first time you are dancing, you have an Honor dance and give something away. Say my grandchild is being initiated, I dance for him and I give money and blankets to whoever I choose. When you have a birthday in Canadian culture, you expect to get something, a gift. In Indian culture, if it's my celebration, I give presents away, that's the philosophy. You could have several Honor dances at a powwow for many different reasons. Money is the best commodity to give away because it helps the dancers. Maybe they get coffee money, maybe a little bit of gas money. In the old days, even if an enemy came to camp, he was helped with food and lodging and then sent on his way after he was OK. Today, even people who don't dance get some money if they come a long way.

MAGGIE BLACK KETTLE

A Blackfoot Indian from Gleichen, Black Kettle is an elder and cultural teacher at the Plains Indians Cultural Survival School. She is also a Traditional Dancer.

How long have you been dancing?

I was around eighteen when I started dancing and now I'm sixty-nine. At first, I didn't really dance like I do now. We didn't have Indian Days back then. We would camp together for four days but we didn't have competition. Now we dance to compete. I really enjoy it. I taught all my grandchildren how to do the steps when they were small. My granddaughter, she dances Fancy, and all my daughters started in Traditional. My boy does Traditional. I think it's fun to be in a powwow

dancing, it seems like there's a bunch of buffalo jumping around. That's how I feel when I'm in a powwow.

Can you describe some of the women's dances?

The way we dance, you have to move your whole body and you have to bend your knees. If you are stiff, it doesn't look good. In Ladies' Traditional, we stand all around in a circle, go to the centre and then move in different ways. Some just dance real hard on the spot. I like to move around the room. In Ladies' Fancy, they move their shawls, and put in all kinds of steps. It is really hard and they get all worked up.

So it is a real workout.

You just sweat out everything that has been bothering you.

Have you ever done singing or drumming?

Before, ladies were not supposed to touch the drum. They stood behind the drum and looked nice in the background, standing behind the men. But now everybody is singing and drumming. We were not allowed to touch the drum; it was precious to the men. Same with their bustles too. We were not supposed to touch the eagle feathers. Now women even wear bustles. Just like the white ladies want the same standing as the men on the job, we native women are just the same.

You attend powwows even if you are not competing. What is the attraction? Why go to all the trouble of travelling around so much?

I like to watch the competition, and see my children and grandchildren dance. My grandson started dancing when he was still in Pampers, we would have to stop him to change him. Now, at the powwow I hold up my great-grandson and he bounces along to the drum.

How do you get there? Does someone pay your way?

We pay for our gas. If you win you are lucky. The men can get as much as a thousand dollars, it is always lower for the ladies, like eight hundred. In Kalispell I won five hundred. That year I was just winning all the time. I've got about forty trophies. We all enjoy powwows, the older people too. We see the people we didn't see all winter in a powwow. It's just like a family. Everyone asks what happened in their lives. I always look forward to going. I like to be with the elders. They say when you feel sick and old, start dancing; then you won't know where you are sore, you forget everything, you just think about old times, and you feel good.

GERALD SITTING EAGLE

Residing on the Blackfoot reserve, Sitting Eagle is director of the Siksika Cultural Center and Alberta representative for the national Native Cultural Centres. He is also president of the A-1 Society, and an active dancer on the powwow circuit.

Has the role of dance changed much in native culture?

The way I understand it, the old dance made you feel good if you were sick or feeling low mentally. There was a power behind the dancing; now the competitiveness has taken most of that away. A lot of people start dancing now without going through the proper channels. When I first started dancing I was about five years old. My parents paid to have a "giveaway." From then on I was told never be shy or let anyone call me down because of my dancing. There are a lot of dancers that just get in for the money part of it, without being initiated. Some people think that as long as they've got a costume they can just go up there and dance.

Is there more meaning than that?

There's more meaning to me. All my kids dance and they have all been initiated properly. I try to teach my kids the Blackfoot type dancing and it's up to them to choose what they want to do. I leave them to do what they like.

What is Traditional Dancing?

To me Traditional Dancing is Chicken Dancing because it is our dance from this area. Traditional Dancing at powwows is the Sioux type traditional dance. They are not doing the Blackfoot traditional dance. When people ask me to teach them dancing I teach them the Chicken Dance. It's up to them to choose whatever type of dance they want to adopt.

How would you describe the Chicken Dance? Does it have a certain set of moves?

It's got its own moves. It is kind of like the Grass Dance but the dress is different. There is a lot of shoulder movement. You try to show as many movements in your body as you can and keep in time with the beat of the drum. The Chicken Dance also has the *shake* and the *crowhop* in the dance itself. I don't know if you've ever seen prairie chickens shake, but it is from them that I adopted my dancing.

Why do people dance these days?

If you are really good you can make a lot of money. Twenty years ago I used to make about ten thousand dollars in three months.

Do you train as a dancer?

I don't train. If I want to learn a new style of dancing, I look at the dancers and buy the drumming tapes. When the southern Fancy Dance first became popular I went to Oklahoma and learned the Oklahoma Fancy Dance. The beat was a lot faster. The first year I didn't place so I bought a southern tape and practised all winter and went back and took first place. I try to steal a little from this person, a little from that person and put it all into one. I always try to develop my own style, especially with the Fancy Dance. It is more free form, you can put any movement in. The trick behind all the dances is that you must keep in time with the drum.

Do the drummers change the beat of the music?

Some of the drummers will try to play tricks and you've got to be able to catch on right away. As soon as I hear a song it is in my head. I know where it's going, when they are going to change in the beat and I know when it's going to stop.

Are there words in the songs?

Traditionally, Blackfoot songs have no words. Words are a new thing that come from the Sioux. So, now when a lot of different tribes compose a song, they put words into them. The beat of the drum is different from when I first started dancing. The songs are longer. Hardly any dancers will get up and dance to the traditional style Blackfoot drumming. The new type of drumming has a *crowhop* beat in just about every verse. Whereas with the Traditional style dancing we do a *crowhop* just when we are going to stop.

Costumes seem to be a really important part of powwows these days, they are so fantastic to look at.

People are using sequins nowadays, so it sparkles a lot. You have to make your costume as stylish as you can and different from everyone else's, so it stands out. When you're dancing you try to move as much of your costume as you can. So when you're making your costume you know that the more fringes it has, the more you look like you're shaking. You try to incorporate every little trick.

Do the designs symbolize anything? Do they have any meaning these days?

Not so much anymore. Most dancers design what we call fire colours, which fade into a fire or something. Most of the outfits I see these days follow that idea. The original Blackfoot designs are a block design. The Cree people have the flower design. A lot of people put these things on because they are available, but they don't follow the proper channels anymore. For example, I'm planning on wearing a headdress that's got a bunch of feathers on top of your head. Because I'm traditional myself, before I put that type of headdress on,

I will take a pipe to the guy who is already initiated. He has the right to give me permission to wear it. Before I started my Hoop Dance, I was initiated into it by asking permission from my friends, up north, who have done it all their lives.

Do you wish that people did things right?

When I go to powwows and see all of the dancers it makes me happy, but what makes me sad is that they are not doing it the proper way. The old people are not teaching the proper way of getting into these dances.

Do you see powwows as maintaining Indian culture?

That, plus the language. People can get back to using their own language and all the different languages. If you lose your language you've lost your culture because a lot of the things we say in English we can explain better in our own language.

ORLANDO CALLING LAST
_____

A Blood Indian, Calling Last is twenty-nine years old and resides on the reserve at Standoff. He is an avid student of traditional native culture, an apprentice of the medicine way, and a practitioner of native religion. He is also a Traditional Dancer on the powwow circuit.

So what's happening right now with you and dancing?

Well, I'm doing pretty good. I took first place in San Francisco in the Men's Traditional category and then I took second place at the University of Seattle. Our Sun Dance is coming up next month.

What's the status of the Sun Dance in Canada?

It's not supposed to be done but we do it anyway on private property, where we pierce. It was supposed to be outlawed because they call it self-torture. To us it's giving flesh offerings. It's hard to explain to somebody why we do this, but there are a lot of reasons. There may be a lot of bad luck running through your family and you would like it to stop, so you ask the creator to help. You give part of your flesh to help him out. You want to bring good luck to the whole reservation. Since we've stopped practising the Sun Dance, alcohol, drugs and suicide have caused problems on the reserve. People don't know if their religion is Catholic or Anglican or Indian. The Indian religion, however, is getting more powerful throughout the Indian Nations in the United States and Canada. It is being recognized that by going back to our ways it is saving our culture and our people.

What's the difference between Traditional and Fancy Dancing?

Fancy has two bustles, a top bustle and a bottom bustle. The drum beat is a lot faster, demanding more footwork. It's more of an endurance test of how fast and fancy you can move within the four push-ups. It also has a lot more beadwork and a lot more colour. The Men's Traditional is very respected because of the eagle feathers we wear. It is also slower. In the Men's Traditional you are telling a story out there while you are dancing. Usually it describes a successful war or anticipates going to war.

Do you borrow movement from the old dances?

Today you can use just about anything you feel comfortable with out there. Powwow is really trying to maintain the Indian culture. I think that if we didn't have powwows the younger people would just forget about it all.

So people dance for more than just prize money?

Yeah. There is still a lot of spirituality involved. There are people who are just there for the money, I call them showboats because they don't dance for themselves. When the emphasis is on costume it kind of bugs me because I'm not wearing a costume. My outfit is a replica of my ancestor's finest regalia. I don't consider myself to be a prize dancer. I just go to local powwows because I want to support them. Prize money brought with it bad relations and jealousy amongst the people, which has hurt us a lot. I can

truthfully say I get jealous too, of dancers who always win. There's another side though. Because of the unemployment on the reservation people have to rely on their skills, like dancing. A lot of powwow people don't have very much money.

Do you train as a dancer?

No, I dance from my heart. I think there are some dancers who practise quite a bit. I just go out there and whatever I feel I do. I don't think about dancing, I just start dancing. When I put my outfit on I am a warrior of the past, no longer a modern Indian with running shoes and blue jeans. I feel like I've just stepped into the past and there are no worries. Everything circulates around the drum and the dancers, without them there is no powwow. I'm the kind of person that hears the drum beat two thousand miles away. I've got to be there. I'm there because I love the powwow.

Has the reason for dancing changed much?

Yes. Today everybody dances whereas before there were only special people who had the right to dance. Today if you feel like you want to dance, you just dance.

And yet even today certain societies have special dances that are just specific to those societies?

Yes. I was home just a couple of days ago and I went to a pipe ceremony called *Long Time Pipe* and saw my father dance with this pipe that must be over nine thousand years old. To see it kind of gave me the chills. Think of all the people who have owned it at one time and danced with it. I watched very carefully to understand a lot more. But there is so much to being an Indian, you need about three lifetimes just to take it all in. But I'll take what I can now.

Is dancing a vehicle into the spirit world?

You could put it that way. I would want to die on the dance floor because I know I would be happy.

Why did you start dancing?

I started dancing when I was three years old. I got sick when I was sixteen and had to stay in the hospital for almost two and a half years. I ended up in a wheelchair. Before that I was a Fancy dancer. My legs and arms gave up on me and through the help of the mystic world I was taken to a Cree medicine man who helped me to regain my walk. Then his spirits told him that I am a dancer. So he encouraged me to keep dancing. I think of dance as a painkiller. I forget about my pain, my aches, and I don't feel sick anymore. About a week after I was doctored there was a powwow held about a mile and a half down the road from my house. I was still in a wheelchair and sat there on the sidelines and heard that drum beat and the medicine man told me to get up and dance. I got up from my wheelchair and started dancing.

The Belly Dance: Ancient Ritual to Cabaret Performance

SHAWNA HELLAND

Enduring time, crossing nations and surviving images ranging from spiritualism to sex, the *danse du ventre* or belly dance has a history as rich and mysterious as the countries of the Far East from which it originates. Although the notion is exotic, our experience is likely less so. It has too often been simplified to a dinner at a Greek or Lebanese restaurant.

Far from just simple entertainment, belly dancing is believed to have originated in the Paleolithic era. Even cursory study reveals its history to be as much that of women as the dance itself. The fact that there is an exotic stigma associated with belly dancing can make it a sensitive subject to discuss. It is a story with a steamy yet compelling past.

It was an early custom to perform the dance around a woman in labour, rendering the birth less painful. This custom is still practiced by many women in North Africa and in parts of the Middle East. Saudi Arabian women cry out sympathetic laments with a woman in labour.

Discoveries in Egypt and India have revealed early representations of full-breasted, pregnant women, painted on stone walls and as terra-cotta statuettes, in positions suggestive of dancing. Archaeologists have dated some of these artefacts to 25,000 B.C. Other accounts of early belly dancing are found in ancient literature. During the first century A.D., the Roman poet Martial described the dancers of Cadiz who used to "swing their lascivious loins in practiced writhings." The Spanish town of Cadiz was colonized by the Phoenicians and Carthaginians who likely brought the dance from North Africa. One might conjecture that the Phoenician traders moved the dance west and that various cultures were interpreting what many practitioners refer to as the "oriental dance," the dance that came from the East.

Ancient dances of India, Africa, Polynesia and Southeast Asia also show resemblance to the belly dance. Their stylistic similarities perhaps result from parallel cultural development rather than the movement of peoples and sharing of culture. Where Polynesian dancing remained close to its ritualistic form with a workable mix of sacred and sexual imagery, belly dancing travelled the rocky road from birthing ritual to cabaret performance.

The U.S. dance ethnologist La Meri, who performed authentic versions of Eastern dance, wrote of her time in Fez, Morocco, in 1929:

> I was told by my teacher Fatma that the "danse du ventre" was of ritualistic origin and was at that time still performed at the bedsides of women in childbirth. She told me that in its ritualistic form, men were not allowed to see the dance.

This is in keeping with the notion that women have long been both feared and respected by men for being able to give birth, for possessing biological and spiritual powers that provide them with what was sometimes perceived as a closer association to the gods.

In *World History of Dance*, Curt Sachs refers to the

dance as a "birth mime." Describing the Bafioti people of West Africa he states, "The purpose of this particular dance is for ancestor worship and the glorification of future generations via the birth process." As a case for parallel cultural development, the Bafioti dance is more likely linked to its own culture's prehistory than to any direct influence of the Middle East. On the other hand, the influence that the spread of Islam had on the world of belly dance cannot be underestimated.

Islam was founded in Mecca by the prophet Muhammad in 569 A.D. and early practitioners undertook a quest to convert whole civilizations to their way of life. The Islamic disciples moved north through India and south through Africa. They spread as far west as Spain and east as Java, prescribing their interpretation of the Koran. Even today, most of the Middle East and North Africa are Muslim countries. While on these crusades dances and dancers were exchanged and both Islam and the danse du ventre moved beyond the shores and deserts of Arabia.

The Islamic practice of polygamy may have given rise to harem life and belly dancing in the Middle East. Confining women in a harem was a way to control and protect the more "delicate sex." The all-encompassing nature of the Islamic faith provides a sense of security for women yet at the same time imposes strict, encumbering regulations. For example, the enforced veiling of women in traditional Muslim society protects them not only from the desert winds but also, symbolically, from the harsh realities of the world. The word harem comes from the Arabic "harim," that which is both sacred and forbidden.

A certain mystique has grown around the image of harem life: that it was a lavish, exotic existence of fine foods, warm baths, oils, incense and oriental dancers. In some cases this was true but in many instances the harem was simply the women and children's quarters. Nonetheless, belly dancing flourished in these harems. It was common for the sultan to call up his chosen dancer(s) to entertain him and his male guests. They are said even to have blind-folded their musicians to

prevent flirtation with the dancer and to ensure the exclusivity of the concubine's beauty.

Given such practices the harem was often viewed as an example of men's enslavement of women. At the same time, it was the place in ancient Islam where women possessed the most freedom. In the harem they were allowed to go unveiled, could share the workload of children and were free to dance. Behind these walls the dance had its own life, it was an art form created by women for personal entertainment and an avenue for sexual expression.

The role of belly dancers in the contemporary Muslim world is ambiguous. On the one hand it is a respected art, part of the cultural heritage. Yet in a more traditional family a father would not tolerate his daughter dancing publicly. Then again he might ask such a dancer to entertain at a family wedding.

Although the spread of Islam helped to introduce the belly dance to new parts of the world, it may have been kept most alive and mobile by a wandering race of people from India known as the Ghawazee (from the Arabic "ghawa" meaning "invaders of the heart"). We know them as Gypsies. It is uncertain what circumstances drove the Ghawazee from India but by the thirteenth cetury A.D. they had left their homeland, populating what is now Afghanistan, Syria and Lebanon. On the shores of the Mediterranean they divided, moving north into Turkey and Greece and south into Egypt, North Africa and Spain.

The Ghawazee had a free-spirited wild-mannered lifestyle which both shocked and fascinated the traditional Muslim world. Draped in colourful fabrics decorated with coins, bangles and glitter, the Gypsies entertained in the market places and began settlements along rivers and the edges of towns and cities. Influenced by the cultures they crossed, the Ghawazee created their own hybrid of the oriental dance. Although gypsy folklore is obscure it is clear they were a very vital part of the diffusion process of the belly dance.

Early in the nineteenth century belly dancing began to be considered disreputable. It underwent a drastic image change as northern armies swept south into

Egypt and belly dancing took on the trappings of bawdy entertainment and prostitution.

As the Middle East was of strategic and commercial importance to the West, military leaders did everything in their command to keep their men from such an enticing pastime. The most extreme case was Napoleon, who in 1830 ordered that four hundred dancing girls be decapitated and thrown into the Nile for causing havoc among his soldiers. Following this incident the Egyptian leader Mohammed Ali banished dancing girls from the Cairo area to a village called Esna. It was not long before Esna was a tourist attraction.

Belly dancing was also popular with artists and statesmen. French and German writers and painters exhaustively depicted the pleasures of the dancing girls. The most reknowned of these performers was Kutchuk Hanem and many celebrities, including Gustave Flaubert, were lured to her bedroom. In a letter to his poet friend Louis Bouilhet, an infatuated Flaubert wrote:

> She is a very celebrated courtesan, large breasted, fleshy with slip nostrils, enormous eyes and magnificent knees. I will spare you a description of her dance for I can find no words to describe it. Her body was covered in sweat. She was tired from dancing. She was cold. I covered her with my fur pelisse and she fell asleep, her fingers in mine. As for me, I scarcely shut my eyes all night.

American journalist and humourist Charles Leland was left less lacking for words, he did well in describing the dance of the Ghawazee:

> The first dancing of all Ghawazee is simply moving about to the music and undulating the body. Then waves of motion are made to run from head to foot and over these waves pass with incredible rapidity the ripples and thrills, as you have seen a great billow in a breeze look like a smaller sea ribbed with a thousand wavelets.

Similarly transfixed, French author Joseph Gobineau wrote:

> Hours pass, and it is difficult to tear oneself away. This is the way the motions of the dancing girls of Asia affect the senses. There is no variety or vivacity and seldom is there a variation through any sudden movement, but the rhythmic wheeling exhales a delightful torpor upon the soul like an almost hypnotic intoxication.

Other travellers, such as Frenchman Gérard de Nerval and American journalist G. W. Curtis, also wrote of travels to the Orient. Their stories followed them into more sober homes and gave rise to a rich and fantastical image of life along the Nile. It was not long before this exotic imagery of the East physically crossed the Atlantic. North America had been well prepared for the arrival of Little Egypt in Chicago for the 1893 World's Fair. The Syrian-born dancer satisfied the yearning of those who could not afford an exotic pilgrimage. Her success at the fair led to Little Egypt imposters across America, dancing in night clubs, performing in carnival settings and rebelling against the restrictive code of behaviour of Victorian England. The belly dance was about to embark on yet another image shift as it took on the tawdry performance style associated with burlesque.

Oriental dancing now conjured up images of scantily clad females and lost its status as a folk art requiring skill and control. In North America the dance no longer had a place among women. It was relegated to strip joints, restaurants and night clubs. In the 1930s and 1940s the dance was further corrupted by its appearance in Hollywood epics. This commercialization of women's oldest dance ritual did nothing but exploit the so-called exotic aspects of belly dancing.

Fortunately the emerging world of modern dance had also found inspiration in the Orient. The imaginations of modern dancers like Ruth St. Denis were stirred by the sensuous spirit and the unfettered serpentine movements of dancers from the East. St. Denis believed that she was an embodiment of Egyptian mystery and created her infamous "Egypta" based on authentic oriental movement. Artistic interpretations of belly dance, performed in a concert dance setting, provided a new context in which to view this dance form. Dance ethnologist La Meri, committed to presenting authentic versions of ethnic dance in a folk art context, also helped to redirect the Western image of the belly dance away from the cabarets.

The show-girl image of belly dancing in North America and the Middle East is thankfully not an exclusive one. Tribes like the Ouled Nail of Algeria continue to relate the dance to its ritualistic and folk roots. A North American return to the dance's origin as a birth ritual blossomed in the 1970s among women's groups. Our public libraries now contain copies of "how-to" books expounding the benefits of this ancient fertility dance. Keeping in shape before, during and after pregnancy by belly dancing created a fresh milieu for the dance. It stressed the universal and timeless element of the dance and its centre of force, the belly.

But for many Western women it is the music which initially draws them to belly dancing. Professional dancers who perform in restaurants and cabarets are often able to work with live musicians and play their hips to the solid rhythms of the jar drum or doumbec. In *The Serpent and the Sphinx*, writer and belly dancer Wendy Buonaventura states:

> If the music is good it inspires certain movements: a plaintive flute solo makes a dancer unwind her veil and twirl it around her; an intense drum solo sets her hips shaking; a rhythmic tapping of the tambourine makes her hips move sharply up and down.

Although it once again holds a great deal of appeal, double standards continue to surround the status of belly dancing. On the one hand, the movements are alluring and seductive; we in the West are unaccustomed to watching a bare-bellied woman gyrate her pelvis and shimmy her breasts. As such, we tend to ignore the skill at work and focus solely on the superficial sexual imagery. In the East, the dance is caught in the maze of what may pass for acceptable behaviour under Muslim law. It is recognized as part of Arabic cultural heritage yet there is still condemnation for the dancer who performs publicly.

A Male View

Born in 1963 in rural Lebanon, Ali Jomma currently resides in Calgary, Alberta where he works as a lawyer. In an interview with Shawna Helland, Jomma expresses his views on belly dancing from a traditional, Muslim male perspective.

Were you familiar with belly dancing when you were growing up?

Belly dancing is not taught in schools in Lebanon. It's not something that is common in the villages or in the rural areas where I grew up. The dance that we grow up with was the debka. It is danced in a circle, holding hands.

But in a city like Beirut are there night clubs with belly dancers?

Put it this way, the nightclubs that feature belly dancing in Beirut are the equivalent to our strip joints here and from a moral, social and religious point of view that's how they are looked at. Canadian high schools don't teach people how to strip tease and they don't teach them to do belly dancing over there. Strip joints are very common here and belly dancing is common there, it's the same kind of thing.

Are both men and women allowed into the nightclubs?

Lebanon is different from most of the other Arab countries. Until the civil war started in 1975 we had the same liberties as in the Western world. In a lot of Arab countries like Saudi Arabia and in some of the Gulf countries nightclubs don't even exist. Neither does belly dancing and sexes don't mix in public.

What do you think of belly dancing? Do you view it as a very old ritualistic dance or a cabaret dance?

To me it's an artistic form of entertainment. To me it doesn't bring to mind a sense of history, although I realize that it has its roots in the Middle East. I think North Americans have mixed messages about our culture from watching movies from the 1950s like *Lawrence of Arabia* and *Ali Baba and the Forty Thieves*. I see that the Western adaptation of belly dancing has taken hold in North America in a very different way than the original idea ever did in the Middle East.

How do you think that Middle Eastern men view belly dancing?

Well I think there are two sides to it. On one hand there is the same sort of sexist attitude as a man viewing a swim suit competition or a strip tease. There's that aspect of it and then there is the artistic, musical and dance aspect of it which, depending on how much credit you want to give to the average male, is more or less present. I think that North American men with a background in Middle Eastern culture see it as exploiting a negative aspect of that culture. There are a lot of rich aspects of our culture which are never exposed and yet here is a quasi-sleazy aspect that the West has decided they want to sensationalize and exploit.

Does it bother you that the belly dance has been misrepresented?

What bothers me is that it is characterized as being an Arabic dance when in fact it's a North American aberration, kind of like chop suey. If I approved of the way it was done it wouldn't bother me, but obviously the fact that it does bother me suggests that there must be some negative aspect of it that causes concern. You don't see men doing it to entertain women. I feel the same way about belly dancing as I do about strippers and the way that they are exploited. It's basically the same thing.

At an Arabic party, if a belly dancer performs, would traditional Muslim men be uncomfortable?

It would offend the typical right-thinking Muslim man, absolutely. My father and anyone like my father would not watch a North American belly dancer. He would find it offensive. In Islam a women is supposed to cover herself, with the exception of her face and her hands. A belly dancer is considered to be naked. In Saudi Arabia, if someone was caught in the street dressed like that they wouldn't hang her but she might get three hundred lashes.

Would your father disapprove of his daughter or wife becoming a belly dancer?

Oh absolutely, as would anyone who has any religious convictions.

All the belly dancers I contacted in Calgary were North American in origin.

That just emphasizes the fact that it really is a North American thing. It has been given this label of being an Arabic dance when in fact it has really been used and popularized in the West.

Interview with a Belly Dancer

Born in Ontario of Ukrainian ancestry, Samea is a professional belly dancer currently working in Alberta. She spoke with Shawna Helland about public and personal perceptions of belly dancers and their art.

What first attracted you to belly dancing?

My sister is a belly dancer. I had two children and did not want to become a full-time housewife. I was trying to find my own thing. Initially I was horrified at what people might think, but the instructor was just a normal person and I fell in love with the music.

What kind of music do you dance to?

I dance to both Greek and Lebanese, but prefer Egyptian music. They are the best composers and singers. They create great mood swings, something that is particularly true of the new style of Egyptian music.

Who becomes involved in belly dancing?

Very few Egyptian or Lebanese women in North America. Although I am treated with respect when I dance at a party I feel that the people are glad it is me and not their daughter. In places such as Cairo dancers are looked down upon when they first begin but if they rise on the ladder they quickly are elevated to the status of queen.

Is belly dancing a part of Muslim culture?

And Christian. Muslims are rather strict, depending on the degree of their religious convictions. They insist that the midriff is covered. When I dance for Muslims I wear a netted dress.

Do Muslim women ever become belly dancers?

Yes, but they will be going against their family. It is a very mixed-up concept. Here, as well as in the Middle East, any belly dancer, Muslim or otherwise, will gain respect if her dance is well-liked.

How many belly dancers are there in Alberta?

There are about six who perform professionally. I do some work with two or three dancers. If someone needs several performers there are people I call on but I prefer to work on my own. It is very personal.

Are there belly dances which are totally choreographed?

Yes, those are the folkloric dances. Something like the Bedouin Wedding Dance is a set piece. However, most dances are very individual. Belly dancers have simply taken the basic steps of folkloric dance, made them more intricate and put them into a cabaret performance. My own dances are largely improvised, drawing on nine years of dance experience.

What is it like to dance in informal places, like restaurants?

I prefer to perform on a stage with a live band. In most Middle Eastern countries dance is performed on a stage. The dancer might go out to the audience to have a bit of fun and interaction. Montreal has about seven Arabic clubs. An evening consists of alternating singers and dancers. On a night when there is no program, the whole audience might get up and dance. It's much like a big party. When I dance it's basically an imitation of that sort of personal exuberance.

Do women come into clubs to watch belly dancers?

Absolutely. The idea is not to get a woman jealous if she is sitting with her boyfriend. If at some point you want to have a bit of fun, you might give the woman a wink, to include her in the game. This is particularly important when dancing for North Americans who often fail to appreciate the dancing. Too many people have the idea that it is sleazy bump and grind because dancers have made it that way. It's a shame. They don't understand where it has come from.

A lot was written about belly dancing in the seventies. Does it paint a true picture of the art?

I think you have to see what it is like in the Middle East. They are very classy people, not at all like the hippy-types in Gypsy costume portrayed in the "how-to" books. That's just not it. That idea has developed along with the North American burlesque appeal. It shouldn't even be called belly dancing. It is more "dance oriental."

Is it an erotic form of dance to you?

No, the dance is definitely sensuous but not erotic. I think of it as almost loving.

Would you like to see the image of belly dancing change?

Yes, definitely. Too often it is seen as something hokey or sleazy. Dancers need to develop a different attitude. It is up to them to research and find instructors who stay true to the art. Publications such as *Arabesque* are invaluable in providing accurate and timely information. If you are truly interested, that is the sort of commitment you must make to yourself and the dance form.

Can a belly dancer have a long career?

It is physically possible. Unfortunately audiences do not often recognize fitness or technique as often as they do personal attractiveness. They forget to appreciate the intricacies of the dance, it is simpler to base criticism in physical beauty.

Is it considered attractive to have a large belly?

Arabs don't like thin dancers. It is considered a good thing to have hips, but you don't have to have a particular look to be involved. I would love to see more people become belly dancers, regardless of their age or ability. Unlike other types of dance, it seems that better understanding and ability comes with age. In Egypt the really big names in the field are around fifty years old.

Have you been to the Middle East to study?

Not yet, but I definitely will. Cairo is where the trends arise, especially the styles of dance and costumes. There is constant change. Belly dancing is very fashion-conscious. One example is the use of castanets, a North American trend which the Egyptians don't favour. I too find them distracting because they take away from the possibility of beautiful hand movements. They can't be used with a lot of the newly composed Egyptian music because it is so erratic. Typically their use is restricted to the performance of slow, folkloric ballads.

How do you keep up with the change?

Belly dancing is a little world of its own. We have a newsletter with information about workshops and who the instructors are. For a beginner I would definitely recommend people in Alberta who can provide lessons but normally I travel to the larger centres, particularly Montreal, to take workshops.

Are belly dancers in touch with any spiritual aspect of the form?

I think it is spiritual if you love the music.

Aside from the music, what is there in belly dancing which holds an appeal for you?

There is a definite power associated with the dance. You can turn an audience on or off almost at will. You can also express emotion in a way that I find very satisfying. It is possible to make the audience almost fall in love with you.

A Chronology of the Belly Dance: History in the Shaking

25,000 B.C. Upper Paleolithic age. Earliest known female figurines of Venus figures date to this time. Earliest indications of a matriarchal dominance in society. Female body worshipped for childbearing capabilities.

5500 B.C. Neolithic era. Mother Goddess religion practiced in the Middle East. Establishment of agricultural societies. Curt Sachs (dance historian) places the beginning of the *danse du ventre* here.

4000 B.C. Suggestive evidence points to earliest invasion of Middle Eastern Goddess-oriented societies by male-dominated tribes of the North.

2300 B.C. Sacred lovemaking widely practiced in the temples in worship of the Mother Goddess. (Caste tribes like the Ouled Nail may have developed at this time.)

1800 B.C. End of the era of matriarchal dominance in Egypt following a series of Northern invasions.

1500 B.C. Egyptian conquest of portions of the Middle East. Egypt sends dancers to other countries and imports dancers from other countries.

960 B.C. Solomon becomes king of Israel. He worships both Jehovah and the Goddess and has a harem of seven hundred wives and three hundred concubines.

ca. 500 B.C. Phoenician finger cymbals used in Carthage.

ca. 60 B.C. Romans import dancers from Syria.

28 A.D. Salome dances before her stepfather, King Herod. He is so pleased that he offers her any request, not knowing that her evil mother, his wife, has already told her to ask for the head of John the Baptist.

300 Closing of Goddess temples begins under the Byzantine emperor Constantine.

450 The Parthenon of the Acropolis, formerly a sacred shrine of the Goddess religion, becomes a Christian church.

527 A celebrated oriental dancer, actress, and alleged courtesan becomes the empress Theodora, wife of Emperor Justinian of the Byzantine empire. As the *de facto* ruler of Byzantium, she is the author of legislation favorable to women's rights.

612 Moors settle in Spain, bringing a dance related to the "oriental form" with "African embellishments." Moorish women typically live in harems.

519 Mohammed's flight to Medina (the Hegira). Beginning of the Muslim calendar.

ca. 622 Mohammed forbids painting or writing about any living things, promotes harems. Beginning of Muslim conquests.

ca. 850 In *Prairies of Gold*, descriptions of qualities of a good dancer are recorded as told by a scholar to the Caliph Mu'tamid.

1096–1300 The Crusades—Christian Europe vs. Muslim Middle East. Middle Eastern dancing girls become influential in Europe when brought back by the soldiers.

1498 Renaissance court dance develops.

1500 Persecution of Moors and other minorities in Spain throws them together in the mountain regions, where the flamenco dance develops.

1798 G. W. Browne reports Ghawazee dancers flourishing as an accepted part of Egyptian society.

1851 Oriental dancers appear at the Crystal Palace Exhibition in London. Queen Victoria is there.

1893 Belly dance movements incorporated into strip tease and vice versa. Many Little Egypts appear. Hootchie Cootchie blends with belly dancing. Modern cabaret costume and high heels introduced.

1906 Ruth St. Denis debuts as an oriental dancer. Not wishing to share billing with a boxer and a herd of trained monkeys, she subsequently rents her own theatre.

1927 Badia Masabni founds Casino Opera in Cairo. Presents shows featuring Tahia Caricoa, Samia Gamal.

1955 Egyptian government requires dancers to cover themselves from shoulders to ankles.

1970 Women's liberation group pickets a performance by Jamila Salimpour's students in Berkeley on the grounds that belly dancing treats women as sex objects and is "antithetical to women's rightful role."

1970–1979 Belly dance movement sweeps U.S.A. Hollywood begins to use real belly dancers and genuine Arabic music.

1975 *Arabesque*, A Journal of Middle Eastern Dance, is founded in New York City.

1978 Thirty conservative members of the Egyptian Parliament call for the belly dance to be banned forever in Egypt.

1979 Belly dancers are still undervalued and underpaid in the United States and subject to political persecution in the Middle East, but look to the future with optimism. The Ayatollah Khomeini bans music on radio and television in Iran.

Changing Images and Shifting Identities: Female Performers in Egypt

KARIN VAN NIEUWKERK

Introduction

In the late eighteenth century, Egyptian female performers, the *awalim,* were described as follows:

> They are called *savantes.* A more painstaking education than other women has earned them this name. They form a celebrated community within the country. In order to join, one must have a beautiful voice, a good possession of the language, a knowledge of the rules of poetry and an ability to spontaneously compose and sing couplets adapted to the circumstances. . . . There is no fete without them; no festival where they do not provide the ornamentation.[1]

While it still holds true today that a celebration without performers is not a real celebration and that entertainers are central to the most important occasions in peoples' lives, female performers are no longer a celebrated community of learned women. On the contrary, in present-day Egypt, female performers are generally regarded as "fallen women." A tailor, talking about female singers, and dancers in particular, told me: "These jobs are shameful and detestable. I don't like it . . . but I do like to watch it. Once in a lifetime we invite them; it is *haram* (taboo), but the fault is theirs."

Only a few women working in the circuit of performing arts—radio, television, and theater—such as Umm Kulthum and the folkloric dancer Farida

Fahmy[2] escape such moral stigma. For most female singers and dancers, however, prostitution is the measuring rod by which they are reckoned.

What are the main reasons for this drastic transformation of the image of female performers from learned women to fallen women? How is this ambivalence concerning women as performers related to cultural constructions of gender? How do female performers relate to these images about themselves?

In this essay, I shall first explore the historical transformations of the image of female performers and clarify the most important reasons for these shifting images. I limit myself to the circuit of weddings and saint's day celebrations, and that of the nightclubs.[3] Secondly, I shall discuss the underlying notions of gender and the image of the female body as one of the main reasons for the moral stigma attached to female performers. Lastly, I shall discuss the manner in which female performers themselves relate to these constructions and the way they try to deconstruct the gendered images.

Changing Images

The entertainment activities of women in the late eighteenth and early nineteenth centuries were confined to singing, dancing, poetry, and music. All acting roles were played by men, even women's roles. The only source of information on female performers of the period—travelers' accounts—is not very reliable, yet it can be reconstructed that there probably existed two broad strata of women performers.[4]

The first stratum consisted of *awalim*, whose main activities were writing poetry, composing music, improvising, and singing. They also danced, but only for other women. They often played instruments to accompany their songs, and they were greatly esteemed for their *mawwal*, or improvised songs. The *awalim* performed for women in the harem. Women's areas for receiving were screened off but overlooked the main, male reception space. The *awalim* were audible, but not visible, to men. These educated *awalim* were highly appreciated for their art, and respected as well, since they did not perform for men.

The second group of female entertainers were the *ghawazi*. They were mainly dancers who performed unveiled in the streets and in front of coffee houses. The *ghawazi* danced especially at saint's day celebrations and migrated from one *mulid* to another. These dancing girls were the most accessible to foreigners since they performed publicly. The most striking element of their appearance was that they were unveiled. Several travelers remarked that the *ghawazi* used to smoke the water pipe and drank considerable amounts of brandy. Due to these associations and the fact that they danced in public for men with unveiled faces, they were generally not regarded as decent women.

There was also a category of female performers between the *awalim* and the *ghawazi*. This group consisted of lower-class singers and dancers, common *awalim* who performed for the poor in working-class quarters. Prostitutes were registered as having a separate profession. However, public dancers could be found who combined dancing and prostitution.

With the opening of the nineteenth century, this group of common *awalim* and the number of dancer-prostitutes seem to have increased. The reasons for these changes in the activity and status of female performers should be understood in the light of political events at the time.

At the end of the eighteenth century, Egypt was divided and politically insecure. Although formally part of the Ottoman Empire, Egypt was in practice ruled by several Mamluk beys who quickly succeeded one another. All had weak internal power bases and had consequently to depend upon their own militias. In order to finance their armies, they levied heavy taxes. During the French Occupation (1798–1801) and the rule of Muhammad Ali (1811–1849) the control over female performers was strict.

Governmental restrictions encouraged many heavily taxed common *awalim* and *ghawazi* to leave Cairo, since state control was less effective outside the capital. Foreigners, who came to Egypt in increasing numbers, provided a new opportunity for employment. Foreigners were mainly interested in dancing. The *awalim* were increasingly described as singers and dancers, the *ghawazi* as dancers and prostitutes. It is not clear whether higher class *awalim* started to work for foreigners, or if women from outside the profession started dancing and singing to earn a living. At any rate, the number of female entertainers who danced and sang for foreigners at the time was considerable.

This new development met with fierce opposition from the religious authorities. In 1834, the ruler, Muhammad Ali Pasha, issued an edict prohibiting public female dancers and prostitutes from working in the capital. Women who were convicted of violating this new law were punished and deported to the south of Egypt. The ban was an attempt to marginalize most public women and to keep them out of the view of foreigners. It proved, however, to be counterproductive. European eyes followed them to the south, to Upper Egypt, where they became the center of attention. There, too, tourists were the main source of income. A number of entertainers turned to prostitution. The move to prostitution was not solely due to the requests of foreigners. It was also caused by the poverty and insecurity performers experienced in Upper Egypt.

The word *alma* (*alima*) lost its original meaning of "learned woman." At the beginning of the nineteenth century, its meaning changed to "singer-dancer." By the 1850s, the word denoted a dancer-prostitute. Dancing sometimes became stripping and dancers increasingly worked as prostitutes. The fading of the distinction between the *awalim* and the *ghawazi* and the growing number of common singer-dancers led to the expulsion of all to the south. The banishment further erased the distinction between performers and prostitutes.

The ban was apparently lifted around 1850. Female performers were allowed to return to Cairo, but not to practice their occupations publicly. For those who once sang and danced in the streets and markets, a new opportunity arose, the *café-chantants*. Female performers were now concealed inside music halls. Gradually these developed into the nightclub circuit.

Performances at weddings had continued through the century. Famous singers were no longer called *awalim*, since the word had become too tainted in the course of the nineteenth century. This word was now used for the group of common singers and dancers who performed in working-class quarters.

The heyday of the common *awalim* was at the beginning of this century.[5] They performed on festive occasions, particularly for other women, as they had done in the nineteenth century. In contrast to that period, however, at the turn of the twentieth century, they increasingly sang and danced for the lower and middle classes. The Westernized elite mostly invited well-known nightclub entertainers to perform at their weddings.

At the beginning of this century, wedding celebrations were still segregated, and for that reason women were prominent in the entertainment market. They formed groups that regularly performed together under the leadership of an experienced performer, the *usta*. She taught the trade to family members and new girls. Female performers often lived in the same house and most *ustawat* clustered together in the same neighborhood of a town. In Cairo, the performers often lived together on Muhammad Ali Street.

At the turn of the century there seems to have been a distinction between the performers for the women's party and those for the men's party. The men's party was not usually attended by *awalim*, who performed mainly for women. From the 1940s onward, however,

the difference between the two groups was only a semantic distinction. The performers for the women's parties and wedding party itself were called *awalim*, whereas the entertainers at the *sahra,* the men's party, were called *artistes*. Most of the older performers I spoke with were both *awalim* and *artistes*, that is, they first performed for the women upstairs and afterwards they sang and danced for the men until the early morning.

In the late 1940s, the *awalim* vanished from urban weddings because the weddings became less extravagant and, more importantly, less segregated. This development was related to social changes in the wider society, where the separation of the sexes became less strict. The separate women's parties lingered on in the countryside, but by the 1960s they had disappeared. Even before that time, people did not hire professional entertainment at the women's party, and often allowed women to be present at the men's party. Women then usually sat apart with the bride and groom, and left early, after which the all-male party continued until dawn. This is still the case with weddings in working-class quarters.

From the 1940s through the 1970s, women of the families of Muhammad Ali Street remained active at weddings and saint's day celebrations. At weddings they chiefly performed as singers and dancers, but several women managed to build up a male clientele as well. Some again resumed the position of *usta*, but their groups less strictly resembled a regular company and performers started working with several male and female employers. Yet entertainers still formed a relatively small society of loosely related groups. During the 1970s, however, these organizational patterns changed.

During Sadat's presidency (1973–1981) Egypt adopted an open-door policy in order to attract foreign investments. With the changes in the economy, a middle class emerged and exploited the new situation. This class of newly rich spent part of their wealth on recreation and brought about a flourishing period for entertainers. The growing demand for entertainers resulted in higher wages. Prices had been on the rise from the 1950s on, but under Sadat they increased tenfold. Not only the wages for entertainment rose, but also the tips.

The increased profits attracted many individuals from outside the profession. They started not only working as musicians, singers, and dancers, but also as impresarios and employers. The band was no longer a group that regularly performed together, sharing experiences and expertise over the years. Instead a group was increasingly composed of individuals working for the highest bidder.

During the late 1970s and the 1980s, the economic boom came to an end. In economic terms, it had benefited only a small segment of society. For most people of the lower and lower middle classes and those living on fixed salaries, such as government employees, the growing inflation and rising food prices caused hardship. The recession has continued up to the present and has negatively affected the entertainment industry.

Muhammad Ali Street performers complain that professional ethics have been abandoned at weddings since their monopoly was broken. Proper conduct of female entertainers with male customers and colleagues used to be maintained by the *usta* and their relatives who also worked in the trade. The older generation claims that presently the women's success is mainly based on fraternizing with customers and wearing scanty costumes, not on their artistry. A few female performers of Muhammad Ali Street decided to leave the trade altogether and most kept their children out of it. Former performers of Muhammad Ali Street were insulted when I asked them whether they had worked in nightclubs. For them, it was synonymous with an accusation of prostitution. But now, with the loss of esteem in the wedding circuits, a number of them try their luck in nightclubs.

The nightclubs started to develop in the late nineteenth century. As a result of the Egyptian government's efforts to institutionalize the entertainment places, in connection with the British presence in Egypt and the expansion of tourism, the existing vari-

ety theaters grew into the present nightclub circuit. The Western cabarets left their mark on their Egyptian counterparts.

In 1910, only three nightclubs existed. The number quickly increased and a concentration of foreign and Egyptian bars and nightclubs developed in the Ezbekiya Gardens in the center of Cairo. The main task of female entertainers was to sit and drink with customers (*fath*). They usually sang first, or danced on the stage, and if they were admired by a client, he ordered them to sit at his table and opened bottles of champagne, whiskey, or beer for them. *Fath* was the most profitable part of the job for the nightclub owner as well as the woman.

Between 1900 and 1956, several laws regulating entertainment places were issued. The laws became more and more severe concerning the moral behavior of the employees. After 1949, the year in which prostitution was made a criminal act, the government tried to purify the nightclubs. Although sitting and drinking with customers was officially forbidden in 1951, *fath* went on, with red lamps and ringing bells warning the women of a vice-squad raid. In 1973, *fath* was eventually abolished. The government initiated a new system of registration and licenses, and checked more closely. To receive a license, the performer had to pass an examination in which she proved herself to be an actual singer or dancer. In addition, she was listed by the police, taxed, and her behavior with customers was closely watched. Moreover, her conduct on stage and costume were prescribed. The belly had to be covered (with netting or material), the slits in her skirts closed, and talking or laughing with customers was no longer allowed.

Some of the cheapest nightclubs, however, still resemble those of the old days of the *fatihat*. The difference is that the socializing is done not by performers but by hostesses or waitresses, who are not allowed to sit with customers at their tables—they must walk around and converse with them while standing. Female performers are still supposed to make longlasting contacts with customers but, in contrast to the past, mainly after, instead of during, working hours. They are expected to have their own customers and bring them to the club. Customers still try to make contacts with female performers. Because they can no longer invite them to their table, they sometimes write their name and address on a tissue and give it to the performer with a tip. Some entertainers, particularly the less talented ones working in the cheaper clubs, use their time on stage for talking, joking, and holding hands, to persuade the men to take out their purses. In the better nightclubs the entrance fee and the wages of the entertainers are much higher. Owners and performers are therefore less dependent on tips. In the course of time, there has thus been a trend toward "respectability" in the nightclubs, but this development has been largely restricted to the five-star nightclubs.

Gender Images

The last two centuries thus witnessed a dramatic change in the status and image of female performers. In the nineteenth century, Western influences were one of the main reasons for the negative changes and loss of esteem. The *awalim* were no longer seen as learned women, and increasingly became common singer-dancers for the lower and lower middle class. In the twentieth century, internal factors caused the disappearance of the *awalim* and the lowering of the common singers' and dancers' reputation. The most important reason for the disappearance of the *awalim* is that weddings are no longer celebrated separately. This means that female performers either sing and dance for mixed parties or for all-male parties. Performing for men stains the reputation. Moreover, while Muhammad Ali Street until the middle of this century formed a tightly knit community with strict social control that protected women's reputations, this is no longer the case. Since the monopoly of the traditional performing families was broken and newcomers entered the trade, the reputation of all entertainers, but especially women, is no longer safeguarded.

In the nightclubs, there has been a tendency toward

"respectability," yet in the eyes of the general public, the attempts have failed. Nightclubs are still perceived as the worst place for women to work, and being a nightclub dancer is almost synonymous with working as a prostitute.

Whereas the changing image from learned women to fallen women can partly be explained by historical transformations and current practices affecting the trade, there is more to it. Female performers were also met with great ambivalence in the past. Only the early *awalim* seemed to have escaped moral stigma, by being talented and educated, and more importantly, by being concealed and invisible to men. The unveiled *ghawazi*, who performed publicly for men, were not respected. Similarly, the *awalim* lost esteem when they started to work for men in the public arena.

At present, all female performers are regarded with ambivalence. Although female singers and dancers working at weddings are considered more respectable than nightclub performers, they are all immoral. Also, the difference between the reputation of female singers and that of dancers was smaller than I had expected. An Egyptian girl remarked, "A female singer at a wedding is also not good. Men at the party are interested in how she moves and what she wears, not in how she sings. For male singers it is no problem, they don't move." Female singers are first assessed visually, and only secondly for their voice. Regardless of their artistic standard they are first and foremost classified as women with (or without) attractive bodies.

I was struck by the fact that female performers working in the respected circuit of "higher" performing arts did not totally escape society's disapprobation. Although female singers working in television are highly esteemed, dancers and folkloric dancers, even those working in theaters, may be regarded with ambivalence. Extremely gifted artists such as Umm Kulthum and the dancer Farida Fahmy were the exceptions who managed to be respected as female artists. Even they had some difficulty in successfully manipulating their image as respectable female artists by creating an aura of simple *baladi* or *fallahi* mores, appearing as women who follow local, conservative values and by covering their bodies accordingly in performances.

The reason that female singers and dancers are generally regarded as immoral is related to the prevailing cultural construction of femininity and particularly of the female body. These constructions of gender and the body are grounded to a great extent in religious discourse.

According to the strictest religious groups, singing by women is *haram*, taboo. One phrase is often cited to discredit female singers—*sawt al-mara'a awra*, "the voice of women is a shameful thing [lit. 'pudendal']." For this reason a *shaykh* I spoke with claimed that even listening to the voice of a woman on the telephone is unlawful. If female singers were concealed, as in the past, they could still seduce the male audience. Presently, they are visible and even more seductive because the excitement aroused by looking is considered more powerful than excitement aroused by listening.[6] Since it is believed that visual rather than aural arousal is more disturbing, the consequences for the various forms of female entertainment differ. Female musicians have an aural audience, female singers have both audience and spectators, whereas dancers are solely viewed, not heard. Thus it is commonly thought in religious opinion—and also in public opinion—that dancing is the most shameful form of entertainment.

Dancers' gravest transgression is that they move. There is a strong association between movement and morality. Lightness of movement stands for lightness in morals.[7] Moving is immoral for women since it draws even more attention to their shameful bodies. When I asked a *shaykh* whether female folk dancers (who wear more clothing than oriental dancers) are less *haram*, he replied resolutely, "No, they also move." Female singers were also described as "moving" in their performances.

Men, as the girl quoted earlier said, do not "move." And even if they do, they are not viewed as having exciting bodies. Male singers and musicians are evaluated with regard to their voices and skills, not their bodies. I asked the same *shaykh* why male dancing is not *haram*. The answer was easy: "A man's body is not shameful

(*awra*)," and regardless of how it moves and shakes, "it cannot excite."

What female performers hold in common is that they are women who use their shameful bodies in public. Their bodies stir others, while male bodies neither move nor stir. Why is the female body considered exciting and shameful?

The discourse on sex and gender in the Muslim world is not an easy thing to describe. It should be borne in mind that there is not just one discourse, and that the multiple discourses do not define actual behavior. In addition, discourses are neither stable over time, nor undisputed. That said, there are two fundamental discourses on gender and sexuality, the orthodox or explicit discourse, and the implicit or erotic discourse.[8] Despite the difference between the constructions of gender and sexuality in the two discourses, it is striking that they converge in their definition of women primarily as bodies, particularly sexual bodies.

According to Leila Ahmed, who traces the varieties of discourses and how they have altered in the history of Middle Eastern Arab women, it was in the Abbasid era that the word "woman" became almost synonymous with "slave" and "object for sexual use." Marketing of women as commodities and objects for sexual use was an everyday reality in Abbasid society. It is no wonder then that Muslim scholars of that period, including al-Ghazali, mainly define women as sexual beings. This period was, however, crucial for the formulation of Islamic laws and thus has had a profound impact up to the present day.[9]

Sabbah argues that Muslim culture has a "built-in ideological blindness to the economic dimension of women, who are ordinarily perceived, conceived, and defined as exclusively sexual objects. The female body has traditionally been the object of an enormous erotic investment, which has clouded (if not totally hidden) woman's economic dimension."[10] In addition, the relations between the sexes are generally eroticized. As a result, women's work outside the home is often considered as erotic aggression.

The definition of women as sexual beings and the female body as enticing is thus a very powerful discourse. It explains why female entertainers are shameful and bad, while, for instance, their male colleagues are not condemned for similar activities. The female body is shameful because it is by definition eroticizing and enticing, whereas the male body has several dimensions and is not seductive by nature. The male body, although sexual in the presence of a female body, has other dimensions—for instance in the economic or political field. The construction of gender and the body explain why the body of male performers is a "productive instrument" whereas that of female performers is by definition a "sexual body."

All women have the power to seduce men by their sexual bodies. Female performers mainly differ from "decent" women because they publicly employ their potential to seduce. Instead of using their feminine power in the legal and private context of marriage, they tempt male customers in public. Female performers are more immoral than other women working in the male public space because in entertainment the bodily dimension is central. They use their sexual bodies as an instrument for earning money. Female performers are perceived as being closely related to prostitutes because both use their sexual bodies in public space to make a living.

Conclusion

The changing image of female performers from learned women to fallen women can partly be explained by historical transformations and current practices in the entertainment trade. Yet, the explanation for the image of the "bad woman" is more profoundly related to the prevailing construction of gender and particularly to the construction of the body. The crux of the gender issue is that women are generally viewed as sexual beings. Their bodies are enticing, regardless of what they do. These constructions of gender and the body pertain to all Egyptian women. Female performers differ from "decent" women because they use their bodies to make a living, instead of hiding them as much as possible. Women who work in male public space are all to some degree suspect. Female performers are more immoral than the other women working in public space because the bodily dimension is central in entertainment. Female performers publicly employ the sexual power of their bodies, hence the poor ranking of entertainment as a field for women to work in.

Female entertainers are ambivalent in their attitude to their bodies. Their femininity and sexuality provide them with a living, yet they pay for it in terms of status and respect. Female performers accordingly try to neutralize and even deny the femininity of their bodies in order to counterbalance the image of looseness or immorality. They try to negotiate the meaning of the body and reduce its sexual dimension by taking on aspects of the male gender in public. For them, their bodies are neutral productive instruments, like the male body.

According to female performers they are women like other women—that is, respectable daughters of the country. Through their self-presentation as ideal housewives and mothers in private, and tough women and "men among men" in public, they try to protect their reputation as respectable women. Female performers consider singing and dancing a livelihood and, for women as well as for men, a respectable trade.

Notes

1. M. Savary, *Lettres sur L'Egypte,* 3 vols. (Amsterdam and Leiden: Les Libraires Associés, 1787), 1:124–125.

2. See the contributions by Virginia Danielson and Marjorie Franken, chaps. 6 and 17 in *Images of Enchantment:* *Visual and Performing Arts in the Middle East,* ed. Sharifa Zuhar (Cairo, Egypt: American University in Cairo Press, 1998).

3. The three main contexts of Egyptian entertainment

are, first, the circuit of weddings and saint's day celebrations; second, the nightclub circuit; and finally, the performing arts circuit, consisting of performances in concert halls and theaters, on radio and television. My research focused on the first two sorts of venues.

4. Karin van Nieuwkerk, *"A Trade Like Any Other": Female Singers and Dancers in Egypt* (Austin: University of Texas Press, 1995; Cairo: American University in Cairo Press, 1996), chap. 2. The main sources for this chapter were W. G. Browne, *Nieuwe Reize Naar de Binnenste Gedeelten van Afrika, Door Egypte, Syrië en le Dar-Four waar Nimmer te Voren Eenig Europeaan Heeft Gereisd-Gedaan in den Jaare 1792–1798* (Amsterdam: Johannes Allart, 1808); J. L. Burckhardt, *Arabic Proverbs, or the Manners and Customs of the Modern Egyptians, Illustrated from Their Proverbial Sayings Current at Cairo* (1875; reprint, London: Curzon Press, 1972); V. Denon, *Reize in Opper-en Neder Egipte Gedurende den Veldtocht van Bonaparte* (Amsterdam: Johannes Allart, 1803); Lady Duff Gordon, *Letters from Egypt* (London: R. Brimley Johnson, 1902); G. Flaubert, *Flaubert in Egypt*, ed. F. Steegmuller (Chicago: Chicago Academy Limited, 1979); E. W. Lane, *Manners and Customs of the Modern Egyptians* (1836; reprint, The Hague: East West Publications, 1978); C. Niebuhr, *Reize Naar Arabië en Andere Omliggende Landen*, 2 vols. (Amsterdam: S. J. Baalde, 1776); M. Savary, *Lettres sur l'Égypte*; M. Villoteau, "De l'état actuel de l'art musical en Égypte," in *Description de l'Égypte XIV* (Paris: Panckoucke, 1822).

5. This information is based upon oral histories collected during fieldwork completed in Egypt between 1987 and 1990.

6. See al-Ghazali on this topic. Looking at female performers is always forbidden whether temptation is feared or not. He reasons that looking at a beardless young boy is only forbidden if there is a danger of temptation. He then likens the lawfulness of listening to a concealed female singer to looking at a beardless young boy. Arousal of temptation is the condition to be avoided, yet only if this state is feared is it unlawful. "Ihya Ulum ad-Din of al-Ghazali," trans. D. B. Macdonald, *Journal of the Royal Asiatic Society* (April 1901): 235–237.

7. Also see W. Jansen, *Women without Men: Gender and Marginality in an Algerian Town* (Leiden: E. W. Brill, 1987), 183. Algerian men are considered to be "heavy," in control of their movements, whereas women have to overcome their natural tendency to be "light."

8. Fatima Mernissi, *Beyond the Veil: Male-Female Dynamics in a Modern Muslim Society* (New York: Schenkman, 1975), and Fatna A. Sabbah, *Woman in the Muslim Unconscious* (New York: Pergamon Press, 1984). Mernissi compares the explicit and the implicit discourses, Sabbah the orthodox and the erotic discourses. The explicit discourse is comparable to the orthodox, while the erotic discourse is an extension, and exaggeration, of the implicit discourse.

9. Leila Ahmed, *Women and Gender in Islam: Historical Roots of a Modern Debate* (New Haven: Yale University Press, 1992).

10. Sabbah, *Woman in the Muslim Unconscious*, 16–17.

Commonalties in African Dance:
An Aesthetic Foundation

KARIAMU WELSH ASANTE

African dance is a complex art in an advanced form. Its development encompasses many forms, including ballet, jazz, and modern dance. Its influence is visible in the highly stylized dances of the Americas such as the samba, rumba, and *capoeira*. The polyrhythmic, polycentric character of African dance is immediately recognizable and distinctive. From the foot-stomping dance of the Muchongoyo of eastern Zimbabwe to the stilt-walking Makishi of Zambia to the masked dance of the Gelede in Nigeria, to the Royal Adowa and Kete of Ghana, to the kneesitting dance of the Lesotho women, to the 6/8 rhythms of the samba from Brazil, to the High Life of West Africa, to the rumba of Cuba, to the Ring Shout dance of the Carolinas, to the Snake dance of Angola, to the jazz dance of Black America, to the Ngoma dance of Kenya, to the Katherine Dunham technique, to the dust-flying dances of the Zulu—and still there are more; in all of these dances a commonality can be established. Intrinsic in this commonality is the ancestral connection to Africa through epic, memory, and oral tradition, even though these dances represent different languages, people, geographies, and cultures.

What this commonality exposes as we examine each dance is a foundation for many African dance techniques. African dance is polyrhythmic, polycentric, and holistic with regard to motion rather than being postural or position-oriented as an essential requisite. Position and posture are integral, but it is the movement that is challenging scholars and choreographers

of African dance to define, structure, and codify it. The genre of African dance has always had technique, indeed, it has enough substance for a hundred techniques. Techniques and qualities from the African dance have been drawn upon by dancers, teachers, and choreographers from all over the world. It is crucial that artists now are organizing, identifying, and codifying some of the techniques that have developed. For example, Dunham and Primus techniques are two of the known techniques. A third technique, following in the tradition of Primus and Dunham, is Mfundalai technique.

African dance is visually stimulating and exciting and capable of arousing emotive responses as well as visual ones. Cultural anthropologists and ethnomusicologists have to date offered insights and research in the field, but lack the expertise and perspective of a trained dancer, choreographer, or dance historian to properly analyze the movements and steps found in the dance.

There are certain foundations which make up the African dance aesthetic which I call senses. They give the African dance its touch, feel, voice, motion. Two of the techniques that I have mentioned: the Katherine Dunham technique, based on Haitian folklore and about forty years old, and Mfundalai, the African dance technique that I began to develop ten years ago based on universal African movement, are both African techniques. They both exhibit the seven senses of the African dance aesthetic and substantiate the evidence for future techniques.

The foundations of an aesthetic can be found in the culture of a society. The value system and religious ethos normally provide and stimulate the creative setting for "stylized art," that is, art which is no longer directly associated with religion or ritual. The particular qualities of an ethnic group provide the ingredients which distinguish the aesthetic and enable individual expression as well as manifest collective expression. All African cultures express themselves through the universals of dance, music, visual arts, and graphic arts. Differences are as varied as the ethnic groups, and it is not the particular artistic qualities of individual African ethnic groups that will be analyzed in this essay, but the aesthetic commonalties of dance in ethnic groups with origins in Africa.

African dance in general has been difficult to categorize because there are thousands of ethnic groups representing 150 million people of African descent in the diaspora (North and South America and the Pacific) and 400 million on the African continent itself. By establishing a definable codification, further scholarship and analysis can be encouraged and techniques and choreography can be improved. By definition, for purposes of clarity, Africans are all people of African descent.[1] An historical, mythological, and religious world view must be undertaken to understand the African aesthetic. Any discussion of African dance must appreciate the role of dance within the African society. Rural dance is traditional dance and traditional dance is rural dance. Traditional dance in urban areas is more stylized, removed from ritual, and influenced by other nationalities. The commonalties discussed here will also cover the creations of contemporary choreography which exhibit the African aesthetic.

The beauty of African aesthetics is in its enormous complexity. Absence of documentation and notation has unfortunately forced students and scholars to rely on performances, oral reports, and scholarship by interested but uninformed persons as the only body of research material. Part of the responsibility for the lack of written documentation and notation is the dominance of the oral tradition, which is an art in and of itself and a form of documentation. An oral tradition, literally a word of mouth phenomenon that preserves history and entertains in African culture, actually appears in all disciplines of the arts as a subtle undercurrent. The "oral narrative" is in effect the story, dance, art, and the speaker becomes the *griot*, dancer, choreographer, or sculptor. And the "oral" becomes the property of the speaker to reshape or to retell within a shape. The boundaries are there in plot, structure, outline, and form, but it is the dancer who breathes new life into the dance and it becomes hers/his for the moment. There are no permanent stamps of the creators, only the changing designs, rhythms, movements that change with the performers. What the work represents is guarded and revered, but not the identity of the creator herself/himself after the creation has been completed even though the profession is respected and acknowledged. The mark of the artist is in her/his creativity, not in time, nor in her/his person. The element of permanence or signature usually deals with the work itself and the culture it represents, not the person of the creator. The oral tradition then is the organic, creative process, evident in all African artists. It is the reason, ironically, that so many impressive works of art are not signed. The signature of the African artist is inherent in the creation and the spiritual or divine creator deserves and is given the credit. It is understood that the artist is a conduit and therefore not responsible for the greatness of the work. This does not mean that the artist is irresponsible, in fact, the responsibility is awesome. Acceptance of the responsibility as a conduit is where the appreciation is acknowledged and the completion of the task is when the applause is given. The artist is considered "chosen" and the rejection of this role is often considered sacrilegious. This is not to be confused with the economics of being an artist when one has to make decisions based on survival, but on the philosophical and spiritual aspect of being an artist.

The oral principle constitutes a fundamental principle in African aesthetics manifesting itself in African dance. It concerns the process of creativity itself and in that respect is a fundamental sense of the African aesthetic. The derivatives of this traditional oral response to the African ethos are seven aesthetic senses: polyrhythm, polycentrism, curvilinear, dimensional, epic memory, repetition, holism.

The first sense, polyrhythm, is the motion sense. Movement and rhythm in the African dance cannot be separated. The rhythmic quality of the aesthetic is the most distinguishable of its qualities. It is the world within another world, the deeper you travel, the more you feel, hear; it is multidimensional. The multiple contractions of dance and polymeter of music best manifest the movement and rhythmic quality. "In a context of multiple rhythmics, people distinguish themselves from each other while they remain dynamically related." This sense of movement, like the other senses I will discuss, refers to qualities which make up the integral composition of the dance and are inherent in all of the dances of Africa, regardless of theme, ethnic group, or geography.

African dance requires a musical sophistication in order to adequately participate within the rhythmic framework of a particular movement. Requirement for participation in such a context is the ability to stand back from the rhythms of the scene and find an additional rhythm which complements and mediates those other rhythms.

The rhythmic sense is evident in all disciplines; particularly in the marriage of music and dance where the sacred circle joins the two. The sense of motion initiates rhythms and then polyrhythms. In fact, the rhythm of one beat after another cannot compete with the complexity of a polyrhythm in which the dancer makes several moves in one beat, simultaneously vibrating hands and head, double contracting the pelvis and marking time with the feet.[2] The performance of this element is crucial if one is to understand polyrhythms as a sense.

The second sense is polycentrism. Movement as defined here is motion spending time, the occupant of a time frame and not the moving from point A to point B.

Robert Thompson cites Richard Alan Waterman in the following statement:

An African learns to be conscious mentally of every instrument employed in an African orchestra and this has a tremendous influence on his dance. All the various muscles of the body act differently to the rhythms of the instruments. One of the terms in the Twi language when speaking musically is to "dance multi-metrically."[3]

Thompson continues to speak about the polycentric sense when he says that "people in Africa further suggest that dance is defined as a special intricacy, built of superimposed motions."[4] Once again, the "extra" or "super" realm is realized and must be taken into account in studying most forms of African dance.[5] It is this multiple existence of polysenses that is the African's signature in dance. The representation of the cosmos in the body is a goal. The myriad possibilities in the universe also exist in the body for the African dancer. The artist has his particular say with the polysense. Multiplication of sound, movement, color, texture, is for us the task which parallels the movement of nature. In the African aesthetic, the polycentric sense allows for both slow and fast (all within the same time frame), with the movements coming from several directions. A readily used principle in African aesthetics is the holism which will be discussed later.

The third sense is the curvilinear as seen in form, shape, and structure. This sense applies to and appears in most African dance. It appears as the antithesis of Western dance, which has a heavy reliance on symmetrical, proportional, and profile-oriented form.[6] Form and shape vary in the arts of Africa with a similarity that occurs frequently enough to make a generalization about the curvilinear quality. The circular quality of the African artists' world is ever apparent. "Let the circle be unbroken" is a creed in the African world. There is "power" in the circle, the curve, the round, supernatural power if you will.[7] The beautiful symmetry of the *chi-wara* heightened by its curvilinear essence contrasts and yet complements the Shona serpentine sculpture where the smooth, round figures curve lines, create circles within circles. Curvilinear qualities of dance, art, and music round, curve, and carve out images that are similar and resemble aspects of African society and mythology, if only in essence. The Watusi in their long sculptured movements carve out half-moons in space and toss their elegant heads, making small circles in the sky. For the dancer, it may be mostly hand movement as in the *Adowa,* or it may be the *Gum-Boot* dance of the Zulu in which the foot stomping focuses the eyes on the energies and messages being sent through the ground and up again as the contact sends sound and dust back to the dancer. The structure is always related to experience, message, theme, and feeling. Structure for structure's sake has been a recent occurrence, and generally it is the result of formal education, outside influences, and urbanization. African dance forms and structures are traditionally, inherently entwined in the work and develop as the idea emerges. There is calculation and methodology as well as precision, but neither masters the artist; rather, they serve the artist and the work of art in expediting the idea.

Some Western writers have misunderstood the essential elements and contributions of the African dance. Lincoln Kirstein has written about African dance:

> From the point of view of actual technique, primitive dancers have not a great deal to offer either in methodology or structure for our theatre. The ends for which they dance are entirely different from ours. Nevertheless, physiologically, as ritual, health, they are fascinating. It is obvious how highly developed the pelvic, visceral and gluteal regions of primitive people are. The movement of the belly is a great aid toward digestion. Exercises of the female pelvis ease birth.[8]

Kirstein's ethnocentrism is understandable. Evaluation by European standards only make Kirstein's statements inaccurate albeit sympathetic. The foundations for African dance techniques have always been present. While the basis for codified and organized techniques have long existed, the need for them and indeed the society that would support that concept does not exist

in traditional Africa. In Western society, dance functions as entertainment and has evolved separately from religious life, but it remains harmonious and functional to Western society where church and state are separate and linear organization is the foundation for most institutions. The function of entertaining becomes paramount in formulating the creation. It is dysfunctional and sometimes contradictory with regard to religious and social goals of the same society, but the coexistence of church and state allows and permits these contradictions. The pelvic development that Kirstein speaks of is correct when he refers to it as a vital instrument in African dance and aesthetics and as physiologically important. What has to be emphasized is that aesthetically there are differences in cultures, but a culture is not void of a technique because it speaks a different language.

The simplicity of form may be regarded as primitive or the busyness of a dance might be interpreted as inspirational but nonstructured. Form produces imagery, and it is the structure and shape that helps to provide the dynamics for the viewers. The images are mirror-like reflections of history, mythology, and literature. Only through memory is the viewer allowed to be an intimate part of the art. The form is paramount in helping the artistic experience along, spurring on the imagination of the participants, viewers, or listeners. The audience engages in a remembrance with the dancer not merely in the mechanical act of seeing and applauding, but through an intimacy that has not escaped documentation.

Alvin Ailey in his magnum opus *Revelations* used contemporary dance language and "epic memory." The presence of the multiple contractions and hip swaying movements were foundations of the dance and the reason for its indelible stamp onto the minds of the dance audience.

The fourth sense is dimensionality. One aspect of depth in the African dance is texture. Music is textured; the dance is textured; the art is textured. The dimensional sense accounts for the fuzziness or graininess that one sees, hears, or feels. Something extra is occurring or existing like that extra contraction or extra beat and three-dimensional essence. Its additional value is entwined and embedded so that its existence becomes inherent. There is a plateau feeling, an area perceived as depth that arises out of African dances. The dimensional aspiration speaks to the supernatural in space, the presence beyond the visual presence. The dimensional aspect is characteristic of all the senses in that it is by definition extrasensory, involving the oral tradition. The texture sense is reverberation. It is interconnected with the first sense. The texture sense is the extrashape and vibration that occurs during a dance. For example, in the movement of the waist and hips of the *Jerusarema* dance of Zimbabwe there are surrounding sounds and motions which are indivisible from the central movement.

In the dimensional sense, there is a human quality, something extra that is present in harmony with the music, dance, or sculpture. It speaks in a physical, three-dimensional sense in Western terminology, but it is not a measured dimension, but rather a perceived dimension. These extra senses, in addition to the universal aesthetics of all cultures, provide the African aesthetic with its complexity and the reasons for its nondocumentability in strictly Western terms. There is great difficulty in documenting an art on the extrasensory dimensions of an art form which is creative by definition, consequently, a changing art form. The nonmeasured, but ultraperceivable senses are difficult to define by virtue of their frequency, complexity, and place in society.

The time and the oral sense contribute to an organic, nonfuturistic perspective that creates and lets be. Preservation and documentation concerns are important to twentieth-century scholars, and the relationship is directly correlated with advances in industry and technology.

Criteria established for the purposes of measuring the value and significance of works of art as they relate to aesthetics must take into account the personal reflection of an entire nation. The historical and social mirror cannot be overlooked. In fact, the particular reflection of the ethnic groups, as well as the collective reflection of the nation, must be considered when considering African aesthetics. There is no universal aesthetic without a personal reflection. In the African aesthetic, imitation is based on sensation, not materialism. The literal or realistic is not prevalent in African aesthetics. For example, the dance of the *chi-wara*, the African half-man, half-antelope, is, in fact, not a realistic representation but a symbol of the feeling of fertility, the relationship of man to the earth, and the harmony that must exist between man and nature for any conception to happen. It is a representation of the mythology behind the reason for "being" for the Bambara people. This is very abstract and yet as a commentary of the Bambara people, it is an accurate idea of how they perceive fertility, but not the actual story of the planting of seeds. The desire to create and be productive in the arts is therefore the artist's personal reflection and a rational contribution to the arts.

Tap dance is an African American art form born of experience. The polyrhythms of a time step of the Cincinnati as danced by Honi Coles are in fact the feet playing multiple rhythms to the inner rhythms of an urban setting, registered in concrete, performed in shoes and props. The relationships are crucial as they provide the sounding board that generates the harmony and "challenge."

Imitation and harmony as reflected and echoed in nature are symptomatic of the "oral" sense, not a materialistic imitation but a sensual one. The imitation of the rhythm of the waves, the sound of the tree growing, the colors in the sky, the whisper and thunder of an elephant's walk, the shape of the river, the movement of a spider, the quiver of breath, the cringing of concrete, the choreography of the expressway become sources of inspiration. The imitation of life is in fact surrealistic, as the Europeans would call it, and as the Africans have interpreted it. Harmony is achieved in the artist so as not to disturb, destroy, disrupt the order of the cosmos, except by permission. The Akan drummer asks the tree before he cuts it to make a drum. Bill "Bojangles" Robinson beseeches his feet, "Feet don't fail me now." "May I?", an African American children's game could well be the collective request of the African people. Harmony does not hurt the earth, land, provider, nor does it retard inspiration and creativity for the artist. This is no longer expressed ritualistically as in the past, but subconsciously in African artists today, particularly in the Americas, there is the "May I?" beneath the skin, above the soul, and in their hearts before they attempt art that achieves harmony. Camara Laye, in the *Radiance of the King,* says it is not merely the skill that makes the drummer, but the history, the memory.[9]

The ontological aspect of African aesthetics is memory. The blues, the presence of memory recreated in the southern United States environment of Africans, and the samba, a 6/8 rhythm in dance, is continued and expanded from memory. The permanence of an art work or creativity is in its harmony with nature, the people, and their god.

In the African sense, the work itself must have life and be worthy of the praises and approbations of an audience. The African aesthetic in the oral element provokes collectiveness in terms of spirit and individuality in terms of artistry. Pride and self satisfaction come from the harmony achieved with the ancestors, nature, family, and village.

The click sound has its counterpart in dance and is another demonstration of the polyrhythmic African sound. In the Xhosa language, the rhythm of the click sound is not unique, it is in the tradition of African culture and consequently African aesthetics. It is not just the pathos (memory) of the Xhosa people singing, but the click itself that renders multiple sounds in one syllable that must be understood. The Khoi Khoi people of Botswana go even further with their language sounding of clicks only. Another example is the Mfundalai poetry verse in seven lines of 5,7,5,5,7,5,7,5 syllables each. This pattern recreates one of the rhythms found among African people.

The epic memory which is the fifth sense contributes to the ideal in the African artistic expression. Perfection cannot be achieved unless the experience or memory sense is drawn upon. It is the "body" of the work itself. In Dianne McIntyre's choreography, the suite *Up North* uses modern dance technique, but it is her epic memory sense that gives *Up North* its complexion and substance. It is not an historical reenactment of blacks coming to the U.S. North from the South, but a memory retrieved that delivers to the viewer the pathos, feeling, and experience without telling the literal story. McIntyre digs for the memory that will jar and reach the audience that she is serving and "universally" compute to any human that is watching. The experience sense is broad, it unearths the emotional feeling realm without limiting the artists or the audience. It is nonspecific, pertaining only to the illusion of experience and not the actuality of it. The experience realm in the arts is the reconciliation of the metaphysical with the physical and plastic.[10] This sense is not, however, the idea or the thought which can merely be an intellectual or mathematical exercise. Rather, it is the image within the structure of the thought that provides for the ethos. There is a spiritual dimension to this concept of experience.

This spirituality is another manifestation of the epic memory. It flows into and overlaps with experience, preceding, feeding, and imprinting the African aesthetic qualities. It is not religious by definition, but can involve ritual; it is the conscious and subconscious calling upon the ancestors, gods, mind, to permit the flow of energy so that the artist can create. It is more than submission to authority, present or ancestral; it is an innate recognition that the creative force is indeed a force and not the person performing the act of creation. The artist can reject it, kill it, or accept it, but the creative energies come from within in response to a spiritual initiator. The spiritual element is embodied in the epic memory sense. The African artist recognizes the "blessings" of the gods for his intentions. Spiritually, the artists' resources are limitless and he draws from the material world and the metaphysical. The spiritual element does not imply that the composition or work of the artist is related to anything metaphysical, extraterrestrial, or supernatural. The process of the creation of the work, not only the manifested work of art, draws upon a spirituality and epic memory that becomes embedded in the work.

The sixth sense I call holistic. In this sense, the parts of a creation are not emphasized or accentuated beyond the whole; neither is the individual. Silence or stillness is as much a part of the music or dance as sound or movement. For example, the ululations performed by the Shona upon greeting each other incorporate silence as part of the rhythm. If you break the silence, you break the rhythm and destroy the good will of the greeting. Attention must be directed at the silence and the stillness if one is to appreciate the full complexity and beauty of the polymultiple experience.

Repetition, the seventh, is a very important sense of the aesthetic in African dance. It is not the refrain or chorus of a movement, but it is the intensifying of one movement, one sequence, or the entire dance. Intensification is not static, it goes by repetition from one level to another until ecstasy, euphoria, possession, saturation, and satisfaction have been reached. Time is a factor, but enough time rather than a set amount of time. A dance that is performed only once is cold, impotent, unable to elicit praise or criticism because of the incompleteness of the dance. Repetition is a constant in African dance. As the artistic director of the National Dance Company of Zimbabwe, I had to prepare traditional dances for the stage, and the first consideration was time. What to do about all these sixty-minute dances? How to condense the dance into seven- and ten-minute versions without losing the intensity? The answer: Warm-up before performance time, so that performers would literally, in the African sense, go on stage dancing.

The oral principle and the seven senses combine to comprise an African aesthetic. The concept is theoretical and does not ignore the myriad attributes and qualities that thousands of ethnic groups and nationalities possess. I speak of African as one speaks of Western, European, Eastern. It is categorical and historical in certain similarities only. The need to understand the various cultures has been largely taken up by historians and anthropologists, but the aesthetics and artistic perspective have been missing and are necessary to properly understand the dance of Africa. The classic, neoclassic, traditional, modern, postmodern forms exist within the confines of the African's own aesthetic and sensibilities. There are schools and differences among the groups within the African culture, but there is a common ground that history, race, and politics contribute to in order to make for collective expression.

The foundation for an African aesthetic has been laid by scholars such as Gayle and Du Bois.[11] African dance offers significant insight into the African culture. This dynamic and organic art form must be analyzed, researched, documented, and preserved so that any contemporary expression in African dance will not be at the expense of traditional dance. African dance encompasses the traditional and contemporary expressions. The thoroughness with which we document and study the traditional dance will directly stimulate and encourage contemporary expressions and techniques.

Notes

1. Tsegaye Gabre-Medhin, "World Dimensions of the Community of Black People," *Proceedings of the First Precolloquium of the Third FESTAC* (Dakar, Senegal: University of Dakar, 1980), 3.

2. Kariamu Welsh, *Mfundalai: A Dance Technique* (Buffalo, N.Y.: School of Movement, 1980).

3. Robert F. Thompson, *African Art in Motion* (Los Angeles: University of California Press, 1974), 16.

4. Ibid.

5. Ibid.

6. Susanne Langer, *Feeling and Form* (New York: Scribner's, 1953), 64–98.

7. See chap. 13 of *African Culture: The Rhythm of Unity*, ed. Molefi Kete Asante (Westport, Conn.: Greenwood Press, 1985).

8. Lincoln Kirstein, *Dance: A Short History* (New York: Dance Horizons, 1969).

9. Camara Laye, *Radiance of the King* (London: Collins, 1956).

10. Maxine Sheets, *The Phenomenology of Dance* (Madison: University of Wisconsin Press, 1967).

11. Molefi Kete Asante, *Afrocentricity: The Theory of Social Change* (Buffalo, N.Y.: Amulefi Publishing, 1980), 1–70.

Invention and Reinvention in the Traditional Arts

Z. S. STROTHER

Coquery-Vidrovitch said fifteen years ago that "no one doubts any longer that precolonial societies had a history." Still, it is one thing to recognize the undeniable, another to give account of it. Models of noncapitalist orders abound, yet few demonstrate their internal capacity for transformation. . . . [H]ow much have we really advanced on our old conception of "traditional" societies, "cold" cultures? Of local worlds trapped in repetitive cycles of structural time . . . [until] they suffer "historical accidents, usually due to contacts with foreign formations"?[1]

In 1990 playwright August Wilson took *The Piano Lesson* to Broadway. Audiences in six major cities across the country had already savored its exploration of the role of history, what he calls "legacy," in daily life. Partway through the play's run in Washington, D.C., the playwright changed the ending to his work.

The first version of the play, built around the story of the struggle between a woman and her brother over ownership of the family piano, left its resolution up to the audience. Spurning the advice of his Yale Repertory and Broadway director, Lloyd Richards, Wilson stuck by his guns: "Having set up the situation in which the question is who gets the piano, in the original ending I never said what happened to the piano. To me, it wasn't important. . . . But I found out that it wasn't over for the audience, which kept saying, 'Yeah, but who gets the piano?'"[2] Wilson recounts that he resisted changing the ending to the play at first because he did not wish to choose between the different positions championed in the play by the sister and brother. With time, he realized that in fact he had chosen between them in the course of writing the script. "So I decided to keep the lights on for another 60 seconds on stage so the audience can see what happens. . . ."[3] The dialogue with the audience and director that Wilson describes is more typical than not of performance arts. Nevertheless, modernist criticism, enamored of the image of the *auteur*, of the lone genius, tends to underplay the importance of such exchanges, if it recognizes them at all.

The standard text of Shakespeare's *King Lear*, for example, is the product of editors who united the substantially different 1608 and 1623 versions of the play, adding text, subtracting text, and choosing among variations on the basis of their own taste.[4] Although one theory claims that the language of the earlier (and longer) version was "corrupted by the faulty memories of actors," it is just as likely that Shakespeare made changes himself in accordance with the responses of both actors and audience.[5] If students of Western cultural studies have turned their sights only relatively recently to the problem of contended readings and to the audience in reader-response criticism, it is not surprising that Africanists have also tended to obfuscate the role of collaboration and dialogue in creativity.

Of late, the problem of an overinsistence on the establishment of rules has been generally recognized in Africanist art studies. Patrick McNaughton has asked: ". . . which is more important to know, the rules or the ways people live them?"[6] Simon Ottenberg has regretted the absence of the lived reality of "conflict, competition, chaos, and disorganization" in art studies, particularly those associated with ritual. He notes: "We prefer to show the positive and cohesive view of African life in the face of so many negative stereotypes in the West. So we often depoliticize African tradition in our writing and our exhibitions."[7] For related reasons, we occlude (often unconsciously) the collaboration, disputes, and changes in African art in order to give it the popular mystique of modernist Western art.

It should be stressed that the problem of opposing a discrete, inert "tradition" to a contemporary reality is not by any means reserved to Africanist art studies. In anthropology, the Comaroffs query: ". . . how much have we really advanced on our old conception of 'traditional' societies, 'cold' cultures? Of local worlds trapped in repetitive cycles of structural time . . . "[8] In Africanist studies, how can we open up our definitions of invention and innovation to include the explosive creativity of teamwork, collaboration, appropriation, and competition? What model can scholars use to explore the processes of transformation within such "traditional arts" as masquerading?

Popular culture is the one branch of cultural studies that has consistently stressed novelty, internal transformations, competition, and dialogue with an audience (market). Within Africanist studies, scholars have tended to locate popular culture in contemporary urban culture, but might it not be possible to consider "tradition" as part of contemporary practice, as part of "popular culture"?[9]

Gindongo (gi)tshi?

Before considering the problem of methodology, let us consider some data from the Central Pende of Zaire, who have a vibrant masquerading tradition that privileges invention and innovation. In the West, a "mask" is usually conceived of as a facepiece; however, in the sub-Saharan context, the concept of "mask" most often includes the overall costume and dance as well as any headpiece. Any study of invention in masquerading must consider the interweaving of these three elements. The story of the creation of one mask genre will demonstrate how complex the situation can be. In the language Kipende, in order to ask who the particular inventor of a mask is, one must ask, "Whose idea [was it]?" (Matangi a nanyi?). In the case of the mask Gindongo (gi)tshi?, adults and children alike will tell you that the idea originated with Gambetshi Kivule of Kinguba. The following is based on his testimony.

Gambetshi grew up in his father's village, Madibu. There one day, around 1970, when Gambetshi was approximately twenty years old, he climbed up a mango tree on the path leading to the fields. Anyone who has been to Zaire knows how choosy people can be about mangos. They insist on fruit at its peak, when it is both sweet and juicy. So, just as Gambetshi was balancing precariously in the tree, stretching to reach that perfect mango, he heard a voice below tell him, "Hey, throw that down for me!" It was a middle-aged woman on her way to the fields. He threw down the fruit and then repositioned himself in the branches to reach out for another fine, juicy mango, when the same scene repeated itself. One after another, each woman who passed wanted him to throw her down a nice, sweet mango.

Finally Gambetshi lost his temper and cried out to a group of petitioners below, "Nu ame, nu aye, gindongo (gi)tshi?" Literally, this translates: "Me and you, which generation?" Gambetshi wanted to complain about how the old always send the young to do things for them. It was a protest against the gerontocracy upon which Pende society is based. He might want to give mangos to a young girl, as a courting gesture, but why should he wish to strain himself to give them to women who were as old as his mother? "Are we dating, that I should gather mangos for you?" The women below laughed.

Nevertheless, each day when Gambetshi climbed the tree, the same scene repeated itself. On the third day, when Gambetshi went to the stream to wash with his buddies, he started to put the words of his complaint to music and to work out a dance. At night, he

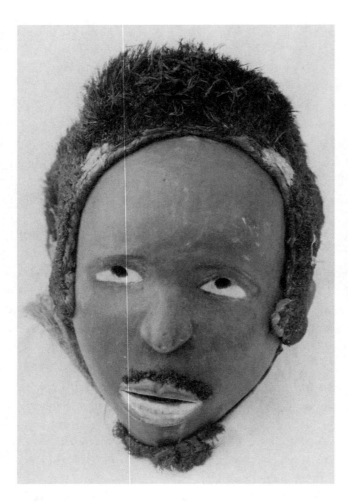

11. Headpiece for the mask *Gindongo (gi)tshi?*, commissioned by Gambetshi Kivule from the sculptor Khumba Gabama of Mubu. Like Matala, it represents a modern young man. Gambetshi, however, directed the sculptor to eschew the features of the standard mask, including the representation of the traditional means of beautification through scarification, camwood makeup, and kaolin enhancement of the hairline. The soft, naturalistic modeling of the face and the painted rather than carved eyes are unique in Pende masquerading. Photo by Z. S. Strother.

taught the song to other young people and refined the dance with their feedback.

Some time later, when a masquerade came up, Gambetshi sought out the master drummer Lutumbu. He sang the song for him and showed him how he wanted to dance, and Lutumbu worked out the rhythms for the drums. At that time, there was no sculptor in Madibu itself, and Gambetshi did not have the means to go elsewhere to commission a headpiece. He adopted a trick used by little children who wish to copy the masks: he took a large calabash and cut out holes for his eyes and used an old burlap sack for his costume.

Despite his meager costume, the dance was a resounding success. Gambetshi is the Fred Astaire of the Central Pende, an extremely gifted dancer who covers the entire dance arena but seems to float effortlessly, without fatigue. His gestures are clear and graceful.

Encouraged by the crowd's response, Gambetshi worked slowly to achieve his vision of the mask. When he had the opportunity, he went to the sculptor Khumba Gabama, who worked in a nearby village, to place his commission. Gambetshi, by this point, had a very clear conception of his character, and he insisted to Khumba that he wanted a mask that looked as much as possible like a "modern" young man.

In Gambetshi's mind, modernity was associated with naturalism (figure 11). He had to insist most emphatically on abandoning the visual codes for which Central Pende masks are known, such as downcast eyes and a continuous brow. The sculptor Khumba considered that the standard physiognomy developed with the mask *Matala* for the genre of the young man would have been far more appropriate. Khumba wished to sculpt the facepiece with sharply chiseled features conveying a young man's taut muscularity, with bulging forehead and disproportionately large eyes and nose. Despite the dispute, the sculptor finally had to bow to the custom of meeting a client's wishes. He then created a work unique in Pende masquerading for its soft modeling, naturalistic proportions, fleshy mouth, and painted rather than carved eyes (figure 11). Gambetshi also insisted on the "retro" hairstyle *(supi)* then popular with young men devoted to up-to-the-minute fashion. To increase the naturalism, Khumba made this in the form of a separate wig.

Bit by bit, Gambetshi accumulated the rest of the costume. He dances *Gindongo (gi)tshi?* with a body suit made from a handsome and rare reddish-striped raffia cloth. He wears a traditional men's wrapper that allows for free striding, rather than the hoop laden with furs and raffia cords. He also invested in a superior (and expensive) pair of foot rattles *(nzuela)*, seeking the cheerful tinkling sound reserved for the most beautiful of masks. Instead of mimicking the red coloration of the other face masks (in reference to the red camwood paste formerly used by Pende as body lotion and make-up), Gambetshi employs a shade closer to actual skin tone. He arrives on the scene with a walking stick and carries a sack made of the same handsome raffia cloth as his body suit. After an initial circling of the arena, he will lay down these props or dance with the cane in the left hand.

Importance of Dance Gestures

To understand the mask *Gindongo (gi)tshi?*, it is crucial to understand the dance gestures. Gambetshi emphasized that the inspiration for the mask lay in a young man's protest against gerontocracy, but Gambetshi is no longer twenty years old. In his early forties now, he is nicely placed in the age hierarchy, and some of the

frustration of youth has been tempered by the privileges of age.

When Gambetshi dances the mask, he will gesture periodically, as he covers the dance arena, in time to the song. He will gesture at a young girl (*Nu aye?* "And you?"), showing her height with his open hand, palm down (figure 12). Then he will turn his hand away, making a gentle wave of negation, responding in gesture to the song "Me and you, which generation?" with "No, you and I are not of the same generation." Like a staircase, his gestures mount in height, until he reaches someone his own size. Then he may nod and lift his hands in a cup shape to indicate: "Yes, this girl has breasts; she is mature enough." At this point, his foot rattles sing out, *cha-cha-cha*, to mark the crescendo of the dance.

Unlike most other masks, *Gindongo (gi)tshi?* completely covers the large dance arena and never stops moving. Gambetshi dances at great speed. Spectators are struck by the beauty and skill of the performance, murmuring comments like: "How light he is on his feet!" *(Gu malu guamuleluga!)*, "Whatever did he put in his foot rattles [to make them sing like that]?" *(Itshi wahatshi mu sambu?)*, or simply "That man knows [how to dance]!" *(Wajiya sha!)*. Many remark on the smoothness and suppleness that make Gambetshi seem as if he is floating above the ground *(kwendesa kosa)*.

It was not long after Gambetshi began to dance his mask that others began to copy it. Very popular with young men, the mask has spread in every direction. That is, the dance has spread in every direction. Not one of Gambetshi's admirers has cared to copy the headpiece that Gambetshi designed, preferring to return to the model that the sculptor Khumba tried to persuade him to wear in the first place.

Even the dance, or more specifically the hand gestures, has undergone some modification. Significantly, the gentle and stylized gestures that Gambetshi uses to say, "I stick with my generation" have been transformed. Other dancers direct their gestures not at young girls but at boys of various heights shorter than the dancer's. Whereas Gambetshi indicated the height and then used a gentle wave to say, "No, we're not of

12. Gambetshi Kivule performs the mask *Gindongo (gi)tshi?* His palms-down gesture is a signature of the dance, which he created himself. The clown Tundu lurks in the background. Nyoka-Munene, Zaire, June 1989. Photo by Z. S. Strother.

the same generation," his followers have reinterpreted that mild negation into a back-handed slap of the hand. "Are we of the same generation?" No?! *Slap!* The message here is: "Then get back in your place."

Each time this gesture is made, it is greeted with uproarious laughter. Amazingly, a mask inspired by a protest against the status quo has come full circle to reinforce its claims.

Analysis

In examining this case study, we can greatly broaden our understanding of how masks develop in Central Pende society and what invention can mean in this context.

As one sculptor, Gitshiola Leon, emphasized: "You can't just invent a mask . . . you need a dance!" It is critical to note that the invention of masks always begins with the dance. The impetus to originate new masks comes almost entirely from young, unmarried men seeking fame, who thus put a priority on novelty. Gambetshi was unusual in working out the dance and the song largely by himself. More often these are team efforts.

Not everyone invents a song or dance from scratch. The competition for laud and acclaim is intense enough to encourage some would-be stars to capitalize on the topicality of popular songs or dances that they import from their neighbors or from urban centers. They then retool the appropriated rhythms and lyrics to the masquerade context. Nonetheless, the story of *Gindongo (gi)tshi?* underscores the lesson that no one man can claim to be solely responsible for the invention of a mask. There must always be at least three men involved: a dancer, drummer, and sculptor. Gambetshi had to seek out both a professional drummer and sculptor.

If dancers usually "invent" (come up with the idea for) the mask, it is hard for Westerners to accept that the sculptor is the last stop in the invention process. Gambetshi went to Khumba with a very clear conception of the character and how he should look. He described to the sculptor that he wanted not just the face of a young man, but that of a "modern" young man with a fashionable coiffure. What is extraordinary is that Gambetshi even insisted on the development of a unique style, apparently connecting naturalism with modernism. Since *Gindongo (gi)tshi?* represents a modern young man, it was important to its dancer that it have a "modern" form.

Anthropologist Roy Wagner has argued in his book, *The Invention of Culture*, that "a great invention is 'reinvented' many times and in many circumstances as it is taught, learned, used, and improved, often in combination with other inventions."[10] Thus, generation upon generation has rediscovered fire, for example, and fitted it to changing contexts as electricity (light), as central heating (warmth), as rocket launcher (energy), as Christmas tree lights (decoration). In the same way, each performer and generation reformulates the masks for evolving social roles. No invention is sacrosanct. Each dancer, drummer, and sculptor who follows contributes to reinventing the mask.

In the project of performing, or reinventing, the mask, audience reaction plays a critical role. Wagner underscores that all invention is predicated upon convention.[11] There is "a dialectic of convention continually reinterpreted by invention, and invention continually precipitating convention."[12] In the case of the performing arts, the audience is capable of reifying the voice of convention that sets the boundaries for what the artist may or may not say, provides his or her

vocabulary, and, in Wagner's terms, provides the actors with their "motivation."[13]

In August Wilson's case, the audience expressed through their disappointment the strong American convention that dramatic tension be resolved at the end of a work. Rather than regarding this negatively, as restricting the artist's liberty, one can consider it in a positive light as forcing the playwright to think through, himself, the very dilemma he had posed for the audience. In the end, Wilson decided that it was not an insoluble problem after all, that he did have a position on the relationship of an individual with his or her history, and certainly the play benefits from this realization.

For *Gindongo (gi)tshi?*, Gambetshi, in an interior dialogue with convention, took the sting out of his own words when he transformed the mask from a protest of youth into a gentle romantic whimsy. His audience (including future dancers of the mask), however, reinterpreted his gestures as a reinforcement of the status quo. At a performance I witnessed by another dancer, not one spectator interviewed was unaware of the implications of the reinvented backhanded slap.

The audience, therefore, plays a crucial role in the development of the mask. The crowd responds positively to some features, and negatively to others. Anyone is free to innovate, but will their invention be deemed worthy of (to use Wagner's term) "reinvention?"

A TV Model

Lest the dynamism of the Pende mask trouble those accustomed to regarding masks through the simile of Western sculpture or painting, let us demystify it by refiguring the model of analysis. What happens if we shift the analogy from Western sculpture to television shows? I choose TV shows rather than film purposely, to stress not only the capacity for internal change but also the critical role of continuing audience response.[14] As in the creation of a TV show, the invention of a mask is a team effort, involving artists of varied visual and acoustic skills. As in a TV show, the "inventor" is usually credited as the person who first came up with the idea, even though the contributions of others, such as producers, actors, musicians, and costume designers, can significantly shape the eventual product.

A familiar example of this kind of teamwork comes from the popular show *Star Trek*. NBC, trying to predict audience reaction, told the "inventor," Gene Roddenberry, that his original idea was "too cerebral" and ordered him to shape the show in the nature of a Western set in space, with lots of physical action. They also told him to get rid of the female first officer that he envisioned, so inappropriate for a Western. The transformation of operational metaphor here is no less significant than for the mask *Gindongo (gi)tshi?*

Once the show was televised, the audience's response to various characters had to be taken into account. For example, although the producers hated the concept of Mr. Spock and told Roddenberry to get rid of him, they had to bow to their audience's enthusiasm. The actors made contributions as well. When James Doohan tried out a Scottish accent, the character of Mr. Scott was born, complete with stereotyped national mannerisms. The point is that we are not so unused to dealing with the collaborative genius of teamwork in the arts as we pretend.

Once we factor audience reaction into our analysis of the masquerade performance, we must begin to consider what historical and sociological factors shape that audience reaction. In this again, popular culture criticism can lead the way. We are not surprised to find television shows like *The Waltons* used to explore changing definitions of the American family, or shows like *Happy Days* analyzed for what they reflect about class consciousness during the recession of the 1970s.[15]

To return to *Gindongo (gi)tshi?*, let us consider audience reaction once again. Gambetshi's followers have turned a beautiful performance into a ludic one. Why those peals of laughter? By slapping the smaller boy, *Gindongo (gi)tshi?* is essentially saying: "You thought that you were entitled to address me as an equal?" *Slap!* "Get back in your place."

I have been referring to this as a confirmation of tra-

ditional gerontocracy, but something more is going on. This is the same kind of derisive laughter with which many young men among the Central Pende greeted Reagan's bombing of Libya in 1986: Khaddafi thought that he could act any way that he liked, he thought that he could claim a political role equal to Reagan's on the world stage, but slap!, he had to get back into his place. (How stupid could he be?) This laughter is a confirmation of the inability of the powerless to change the system.

This kind of slapping down, in fact, is not typical of the consensual society that Pende traditional culture encouraged. It is, however, typical of the political experience of both the colonial and postcolonial regimes. The entire political climate has been shaped by the big man/little man metaphor, where the bigger will never allow the smaller to move up and share power.

The cynicism of *Gindongo (gi)tshi?*'s reinvented slap was reflected in a witticism widespread in Pendeland in 1987–89, having to do with "Article 15." In this oft-repeated joke, the national constitution secures various rights, useless in a smashed economy where survival can be the only preoccupation, finally decreeing in the putative 15th article the right to "Débrouillez-vous" (Hustle for yourself).[16] Individuals, especially young men, facing hard times would tell each other "Article 15" as a shorthand for "The times are rough and no one above, much less the state, is going to help." The reformulated *Gindongo (gi)tshi?*, like the witticism about "Article 15," equips its audience to face the situation with humor and resolve.

In judging audience reaction, we must consider as well the historical, even political, climate active at the time of inception and at subsequent performance. Despite the volatility of Central Pende masquerading, some masks do endure. Whether a mask stands the test of time depends in part on whether it can outlive its topicality to be reinvented for new contexts. With the changes fast overtaking Zaire, we will have to see if the mask *Gindongo (gi)tshi?* retains its comedic appeal.

What Is Popular Culture?

The connection between *Gindongo (gi)tshi?* and its political, social context raises the question of how valid is the analytical distinction separating "traditional art" from the new arts springing up in the cities. Anthropologist Johannes Fabian questioned this comfortable division operating in his own analysis, wondering how much the concept of popular culture may "reflect, and perhaps, exaggerate the gap between rural and urban African masses."[17] In his essay in *Africa* he endeavors to uncover the "common, shared discourse" (in a Foucauldian sense) underlying three different facets of popular culture (music, religion, painting) in the Shaba province of Zaire.[18] Michel Foucault discovered that contemporary scholars from many different disciplines "employed the same rules to define the objects proper to their own study."[19] This section will consider whether there might not be such a "shared discourse" operating between two discrete social practices, Central Pende masquerading and Zairian painting, the former classed as "traditional" and the latter as "modern."

The most common understanding of popular culture is that of "contemporary cultural expressions carried by the masses in contrast to both modern elitist and traditional 'tribal' culture."[20] As a concept it irritates many social scientists because of the term's historical dialectical tension with its pendant category, the "fine arts," hence issues of quality.[21]

At the moment there are vociferous debates swirling around "popular culture." For example, who constitutes the "masses"? Would "consumer culture" be a better description? Does the motor for cultural formations come from the capitalist world market or from marginalized subcultures? Karin Barber gives an excellent overview of some of the concerns special to Africa.[22] For the purposes of this piece it is not necessary to enter into this definitional debate. I merely wish to stress two widely recognized qualities of popular culture that are worth examining in the traditional arts: its nature as an open text and its appeal to a wide audience that cuts across societal divisions.

Roy Wagner posits a very useful formulation deriving from music criticism. "Popular culture" is "interpretive culture" allowing for the free "reinvention of the subject."[23]

> Thus we define "popular music" as that which, unlike "classical music," admits of interpretive changes according to the performer's "style." When a piece by Beethoven, Rossini, or Rimsky-Korsakov is "interpreted" by resetting the words, retooling the orchestration, we say that it has been "popularized," "jazzed up," that it is now a "popular" piece.[24]

The receptivity to change and reinterpretation that Wagner identifies is, of course, exactly what once charged the term with a negative valence in opposition to the presumed universality of "high culture." Today, in the wake of the dissolution of faith in universals, this same receptivity to change is precisely what charges the term with a positive valence and makes it an attractive focus of academic research.

The other way I will be referring to the term will be as cultural forms appealing to an audience spanning societal divisions. By "mass" audience, I will not mean "proletarian" audience. In fact, although "high" art forms often do not appeal to the masses because they require a specialist education, "popular" art forms are consumed by everyone, although in some cases their generation may be localized in a particular class or segment of society. Consider television, opera in its heyday, or comic books. Does the Beatles' audience know social class?

Collective Memory

In regarding Zairian painting, Westerners are sometimes distressed to discover that artists routinely paint many different versions of the same theme. Because these artists work in a familiar medium, people tend to transfer their expectations from the late-twentieth-century Western art world, where they think in terms of "prime objects" and "copies." In a brilliant essay Bogumil Jewsiewicki deconstructs such expectations. He notes that in fact the artist Chart Samba is not content until he has worked several renditions on a theme.[25] He writes that these themes may be considered in the light of improvisations on familiar subjects whose very familiarity "invites the participation of all present."[26] These works are not copies, since their goal is not exact duplication. They are executed from memory or, perhaps, from the same original, but rarely from a preceding work.

Jewsiewicki observes that some themes disappear after only one effort if they do not find customers. The painters are "very sensitive to the reactions of their public."[27] This is not true solely because of financial dependence; they also desire popular approval.

Jewsiewicki's description echoes the structures of masquerading.[28] The dancer coming to the sculptor to commission a mask operates with the same expectations of familiarity and reinterpretation. The dialectic between "repetition" and "diversification" is the same.[29] And most important, there are the same close ties with the audience. A new theme will not fly without the approbation (hence understanding) of the clientele.

In his essay on collective memory, Jewsiewicki identified its major theme (expressed in either painting or contemporary biographies) as the expression of domination in Zairian power relationships: "As 'laicon' of social practices, one's first reaction when confronted with power is passive submission, silent suffering, and/or flight. Revolt is represented in historical accounts as some foolish gesture. . . ."[30] The response to power that he outlines is exactly the theme articulated in the transformed *Gindongo (gi)tshi?* Jewsiewicki further emphasizes the fact that the "indigene hierarchy" is as implicated as the state in the oppressive vision of power.[31] In this elegant juxtaposition of state and local oppression, Jewsiewicki reveals the line of connection between the urban and rural masses.

Zairian Popular Culture Writ Large

Although (at least before the current crisis) Kinshasa, Lubumbashi, and other centers are developing true urban classes of four generations or more, the constant movement between city and country of very large segments of the population calls into question any facile divisions between urban and rural populations. The financial base for many urban families in Kinshasa lies in the countryside, where they utilize family and ethnic ties to pursue trade. In Pendeland it is difficult to meet a man who has not at some time visited the "big city," whether Kinshasa, Kikwit, Tshikapa, or Ilebo. Because Pendeland lies within reasonable distance of several urban centers, a fair number of women also travel from time to time, either for trade or for family funerals. A large percentage of young men today try to make a go of it in the city or in the diamond mines near Tshikapa. When their dreams crash, they are forced to return home to the village. Their fathers and grandfathers traveled to Djoko Punda, the great palm plantations, or Tshikapa.

These young men constitute a recognizable cluster in the village, where they try to preserve as much of urban culture as possible. Their income goes overwhelmingly to acquiring the fashionable attire of the well-dressed *Kinois*, for which prominent display of a watch is deemed essential. Their lives revolve around leisure activities of conversation, urban music (through the radio), soccer, and seduction, while they wait for the opportunity to return to the city.

They prefer Kinshasa's bottled beers to the local palm wine. Because they perceive their stay as temporary, they put off marriage and house construction. Consequently they are forced to use their bedrooms as their *salons*, which they decorate along *Kinois* principles, with photos torn from rare magazines substituting for paintings. Literate and francophonic, in their self-perceived alienation from their fellows they bear an amazing resemblance to the *flaneurs* who emerged in Paris in the nineteenth century. For one and all, part

13. Mukedi of Ngunda performs Matala, the modern young man, at the "Festival de Gungu." Note the vainglory of his costume with checked vest, voluminous tutu, and exaggerated arm tufts. His "retro" hairstyle surpasses all others' and expresses his commitment to fashion. Gungu, Zaire, May 1989. Photo by Z. S. Strother.

of the appeal of the city lies in the opportunity to escape the threat of sorcery and the constant nagging responsibility to the extended family.

It is this self-styled "modern" young man, baptized a *sapeur* since the 1980s, who is represented in many urban commercial signs. It is the same *sapeur* who appears in the village masquerades in the genre of the chic young man, as Matala (figure 13), *Gindongo (gi)tshi?,* and others. What Jewsiewicki calls "theme," Fabian posits as "genre," which he defines as "complexes of form, content and presentation," allowing the placement of almost any painting into a category la-

beled often by the clientele.[32] Fabian's preliminary list of genres in painting[33] bears witness to many of the same preoccupations as the genres in Central Pende masquerading, although they are expressed in radically different forms.

The synthesizing theme of dominant, exploitative, inescapable power underlies much Zairian painting, developed since Independence in 1960, and twentieth-century masquerading among the Central Pende. While paintings express this concern frequently through quasi-historical images (as in the genre Colonie Beige), Fabian explains that they also do so through depictions of the devouring mermaid and powerful animals.

In the masquerading milieu, there is an occasional mask that addresses the power of the state directly through depictions of its agents (e.g., *Galubonde, Gikitshikitshi*), but in general the predominant mode is to present the image of devouring power through depictions of agents of sorcery. Thus, one notes the development, at the beginning of the colonial era, of a new category of masks: the *mbuya jia mafuzo*, which represent dangerous animals of the bush (the familiars of the chief and other sorcerers), as well as sorcerers' dolls (*Kolombolo*, etc.) and other strange and threatening apparitions. *Nganga* (the sorcerer), *Gatomba* (the bewitched), and many other masks invented during this century express this theme as well. Since Independence the *Gikalambandji*, in a new synthesis of dance and masquerading, has presented a stereotyped performance of costumed actors in a representation of a nefarious sorcerers' reunion.

While there are other motifs operating in the masquerades as well, the presence of these dark themes is inescapable. In his social history of frothy Offenbach operettas, Siegfried Kracauer demonstrated how in a period of rigid censorship and political oppression, popular culture forms like operetta can flourish as an indirect means of criticism against the government.[34] T. O. Ranger found that the Beni *Ngoma* dance performed that function in Tanzania.[35] Zairian urban painting and Central Pende masquerading have filled the same role.

During the 1987 discussion of the popular arts in the *African Studies Review*, Mary Jo Arnoldi remarked:

> Before we eliminate "traditional" expressive forms from our definition of popular arts we must ask if indigenous forms with the same concern for playfulness, dynamism, innovation, fashion and topicality, which Barber identifies as the defining features of contemporary urban popular arts, exist outside the urban setting or have existed in multiple settings in the past.[36]

Certainly, the story of the mask *Gindongo (gi)tshi?* demonstrates all of these characteristics.

Examining traditional arts such as masquerading through the lens of popular culture studies is valuable for several reasons. First, it allows us to consider rural and urban dwellers as inhabiting the same world and time, as grappling with many of the same problems. It allows us to consider the cultural sub-strata disguised in the urban arts by the appropriation of European modes or market goods. Second, it allows us to assume and search for a topicality that may be political and contended, as in the message of *Gindongo (gi)tshi?* Third and most important, considering the history of scholarship on the traditional arts, this approach assumes constant change rather than stasis marked by drift or by "influence" from outside. It stresses invention, collaborative teamwork, competition, and dialogue with convention through the audience.

Fourth, popular-culture studies have also pointed out the "porous" nature of cultural categories.[37] Thus, Shakespeare, experienced very definitely as popular culture in nineteenth-century America, has migrated into the "high" or "serious" art bracket today. Lawrence Levine makes similar arguments for Charlie Chaplin, Fred Astaire, and Louis Armstrong.[38] On the other side of the coin, chromolithography has lost its position as part of the "fine arts."[39] This consideration of how art forms can gain or lose mainstream appeal is another vital point for Africanists to explore.

For example, among the Eastern Pende, masquerade is losing mainstream appeal. Whereas it once filled the role of both community ritual and popular entertainment, it is now in the process of ossifying into a religious practice that is of interest predominantly to older citizens. No one invents masks any longer among the Eastern Pende, and the corpus is steadily dwindling into two or three of the most important characters. More serious yet, once classed strictly as religious (and infrequent), masquerade is losing its drummers, who are attracted to the steadier income provided by Christian churches. In contrast, Central Pende masquerades have almost entirely lost their religious function and have expanded their traditional popular entertainment role so that key dancers may appear on Zairian television, perform at festivals, or travel abroad.

Finally, the very topicality stressed in studies of popular culture provides much-needed evidence for exploring the historical experiences of groups silenced in dominant political discourse.[40] Masquerades, the popular culture of the rural Central Pende, proved responsive to eloquent if disguised expressions of discontent and suffering during the colonial era (above all, in the *mbuya jia mafuzo*) and in the postcolonial regime. Even the light-hearted *sapcur* of *Gindongo (gi)tshi?* cannot escape the web of power relations. As reinvented by Gambetshi's audience, he must learn that wherever he goes, he must slap or be slapped into place. All that remains is the infamous Article 15: *Debrouillez-vous.*

Notes

My research was supported by three Fulbright-Hayes dissertation grants, from 1987 to 1989, in Zaire [Congo]. I particularly wish to thank master dancer Khoshi Mahambu for shepherding the project.

1. Catherine Coquery-Vidrovitch, "The Political Economy of the African Peasantry and Modes of Production," in *The Political Economy of Contemporary Africa,* ed. P. Gutkind and I. Wallerstein (Beverly Hills, Calif.: Sage, 1976), 91; quoted in John Comaroff and Jean Comaroff, *Ethnography and the Historical Imagination* (Boulder, Colo.: Westview Press, 1992), 24.

2. August Wilson, quoted in Mervyn Rothstein, "Round Five for a Theatrical Heavyweight," *New York Times,* 1990, sec. 2:1, 8.

3. Ibid.

4. Alfred Harbage, *William Shakespeare: The Complete Works* (New York: Viking Press, 1969), 1064, 1104.

5. Ibid., 1064.

6. Patrick McNaughton, "Theoretical Angst and the Myth of Description" (dialogue), *African Arts* 26, no. 1 (1993): 83.

7. Simon Ottenberg, "Where Have We Come From? Where Are We Heading? Forty Years of African Art Studies," *African Arts* 26, no. 1 (1993): 73.

8. Comaroff and Comaroff, *Ethnography and the Historical Imagination,* 24.

9. See Karin Barber's overview, "Popular Arts in Africa," *African Studies Review* 30, no. 3 (1987).

10. Roy Wagner, *The Invention of Culture,* rev. ed. (Chicago: University of Chicago Press, 1981), 136.

11. Ibid., 51–52.

12. Ibid., 69.

13. Ibid., 51.

14. Filmmakers have long attempted to use previews to recapture some of the freedom of television producers (or playwrights like August Wilson) to respond to audience reaction. Lawrence Levine recounts several examples of acclaimed directors who made substantive changes in response to their preview reception. In a famous recent example, initial preview disappointment was responsible for a drastic reworking of the ending to the film *Pretty Woman.* Lawrence Levine, *The Unpredictable Past* (New York: Oxford University Press, 1993), 16–17.

15. Horace Newcomb, *Television: The Critical View,* 3d ed. (New York: Oxford University Press, 1982), 77–78, 198–205.

16. Allen F. Roberts, "The Ironies of System D," in *Recycled, Reseen: Folk Art from the Global Scrap Heap,* ed. C. Cerny and S. Sheriff (New York: Harry Abrams for the Museum of International Folk Art, Santa Fe, 1996).

17. Johannes Fabian, "Popular Culture in Africa: Findings and Conjectures," *Africa* 48, no. 4 (1978): 329.

18. Ibid., 316.

19. Michel Foucault, *The Order of Things: An Archaeology of the Human Sciences* (New York: Vintage Books, 1973), xi.

20. Fabian, "Popular Culture in Africa," 315.

21. See Bogumil Jewsiewicki, "Painting in Zaire: From the Invention of the West to the Representation of Social Self," in *Africa Explores: 20th Century African Art,* ed. Susan Vogel (New York: Center for African Art, 1991), 151, n. 3.

22. Karin Barber, "Popular Arts in Africa," *African Studies Review* 30, no. 3 (1987).

23. Wagner, *The Invention of Culture,* 61.

24. Ibid., n. 4.

25. Jewsiewicki, "Painting in Zaire," 131.

26. Ibid., 130.

27. Ibid., 134.

28. I am not arguing that Central Pende masqueraders "influence" painters, or vice versa, but that both practices emerge from a shared cultural matrix. Susan Vogel has come to a similar conclusion: "Like nineteenth-century traditional art, virtually all strains of twentieth-century African art are client or market driven. . . . Today, the interaction between African artist and patron in general continues the traditional relationship between artist and client, and between the artist and the work." Susan Vogel, "Introduction: Digesting the West," in Vogel, *Africa Explores,* 20–21.

29. Jewsiewicki, "Painting in Zaire," 130.

30. Bogumil Jewsiewicki, "Collective Memory and the Stakes of Power: A Reading of Popular Zairian Historical Discourses," *History in Africa* 13 (1986): 211.

31. Ibid., 219.

32. Fabian, "Popular Culture in Africa," 1.

33. Ibid., 4.

34. Siegfried Kracauer, *Orpheus in Paris: Offenbach and the Paris of His Time,* trans. Gwenda David and Eric Mosbacher (New York: Alfred A. Knopf, 1938).

35. T. O. Ranger, *Dance and Society in Eastern Africa, 1890–1970* (Berkeley: University of California Press, 1975).

36. Mary Jo Arnoldi, "Rethinking Definitions of African Traditional and Popular Arts," *African Studies Review* 30, no. 3 (1987): 80.

37. Lawrence Levine, "William Shakespeare and the American People," in *Rethinking Popular Culture,* ed. Chandra Mukerji and Michael Schudson (Berkeley: University of California Press, 1991), 188; and Lawrence Levine, *Highbrow, Lowbrow: The Emergence of Cultural Hierarchy in America* (Cambridge, Mass.: Harvard University Press, 1988), 234.

38. Lawrence Levine, "William Shakespeare and the American People," in Mukerji and Schudson, *Rethinking Popular Culture,* 189.

39. Ibid., 187–188.

40. See Kracauer, *Orpheus in Paris;* Ranger, *Dance and Society in Eastern Africa;* Karin Barber, "Popular Arts in Africa," *African Studies Review* 30, no. 3 (1987); and George Lipsitz, *Time Passages: Collective Memory and American Popular Culture* (Minneapolis: University of Minnesota Press, 1990).

Headspin: Capoeira's Ironic Inversions

BARBARA BROWNING

Capoeira is a game, a fight, and a dance, composed of kicks, acrobatics, and traditional Kongo dance movements. One doesn't speak of "dancing" or "fighting" capoeira but rather of "playing": *jogar capoeira*.[1] Or one can eliminate the substantive and use the simple verb *vadiar*: to bum around. And yet capoeiristas universally take the game very seriously. Most, when asked to define it in a word, call it an art.[2] In New York I once saw a capoeirista wearing a button that said "Doing strange things in the name of art." And it's true, they will go to extremes.

While some people will tell you there are two basic styles of capoeira,[3] there are in fact as many as there are great capoeiristas. But certain generalizations apply. Capoeira is always played in a *roda*—the same circle formation that delimits all traditional Afro-Brazilian dance. Two players enter the roda at a time, and their focus remains on each other, while they may pivot either clockwise or counterclockwise throughout the game. Motion is generally circular. Kicks and sweeps are more often than not arched or spinning, and they loop together in a series of near misses. The ideal is to keep one's eyes fixed on one's opponent. At times this necessitates having eyes in the back of one's head. But the relative placement of body parts or facial features seems to be constantly ridiculed anyway. The capoeirista spends a good deal of time inverted, with hands planted firmly like feet on the ground, feet slapping happily like palms in the air. The upside-down face, like those magical cartoons from our childhood where

the hair became a beard and the creased forehead a smirking, lipless mouth, grins at your attempts to fix it. And still, those eyes are on you.

How do I reconcile this silly picture with what I want to communicate of capoeira's elegance and even gravity? The game can be humorous, but it is not self-ridiculing—at least not simply so. This is partly because of the obvious physical prowess involved, but even more because of the understanding of the role of capoeira in popular histories.

As usual, a linear history of capoeira is far from satisfactory. The popular histories which circulate most commonly seem to pit forces of influence against each other in a struggle for control of the game: African versus European or Asian values and gestural vocabularies, ruffianism versus links to the military police, tradition versus corruption, chaos versus discipline. Depending on one's perspective, these influences may seem to be playing out a struggle between good and evil. But capoeira, whatever one's style or perspective, always ironizes the notion of Manichean extremes. Just when you think you've determined who are the good and the bad, it all suddenly strikes you rather as an aesthetic issue, excepting that you can't tell anymore what is ugly and what is beautiful. And an upside-down mug is grinning at you, pug-ugly, gorgeous.

Nobody generally "wins" a game of capoeira—although in recent years there have sprung up various tournaments and other events—but that's all part of the story. There are takedowns, and certainly the ability to apply them effectively adds to one's prestige as a capoeirista. But gratuitous, unprovoked violence or even humorless humiliation of one's opponent (or partner?) is never admired. The question is at what point provocation occurs. In a tight, "inside" game *(jogo de dentro)* when the players are interweaving spinning kicks, the agility and precision of one opens a precise space for the elegant partnering of the other. But there may be a moment imperceptible to a spectator when somehow synchronicity shatters and there are in fact two opposing forces. Someone provoked. Someone sprung malice, which was always inherent in the moves.

However they have developed, the question of where these moves originated is one that inspires impassioned arguments from most capoeiristas. Capoeira is decidedly an Afro-Brazilian art, but which half of this term should be weighted? The simplest little narrative in circulation is something like this: prior to their captivity and enslavement in Brazil, the people of the Kongo-Angola region practiced certain kicking games for sport and recreation. In Brazil, the games were prohibited for all too obvious reasons. But the Kongo people continued practicing their games in seclusion. The roda was formed as a protective circle, and the choreographic elements—as well as music—were added to disguise a fight as a dance. Repression of the practice continued even after abolition. The players invented a special rhythm, *cavalaria*, an imitation of the sound of approaching horses' hooves, to warn each other of police surveillance, and on that cue the capoeira became an "innocent" samba. In other words, capoeiristas generally acknowledge that a martial arts technique and choreographic and rhythmic vocabularies were brought from Africa. But the strategic blending of fight and dance occurred in Brazil, under specific pressures. And while this strategy appears to have been directed against forces outside the roda de capoeira, it became the fundamental strategy *within* the game. Dance—as seduction, illusion, deception—became dangerous, and kicks became elements of choreography. The Portuguese tolerated the roda de capoeira because it was

merely dance—perceived as motion without purpose or effect, other than aesthetic. And within the circles, Africans in Brazil trained like fighters in the art of dissimulation—how to grin upside down.

This story is typical of those recounted in the capoeira community—although there are variations placing greater and lesser emphasis on tradition or change, on Africanness or Brazilianness. Ethnographic narratives of origin also vary, although the most powerful arguments come from scholars who view themselves as advocates of African diasporic culture. Righteously countering centuries of European dismissal of sophisticated African traditions, scholars like Robert Farris Thompson, Kenneth Dossar, and Gerhard Kubik,[4] have given a strong case for the ever-fresh inscription of Kongo cosmology in capoeira's designs. I find these arguments powerful not simply because of their convincing "evidence" but because of their commitment to the principles of resistance which are at the heart of capoeira.

More politicized capoeiristas in Brazil also tend to emphasize African sources. If the seeds of the game existed in Angola but the intention or strategy developed in Brazil, then it would appear that capoeira must be acknowledged as an authentically Afro-Brazilian form. But when black nationalist Brazilians regard capoeira as an African form, their argument is strong. If one recognizes that Bahia, the capital of capoeira and Afro-Brazilian culture generally, resembles a West African port city much more than it does any city in Latin America, the gap of the Atlantic begins to seem quite incidental. The historical fact of forced migration is not forgettable, but the racial and cultural constituency of Bahia is overwhelmingly African. The dance forms which developed there were influenced by Europeans and indigenous Brazilians, but they developed in a culturally African metropolis.

Gestural vocabularies, as I noted, are difficult to trace, so arguments regarding the history of capoeira frequently rest on linguistic etymologies. The etymological debate has been characterized by one historian as "a linguistic version of antiquarian disputes over empirical details in history."[5] There is something oddly literal-minded about this line of research, considering that capoeira's own strategy is founded on irony: saying one thing and meaning another. Capoeira, like samba, is an alternative language to the dominant one. Gerhard Kubik[6] suggests a Bantu derivation of the term, and given the general acceptance of the largely Kongo-Angolan roots of the game, it's surprising this argument hasn't gained greater currency. But etymological hypotheses are also narratives, and they have political significances.

In contemporary usage, the word *capoeira* refers most often to the game, but there are two other meanings in standard Brazilian Portuguese: bush and chicken coop. The latter meaning derives from the Portuguese word *capão*, which means rooster and is related to the English word *capon*. Some suggest that the game resembled a chicken fight, the scrambling of two birds in a cage. Whether the term would have been applied in this case by Portuguese observing the practice or ironically by capoeiristas themselves is not clear. Another suggestion is that the chicken coop label was attached metonymically rather than metaphorically: it was the Africans taking fowl to sell at the markets who practiced the game in public plazas, transferring the name of their merchandise to their pastime.

Capoeira as "bush," or wild space, is said to derive from Tupi roots (*caá*: forest, *puêra*: extinct). Again, the etymology may be "true" or "false"—although its accuracy is less interesting than the association of a term for wildness with the indigenous Brazilian. The figure of the "Indian" or *caboclo* absorbs wilderness from both Portuguese and African imaginations in Brazil. While no explicit connection is indicated between indigenous games or dances and capoeira, the caboclo figure bears certain similarities to the capoeirista. The caboclo is an emblem in Afro-Brazilian culture of the refusal to be or remain a captive. One popular conception of capoeira is that it was developed as a means of self-defense for slaves hoping to escape to independent black communities in the backlands of the agricultural states. These communities, *quilombos,* have been documented as re-

markably developed urban centers with organized political and market systems.[7] The best known was called Palmares, in the interior of the state of Alagoas. Capoeiristas insist that it was the art of capoeira which defended Palmares against repeated attempts to dismantle it and return its residents to captivity.

The efficiency of capoeira in defending a community against mounted, armed invasions is questionable, and this part of the story may well have been inflated over the years.[8] Brazilian director Carlos Diegues's 1984 film, *Quilombo*, showed highly romanticized scenes of young boys practicing cartwheels in training for the defense of their society. But to return to the etymological significance of the bush, the wild place, the caboclo's terrain—one thing should be mentioned. Capoeira is an urban phenomenon. It has always flourished in high-density areas: Salvador, Bahia; possibly Palmares; New York City. The urban bush. The notion of its wildness, even the animality of its motion, doesn't mean it came organically from an uncivilized, un-Europeanized space. It was constructed specifically to counter European pressures.

Most capoeiristas and historians are in agreement on most of the details of this account of capoeira's origin. But its consequent developments are contested. The roda de capoeira ostensibly began as a protective circle enclosing the capoeiristas who were in training— in the process—of an organized transmission of techniques of resistance. But capoeira's bright image as a system of righteous defense becomes confused in the eighteenth century with boundless, undirected, or uncontrolled violence. In the major cities, gangs known as *maltas*, largely composed of mixed-race, impoverished free men, we are told,[9] used capoeira technique in general looting and gang fighting. Under such circumstances, they dispensed with the roda, as well as the dance.

This is the beginning of capoeira's association with ruffianism—an association which continued to have currency, to varying degrees, over the years. But the idea of breaking out of boundaries, of getting out of control, is not only figured in the broken circle, the shattered roda where dance explodes into class unrest and violence. Ostensibly, racial borders as well were being broken. The so-called *mulato* capoeirista is a figure moving between categories. He exists at the anxious point of contact between blacks and whites. And while that point of contact was sexualized in the body of the *mulata* sambista, it is made violent in that of the capoeirista. In fact (as is the case with the crack sambistas as well), while they may be narrated as embodying the mixture of races, capoeiristas are in the majority black. But in the period immediately preceding and following slavery's abolition in 1888, they absorbed some of the racial fears of a society in transition.

The music stopped—at least on the soundtrack of the romanticized, cinematic version of the story. But there is something suspect in the suggestion that the intention of capoeira had essentially changed. Was it a black dance when contained within the roda, when it expressed self-irony, restricted to black-on-black aggression? Even on the quilombos, the roda de capoeira as a training ground for defense seems ultimately unthreatening to white authority, because it is isolated. The quilombos were remarkably successful, but basically self-contained. That may be what allows for their romanticization in retrospect: Palmares has come to represent a never-never land where racial injustice didn't have to be dealt with as long as there was minimal contact with white society.

During the "ruffian" stage, it's said that capoeira was still occasionally played in the "old style"—as a dance, a game, a diversion. But this qualitative difference may not have been so much a change in style or form as a change in perspective and context. Capoeira, however dissimulating, has always held violent potential. It has also long maintained an ambiguous relationship to white authority. In the early nineteenth century, at the start of Dom João VI's monarchy, the first official police force was instituted in Brazil, and the head of the Royal Guard, a Major Vidigal, is supposed to have been a powerful capoeirista. He is also supposed to have been charged with keeping the ruffian capoeira contingent in line.

Capoeiristas were absorbed into the order during the brief war with Paraguay in 1865. They were forcibly recruited and are said to have fought valiantly. A number of traditional capoeira song lyrics refer to this event. The capoeiristas returned to the cities of Salvador and Rio with renewed prestige, although the situation was short-lived. When the roda, the circle of control, could not be maintained, capoeira was again perceived as a threat. The Penal Code of 1890 legislated corporal punishment or forced exile for the practitioners of capoeira. Even early in this century, according to the great fighter Master Bimba,

> the police persecuted a capoeirista like you chase after a damn dog. Just imagine, one of the punishments they gave capoeiristas that were caught playing was to tie one wrist to a horse's tail, and the other to another horse. The two horses were sent running toward the police station. We even used to make a joke, that it was better to play near the police station, because there were many cases of death. The individual couldn't support being pulled at high velocity along the ground and died before arriving at his destination.[10]

But it was Bimba, in fact, who initiated certain changes so that, in time, capoeira began to be tolerated as a game—under certain circumstances. It was more or less institutionalized. And you still find in Brazil the popular conception that street capoeira is for troublemakers, and the only respectable place for the game is in the capoeira "academies."

If the joke was that it was better to play near the police station, the academicization of capoeira in some ways realized such an approximation. The academy became the controlled space. It was a structure of containment, not a protective circle like the roda. And yet ostensibly the academy serves the function of an educational space. Politicized black parents today send their children to capoeira academies to learn about their cultural heritage.

As an initiate in the U.S. "academy," I am always particularly interested in notions of pedagogy in the

Afro-Brazilian context. The "alternative" pedagogical institution may appear to be a simple ironic response to dominant, repressive, or exclusionary institutions: the capoeira academy in opposition to the police academy, or the samba school in opposition to an educational system which denies the cultural validity of one's African heritage. But it isn't that simple. The phrase *escola de samba* is popularly held to derive from the schoolyard location of the first group's early rehearsals. That metonymic explanation doesn't preclude irony, but the Rio samba schools can't really be held up as shining examples of antihegemonic, popular education.[11] The twitching white soap-opera star who crowns a Rio carnaval float is the same schoolmarm as that of the national broadcast which portrays whiteness as desirability. The lesson is the same. The capoeira academies also reiterate, sometimes, rigid, linear pedagogical technique which seems bought wholesale from the police academy. Still, there are valuable lessons of African history and aesthetics. I take all this to heart as an educator who attempts to transmit non-Western culture through historically Eurocentric institutions.[12] Certainly the *way* we read, teach, and write about culture is as important as the particular manifestations we're considering. The capoeira academies demand that we rethink inclusion and exclusion, cultural containment and liberational pedagogy.

In a world of ironic inversions, which way is up? Perhaps the most beautiful *ladainha,* or extended, plaintive solo lyric of capoeira, was sung by Mestre Pastinha:

> Already I'm fed up
> of life here on the earth.
> Oh mama, I'm going to the moon,
> I talked to my wife about it.
> She answered me,
> we'll go if God wills it.
> We'll make a little ranch there,
> all full of greens.
> Tomorrow at seven o'clock,
> we'll have our breakfast.

> I really can't abide
> people who tell unbelievable stories.
> Eh, the moon comes to the earth.
> Eh, the earth goes to the moon.
> All this is just talk,
> now let's get to work. . . .[13]

Upside down, the sky is the ground beneath your feet, and the only heaven is the earth to which you are bound. It's an unbelievable story, but true. The plaintiveness of the ladainha is that that upside-down world is a better one than this one. It is a world where there will always be food to put on the table. But the song stops itself: all this lyricism is just talk. And the call to get to "work" is a call to action—a call to begin the game, to come back *through* the game to the ground of significance, of political reality, and of the fight.

That doesn't mean the music has to stop, nor the dance. The fight is in the dance, and the music itself, even this kind of lyricism, can be a weapon, and can be pointedly, politically significant. The *berimbau* is a hauntingly beautiful instrument. It consists of a curved wooden bow strung with a single wire cord, and with a resonating gourd attached at the base. The gourd pressed against his belly, the player strikes the cord with a small stick while simultaneously varying the pitch by manipulating a small stone or coin near the base of the instrument. Effectively two notes are achieved, although variations in pressure allow for a much wider spectrum of sounds. The sound emitted is an eerie twang. There is something deeply sad and mysterious about berimbau music. It is said to be an instrument of communication with the dead. There are various rhythms played for capoeira, and in this century they have been classified and categorized ad infinitum by different masters.[14] But unlike most of the highly sophisticated rhythmic patterns of African Brazil, capoeira music doesn't dictate stepping on a certain beat. Rather, the music dictates the emotional tenor of the game and its intent. The moves themselves move in and out of synchrony with the berimbau.

The rhythm isn't the only thing hard to pin down

about the berimbau's sound. Pitch, too, is neither here nor there. Lewis describes this accurately:

> For some time I assumed that the interval between stopped and unstopped strings on the *berimbau* was in fact a whole tone, but upon closer listening, and comparing several bows, I realized that the interval was usually somewhat less than a whole step but more than a half-step. In Western musical terms this kind of pitch is sometimes called a "quarter tone" or (more generally) a "micro-tone," and the effect in this case is that the interval can be heard (by Western ears) either as a major second (whole step) or a minor second (half-step). In practice this means that *berimbau* music can be used to accompany songs in various modes or scales, with either a major or minor feel, but always with a slight dissonance.[15]

Lewis suggests that this indeterminacy might be a way of explaining the "call" of the berimbau—that quality which seems to summon a listener to participate in its musicality. As in my own earlier discussion of "bent" rhythms in the samba, the "micro-tone" explanation—enlightening as it is—is probably not quite as satisfying as the acknowledgment of *axé*, or spiritual energy.

A capoeira song says, "the berimbau is an instrument / that plays on just one string. / It plays angola in C-major. / But I've come to believe, old pal, / berimbau is the greatest / comrade." The simplicity of the berimbau is misleading. Pastinha said:

> A lot of people say that it's an instrument—berimbau berimbau berimbau, it's music, it's an instrument. Berimbau, then, is music, it's a musical instrument—it's also an offensive instrument. Because on the occasion of happiness, it's an instrument—we use it as an instrument. And in the hour of pain, it stops being an instrument and becomes a hand weapon.[16]

The use of the thick wooden bow as a weapon is not taught in capoeira academies. But if the wood is in hand and the occasion for violence arises, it is not diffi-cult to imagine that uses other than musical might be made of the berimbau.

In capoeira, apparent musicality always contains violent potential, and all aggression is transformed into dance. That is why the simple opposition of categories seems to me clearly unsatisfactory. Regional and angola styles strike me rather as in dialogue with one another, and speaking, finally, the same double-talk, whether or not you call it "up-to-date." And while most scholars of the art have come down on one side of the fence (with Lewis an exception), the majority of capoeiristas, at least until very recently, did not necessarily ally themselves with one camp—including "atual." How do you make rigid alliances in a world where you must trust everyone but can't trust anyone?

How could you classify capoeira as a dance or a fight? One seldom strikes a blow to hit—more often to demonstrate the beauty of the movement, and to harmonize it with the movements of the other. And the most powerful players are those who incapacitate their opponents by doing some stunning trick of pure gorgeousness: a flip, a slow, twisting cartwheel, a headspin, or just a graceful *ginga,* the swaying dance step that comes between blows. A capoeirista can have such a pretty ginga, arms twisting in impossible beautiful waves, that it *confuses.*

It was my first master who taught me the philosophical implications of the beauty and illusion of capoeira. That's why I came to syncretize, in my mind, Boa Gente with Nietzsche—and, of course, Exú. In the Catholic context, Exú has defied syncretism. His pairing with the devil is misleading. Exú is more playful than evil. Jorge Amado says he is "just a deity in constant motion, friend of fracas, of confusion, but, in his heart of hearts, an excellent person. In a way he is the No where only Yes exists."[17]

Exú, Boa, Friedrich: they make up a trinity. They are the No in the Yes, the Falsehood in Truth, the big mixup, the good laugh. It's an inverted trinity, just as the sign of the cross is inverted in the roda.

Many of capoeira's maneuvers are inversions, whether literal or ironic, physical or linguistic. One of the most basic blows is called the *benção* (blessing or benediction).[18] But instead of giving a good word or extending a pious hand, the capoeirista "blesses" with the sole of his foot, shooting it forward toward the other player's chest. The move is at least physically perfectly straightforward. But the response to it is usually an exaggerated pantomime of getting clobbered: part of the defense actually might be to fake getting hit, although that rarely happens. The one receiving the blow may even issue an ear-piercing shriek, snapping back his head in mock deflection of the kick. Sometimes this kind of defense is more dramatic, more satisfying than the blow itself.

Capoeira defensive moves are not so much blocks or even counterattacks as they are ironic negations of the offense.[19] The basic defensive position is called, in fact, the *negativa*. The player squats, one crooked leg extended, and leans forward and across this leg, pressing the side of his head toward the ground. To the uninitiated, it feels like an almost impossibly uncomfortable, impractical, and vulnerable position. But it is the ground zero from which a vast number of deep maneuvers can be deployed.

The low-to-the-ground moves are the ones most often used in capoeira angola. They don't look efficient—who would think to bend over and look through his legs in order to fight? But they are wily and sly. Many moves are named after animals, such as the stingray-tail, an unexpected backlash, or the monkey, a lopsided back flip. The apparent impracticality of these acts has to be understood within the context of creating irony. To regard the animal references as evidence of the "natural" origins of capoeira seems to me a limited idea. Rather, these references seem to be in part ironic responses to projections on black culture in Brazil of stereotypes of innocence. A 1980 ethnography[20] cited an Angolan informant who suggested that capoeira had developed from an ancient Angolan ritual called "the dance of the zebra," in which young men imitated a mating ritual of zebras, fighting to win first choice of the young marriageable women. This document was quickly absorbed by some members of the capoeira angola contingent who began circulating the story. It is not unreasonable to suggest that some of the maneuvers of capoeira were inspired by animal motion. But I have also heard of a dubious older *angoleiro* who, on hearing this story, shook his head: "The only 'dance of the zebra' I ever saw was in the zoo, and it was two zebras fucking."

That kind of cynicism isn't a self-wounding rejection of Africa. And maybe a romanticized version of Africa has to exist on a certain level in capoeira history. But when it is ridiculed, it is also an affirmation of the developments of black culture in urban Brazil. Regional moves are self-ironizing as well. Bimba himself had a trick of "modernizing" capoeira while simultaneously making fun of modern technologies and of Western influences. He developed a sock to the head which set the ears ringing and called it the "telefone." That joke strikes me as remarkably reminiscent of the Nigerian "naive" (ironic!) novelist Amos Tutuola who introduces a character with a "voice like a telephone" in the middle of the wildest, deepest, most "African" bush, residence of ancestral spirits.[21] Another of Bimba's head-banging techniques was a knockout punch called "godême," his phonetic transcription of the "God damn it" gasped by a U.S. marine who got busted in his challenge to the master. If people complained he was incorporating boxing techniques, he Brazilianized those blows and made them capoeira.

A friend sighed to me recently, watching a rapid-fire, exquisitely executed regional game, "capoeira has really developed into a sophisticated art over the last twenty years." It's true that some regionalistas are remarkable athletes. Their speed, flexibility, precision, and strength seem in perfect harmony. But for all that I will defend the validity of their modifications on the game—they continue cannibalizing gymnastics, kick-boxing, ballet, and, in the '80s, break dancing (a form that some have speculated was at least partly derived from or inspired by capoeira)[22]—it is still an old-fashioned, flatfooted, earthbound game of angola that brings tears to my eyes. Capoeira angola's wit is defter and more stunning than any feat of athleticism. I'm certainly not alone. Perhaps the most sought-after master in

New York today is João Grande—Big John—an old-guard angoleiro of Bahia, former student of Pastinha.

It isn't just a question of wit. Nor is it just that an angoleiro's play is funky with wisdom that's been fermenting for centuries. Young, politicized angoleiros have a point. It is important to reaffirm constantly the history of capoeira as an art of resistance. Hot dog regionalistas can spin so fast they sometimes lose sight of the past, and the present. The postmodern cultural critic must acknowledge that she, too, is a product of the times. We're sometimes giddy with the new language available to us for expressing our enthusiasms for cultural cross-fertilization. But in rejecting a restrictive, static notion of cultural authenticity, we risk losing some of the political potential of rootedness, of respect for deep funk, of the eloquence of an old man's body in motion.

Beyond the issue of tradition and modification, capoeira also raises the more general problem of "playing" politics. The black consciousness movement in Brazil has been hampered by conflicting strategies. But both traditionalist and syncretic enclaves might appear, to North American eyes, to fall prey to an overly aestheticized idea of activism. It's true of the class struggle as well. Every political rally in Brazil degenerates (explodes?) into music minutes after its inception. Everybody is in motion—but is it progressive motion or simply a circular dance which expends energy without changing the world? That's the familiar question asked of carnaval.[23] To an outsider, capoeira may appear particularly ineffective as a martial art, since so much of its energy is expended on dance—on motion for the sake of pleasure.

But the capoeiristas say that in life, as in capoeira, you have to keep doing the ginga, dancing between the blows. Maybe it's true. The political and economic situation in Brazil has been so bad for so long, sometimes it seems inevitable that these people will get disheartened. What hope would be left if there weren't that distant, exciting rumble, of the samba and the scratchy voice of Boa Gente on the air? I wish, in fact, his voice could carry across the water and make us feel watched over here in New York. I miss Loremil terribly. I feel like when he went sky-rocketing out of here, he burst a hole in the electrified firmament. It's 3 A.M. in another city that is part war zone, part ecstatic celebration.

I imagine Boa Gente could be on the air now, live from the Valley of Pebbles. And he could be saying the words of Nietzsche's *Zarathustra*:

> Lift up your hearts, my brethren, high, higher! And do not forget your legs! Lift up also your legs, ye good dancers—and better still if ye stand also on your heads!

Notes

1. The English verb *to play* can be translated three ways in Portuguese: *brincar* (intransitive) = to play freely, like a child; *jogar* (transitive) = to play a sport or game; or *tocar* (transitive) = to play a musical instrument. Capoeira may appear to be a physical game or sport, but, as John Lowell Lewis has pointed out, all three kinds of play are demanded of the capoeirista, who must be an athlete, a musician in his own accompaniment, and—at the highest levels—a master of childish imagination. See Lewis, *Ring of Liberation: Deceptive Discourse in Brazilian Capoeira* (Chicago: University of Chicago Press, 1992), 2.

2. See, for example, Bira Almeida, *Capoeira, a Brazilian Art Form* (Palo Alto: Sun Wave, 1981).

3. I discuss later in this chapter the distinction between *angola* and *regional* styles, as well as the counterarguments to their division.

4. See Robert F. Thompson, "Capoeira," New York, Capoeira Foundation, 1988; Kenneth Dossar, "Capoeira Angola: Dancing between Two Worlds," *Afro-Hispanic Review* 11, nos. 1–3 (1992): 5–10; and Gerhard Kubik, "Angolan Traits in Black Music. Games and Dances of Brazil: A Study of African Cultural Extensions Overseas," *Estudos de Antropologia Cultural*, no. 10 (Lisbon, 1979): 7–55.

5. Thomas H. Holloway, "'A Healthy Terror': Police Repression of *Capoeiras* in Nineteenth-Century Rio de Janeiro," *Hispanic American Historical Review* 69 (1989):

643. Waldeloir Rego, *Capoeira Angola, ensaio socio-etnográfico* (Salvador: Editora Itapuã, 1968), 17–29, gives a fairly extensive account of the debate, which is summarized and modified in Lewis, *Ring of Liberation*, 42–44. See also Almeida, *Capoeira*, 17–20.

6. Kubik, "Angolan Traits," 29.

7. See Décio Freitas, *Palmares, a guerra dos escravos* (Rio de Janeiro, 1982).

8. Lewis, *Ring of Liberation*, 38, expresses skepticism about this historical narrative while acknowledging its cultural significance.

9. See Almeida, *Capoeira,* and Rego, *Capoeira Angola.*

10. Quoted in Raimundo Cesar Alves de Almeida, *Bimba: Perfil do mestre* (Salvador: UFBA, 1982), 13–14.

11. Alma Guillermoprieto recounts a disturbing history of political and financial manipulation and corruption at the leadership level of the samba schools in Rio. See her *Samba* (New York: Knopf, 1990).

12. John Guillory's considerations of multiculturalism and canon formation are most instructive on this point. He warns that limiting the discussion to what is included in or excluded from the canon can obfuscate the greater question of pedagogy: "To have drawn up a new syllabus is not yet to have begun teaching, nor is it yet to have begun reflection upon the institutional form of the school." Guillory, "Canon, Syllabus, List: A Note on the Pedagogic Imaginary," *Transition* 52 (1992): 54.

13. Pastinha, LP recording.

14. For a sample of the wide variety, see Almeida, *Capoeira.*

15. Lewis, *Ring of Liberation*, 159.

16. Pastinha, LP recording.

17. Jorge Amado, *Bahia de Todos os Santos* (Rio de Janeiro: Record, 1980).

18. See Barbara Browning, *Samba: Resistance in Motion* (Bloomington: Indiana University Press, 1995), chap. 1.

19. Lewis writes that the taxonomy of "attacks" and "defense moves" is never clear. Many moves "can function *either* as attacks or defenses, or even as *both* at the same time!" Lewis, *Ring of Liberation*, 98.

20. Jaír Moura, "Capoeiragem—Arte e malandragem," *Cadernos de Cultura*, no. 2 (Salvador, 1980): 15–16.

21. Amos Tutuola, *The Palm-Wine Drinkard* (New York: Grove Press, 1984), 35.

22. Kenneth Dossar, "Capoeira Angola: An Ancestral Connection?" *American Visions* 3, no. 4 (1988): 38–42.

23. See Browning, *Samba: Resistance in Motion,* chap. 4.

Epitome of Korean Folk Dance

LEE KYONG-HEE

The dancer is seated on the stage, with her face and torso bent deep, almost touching the floor. She begins to move from the shoulders, slowly and mysteriously. In a dramatic and solemn gesture, she faces upward, turning her torso to the left and then to the right. Her movements are delicately restrained, but unusually powerful.

As she stands up, the dancer throws up the long sleeves of her white silk gown, drawing a magnificent circle in the air. Her face, half hidden in the white conical cap of a nun, bears a slightly pathetic expression.

The nun's dance, or *sungmu* in Korean, contains all the essential elements of Korean native dance as handed down among the general populace. It stands for the quintessence of the dance traditions of the Korean public, both emotionally and technically.

"I believe that the nun's dance embodies not only the basic structure of Korean traditional folk dance but also the stream of our national history itself," said Lee Ae-ju, a leading *sungmu* performer and professor of Korean traditional dance at Seoul National University. "Whenever I prostrate myself on the stage to begin this dance," she noted, "I feel as if I am turning into a small seed buried in the ground, or an embryo in the womb."

She envisions the seed sprouting and growing into a big tree. After a thriving summer, the tree will wither in accordance with the laws of nature and, eventually, the leaves will fall, signifying the finale of an era. "And my dance will also come to a close," she said.

Prof. Lee went on to explain that, like most theorists in Korean native dance, she feels there is little religious influence of Buddhism in the nun's dance, in spite of its title and the costume of the dancer.

"If we have to discuss the religious aspect of this dance," she said, "I'd rather say that it has more shamanistic influences than Buddhist."

It is generally agreed that the nun's dance attained its present style at the turn of the century, owing mostly to the genius of Han Song-Jun, a master dancer and musician as well as a prominent teacher.

Han adapted a number of traditional Korean dances to be performed in theaters instead of village squares or the courtyards or banquet halls of kings and noblemen. At the same time, he also trained many outstanding dancers. Among his beloved students was his granddaughter, the late Han Yong-suk, who was the teacher of Lee Ae-ju.

"My grandfather seemed determined to teach me everything he knew," Han recalled during an interview a few years before her death in 1989 at the age of sixty-nine. She learned from him a wide variety of folk dances as well as musical instruments.

Han's presentation of the nun's dance drew much acclaim. Blessed with an exquisite physique ideal for the unique expression of the dance, her name itself symbolized the beauty of the dance for almost half a century.

Prof. Lee, whose dance education began at the National Classical Music Institute when she was seven years old, became a student of the late Han in the early

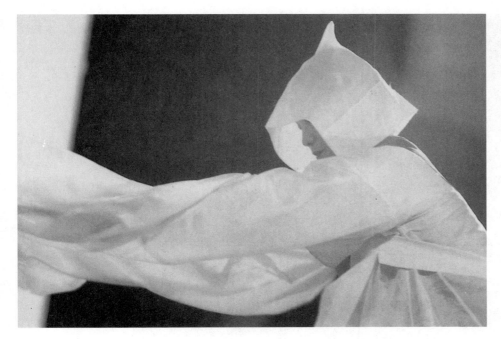

14. Lee remarks that the nun's dance symbolizes the Korean traditional concept of harmony between heaven and earth. Photo by Chang Young-joon.

1970s. At the time she was taking a graduate course in Korean classical literature at Seoul National University in order to study the literary background of the nation's dance heritage after graduating from the university's department of physical education.

"My teacher was a brilliant dancer, in a word," Lee said. "She couldn't explain her dance theoretically because she didn't have much school education. But once on the stage, she proved eloquently that she didn't need words at all."

If the late Han was an accomplished dancer with no peers for her artistic expression in her days, Lee seems to be capable of inheriting her teacher's performing style and skills as well as being able to theorize on the historical and aesthetical characteristics of the dance she performs.

Lee explains that sungmu has a much deeper meaning than most people believe nowadays. "There is no doubt that the dance represents the folk dance traditions of the Koreans, including all important movements and symbolizing all inherent emotions," she said.

"And it is a very philosophical dance, too," she em-phasized. "It stands for our traditional philosophy of heaven and earth, and their harmony."

She went on to note that whenever she positions herself on the stage to begin her performance, she always tries to feel that she is becoming "one with the earth." And when she throws up her long sleeves in the air, she said that she feels an invisible extension of her movement "reach the heaven."

In this sense, the spiritual origin of the dance antedates the introduction of Buddhism into Korea, with its remote roots in the primitive religious faith of the Korean people. Lee argued, "I believe that the dance continued to evolve through our history, absorbing shamanistic elements and finally borrowing Buddhist-style props in later centuries, probably during the Choson period," she said.

During the Confucian-dominated Choson Dynasty (1392–1910), its ruling elite persecuted Buddhism, causing a remarkable degeneration of the religion. Buddhism, which turned largely into a religion of women and the less educated, had to resort to music and dance as a popular means for propagation.

15. The nun's dance encompasses the full range of sentiments innate in human beings, according to Lee. Photo by Chang Young-joon.

Monks needed training in the musical chanting of scriptures and dance performance in order to appeal to a broader public. Naturally, music and dance came to form an important part of rituals in the temple. Such a tradition is believed to have contributed to the development of the monk's dance, or the nun's dance when it is performed by a female dancer.

Prof. Lee said she believes that sungmu encompasses all kinds of sentiments innate in man, such as joy and sorrow, hope and frustration, agony and pleasure, and so on. Therefore, she strongly repudiated the popular explanation that the dance depicts the inner conflict of an apostate nun, or the sorrow of a beautiful woman who has renounced the world to forget her past.

In spite of her objection, the late Han Yong-suk once said, with an unmistakable air of pride, that her dance inspired the poet Cho Chi-hun to write his widely appreciated poem, *Sungmu.*

"The poet watched me dance many times before he wrote the piece," she reminisced. "It was, of course, when I was young and pretty."

It was either the poet's limited understanding or his freedom of imagination, or both, to depict the dance with an obviously sentimental and even vaguely erotic undertone. But there is no doubt that Cho's poem greatly contributed to the popularization of the dance among modern-day Koreans. The poem, written in the late 1930s, reads as follows:

The white silk cowl folded gently
wavers like a butterfly.
A bluish head, shaved close
veiled under the fine cowl.
The glow on her cheeks
pretty as a sorrow.
A candlelight burns silently
on an empty altar.
The moon sinks into
every paulownia leaf.
Her long sleeves flow up
against the vast heaven.
Oh, how her shapely white socks
turned up so slightly
as if flying on the wing.
Raising her dark eyes softly,
she gazes at a single star
in the far-off sky.
Her fair peach blossom cheeks
adorned with a teardrop or two.
Like a star shine her agonies
if painful are her worldly cares.
Swaying, bending and folding again
her hands are stretched out
as if telling of a devout prayer in her heart.
As the crickets cry away the night
her white silk cowl folded gently
wavers like a butterfly.

The Many Faces of Korean Dance

JUDY VAN ZILE

On October 16, 1990, I sat in the Munye Theatre watching a performance that was part of the twelfth Seoul Dance Festival. Initially I was struck by the stage set—a backdrop of three-dimensional, quite realistic trees. At first they swayed gently; then they became agitated, as if rustling in a winter storm; the lighting changed to red while crackling sounds contributed to the effect of a forest fire; and finally, all became calm again.

A lone male dancer, clad in pants and jacket clearly inspired by the attire of aristocrats of former times (*yangban*), appeared to wander through a forest. His movements could have come from anywhere—England, the United States, Japan. But in a moment I was very definitely in Korea; the meandering stopped as the dancer placed both feet together, torso tilted forward a bit and knees slightly bent. As he faced the corner of the stage he straightened one knee and lifted the other forward, ankle bent and toes turned up. With one arm he delicately grasped the edge of his jacket and pulled it back just a little. The other arm reached forward creating a counterpoint to the lifted leg that forced the torso to twist. The movement was held in animated suspension. Amidst the contemporary realistic stage set and movements that could have emanated from almost any geographic locale, I was suddenly in the heart of older Korean dances—watching a movement that can be seen again and again in *sйngmu*, often referred to in English as the Monk's Drum Dance, and *salp'uri*, a type of dance believed by many to be rooted in shaman ritual.

The diverse forms of dance that can be seen in Korea today run the gamut from traditional dances to ballet, modern dance, experimental choreography, and hip-hop and disco dancing.[1] The discussion here focuses on older, more indigenous dance forms and some developments beginning in the twentieth century. It is important to keep in mind that Korea is now politically divided. The focus here is on dance in the Republic of Korea, commonly referred to today as South Korea. While some historical information relates to Korea in the days when it was unified, the inaccessibility of information on dance in North Korea (Democratic People's Republic of Korea) requires the emphasis taken here.

The Heritage of the Past: Traditional Dance

The variety of dances classified by Koreans as traditional dance (*chônt'ong muyong*) differ in both the contexts and manner in which they were originally performed. What unifies them in the minds of Koreans is the belief that most have been passed on over a long period of time and that they reflect the uniqueness of Korean culture. One key to former support for many of these kinds of dances was the royal court, which, at different times, nurtured some dances for entertainment and others for ritual purposes. In the context of entertainment, dances were performed for the pleasure of local and visiting dignitaries. Elaborate palace banquets included grand spectacles that not only entertained but also demonstrated wealth and power. Extant paintings and written texts portray large numbers of dancers clad in rich, colorful costumes moving through precise geometric formations to the accompaniment of music played on diverse and elaborate instruments. During some periods the dancers portrayed were men, but more frequently they were women.[2]

Court entertainment dances are generally classified into those said to have originated in Tang dynasty (618–907) China (*tangak chôngjae*) and those said to have originated in Korea (*hyangak chôngjae*). This classification is a reminder of early political interactions between China and Korea, which included a visit by a group of Korean performers sent to China during the Unified Shilla period (668–935) who returned with musical instruments, dance properties, and costumes. Later, in 1116, a complete music and dance ensemble from the Chinese court visited Korea. Although such interchanges might suggest substantive differences in the two kinds of dance, documents such as the 1493 *Guide to the Study of Music* (*Akhak kwebôm*; music was assumed to include dance), which contains detailed dance descriptions, and the manner in which the dances are performed today attest to a difference in overall format but little difference in the movements themselves. In the dances of Chinese origin, a formal procession by individuals holding various kinds of standards precedes and follows the dance, the dance name is announced, and the dance is interrupted for a brief song sung in Chinese by the dancers; in dances of Korean origin, the dancers begin with a bow to the king and brief song in Korean praying for his happiness, and end with a bow to the king, but there are no standard bearers or processions. Any early movement differences between the dances of Chinese origin and those originating in Korea no longer exist.

Most of the court dances performed today involve large numbers of dancers moving elegantly through circle, square, and line formations. They generally wear colorful costumes in bright hues reserved, in the past, for royalty. The long sleeves of stiff, multicolored silk which reach almost to the ground are considered by some to be related to the long sleeves used in Chinese opera forms. With arms frequently extended sideward, the dancers walk, almost as if floating, while gently bending and extending their knees. They punctuate their movements with flicks of the wrist that gently propel their sleeves upward and outward.

The ensemble that provides accompaniment for court dances is comprised of traditional wind, string, and percussion instruments. (Although many instruments used in the court originated in China, they became so integral to Korean music that they are often considered Korean.) The conductor plays an instrument with six slats of wood fastened at one end with a leather thong (the *pak*). He contributes to the visual picture, standing motionless at the side of the performing space, and moving only when necessary to signal the beginning and ending of a piece and transitions between sections by spreading the slats apart and then snapping them shut to provide a loud clap.

The movements of some court dances are literal, as in Beautiful Women Picking Peonies (*Kain Chônmoktan*). Said to depict the pastimes of court women, the dancers move around a large vase containing flowers that they eventually pick and hold while dancing. Another court activity is depicted in the Ball Playing Dance (*P'ogurak*). This time the dancers try to throw small, pincushion-like balls through a hole in a simulated gate. Those who succeed are rewarded with a flower; those who fail receive a black stripe painted on the cheek.

Many court dances are more abstract. The Nightingale in Springtime (*Ch'unaengjôn*), one of only two solo court dances performed today, suggests the quality of a nightingale through its delicate movements; the gentle, sometimes wave-like motions of the arms, often extended sideward, are bird-like, but there are no movements that mime the flapping of wings or the soaring of a bird.

Two of the court dances performed today are quite distinctive because the dancers wear masks—the Crane Dance (*Hakch'um*) is believed to have ritualistic origins.

For Koreans, the crane is a symbol of longevity that figures prominently in paintings and embroidery. In the version of this dance performed today, two dancers in realistic crane costumes that extend over their heads to form a kind of headdress—concealing the entire torso, arms, and head—execute pantomimic movements of flying, roaming through fields, and pecking at food. Historical sources indicate the Dance of Ch'ôyong (*Ch'ôyongmu*) was also once part of rituals—specifically to expel evil spirits at New Year—and that it was performed out-of-doors. Five dancers said to represent the directions (north, south, east, west, and center) wear large masks suggestive of Ch'ôyong, a son of the Dragon of the Eastern Sea. At some time the Dance of Ch'ôyong was brought into the court, where it was transformed into a dance done purely for entertainment and became part of a suite of dances that included the Crane Dance.

Today Korea is governed by a political system with a president at its head, and there is no longer a royal court. Court dances are still done, however, but in theatrical concert setting where they both entertain and remind people of the heritage of the past.

Besides dances for entertainment, the royal court also supported dances that continue, today, to serve ritual purposes associated with Confucianism—again a reminder of influences from China. Although Confucianism entered Korea from China as early as the fourth century A.D., it did not become official orthodoxy until the Chosôn dynasty (1392–1910), when it replaced Buddhism as the state's main philosophical tenet. Although Confucian dances are sometimes categorized as ritual dances because of the occasions on which they are performed, many Koreans prefer to identify them as court dances because of their early sponsorship. Confucian dances were originally performed several times a year at memorial services. Today these dances take place three times a year: twice (in the second and eighth months of the lunar calendar) to honor Confucius, and once (in May) to honor the spirits of the Chosôn dynasty rulers.

Despite the slightly different reasons for which these dances were traditionally done, there is little difference in their performance today. Dancers perform in a square formation of precise rows and columns, today usually eight rows and eight columns, or sixty-four performers in all. The number of performers was originally dependent on the rank of the individual in the audience for whom the dances were performed: sixty-four dancers for an emperor, thirty-six (six rows and six columns) for a feudal lord or baron, four (two rows and two columns) for a ranking governing official or lesser aristocrat. The dancers execute simple arm movements and bows to a slow, consistent tempo. The stark movement simplicity and ponderous tempo contribute to a meditative and highly ritualistic atmosphere. The performers hold symbolic implements: for dances classified as "civil" (*munmu*), a stick with a dragon's head and pheasant feathers in one hand and a flute in the other, symbolizing peace and prosperity; for dances classified as "military" (*mumu*), an ax and mallet or wood sword and spear, symbolizing war.

Masked dance-dramas (*t'alch'um*) were at one time associated with the court, but originated in conjunction with village shaman rituals and eventually became largely an entertainment form for commoners. They evolved to cleanse houses and villages, afford protection from calamities, and assure good crops. Their support from the court varied: during the Koryô dynasty (919–1392), the court maintained an Office of Masked Dance-Drama (Sandae Togam) and some dances were performed at royal banquets; during the Chosôn dynasty (1392–1910), possibly because of the new importance of Confucian values, the office was abolished. Despite former occasional affiliations with the court and frequent performance today in large cities, masked dance-dramas are still closely associated with villages. There are many regional variants, but most revolve around humorous themes that allowed the people of former times the opportunity to poke fun at things they would normally not discuss in public: liberties taken by ostensibly serious, wholesome monks; frivolous rompings of upper class noblemen; and bawdy activities of matchmakers. As performed today, masked dance-dramas perpetuate the traditional satirical stories of the past but also occasionally incorporate references to important contemporary individuals or events. Performers serve as caricatures who strut and dance as they sing and engage in sometimes risqué dialogue that creates a lively atmosphere in which audience members shout their delight at peak moments.

Although masked dance-dramas are most frequently performed today in formal settings by government-recognized master performers and their students, they are a popular activity among university students, who sometimes perform them on campuses. This interest originated with the student nationalism of the 1980s, one aspect of which was a movement to heighten Korean cultural consciousness and revive or strengthen the performance of traditional dance forms. Masked dance-dramas are also sometimes used to make political statements during times of unrest.[3]

Farmers' band dance and music (*nongak*)[4] is another traditional form with strong connections to villages. Believed by some to be the oldest form of dance in Korea and to have shamanic origins, this is a loud, extremely vigorous performing tradition originally engaged in by farmers, in conjunction with agricultural events. Performers paraded through villages, then stopped in large open areas to perform, while playing wind instruments, drums, and gongs that created a piercing cacophony as they danced. In farmers' band dance and music, as in many Korean dance forms, the interplay between dance and music, and dancers and musicians, is particularly important: dancers play musical instruments and musicians perform highly stylized movements. Dancers play several varieties of drums, ranging from a small hand-held drum (*sogo*) to a large hourglass-shaped drum (*changgo*), the latter fastened to their bodies with sashes around the waist and shoulder. A musician playing a harsh-sounding brass gong (*kkwaenggwari*) skips and leaps at the head of the group as the ensemble's conductor. A highlight of farmer's band dance and music is the performance of an individual wearing a tightly-secured hat with a small flexible rod (*sangmo*) in the top that can revolve.

Affixed to the rod is a very long streamer. With continuous small, strong, abrupt movements, the dancer rapidly tilts his head forward, to one side, backward, and then the other side, causing the streamer to whip through the air as it traces large circular designs in space. He may also play the small hand-held drum and fly through the air in gymnastic aerial turns—all simultaneously.

Today farmers' band dance and music, like masked dance-dramas, is performed by governmentally recognized masters and their students, by groups of villagers who gather for entertainment and to maintain community spirit, and by students from elementary through university levels. It has also been used for political purposes by labor unions and campaigning politicians.

The shamanism that contributed to the development of masked dance-drama and farmers' band dance and music also gave rise to dance and stylized movement that remain a part of shamanic rituals. Although not always looked on favorably by the government, shamanism has never completely disappeared and is practiced today in both villages and large cities. "Clients" who enlist the services of a shaman to heal the ill, appease the spirits of the deceased, or thwart other negative forces, participate in elaborate rituals including food and monetary offerings, singing, and dancing. Singing is generally done by the shaman, who in most regions is female, and who also engages in various forms of structured movement.[5] Stylized movements are often used when the invoked spirits descend and speak through the shaman, or when the shaman approaches clients while holding out a fan to solicit monetary offerings. At climactic moments the shaman will insist that the client don special clothing, execute movements similar to those of other traditional dance forms, and jump up and down. As in masked dance-dramas, regional variants of the rituals and movements used in shamanic activities abound. Shaman dances are still performed by practicing shamans in the context of rituals. Even though the values of a highly modernized society tend to reject shamanistic practices, at the end of the twentieth century women wearing the highest fashions of Europe and businessmen in sleek western suits sometimes consult a shaman. Many Koreans believe shaman movement has had the most pervasive impact on all types of traditional Korean dance, a view that may be rooted in nationalistic perspectives emphasizing the uniqueness of Korean shamanism as a way to separate Korea culturally from Japan.[6]

Formalized movements are also found in the traditional dances of Buddhist rituals. Like Confucianism, Buddhism was introduced from China in the fourth century A.D. It became the official national religion during the Unified Shilla period (668–935). Buddhist dances were originally performed by monks, usually in large open courtyards at shrines, to the accompaniment of ritual chant and recitation (*pômp'ae*) originating in India, the homeland of Buddhism. Only four Buddhist dances are performed today. The Butterfly Dance (*Nabich'um*) is believed by some to be symbolic of the spreading of the Buddha's will in all directions. Performing either solo or as a duet, the dancers wear white cloaks with extremely long sleeves. They move slowly, bending and extending their knees as their lifted arms sweep gently forward and backward like the wings of a butterfly in slow motion. The Cymbal Dance (*Parach'um*) is also said to spread the word of the Buddha. This dance is most often performed by four dancers who, as in farmers' band dance and music, function as musicians, in this case each manipulating a pair of large cymbals. While playing the cymbals, the dancers turn in various directions, bend and extend their knees, and rotate their arms overhead so that the cymbals contribute to the overall visual design as well as produce sound. The Monk's Drum Dance (*Pôp-koch'um*) is a solo, and the dancer again functions as a musician. He performs highly stylized movements as he plays a drum mounted in a tall wooden frame. (Originally, the drum was extremely large; nowadays, it is often small to facilitate transporting it to performance locations.) In the Dance of the Eightfold Path (*T'aju*), an octagonal box with inscriptions on each side—representing the eightfold way of the Buddha—is placed on the ground between two dancers. Each

holds a long, thin stick, and gently taps the top of the box as he moves around it.

Buddhist dances are performed today primarily by male monks, most often at the Pongwôn Temple in central Seoul on traditional religious occasions, but occasionally at other temples and for other events.

Characteristics of Traditional Dance

No discussion of traditional Korean dance would be complete without mention of *môt* and *hûng*. Among the more difficult of Korean words to translate, these terms refer, respectively, to an inner spiritual quality of charm or grace and a feeling of lively animation or enthusiasm, both of which lead to an almost irrepressible joy or giddiness. This is described by Koreans as the ultimate quality the Korean dancer strives to achieve in folk dance, and specific movement characteristics either contribute to achieving this desired state or are the physical manifestation of its having been achieved. *Môt* and *hûng* are not usually used to describe court dance because of the influence of Confucianism on these dances. Confucian ideals of femininity would not allow for the kind of frivolity suggested by *môt* and *hûng*, and since court dancers were most often women, these qualities would have been inappropriate. Such behavior was also likely inappropriate for men in the context of official court ceremonies, which called for dignity and propriety. Many of the movement characteristics contributing to the qualities to which *môt* and *hûng* refer, however, are present in all traditional dances of Korea, their dynamics are simply changed to make them appropriate for particular kinds of dance.[7]

One of these movement features is an emphasis on verticality. Throughout much of traditional Korean dance there is a persistent alternation between up and down actions, seen in several different ways. In the slower forms, such as the court and Buddhist dances, the dancers regularly alternate between bending and extending their knees. Hence, the whole body lifts and lowers. In the faster, more vigorous dances, such as the farmers' band dance and music and the masked dance-dramas, the bending of the knees serves as a preparatory push that propels the body into a jump, enlarging the up and down action. This is also prevalent in shaman dancing when the spirits take over the shaman's body, resulting in vigorous jumping.

The upward-downward action is also emphasized in a smaller, but very important way in the "dance of the shoulders" (*ôkkae ch'um*). Movement is often initiated in the chest area with what appears to be a quick inhalation of the breath that causes the spine to lengthen upward and eventually forces the shoulders to rise. This movement is then released as the shoulders and spine relax, creating a kind of visual "sigh of relief." In court dances this movement is extremely subtle, but in such genres as the farmers' band dance and music and the masked dance-dramas, it can become a very obvious, exaggerated shoulder shrug. What is important in this movement, however, is that it emanates from an internal feeling (generally manifest in the flow of the breath) rather than from a conscious, mechanical action of the shoulders.

Another distinguishing feature that pervades many forms of traditional dance is a feeling of suspension. The dancer begins a movement that rises, in some fashion, and then appears to stop abruptly. The dancer briefly remains poised, as if deciding whether to lift even higher or to move on to something else. As the contained energy verges on explosion, the performer quickly rises just a bit higher, almost like a small hiccup, before releasing everything into a gentle downward movement. This moment of suspension, a delicate hovering, provides a strong, dynamic tension for the viewer and contributes to the visual sigh of relief created by the shoulder dance.

Yet another distinctive feature of traditional dance is a particular way of using the foot. Koreans are quick to point out that their dance is characterized by walks in which the dancer steps first on the heel rather than the toe or the ball of the foot. But what is unique in this movement is the way in which dancers seem to almost caress the floor with their feet, curling their toes upward before placing the heel on the floor and then gently rolling the entire foot down. This action is enhanced by the tight-fitting padded "socks" with upturned toes (*pôsôn*) that most dancers wear. Whether done slowly or quickly, the overall effect is as if the dancer is walking on something quite delicate, contributing to the feelings of *môt* and *hûng*.

In many Korean dances the arms frequently extend sideward at shoulder height. They are turned inward so the thumb surface of the hand points forward, and the wrist is relaxed, allowing the fingertips to point gently downward. There are many movements in which the wrist is flicked to manipulate a long sleeve or scarf, and then the sleeve or scarf and fingertips all finish pointing downward. This same movement is also done when there is no sleeve or scarf to manipulate. Additionally, the arm often rotates outward and then inward, concluding with a relaxation of the wrist that returns the fingertips to their downward orientation.

All of these elements contribute to an emphasis on motion rather than isolated positions or posturing. In fact, Koreans sometimes describe their dance as "motion in stillness" (*chông-jung-dong*).[8] The fluid, ongoing movements that appear to stop are, in reality, simply collecting energy that ultimately gently explodes, or runs over, into the next series of fluid actions. Korean dancers move *through* positions rather than arriving at them, creating curvilinear shapes as well as a rounded, ongoing quality of energy use.

The skillful manipulation of costume components or hand-held implements and the playing of musical instruments are also features of many traditional Korean dances. In court and masked dance-dramas performers manipulate long sleeves that are a part of their costumes; in Buddhist dances musical instruments are manipulated; and in many kinds of dance the performers play one or more of a wide variety of drums.

One final feature prevalent in many traditional dances is an emphasis on compound meters. Movement phrases are choreographed in three-beat units, and underlying musical pulses are often further subdivided into units of three. This triple-meter emphasis frequently ties in with the emphasis on verticality and suspension: the rising action that leads to a brief suspension on the first two pulses and a slight accent at the end of the second pulse just before the downward release on the third pulse.

Derived Dance Forms

The various dances described thus far, whether originally supported by religious institutions or the former court, whether done for entertainment or as part of ritual, and whether performed by highly trained specialists or common villagers, are considered by Koreans to be traditional dances, and are readily identifiable as being Korean. Although many are said to trace their roots to earlier eras, as performed today the dances are believed to be akin to those practiced during the Chosôn dynasty (1392–1910). But as the country once known as the Hermit Kingdom opened its doors to the rest of the world in the late nineteenth century, and as various kinds of interactions (both peaceful and otherwise) developed with close geographic neighbors and countries considerably further away, significant changes began to occur in dance.[9] In some instances choreographers looked to their traditional heritage as a source of inspiration for new creations that retained strong ties to the past. In other instances a conscious effort was made to merge features of traditional dances with those of dance forms introduced from other cultures. In some instances the newly-created dances were still recognizable as emanating from Korea; in others, the departure was sufficiently great as to raise questions regarding a specific cultural tie. Several of the new dances with clear roots in older dance forms eventually became so significantly representative of Korea that Koreans added them to their traditional category, even though they evolved in more recent times than others in this grouping. Some dances led to the development of new categories and ways of conceptualizing Korean dance.

It is often difficult to draw clear boundaries between the kinds of dances that began to develop. Because of the inspiration and movement characteristics drawn from older Korean dances, I believe many of the new dances can be described most easily as "derived dances": their movements and over-riding qualities clearly emanate from those of the more distant past. Choreographers also adapted older dance movements; for performance on a western, proscenium-arch stage, rather than in a royal palace, temple courtyard, or outdoor setting, and in a context of theatrical entertainment, rather than entertainment at a royal banquet or as part of a ritual occasion. During their early development, some of the derived dances done to entertain were performed in the more intimate settings of restaurants or bars.[10]

There are many complications preventing an entirely clear elucidation of the visual manifestation of some of the early derived dances. Because of political circumstances and the lack, until very recently, of good dance documentation, little remains of some developments, beyond vague verbal descriptions. Contributors to what led to the changes creating these dances, however, *are* clear. First, following several wars, Korea became a colony of Japan in 1910. From that time until independence in 1945, there were periods in which Japan made every effort to obliterate traditional Korean culture and times when the prevailing government authorities allowed Koreans to assert their identity in specific contexts. Independence was followed quickly, however, by the Korean War (1950–1953), which ultimately divided the Korean peninsula into two political entities that have had minimal interaction ever since. Thus, political upheavals contributed to fluctuating opportunities for dance to occur and fluctuating amounts and nature of support for it.

Second, with the colonization of Korea by Japan came the end of the royal court. Around the same time, western-style theatres began to appear in Seoul.[11] The tradition of female court entertainers was transformed as dancers began to perform in restaurants and for parties among the common people and in the newly-built theatres. Thus, new contexts and physical environments in which dance occurred contributed to changes.

Third, Korea's increasing contact with other cultures brought increasing contact with different kinds of dance, some of which contributed to conscious changes and some of which contributed to a gradual "filtering in" of outside influences.

Some of the derived dances, together with the older traditional dance forms, have become symbols of Korea. They are used to officially represent the country at international events, to adorn posters intended for tourists, and in television commercials advertising such things as the wares of a traditional medicine manufacturer.[12] One such dance, often described as representing the epitome of Korean dance features, is salp'uri.[13] There are many versions of this dance performed today, but certain elements characterize most of them. Salp'uri is a solo dance, generally performed by a woman, but occasionally by a man. It starts very slowly, sometimes with the performer facing away from the audience. The dancer wears the traditional Korean garment of women, which includes a floor-length full skirt that billows out from just below the breast area and a short jacket-type top with sleeves extending to the wrist in a soft, full curve under the arm. (When performed by a man the dancer typically wears traditional baggy pants and either a vest or long, light-weight coat.) The garment is most often white or a very muted color. In most salp'uri the dancer carries, in one hand, a long white scarf, made of a very light-weight silk.

As the dance progresses the performer traces circular pathways, turns around herself, and manipulates the scarf so that it, too, flows in graceful curves. The movement characteristics of traditional dances described earlier are highlighted, with many alternations between moments of suspended action and a kind of hurrying as the dancer resolves the suspension into a series of rapid steps. At one moment the dancer gently throws the scarf and it wafts to the ground. She lowers herself to a kneel and hovers over it, almost caressing it before retrieving it and returning to her standing dance.

Although dancers and dance teachers today consistently point out that the roots of salp'uri lie in shamanism, the basis of the concert form of the dance seen today is generally attributed to Han Sông-jun

(1874–1942), who is said to have choreographed it in Seoul in the mid-1930s, and to have named it after a rhythm and dance used in shaman rituals in South Chôlla Province.[14] Other theories attribute the dance to female entertainers of the twentieth century, claiming that the only tie to shamanism is the dance's name, which is usually described as meaning "to expel evil spirits."

Salp'uri is still very popular, and despite the relative newness of its origin as a concert dance form, the quality of a traditional dancer today is often determined by how well she can perform this dance. Many say that salp'uri embraces the essence of *han*—a term translated variously as sorrow, bitterness, or unsatisfied desire.[15] Salp'uri's close movement ties to older Korean dances clearly show its derivative nature.

Another popular derived dance is sûngmu, which, like salp'uri, has many variations. Although sûngmu is usually identified in English as the Monk's Dance or the Monk's Drum Dance, this gloss leads to confusion since it is the same name given to a traditional Buddhist dance. It is the Korean terms, *Pôpkoch'um* for the Buddhist dance and *sûngmu* for the derived dance, that clarify which dance is being described. Recall that the original Buddhist dance (*Pôpkoch'um*) was performed as a solo by a monk in conjunction with temple ritual. During the dance the monk plays some relatively simple patterns on an extremely large double-headed drum suspended in a standing frame. Sometimes a second monk plays a steady pulse on the opposite side of the drum. Early in the twentieth century, choreographers elaborated on this dance and created an adaptation of it for performance in a concert setting. Sûngmu, as the adaptation and any of its variants is known, generally begins with a somewhat lengthy, slow introduction that does not involve playing the drum but rather the manipulation of extremely long sleeves. This is then followed by a section in which the dancer pulls his or her arms through openings in the long sleeves near the base of the arm and, using drumsticks originally concealed inside the sleeves, executes intricate rhythmic patterns on the surface of the drum (which is generally smaller than that originally used in Buddhist rituals), on the wooden frame of the drum, and by beating the drumsticks themselves together. Stories attribute the origin of this dance to a monk trying to drive out the temptation of a young woman or exuding the ecstasy experienced during enlightenment. Both the stories and the playing of a drum in a standing frame during the dance reflect its derivative nature. Much of the movement, particularly in the danced portion preceding the drum-playing, constitutes a considerable departure from the original Buddhist dance.

There were many other drum dances created in the early and mid-twentieth century that are also derivative in nature. Borrowing the hourglass-shaped drum tied to the dancer's body in the farmers' dances, virtuosic dances, known as changgoch'um (*changgo* dance) were choreographed. The traditional Buddhist drum dance (*Pôpkoch'um*) was adapted beyond sûngmu to incorporate three, five, seven, and occasionally as many as nine drums. One small drum in a standing frame was placed upstage, parallel to the audience. One or more drums were then placed perpendicular to it and extending toward the audience to form a kind of alley way in which the dancer performed. She progressed up and down the alley way as she played on various parts of the drums, sometimes facing one drum but bending backward to play on the surface of the opposite drum. Several such drum formations might be placed on the stage at once, with a group of dancers creating a dynamic dancing percussion ensemble. Again, movements derived from older traditional dances fueled the imaginations of choreographers to create new works intended to entertain.

Similar derivative entertainment dances were created based on shaman rituals. The jumping performed by shamans when they were taken over by spirits became codified and choreographed into theatrical depictions of shamans on concert stages. Carrying fans, bell trees, scarves, and other implements typically manipulated by shamans, professional dancers created dances representing shamanism rather than trying to depict actual rituals on stage.

In derived dances choreographers look both back to their traditional heritage and forward to creating new works based on that heritage. While new versions of these dances continue to be choreographed at the end of the twentieth century, the creativity employed remains within the boundaries of the models established for these dances in the early and mid-twentieth century. The aesthetic of these derived dances is based on presenting the beauty of the dancers' movements by rearranging, in a homogeneous fashion, many of the movement patterns of older dances.

Major Contributors to Dance in Korea Today

Although dance has played an integral role in various facets of Korean society for centuries, and has been supported by the court and religious institutions to greater and lesser extents at different times, the traditions of the past have been carried on at the same time that changes have occurred and new forms developed. Ballet was first seen in Korea around 1917, and the tradition, as established in the West, became firmly entrenched by the middle of the twentieth century with the establishment of a national ballet company. Today, there are many ballet studios and numerous ballet companies.

Modern dance was first introduced to Korea in the late 1920s via a Japanese dancer who was most strongly influenced by the European tradition. It later became solidly established based on the Martha Graham style, and subsequently was influenced by many styles from both Europe and the U.S.

Since the 1970s, there has been a phenomenal dance boom in Korea. This boom is manifest in both the variety and quantity of dance activities. Dance offerings in higher education have increased, dance studios have been established throughout the country, dance students and performers have gone abroad to perform and to study, and professional dance organizations have been created. During the ten years from 1980 to 1990, the number of dance performances per year increased from forty to four hundred, and in 1994 there were almost one thousand dance performances in Korea and abroad; in 1989 twenty dance theory books were published, approximately seven times the previous average of three books per year; in 1990 alone, six new dance companies were formed.[16] By 1997 twenty-eight universities and eight junior colleges had established dance departments, with most retaining four to seven full-time professors and three to eight part-time instructors.[17] And in 1998 there were forty-five dance departments in universities and more than 150 dance companies.[18]

I believe four forces have contributed significantly to this growth: the Dance Department at Ewha Woman's University, the Korea branch of the American Dance Festival, increased financial support in the form of grants from government agencies and private corporations, and Korea's National Treasure System.

Originally begun as part of the physical education program in the 1950s (a genesis parallel to the beginnings of dance in higher education in the United States), in 1963 Ewha Woman's University became the first four-year university in Korea to establish an independent dance department (again following a pattern common in the United States).[19] At the end of the twentieth century the curriculum offered both bachelor's and master's degrees in one of three emphases: Korean dance, ballet, and modern dance. Graduates have contributed to virtually every facet of dance in Korea—founding their own companies, establishing dance programs in other universities and colleges, opening studios, going abroad to further their education, and participating in festivals. Probably not until later this century will Korea see dancers who were not, at some point, involved with the Ewha program.

A reflection of the growth of dance in academic institutions in Korea is the Ministry of Culture and Sports's 1992 establishment of the Korean National University of Arts, the first Korean university arts program emphasizing a conservatory approach. The institution-wide focus is on performance and profes-

sional training. The School of Dance opened in 1996, and includes performance, choreography, and dance studies (theory) departments. The performance department maintains the Korean dance, ballet, and modern dance sectional model initiated by Ewha. It will take some time before the impact of this program is felt, but the fact that it is governmentally supported reflects a significant national contribution to dance.

A second important influence on dance was the establishment of a Korea branch of the American Dance Festival. The festival, a United States–based administrative body that facilitates the creativity of modern dance choreographers and fosters the appreciation and awareness of dance, began in the United States in 1934.[20] Its goals are achieved through intensive summer classes, workshops, and performing opportunities for faculty and students. The success among Americans of Festival-sponsored activities in the United States eventually led to participation by foreigners, and subsequently to the establishment, by Festival administrators, of branch programs abroad. In 1980 Yuk Wan-sun, modern dance teacher formerly affiliated with Ewha University and the woman largely responsible for the beginnings of modern dance in Korea, brought forty Korean students to the Festival in the United States. The participation of Korean dance students continued, and Yuk was ultimately instrumental in the establishment, in 1990, of the Korea branch of the Festival. From July 30 to August 11 of that year, 487 students in Seoul participated in classes taught by visiting American modern dance instructors as well as several Korean instructors. The event continues to be extremely popular and contributes substantially to the awareness in young dancers of what is being done in modern dance in other parts of the world. The long-range impact of the American Dance Festival in Seoul on the development of modern dance in Korea remains to be seen, but it has clearly contributed to training and motivating young modern dancers.

The third major impact is the increased financial support for dance. Prizes awarded by the Ministry of Culture at dance competitions and outright grants from government and non-government agencies afford dancers the means to pay for costumes and to rent performing spaces, and offer individuals financial support while they develop skills and rehearse. So substantial have both the number of dance activities and the nature of support for them become that the government declared 1992 the Year of Dance, and featured performances, workshops, and symposia. In 1996 the government was reported to have paid 530 million wôn (almost $628,000 U.S., based on the average exchange rate for the year) for international exchange through dance performances, and in 1997 an equal amount was spent for the cultural promotion of dance.[21]

The fourth contributor to dance in Korea today is the government's National Treasure System. A formalized procedure for identifying important dances and dance masters, the system provides for the preservation of distinctive traditional dances by supporting research, documentation, and teaching and performing opportunities.[22]

But the dance boom may be short-lived. Serious financial changes in Korea at the end of 1997 will likely have a critical impact. The economy plunged, businesses declared bankruptcy, and countless individuals lost their jobs. In times of financial constraints the arts are typically among the earliest, and most profoundly, affected in negative ways. The future of dance in Korea, which once played an important role in many facets of life, remains to be seen.

Notes

1. The concepts of "tradition" and "traditional" are complex, and the terms are not universally defined. For a summary of some meanings associated with them, see Andrew P. Killick, "The Invention of Traditional Korean Opera and the Problem of the Traditionesque: *Ch'angguk* and Its Relation to *P'ansori* Narratives" (Ph.D. diss., University of Washington, 1998). I use "traditional" here because it is the most common gloss of the term used by Koreans for a particular kind of dance. In many traditional performing art forms in Korea what are commonly compartmentalized in the west into such things as music, dance, drama, and acrobatics are conceived of as a single entity. This is particularly apparent in, for example, the many "drum dances." Additionally, the playing of many musical instruments incorporates highly choreographed, or structured, movement sequences. Since the focus here is on dance, music is only briefly touched on.

2. The men were known as *mudong*, the women as *kisaeng*. Although a law was passed in 1477 to replace female dancers with young boys, it was unsuccessful (Alan Heyman, *Dances of the Three-Thousand League Land* [New York: Dance Perspectives, 1964], 11, 14). During the mid- and late-Chosôn dynasty (1392–1910) boys performed for kings, princes, and guests, and women for queens, princesses, and occasionally male members of the royal household (ibid.,

14). For an overview of the *kisaeng* tradition see Christine Loken-Kim, "Release from Bitterness: Korean Dancer as Korean Woman" (University of Michigan Ph.D. diss., 1989), 36–51, 65–69; and Byong-won Lee, "Evolution of the Role and Status of Korean Professional Female Entertainers," in *The World of Music* 16, no. 2 (1979).

3. For discussions of political uses of masked dance-drama and other traditional dance forms see Chungmoo Choi, "The Minjung Culture Movement and the Construction of Popular Culture in Korea," in *South Korea's Minjung Movement Culture and Politics of Dissidence*, ed. Kenneth M. Wells (Honolulu: University of Hawaii Press, 1995), 105–117; and Jong-sung Yang, "*Madangguk*: The Rejuvenation of Mask Dance Drama Festivals as Sources of Social Criticism" (master's thesis, Indiana University, 1988); and Jong-sung Yang, "Folklore and Cultural Politics in Korea: Intangible Cultural Properties and Living National Treasures" (Ph.D. diss., Indiana University, 1994).

4. *Nongak* literally means "farmers' music." Koreans often refer to this genre in English as "farmers' music" or "farmers' dance." Ethnomusicologist Keith Howard (see especially chap. 2 of *Bands, Song, and Shamanistic Rituals: Folk Music in Korean Society* [Seoul: Royal Asiatic Society, 1990]) glosses the term "farmers' band music" or "percussion band music." Because the genre to which I refer throughout this essay is

comprised of choreographed, or structured, movement as well as percussion music, I have chosen to gloss the term in a way that reflects both of these important ingredients—hence, "farmers' band dance and music."

5. Defining "dance," as opposed to movement systems that are structured but not considered dance, is a task that goes beyond this volume. For discussions of the topic see, for example, Judith Lynn Hanna, *To Dance Is Human: A Theory of Nonverbal Communication* (Austin: University of Texas Press, 1979); Adrienne Kaeppler, "Dance," *International Encyclopedia of Communications* (New York: Oxford University Press, 1989); and Joann Kealiinohomoku, "An Anthropologist Looks at Ballet as a Form of Ethnic Dance," reprinted in part I of this reader.

6. See Jong-sung Yang, "Folklore and Cultural Politics in Korea," 25.

7. For discussions of *môt* in relation to many aspects of Korean culture, see the autumn 1998 issue of *Koreana*.

8. In a January 1998 lecture in Hawai'i, Korean musician Yi Chi-yông described the importance of the curved line in traditional Korean music when discussing the way pitch changes are made. She also commented that one way to show the beauty of this line was by a momentary stopping, or suspension, of the tone, or by showing "empty space." This suggests that a suspension, or pause (the "motion in stillness" in dance), is a shared feature of dance and music.

9. Except for limited interactions with China and Japan, its closest neighbors, for many years the Korean government sustained a strong isolationist policy, contributing to much of the western world's identification of the country as the Hermit Kingdom. An 1876 treaty of amity with Japan was followed shortly by commerce and navigation treaties with the United States, Great Britain, Germany, Russia, and France, hence opening Korea to the rest of the world and making the appellation of the Hermit Kingdom no longer relevant.

10. Loken-Kim ("Release from Bitterness: Korean Dancer as Korean Woman," 81) presents a somewhat similar classification scheme to that presented here in which she identifies three categories: traditional, transitional, and modern. Her system, however, was delineated to describe the way in which dancers were trained, rather than the dances themselves; it only relates to the dances by implication. She labels those dancers "traditional," who received their training in *kwônbôn* [schools for female entertainers],

chaeinchong [*chaeinch'ông*—schools for traditional artists], or privately from family members or pre-theatrical troupes. "Transitional" dancers are those who have received their training in private studios, often from traditional dancers, but have adapted the dances for the stage. "Modern" dancers are those who have attended high school or colleges where they were exposed to non-Korean forms of dance such as ballet and modern (ibid.).

Robert J. Fouser ("Kim Young-dong and the Dilemma of Koreanesque," in *Korean Culture* 15, no. 1 [spring 1994]: 4–11) uses the term "Koreanesque" to identify a category that exemplifies some of the characteristics in what I describe here as "derived," and Killick ("The Invention of Traditional Korean Opera and the Problem of the Traditionesque") introduces the term "traditionesque." It is also possible to identify this "derived" category as "modern dance," since in many cases its intent was to modernize the traditional. See also Jack Anderson, *Art without Boundaries* (Iowa City: University of Iowa Press, 1997), 272–290.

11. The first such theatre is generally identified as Hyômnyulsa, built in 1902 and later renamed Wôn'gaksa. Killick, however, states that this theatre was originally known as Hûidae, and that there may have been other indoor theatres prior to 1902. See Killick, "The Invention of Traditional Korean Opera and the Problem of the Traditionesque," 54–58.

12. Yang Jong-sung describes the use of sûngmu in such a television commercial (Jong-sung Yang, "Folklore and Cultural Politics in Korea," 36).

13. Because there are many different dances identified as salp'uri, I use this term with a lower-case "s" to refer to them generically. This format is also followed for sûngmu and changgoch'um, discussed shortly.

14. See Christine Loden-Kim and Juliette T. Crump, "Qualitative Change in Performances of Two Generations of Korean Dancers," *Dance Research Journal* 25, no. 2 (fall 1993): 14; Hee-seo Ku, "Masters of Traditional Dance," in *Korean Cultural Heritage*, vol. 3: *Performing Arts*, ed. Joungwon Kim (Seoul: Korea Foundation, 1997), 156; and Kyoung-ae Kim, "Dance since 1945," in Kim, *Korean Cultural Heritage*, vol. 3, p. 178. Han Sông-jun began his performing studies under his grandfather, learning tightrope walking, drumming, and some southern styles of village dances, including shaman dances. While he was teaching female entertainers (*kisaeng*), he recreated and arranged many village folk dances for the-

atrical performance (Hae-ree Ch'oi, "*Ch'angjak Ch'um:* History and Nature of a Contemporary Korean Dance Genre" [master's thesis, University of Hawai'i, 1995], 173).

15. *Han* is a particularly important emotion in Korean culture, often said to be the result of the country's continual involvement in war. Hyun Young Hak (*sic*), a Korean theologian, describes it as "a sense of unresolved resentment against injustice suffered, a sense of helplessness because of the overwhelming odds against, a feeling of total abandonment . . . , a feeling of acute pain and sorrow in one's guts and bowels making the whole body writhe and wriggle, and an obstinate urge to take 'revenge' and to right the wrong all these constitute" (in Chung Hyun-kyung [Chông Hyôn-gyông], *Struggle to Be the Sun Again: Introducing Asian Women's Theology* [New York: Orbis Books, 1990], 173).

Korean writer Elaine H. Kim states it is "the anguished feeling of being far from what you wanted, a longing that never went away, but ate and slept with you every day of your life . . . by no means a hopeless feeling, however" ("War Story," in *Making Waves: An Anthology of Writings by and about Asian American Women*, ed. Asian Women United Collective [Boston: Beacon Press, 1989], 82–83).

16. See Seong-kon Kim, "On Native Grounds: Revolution and Renaissance in Art and Culture," in *Korea Briefing,* *1990*, ed. Chong-Sik Lee (Boulder, Colo.: Westview Press, 1991), 113; T'ae-won Kim, "III. 1981–1997: The Rapid Growth of Creative Activity and the Appearance of New Dance Genres and Generations," in *Korean Performing Arts. Drama, Dance and Music Theater*, Korean Studies Series no. 6, ed. Hye-suk Yang (Seoul: Jipmoondang, 1997), 151; *Korea Annual* (1990), 280; and *Korea Annual* (1991), 29.

17. T'ae-won Kim, "III. 1981–1997," 150.

18. See Kyoung-ae Kim, "To Join with the World of Dance," *DanceForum* 1, no.1 (winter 1998): 4.

19. See Kyunghee Kim, "The Status of Dance in Korean Higher Education" (Ph.D. diss., Texas Women's University, 1993), 42.

20. The Festival originally took place in Bennington, Vermont. It relocated in 1948 to the campus of Connecticut College in New London, and in 1978 to its present home at Duke University in Durham, North Carolina.

21. T'ae-won Kim, "III. 1981–1997," 151.

22. For a discussion of Korea's National Treasure System see Judy Van Zile, "How the Korean Government Preserves Its Cultural Heritage," *Korean Culture* 8, no. 2 (summer 1987): 18–19; Jong-sung Yang, "*Madangguk*" and "Folklore and Cultural Politics in Korea."

Writing Dancing, 1573

MARK FRANKO

> *Figure porte absence et présence, plaisir et déplaisir.*
> The figure brings absence and presence, pleasure and displeasure.
>
> BLAISE PASCAL, Pensées

At the dawn of theatrical dance in France, choreography was frequently likened to, and indeed contrived to suggest, a written text.[1] One genre in particular—geometrical dance—pushed the conceit of a bodily writing to its ultimate visual consequences. This [essay] outlines the various ways that the body—within its very presentation as a spectacular entity—was also identified as a textual entity. By becoming textual at the time of its deployment within the theatrical sphere, dancing became identified with highly rhetorical forms of late Renaissance culture.

Geometrical dance made extensive use of what were called "figures." The term *figure* could designate tableau vivant as well as choreographic path. That is, it referred to both the static and mobile aspects of pattern making in choreography.[2] A formation was occasionally set in motion while maintaining its fixed, or structural, characteristics. For instance, dancers could move along the circumference of a spherical path while still maintaining the clarity of that path's spherical shape. Whether still or active, the choreographic figure presented bodies as physical metaphors of written characters or symbolic designs. The first traits of theatrical choreography show that dance aspired to be textual or discursive in this very palpable sense. A gratuitous plasticity frequently associated with the appearance of spontaneity in dancing was thus originally diverted toward the body's capacity as a figure to enter into symbolic relation with words or written symbols, especially the shaping of massed bodies in collectively written characters. The choreographic impersonation of characters was interspersed with a physical lightness and postural erectness typical of courtly social dance.[3] Yet by dancing, the body was engaged in a process that eliminated the exhibition of an individual's intent or personal message.

Quintilian's analogies between rhetoric and the body in the first century are pertinent to this discussion because sixteenth-century geometrical dance used choreographic figure to produce meaning. The later choreographic meanings of the term *figure* parallel its earlier rhetorical ones. Or, put otherwise, a notion of choreographic form was developed in the early modern period out of the rhetorical refinement of the term *figura*.[4] Quintilian's first and simplest definition of *figura* in its rhetorical context recalls unintentional pattern, the simple plastic necessity of outward form. He applies the term to "any form in which thought is expressed, just as it is to bodies which, whatever their composition, must have some shape."[5] This is the historical root sense of figure that Auerbach calls "plastic form" or "perceptual shape."[6] Quintilian employs the upright body showing no postural distortion as a figure to express the meaning of the rhetorical term figure itself.[7] Moreover, the more complex sense Quintilian gave to a subcategory of the figure he called *schema* led him to employ an image of physical alteration: "It [*schema*] means a rational change in meaning or language from the ordinary and simple form, that is to say, a change analogous to that involved by sitting, lying down on something or looking back."[8] If the *figura* is analogous to upright posture and the very fact of language itself, a kind of natural starting point or raw material of utterance, the movement involved in changing positions is analogous to rhetorical and choreographic form: *schema* indicates ways to generate nuanced meanings by inflecting those fundamental "figural" givens. Nevertheless, in both *figura* and *schema*, Quintilian stresses the body's physical repose or relative stillness rather than its motion. While *schema* suggests change, it is a change to another position, not the motion operative in effecting that change. Similarly, in geometrical dance, it was frequently necessary to strike a significant stillness at the heart of motion, a posed quiescence in dynamic stasis, in order to assure the legibility of the pattern or the characters to which the pattern gave rise.[9] In ancient Greek, *schema*, which adds significance to outward shape, also meant pose. Furthermore, there is a conceptual and technical precedent for the physical techniques of geometrical dance in Roman pantomimic dancing of the second century.[10] Thus, while geometrical dance drew on the dance vocabulary of Renaissance courtly social dance, its theory was derived from classical sources.

Choreographers certainly used, even lavishly used, geometrical figures before and since the period under discussion.[11] But late Renaissance choreography distinguished itself by its professed intent to practice a hermetic symbolism in visual effects. The audience was called on to decipher or, in some sense, to read choreographic patterns.[12] Viewing a group of dancers as a living alphabet, and dancing bodies as letters, the spectator would reassemble each sequence of letters as a word, and each sequence of words as a phrase. For example, in *Le Ballet de Monseigneur le duc de Vandosme* (Paris, 1610), twelve knights, transformed into twelve nymphs, signal their metamorphosis to the audience by the choreographic spelling of an enchantress's name.

"[Elles] formoient ceste premiere figure, A: puis la marquoient durant une cadance, moitié en avant, moitié en arrière, et de ceste seconde, L . . . " ("[They] formed this first pattern, A: they held it for a beat, half facing front, half facing back, and from this first one they moved into a second one, L . . ."). Eventually, the letters A L C I N E are read.[13] This simulated text indexed their metamorphosis into nymphs, their captivity in bodies other than their own. Thus, much like the *alfabeto figurato* created by Braccelli in 1624,[14] the body was used as a figure of language. Sometimes messages were indexed with geometrical shapes, which thus constituted spontaneous hieroglyphs—symbols whose explanation could be derived from a reading of the libretto, which was always distributed beforehand. For example, the patterns formed by the knights in the final grand ballet of *Monseigneur le duc de Vandosme* are illustrated in the libretto as letters of an ancient Druidic alphabet. Each letter's meaning is explained in the libretto. As in the contemporaneous pictorial work of Arcimboldo, there is a time lapse between what things look like and the message they contain. Baroque choreographers thus experimented with choreographic pattern as index through a legible text or interpretable hieroglyph.[15]

Geometrical dances were usually placed at the end of court ballets and constituted the grand ballet. Most often, female dancers personified nymphs, and male dancers knights.[16] Sometimes, dancers stood for heavenly bodies. Whether as nymphs, knights, or celestial bodies, dancers portrayed pure and elevated beings. For example, in the *Balet représenté devant Madame, à Pau* (1593), the nymphs were followers of Diane, and therefore proponents of chastity, armed with spears and bows to resist "Amour."[17] In a 1622 ballet, the character of "Love" describes the nymphs as pure, yet condemned to succumb to love's power.[18] On occasion, their allegorical content served other themes, as in Colletet's *Ballet de l'harmonie*, where they appear as six notes of music following Orpheus.[19] Their character is occasionally colored by moral ambivalence as they represent chaste yet provocative Petrarchan love goddesses whose eyes emit dangerous rays. In *Les Nymphes bocageres de la forest sacrée* (Paris, 1627):

> Les Nymphes qui gardent ces bois
> N'espargnent pas les plus grands Rois:
> Tout fleschit sous leurs beautez,
> Tout ressent leurs cruautez. (L, 4:49)

> The Nymphs whose woods these are
> Do not spare the greatest Kings:
> Everything yields to their beauties,
> All are made sensitive to their cruelties.

Brantôme writes, "Bien heureux estoit-il qui pouvoit estre touché de l'amour de telles dames, et bien heureux qui en pouvoit *escapar*" ("He who could be touched with the love of such ladies was very fortunate indeed, but also fortunate was he who could *elude* it"). He calls them "creatures plustost divines que humaines" ("more divine than human creatures") and repeatedly stresses the sexual attraction they exerted when dressed "à la nimphale," with legs, calves, and feet exposed.[20] The audience may have responded to these characters on a somewhat visceral level, but the patterns formed by the dancers were meant to appeal to the intellect.

Geometrical dance, indeed, acquired its name from geometrical and symbolic patterns that were designed to be seen from above as if they were horizontal or flat on a page. From an elevated view, the spectator succumbed easily to an optical illusion whereby the far end of the stage would seem to slant upward toward him or her. Once dancers assumed a patterned configuration, they created an effect of flattened or foreshortened space. Each body became transformed into a point in space at the most fundamental visual level: the body loses its human resonance when it becomes a marker of geometrical position.[21] The performing area, dotted with bodies marking points, thus appeared to be a flat backdrop replacing three-dimensional space. Then the eye, picking out a configuration of points and the proportionate space lying between them, was sensitive above all to the potential for pattern suggested by the distance between the dancers. It was under these conditions that a text emerged from choreographic pattern.

The most valuable description of a geometrical dance is to be found in the *Balet des Polonais*, which was written in Latin by Jean Dorat and printed as *Magnificentissimi spectaculi* in 1573.[22] While the libretto is hardly unknown, the passage most relevant to dancing has essentially been overlooked by serious commentators. It is, in fact, the single most revealing description that survives and merits being cited in its entirety. Dorat's "Chorea nympharum" ("Dance of the Nymphs") describes all the modalities of geometrical dance that will subsequently be displayed in later court ballets:

> Carmine finito nunc incipit ecce Choreas
> Nympharum ad certos grex agitare modos.
> Et sua testatur numeroso gaudia gestu,
> Henrico lecto quae modo Rege, capit.
> Nunc veluti totidem Reginas ire putares,
> Quot Nymphas: lenta sic gravitate decent.
> Nunc veluti totidem Delphinas in orbe natantes
> Ludere: tam facili mobilitate micant.
> Mille breves cursus iterant & mille recursus:
> Mille fugas miscent, mille pedumque moras.
> Nunc haerent ut apes manibus per mutua nexis,
> Nunc in acumen eunt ut sine voce grues.
> Nunc aliis aliae transuerisis nexibus haerent
> Implicities sepes qualis ab arte rubis.
> Nunc hanc, nunc illam, variant per plana figuram:
> Descripsit plures nulla tabella notas.
> . . . Non Labyrinthaei tot erant curuamina tecti:
> Non Maeandreae sic sinuantur aquae . . .
> Dum simulat fictis praelia vera modis.
> Sic nunc in frontem, nunc in latus agmina ducunt:
> Sic nunc incurrunt, nunc fugiuntque leves.
> Sed iam composita veluti post praelia turma
> Incedunt, Regum praeter & ora meant,
> Dumque meant sua quaeque ferunt Regalia dona
> Aurea, quae spectans acutula parva putes.
> Er sua cuique super scuto caelata figura
> Nescio quod laetum Regibus omen habet.[23]

16. A geometrical figure from "Chorea nympharum" in *Le Balet des Polonais* (1573). Cliché Bibliothèque nationale de France, Paris.

Once the song was finished the dance began
Of the Nymphs moving in certain ways like troops
And their rhythmical gestures gave witness to their
    joy
Which Henry grasped, reading them, in the way
    kings can.
Now you would think you saw as many queens
    moving
As Nymphs: they were proper, slow to the point of
    graveness
Now, so many Dolphins swimming on the heav-
    enly waves
They play: they quiver with such easy mobility

They repeat many brief trajectories and many
    returns
They blend a thousand flights with a thousand
    pauses of the feet
Now they stitch through one another like bees by
    clasping hands
Now they form a point like a flock of voiceless
    cranes.
Now they draw close intertwining with one an-
    other
Creating an entangled hedge like a kind of bramble
    bush.
Now this one and now that switches to a flat figure

Which describes many letters without a tablet.

. . . The curves of a weave have not as many
    labyrinths

Water's meanders have not so many sinuosities . . .

They feign truthful battles with fictive means.

Now they lead the movement head on, now to the
    side

Now they rush forward, now they flee back lightly

But now gracefully just as the troops after the com-
    bat

They march along, moving in front of the faces of
    Kings.

And as they move they bear royal gifts of gold

Which, looking at, you could take for trifling
    things

And whose celestial figures engraved upon a shield

Have I know not what good omen for Kings.

There are three references to reading in Dorat's text. In the first, the verb *lego, legere* maintains its varied meanings: to collect, to gather together, pick, survey, scan, read, peruse. ("Henrico lecto quae modo Rege, capit"—"Which Henry grasped, reading them, in the way Kings can.") The connection between visual apprehension (scanning, gathering within a field of vision) and the decisive intellection of capit ("he grasps") is portrayed as inherently mysterious because of being proper only to Henry as King ("Henrico . . . modo Rege"). The final allusion to the happy omens (*laetum omen*) signified by the devices that dancers presented to Henri III also implies that the profane observer of the ballet cannot read (*nescio*) over the king's shoulder, as it were. Henry can read the true meaning of the action for himself, but the audience is destined to observe it crudely as an event of visual splendor. At this early stage of experimentation, the spectacle empowered the monarch as reader. Furthermore, his dancing subjects were his text.

The last reference to reading in Dorat's "Chorea nympharum" suggests bodies forming letters or words: "plures nulla tabella notas" ("many letters without a tablet"). Here, we come upon the unique nature of

dance textuality. The "readable" figures are clearly the static part of the performance text. Motion, however, is present in the forming as well as in the undoing of the figures. In Dorat's description, the alphabetic figure is arrived at through an entangling, intertwining movement likened both to a bramble bush and a swarming of bees. These last two images are not figures, they are descriptions of figureless flux. If they are figures at all, they are maze figures in that their legibility is seriously compromised.[24] It is interesting that among these figures of flux, the pointed formation of the "flock of voiceless cranes" directly preceding the latter two examples does suggest geometrical shape. Similarly, in Ronsard's forty-ninth sonnet, one of the figures described is the very figure of flight: "Ores il [le ballet] estoit rond, ores long, or' estroit / Or' en pointe, en triangle en la façon qu'on voit / L'escadron de la Gruë evitant la foidure" ("Now it [the ballet] was round, now long, now narrow / Now in a point, in a triangle as one sees / The squadron of the Crane escaping the cold").[25] The crane squadron is, on the one hand, a euphemism for what Brantôme called *l'escadron volant* ("the flying squadron"): the ladies in waiting to Catherine de' Medici who performed those very geometrical dances at the Valois court. On the other hand, the conceit of flight is contrary to the positionality of the figure. It seems strange that flight should obtain figural form. If one adds voice to Dorat's "flock of voiceless cranes," one thinks of Dante's second circle of hell ruled over by Minos, the commissioner of the labyrinth's construction. In that passage of *Inferno*, the lustful "che la ragion sommettono al talento" ("who subject reason to desire") are whirled about by the wind "Di qua, di là, di giù, di su le mena; / nulla speranza li conforta mai, / non che di posa, ma di minor pena" ("Hither, thither, downward, upward, it drives them; / no hope ever comforts them, / not to say of rest [*posa*], but of less pain").[26] The wailing flight of these damned souls depicted as both writhing in space and propelled inevitably forward is likened by Dante to a squadron (*briga*) of cranes: "E come i gru van cantando lor lai, / faccendo in aere di sè lunga riga" ("And as the cranes go chanting their lays, / making of themselves a long line in the air").[27] These references suggest that the triangle may have been the only displaceable figure in the geometrical dance tradition and one whose pointed direction suggested flight and greater individual plasticity for each dancer. The triangle's point is the figure of the nonfigure or of escape from the labyrinth, loss of sovereign reason, and potentially chaotic transfer of the body between the shores of two theses or positions. Nonfigurative or labyrinthine transitions should also be considered as part of the text, albeit its unsymbolic component.[28]

Thought of in its entirety, geometrical dance stages the appearance and disappearance of writing in space. Writing, of course, must disappear in order to reappear: each character is produced by a series of subsidiary motions that themselves cannot accede to meaning. But the vanishing of figure implicit in writing's temporary disappearance also partakes of textuality. Flight is part of the writing process. Thus, geometrical dance could be thought to provide two different, even opposed, though interdependent, textual models: one founded on the hieroglyph, the other on the labyrinth; one an obedience, the other an escape; one a discursivity, the other a madness.

The choreography of geometrical dance employs stable positioning, patterned movement, and patternless flux. It is pattern that alters the perception of the performance space, transforming it into a flat or two-dimensional environment. In contrast, the movement out of pattern allows the space to reassert its depth and volume. The dissolves, or *melanges geometriques*, as Beaujoyeulx named them, most likely occasioned the resumption of a three-dimensional space out of what had appeared to be a two-dimensional surface plane.

Descriptions of geometrical dances also suggest a dichotomy between movement and pose, or between stasis and flux. Self-contained suspension of movement contrasted with buoyant lightness and speed: "They keep movement in repose / and their moving is in repose concealed."[29] While this aesthetic could have a dynamic power when applied to sculpture because it

introduces movement into stillness, it privileges tension or denial when deployed by dancers because it introduces stillness into movement. Yet there was movement in geometrical dance. There are a fair number of scattered references to *marquer* ("holding") and *rompre* ("breaking away") in the literature. Dorat writes of both "a thousand flights" and "a thousand pauses," whereas Brantôme's description of *Le Balet des Polonais* uses the terms "confrontations and stops" as well as "turns, contours and detours," and "interweavings and blending."[30] If the holding of a pattern was characterized by a solemn immobility, the ensuing transition could appear by contrast quite chaotic and, conceivably, rapid. Descriptions indicate that geometrical dances contained brusque transitions from a serious and solemn demeanor to a playful and lively one. Dorat mentions "moving slow[ly] to the point of graveness" and, soon after that, quivering "with such easy mobility."[31] The twelve nymphs in one of the geometrical dances from *Le Ballet du Monseigneur le duc de Vandosme* dance "tantost par haut, tantost par terre d'un pas ores leger, ores grave" ("at times high and at times low, with a step by turns light and solemn").[32] Most striking in this juxtaposition of movement and figure is the lack of connective borders linking them, the absence of an aesthetic to render them organic extensions of one another allowing them to appear to remotivate one another.

There is evidence to maintain that transitions between figures were based on earlier dance forms called hays, or *chaînes*, an interlacing serpentine trajectory. In Dorat's "Chorea nympharum," for example, the trajectory lacked choreographic shape thanks to the weaving of bodies around one another: a voluminous massing rather than the very linear spacing needed for pattern making.[33] Brantôme's description of *Le Balet des Polonais* indicates that impressions of chaos and discipline succeeded one another: "Tout le monde s'esbahit que, parmi une telle confusion et un tel desordre, jamais ne faillirent leurs ordres, tant ces dames avoient le jugement solide et la retentive bonne" ("Everyone was amazed that amidst such confusion and disorder they never broke their ranks, these ladies having such solid judgement and good memory").[34] The decipherable figure contained in pause and pattern and, alternately, abandoned in voluminous space together comprise the text of the dance. That is, the body moves in and out of the verbal grid. One can say, without being overly metaphoric, that one of choreography's goals was to *inscribe* dance in theatrical space. The textuality of dance was not limited to figural inscription: textuality encompassed the motion with which an act of inscription is accomplished. The movements attendant to the act of writing itself are not inherently significant or legible in any conventional sense. In fact, they are roughly equivalent to the semiotic process against which symbolic pattern making flashed forth as *idea*: the *chora* which underlay *choreia*.[35] In other terms, the ideological impulse behind geometrical dance could only achieve a partial colonization of space by the verbal/figural text. It had necessarily to share that space with motion productive of the text. The human action needed to produce the figure could not itself submit to figurality. Thus, the monarch's control of geometrical dance was, of necessity, partial and incomplete.

Notes

1. Frances A. Yates endows the chivalric traditions of tournaments with enormous importance in the development of court ballet (*The Valois Tapestries* [London: Routledge & Kegan Paul, 1975]). This tradition was doubtless transmitted most directly to court spectacle through the chess game conceit that does suggest geometrical formations. Margaret McGowan dates the earliest literary manifestation of geometrical dance as 1499. She refers to Francesco Colonna's *Hypnerotomachie*, originally published in Italian and translated into French in 1546. See her *L'Art du ballet de coeur en France, 1581–1643* (Paris: Centre Nationale de la Recherche Scientifique, 1963), 36. Another example that merits mention is the detailed description of a ballet as tournament in Rabelais's *Le Cinquiesme livre*, first published in 1564. See Rabelais, *Oeuvres complètes* (Paris: Gallimard, 1955), chaps. 24 and 25, 814–822. The metaphor of chess and games in general is present in several burlesque ballets as well. Yet from a purely choreographic standpoint, the tradition of *ars amandi* is also an important source for the alphabetic conceits of geometrical dance. Dance was often close to the subject of gallantry, and on those occasions the calligraphic metaphor had an erotic dimension as well. Sexual activity was likened to writing by Angot de l'Eperonnière in his 1626 *Exercices de ce temps*: "Que la mode est d'apprendre en l'Amour les mysteres, / Et sur parchemin vierge escrire caracteres . . . / " ("The fashion is to learn the mysteries of Love, / And to write characters on virgin parchment . . . / "). Cited in René Pintard, *Le Libertinage érudit dans la première moitié du XVIIe siécle* (Geneva: Slatkine, 1983), 14.

2. For example, some of the patterns of the knights' Druidic alphabet in *Le Ballet de Monseigneur le duc de Vandosme* were moving ones: "Les susdites figures se moquoient chacune d'une cadence entiere, tournant ou retournant en leur mesme place" ("The above mentioned patterns each occupied a full cadence, turning one way or another in place"). See *Le Ballet de Monseigneur le duc de Vandosme, dancé le douziesme en la ville de Paris, dans la grande salle de la maison Royalle du Louvre* (Paris, 1610), Bibliothèque nationale: Yf. 7853; Bibliothèque de l'institut: 34613, 24 pièce 19, 35, reprinted in *Ballets et mascarades de coeur, sous Henri IV et Louis XIII (de 1581 à 1652)*, ed. Paul Lacroix, 6 vols. (Geneva: J. Gay et fils, 1868–70; reprint, Geneva: Slatkine, 1968), vol. 1, 237–269. This libretto will be referred to hereafter as *Vandosme*.

3. In this sense, rhythmic movement was assimilated to posing. But there was also a more radical sense to motion that escaped theorization but was also implicit in the term "figure" as changing form. There always seems to be an outward form to movement. But I will be interested in movement that constitutes its own radical identity as *figureless*, wholly lacking in meaningful form. This too occurs in the interstices of geometrical dance. In the very attempt to eliminate motion as self-defining, to saturate it with preordained meaning, geometrical dance unwittingly opens a breach in pose-oriented performance.

4. On the development of the concept of the figure, see Erich Auerbach, "Figura," in *Scenes from the Drama of European Literature* (Minneapolis: University of Minnesota Press, 1984), 11–76.

5. See Quintilian, *The Institutio Oratoria of Quintilian*, bk. 9, 353 (Cambridge, Mass.: Harvard University Press, 1976). Auerbach explains that the Latin *figura* develops from the Greek *schema*. Nevertheless, Quintilian chooses to use both Latin and Greek terms in his Latin text.

6. Auerbach, *Scenes*, 11–16.

7. Quintilian thereby demonstrates how close dance and rhetorical action were in Christian antiquity and would continue to be throughout the Renaissance. See Mark Franko, "The Mythological Intertext: Language," in *The Dancing Body in Renaissance Choreography (c. 1416–1589)* (Birmingham, Ala.: Summa Publications, 1986), 14–23.

8. Ibid.

9. Geometrical dance was modeled on the precedents of the cosmic dance as described by Plato and elaborated on by Plotinus and later Neoplatonists. Geometrical dance was thus clearly an expression of Renaissance Neoplatonism. See James Miller, *Measures of Wisdom: The Cosmic Dance in Classical and Christian Antiquity* (Toronto: University of Toronto Press, 1981). Geometrical dance was also the first truly public construction of cosmic dance, earlier confined to religious mysteries and philosophical speculation.

10. See James Miller, *Measures of Wisdom: The Cosmic Dance in Classical and Christian Antiquity* (Toronto: University of Toronto Press, 1981), on how holding the pose established meaning and constituted animation in Roman pantomime: "Pantomimic dancing was an art not only of changing and forming but also of holding poses: the dancer moved, and froze, and moved, and froze, constantly punctuating the flow of his performance with set poses (known technically as 'scheseis' or 'schemata') which displayed his supple limbs in various symmetrical configurations. . . . The spectators fixed their attention not so much on the dynamism of the dance as on its static poses, which they would read one by one like words in a sentence or glyphs in an inscription" (228). It is not surprising that Roman pantomime stands in the background of Neoplatonic dance since pantomime was the dance witnessed by the first Neoplatonist, Plotinus (see ibid., 528). Plotinus transmits the Platonic tradition to a Renaissance equally immersed in rhetorical tradition stemming from the same period. Further work remains to be done on the conceptual links between Roman pantomime and oratorical action. For Plotinus's theory of dance as pose, see his *Enneads* 3:2:16 and 4:4:33 (trans. A. H. Armstrong [Cambridge, Mass: Harvard University Press, 1984]).

11. Geometrical or horizontal dances were a choreographic feature of some of the earliest court ballets in France since Beaujoyeulx's *Le Balet des Polonais* (1573) and *Le Balet comique* (1581). Although Florentine theater dance contained geometrical dances, there is much less emphasis in Italy on a succession of shapes containing a hermetic meaning. Geometrical dance is present in the first intermezzo of the 1589 *intermedii*. There, fifteen "serene Celesti" represented universal harmony guiding the movement of the spheres. See Aby Warburg, "I Costumi teatrali per gli intermezzi del 1589," in *Atti dell'Accademia del r. istituto musicale di Firenze anno XXXIII: Commemorazione della riforma melodrammatica* (Florence: Galletti e Cocci, 1895), 19–20. In the sixth and last intermezzo, "o che nuovo miraculo," there is a crescent-moon shape and four lines (*schiere*). See Cavalieri's choreography in the ninth partbook of Cristofano Malvezzi, *Intermedii et concerti* (Venice, 1591; reprint, *Musique des intermèdes de "La Pellegrina,"* ed. D. P. Walker [Paris: C.N.R.S., 1962], lvi–lvii). Alesandro Giudotti's preface to Cavalieri's *Rappresentatione di anima et di corpo* (Rome, 1600) mentions a final "ballo formato." See Angelo Solerti, *Le Origine del melodramma* (Turin, 1903), 3. Cavalieri also mentions it himself in the text as a choreographic possibility. Cesare Tinghi's description of *Mascherata di Ninfe di Senna* (ca. 1611) mentions the spelling out of words with bodies: "Fecero un balletto di molto studio et molto vago, figurando le lettere che dicevano *Cosimo et Maddalena*" ("They performed a difficult and beautiful ballet forming the letters of *Cosimo and Maddalena*"). See Solerti, *Gli Albori del melodramma* (Milan, 1905), vol. 2, 263. The ballet of the nymphs in *La Rappresentazione di Mantova dell'Idropica* (1608) describes qualities central to French horizontal dance: *l'ordine* ("order") and "molti intrecciamenti" ("many interweavings") (ibid., vol. 3, 229). Cesare Negri's "Brando" uses spherical shapes, notably "in foggia d'una meza lune" ("in the shape of a crescent moon") danced by four shepherds and four nymphs. See *Le Gratie d'amore* (1602; reprint, Milan: Forni Editore, 1969), 291–293. More isolated examples of geometrical patterning are also to be found later in the seventeenth century. Menestrier relates that a ballet performed in Parma in 1667 included the spelling of the name "MARIA" (see *Des Ballets anciens et modernes selon les regles du theatre* [Paris: René Guignaud, 1682], 177–178).

12. A similar phenomenon could be examined from an art historical perspective in which the body has much in common with the image. Norman Bryson has analyzed Western art history in terms of a conflict between interpreting word and autonomous image, a conflict in which the discursive repeatedly gains ascendancy over the figural. See his *Word and Image: French Painting of the Ancien Regime* (Cambridge: Cambridge University Press, 1981). In geometrical dance, however, the power of the discursive assembles the very figurality of the body as image in order to project its legend or text from within rather than imposing a semantic relation from without. In other terms, the hackneyed distinction between the dancer and the dance seems reinvested with new meaning here. At the same time, there was also a discursive ambiguity inherent in some of the figures of geometrical dance, an ambiguity that stressed the effort to read their meaning over the certainty of their content.

13. This geometrical dance is called "Ballet des douze nimphes transformées." See *Vandosme,* in Lacroix, *Ballets et mascarades de coeur,* 237–269. It is clearer in the *Dessein du balet de Monseigneur le duc de Vandosme* than in the actual libretto that the nymphs are actually the transformed knights: "Alcine faict sortir d'un bois enchanté les Douze Chevaliers susdicts sous des estranges formes, qu'elle transmuë en douze Nayades, lesquelles dancent quatre à quatre, et puis toutes ensemble" ("Alcine has the knights, strangely transformed into Naiads, come out of the enchanted wood; they dance four by four and then all together") (ibid., 202).

14. Giovanni Battista Braccelli, *Bizzarie di varie figure* (Paris: Brieux, 1963).

15. Margaret McGowan claims that geometrical dance remained in style until approximately 1640 when the stage became elevated and its patterns could no longer be viewed from above. See *L'art,* 37. While this may be so, one of the last librettos containing what can unequivocally be called a geometrical dance is the *Ballet du soleil pour la reyne* (Paris: Nicolas Rousset, 1621), Bibliothèque nationale: Yf 8142, in 8 pièce. Although none of the patterns is described in the libretto, the cast of characters—stars, sun, and the hours of the day—makes it likely they existed there. In a similar manner, Guillaume Colletet's *Ballet de l'harmonie* (Paris, 1635) may also have contained a geometrical dance. Its allusions to late Renaissance concepts of harmony would suggest this theory although it, too, did not describe the patterns. Similarly, *Le Balet du roy ou la vieille cour* (Paris, 1635)

may have included a geometrical dance as it harks back nostalgically to an earlier period. The libretto only mentions "des figures que representoient ces seize divinitez dont il estoit composé" ("the figures that these sixteen divinities represented of which it [the ballet] was composed"). See Lacroix, *Ballets et mascarades de coeur,* vol. 5, 67.

16. In *Le Paradis d'amour* (1572), which precedes Beaujoyeulx's two other ballets, the final grand ballet was danced by men *and* women. Yet nothing in the description we have of it clearly indicates that they performed a geometrical dance: "Lors les trois chevaliers se levèrent de leurs sièges, et traversans le Paradis, allerent aux champs Elysees quérir les douze Nymphes, lesquelles ils menèrent au milieu de la salle ou elles se mirent à danser un bal fort diversifié, et qui dura plus d'une grosse heure" ("Then the three knights arose from their chairs, and crossing Paradise, they sought the twelve Nymphs in the Elysian fields, leading them to the center of the room where they began a dance full of variety which lasted more than a full hour"). Pierre de l'Estoile, *Mémoires-Journaux de Pierre de l'Estoile* (Paris: Alphonse Lemerre, 1888), vol. 1, 269r. On this event, see also Yates, *The Valois Tapestries,* 61–63. It is tempting to see a transition in *Le Paradis d'amour* between French couple dance and geometrical dance but, until now, there has been insufficient evidence to sustain the hypothesis. Brantôme mentions a comedy entitled *Le Paradis d'amour* given in the Salle de Bourbon, in his *Les Dames galantes* (Paris: Garnier, 1955), 344. The two plots, however, do not match up. Four knights and four nymphs dance a grand ballet at the conclusion of *Au ballet de Madame de Rohan* (Tours, 1593) in Lacroix, *Ballets et mascarades de coeur,* 134. Not every grand ballet, however, is necessarily a geometrical dance.

17. "Les Nymphes entrans tendans en la main droite un javelot, et en l'autre leurs arcs, et dançans une forme de balet" ("The Nymphs entering holding in their right hand a spear and in the other their bows, and dancing a kind of ballet"). Catherine de Parthenay, douane de Rohan, *Ballets allégoriques en vers, 1591–1593,* ed. Raymond Ritter (Paris: E. Champion, 1927), 11–12. These three ballets are also reproduced in Lacroix, *Ballets et mascarades de coeur,* vol. 1, 91–134.

18. See *Le Magnifique et royal ballet danse à Lyon en présence de deux roynes, sous le nom de l'Aurore et Céphale* (Paris, 1622), Bibliothèque de l'institut: 357262 27e, 10.

19. "L'On voit paroistre ensuite le mesme Orphee, suivi

de six Nymphes, qui sont les six notes de la musique." Lacroix, *Ballets et mascarades de coeur*, vol. 4, 213.

20. Brantôme, *Oeuvres complètes* (Paris: Foucault, 1823), vol. 5, 76–77. Much costume information on the female dancer is to be culled from *Les Dames galantes,* particularly on 196–197, 198, and 448 of the edition cited. It is characteristic of Brantôme to stress sexual excitement at the sight of exposed legs, calf, and feet (200–201). See also Mary Newton Stella, *Renaissance Theatre Costume and the Sense of the Historic Past* (London: Rapp & Whiting, 1975).

21. There is only one geometrical dance, to my knowledge, that has dramatically motivated transitions. In the *Receuil des vers du balet de la Royne* (Paris, 1609), the knights, free of their enslavement to love, describe their transitions as a dodging of Cupid's darts:

> Car, en changeant toujours de lieu
> Nous n'empeschons si bien ce Dieu, [Cupidon]
> Qu'il ne peut s'asseurer des coups
> Qu'il pense tirer contre nous.

> For, in always changing places
> We prevent this God [Cupid]
> From sending his blows against us
> With great assurance.

See Lacroix, *Ballets et mascarades de coeur,* vol. 1, 176.

22. See Jean Dorat, *Magnificentissimi spectaculi a regina regum matre in hortis suburbanis editi in Henrici regis Poloniae invictissimi nuper renunciati gratulationem descripto* (Paris: Frederic Morel, 1573), B.N.: Rés. p. 5c. 1845 (1). This edition contains a translation of the discourse of the French nymph by Ronsard and of the Angevin nymph by Jamyn. When compared with Ronsard's forty-ninth sonnet of the *Sonnets pour Hélène* ("Le soir qu'Amour vous fist en la salle descendre"), Dorat's "Chorea nympharum" indicates that *Le Balet des Polonais* was a choreographic study for the geometrical dances of *Le Balet comique*. The poem appeared in 1578: five years after the first ballet and three years before the second. Yates shows that Hélène de Surgères, to whom Ronsard's sonnet was addressed, danced in Beaujoyeulx's ballets and argues convincingly that *Le Paradis d'amour* of 1572 was also, in many respects, a preliminary study for *Le Balet comique*. Ronsard's fragments "Dialogue pour une mascarade" and "Monologue de Mercure aux dames" seem to be part of *Le Paradis d'amour*, indicating that he was close to all of Beaujoyeulx's work. See Pierre de Ronsard, "Les Mascarades, combats et cartels," in *Oeuvres complètes,* ed. Gustave Cohen (Paris: Gallimard, 1950), vol. 1, 1025–1027. Furthermore, certain phrases from the forty-ninth sonnet are close in descriptive content to Dorat's "Chorea nympharum": "Le ballet fut divin, qui se souloit reprendre, / Se rompre, se refaire, et tour dessus retour / Se mesler, s'escarter, se tourner à l'entour, / Contre-imitant le cours du fleuve de Meandre" ("The ballet was divine which was accustomed to repeat itself, / To break itself, redo itself, and turn upon return / To mix, withdraw, and turn about its confines, / Counterfeiting thereby the course of the river Meander"). For further description of dancing forms in the literature of the late French Renaissance, see Margaret M. McGowan, "Dancing Forms," in *Ideal Forms in the Age of Ronsard* (Berkeley: University of California Press, 1985).

23. Dorat, *Magnificentissimi spectaculi,* fol. C.

24. See Penelope Reed Doob, *The Idea of the Labyrinth from Classical Antiquity through the Middle Ages* (Ithaca, N.Y.: Cornell University Press, 1990).

25. Ronsard, *Oeuvres complètes*, vol. 1, 262.

26. Dante, *The Divine Comedy*, trans. John D. Sinclair (Oxford: Oxford University Press, 1982), vol. 1, canto 5, pp. 74–75.

27. Ibid.

28. On the relationship of the labyrinth to textuality, see Doob, *The Idea of the Labyrinth*. In his unpublished paper, "On the Bed of Polyclitus: Ancient Sculpture and Renaissance Aesthetics" (read at the conference "Mannerism at the Crossroad: Eccentricity and Interdisciplinarity," Indiana University, Bloomington, March 28, 1990), Leonard Barkan suggested that the human figure subsumed by geometrical patterning in Renaissance art signifies a move toward "decorative independence." He also proposed that geometry was later replaced by a turned or twisted body. Both of these ideas confirm my findings in contemporaneous court ballet. Although both geometry and writing—of which one can already see a hint in the chaotic meandering of the transitions in geometrical dance—come about in fine art through quotations of classical sources, they also intentionally ambiguate the narrative content of those sources, thus shaping an autonomous, self-reflected history within the art work. We shall see in what follows that the turned and twisted body is essential to the choreographic aesthetic of burlesque ballet. It already exists in embryo in geometrical dance.

29. Bocangel on movement in sculpted human figures, quoted by José Antonio Maravall, *Culture of the Baroque: Analysis of a Historical Structure,* trans. Terry Cochran (Minneapolis: University of Minnesota Press, 1986), 176.

30. See Brantôme, *Oeuvres complètes,* vol. 5, 59.

31. Librettos indicate that such disjointed transitions are a feature of much court ballet choreography and are not limited to geometrical dances alone.

32. *Vandosme,* 24.

33. *Chaînes* ("chains") are mentioned in *Le Balet comique, Le Ballet de Monseigneur le duc de Vandosme, Le Balet de la reyne* (1609), *Le Ballet du veritable amour* (1618), and *Le Ballet de la Royne representant la Beauté de ses nymphes* (1619).

34. Brantôme, *Oeuvres complètes* (Paris: Foucault, 1823), vol. 5, 59.

35. See Julia Kristeva's theory of the semiotic *chora* in *Revolution in Poetic Language,* trans. Margaret Waller (New York: Columbia University Press, 1984). Kristeva adapts the term *chora* from Plato's *Timaeus* (50e–51b), a text that is also at the origin of what James Miller calls the "*choreia topos*" (40c–d).

Beyond La Danse Noble: Conventions in Choreography and Dance Performance at the Time of Rameau's *Hippolyte et Aricie*

CATHERINE TUROCY

Conventions in choreography and dance perform-ance at the time of Jean Philippe Rameau have been subjects of study for me over the last twenty-six years. The problem is that there are no period nota-tions of the choreography for his operas. Books like Jean Georges Noverre's *Les Lettres sur la danse et les ballets*[1] certainly describe what people thought could be improved upon in the art of dance, but these books do not systematically outline the complete picture of the-atrical conventions and how they were employed.

In attempting to realize a major work of Rameau's today it is important to study and analyze, first, the concrete evidence of the period dance notation[2]; sec-ond, the different genres of dance and their context within the *tragédie lyrique*[3]; and finally, the period act-ing treatises and how they pertain to the dance. One must also search for the dance in the arts of painting, sculpture and drama. Period concepts of "natural," and "beautiful" can be understood more fully today if the arts are studied as a whole and not as independent sub-jects. In their own day, both Noverre and the English dancing master John Weaver[4] implored dancers to study painting and sculpture in order to portray ex-pressive gesture in a well-crafted pose.

This essay will use Rameau's first full-length stage work, *Hippolyte et Aricie*, premiered at the Paris Opera in 1733, as an example when referring to dance in the context of an opera. The work consists of a prologue and five acts and is based on the Greek legend of Phae-dra and Theseus. Some 30 percent of the music is des-ignated for the dance.

Before looking at the notation, the reconstructor needs to familiarize himself with descriptions of the dance left to us by people like Cahusac,[5] Gallini[6] and Diderot[7] in which we discover philosophical principles and aesthetic theory. Through letters, treatises, reviews and reports we can build a social/political context for the works to be reconstructed and interpreted. Period dance dictionaries link contemporary art with its history, placing dance's roots in ancient Greek and Roman cul-tures. For example, Charles Compan's *Dictionnaire de Danse*[8] has listings which give us insights into the dra-matic adaptation of Greek traditions by eighteenth-century librettists. One is a description of the *archimime*, in the context of funeral rites. Gluck's *Orfeo* opens with a dance for the *archimime* as Orfeo calls to the spirit of Euridyce. Another is a vivid description of the *Dance de L'Innocence* of the Lacedemonians danced by young women honoring the goddess Diana. Rameau com-posed his own *Dance de L'Innocence* in act 1, scene 2 of *Hippolyte et Aricie*, when the priestesses of Diana enter singing: "*Dans ce paisible séjour regne l'aimable inno-cence*" and the music for the dance suggests a purity of mind as well as spiritual ecstasy.

After studying some three hundred published notations in the Feuillet system, the concrete evidence, one can discern formulas for choreography used during the eigh-teenth century. I have observed the following principles:

1. The dancer(s) begin upstage center and then proceed downstage toward the audience in a presentational or introductory passage (the first "figure" of the dance).

2. The following figures develop the subject as the dance expresses itself through both the symbolic geometry of the dancer's path and through the steps.

3. The patterns the dancer traces along the floor are balanced around a strong center line running up and downstage, dividing the stage in half. For example, if one dances in a circular path on stage right, one would later cross the center line and make another circular path on stage left.

4. With a dance other than a solo, both mirror symmetry and irregular symmetry keep the dancers in a geometrical pattern filled with inner tensions.

5. The geometrical track or floor pattern the dancer traces corresponds with the length of the musical phrase and serves as a visual architecture.

6. The cadences in the music are marked by the completion of the dancer's geometrical pattern. It seems that the dancer assumes an expressive pose at this moment to crystallize the passion which had just been explored or to introduce the next subject.[9]

7. The dance closes with a leave-taking of the audience as the dancer retreats upstage center, ending where the dance began.

Performing the notated dances in a period theater with a raked stage reveals even more properties of period choreography. The upstage position for the opening and closing of a dance puts the dancer in a distant visual realm, removed from the spectator's immediate reality. With the forced perspective of the set design, the dancer's figure seems to grow upon descending toward the spectator. Often the most downstage part of the floor is leveled out. This leveling of the floor gives the illusion that the dancer has arrived into the world of the spectator. Any leaps downstage take on an acceleration and augmentation from the rake. Running motions upstage demand more physical effort and amplify the distance between the performer and the spectator. In the context of a *tragédie lyrique*, the motion of the dancer balances the lack of motion in the declamatory style of the singers who remain in the more downstage areas. The leave-taking of the dancer at the end of the dance can be grand and mysterious as it is enhanced by the rake. In today's modern theaters where stages are not raked, the choreographer/reconstructor can coax the dance into a raked effect by nuances in the efforts and *épaulement*[10] of the dancer.

Now let us look at the placement of dance within the *tragédie lyrique*. A well-composed theatrical spectacle balances the spectators' focus on the aural, visual, emotional and philosophical elements. The senses are not fatigued by a long spectacle, but rather enlivened as a rhythm is established with the unfolding of the plot. The story alternates between the recitative and solo air, the chorus and the dance, and instrumental passages in the orchestra, keeping the aural and visual senses of the spectator alert.

The purpose of any dance is defined by its placement in the context of the opera. By its very nature, the opera requires different kinds of dance, not just the *danse noble* style. In act 3 for instance, there is a danced *fête* for sailors to honor the return of Theseus. The dramatic conflict is heightened by the juxtaposition of this *fête* to the previous scenes where the tragic discovery of suspected incest turns Theseus's world upside down. His confused thoughts at the end of scene 6 are interrupted by the entrance music of the sailors, calling him to his public appearance at the *fête* in scene 7. To assume blithely that *danse noble* would suffice for every scene clearly makes no sense as here, to be sure, the drama calls for a faster, joyful dance of the people in celebration of the returning king and hero. Equally, the dance is crucial to the staging of the conflict between public life and private life, duty and passion, Theseus as a king and Theseus as a man. To treat the dance as a superfluous *divertissement* would weaken the opera tremendously while lessening the power of the dance.

This example of the sailor dances leads us to the question of the many categories[11] in eighteenth-century dance. Briefly, they can be characterized as follows. *La simple danse* is movement which expresses nothing and stays close to the ground, but is graceful and is used exclusively in the ballroom.[12] *La danse noble* is a noble, majestic style following classical principals of beauty. It is common to both the ballroom and the stage. *La danse en haut* or *la danse haute* is restricted to the theater and involves vigorous, high jumps and virtuosic dancing. *La danse sérieuse et héröique* is also designated for the stage and expresses proud, noble sentiments and can involve virtuosic dancing. *La danse grotesque*, only for stage dancing, involves exaggerated motions, outside the noble definition of proportion. Some dancing masters put the dance for the furies in this category while others group only the vulgar and comedic dances here.[13] *La danse demi-caractère* expresses tender and convivial sentiments of the common man and is designated for the stage.

Carriage of the body and step vocabulary varied according to these styles. Details of step execution and height of arm motion were dictated by the category. For example, *la danse noble* employed a regal carriage balanced with decorative and expressive arm gestures. The essence of this style was a contained spirit filled with all the passions of mankind. *La danse grotesque*, in contrast, could be executed by a gnarled body carriage with twisted arm gestures low and close to the body. Accompanied by a flailing spirit of unconfined wrath, the body could be thrown into the type of acrobatic dancing usually associated with the carnival.

It is clear to me that all of these dance categories are called for in a historically informed revival of Rameau's *Hippolyte et Aricie*. He balances the strength and pride (*la danse noble*) of Diana's followers in the Prologue with the spiritual and emotional questioning (*la danse sérieuse*) of the Priestesses as Aricie enters the temple of Diana in act 1. The *grotesque* dancing of the Furies in act 2 finds its contrast in the *demi-caractère* sailor dances of act 3. Remaining in the *demi-caractère* style the dance continues with the entrance of the hunters in act 4 and then returns to *la danse noble*, with the musette reuniting Aricie and Hippolyte in act 5. The musette typically represents a utopian Arcadia where Nature and Love reign. The final chaconne is a noble reflection on the drama, the ground bass representing Time and Fate.

Variety is the key to a successful choreography in this period, as in any period, and an effort is made by Rameau to provide for all facets of dance, not just the *danse noble*. A good example of the varied dance genres can be found in Gregorio Lambranzi's book *The New and Curious School of Theatrical Dancing*,[14] published in Nuremberg in 1716, where he records over one hundred dances described as *Delicium Populi*. These dance ideas are extremely useful to a choreographer/reconstructor today as they illustrate dances for sailors, hunters, tradesmen, *commedia dell'arte* figures, a few noble dances and absurd subjects such as dancing hats. The dances are not notated, but rather sketched out verbally. In some instances it is stated that the dancers mimed as they danced. Gennaro Magri's *Trattato Teorico-Prattico di Ballo*[15] (Naples, 1779) also gives a dancer's perspective on these different categories.

It is typical of the *tragédie lyrique* that dancers are paired with the singing chorus and appear as "the people," echoing the function of the Greek chorus in ancient tragedy. But the dancers would wear their customary mask, which was not discarded in France until the end of the eighteenth century and whose custom also harkens back to Greek tragedy. The spectator looks to the dance for the "picture" to illuminate an essence of an emotion.

The use of the mask in today's revivals of the works of Rameau is a key to understanding the theatrical performance of the period. The wearing of the mask was well documented and masks were certainly worn in Rameau's operas on the Paris stage. Although Marie Sallé[16] and Noverre later pushed to discard the mask for the freedom of an expressive face (a mobile mask), their own training was with the mask. This is an important issue as the mask does affect the way both the performer and the spectator perceive gesture.

Today, when one dons a mask in rehearsal, one is struck by the fact that any movement of the shoulders or head is no longer an abstract action, but rather a dramatic gesture with a specific meaning. The dancer becomes aware of the body as a gestural instrument. The words of Claude François Ménestrier[17] from his book *Des Ballets anciens et modernes selon les règles du théâtre* (Paris, 1682) take on a new meaning:

> Ballet imitates not only actions, it imitates according to Aristotle the passions and the manners, this is more difficult than the expression of actions. This imitation of manners and affects is based on the impressions that the soul naturally makes on the body, and on the judgment that we make of manners and observations of persons based on these exterior movements. . . . As in Oratory, there are certain figures that seem to make obvious the things the orator speaks of; one must do these same movements in the ballets.[18]

This quotation refers to the style of dance developed during Lully's time which was the basis of good training for Rameau's dancers. Indeed, the singer and dancer during Rameau's time are often referred to as *l'acteur chantant* or *l'acteur dansant*. The performance of the solo singer and dancer is united in the acting technique of the period.

Although our historical dance field has been reluctant to apply acting theory to theatrical dance, Weaver[19] and Taubert[20] reveal in their treatises from the first half of the eighteenth century that the ballroom dance and stage dance differed. Indeed, it is difficult to ignore the book of Charles Pauli, *Elémens de la Danse*, published in Leipzig in 1756, where he discusses the differences between *la danse haute* (virtuosic theatrical dance which called upon the art of gesture) and *la danse simple* (dance style of the ballroom). He clearly states: "*L'Art d'écrire la danse* (referring to Feuillet's *Chorégraphie*) only covers *la danse simple*, and not the art of gesture . . . and can be seen as the base and the-

ory of *la danse simple*."[21] This statement puts Feuillet's notation treatise in perspective, inferring that the dance of the theater requires further study and explanation beyond the scope of Feuillet's work.

In speaking of *la danse sérieuse*, and specifically chaconnes and passacailles, John Weaver's *An Essay towards an History of Dancing* (London, 1712), praises the French dancer, Desbargues: "who had a certain address and artfulness in his gestures, which, as they are the most material articles, and qualifications of the Arts; so, who excels in them, ought I think to be esteemed the greatest Master." Clearly, it is in the first quarter of the eighteenth century, and not only with Noverre's inventions, as dance historians have often written, that the art of gesture was required in *la danse sérieuse* and in the dance of the theater in general.

Allow me to clarify the word "gesture." When dancing masters write about the motions of the arms, they make a distinction between movement of the arms and expressive gesturing with the arms. In the context of his full essay, Weaver's reference to "a certain address and artfulness in his gestures" refers to an expressive attitude of the body and expressive use of the arms. The word "expressive" is not to be confused with the act of miming or with pantomimic dance, an entirely different subject.

Going beyond notation, today's choreographer/reconstructor must turn to the acting technique to discover a common ground between the actor and the dancer. In looking more closely at Ménestrier's words, "and as in Oratory there are certain figures that seem to make obvious the things the orator is speaking about, it is necessary that the movement do the same in ballet," today's reconstructor should be encouraged to study the abundant acting treatises in this period.

Published in 1806, but reflecting back on the second half of the eighteenth century, Reverend Gilbert Austin's *Chironomia*[22] offers an analysis of attitude and gesture which can be directly related to the dance. The same theories presented in this book are reiterated and are perhaps the basis of the methods of Delsarte, Ted Shawn[23] and Doris Humphrey.

17. The New York Baroque Dance Company in *El Sarao de Venus*. In photo, Carlos Fittante and Catherine Turocy. Photo by Stephen Cowles.

In studying *Chironomia* I was struck by five concepts which directly relate to the dance.

1. Austin defines a sphere around the body which is the actor's expressive space.

Much like Rudolph von Laban's kinesphere, this sphere vibrates with a dramatic and physical tension. In my lectures I often refer to this sphere as the "Baroque Bubble." Each performer's bubble maintains a polite distance from others sharing the space on stage. The Baroque Bubble also contains the character's full range of dramatic and psychological energy. If the bubble is pressed by another performer's presence, a relationship of intimacy or conflict is immediately perceived by the audience.

2. The shifting of the body weight within the sphere carries dramatic implications just as the motions in the geometric path of the dance color the symbolism of the dance.

Austin notates a poem, *The Miser*,[24] and clearly indicates the actor's shifts of weight within the sphere as the drama unfolds. The dancer, while moving, can also utilize these same shifts of weight in the carriage of the body while in motion on the track of the choreography. One might visualize Austin's actor shifting his body in the sphere and gesturing dramatically as his legs dance upon the track of the choreography. I suggest this image as an attempt to understand the nature of expressive dance (not pantomime) in Rameau's time.

3. Austin's definition of "attitude" is the same as that used in dance dictionaries of the period: "The painter is struck by the boldest and finest of the significant gestures which are called attitudes, and he records them; they are the proper objects of his art; they are striking and less evanescent than the other gestures, which pass unnoticed by him, although they make up by far the greater and more important part of the gestures requisite for illustrating the sentiments."[25]

Compare this quotation to that of Gennaro Magri in his *Trattato Teorica-Prattico di Ballo*:

> The true theatrical attitude does not consist of a single and simple gesture, but it is a union of several poses, being an accompaniment of the arms, the legs, the head, the eyes, which must express in which emotional state the person is found.[26]

In an effort to physically understand the difference between gesture and attitude as both these men describe the terms, one discovers the fourth important lesson from Austin's book:

4. Gesture has a complex relationship to attitude and they both depend upon one another as the body transforms to another attitude through a series of gestures.

It is the artful dynamic manipulation of motion from gesture resolving in attitude that ties dance to oratory as earlier described by Ménestrier.

5. Finally, the duration of declamatory gesture can be related to the phrasing of the dance steps.

Again, in Austin's notated *The Miser*, the actor shifts his weight forward and backward in the sphere as the drama of the poetry is emphasized, much as the dancer will advance or retreat in the space, in measured phrases, as the choreography unfolds. It is beyond the scope of this paper to go into a full discussion of dance as *mute rhetoric*. However, Patricia Ranum in her article for *Early Music Magazine* (February 1986) offers convincing evidence outlining the links between French poetry, music and dance. She says:

> Pomey's precious document . . . provides sufficient information to permit some study of the dance as a unitary experience, that is, a study not only of the notes and lyrics, but of gesture as well, in the light of the rhetorical theory of the period. The analysis of all these dimensions is inspired by numerous statements in rhetoric handbooks of the period, which likens dance steps to the individual syllables of a song, the complete lyrics of that song to an oration, and the actor's expressive gestures to the orator's figures of speech.[27]

Exploring the concrete evidence of the dance notations and treatises published in the period, understanding the different genres of dance and their use in staged works, and gaining a physical knowledge of the acting technique and its application to dance, all aid toward illuminating the nature of eighteenth-century dance. The conventions of choreography and dance performance at the time of Rameau were highly sophisticated structures in tune with the other arts and can be understood at an elemental level in our laboratory of dance analysis. But like an element, the discovery of its nature is most exciting and meaningful when viewed in the larger context. And as in any science, there are yet other avenues waiting to be explored by the next generation of dance history scholars!

Notes

1. Jean Georges Noverre, *Les Lettres sur la danse et les ballets* (Lyon, 1760).

2. Pierre Beauchamp and Raoul Auger Feuillet, among other dancing masters, developed an abstract notation system for the dance. The first book published on this system and its application is *Chorégraphie* by Feuillet (Paris, 1700). Feuillet, much to the dismay of his colleagues, alone, retained the copyright of this seminal work.

3. *Tragédie lyrique* is a genre of French opera from the seventeenth and eighteenth centuries. It consists of a prologue and five acts. The libretto is based in ancient Greek or Roman history. Dance plays an important role in the development of the plot.

4. John Weaver, *Anatomical and Mechanical Lectures upon Dancing* (London, 1721), 145–146.

5. Louis de Cahusac, *La Danse ancienne et moderne ou Traité historique de la danse* (La Haye, 1754).

6. Giovanni-Andrea Gallini, *A Treatise on the Art of Dancing* (London, 1762).

7. Denis Diderot and Jean le Rond D'Alembert, *Encyclopédie* (Geneva, 1765–72).

8. Charles Compan, *Dictionnaire de Danse* (Paris, 1787).

9. The notation does not indicate a picture of a pose, but rather the dance step resolves in a corresponding physical cadence with the end of the musical phrase. In compliance with the rules of declamation, it seems the notation implies assuming a dramatic attitude at these cadences.

10. By *épaulement* I mean the shifting of the shoulders in opposition to the hips and other more subtle changes in the angles of the shoulders and chest. I am referring to *épaulement* in the more general sense and not with a strict classical ballet technique in mind.

11. For a complete explanation of dance categories please refer to *Dictionnaire de la musique en France aux XVII et XVIII siècles* under the direction of Marcelle Benoit (Paris: Fayard, 1992).

12. Claude François Ménestrier, *Ballets anciens et modernes selon les règles du théâtre* (Paris, 1682): "La simple danse est une mouvement qui n'exprime rien, et observe seulement une juste cadence avec le son des instrumens par des pas et des passages simple ou figurez, au lieu que le Ballet exprime selon Aristotle les actions des hommes, leurs moeurs, et leurs passions" (158).

13. Gennaro Magri, *Trattato Teorico-Prattico di Ballo*, trans. Mary Skeaping (Naples, 1779; London: Dance Books, 1988): "To do an attitude in the manner of a fury, the same arm and the leg which is in the air will be lifted high beyond measure with the fingers held with the said regularity, expressing the kind of rage which makes all the limbs of the body rigid, with scintillating eyes, gnashing teeth, like mastiff dogs, and everything else which can characterize their embittered, vicious and spiteful character; for

regularity should never be observed in them but only a skillful speed in gesturing" (149).

14. Gregorio Lambranzi was a Venetian dancing master who later lived and worked in Nuremburg. Not much is known about his life; however, judging from his book, he had a keen sense of humor and knowledge and a compassionate heart for those dancing masters who were fervently looking for new ideas to please their audiences!

15. Gennaro Magri (birth and death dates unknown) lived in the second half of the eighteenth century. The majority of his professional life was in Naples. His book is one of the few treatises of this period which is written by a dancer for dancers. He, himself, excelled in the grotesque style.

16. Marie Sallé (ca. 1707–1756) was known for her expressive dancing. Noverre was one of her students and he carried on innovations she had started such as dispensing with the mask, more realistic costuming and using the dance to tell the entire story of the ballet rather than depending on a sung libretto. She was the choreographer for Handel's operas in London, performing with her own troupe of dancers. She was also a good friend of Voltaire's. As she did not publish a treatise on dance, her accomplishments often go uncredited. Descriptions of her dancing are to be found in the *Mercure de France,* January and September 1732; July 1756.

17. Claude François Ménestrier (1631–1705) was a Jesuit priest, dance theoretician, dance producer and one of ballet's first historians. He worked at the Collège de la Trinité in Lyon and was responsible for public celebrations and spectacles. A wonderful account of Jesuit involvement with dance and its development as a theatrical form can be found in Judith Rock's book, *Terpsicore at Louis-le-Grand, Baroque Dance on the Jesuit Stage in Paris* (St. Louis: Institute of Jesuit Sources, 1996).

18. "Le Ballet n'imite pas seulement les actions, il imite encore selon Aristotle les passions et les moeurs, ce qui est plus difficile que l'expression des actions. Cette imitation des mouers et des affections de l'âme est fondée sur les impressions que l'âme fait naturellement sur le corps, et sur le jûgement que nous faisons des moeurs et des inclinations des personne sur ces mouvemens, extérieurs . . . et comme dans l'Eloquence il y a certaines figures, qui semblent mettre sous les yeux les choses dont L'Orateur parle, il faut que

les mouvemens fassent la meme chose dans les Ballets" (159).

19. Please see Richard Ralph's comprehensive book on Weaver and his writings: *The Life and Works of John Weaver,* an account of his life, writings and theatrical productions, with an annotated reprint of his complete publications (New York: Dance Horizons, 1985).

20. Gottfried Taubert, *Der Rechtschaffener Tanzmeister* (Leipzig, 1717).

21. "*L'Art d'écrire la danse* ne s'étend que sur la danse simple, et non pas sur l'art des gestes . . . et peut attire regardé comme la base et la théorie de la danse simple" (53).

22. Reverend Gilbert Austin, *Chironomia; or, A Treatise on Rhetorical Delivery; comprehending many precepts, both ancient and modern, for the proper regulation of the voice, the countenance, and gesture (Together with an investigation of the elements of gesture, and a new method for the notation thereof; illustration by many figures)* (London, 1806). Austin developed a notation for gesture which he explains in this book.

23. It is very interesting to compare Austin's book with Shawn's *Every Little Movement* (Lee, Mass., 1954).

24. *The Miser and Plutus,* described as a fable by Gay, *Chironomia,* 368.

25. Ibid., 497.

26. *Trattato Teorica-Prattico di Ballo,* chap. 58, 148, of the Skeaping translation.

27. Patricia Ranum, "Audible Rhetoric and Mute Rhetoric: The Seventeenth Century French Sarabande," *Early Music* 14, no. 1 (February 1986): 24, citing Father François Pomey, *Dictionnaire royal* (Lyon, 1671).

The Travesty Dancer in Nineteenth-Century Ballet

LYNN GARAFOLA

More than any other era in the history of ballet, the nineteenth century belongs to the ballerina. She haunts its lithographs and paintings, an ethereal creature touched with the charm of another age. Yet even when she turned into the fast, leggy ballerina of modern times, her ideology survived. If today the art of ballet celebrates the *danseur* nearly as often as the *danseuse*, it has yet to rid its aesthetic of yesterday's cult of the eternal feminine. Like her nineteenth-century forebear, today's ballerina, an icon of teen youth, athleticism, and anorexic vulnerability, incarnates a feminine ideal defined overwhelmingly by men.

The nineteenth century did indeed create the mystique of the ballerina. But it also gave birth to one of the more curious phenomena of history. Beginning with romanticism, a twenty-year golden age stretching from the July Revolution to about 1850, the *danseuse en travesti* usurped the position of the male *danseur* in the *corps de ballet* and as a partner to the ballerina. Stepping into roles previously filled by men, women now impersonated the sailor boys, hussars, and toreadors who made up "masculine" contingents of the *corps de ballet*, even as they displaced real men as romantic leads. Until well into the twentieth century, the female dancer who donned the mufti of a cavalier was a commonplace of European ballet.

In real life, donning men's clothing meant assuming the power and prerogatives that went with male identity. Cross-dressing on the stage, however, had quite different implications. Coming into vogue at a time

of major social, economic, and aesthetic changes, it reflected the shift of ballet from a courtly, aristocratic art to an entertainment marketplace and the tastes of a new bourgeois public.

Thus the *danseur* did not vanish in Copenhagen, where August Bournonville guided the destiny of the Royal Theater for nearly five decades, or at the Maryinsky Theater in St. Petersburg, where Marius Petipa ruled the Imperial Ballet for a similar tenure. On these courtly stages the male remained, even if eclipsed by the ballerina.

Where he fought a losing battle was in those metropolitan centers that stood at the forefront of the new aesthetic—Paris and London. At the prestigious cradles of ballet romanticism in these cities, the Paris Opéra and King's Theatre, he was edged gradually but firmly from the limelight by a transformation in the social relations of ballet as thoroughgoing as the revolution taking place in its art.

Unlike the theaters of the periphery, where government control of arts organization remained intact, those of the European core operated, or began to operate, as private enterprises.[1] Entrepreneurs stood at the helm, with subscribers paying all or a substantial share of the costs—even at the Paris Opéra which continued to receive partial subsidy from the government after losing its royal license in 1830. This change in the economic structure of ballet placed the audience—particularly the key group of monied subscribers—in a new and powerful position. It led to a new kind of star system, one based on drawing power rather than rank, while eliminating, for purposes of economy, the pensions and other benefits traditionally accruing to artists in government employ. The disappearance of the male dancer coincided with the triumph of romanticism and marketplace economics.

The ban on male talent was not, strictly speaking, absolute. Even in the second half of the century in England and on the Continent, men continued to appear in character roles such as Dr. Coppélius, the doddering, lovestruck Pygmalion of *Coppélia,* parts that demanded of dancers skill as actors and mimes and could be performed by those long past their prime. Men on the ballet stage were fine, it seemed, so long as they left its youthful, beardless heroes to the ladies and so long as they were elderly and, presumably, unattractive.

Initially, then, the "travesty" problem defines itself as one of roles, specifically, that of the romantic hero, who incarnated, along with his ballerina counterpart, the idealized poetic of nineteenth-century ballet. In the new era opened by the July Revolution, this aesthetic and the styles of masculine dancing associated with its expression became gradually "feminized." Scorned by audiences as unmanly, they became the property of the *danseuse en travesti,* that curious androgyne who invoked both the high poetic and the bordello underside of romantic and post-romantic ballet.

Although travesty roles were not unknown before 1789, they were rare, especially in the so-called *genre noble,* the most elevated of the eighteenth century's three balletic styles.[2] Indeed, its most distinguished exponents were men, dancers like Auguste Vestris, who brought a supreme elegance and beauty of person to the stage and majestic perfection to the adagios regarded as the touchstone of their art. No one embodied more than the *danseur noble* the courtly origins of ballet, its aristocratic manner, and the masculinity of a refined, leisured society.

Already by 1820, the *danseur noble* appealed to a very limited public—connoisseurs and men of refined tastes. To the increasing numbers from the middle classes who began to frequent the Paris Opéra in the later years of the Restoration, his measured dignity and old-fashioned dress betrayed, like the *genre noble* itself, the aristocratic manner and frippery of the Ancien Régime.

In the changing social climate of the 1820s, then, a new kind of gendering was under way. The men about town who formed the backbone of the growing bourgeois public saw little to admire in the stately refinements of the *danseur noble.* Their taste, instead, ran to the energized virtuosity of a *danseur de demi-caractère* like Antoine Paul whose acrobatic leaps and multiple spins offered an analogue of their own active, helter-skelter lives. The high poetic of ballet, the loftiness of feeling embodied by the *danseur noble,* came to be seen as not merely obsolete, but also unmanly. With the triumph of romanticism and the new, ethereal style of Marie Taglioni in the early 1830s, poetry, expressiveness, and grace became the exclusive domain of the ballerina. At the same time, advances in technique, especially the refining of *pointe* work, gave her a second victory over the male: she now added to her arsenal of tricks the virtuosity of the *danseur de demi-caractère.* By 1840 a critic could write, "If male dancing no longer charms and attracts today, it is because there is no Sylphide, no magic-winged fairy capable of performing such a miracle and doing something that is endurable in a male dancer."[3]

In appropriating the aesthetic idealism and virtuoso technique associated with the older genres of male dancing, the ballerina unmanned the *danseur,* reducing him to comic character and occasional "lifter." But her gain had another effect, more lasting even than the banishment of the male from the dance stage. Beginning with romanticism and continuing throughout the nineteenth century, femininity itself became the ideology of ballet, indeed, the very definition of the art. Ideology, however, turned out to be a false friend. Even as nineteenth-century ballet exalted the feminine, setting it on a pedestal to be worshipped, its social reality debased the *danseuse* as a worker, a woman, and an artist.

From the romantic era with its triumphant bourgeoisie and market ethos came the dual stigma of working-class origins and sexual impropriety that branded the woman dancer well into the twentieth century. The great ballerinas continued, by and large, to emerge from the theatrical clans that had survived from the eighteenth century, a kind of caste that trained, promoted, and protected its daughters. (Taglioni, for instance, arrived in Paris in 1827 with a brother to partner her and a father who coached her, choreographed for her, and acted as her personal manager.) The rest, however, belonged to the urban slums. "Most of the dancers," wrote Albéric Second in 1844, "first saw the light of day in a concierge's lodge."[4] Bournonville summed up the lot of the majority succinctly—humble origins, little education, and wretched salaries.[5]

Poverty, naturally, invites sexual exploitation, especially in a profession of flexible morals. (Liaisons sweeten almost every ballerina biography.)[6] In the 1830s, however, the backstage of the Paris Opéra became a privileged venue of sexual assignation, officially countenanced and abetted. Eliminating older forms of "caste" separation, the theater's enterprising management dangled before the elect of its paying public a commodity of indisputable rarity and cachet—its female corps of dancers.

Imagine for a moment the inside of the old Paris Opéra. Descending tier by tier from the gods, we move up the social scale, until, finally, we stand at the golden horseshoe of wealth, privilege, and power where, in boxes three-deep on either side of the proscenium, sit the pleasure-minded sportsmen of the Jockey Club.

As the Opéra's most influential *abonnés*, the occupants of these *loges infernales*—all male, of course—enjoyed certain privileges: the run of the *coulisses*, for example, and entry to the Foyer de la Danse, a large room lined with barres and mirrors just behind the stage. Before 1930, lackeys in royal livery had warded prying eyes from this warm-up studio. When the new regime turned the Opéra over to private management, the Foyer de la Danse acquired a different function.[7] No longer off limits to men of wealth and fashion, before and after performances it became an exclusive

maison close, with madams in the shape of mothers arranging terms. Nowhere was the clash, evoked time and again in lithographs and paintings, between the idealized femininity of balletic ideology and the reality of female exploitation so striking as in the Opéra's backstage corridors.

The commerce in dancers' bodies was not peculiar to Paris. In London, remarked Bournonville, it lacked even the pretension of gallantry that accompanied such exchanges across the Channel. To be sure, some dancers did eventually marry their "protectors." Many more bore children out of wedlock, sending them in secrecy to distant relations or country families to be reared. Nor did marriages between dancers fare well in this atmosphere of libertinage: one thinks of the choreographer Arthur Saint-Léon, Fanny Cerrito's on and off-stage partner, who, jealous of the gifts showered on his beautiful and brilliant wife (which he could neither duplicate nor reciprocate), left the field of battle to his competitors.[8] The association of ballet and prostitution was so pervasive that Ivor Guest in his history of ballet under the Second Empire makes a special point of noting the Opéra's good girls—model wives, midnight poets, authors of books of religious reflections. But such cases were only exceptions. For pleasure-loving Paris, dancers were the cream of the *demi-monde*.

Aesthetics today stresses the dancer's symbolic function: it views physical presence as the form of dance itself. In the nineteenth century, however, the *danseuse* was first and foremost a woman. Like her audience, she saw the task of ballet as one of charming the sensibility, not elevating the mind. Tilting her face to the *loges infernales*, flashing the brilliants of her latest protector, making up with coquetry the shortcomings of technique, she presented herself as a physical synecdoche, a dancer without the dance. For the nineteenth-century public, ballet offered a staged replay of the class and bordello politics that ruled the theater corridors.

Conventional wisdom has it that there were two sorts of romantic ballerinas: "Christians" who evoked romanticism's spiritual yearnings and supernal kingdoms, and "pagans" who impersonated its obsession with exotic, carnal, and material themes.[9] But this paradigm, invented by Théophile Gautier to describe the contrasting styles of Marie Taglioni and Fanny Elssler, is at best misleading. For no matter how patly the virgin/whore scheme seems to fit the ideology of romanticism, it ignores both the dancer's totemic reality—her position within the social order of ballet—and that troubling third who articulated the common ground of the period's balletic avatars of Eve. As an emblem of wanton sexuality, feminized masculinity, and amazon unviolability, the *danseuse en travesti* symbolized in her complex persona the many shades of lust projected by the audience on the nineteenth-century dancer.

Unlike the older genre distinctions based on body type, movement, and style, romanticism's female tryptich aligned balletic image with a hierarchy of class and sexual practice. If Taglioni's "aerial, virginal grace" evoked romanticism's quest for the ideal it also summoned to the stage the marriageable *démoiselle*, chaste, demure, and genteel. So, too, Elssler's "swooning, voluptuous arms," like her satin, laces, and gems, linked the concept of materialism with a particular material reality—the enticing, high-priced pleasures of a *grande horizontale*.

The travesty dancer practised none of these symbolic feminine concealments. As shipboys and sailors, hussars and toreadors, the proletarians of the Opéra's *corps de ballet* donned breeches and skin-tight trousers that displayed to advantage the shapely legs, slim corseted waists, and rounded hips, thighs, and buttocks of the era's ideal figure. Like the prostitutes in fancy dress in Manet's "Ball at the Opera," the *danseuse en travesti* brazenly advertised her sexuality. She was the hussy of the boulevards on theatrical parade.

The masquerade of transvestism fooled no one, nor was it meant to. The *danseuse en travesti* was always a woman, and a highly desirable one (a splendid figure was one of the role's prerequisites). She may have aped the steps and motions of the male performer, but she never impersonated his nature. What audiences wanted was a masculine image deprived of maleness,

an idealized adolescent, a beardless she-man. Gautier, in particular, was repelled by the rugged physicality of the *danseur*, that "species of monstrosity," as he called him.[10] "Nothing," he wrote, "is more distasteful than a man who shows his red neck, his big muscular arms, his legs with the calves of a parish beadle, and all his strong massive frame shaken by leaps and *pirouettes*."[11]

His critical colleague, Jules Janin, shared Gautier's prejudices: even the greatest of *danseurs* paled against the delicate figure, shapely leg, and facial beauty of the travesty dancer. Janin, however, added another element to Gautier's list of characteristics unbecoming in a male dancer—power. No real man, that is, no upstanding member of the new bourgeois order, could impersonate the poetic idealism of the ballet hero without ungendering himself, without, in short, becoming a woman in male drag. Janin's remarks, published in the *Journal des Débats*, are worth quoting at length:

Speak to us of a pretty dancing girl who displays the grace of her figure, who reveals so fleetingly all the treasures of her beauty. Thank God, I understand that perfectly, I know what this lovely creature wishes us, and I would willingly follow her wherever she wishes in the sweet land of love. But a man, as ugly as you and I, a wretched fellow who leaps about without knowing why, a creature specially made to carry a musket and a sword and to wear a uniform. That this fellow should dance as a woman does—impossible! That this bewhiskered individual who is a pillar of the community, an elector, a municipal councillor, a man whose business it is to make and unmake laws, should come before us in a tunic of sky-blue satin, his head covered with a hat with a waving plume amorously caressing his cheek, a frightful *danseuse* of the male sex . . . this was surely impossible and intolerable, and we have done well to remove such . . . artists from our pleasures. Today, thanks to this revolution we have effected, woman is the queen of ballet . . . no longer forced to cut off half her silk petticoat to dress her partner in it. Today the dancing man is no longer tolerated except as a useful accessory.[12]

As the concept of masculinity aligned itself with productivity, the effeminate sterility of the *danseur* became unacceptable to ballet's large male public.

But in defining power as male, Janin implicitly defined powerlessness as female. In photographs of the *danseuse en travesti* posed with her female counterpart, the modern eye notes a curtailment of scale, a reduction not only in the height and girth of the masculine figure, but in the physical contrast of the imagined sexes. What is missing, above all, is the suggestion of dominance, that intimation of power that even the most self-effacing *danseur* communicates to his audience. In appropriating the male role, the travesty dancer stripped that role of power.

In eliminating the *danseur*, ballet turned out the remaining in-house obstacle to sexual license. With the decline of the clan, only his lust, that last bastion of power, stood between the *danseuse* and the scheme so artfully contrived by the entrepreneurs of ballet for the millionaire libertines of the audience. For what was the Opéra if not their private seraglio? Thanks to the travesty dancer, no male now could destroy the peace of their private harem or their enjoyment of performance as foreplay to possession.

In appearance, the feminine androgyne laid claim to another erotic nexus. Tall, imposing, and majestic, she added to the charm of wantonness the challenge of the amazon, that untamed Diana who so fascinated the nineteenth-century imagination. In Gautier's description of Eugénie Fiocre as Cupid in *Néméa*, note the sapphic allusions.

Certainly Love was never personified in a more graceful, or more charming body. Mlle. Fiocre has managed to compound the perfection both of the young girl and of the youth, and to make of them a sexless beauty, which is beauty itself. She might have been hewn from a block of Paros marble by a Greek sculptor, and animated by a miracle such as

that of Galatea. To the purity of marble, she adds the suppleness of life. Her movements are developed and balanced in a sovereign harmony. . . . What admirable legs! Diana the huntress would envy them! What an easy, proud and tranquil grace! What modest, measured gestures! . . . So correct, rhythmical and noble is her miming that, like that of the mimes of old, it might be accompanied by two unseen fluteplayers. If Psyche saw this Cupid she might forget the original.[13]

Fiocre, an exceptionally beautiful woman who created the role of Frantz in *Coppélia*, was one of the most famous travesty heroes of the 1860s and 1870s. Like a number of Opéra dancers, she shared the boards with a sister, whose shapely limbs commanded nearly as much admiration as her sibling's. By far, the most fascinating sister pair of the century were the Elsslers— Fanny, the romantic temptress with the body of a "hermaphrodite of antiquity,"[14] and Thérèse, her partner and faithful cavalier. For over ten years they danced together, lived together, and traveled together. On stage they communicated a veiled eroticism, while offstage their relationship suggested a feminized relic of the older clan system.

A giraffe of a dancer at five foot six inches, the "majestic" Thérèse served her diminutive sister in the multiple roles reserved in an older era for the ballerina's next of kin. She handled all of Fanny's business affairs, decided where and what she should dance, and staged, without credit, many of the ballets and numbers in which they appeared. As a woman, however, Thérèse lacked the clan's patriarchal authority, while as a dancer, she would always be without the wealth and power of the "protectors" who increasingly materialized behind the scenes— promoting favorites, dispensing funds as well as maintaining dancers and their impoverished families. Indeed, one such protector, the self-styled Marquis de La Valette, who became Fanny's lover in 1837, eventually destroyed the sororial ménage: his scorn for the ex-dancer who shared her bed forced Thérèse to leave.

One expects that the likes of the Marquis de La

Valette relished the sight of his Elssler girls charming confreres of the *loges infernales*. But one also suspects that the travesty *pas de deux* was not so completely un-sexed as the household he ruled. Certainly, it had been neutered by the substitution of a woman for the man, but that hardly means it was devoid of erotic content. Might not audiences have perceived in the choreographic play of female bodies, something other than two women competing to whet the jaded appetites of libertines? Consider Gautier's account of a duet performed by the two Elsslers:

> The *pas* executed by Mlle. T. Elssler and her sister is charmingly arranged; there is one figure in particular where the two sisters run from the back-cloth hand in hand, throwing forward their legs at the same time, which surpasses everything that can be imagined in the way of homogeneity, accuracy, and precision. One might almost be said to be the reflection of the other, and that each comes forward with a mirror held beside her, which follows her and repeats all her movements.
>
> Nothing is more soothing and more harmonious to the gaze than this dance at once so refined and so precise.
>
> Fanny, to whom Theresa has given as ever the more important part, displayed a child-like grace, an artless agility, and an adorable roguishness; her Creole costume made her look ravishing, or rather she made the costume look ravishing.[15]

Thérèse had choreographed *La Volière* ("The Aviary" in English), which like her other ballets and dances made no use of men: she cast herself in the masculine role. Yet despite the differences in their attire, what struck Gautier was the oneness of the pair: he saw them as refracted images of a single self, perfect and complete. In evoking an Arcadia of perpetual adolescence untroubled and untouched by man, the travesty duet hinted at an ideal attainable only in the realms of art and the imagination—not the real world of stockbrokers and municipal councillors.

But dancing by its very nature is a physical as much as symbolic activity. In the formalized mating game of the travesty *pas de deux*, two women touching and moving in harmony conveyed an eroticism perhaps even more compelling than their individual physical charms. The fantasy of females at play for the male eye is a staple of erotic literature, a kind of travesty performance enacted in the privacy of the imagination. Ballet's travesty *pas de deux* gave public form to this private fantasy, whetting audience desire, while keeping safely within the bounds of decorum. For ultimately, sapphic love interfered with the smooth functioning of the seraglio as much as the obstreperous male. In the case of the Elsslers, where Thérèse seems to have animated her choreography with something akin to personal feeling, the incest taboo coded as sisterly devotion what might otherwise have been construed as love. And one cannot help thinking that the buxom travesty heroes of the Second Empire and subsequent decades flaunted an outrageous femininity to ward off the sapphism immanent in their roles. In so doing, however, ballet robbed the *danseuse* of erotic mystery.

Today, thanks to the example of the Ballets Trocadero, we are apt to think that travesty in dance inherently offers a critique of sexual role playing. But the travesty dancers of nineteenth-century ballet offered no meditation on the usages of gender, no critical perspective on the sexual politics that ruled their lives, no revelation of the ways masculine and feminine were imaged on the ballet stage. What they exemplified was the triumph of bordello politics ideologized as the feminine mystique—a politics and an ideology imposed by men who remained in full control of ballet throughout the century as teachers, critics, choreographers, spectators, and artistic directors.

The advent in 1909 of Diaghilev's Ballets Russes with its dynamic new aesthetic shattered the travesty paradigm. Seeing real men on the stage in choreography that exploited the strength, athleticism, and scale of the male body simply electrified audiences, causing them to look anew at the travesty dancer. But the audience itself had changed dramatically. The new following for ballet came from the highly sophisticated milieu of *le tout Paris*. The great connoisseurs, collectors, musical patrons, and salonnières of the French capital—many of whom were women—replaced the sportsmen and roués of the *loges infernales*. At the same time a new androgynous thematic and iconography,

particularly evident in works created for Nijinsky where images of sexual heterodoxy transgressed rigid categories of masculinity and femininity, regendered the ideology of ballet, ending the reign of the feminine mystique. The era of the *danseuse en travesti* had come to an end.

Notes

1. For the dramatic changes in the organization of the Paris Opéra after the Revolution of 1830, see Ivor Guest, *The Romantic Ballet in Paris,* forewords by Ninette de Valois and Lillian Moore, 2d ed. rev. (London: Dance Books, 1980), 22–25. In England, nineteenth-century ballet appeared exclusively in a commercial setting. John Ebers, a former ticket agent, assumed the management of the King's Theatre in 1820, an association that ended in bankruptcy in 1827. He was succeeded in 1828 by Pierre Laporte, who, with the exception of the 1832 season, controlled the opera house until his death in 1841, whereupon Benjamin Lumley, in charge of finances since 1836, assumed the theater's management. In the hands of this solicitor/impresario, Her Majesty's (as the King's Theatre had been renamed) entered upon an era of glory. In the 1830s and 1840s, under the management of Alfred Bunn, the Theatre Royal, Drury Lane became another important venue for ballet. During the latter part of the nineteenth century up to the eve of World War I, ballet lived on in the music-halls, above all, the Empire and Alhambra. Ivor Guest, *The Romantic Ballet in England: Its Development, Fulfilment and Decline* (London: Phoenix House, 1954), 33, 46, 83–87, 128–131; *The Empire Ballet* (London: Society for Theatre Research, 1962); "The Alhambra Ballet," *Dance Perspectives* (autumn 1959).

In France, it should be noted, the commercial boulevard stage was the breeding ground for theatrical romanticism. Long before the Paris Opéra's *Robert le Diable,* usually considered the official point of departure for romantic ballet, spectacular techniques and supernatural effects were commonplace in the melodramas and vaudevilles of the popular theater. Ballet was an important component of these spectacles. Indeed, it was at theaters like the Théâtre de la Porte-Saint-Martin, which maintained a resident troupe and regularly presented new ballets and revivals, that the aerial style

of dancing associated with romanticism began to crystallize early in the 1820s. Among the talents associated with the flowering of romantic ballet at the Paris Opéra who gained early experience on the boulevard stage was Jean Coralli, who produced several ballets at the Théâtre de la Gaîté. Guest, *The Romantic Ballet in Paris*, 4–5, 13–14, 16, Appendix D, 272–274; Marian Hannah Winter, *The Pre-Romantic Ballet* (London: Pitman, 1974), 178–179, 193–197.

2. Some instances of gender swapping prior to the nineteenth century are Marie Sallé's appearance as Amour in Handel's *Alcina* (which Sallé choreographed herself) and the three graces impersonated by men in *Plathée*, Jean-Philippe Rameau's spoof of his own operatic style. The lover in disguise à la Shakespeare's *Twelfth Night* was a popular conceit that called for cross-dressing. I am grateful to Catherine Turocy for this information. For the response of the London audience to Sallé's performance, see Parmenia Migel, *The Ballerinas from the Court of Louis XIV to Pavlova* (1972; reprint, New York: Da Capo, 1980), 25.

3. *Le Constitutionnel,* quoted in Guest, *The Romantic Ballet in Paris*, 1.

4. *Les Petits Mystères de l'Opéra,* quoted in Guest, *The Romantic Ballet in Paris*, 25.

5. August Bournonville, *My Theatre Life,* trans. Patricia N. McAndrew (Middletown, Conn.: Wesleyan University Press, 1979), 52.

6. Fanny Cerrito's liaison with the Marqués de Bedmar, Carlotta Grisi's with Prince Radziwill, Fanny Elssler's with the Marquis de La Valette, Pauline Duvernay's with (among others) Valette and Lyne Stephens, and Elisa Scheffer's with the Earl of Pembroke are a few of the romances that dot the ballet chronicle of the 1830s, 1840s, and 1850s.

7. For the changes introduced by Dr. Louis Véron at the Paris Opéra after the Revolution of 1830, see Guest, *The Ro-*

mantic Ballet in Paris, 28. Under Ebers, the Green Room built at the King's Theatre performed a similar function as the Foyer de la Danse, while at Drury Lane, Bunn allowed the more influential patrons the run of the *coulisses*. Procuresses "of the worst type" circulated backstage at Drury Lane, among them the blackmailing beauty specialist known as Madame Rachel. Guest, *The Romantic Ballet in England*, 36–37, 113.

8. Migel, *The Ballerinas*, 218. Married in 1845 (to the chagrin of Cerrito's parents, who had hoped for a son-in-law with a fortune or at least a title), the couple broke up in 1851. Shortly thereafter, her liaison with the Marqués de Bedar became public knowledge. When rumors began to circulate in 1844 about Cerrito's impending marriage to Saint-Léon, the ballerina's London admirers, headed by Lord MacDonald, created a public disturbance when Saint-Léon appeared onstage. During one performance, the dancer stopped before their box and with a "sarcastic grin" and an "indescribable gesture" hissed menacingly at Lord Mac-Donald. The word *cochon* was heard to leave Saint-Léon's mouth, a gross impertinence coming from a dancer. Saint-Léon's written apology appeared in the *Times* a few days later. Ivor Guest, *Fanny Cerrito: The Life of a Romantic Ballerina*, 2d ed. rev. (London: Dance Books, 1974), 85.

9. "Fanny Elssler in 'La Tempete,'" in *The Romantic Ballet as Seen by Theophile Gautier*, trans. Cyril W. Beaumont (London, 1932; reprint, New York: Arno Press, 1980), 16.

10. "Perrot and Carlotta Grisi in 'Le Zingaro,'" in ibid., 44.

11. "The Elsslers in 'La Volière,'" in ibid., 24.

12. March 2, 1840, quoted in Guest, *Romantic Ballet*, 21.

13. Quoted in Ivor Guest, *The Ballet of the Second Empire* (Middletown, Conn.: Wesleyan University Press, 1974), 200.

14. "Fanny Elssler," in *The Romantic Ballet as Seen by Theophile Gautier*, 22.

15. "The Elsslers in 'La Volière,'" 24.

Interrupted Continuities: Modern Dance in Germany

SUSAN ALLENE MANNING AND MELISSA BENSON

Editor's Note: This photo essay was originally an exhibition displayed in the Brooklyn Academy of Music lobby lounge from 1 October to 8 December 1985 as part of the Next Wave Festival humanities program. Dance historian Susan Manning curated the exhibition with the technical assistance of Melissa Benson.

The roots of today's modern dance first appeared in Germany and America. In the decade preceding World War I, American and German dancers independently evolved new dance forms that opposed the tradition of narrative and spectacular ballet. Yet the new forms probably would not have developed if the two traditions had not come into contact. When American dancers Isadora Duncan and Ruth St. Denis appeared in Germany after 1900 they became immediate sensations and catalysts for German dancers. In the twenties, the movement known as *Ausdruckstanz* (literally "dance of expression") came to dominate the German concert stage and opera house.

Under the Third Reich, ausdruckstanz lost its artistic vigor, and the direction of influence reversed. Many German dancers emigrated to America in the thirties and contributed to the establishment of American modern dance. After World War II ausdruckstanz nearly disappeared in divided Germany, while American modern dance achieved a worldwide reputation.

Beginning in the late sixties, modern dance reappeared in Germany as *Tanztheater* (literally "dance theater"). Taking ausdruckstanz as precedent, the choreographers of tanztheater elevate expression over form and view dance as a mode of social engagement. Their aesthetic opposes the formalism of both classical ballet and postmodern dance. Last season's appearances by Pina Bausch, Reinhild Hoffmann, and Susanne Linke at the Brooklyn Academy of Music continued the encounter between German and American modern dance.

The Solo Form: New Roles for the Sexes

The dancer of the future . . . will dance not in the form of nymph, nor fairy, nor coquette, but in the form of woman in her greatest and purest expression. She will realize the mission of woman's body and the holiness of all its parts. . . . She will dance the freedom of woman.
—Isadora Duncan, *Der Tanz der Zukunft* ("The Dance of the Future"), 1903

The new dance that appeared at the turn of the century involved a new sociology of the dance scene. While the narrative and spectacular ballet of the nineteenth century required large, expensive companies and authoritarian company managers, the new form required little more than a dancer, an accompanist, and an empty stage. In the nineteenth century the dancer was rarely presented alone but rather served as the focal point of spectacle. The dancer was almost always female, who had come to embody the Victorian conception of woman: either an ethereal ballerina—woman as angel—or an overstuffed chorus girl—woman as whore. She did not choreograph her own movement; rather, she executed the steps arranged for her by the ballet master, who was, without exception, a man.

In the twentieth century dancers rejected this institutional setup. The male dancer made a comeback. Whether male or female, dancers turned toward solo forms. The dancer became at once choreographer, performer, and manager; dance became an intensely personal expression of the self. The new dance freed men and women to experiment with the wider range of sexual roles then possible after the demise of Victorianism. Female soloists such as Isadora Duncan and the Wiesenthal sisters appeared as images of the new woman—independent of a male partner and free to create her own identity. Male soloists such as Alexander Sacharoff appeared in a variety of androgynous roles, no longer limited to the role of partner to the ballerina.

Physical Culture and the Avant-Garde

I want to raise rhythm to the status of a social institution, and prepare the way for a new style . . . that may become the basis for a new society.
> —Emile Jaques-Dalcroze, letter to philanthropist Wolf Dohrn, 1909

The new dance paralleled the popular physical culture movement. Women especially took to exercise as a means to physical and psychological health. Many dancers opened schools geared toward laymen that emphasized the artistic potential of physical culture.

The institute founded by Emile Jaques-Dalcroze at Hellerau in 1910 mingled the influences of physical culture and art. Dalcroze, a musician by training and an educator by inclination, set out to develop a method of teaching musical concepts through movement. His method, today called eurhythmics, drew on the principles of physical culture. He also devised a new performance form based on a closer integration of movement and music. To demonstrate his ideas he collaborated with Adolphe Appia to stage Gluck's *Orpheus* in 1912 and

1913. The demonstrations struck a responsive chord among visual and theatrical artists, who heralded *Orpheus* as the sign of a new union of the arts. At Hellerau ideas drawn from popular culture and the avant-garde intersected and pointed the way toward ausdruckstanz.

Ausdruckstanz in the Weimar Republic: Rudolph Laban and Mary Wigman

The dancer in a movement choir discovers an awakened sense of movement in his inner being by representing himself not as an individual but as part of a greater living group.
> —Rudolf Laban, "Vom Sinne der Bewegungschöre" ("On the Meaning of Movement Choirs"), *Schriftranz*, June 1930

My group does not dance feelings. Feelings are far too precise, too distinct. We dance the change and transformation of spiritual states as variously manifested in each individual.
> —Mary Wigman, "Tanzerische Wege und Ziele" ("The Ways and Goals of the Dancer"), *Neue Rundschau*, November 1923

Rudolf Laban opened a school in Munich in the same year that Dalcroze founded Hellerau. A prolific writer, Laban gave theoretical definition to ausdruckstanz. He believed that modern industrial society divided man against himself and that dance could restore man's original harmony with the cosmos, hence restoring the natural bonds of community. To facilitate this process he innovated a form suitable for large groups of amateurs, the "movement choir." He saw the movement choir as a means of promoting a sense of community among members of a fragmented society.

Laban also established the formal basis for ausdruckstanz with his concept of "free dance." This concept emphasized the spatial dimension of movement and was performed without music or to a simple rhythmic accompaniment. Laban's formulation was shaped by his work with dancers at the Monte Verita

18a and b. The *Visions* cycle (1925–28) marked the high point of Mary Wigman's solo choreography. Pictured are (a) *Dream Figure* (1927) and (b) *Space Shape* (1928). Her costumes became masks as the persona of a transformed self eclipsed her everyday self. Her solos were neither autobiographical nor overtly feminine, as were Isadora Duncan's; rather, she projected an image of gender that escaped and confounded the conventional distinctions between masculinity and femininity. Photos by Charlotte Rudolph, © 2000 Artists Rights Society (ARS), New York / VG Bild-Kunst, Bonn.

artists' colony in the Swiss Alps. An exceptional group of dancers gathered there, including Mary Wigman. She was a former student of Dalcroze who became Laban's closest collaborator during World War I.

After the war Wigman toured Germany and gained an immediate following. Her dances embodied the spirit of expressionism, its pervasive angst, and escape into ecstasy. For Wigman, the soloist's projection of the spontaneous self no longer sufficed. She required a form that transcended the individual, a requirement fulfilled by her use of masks, and by her all-female group. Her dances revolved around the relationship of the leader and the group.

Laban's ideology and Wigman's example dominated German dance in the twenties. Laban founded more than twenty-five schools across Germany while Wigman established a Central Institute in Dresden and several branch schools. As a term, ausdruckstanz signified the styles and forms of dance propagated by their many students and followers. Their followers, fiercely partisan, debated the merits of one approach over the other. Laban advocated egalitarianism and the desire to make dance accessible and integral to everyday life. Wigman espoused elitism and the belief that only a chosen few could communicate the spirit of the time through dance. Their aesthetics defined the end points of the ausdruckstanz continuum.

Alternate Visions: Valeska Gert, Oskar Schlemmer, Jean Weidt, and Kurt Jooss

Because the average German has no self-confidence, he considers great art only that which he does not understand and which bores him. Mary Wigman fulfills these expectations of the educated middle class and therefore has acquired a national reputation.
—Valeska Gert, "Mary Wigman and Valeska Gert," *Der Querschnitt*, May 1926

The dance entitled The Worker involved hard work. I was myself a worker, a gardener who plied his trade

eight to ten hours a day, and my limbs sensed the fatigue. But I did not want to represent the worker as he toiled, rather the worker as he made life more beautiful.
—Jean Weidt, *Der Rote Tänzer*, 1968

Only a few dancers stood apart from the dominant aesthetics of Wigman and Laban. One was Valeska Gert, a Berlin cabaret dancer who also appeared in films and on the stage. Gert knew Bertolt Brecht, and her theory of the social function of dance in many ways paralleled his theory of theater. Once she asked Brecht to define epic theater. He replied, "What you do."

Gert employed stereotyped roles and forms drawn from popular entertainment—*Tango, Charleston, Variety, Circus, Sport, Clown.* Her deadpan expression distanced her self from her performance; in this way she mocked and commented on the forms she used. Gert called the dancer a transition between the old theater and the new and believed that new forms could arise only from the breakdown of old forms. She considered the movement choir a false path toward the theater of the future because it posited a sense of community where none existed.

Oskar Schlemmer presented another alternative. He organized a stage workshop at the Bauhaus in which students experimented with a new form of abstract theater. Like Gert, Schlemmer parodied pre-existing dance forms, but his satire was mixed with an exploration of form for its own sake. He masked his dancers in body-distorting costumes as a way of exploring the body's spatial configurations. In Schlemmer's works the dancer functioned like a puppet or puppeteer; the performer's expressive self disappeared.

Dancers by and large remained aloof from national political issues, for their conception of dance's social function derived from the utopian humanism of Dalcroze and Laban. As political factionalism intensified during the closing years of the Weimar Republic, however, a few dancers finally felt compelled to take sides.

Jean Weidt dedicated his career to furthering the proletarian cause through dance. First in Hamburg and

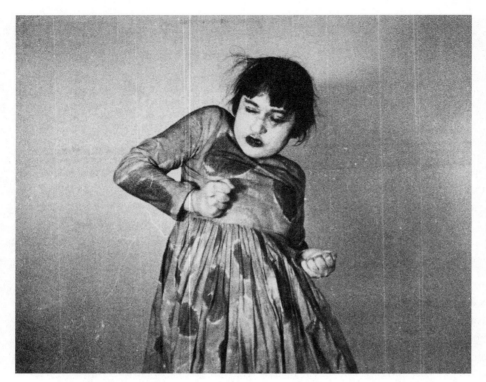

19. Like Mary Wigman, Valeska Gert confounded the conventional image of femininity projected by Isadora Duncan and other female soloists, but she did so in the spirit of satire and parody rather than as a means for transcending everyday reality. Photo courtesy of the Dance Division, The New York Public Library at Lincoln Center, Astor, Lenox and Tilden Foundations.

later in Berlin, he organized dance troupes of young workers that performed both on the concert stage and at Communist Party rallies. Known as the Red Dancer, Weidt went into exile when Hitler came to power.

Kurt Jooss was another dancer who took sides, although he never explicitly supported any one party. Originally a student of Laban, Jooss employed sharply-observed social caricature in his works beginning in the mid-twenties. Not until the early thirties did he create an explicitly political work: *The Green Table* was an anti-war ballet. Like Weidt, Jooss went into exile once Hitler rose to power.

1930 Dancers Congress

The chief opposing camps are headed, respectively, by Mary Wigman and Rudolf Laban, but there are innumerable lesser divisions and alliances. In fact, there is apparently a great game of politics being played which is at least as absorbing as the business of making and performing dances.
—John Martin, "A Futile Congress," *New York Times*, 20 July 1930

Dancers began to organize themselves in the late twenties. The 1930 Third Dancers Congress drew fourteen hundred participants, including dance critic John Martin. The Congress marked the high point of the German modern dance movement as well as its demise, for strident debate threatened the unity the Congress intended to create. At issue were the relations between professional and lay dance, the role of dance within the theater and opera house, and the social function of the dancer.

In collaboration with poet Albert Talhoff, Wigman staged *Totenmal* at the Congress. Wigman and Talhoff intended the work, a memorial to the fallen of World War I, to point the way toward a new form of dance

20. *The Green Table* (1932) is a dance of death led by a martial figure personifying war. The masked diplomats who frame the scenes are exempted from death, suggesting their culpability in the perpetuation of war. Photo courtesy of the Dance Division, The New York Public Library for the Performing Arts, Astor, Lenox and Tilden Foundations.

theater above politics. In the end, however, the work became mired in political ambiguity. As one critic said, it "affected both sides, both pro-war and anti-war."

Nationalist and socialist factions polarized the Weimar Republic. The ambivalence of Germans caught in the middle rendered them politically ineffectual. The Dancers Congress mirrored the factionalism of Weimar politics and *Totenmal* its ambiguity.

The Third Reich

State certification is required for all dancers. . . . Candidates of Aryan origin are eligible to take the state examination upon reaching age 18. In addition to possessing a middle school certificate, they must present a certificate of good health signed by a state doctor, a certificate of good conduct issued by the police, a written biographical statement, and proof of at least one year's study at a dance school certified for the Ministry for Popular Enlightenment and Propaganda.

—Ministry for Popular Enlightenment and Propaganda directive, No. 26, 29 July 1934

In the Third Reich dance came under the authority of Josef Goebbels' Ministry of Culture, which issued a stream of directives setting standards for prospective dancers, including proof of Aryan origin. The Ministry sponsored large-scale dance festivals in Berlin in 1934, 1935, and 1936. In addition, the Ministry established a Central Institute for Dance in Berlin, which dictated a

21a and b. (a) Aerial shot of the Olympic stadium, Berlin, and (b) view of dancers on the field. *Olympic Youth* (1936) worked on two levels. On one level, the spectacles glorified athletics and youth by presenting the familiar motifs of the Olympic Games—the interlocking circles, the flags, the torch's flame. But on another level, the spectacle glorified the offstage presence of Hitler, who became the focal point for the discipline and devotion exhibited by the unison ranks of dancers. Photos from *The XIth Olympic Games in Berlin 1936: Official Report*, Rare Book and Manuscript Library, Columbia University.

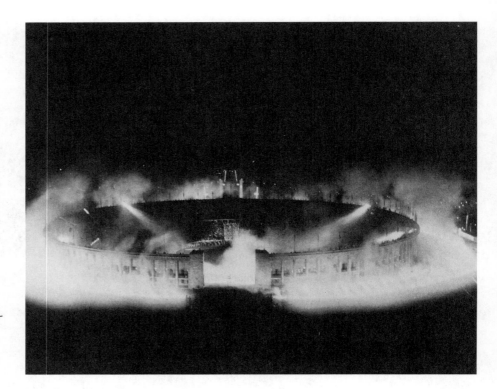

standardized curriculum of ballet, folk dance, and "German Dance," as ausdruckstanz was now called. Never before had dance received such recognition or subsidy on the national level. While the National Socialists branded modernist movements in the other arts as degenerate, they appropriated ausdruckstanz with the dancers' passive support.

The Nazis staged immense spectacles by enlarging the scale of the movement choir, as in *Olympic Youth*, the opening night presentation of the 1936 Berlin Olympic Games. Wigman, Harald Kreutzberg, Gret Palucca, and other modern dancers participated along with thousands of Berlin schoolchildren, who executed precision patterns on the field of the Olympic stadium. Moving in unison ranks, the boys and girls glorified the presence of the Führer, who reviewed them from the stands. The movement choir had become the basis for mass propaganda.

The Survival of Ausdruckstanz and the Emergence of Tanztheater: Pina Bausch, Reinhild Hoffmann, and Susanne Linke

The question I ask myself is how this "nation of poets and thinkers" could have started two world wars. These are the problems I am constantly exploring on the stage and in the work with my dancers.
    —Johann Kresnik, "Politician of Dance Theatre," *Ballett International*, May 1985

I am not so much interested in how people move as in what moves them.
    —Pina Bausch, quoted in *Pina Bausch Wuppertal Dance Theater, or the Art of Training a Goldfish*

Its association with National Socialism drained ausdruckstanz of artistic vigor. Hence it is not surprising that ballet came to dominate both East and West Germany after World War II. Ironically enough, it was the Nazi promotion of ballet as light entertainment that made the ballet boom possible.

As West Germany turned toward reviving the classics and rebuilding the network of municipal repertory theaters, modern dancers received less and less recognition. Without fanfare Wigman opened a studio in West Berlin, and Jooss resumed his teaching position at the Folkwang School in Essen. For the few young dancers desiring an alternative to ballet, the Folkwang School provided the only opportunity for formalized training. One of the few was tanztheater choreographer Pina Bausch, who entered the Folkwang School in 1955 at age fifteen.

Ausdruckstanz fared somewhat better in East Germany than in West Germany, for dance pedagogy integrated modern dance techniques with Soviet methods for ballet training. Weidt returned from exile to East Berlin and worked to establish an amateur dance movement. Palucca, originally a student of Wigman, reopened her school in Dresden under government sponsorship and trained a generation of choreographers.

Stirred by the student movement of the sixties, young dancers in West Germany became dissatisfied with the orthodoxies of ballet technique and the hierarchies of ballet companies. Fusing techniques drawn from experimental theater and American modern dance with ballet, they called their work tanztheater to differentiate it from *opernballett*.

Johann Kresnik, a dancer with the Cologne Opera Ballet, was one of the first to assert choreographic rebellion by creating dances as political agit-prop. His career represents one extreme of the sociology of the current dance scene: as director of the Bremen Ballet until 1980 and of the Heidelberg Ballet today, he works within the system of well-subsidized municipal ballet companies established during the fifties. Yet the fundamental premises of his work agitate against the world view of the traditional ballet audience. In his tanztheater, the subversion of the system becomes content and form.

Another early tanztheater choreographer was Gerhard Bohner, a ballet dancer who had also studied with Wigman. In contrast to Kresnik, his career reflects the other extreme of the current scene, the situation of the "free dancers" who find their vision unrealizable within

22. Pina Bausch's *He Takes Her by the Hand and Leads Her into the Castle, the Others Follow* (1978). Like Kresnik, Bausch interweaves the political and the psychological. The spectator never knows if the images are intended as psychological projection or exaggerated realism. Photo by Gert Weigelt.

the municipal repertory system. Bohner's agitation for reform with the Berlin Ballet in the sixties led to his dismissal. Since then he has worked as a freelance choreographer. Because West Germany provides almost no patronage for dancers outside the repertory system, Bohner is one of the few dancers who manage to survive on their own.

Like Kresnik, Pina Bausch directs one of the few municipal repertory companies receptive to tanztheater. Her Wuppertal Dance Theater is unique among German troupes in that it performs twice as much abroad as at home. Hence it is not limited by the demands of a local repertory theater audience, and in this way recalls the touring soloists and companies of the ausdruckstanz era.

In contrast to the "poor theater" of ausdruckstanz, Bausch's dances employ a visually rich production style. And yet, like dance in the twenties, her work elevates expression over form. Her association with the Folkwang School directly connects her to the tradition of ausdruckstanz, and her work continues Jooss's vision of a socially critical dance theater. Whereas Jooss focused on the public issue of the corruption of power, Bausch turns to the more private issue of relations between men and women. However, she does not ignore the sociological dimension of the psychology of gender. Indeed, the feminist subtexts of her works call attention to the politics of the personal.

Reinhild Hoffmann and Susanne Linke share Bausch's concern with feminist issues and the female perspective. Significantly, they too have worked at the Folkwang School. Their work also exhibits similarities to the ausdruckstanz tradition: the revival of the solo form, the use of the costume as mask, and the emphasis on expressive abstraction.

Dance is the only West German art today in which female artists play a leading role. Why this is so remains a provocative question.

World Dance Traditions: Further Readings

Asante, Kariamu Welsh, ed. *African Dance: An Artistic, Historical, and Philosophical Inquiry.* Trenton: Africa World Press, 1996.

———. *Mfundalai: A Dance Technique.* Buffalo, N.Y.: School of Movement, 1980.

Asante, Molefi Kete, and Kariamu Welsh Asante. *African Culture: The Rhythms of Unity.* Westport, Conn.: Greenwood Press, 1985.

Balasaraswati. "Bala on Bharata Natyam." *Sruti* (March 1984).

Bandem, I. Made, and Fredrik Eugene deBoer. *Kaja and Kelod: Balinese Dance in Transition.* 2d ed. New York: Oxford University Press, 1995.

Bennahum, Ninotchka. *Antonia Mercé la Argentina: Flamenco and the Spanish Avant-Garde.* Hanover, N.H.: Wesleyan University Press, 2000.

Black Elk. *The Sacred Pipe: Black Elk's Account of the Seven Rites of the Oglala Sioux.* Ed. Joseph Epes Brown. Norman: University of Oklahoma Press, 1953.

Bowers, Faubion. *Theatre in the East: A Survey of Asian Dance and Drama.* New York: Grove Press, 1956.

Browning, Barbara. *Samba: Resistance in Motion.* Bloomington: Indiana University Press, 1995.

Buonaventura, Wendy. *Belly Dancing: The Serpent and the Sphinx.* London: Virago Press, 1983.

Dunham, Katherine. *Dances of Haiti.* Los Angeles: University of California Press, 1983.

———. *Island Possessed.* Chicago: Doubleday, 1969.

Foster, Susan. *Choreography and Narrative: Ballet's Staging of Story and Desire.* Bloomington: Indiana University Press, 1996.

Franko, Mark. *Dance as Text: Ideologies of the Baroque Body.* New York: Cambridge University Press, 1993.

Friedlander, Shems. *The Whirling Dervishes.* Albany: State University of New York Press, 1992.

Friedler, Sharon, and Susan Glazer. *Dancing Female: Lives and Issues of Women in Contemporary Dance.* Amsterdam: Harwood Academic Publishers, 1997.

Garafola, Lynn. *Diaghilev's Ballets Russes.* New York: Oxford University Press, 1989.

———, ed. *Rethinking the Sylph: New Perspectives on the Romantic Ballet.* Hanover, N.H.: Wesleyan University Press, 1997.

Gaston, Anne-Marie. *Siva in Dance, Myth and Iconography.* Bombay: Delhi University Press, 1982.

Heth, Charlotte, ed. *Native American Dance: Ceremonies and Social Traditions.* Washington, D.C.: Smithsonian Institution, 1992.

Holborn, Mark. *Butoh: Dance of the Dark Soul.* New York: Aperture, 1987.

Huet, Michael. *The Dances of Africa.* New York: Harry N. Abrams, 1996.

Jonas, Gerald. *Dancing.* New York: Harry N. Abrams, 1992.

Kliger, George, ed. *Bharata Natyam in Cultural Perspective.* New Delhi: Manohar American Institute of Indian Studies, 1993.

Laubin, Gladys, and Reginald Laubin. *Indian Dances of North America: Their Importance to Indian Life.* Norman: University of Oklahoma Press, 1977.

Lewis, John Lowell. *Ring of Liberation: Deceptive Discourse in Brazilian Capoeira.* Chicago: University of Chicago Press, 1992.

Manning, Susan. *Ecstasy and the Demon: Feminism and Nationalism in the Dances of Mary Wigman.* Berkeley: University of California Press, 1993.

Mukherjee, Bimal, and Sunil Kothari, eds. *Rasa: The Indian*

Performing Arts in the Last Twenty-Five Years. Calcutta: Anamika Kala Sangam Research and Publications, 1995.

Nettleford, Rex. *Dance Jamaica: Cultural Definition and Artistic Discovery.* New York: Grove Press, 1985.

Preston-Dunlop, Valerie, and Susanne Lahusen. *Schriftanz: A View of German Dance in the Weimar Republic.* London: Dance Books, 1990.

Ramnarayan, Gowri. "Bala, My Guru," *Sruti* (March 1983).

———. "Rukmini Devi: Restoration and Creation." *Sruti* (August 1984).

Savigliano, Marta. *Tango and the Political Economy of Passion.* Boulder, Colo.: Westview Press, 1995.

Taylor, Julie. *Paper Tangos.* Durham, N.C.: Duke University Press, 1998.

Thompson, Robert F. *African Art in Motion.* Los Angeles: University of California Press, 1974.

Van Nieuwkerk, Karin. *A Trade Like Any Other: Female Singers and Dancers in Egypt.* Austin: University of Texas Press, 1995.

Vatsyayan, Kapila. *Indian Classical Dance in Literature and the Arts.* New Delhi: Ministry of Information and Broadcasting, 1968.

———. *Indian Classical Dance.* New Delhi: Ministry of Information and Broadcasting, 1974.

Zeami. *On the Art of the No Drama.* Trans. J. Thomas Rimer and Yamazki Masakazu. Princeton, N.J.: Princeton University Press, 1984.

PART THREE

America Dancing

Historical Moments: Rethinking the Past

Virginia Tanner's Children's Dance Theatre performed at the Jacob's Pillow Dance Festival in July 1953, dancing on an outdoor stage against a backdrop of moonlight, fireflies, and the Berkshire Mountains. The children, girls from eight to eighteen, improvised about rhythms and water rushing over Niagara Falls and danced to carols and poems about animals and babies. They danced, according to critic Walter Terry, with a "vital innocence," performing children's versions of the runs, leaps, and spiraling turns Tanner learned from Doris Humphrey. Terry closed his review with these remarks:

> Other children have danced such themes and there are other children . . . who have performed with . . . far more precociousness of a technical nature but none, I think, have conveyed so perfectly the bright (not pallid) purity of child-dance. It is difficult to describe even the most potent intangibles and the best I can do is to say that the children danced as if they had faith in themselves, had love for those of us who were seeing them, actively believed in their God and rejoiced in all of these.[1]

This performance of Virginia Tanner's Children's Dance Theatre is the kind of moment that historians hope to find, a moment that is rich with imagery and suggested complexity. The natural beauty of this scene and the innocence of children giving themselves passionately to dancing make this an appealing moment in American dance. It is also a moment when the cultural importance of dance becomes clear, even in a place where the artistic nature of dance is celebrated. Such moments become nuclei around which to weave stories of dance as art, culture, history, and personal testimony.

Jacob's Pillow is one of America's biggest summer dance festivals. This performance was held during the 1950s heyday of modern dance and in the presence of important modern dance personages. Doris Humphrey, José Limón, and Ted Shawn all attended. Yet at this performance, the nature of modern dance as individual artistic expression shifts over to reveal its cultural underpinnings. We see a modern dance that is not just individually expressive, but expressive of community values and religious belief. (Tanner's company was based in Salt Lake City, Utah, and Tanner and many of the children were members of the Church of Jesus Christ of the Latter-day Saints.) We are reminded that modern dance was nationally important as part of American physical culture, in colleges and universities and at summer dance schools and festivals. These include Jacob's Pillow where this performance occurred, the programs at Bennington and Connecticut colleges and the Perry-Mansfield Camp in Steamboat Springs, Colorado, where Tanner first trained with Humphrey.

We see modern dance used, as Isadora Duncan hoped to use her expressive dancing, to train children. Within Tanner's company and school, learning to dance was learning to be a supportive, creative part of a group. Dancing was affirmed by a Mormon belief that people should give of themselves creatively, sharing that which is "virtuous, lovely, or of good report or praiseworthy."[2] But dancing also offered a different vision of the world, and a larger sense of personal possibility than that offered by many Mormon households in the 1950s, where women were encouraged not to venture into any public sphere but to make their contributions as wives and mothers.

"America Dancing" is a collection of articles that form a rough chronology of dance in the United States from mid-nineteenth through mid-twentieth centuries. Throughout this section we are consciously trying to interweave the story of American concert dance, a tradition that informs most university dance programs and is familiar to students through choreography classes and traditional dance history classes, with the stories of other American dance forms. We've chosen articles that simultaneously construct a critical awareness of the issues of racism and elitism imbedded in much early American concert dance and refigure and reframe that tradition, hoping that its vital energy will continue to inspire and inform dancers.

Taken as a whole the articles provide a sense of the scope of American dance heritage and the potential of studying American dance as a distinct phenomenon, as opposed to studying American dance as the continuation of practices begun elsewhere. In reading across the articles, several ideas about American dance become clear.

First, underscored again and again is the breadth of activity that might be examined as American art forms or as capturing American character. This sweet picture of girls dancing in the summer air, for example, replicates a familiar American dance image. The innocent young (white) girl enjoying the outdoors was a popular dance image throughout the twentieth century, repeated in relationship to Delsarte practice and in images of Isadora Duncan and the Isadorables. A *Life* magazine spread done in the 1950s about Virginia Tanner's Children's Dance Theatre was full of these images, especially the cover image of two blond "Mormon angels" dancing and inspecting shells on a beach. Richard Paul

Evans's *The Dance*, a currently popular children's book, is graced with an image of a blond girl skipping in a garden.[3] (And this book was recently done in dance form by the still-existing Children's Dance Theatre.)

But there are many equally American dance images. Consider these excerpts from the readings, included here to jar any habit of thought that centralizes particular dance practices:

- an image of a Hopi snake dancer who "smooths the rattlesnake and carries him in his mouth, to send him back into the dark places of the earth, an emissary to the inner powers."
- an image of Snake Hips Tucker in a "sequined girdle supporting a seductive tassel," dancing a move "known among dancers as the Belly Roll . . . a series of waves rolling from pelvis to chest—a standard part of a Shake dancer's routine, which Tucker varied by coming to a stop, transfixing the audience with a baleful, hypnotic stare, and twirling his long tassel in time with the music."
- the image of Lincoln Kirstein, persuading a friend to help fund the future of American ballet by bringing George Balanchine to America: "We have a real chance to have an American ballet within 3 yrs. time. When I say ballet, I mean a trained company of young dancers—not Russians—but Americans. . . . We have the future in our hands. For Christ's sweet sake let us honor it."
- the image of Trisha Brown helping a classmate complete a three-minute dance, an assignment from Robert and Judith Dunn's choreography class. Brown remembers that "Dick Levine taught himself to cry and did so for the full time period while I held a stopwatch instructed by him to shout just before the time elapsed, 'Stop it! Stop it! Cut it out!' both of us ending at exactly three minutes."

If there's anything that captures the nature of Americans dancing, it is a quality of negotiating between various influences and needs, between tradition and change, heritage and class mobility, regional interest and the influence of mass culture.

Second, we need more studies about dance as an agent of cultural convergence, assimilation, or resistance in American culture. This strategy is provocatively employed by several authors included here. Sharyn Udall in "The Irresistible Other: Hopi Ritual Drama and Euro-American Audiences," uses analysis of images and written documents to discuss the history of Euro-American spectatorship for the Hopi Snake Dance. She allows her readers a glimpse of the dance at several points in history and discusses the impact of various kinds of people—government officials, tourists, visual artists, and filmmakers—on the ritual and on public perception of the Hopi. Udall investigates the costs and benefits of Euro-Americans making art about a Hopi ritual. Artists might be seen as misrepresenting the Hopi or as indulging in cultural banditry, but their work also prompts discussion about commonalities in art and experience across cultures.

Marian Hannah Winter, in "Juba and American Minstrelsy," discusses the development of dances by African slaves in the American South, then the importance of professional entertainers such as William Henry Lane to American minstrelsy. A complicated tradition, minstrelsy included both black performers and white performers performing in blackface and involved the use of stereotypes (African American men were either slick dandies or inarticulate fools) as humor. The dances of minstrelsy, however, provided a vehicle for some African American performers to achieve international recognition.

Brenda Dixon Gottschild, in "Stripping the Emperor: The Africanist Presence in American Concert Dance," discusses the use of Africanisms—angular arms and hands, an articulate pelvis, percussive attack—in jazz performers of the 1920s such as Snake Hips Tucker and in the work of ballet choreographer George Balanchine. She presents written evidence of Balanchine's interest in African movement and jazz and her own descriptions of African elements in Balanchine dances, leaving her readers with a vision of what might have happened in American ballet had the prohibitions of racist America not limited his choreographic vision.

Gottschild's article is especially interesting to read along with Nancy Reynolds's "In His Image: Diaghilev and Lincoln Kirstein." Reynolds emphasizes Kirstein's fascination with Serge Diaghilev's vision of ballet as a synthesis of the arts, his early creative role in the productions of Ballet Caravan and Ballet Society, and his prolific writings. Kirstein's reinvention of the Diaghilevian model—lush works that brought together painters, musicians, and choreographers—was abandoned as Balanchine's sparser style won public favor. Both Gottschild and Reynolds discuss Balanchine's work *Agon*, Gottschild for its jazzlike qualities, and Reynolds as Balanchine's most radical work, "stripped, reductive, and musically uncompromising." If, as Reynolds states, *Agon* was well received by both critics and the general public, which quality was responsible for its success?

Julie Malnig, in "Two-Stepping to Glory: Social Dance and the Rhetoric of Social Mobility," explores the "modern" ballroom dances of the Progressive Era. These dances supported and enabled the transformation of workers flocking into American cities from other countries and from rural America into modern, urban Americans. Social dancers were taught in environments that were open to many people, yet safely overseen by society ladies. The dance environment supported by successful exhibition ballroom teams such as Vernon and Irene Castle and by images in mass-marketed magazines and newspapers, helped newcomers learn social niceties and to mold themselves, through new clothing and postures, into appropriate men and women.

These writings and others in this section suggest an extended study of the convergences of various cultures on American soil as a way to think about American dance. We don't know, for example, why Native Americans and African Americans were exoticized in such different ways. How might this be connected to the influences each group has had on American life, and how did this relate to the assimilation or resistance of each group to mainstream culture? We also know too little about European vernacular dance in America. In the late twentieth century, people took up traditional social dancing as a way to affirm and reclaim heritages (or adopt new identities) that seemed more satisfying than American popular culture. But what happened to these forms when people immigrated to America? We know little about how various dance forms either helped settlers maintain their identities or, moving with members of their communities from other parts of the world, create our regional dance forms. How exactly did Zydeco dancing, Appalachian clogging, and Western square dancing come to be? Dance may be the ultimate mover of American cultural history, as we engender social and political change in our taking on of dance moves and bodily attitudes.

Third, when we study dance as culture, we're constantly forging new conceptual territory. One of the reasons so many writers begin with an event, a moment that is then explicated through writing, is that there is no other focal point that holds this material together. Thinking about the functions of dance, about dance as a socializing agent or religious or theatrical expression, is helpful until it blinds us to seeing that dance can be simultaneously social and theatrical. Thinking about dance as a cultural tradition is useful until it keeps us from seeing the convergences and influences between forms. Looking from the traditions of American history is just as blinding if we try to see dancing as only a reflection of events or attitudes such as American cultural imperialism or racism. Nor can we fully explain a dance by excavating only its connections to cultural forces such as attitudes about race, ethnicity, class, gender, sexuality, or religious belief. As the articles in this section illustrate, dance sits in between these things.

Jane Desmond, in "Dancing Out the Difference: Cultural Imperialism and Ruth St. Denis's *Radha* of 1906," is particularly careful and explicit about mixing an investigation of artistic practice with readings of cultural meaning and critique. She starts by describing *Radha*, then enriches this with discussions of St. Denis's background in aesthetic dancing and American

Delsarte practice. Building conceptual framings, she then explicates the viewing of *Radha* within Orientalist assumptions about women and skin color and as a "confession" that allows viewers to witness, but not negatively label, dancing that is both sensual and sexual. Her article serves as a valuable template for thinking about the conceptual unturned stones of dance scholarship.

In her article, "The Dance Is a Weapon," Ellen Graff discusses dance as a vital part of a search for economic and social equality in the midst of the Great Depression. Some dancers of this era were caught between their political ideals (either communist or sympathetic to the social and economic implications of communism) and the artistic ideals of the equally revolutionary, but nonpolitical, modern dance movement. Should leftist choreographers borrow the aesthetics of bourgeois choreographers such as their use of trained dancers and sophisticated choreographic methods? Or should the dances of the left reflect the aims of revolutionary struggle and be easily understandable? Graff's discussion forces the reader to rethink modern dance as a revolutionary movement by critiquing its elitism.

The modern dancers and choreographers stand in contrast to those who thought art should be easily accessible and suit mass tastes. Because modern dance is often thought of as individual presentations of universal themes, it's interesting to go back now and think about the cultural moorings of these dances. Both Martha Graham and Doris Humphrey forged movement and choreographic languages that allowed them to make personal connections to literature, history, the other arts, and to their American heritages. Their references were not blatant, but realized through the abstraction of gesture, line, and energy. Marcia B. Siegel, in "The Harsh and Splendid Heroines of Martha Graham," discusses Graham as especially attuned to the trials, emotions, and characters of women. The Brontë sisters were Graham's inspiration in her *Deaths and Entrances*, and Emily Dickinson inspired her *Letter to the World*. She imagined a female antagonist for the Minotaur in *Errand into the Maze*.

Doris Humphrey worked more architecturally. Deborah Jowitt discusses Humphrey in "Form and Human Perfectability," explaining how the choreographer could, through a single spatial form such as the wagon wheel (or "whirling" or Texas Star), get at multiple human situations and emotions. Jowitt describes how Humphrey used double stars in *The Shakers*, one for men and one for women, placing each on opposite sides of the stage. As the stars whirled, men and women reached out for each other, their longing kept in check by the turning momentum of the group. A single star moving around a central pile of boxes was used in "Variations and Conclusion" from *New Dance*, to suggest a courteous community forming aisles down which soloists could move.

Fourth, and last, these articles are rich with ideas for physical study. For many young dancers, postmodern dance means the minimalism of Yvonne Rainer's *Trio A*. In "Choreographic Methods of the Judson Dance Theater," Sally Banes discusses a wide variety of movement studies and dances performed as part of Robert and Judith Dunn's choreography classes and at Judson Dance Theater performances. In these studies are connections to current performance, especially the use of film, alternative spaces, collage structures, music and physical imagery from various dance cultures, and political commentary.

Few choreography students investigate the choreographic potential of varied bodies, as many choreography teachers skip a discussion of body size, fitness, race, and gender as contributing to meaning. Too often, there is an assumption that all dancers should look a particular way, rather than thinking about the expressive, and political, potential of differing bodies. Many of these articles discuss the look of the body as contributing to the meaning of dances. In "Simmering Passivity: The Black Male Body in Concert Dance," Thomas DeFrantz explores Helmsley Winfield's solo, *Bronze Study*. DeFrantz explains how Winfield renamed skin color, pointed to its variations, and to variations in strength and flexibility as a way of subverting dance critics' repeated discussions of "exemplary"

strong, black male bodies. In "Chance Heroes," Deborah Jowitt describes the tall, cool look of Cunningham dancers, as contributing to the polite, unruffled feel of the dancing. Ann Daly broadens the look of the body to costuming and stance. In "The Natural Body," she investigates how Isadora Duncan's Greek clothing and the stances she adopted from Greek sculpture allowed her a public persona that mixed high art with the freedom of nature.

One of our goals in "America Dancing" was to refigure the history of American concert dance. Ellen Graff, through her discussion of dance and politics in the 1930s, and Thomas DeFrantz, through his discussion of African American male concert dancers, have opened up a broader understanding of dance activity in America, and of the dancers whose energy motivated that activity. There are many, many more American dancers whose work might be meaningfully investigated. In the course of research on Virginia Tanner, for example, I learned of Tanner's first teacher of modern dance, Washington, D.C. dancer, teacher, and choreographer Evelyn Davis. Beginning in the early 1930s, Davis ran a dance studio, directed a professional modern dance company, founded several summer dance programs, and eventually founded her own studio theater. One moment from my research stands out. I called Elizabeth Burtner, a former George Washington University faculty member and member of Davis's company, to ask her about Davis. Burtner described her as a "Humphrey-Weidman-Graham peer, working in Washington."[4] My vision shifted. Modern dance outside New York City in 1933? Humphrey-Weidman-Graham peer? The priority given to white modern dancers of this period was already clear to me, but I had never questioned the idea that New York was the cradle of early modern dance activity. I tended to see the people who sponsored performances of the Humphrey-Weidman company and other modern dance groups in towns across America as well-wishers, not as peers with functioning companies, studios, and concert seasons of their own. Who else was out there? How were they trained? In what way were they "modern"?

In "America Dancing," you'll read about some of the mainstays of modern dance history such as Isadora Duncan, Ruth St. Denis, Martha Graham, Doris Humphrey, and Alvin Ailey. Others from that canon are missing or barely mentioned, including Ted Shawn, Helen Tamiris, Charles Weidman, Paul Taylor, Alwin Nikolais, and Erick Hawkins. You'll read of the work of dancers often left out of traditional histories, such as Anna Sokolow, Edith Segal, Miriam Blecher, Nadia Chilkovsky, Edna Guy, Add Bates, Helmsley Winfield, and Randolph Sawyer. But this figuration is just our momentary framing of dance history. Dancers like Evelyn Davis, and many others who started dance companies or founded college and university dance programs in cities across the United States, have the power to again reshape our visions of "America Dancing."

Notes

1. Walter Terry, "A Dance Pilgrimage," *New York Herald Tribune,* July 26, 1953, n.p. [clipping], Virginia Tanner Papers, 1945–79, Box 3, Folder 4, Jackson Library, University of North Carolina at Greensboro.

2. From the Thirteenth Article of Faith, written by the prophet Joseph Smith, as explained to Ann Dils by Marilyn Berrett, August 19, 1998.

3. "Little Angels from Utah: Mormon Children Make a Triumphant Ballet Junket," *Life* [feature story and photo spread], August 24, 1953; Richard Paul Evans, *The Dance* (New York: Simon & Schuster Books for Young Children, 1999).

4. Elizabeth Burtner, personal communication to Ann Dils, August 15, 1998.

The Irresistible Other: Hopi Ritual Drama and Euro-American Audiences

SHARYN R. UDALL

No one knows how long the Snake Dance Ritual has been performed at the mesa-top Hopi villages in northern Arizona. Buried in prehistory, its origins long precede written records. But as part of the cycle of ritual dramas intended to benefit the Hopi people through weather control, fertility, and health, the Snake Dance speaks of collective needs both ancient and perennial.

Sixteenth-century visitors to the Southwest recorded ceremonies that may be antecedents of the modern Snake Dance. Both Hernan Gallegos in 1581 and Antonio de Espejo in 1582 reported seeing rattlesnakes used in rain dances in central and southern New Mexico.[1] But material evidence suggests that Snake Dance origins among the Hopi may go back well beyond the period of early Spanish contact. University of Chicago anthropologist Elsie Clews Parsons conjectured in 1940 that the design of a fourteenth-century Jeddito bowl represented a Snake Dance subject.[2]

It was Parsons, in her *Pueblo Indian Religion*, who posited a relationship between ritual and creativity among the Pueblo people. In an effort to control the unpredictable forces of nature, she wrote, Pueblo arts employed "poetry and song, dance and music and steps, mask, figurine, fresco and ground painting, beautiful featherwork, weaving and embroidery [as] measures to invoke and coerce, to gratify or pay, the Spirits."[3]

In ritual dramas such as the Snake Dance, a rich orchestration of color and rhythm echoes the larger rhythm of nature that governs the Hopi cosmos and, indeed, their whole existence. Each season and its attendant ceremonies address certain communal needs, with the summer ceremonies largely devoted to the perennial need for rain. Anthropologist J. Walter Fewkes described the Snake Dance as "an elaborate prayer for rain, in which the reptiles are gathered from the fields, intrusted with the prayers of the people, and then given their liberty to bear these petitions to the divinities who can bring the blessing of copious rains to the parched and arid farms of the Hopi."[4]

Much of the ritual Snake Dance activity has always been closed to outsiders. The first eight days of the nine-day ceremonial were traditionally private, reflecting the widespread Pueblo ambivalence towards strangers in cosmic or tribal space and the possible introduction of evil accompanying their presence.[5] It is not possible to discuss complex implications of Hopi epistemology here, except to note that historically such questions of openness and secrecy have been central but at the same time unresolved and often unenforced among the Hopi.

At the First Mesa village of Walpi, where the Snake Dance was long performed during odd-numbered years, private ritual activity centered in five rectangular kivas built into the rock. Entered by ladders from above, these kivas were usually, but not rigidly, off-limits to Euro-American eyes and cameras.[6] For most visitors, the mystery surrounding the rites only enhanced their appeal. They focused their curiosity on the ninth, or public, day of the performance. Towards the end of the eight-day private period visitors began to arrive—a trickle before 1890, in later years a flood—to witness, discuss, sketch, photograph, and record rites unlike those performed anywhere else in the United States. Most did not mind the long, jolting wagon ride over the seventy or eighty miles of corrugated roads leading from the rail points at Holbrook, Winslow, or Canyon Diablo, Arizona. After the turn of the century, when roads improved somewhat, intrepid motorists drove their cars the greater distances from Phoenix, Albuquerque, Santa Fe, or Taos. They camped below the villages, seeing what they could of the snake-gathering, waiting for the public culmination of ritual activity.

The appeal of the Snake Dance for late-nineteenth-century Americans is not difficult to understand: accompanying the disappearance of their own vanishing western frontier, Euro-Americans glimpsed the coming demise of the much-romanticized Indian. By 1890 the Indian's geographic containment by white political authority had already produced a tamer West, an expanded arena for the exercise of white territorial ambitions. But it was also a diminished West, whose excitement, exoticism, and dangers were swallowed up in the web of rail lines and roads flung over it. Year by year its openness and imagined freedom receded, until only vestiges of its former wildness remained.

Scholarly and Scientific Accounts

Because of their relative isolation from sustained Euro-American contact, the Hopi and their ceremonials were widely regarded by scholars and artists as unbroken links to an ancient past—a past that anthropologists like Fewkes and Adolph Bandelier were trying to reconstruct. But beyond their historical appeal, remote and ancient ceremonials like the Snake Dance allowed early artists and ethnologists to glimpse cultural features so exotic that they could not be forced into an Anglo-Saxon mold. Fewkes, reporting on preparations for the 1891 Snake Dance at Walpi, commented on the attraction of the rites as exotic spectacle. In language

that reveals the nearly ubiquitous ethnocentrism of his day, he recalled:

> The sight haunted me for weeks afterwards, and I can never forget this wildest of all the aboriginal rites of this strange people, which showed no element of our present civilization. It was a performance which might have been expected in the heart of Africa rather than in the American Union, and certainly one could not realize that he was in the United States at the end of the nineteenth century.[7]

Fewkes was by no means the earliest Euro-American visitor to record the Snake Dance: many outsiders, of diverse backgrounds and purposes, had preceded him to Hopi. Following an 1879 notation in *Masterkey* (perhaps the first written mention of the Snake Dance in modern times), word of the Snake Dance spread among the scholarly community.[8] Many felt curious enough to make the long trek to see it for themselves.

In 1881, a party led by Captain John G. Bourke witnessed the Walpi Snake Dance. This army expedition, sent to investigate ethnological aspects of the Pueblo Indians, resulted in Bourke's well-known book *The Snake-Dance of the Moquis of Arizona.*[9] Bourke used illustrations by a member of the party, Sgt. Alexander F. Harmer (1856–1925), who had studied at the Philadelphia Academy of Fine Arts. Harmer's illustration, dated 12 August 1881, may qualify as the earliest visual record of the Snake Dance (figure 23). Into one illustration Harmer has massed a great deal of visual information, crowding the Walpi plaza with dozens of dancers (adults and children), onlookers, and animals. Harmer compressed the visual depth of the site, placing the mushroom-shaped snake rock, the *kisi* or *bosque* (a conical enclosure of leafy saplings wrapped by hide, where the snakes were kept just prior to the dance), and the dancers much closer together than they appear in contemporaneous photographs. By doing so, he was able to make his figures of relatively similar sizes, with nearly equivalent visible detail. Harmer added dozens of Indian observers, who look on from vantage points on walls, roofs, or along the perimeter

23. Alexander F. Harmer, *Snake Dance of the Moquis Pueblo of Hualpi, Arizona* (August 12, 1881). Plate 2 from John G. Bourke, *The Snake Dance of the Moquis of Arizona* (Glorieta, N.M.: Rio Grande Press, 1962 [1884], n.p.). Photo courtesy of the Laboratory of Anthropology, Museum of New Mexico, Neg. No. 132364.

of the plaza. (These he could have drawn at leisure before the appearance of the Snake Dancers.) Bourke estimated that perhaps 750 persons (including only a half-dozen Anglos) assembled for the Walpi Snake Dance that August day in 1881.[10]

Besides his collective view of the ceremonial, Harmer prepared illustrations of some of its individual participants. His *Dancer Holding Snake in Mouth* is attired in full dance regalia: from shoulder bandelier to turtle-shell knee rattle, to fox skin and body paint, the dancer—with requisite snake in his mouth—presents a complete picture.

For early artist-illustrators like Harmer, the rush to record accurate details would have necessitated frantic sketching; the Snake Dance itself lasted only forty-five minutes or so. That Harmer was able to produce more than a dozen illustrations of various aspects of the

snake ceremony is a tribute to his rapid, disciplined drafting. But, he also made careful notes, which later enabled him to transcribe sketches and descriptions into highly finished oils and watercolors.[11]

Serenely confident of their right as government-approved "scientific" observers to make a visual record of all aspects of the ceremony, it would never have occurred to Harmer or Bourke that there was anything improper about their activities at the Snake Dance. In the absence of objections from the Hopi themselves, they saw no reason to limit their investigations.

Early Snake Dance illustrations were prized as visual documents to accompany ostensibly objective ethnographic records. Yet the accounts were often tinged with Eurocentric bias: Bourke's book was subtitled "A Description of the Manners and Customs of this peculiar People, and especially of the revolting religious rite, the

Snake-Dance." But as attitudes towards Native Americans began to change, the terminology of the accounts and the visual interpretations changed as well. A growing cultural relativism was beginning to find in Native lifeways certain superior values antithetical to the consuming Anglo notions of progress and capitalism. Now cast in a more positive light, the "wildness" and "primitivism" of tribal life invited scholars (as well as artists and writers) to discard such adjectives as "peculiar" and "revolting" and to invent, instead, a new poetics of the exotic. Sociologist Mary Roberts Coolidge, who visited the 1913 Snake Dance at Walpi, expressed this view of the Pueblo people: "Their clear, brown skins, their quiet voices, their simplicity and reticence and dignity, their astonishing endurance, are a sharp contrast to our haste, excessive energy and restless search for novelty."[12]

Popular Accounts

But the appeal of the Snake Dance soon reached beyond scholarly circles, entering the American imagination through the fine arts and popular literature. To Hamlin Garland, the keen and sympathetic observer of Native American life at the turn of the century, the Snake Dance represented "the most complete survival of the olden days to be found among American Indians."[13] Just whose "olden days" they were did not seem to matter much. The "discovery" of the Snake Dance coincided perfectly with an accelerating American search for national identity. Hungry for a cultural past distinct from that of Europe, Americans had begun to look among the indigenous peoples of their own continent. Onto ancient American roots (surviving visibly in Native American ceremonials like the Snake Dance) Euro-Americans began to graft their aspirations for a noble past.

At once exotic and authentically American, the Snake Dance (already valorized by the scholarly community) was ripe for appropriation—and frequent exploitation—by popular image-makers. The scores of painters, photographers, and illustrators who began to flood into the Snake Dance plazas fed the curiosity of a distant public, most of whom would never see the dances firsthand. Beginning about 1882, wide-circulation magazines, often illustrated with woodcuts and chromolithographs, carried stories of the Snake Dance. Trader Thomas V. Keam's account appeared in 1883 in *Chambers's Journal*, and Bourke's well-illustrated volume was widely reviewed in newspapers and popular journals following its appearance in 1884.[14] The *Saturday Review*, in an extravagant exercise of American culture-boosterism, linked the Snake Dance to distant classical prototypes: "Athens, like a Moqi village, was accustomed to the spectacle of dancers waving snakes in the midday streets."[15]

Over the next decade the major newspapers of the United States carried stories about the ceremonies. Chicago, New York, Washington, San Francisco, Los Angeles, Philadelphia, St. Louis, Cincinnati—all ran accounts, often sensationalized, of the Snake Dance.[16] They speculated on its dangerous, "primitive" aspects: How often were snake priests bitten? Did they possess an antidote? Had the snakes been devenomized before the ceremony? Why were emetics used at the end of the dance? Since even scientific accounts of those years carried conflicting interpretations of these aspects of the ritual, it is little wonder that the popular press seized upon every exotic detail and embellished at will.

Snake Dance Photography

Once painters, illustrators, and photographers began visiting the Hopi Villages, a steady stream of visual representations flowed from their brushes, pens, and darkrooms. Starting about 1883 photographs of the Snake Dance had been made by Ben Wittick, then by W. Calvin Brown of Albuquerque (1885), and by Cosmos Mindeleff of the Smithsonian Institution (1885).[17] From Mindeleff's photographs Cincinnati artist Henry F. Farny (who never visited the Southwest) created a full-page illustration for *Harper's Weekly*—the first such visual representation to appear in a magazine of national circulation.[18] Clearly feeding the appetite of its readers for action and excitement, the *Harper's* illustration intrudes unapologetically into the midst of the Snake Dance. With dancers arrayed on all sides, Mindeleff's camera-eye, mediated by Farny's pen, brings the viewer within inches of dangerous snakes. Safe at home in an armchair, Farny's viewer can almost taste the dust, feel the thud-thud of padded feet, and savor, vicariously, the adventure of the Snake Dance. By contrast, Harmer's illustration, only four years earlier (figure 23), is orderly, closed, and sedate.

Between 1885 and 1913, thousands of photographs were made of the ceremonials at Hopi. Besides the Snake Dance, the year-round Hopi religious cycle includes the Bean, Flute, and masked Kachina ceremonies. Though not the most important to the Hopi, the Snake Dance—in part because of its summertime occurrence, in part because of its vaunted danger and excitement—attracted the largest number of spectators. "From the 1890s on," writes William Truettner, "the Snake Dance was the most frequently described and photographed Indian ceremony in the Southwest."[19]

Whether professional or amateur, the camera-wielding Snake Dance visitors increased annually, in numbers and boldness, until few ritual secrets remained unphotographed. By 1901 the hordes of invading spectators, painters, and photographers threatened to impede performance of the rituals. George Wharton James, one of the photographers whose images appear in Walter Hogue's *The Moki Snake Dance* (1898), described the overeager photographers: "[E]very man had chosen his own field, and moved to and fro wherever he liked—in front of his neighbor or someone else; kicking down another fellow's tripod and sticking his elbow in the next fellow's lens."[20]

What James did not address were the potentially negative effects of so much camera intrusion into the ritual. But local officials could scarcely ignore the camera free-for-all. Recognizing that disruptive documentation had to be controlled, they decided about 1901 "that the photographers present—and they were legion—must be kept within a certain line, and that no one without a camera would be permitted in their pre-serves."[21] Photographs made after 1900 sometimes show the roped-off area for photographers.

Competing with James and his fellow still-photographers for prime vantage points at the 1901 Walpi Snake Dance was a new breed of imagemaker. That year, for the first time, the ritual was recorded on motion picture film by one of Thomas A. Edison's crews.[22] A few years later Edward S. Curtis brought his own movie cameras to film the Hopi rituals. Engaged in his monumental study *The North American Indian* (1907–1930) Curtis had begun to visit Hopi in 1900 and continued to do so every few years until the early 1920s.[23]

Abuses by photographers led to severe restrictions on Snake Dance photography beginning in 1913. Luke Lyon notes that an edict that year from the Commissioner of Indian Affairs in Washington had prohibited Snake Dance photography for commercial use. But when the local Indian agent, Supt. Leo Crane, arrived at Walpi that August day, he found two unauthorized movie crews. Crane promptly demanded written promises that their films would be used solely for historical documentation. One crew complied; the other sought to evade such restrictions. Their filming completed, the latter attempted a nighttime escape through the rough country of the Hopi and surrounding Navajo reservations. Whether due to Hopi imprecations or because of violent thunderstorms which often occur in the August rainy season, the furtive crew was soon trapped by flash-flooded arroyos. In short, as Lyon relates, they were summarily arrested and their film confiscated. Thoroughly piqued at the flagrant disregard of his partial ban, the commissioner pronounced an even sterner edict. Thenceforth, no photographs—whether "still, animated or out of focus"—would be permitted at the Snake Dance. This is not to say that photography at the Snake Dances ceased at once and altogether. A considerable number of photographers circumvented the restrictions into the 1920s, when stricter enforcement finally reduced the production of images.

Because many painters relied on photography as an

24. William P. Henderson, *Walpi Snake Dance* (1920), oil on canvas 41 x 53 inches. Private collection. Photo courtesy of the Museum of New Mexico, Neg. No. 20117.

aide-mémoire, they too were affected by the ban on photographing the Snake Dance. Santa Fe painter William Penhallow Henderson (1877–1943) attended the Walpi Snake Dance, probably in 1919 during a three-week trip by train, automobile, and horseback through much of the Navajo and Hopi country. Accompanied by his friend Carter Harrison, the colorful arts patron and ex-mayor of Chicago, Henderson visited Canyon de Chelly, Chaco Canyon, and the western pueblos of Laguna and Acoma. By the time of their arrival at Walpi they had seen and experienced much. But even frequent attendance at other Indian dances had not prepared Henderson for the arresting visual drama of the Snake Dance. Like a growing number of sensitive artists, he bowed willingly to the prohibitions against sketching and photography, recording visual impressions only with his mind's eye. His resulting *Walpi Snake Dance* (figure 24), painted from memory some months later, has a limited amount of detail but a flood of vibrant color and remembered rhythm. When this painting was shown with a group of Henderson's

other dance paintings at the Santa Fe Fine Arts Museum in 1921, Carl Sandburg wrote a foreword to the catalog. Henderson, wrote the poet,

> spent his best years mixing with the material here dealt with and was spiritually mortgaged to the still and living objects, the forms and gestures, colors and shadows. [. . .] He pays them for what they gave him by a setting forth of fine human and cosmic implications that rise behind and out of the portrayed Indians, mountains, houses, sparse trees. [. . .] Yes, the inevitable is over this work.[24]

Sandburg was not the only major literary figure to respond to the Southwest's Indian ceremonials. In 1924 D. H. Lawrence, by then many months in New Mexico, was taken by his hostess, Mabel Dodge Luhan, to the Snake Dance at Hotevilla. Lawrence, who wrote sensitively about many aspects of Indian life, had already been impressed by the big ceremonials at Santo Domingo and Taos. Now, with a legion of the curious 3,000 strong, the Luhan-Lawrence party rumbled across the thirty miles beyond Walpi to Third Mesa. Watching the ritual—a dozen or so dancers whose every move was devoured by thousands of hungry eyes—Lawrence could not screen out the context to focus on the ceremony itself. What he perceived was the ghastly transformation of ritual drama into public spectacle. On the return to Taos he wrote down his impressions, mostly a biting characterization of the whole experience as a tawdry circus performance: "Oh, the wild west is lots of fun: the Land of Enchantment. Like being right inside the circus-ring: lots of sand, and painted savages jabbering, and snakes and all that."[25]

Mabel Dodge Luhan complained. Lawrence, she said, had written an account that was itself a dreary mockery of the performance. Apparently chagrined, he started over, producing a longer meditation on the Snake Dance. In a milder tone he repeated his denunciation of the sideshow atmosphere. But he acknowledged that behind it, discernible to the seeker, lay an ageless animistic religion whose only commandment was (as Lawrence had once written), "Thou shalt acknowledge the wonder." "We dam the Nile and take the railway across America," he now wrote. "The Hopi smooths the rattlesnake and carries him in his mouth, to send him back into the dark places of the earth, an emissary to the inner powers."[26]

The dark mysteries of the Snake Dance held less appeal for many Americans than for Lawrence and Luhan. For decades government Indian agents objected to the Snake Dances on the grounds that they kept the Hopi from "productive" agricultural pursuits during the weeks of training and preparation before the dances. As early as 1891 artist Julian Scott noted that the Hopi had been warned of the government's intention to stop the Snake Dance.[27]

But many artists and writers spoke out in opposition to the government's position, and their arguments were heard far beyond the boundaries of the Southwest. Novelist Alida Sims Malkus, writing in the *New York Times*, deplored the proposed halt.[28] In a 1924 article, painter John Sloan delivered a stinging reply to those who charged that the Indian dances were

"degrading" and "demoralizing," "orgies" attended by "writers and artists, greedy for the retention of these dances for their own personal advantage."[29] Sloan cheerfully pled guilty to being one of those artists, adding, "I am truly sorry that there are not more people who have the same interest in the ceremonials, to write about them and paint them, for they have already proved a fine and refreshing influence for American art."

Sloan's interest in the dances was not limited to aesthetic appropriation. He tried to see beyond the confines of Euro-American paternalism to a respect for the deeply religious nature of the rituals. In short, he advocated a hands-off government policy with regard to the ceremonial life of the Indians so that "what is left of a beautiful, early civilization will be allowed to survive with its *soul* as well as its body intact."[30] Dismissing as "piffling absurdities" charges that the dances were somehow offensive. Sloan worried instead about the negative effect of Euro-American life in the 1920s on the relatively uncorrupted Indian: "There can be no question but what these same Indians are profoundly offended with certain elements of our jazz dancing— dances which certainly have no beauty and no religious significance."[31]

To point out the contrast between what he called the "aesthetic quality of Indian culture" and the excesses of the Roaring Twenties, Sloan caricatured the voracious, insensitive ceremonial visitors in several etchings made in the mid-twenties. In *Knees and Aborigines* he portrayed as ludicrous the flappers and flivvers at a ceremonial, while in his 1927 *Indian Detour* crowds of desultory tourists wander about a pueblo plaza where a circle of aggressive tour buses, like some maddened modern-day wagon train, crowds in upon the handful of Indian dancers.

Paradoxically, the 1920s effort by artists and writers to preserve the dignity and mystery of the Indian ritual wrenched the Snake Dance out of its remote desert venue into the glare of Washington. As if absolute decontextualization would once and for all prove their harmlessness, a group of Hopi Snake dancers was brought to the nation's capital in 1926. There they performed before Vice President Dawes, Alice Roosevelt Longworth, and 5,000 other onlookers. Dancing in the white man's plaza, caught in the gaze of cameras and reporters, the five dusky snake priests seemed far less threatening to Euro-American values than their detractors had argued. Arizona's Senator Cameron, echoing John Sloan's contention, remarked to the *Washington Post* and *New York Times* that the Snake Dance was not as bad as the Charleston.[32]

Once the threat of its suppression was past, the Snake Dance slipped from notoriety back to the relative obscurity of the far-off Southwest. But if its political currency was spent, the Snake Dance continued to exercise its fascination for Euro-American artists. Each August brought a new group of spectators, struck by the austere setting, the costumes, body painting, and measured rhythms of the dance. Jan Matulka, Emil Bisttram, Leon Gaspard, Frank Applegate, Tom Lea, Will Shuster—these and countless others have recorded their visual responses to the experience in every imaginable medium and style. Among the most powerful of these responses is *Snake Priest* by Canadian-born printmaker Frederick O'Hara (1904–1980). O'Hara's 1957 monoprint has a simultaneous sophistication and primordial quality: deliberately crude, distorted, richly textured, it is a figure outside the bounds of ordinary perception. It is a heroic, monumental being charged with the power of ritual. But O'Hara is a respectful keeper of secrets; his is a sensitive handling, purged by intent and technique of the literality that offends.

Other artists have been content to watch and listen, knowing that their visual interpretation could add nothing to a ceremonial expression complete as an aesthetic as well as a ritual act. Georgia O'Keeffe found the Snake Dance compelling, but she was, after all, not a figure painter. The closest she came to recording Hopi ceremonial life were her 1930s renderings of some kachina *tihus*, those spirit likenesses carved by the Hopi for teaching purposes.[33]

A case apart is Fred Kabotie's watercolors of the Snake Dance, because they are renderings of Hopi ritual by a Hopi painter.[34] Born at Shungopavi at the turn of the century, Kabotie was encouraged in his artistic talent by Dorothy Dunn at the Santa Fe Indian School Studio. There he learned the studio's pictorial manner: flat application of decorative color, delicate linear separation of form, and overall attention to detail in the patterns of dress and body painting. In Kabotie's Snake Dance paintings these formal conventions dictate more than the *look* of the painting; they also affect meaning. Since no one detail is emphasized more than others, Kabotie's paintings (unlike most Euro-American paintings of the Snake Dance) sidestep the sensational visual focus on snakes carried in the dancers' mouths. To Kabotie, the snakes are only one of many visual incidents within a composition that emphasizes the communal value of the dance.

In Kabotie's Snake Dance paintings we also see the studio's pan-Indian landscape manner. Nature here is merely symbolic; the ritual kisi, itself a constructed form, is the sole allusion to landscape. Nothing else—no ground line, no architecture, no stray shrubs—anchors the composition in temporal reality. Kabotie's imagined re-creation of a timeless ritual act occurs outside measurable space and time, in a void that corresponds to the gap between the Hopi and Anglo worlds.

It is precisely there, in Kabotie's void, that certain troubling notions collide. He is, after all, Hopi. And even though his Snake Dance paintings may appear detached from life, his creative act was not. Kabotie's own experience—learning to move between the Anglo and Hopi worlds—was conditioned by Anglo economic support, first at the Studio itself, later when he filled many commissions to record ceremonies and lore of the Hopi in murals and in easel paintings. For better or worse, well-meaning Euro-American patronage has often produced changes in both the content and form of Native American art. For Kabotie, and for many Native artists since, satisfying the twin demands of tradition and audience has been problematic. Nelson Graeburn, in his discussion of fourth-world arts (usually produced, like Kabotie's, for outside consumption), describes the frequent double-coding in work that must respond to "more than one symbolic and esthetic system."[35]

Conclusion

Because it has been so well documented, the Snake Dance provides a useful historical example of the dissemination of cultural meaning through ritual and art. Subjected to sustained outside approaches for well over a century, it has been described, photographed, painted, and satirized beyond counting. Admittedly, outside attempts to grasp its significance have focused all too often on its exoticism, constructing differences based on subtly ethnocentric systems of value.

Today's postmodern preoccupation with the twin crises of meaning and representation complicates issues that went virtually unnoticed when Kabotie (and Euro-American artists) was recording the rituals of the Hopi. Now, in the 1990s, anthropologists and artists struggle with questions of conquest, neocolonialism, and visual appropriation. New consciousness of symbols and acts sacred to others has made visual artists question the very basis of their representations and has made museum curators acutely aware of past offenses. But amid these newfound concerns we must keep in mind that the interplay of visual referents, ritual, and decoration has undergone profound changes during more than a century of Snake Dance representations. Between Moran's sketches and the expressionist interpretation of Frederick O'Hara lie differences as vast as those between the covered wagon and the jet airplane. As we think about contextual differences, one caveat emerges clearly: We must be careful not to judge the artistic acts of past decades solely by the imperfect standards of our own.

What about the very act of writing about Snake Dance—by early ethnologists, by D. H. Lawrence, or John Sloan, or in articles such as this one that reconsider past images and texts? If such discussions are aimed at a Euro-American audience, do they necessarily perpetuate asymmetrical power relations between dominant and subject cultures? Will appropriation and neoprimitivism necessarily continue to naturalize the entrenched self/other dichotomy? Yes, many scholars argue, if the discussion is framed in terms of Euro-American needs and values. To Robert F. Berkhofer Jr., there is no clear way out. In *The White Man's Indian* he has written that the *idea* of the Indian is destined to remain appropriative, part of what he calls "the recurrent effort of Whites to understand themselves, for the very attraction of the Indian to the white imagination rests upon the contrast that lies at the core of the idea."[36]

Lucy Lippard takes a slightly different view. In summarizing some of the pitfalls Euro-Americans have faced in addressing other cultures, she cautions, "Well-meaning white artists and writers who think we are ultra-sensitive often idealize and romanticize indigenous cultures on one hand, or force them into a Western hegemonic analysis on the other hand." But she stops short of advocating a strict hands-off policy: "I am not suggesting that every European and Euro-American artist influenced by the power of cultures other than their own should be overwhelmed with guilt at every touch." But they should, concludes Lippard, maintain "an awareness of other cultures' boundaries and contexts" as one way of respecting "the symbols, acts or materials sacred to others."[37]

Lippard's admonitions reflect contemporary multicultural consciousness, as well as the perennial desire to find meaning through art and ritual. That desire, given free rein in the past, has been at the heart of the problem: Hopi "boundaries and contexts" have repeatedly been violated, often by persons oblivious to the negative effects their presence and representations generate. One poignant example is that of missionary and amateur anthropologist H. R. Voth, who lived at Hopi during the early years of the century. Over a period of years he photographed and described their ceremonial life in great detail. Voth was long thought (by white colleagues) to have the complete trust of the Hopi because he was allowed to enter kivas freely and to "collect" ceremonial images. Only later, in an autobiography of a Hopi leader, was it revealed that Voth's intrusions were blamed for a crippling drought among the people.[38]

More recently, media attention accompanying celebrated visitors (amplified a thousandfold since Theodore Roosevelt's 1913 visit) has nearly swallowed up Snake Dance performances in a sea of hype. Worse, it has again threatened access (reprising G. W. James's 1902 account) by the Hopi themselves to the dance's ritual significance. When Johnny Carson visited, one Hopi told me, it was the last straw. D. H. Lawrence's worst fears were realized: what began as ritual performance had been reduced to public spectacle, finally to a media circus.

In an effort to prevent the irretrievable loss of their ceremonial life (predicted almost a century ago by J. Walter Fewkes) the Hopi have closed the Snake Dance to visitors in recent years. Today it survives in much-reduced form, a casualty of the impact of the twentieth century on the beliefs and ceremonial systems of the Hopi. Factionalism within the 7,600-member tribe has also affected the performance of the ancient ritual dramas. Tribal government, since 1936 in the hands of elected political leaders, has favored economic development and jobs over traditional religious concerns. In 1989, for example, the tribal council hired an Albuquerque construction company to build a road that destroyed part of the habitat for snakes used in the Snake Dance. Hopi traditionalists have called for, but not yet received, reparations.[39] Even if paid, monetary compensation could not replace land long sacred to the Hopi belief system.

Many factors have undermined performance of the Hopi Snake Dance. That it survives at all is testimony to the richness and meaning of the ritual to the Hopi themselves. To generations of outsiders who have been drawn to it, that ritual significance can never be experienced in precisely the same way. But to admit that is not to deny other levels of experience and meaning within the Snake Dance. As Susan Sontag argues, "meaning is never monogamous."[40] One person's meaning is never precisely that of another. Besides, there is a critical difference between finding "meaning" and "a meaning," a distinction which Roland Barthes made in discussing the aim of literature, but which applies equally to visual art.

Finally, if Carl Jung was right—that meaning exists only when shared—then the Snake Dance experience has the potential of enriching constantly enlarging circles of perception.[41] And, one wants to ask, isn't there meaning enough in the Snake Dance to go around? If so, the long fascination of the Snake Dance performance, particularly to visual artists, has created meaning that extends well beyond the Hopi dance plazas. Their representations can thus be construed less as cultural robbery, more as openness—even homage—to alternative aesthetic and communal values.

But the Snake Dance representations have signified more than that. The rich variety of visual responses to a common experience has helped artists to rethink old questions of perception. And from their insistent urge to situate meaning in ritual and in art have sprung images that engage issues common to Hopi cosmology and to human artistic endeavor generally: a search for order in the natural world, the relationship of art and ritual, and the linkage of individual creative acts to beliefs about primal acts of creation.

Notes

1. On Gallegos, see Don Roberts, "The Ethnomusicology of the Eastern Publos," in *New Perspectives on the Pueblos*, ed. Alfonso Ortiz (Albuquerque: University of New Mexico Press, 1972), 243–255. For Espejo's note of a dance at Acoma "con vivoras vivas," see Walter J. Fewkes, "The Snake Ceremonials at Walpi," *Journal of American Ethnology and Anthropology* 4 (1894). Adolph F. Bandelier, *The Delight Makers* (New York: Dodd, Mead, 1916), notes a pictograph at Abo, a possible image of the Snake Dance in earlier times. Snake legends from Mexico and Central America, combined with sculptural representations of serpents at temple pyramids of Teotihuacan, Tenayuca, and at Copan

encourage attempts to link the plumed serpents of Hopi religion with those from the South.

2. Elsie Clews Parsons, "A Pre-Spanish Record of Hopi Ceremonies," *American Anthropologist* 42, no. 3 (July–September 1940): 541–542.

3. Elsie Clews Parsons, *Pueblo Indian Religion*, 2 vols. (Chicago: University of Chicago Press, 1939), xi.

4. Walter J. Fewkes, "The Snake Ceremonials at Walpi," 124.

5. Alfonso Ortiz, *New Perspectives on the Pueblos* (Albuquerque: University of New Mexico Press, 1972), 145.

6. Exceptions were sometimes made in the case of certain visitors, such as anthropologist J. Walter Fewkes, who with his party was allowed into the kivas in 1891 and 1893. Certain photographers, for example George Wharton James in 1896, likewise were allowed access to the kivas. Fewkes mentions the efforts of uninvited white spectators to enter kivas during the Snake Dance of 1891 ("The Snake Ceremonials at Walpi," 5).

7. Fewkes, "The Snake Ceremonials at Walpi," 84–85.

8. W. R. Mateer, *Masterkey* 8, no. 4 (October 10, 1879): 150–155.

9. Most early accounts use the name Moqui or Moki. Only later did anthropologists adopt Hopi, the name the Indians called themselves. See John G. Bourke, *The Snake-Dance of the Moquis of Arizona* (1884; Glorieta, N.M.: Rio Grande Press, 1962).

10. Ibid., 156–157.

11. Robert Taft, *Artists and Illustrators of the Old West, 1850–1900* (Princeton, N.J.: Princeton University Press, 1953), 348.

12. Mary Roberts Coolidge, "The Glamour of the Southwest," In *Santa Fe New Mexican*, Artists and Writers Edition (June 6, 1940).

13. Hamlin Garland, *Hamlin Garland's Observations on the American Indian, 1895–1905*, ed. Lonnie E. Underhill and Daniel F. Littlefield Jr. (Tucson: University of Arizona Press, 1976), 103.

14. Thomas V. Keam, "An Indian Snake Dance," *Chambers's Journal* (1883): 14–16.

15. E. B. Tylor, "Snake Dances, Moqui and Greek," *Saturday Review*, October 18, 1884, p. 10.

16. See, for example, the bibliography in Fewkes, "The Snake Ceremonials at Walpi," 124–126.

17. Luke Lyon, "History of Prohibition of Photography of Southwestern Indian Ceremonies," in *Reflections: Papers on Southwestern Culture History in Honor of Charles H. Lange*, ed. Anne van Arsdall Poore, Papers of Archaeological Society of New Mexico 14 (Sante Fe: Ancient City Press, 1988), 261.

18. Farny had earlier made illustrations for *Century* magazine to accompany Frank Hamilton Cushing's account of his years at Zuni. These Zuni illustrations were likewise based on photographs, in that instance those of John K. Hillers.

19. Charles Eldredge, Julie Schimmel, and William H. Truettner, *Art in New Mexico 1900–1945: Paths to Taos and Santa Fe* (New York: Abbeville Press, 1986), 89.

20. G. Wharton James, "The Snake Dance of the Hopis," in *Camera Craft* 6, no. 1 (1902): 7–8.

21. Ibid.

22. Information on this film and references to subsequent Snake Dance films are found in Luke Lyon, "History of Prohibition of Photography of Southwestern Indian Ceremonies," 238–272.

23. Edward S. Curtis, *The North American Indian*, 20 vols. with photograph supplements (Norwood, Mass.: Plimpton Press, 1907–1930).

24. Carl Sandburg, Foreword, *William Penhallow Henderson, 1877–1943*, Retrospective exhibition catalog (Santa Fe: Museum of New Mexico, Fine Arts Museum, 1921).

25. D. H. Lawrence, "Just Back from the Snake Dance—Tired Out," *Laughing Horse II* (September 1924).

26. In *D. H. Lawrence and New Mexico*, ed. Keith Sagar (Salt Lake City: Peregrine Smith, 1982), 72.

27. Thomas Donaldson, *Moqui Pueblo Indians of Arizona and Pueblo Indians of New Mexico, Extra Census Bulletin, Eleventh Census of the United States* (Washington, D.C., 1893).

28. "Those Doomed Indian Dances," *El Palacio* 14, no. 10 (May 15, 1921): 149–152. Reprinted from the *New York Times*.

29. Sloan was one of the American artists who worked most actively to preserve and champion Native American art, encouraging its elevation from craft to fine art. He served as president of the 1931 Exposition of Indian Tribal Arts, a major New York showing of high-quality Native American work presented as art.

30. John Sloan, "The Indian Dance from an Artist's Point of View," *Arts and Decoration*, January 1924, 17, 56.

31. Ibid., 56.

32. Luke Lyon, "History of Prohibition of Photography of Southwestern Indian Ceremonies," 245. Between 1924 and 1930 these snake dancers toured the United States, organized by M. W. Billingsley and accompanied by lectures and demonstrations.

33. Laurie Lisle, *Portrait of an Artist: A Biography of Georgia O'Keefe* (New York: Seaview Books, 1980), 225.

34. Kabotie is not the only Hopi artist to make Snake Dance paintings or drawings; others include Otis Polelomena, Gilbert Naseyowma, and Lawrence J. Outah.

35. Nelson Graeburn, *Ethnic and Tourist Arts: Cultural Expressions from the Fourth World* (Berkeley: University of California Press, 1976), 2.

36. Robert F. Berkhofer Jr., *The White Man's Indian: Images of the American Indian from Columbus to the Present* (New York: Alfred A. Knopf, 1978), 111.

37. Lucy Lippard, *Mixed Blessings: New Art in a Multicultural America* (New York: Pantheon Books, 1990), 9.

38. Don Talayesva, *Sun Chief*, ed. Leo W. Simmons (New Haven, Conn.: Yale University Press, 1942), 252.

39. "Hopis Must Oust Council on Their Own," *Albuquerque Journal*, April 4, 1991, D.1.

40. Susan Sontag, ed., *A Barthes Reader* (New York: Hill & Wang, 1982), 12.

41. Carl Jung, "The Pueblo Indians," in *The Spell of New Mexico*, ed. Tony Hillerman (1963; Albuquerque: University of New Mexico Press, 1989), 37–43.

Juba and American Minstrelsy

MARIAN HANNAH WINTER

The history of Negro dance and its music in North America is fundamentally so integrated with our entire music and dance history that it may seem curious here to isolate or limit its boundless divergences. However, no sequential survey has been made in any general history to date, and episodic treatments can give no concept of the Afro-American contribution in continuity or importance. Hazards are always involved when social and economic problems inexorably impinge on any phase of Negro cultural history, and objectivity becomes an elusive lodestar.

This is in part the saga of William Henry Lane, known as Master Juba. This most influential single performer of nineteenth-century American dance was a prodigy of our entire theatre history. Almost legendary among his contemporary colleagues, the Juba epic dwindled into oblivion. Negro historians, intent on apotheosizing Ira Aldridge, the African Roscius, ignored him. Yet this is equivalent to writing a twentieth-century theatrical history of the Negro mentioning only Paul Robeson and omitting Bill Robinson, the great Bojangles. It is more outrageous in that Robinson has embellished an already established form, whereas Juba was actually an initiator and determinant of the form itself. The repertoire of any current tap-dancer contains elements which were established theatrically by him. Herein is the cornerstone of his memorial.

Negroes were first brought to America in the sixteenth century. They came principally from the Gold Coast, Ivory Coast, Congo, Angola, Benin, Gambia, Senegal, Nigeria, Dahomey, and Togoland. Conditioned physiologically and psychologically to elaborate, legalistic tribal ritual and the extrovert, centrifugal community ring-shout, then to the restricted disorder of slave-ship holds, plantation huts, and enforced dissolution of their cultural traditions, with only the slightest elements of Western European tradition to draw upon, they evolved art forms which became indigenous manifestations of American culture.

That Negro music-making survived is miraculous when we consider the Slave Laws of 1740, which remained among the basic regulatory laws for Negroes during the subsequent century and a quarter. These were promulgated after the Stono Insurrection of 1739, in South Carolina. A group of slaves attempted an escape to Florida, got hold of some rum en route, stopped to celebrate with a song and dance bout, and were captured in a bloody charge. They had marched "with colors flying and drums beating." The laws of 1740 stringently prohibited any Negro from "beating drums, blowing horns or the like which might on occasion be used to arouse slaves to insurrectionary activity." Since most states patterned their slave laws after those of South Carolina and Virginia, the effect of these prohibitions would have discouraged any people inherently less musical.

Substitutions for the forbidden drum were accomplished with facility—bone clappers in the manner of castanets, jawbones, scrap iron such as blacksmiths' rasps, handclapping, and footbeats. Virtuosity of footwork, with heel beats and toe beats, became a simulacrum of the drum. In modern tap-dancing the "conversation" tapped out by two performers is a survival of African telegraphy by drums. Since African dance had already developed rhythms stamped or beat out by dancers as counterpoint to antiphonal musical accompaniment, and solo dances set against the communal ring-shout, the formal source material surmounted any restrictions. The slave created the *bonja* too, made from a hollow gourd without resonance board, slack strung, which developed into the banjo of minstrelsy and jazz.

The Juba dance (simplified from *giouba*) was an African step-dance which somewhat resembled a jig with elaborate variations, and occurs wherever the Negro settled, whether in the West Indies or South Carolina. One variation—crossing and uncrossing the hands against kneecaps which fanned back and forth—was incorporated in the Charleston of the 1920s. Juba and Jube are recurrent slave names with particular association to dancers and musicians. Juba also occurs as the name of a supernatural being in some American Negro folklore, and became the popular name for an expansive weed, the Juba's bush or Juba's brush.

The Negro dancer on the American stage was originally an exotic, much the same as blackamoors in a Rameau ballet-opera. Blackface "Negroes" appeared in eighteenth-century Captain Cook pantomimes and Sheridan's *Robinson Crusoe* (New York, 1785). In 1791 a Negro troupe of comedians and entertainers, under the direction of one Louis Tabary, gave performances in New Orleans. A typical playbill announcement offers *Paul and Virginia*, with music by Mazzinghi and Reeve, and accompaniments by James Hewitt, featuring a "NEGRO DANCE by Monsieur Labottiere and Mrs. Darby" (New York, 1805). By 1810 the singing and dancing "Negro Boy" was established with the traditional clown as a dance hall and circus character. These blackface impersonators simply performed jigs and clogs of Irish or English origin to popular songs with topical allusions to Negroes in the lyrics.

Blackface minstrel songs, to the accompaniment of a genuine Negro instrument, the banjo, abetted by tambourine and bone clappers, were popular by 1820, but genuine Negro performers continue to appear only in sporadic interludes. The African Company gave a New York version of the London burletta *Tom and Jerry* in 1821, but the comic dance by the characters African Sal and Dusty Bob had long been performed in blackface.

"Daddy" Rice, the famous, original "Jim Crow," was a blackface performer who first definitely used a Negro work song. Picked up from a livery stable porter, this monotonously cheerful refrain—"spin about and turn about and jump Jim Crow"—with accompanying jig and shuffle, focused attention on the Negro as theatrical source material in 1829. Traditional Anglo-American fiddle break-downs, such as *Turkey in the Straw*, and popular ballads as well, were absorbed into the minstrel amalgam. The minstrel show, as a unit of songs, dances, and jokes, crystallized in the 1840s. Although the stock "Negro" was already formed, there was some slight effort initially to approximate Negro music. But Negro qualities of minstrel music dwindled, and even the adapted Negro techniques of performance which had been taken over grew vague and sloppy, save in rare instances. Yet because of the vast influence of one Negro performer, the minstrel show dance retained more integrity as a Negro art form than any other theatrical derivative of Negro culture.

Juba, born William Henry Lane, circa 1825 or later, seems to have sprung full-panoplied from the brow of Terpsichore. Probably a freeborn Negro, and from the first records of his appearance at about fifteen, unencumbered by family, he was generally adopted by the entire fraternity of white minstrel players, who unreservedly recognized his genius. He had supposedly learned much of his art from "Uncle" Jim Lowe, a Negro jig and reel dancer of exceptional skill, whose performances were confined to saloons, dance halls, and similar locales outside the regular theatres. By 1845 it was flatly stated by members of the profession that Juba was "beyond question the very greatest of all dancers. He was possessed not only of wonderful and unique execution, but also of unsurpassed grace and endurance." *A New York Herald* feature-writer has left us a description of his early extra-theatrical performances.

At the time when he performed at Pete Williams', in Orange Street, New York, those who passed through the long hallway and entered the dance hall, after paying their shilling to the darky door-keeper, whose "box-office" was a plain soap box, or a wooden one of that description, saw this phenomenon, "Juba," imitate all the dancers of the day and their special steps. Then Bob Ellingham, the interlocutor and master of ceremonies, would say, "Now, Master Juba, show your own jig." Whereupon he would go through all his own steps and specialities, with never a resemblance in any of them to those he had just imitated.

The best in the profession danced there, as well as Juba. A most amusing feature of the entertainment was the comic "walk-around," given in true darky style, with the lean, the fat, the tall, the short, the hunchbacked and the wooden-legged, all mixed in and hard at it. It was from a one-legged performer there, whose second leg was a wooden one, that Dave Reed learned his celebrated "stiff" leg steps.

(This reminds one of Peg-Leg Bates, whose handicap turned him into an amazing virtuoso performer among our current dancers.) Negro art forms always reached the public, in the popular dance halls, even when the legitimate theatres were closed to them.

Juba's fame was already so legendary that by 1845 he achieved the unprecedented distinction of touring with four white minstrels and received *top billing!* When Juba next toured with the Georgia Champion Minstrels in the New England states, he was entitled to this billing: "The Wonder of the World Juba, Acknowledged to be the Greatest Dancer in the World. Having danced with John Diamond at the Chatham Theatre for $500, and at the Bowery Theatre for the same amount, and established himself as the King of All

Dancers. No conception can be formed of the variety of beautiful and intricate steps exhibited by him with ease. You must see to believe." (The word "beautiful" was almost never used to describe minstrel dancing.)

Working an almost superhuman schedule, thoroughly enjoying his work, and reacting normally to the excitement of his triumphs, Juba burned up his energies and health. In America a pious commentator and theatre historian, Allston Brown, smugly noted that "Success proved too much for him. He married too late (and a white woman besides) and died early and miserably."

From the age of fourteen Juba seems to have danced for his supper; at that time the standard culinary recompense "on the house" where he danced was a dish of fried eels and ale, which was scarcely a balanced diet. That Juba worked both night and day, consistently, from 1839 to 1850, is record. Small wonder if years of irregular food, irregular sleep, and regular strenuous physical exertion finally produced a breakdown, which had nothing at all to do with "success proving too much for him." His greatest white contemporary—John Diamond—had a somewhat similar background, was an acute dipsomaniac and melancholic, and also died prematurely—in Philadelphia.

It was Juba's influence primarily which kept the minstrel show dance, in contrast to the body of minstrel show music, in touch with the integrity of Negro source material. There was almost a "school after Juba." Certain of these white performers maintained his tradition with integrity and were worthy artists.

The entire dance repertoire finally became synthesized in the so-called "essence" dances, made famous by Billy Newcomb. The music for these drew upon folk fiddle tunes, enhanced by the Negro's rhythmic gift and development of the offbeat which is the syncopation of jazz. Southern mountain songs—*Cotton Eyed Joe, Cripple Creek*, and popular traditional jigs and hornpipes—*Turkey in the Straw, Old Zip Coon*, and *Durang's Hornpipe*, were incorporated. In turn, many square dances of the South and Southwest used or adapted minstrel songs—*Old Dan Tucker, Buffalo*

Girls, and Botkin notes that the *danse aux chansons* of American play-party games had "songs often sung by the non-dancing part of the party to mark the rhythms—much, it might be added, after the fashion of patting out the rhythm in Negro dances" (*American Play-Party Song*, cf. Hudson).

Against this musical mélange was set minstrelsy's most famous dance—*Essence of Old Virginny*—performed initially in the make-up of a decrepit and tatterdemalion darky, but soon turned into a flashy young dude number. Based firmly on Negro source material, this theatrical showpiece was made famous by several excellent blackface performers. W. W. Newcomb is credited as its originator; his style was called "quintessence" and was done in rather fast time. In contradistinction Dan Bryant, its most famous exponent, who made important technical advances in the development of clog dancing, performed his famous *Essence* very slowly. George F. Moore originated the noiseless, soft-shoe *Essence* about 1875, and the last, whirlaway performance was that of Eddie Girard.

At this point, after looking at the blackface masks, it is necessary to evaluate the Negro position. By the 1870s there was a relentless, and impalpable, pressure to stereotype the stage Negro completely. Although groups such as the Fisk Jubilee Singers toured America and Europe they reached only a small minority of the general audience. Increasingly the Negro was forced into his caricature. Lack of education had caused the Negro to retain, through word of mouth retelling, innumerable superstitions which had been commonplaces among the white settlers in the seventeenth and eighteenth centuries, ergo superstition and fear were "Negro peculiarities," and an adjunct of Negro "make-up" was the "shock" or "fright" wig, listed in the old theatrical catalogues, which could be made to rise and stand on end. Ignorance, vanity, and childlike display of emotions constituted other characteristics which writers of that period continually referred to as "peculiar to the Negro." This last stricture is particularly interesting in view of an analysis by Herskovits (in *Freudian Mechanisms in Negro Psychology*) of the African "insult" song and dance,

which are used as "socially institutionalized release." According to West African ritual, repressing emotions such as anger and hate is considered a primary cause of insanity; hypocrisy is a cause of illness, and the person who practices it gradually sickens. Thus there was a traditionally rather sound and healthy basis for emotional display, which was caricatured out of all proportion into a component of the cliché.

The Negro performer found that unless he fitted himself into the mold cast for him as typical he could get no work. This represents one facet of a vast attempt at justification of the slave system long propounded—the cliché that plantation life for the Negro had been a joyous lark, that happy, lazy Negroes spent their days dancing, singing, and indulging in childish pranks, with occasional spells of cotton-picking, and that the Negroes were wistfully lonely to be back at said plantations, which they were convinced constituted the happy land of Dixie. A Negro who had left the plantation or local mill was selected as a butt of ridicule—in the character of the "dandy nigger"—who squandered his earnings on flashy clothes and scorned his own people. Particular emphasis was always placed on class distinctions among the Negroes themselves, which were the basis for countless skits and dialogues.

Another curiosity was the extremely successful attempt to reintroduce the Negro as an exotic, attempted about 1883 by the Callender-Kersands company. The dancers' drill, a nineteenth-century theatrical fashion, which had its inception in classic ballet, was popularized in France, and taken over by England and America for all types of extravaganza. There were drills of Tartars, Amazons, Naiads, Turks, Brigands, Airy Sprites, and Skeletons. The Zouaves, with their colorful red and blue costumes and dark complexions, were a "natural" for the Negro dancers. Even as the Negro performer was at the threshold of his first great "period" theatrically, which might be generally characterized as the Williams and Walker era, concerted efforts were made to place every difficulty athwart his path.

Since the opportunity for literal, literary presentation was not afforded, nor any representation of Negro humor save the "unconscious" humor of an outsider having difficulty with an alien tongue (and how many thousands of blackface dialogue "sermons" there were!), it was only in the field of music and dance that the Negro might really leave an impress. An interesting note on the way in which the restrictions of the stereotype finally helped kill off the minstrel show itself was sounded in an interview by Lew Dockstader in 1902, when he told a *Sun* reporter that the Negro had so advanced that the dialects and material for the old-fashioned take-offs were already lacking, and so the "Negro character" was being invalidated, bringing to a close one phase of Negro contribution to the American stage. The clichés and stereotypes persisted of course, to this day, even among Negro performers. Yet during the latter days of the minstrel shows and the transition period of the nineties, when Negro dance and music in the theatre seemed to be losing their identity, the real Negro art kept alive and re-entered through another channel—the social dance—as well as through a medium which we might call a type of highly specialized social entertainment.

We have seen that the Negro as entertainer and musician was long welcome in saloons and dance-halls, even when the theatres were difficult for him to attain. This was equally true of bawdy-houses. And in such milieus, where there was no interest in imposing extraneous artistic standards, the Negro musician was empowered to create and perfect his own art. In dance halls and barrooms of New Orleans, St. Louis, Chicago, and the Barbary Coast, small Negro orchestras, now with a full complement of instruments, further developed that music which was to sweep the world. Syncopated off-beats, which had been known to western musicians for centuries, became a particular earmark associated almost exclusively with Afro-American music. The sense of timing and rhythmic "breaks" were equally a part of the dance. A great exhibition dance, the cake-walk, was also developed, with such superb theatrical potentialities that it served as a Negro re-entry permit to the stage. In the declining days of minstrelsy it was incorporated in finale "walk-arounds," an authentic American note at a period when imported operetta and extravaganza were eclipsing most of our indigenous theatrical forms.

Although handled with the bad taste of a supercolossal raree-show, *Black America*, presented in 1894 by Buffalo Bill's impresario, Nate Salsbury, was a first effort to make some presentation of the Negro as a person. Salsbury, a kindly man, who had offered such exotics as Pawnee Indians to the public, felt warranted in presenting the Negro in what was considered his native habitat—a plantation village. Large acreage, such as Ambrose Park in Brooklyn or the Huntington Avenue grounds in Boston, was made the site of a "Negro village," in which cabins and general living quarters were set up, with preacher and meeting house, mules, washtubs, and hay-wagons included, so that visitors might have occasion to see "the unconscious humor of darkies" (publicity release). Salsbury had gathered a choir of five hundred untrained voices, belonging, as a Boston newspaper touchingly explained, "to black men, women, and children, who themselves are devoid of culture." According to the *Illustrated American*: "They were recruited among the farm and mill hands of Georgia, Alabama, and Florida, with a view to securing perfect Negro types, rather than theatrical or musical talent. They arrived in New York ten days previous to the opening of the show, when a Negro minstrel stage manager took them in hand, and, building upon a foundation of inborn imitative aptitude, taught each what he or she was expected to do."

The spectacle itself had a brief introduction of "African tribal episodes and war dance," followed by interludes of song and dance, including a grand cakewalk contest. In every review it is immediately apparent that no audience was able to resist the beauty of Negro music. Again and again there is the same amazement at the beauty and technical ability of these untrained singers. Perhaps this admiration wrested from general audiences, in contrast to the select concert public of the Fisk Jubilee Singers, made this venture something of a triumph in spite of all the tawdry antics which were attendant to it.

In 1897 a brilliant period for Negro entertainment, lasting something more than a brief decade, was inaugurated. It produced musical comedies or extravaganzas which assembled the talents of Will Marion Cook, Ernest Hogan, Will Vedry, Paul Laurence Dunbar, Aida Walker, Jesse Shipp, Bob Cole, and many others. Their bright particular stars were the famous team of Williams and Walker.

The titles of many of these shows—*Senegambian Carnival, A Trip to Coontown, The Sons of Ham, In Dahomey, The Smart Set, In Bandana Land, Abyssinia, Shoofly Regiment, Rufus Rastus*—have a close relationship to the minstrel show stereotype, and the comedians wore the burnt cork and enormous painted mouth which were de rigeur for Negro comics. But the music and dances were unfettered by past conventions, and the raw elements of twentieth-century popular music acquired a style which would supersede the schottisches, waltzes, and cotillions of the nineteenth.

The transition did not come at the turn of the century, but with the First World War. It was a Negro composer, Ford Dabney, working with Vernon and Irene Castle, who set a general pattern both for social dance and theatrical forms. In its purest form hot music is essentially for listening. The great soloists of jazz, the improvisations of the jam session, demanded as much concentrated attention as any other piece of chamber music. Dabney, as accompanist, composer, and collaborator with the Castles, was initiator and popularizer of a new dance music.

Ford Dabney came to New York in 1900 with James Reese Europe, the noted band-leader, to appear at the Ziegfeld Roof. From 1904–1907 he was official pianist to the President of Haiti. He knew at first hand the unusual rhythms of the *tambours*, and of heel-beats against smooth earth. He listened to and remembered African ceremonial melodies, many of which the Haitians had preserved unchanged. On his return to New York he became one of that talented group of Negro musicians known as the Clef Club. In 1913 he met the Castles and worked with them until Vernon's untimely death. He was the alchemist who fused the diverse jazz elements into a popular style.

Master Juba had imposed the Negro tradition on tap-dancing. Ford Dabney, with his musical *Rang Tang*, consolidated Negro traditions theatrically as he had done socially. Negro music and dance, which had a virtuosity supported by native vitality, making them difficult to adapt, were finally integrated in the complete panorama of American music and dance.

Dancing Out the Difference: Cultural Imperialism and Ruth St. Denis's *Radha* of 1906

JANE DESMOND

Introduction

An analysis of the mechanisms through which meaning is generated is central to any re-evaluation of dance history and its canon. I will be arguing in this essay for the application of poststructuralist theory to the writing of dance history and also for the wider opening of feminist scholarship to considerations of live performance.[1] Women's studies, although it has generated a great deal of scholarly writing on the social construction of gender and the visual and verbal representation of women in literature, visual arts, and the mass media, has yet to engage fully with the specific richness of performance. Study of performance can include not only historical analysis of visual representations, their construction and reception, but also consideration of the special case of construction of meaning through display of the body—a body that is at once "real" and "representational" as it exists in performance. If "the feminine" itself can be conceived of as a socially constituted masquerade, as Mary Ann Doane and others have noted, then an analysis of performance has wide potential application for work in feminist studies.[2]

Dance Spectacle

Although dance scholarship has expanded dramatically in the last fifteen years or so, it remains far behind related fields of arts criticism both in the amount of work and in the level of analysis. Within the bounds of traditional history and criticism, several excellent scholars have emerged in the last two decades,[3] but the discipline as a whole is still waging a battle for acceptance within the academy and remains relatively closed to current work in related fields such as literary theory. There are many reasons for this: as the most ephemeral of all the arts, dance leaves the fewest traces (most dances have not been recorded in any way), making historical reconstruction and analysis exceedingly difficult. And, because it deals most directly with the mute (and most often female) body, dance remains suspect in institutions of higher learning.

Most dance writing is still concerned with technical and artistic judgment, historical reconstruction, reportage, and description, or even social history; but deeper analyses of the ideological functions of dances as works of art are still relatively rare. Only in the last few years have dance critics and historians begun to consider issues that have engaged literary critics and feminist scholars for much more than a decade. Gender, while it may be noted, is rarely analyzed as a constitutive factor.[4]

Furthermore, we are still in the early stages of developing theoretical tools suitable for our object of investigation: the human body, most often the female body, moving in performance. I want to show how theoretical tools drawn from other disciplines can be adapted to dance criticism, as well as how any investigation of gender in dance must be linked to concurrent analysis of other markers of cultural otherness, such as race and class. I hope that in return the particular structure of dance as live performance will open new avenues of theoretical investigation, furthering development of current theories about perception, pleasure, and the mapping of meaning onto the gendered body.

Ruth St. Denis

My object of analysis is an important 1906 piece, *Radha*, choreographed and performed by Ruth St. Denis. St. Denis is usually presented as one of the major figures in the history of American dance, and she is always cited, along with Loie Fuller and Isadora Duncan, as one of the three "mothers" of modern dance. Any re-evaluation of the dance history canon must consider St. Denis's work.

With her husband, Ted Shawn, she started the Denishawn school of dance, one of the first professional schools of "aesthetic" dancing, in 1915, and toured throughout the country in the early decades of this century. Doris Humphrey, Charles Weidman, and Martha Graham, the leading choreographers of the next generation, all served an apprenticeship with Denishawn. St. Denis's work was seen on the vaudeville circuit (often the first professional aesthetic dancing that many Americans encountered) and was performed in elite theaters as well. The bulk of her repertoire, which she continued to perform well into the 1960s, consisted of dances inspired by ethnic styles ranging from American Indian to Japanese. The scale of the works varied from solo pieces to large spectacles. Denishawn dancers even appeared in D. W. Griffith's 1916 film, *Intolerance*. In the 1920s St. Denis's company toured Asia, presenting its orientalia to enthusiastic crowds. Although St. Denis's aesthetic was largely rejected as too decorative by Humphrey and Graham, and her works are not regularly performed today, her contribution to the rise of modern dance in America cannot be denied.

Most dance histories discuss St. Denis's "showmanship" and refer to her dances as part of the turn-of-the-century American passion for exotica.[5] But such observations do not take us deeply into the ideological structure and function of the work itself. While we can never imagine with certainty the meaning of an art work for a particular audience, we can venture an analysis of its structures of meaning. I will argue that by adapting contemporary insights drawn from literary criticism, film theory, and work on race and colonialism, we can come closer to understanding not only what *Radha* means, but how its range of meanings may be produced. I will argue that *Radha* presents a hyperbolization of categories of otherness, mapping markers of race, orientalism, and sexuality onto the white middle-class female body. Thus, *Radha* can be said to function as a site of condensation and displacement of desire.

Radha

Spectacle

The dance opens and closes with visions of the Hindu goddess Radha posed in spiritual contemplation, partially hidden by a screen. The longest portion of the dance, however, consists of five variations celebrating the pleasures of the senses, and a whirling "delirium of the senses" episode that plunges the dancer into postorgasmic darkness. In both its theatrical structure and its visual arrangement on the stage, *Radha* is a spectacle displaying the female body.

It is spectacular first in the sense of not being narrative. Although there is a thin story line to the dance, and it fits the barest requirements of narrative—stasis, disruption, stasis—the majority of stage time is devoted to the display of the body in a way that does not drive a narrative forward by providing new information or character development.[6] Second, the spectacular aspects of the dance are enhanced by an emphasis on surface decoration. The stage is set with soft amber lighting, wisps of incense, and an ornate backdrop (or—in a later version—a stage set) representing a Jain temple. St. Denis's costume, a short jacket and gauzy skirt, is accented with "jewels" and trimmed with shiny material. Flowers adorn her hair and jewelry her ankles and arms. Midriff and feet are bare. That a critic for

25. Ruth St. Denis in *Radha* (1906). Reprinted courtesy of the Dance Division, The New York Public Library for the Performing Arts, Astor, Lenox and Tilden Foundations.

Variety referred to the "semi-nudity of the woman" tells us how this costuming was perceived at the time.[7]

The choreography itself reiterated the decorative aspect of the design. As Suzanne Shelton notes, St. Denis believed that "each gesture and pose should objectify an inner emotional state," and *Radha* was conceived as "an elaborate network of spatial and gestural symbols" connoting such feeling states as rapture, despair, or inspiration.[8] Authorial intent aside, *Radha*—having been blocked out with saltcellars on the kitchen table—was a series of simple circular or square spatial patterns composed of relatively simple movements.

These movements were the turns and flourishes of the skirt dancer's repertoire mixed with a smattering of balletish steps and Delsartean limb movements. Never

having studied Indian dance, St. Denis drew on the images of India available to her in books and punctuated her simple phrases with poses that recalled oriental icons and "popular images of the late Victorian era," such as the femme fatale.[9] Many of these poses were performed in profile, enhancing the two-dimensional quality of the figure-ground relationship. Radha, brought out of her ornate enclosure like a precious jewel, becomes a moving ornament against an elaborately decorated backdrop until, after displaying her valuable beauty, she is enclosed again, still tantalizingly visible but unattainable, within the carved fretwork of her diadem. Every aspect of staging can be seen as contributing to this fetishistic display. A closer look at the choreography will clarify the presentation.

Description and Close Analysis

The curtain rises to reveal the goddess Radha sitting in the lotus position on a pedestal.[10] (In later versions she is partially hidden from view behind an ornately carved screen, which will be opened by the head priest.) A procession of Brahman priests enters, carrying sacrificial offerings. (The priests were performed by Indian sailors and clerks rounded up for the purpose.)[11] When the priests are seated in a semicircle, framing a space for Radha to enter, she comes to life. Watched by her priests, she enters the sacred space to begin the dance of the five senses. In a progression from the senses of far distance to the more intimate ones (taste and touch), Radha dances to music from Delibes's orientalist opera, *Lakme*.

In the opening dance of sight, Radha holds a strand of pearls in each hand as she revolves in place. Then, in small steps phrased to the music, she moves from side to side in front of her watching priests, posing occasionally with one leg gently lifted to the front. Exchanging the pearls for bells, she begins the playful, rhythmic dance of hearing during which she surrounds her body with a cascade of sounds. Throbbing music initiates the dance of smell as Radha manipulates a garland of marigolds in a series of simple waltzing steps and poses. At the close of the section she arches back, trailing the blossoms along the front of her body, one hand crushing the flowers to her face. So far we have seen the dancer's body in association with nature and signs of luxurious ornamentation.

Things heat up for the dance of taste, which follows. Drinking deeply from a simple clay bowl, she whirls with abandon, ending in the seductive vulnerability of a deep back bend before she falls to the ground. Kneeling, with her skirt spread around her, she starts the dance of touch by caressing one hand with the other. Languorous music accompanies her movements as she slides her hands voluptuously over her body, ending with fingertips to her lips.

After the "foreplay" of the preceding episodes, the "delirium of the senses" section unfolds, the music

quickening to a frenzied tempo. Spinning, possessed, Radha whirls with her skirts swishing wildly until she suddenly falls to the ground, and "writhes and trembles to a climax, then lies supine as darkness descends."[12] The lights come up on a chastened Radha, lifting her arms in supplication. After tracing the petals of a lotus blossom on the floor, she withdraws to her shrine. The final image shows her sitting on her pedestal, transformed by *samadhi*, self-realization.

Aesthetic Dancing

St. Denis's aesthetic dancing arose during a time of complex social change in America. At the turn of the twentieth century, changing gender roles joined with racial and ethnic differences and class antagonisms to create a volatile social mixture.[13] To contextualize St. Denis's work, I will consider two aspects of turn-of-the-century culture: changing social attitudes toward the body, and popularization of the "exotic" in cultural forms.

American Delsarte Movement

In the latter decades of the nineteenth century, a growing emphasis on "physical culture" was allied with a number of reform and educational movements, such as women's dress reform and physical education.[14] Prominent among these physical training regimes was the American Delsarte movement, based on the teachings of French music and drama teacher François Delsarte (1811–1871). Seeking to analyze and classify human expression, he developed a technical training system based on "an elaborate and mystical science of aesthetics deriving from his personal interpretation of the Christian Trinity."[15] In the Delsarte system, the codification of gesture was linked to "a spiritual labeling of every part of the body according to certain zones— Head, Heart, and Lower Limbs, which corresponded to Mind, Soul, Life."[16]

Although intended for the elocutionary training of professional speakers and actors in the 1870s, the expressive principles of Delsarte's aesthetic theory were being practiced throughout the United States by the late 1880s, especially by women, in the drawing rooms of middle- and upper-class households. American proponents of Delsartism stressed relaxation techniques, "energizing" exercises, rhythmic gymnastics, "natural" movement based on spiralling curves, statue-posing, and pantomime. Statue-posing and pantomime were deemed "the ultimate in refinement and gentility" and helped open a "wedge for the entrance of respectable women into the field of theatrical dance" at a time when the theater was regarded in the United States as morally suspect.[17]

Through Delsarte, movement was analyzed and linked to meaning and morality. "Natural" movement was thought to provide authenticity of expression. The body became a signifier of Truth. Writing in 1954 about the Delsarte system, Ted Shawn, St. Denis's life-long partner, states, "The spontaneous movements of the body cannot lie . . . all human beings move under the government of universal laws, and gesture is the universal language by which we can speak to each other with immediacy, clarity, and truth, and which no barrier of race, nationality, language, religion or political belief can diminish in communicative power."[18]

The changes in American society at the turn of the century coincided with massive colonial expansion in which Europe consolidated control of most of what is now known as the Third World. During this time, a popular and elite fascination with non-European cultures coincided with a rise in such "sciences" of codification as ethnography. The "exotic" was extremely fashionable in scholarly endeavors as well as "high" art and "low" art forms.

In some high art contexts, the exotic was cast as a utopian vision of the past glories of classical civilizations. The past seemed to offer an antidote to the chaotic urban conditions that threatened the middle and upper classes. At the 1893 Chicago Columbian Exposition, the monumental White City, built in neoclassical style, typified this urge in elite cultural production.[19] Popular images of the exotic, however, were less utopian and were perceived by the cultural elite as merely gratifying the senses rather than providing spiritual uplift. For example, historian John Kasson describes the exposition's Midway as "exuberant chaos," and a "hurlyburly of exotic attractions: mosques and pagodas, Viennese streets and Turkish bazaars, South Sea Island huts, Irish and German castles, and Indian tepees."[20] A prime attraction was the Persian Palace of Eros where Little Egypt and her cohorts danced the hootchy-kootchy. Described at the time as a "suggestively lascivious contorting of the abdominal muscles" that was "almost shockingly disgusting," this attraction proved immensely popular.[21]

Exotic popular amusements like the Midway and Luna Park on Coney Island, which attracted both middle- and working-class patrons, supplied an ornate aesthetic that Kasson has termed the "oriental orgasmic." The essentialist strains of Delsartism and orientalism mixed well. St. Denis's achievement in *Radha* was to combine the oriental orgasmic with Delsartism's transcendent spirituality into a spectacular form that could play successfully not only on the vaudeville circuit but also at the garden parties of the elite and in the art theaters of America and Europe.

Ruth St. Denis and Radha

The multiple strains of orientalism, popular culture, and artistic spiritualism that are found in St. Denis's work have their beginnings in her childhood. The daughter of a well-educated progressive mother, she was drilled in Delsarte exercises and exposed to Eastern spiritualism through theosophy and through the orientalist performance of leading American Delsarte exponent Genevieve Stebbins. As a young adult, St. Denis became a believer in Christian Science, and throughout her career she combined the spirituality of the Delsarte system with her own adaptations of Christian Science teachings, which emphasized that "spirit is the immortal truth; matter is mortal error."[22]

Some scholars have seen a feminist dimension in Christian Science, founded by Mary Baker Eddy, because it asserts the androgynous nature of God. In the social sphere, this concept means that in order to be complete persons, both men and women had to have "a harmonious balance of masculine and feminine traits."[23] But equally important to Christian Science were notions of morality that promoted "purity" and chastity.[24] Inheriting the traditional Christian dualism between the spiritual and material realms, Christian Science did away with the hierarchy of that dualism by denying the material world altogether, subsuming it into a monism of Spirit. As Susan Hill Lindley has argued, the feminism of Christian Science was "ambiguous," and Eddy's resolution of this dualism that traditionally denigrated both women and the material "was no real solution to the tension, for it denied rather than redeemed the 'lost half.'"[25]

But, the spiritualism of Christian Science combined with the Delsarte system, which allowed women a new freedom of expression through movement, may have provided St. Denis a way "around" the strictures associated with the body's materiality and sensuality. While building a career on her own physical display, she steadfastly asserted her identity as a mystic and her dancing as spiritual uplift. In a poem titled "White Jade" describing an early dance of the same name, St. Denis writes, "My own body is the living Temple of all Gods. The God of Truth is in my upright spine. The God of Love is in the Heart's rhythmic beating. The God of Wisdom lives in my conceiving mind. . . . The God of Beauty is revealed in my harmonious body."[26] In this rhetorical fiat, the material body is not so much denied as transposed into the figuration of transcendental values.

Through her dance, St. Denis declared that she was presenting the mystic's experience of unity with God. In preparation for each performance of *Radha,* St. Denis writes, she would meditate for half an hour to "realize my contact with the one Mind," so that by the time she stepped onstage, she felt she was truly the priestess in the temple."[27]

Just as in Christian Science the body was subsumed into Spirit, St. Denis subsumed the sensual aspects of her dancing into a vaunted mysticism framed both as

religion and as art. In doing so she, like her contemporary Isadora Duncan, was able to extend the bounds of propriety in the public display of the partially clothed female body. At a time when bare feet were cause for shock, St. Denis in her revealing costume earned reviews declaring, "Every lascivious thought flees shy into the farthest corner. . . . [She has] freed our souls from the clutches of everyday life."[28]

St. Denis's dancing was not always so uplifting. With the support of her mother, who accompanied her to New York, she got her start at the age of fifteen as a skirt dancer in a dime museum variety show. Surrounded by specimens like triple-headed calves, she danced six shows a day, punctuating her routines with acrobatic roll-overs and her specialty, the slow-splits. On the bill with St. Denis one week in 1894 were an albino musician and Lillie the Trick Dog. This may not seem an auspicious start for a dancer who was later to be hailed as the solution to "the world's enigma," but it provided the basis for an artistic savvy that "aspired to the loftier echelons of fine art" while never losing the "genius of lowbrow."[29]

The myth surrounding St. Denis's first moment of choreographic revelation combines mass consumer culture with the spiritual aspirations assigned to high art. In 1904, while on tour in a David Belasco production of *DuBarry,* St. Denis was struck by a drugstore poster advertising Egyptian Deities cigarettes: the barebreasted goddess Isis sat surrounded by huge columns and flowering lotus. An inscription carved in stone above her head assured the buyer that "No Better Turkish Cigarette Can Be Made." St. Denis later wrote, "My destiny as a dancer had sprung alive in that moment. I would become a rhythmic and impersonal instrument of spiritual revelation. . . . I have never before known such an inward shock of rapture."[30]

In dance histories, this incident is usually repeated and valorized as a moment of artistic inspiration. What should be noted, however, is how it reveals the forces of commodification, appropriation of the exotic, rapturous denial of the physical in favor of the spiritual, and display of the female body as a site of revelation that were to mark St. Denis's work throughout her career. All of these are exemplified in *Radha*.

The dance (*Egypta*) that the poster inspired was not completed until several years later, but the idea of an Eastern goddess was transposed into an Indian setting for *Radha*, which catapulted St. Denis into the artistic circles of the cultural elite. First publicly performed in 1906, *Radha* played in New York at Proctor's vaudeville house on Twenty-third Street,[31] with St. Denis appearing between acts by a pugilist and a group of trained monkeys.[32] Soon, however, a New York socialite and oriental enthusiast, Mrs. Orland Rowland, took an interest in St. Denis's work and arranged a private matinee for her society friends. *Radha* became a hit. Newspaper notices assured her success with headlines such as "Yes, Society Did Gasp When Radha in Incense-Laden Air 'Threw Off the Bondage of the Earthly Senses,'" and hundreds of eager spectators were turned away from subsequent performances.[33] St. Denis was launched on the high art circuit and soon found an influential supporter in Stanford White, but her work never lost its cross-class appeal. Lean times periodically sent her back to vaudeville to finance her work.

By thus contextualizing *Radha* in terms of the popularity of exotica at the turn of the century, the rise of "barefoot dancing," and various strains of spiritualism, I have touched on issues of gender, orientalism, and changing representations of women. Many dance historians stop their analysis at this point. But I still want to consider in detail the ideologies of these various discourses and their mode of activation in the construction of *Radha*.

"Orientalism"

Edward Said defines "orientalism" as "a political vision of reality whose structure promoted the difference between the familiar (Europe, the West, 'us') and the strange (the Orient, the East, 'them')."[34] Through an act of "imaginative geography,"[35] it both created and then served the maintenance of the two worlds. It articulates a "relationship of power, of domination, and of varying degrees of cultural hegemony."[36] "Orientalism" in Said's usage refers not only to the changing political-historical relations between Europe and Asia but also to the discovery and study of various oriental cultures by Westerners and to a body of assumptions, images, and fantasies held by Westerners about the Orient.[37] It is this latter category that is my concern here. Although Said traces historical changes in the specific constitution of these images and fantasies, he maintains that a pervasive "latent Orientalism," circulating both inside and outside of scholarly disciplines, has remained remarkably consistent for several hundred years.[38]

Above all, the Orient is conceived of as unchanging and eternal. Occasionally these characteristics are valorized as "seminal" and "profound," as in reference to "the wisdom of the East."[39] Yet, most of the attributes assigned to the Orient are opposite to those valorized in the West. The East is primitive, childlike, and backward; it is eccentric, irrational, chaotic, and mysterious; it is sensual, sexual, fecund, and despotic. Most important, the Orient is deemed incapable of speaking for itself. It is not Europe's "interlocutor, but its silent Other."[40] The Western orientalist, as artist or scholar, "makes the Orient speak, describes the Orient, renders its mysteries plain for and to the West."[41]

By the end of the nineteenth century, the East was clearly constructed as a site requiring explication, investigation, illustration, discipline, reconstruction, or redemption.[42] The East's otherness offended European standards of sexual propriety, threatened domestic seemliness, and "wore away Eastern discreteness and rationality of time, space, and personal identity. In the Orient, one was suddenly confronted with unimaginable antiquity, inhuman beauty, boundless distance."[43]

By the last decades of the nineteenth century, the "unchanging" nature of the East was seen as a source of regeneration for a Western world caught in an unsettling rise of industrialism and materialism.[44] Said has characterized this idea of regeneration as a secular post-Enlightenment myth based on Christian imagery of death and rebirth through salvation.[45] In *Radha*, St.

Denis acts out a similar scenario of redemption within the imaginative geography of the Orient.

Following Said, we could thus look at *Radha*, with its cresting tide of physical excitement overcome by spiritual purification, as illustrating the threatening chaotic sensuality of the East and its ultimate discipline and redemption through the triumph of spirituality or the law of ultimate truth. From this point of view, *Radha* projects a vision of the East as a site of imaginary pilgrimage both for sensual indulgence and physical awakening (the same notion later popularized in E. M. Forster's *Passage to India*) and for spiritual rejuvenation of an America in the throes of change.

But if *Radha* is "about" the East, it is even more about the West. As James Clifford has noted in his criticism of Said's book, Said's argument at times suffers too much from the dichotomy we/they he attempts to describe.[46] In fact, Western discourse about "the East" reflects a continually changing historical process of self-definition by "the West." We can see *Radha* as a portrayal of Western desires and ambivalences displaced onto an orientalized, gendered body. The association between the cultural otherness of the Orient and the construction of gender in the West is the key to this linkage.

Orientalism and the Otherness of Gender and Race

As a site of unlimited desire and deep generative energies, the Orient is figured as female.[47] Trinh T. Minh-ha describes the construction of the feminine in Western culture in practically the same language Said uses in depicting the Orient. "Woman," she says, "can never be defined. . . . She wallows in night, disorder, immanence, and is at the same time the 'disturbing factor (between men)' and the key to the beyond."[48]

Both "woman" and "the East" are constructed by Western patriarchy as "natural" categories of difference requiring explication, investigation, illustration, discipline, reconstruction, or redemption. Knowledge of both is eroticized as a stripping bare, an exposing of

hidden meaning. The vocabulary itself reveals a scopic economy of difference in which the act of seeing is equated with mastery. As Said notes, a recurrent motif in nineteenth-century writing is the "vision of the Orient as spectacle, or tableau vivant."[49] That both the Orient and woman are cast as speechless renders self-narrative and history impossible and creates the necessary conditions for visual spectacle as site or source of knowledge. These double specular economies of difference come together in St. Denis's performance of *Radha*. Here the mute colonized female body represents the sensuality of both the "female" and the Orient. Similarly, the higher spirituality attached to the "wisdom of the East" meets current notions of the women's sphere as the province of moral guardianship.

Radha is thus doubly sexualized and doubly chaste. The tensions between these seemingly incommensurable attributes—goddess/whore, Eastern/Western, and sexual/chaste—are all articulated across the material presence of the female body. The dance signals the underlying dialectical relation of opposites in any binary construction. It also points to the changing dimensions of women's roles at the turn of the century and the reconstruction of female physicality as it was reflected in the health reform movement.

Freud's description of woman's sexuality as the dark continent reminds us of the intimate relationship among orientalism, gender, and a third register of otherness: race. In discussing this phrase, Sander Gilman asserts that Freud "ties the image of female sexuality to the image of the colonial black and to the perceived relationship between the female's ascribed sexuality and the Other's exoticism and pathology."[50] The reason Freud's statement was legible to his contemporaries is that, like female sexuality and the imaginative geography of colonialism, the "dark races" were represented as objects to be illuminated, mapped, and controlled.

Early nineteenth-century race theory[51] joined with social Darwinism in the latter half of the century to provide intellectual currency for white ideas about the biological basis of racial inequality.[52] Like gender, the concept of race entailed notions of difference that were seen as irreducibly linked to the body and, therefore, as "natural." Both women and non-whites were thus consigned to the "lower" realm of nature. The same dynamic of dominance based on natural difference that was exemplified in white colonialism also undergirds patriarchy.

Reading *Radha*

In *Radha* I find a construction of meaning that depends on manipulating these codes of difference into an overlapping structure. Race, gender, and cultural otherness double one another, with each register reinforcing the next to produce a hyperbole of "Otherness." Dancing, as a nonverbal display of the body—most often the female body—provides an especially rich mode of articulation for this process.

As I have noted in the preceding discussion, orientalist thought has constructed the East as feminine. Racial thinking has similarly tied otherness to the body. Display of the "colored" Eastern female body then carries with it a surplus of signifiers of difference. The litany of difference can be summarized as sexual (i.e., desirable yet terrifying), mute, natural, essential, universal, unchanging, and visually knowable. The female body is the nodal point that interpolates racial and cultural difference in *Radha*. Its investigation is also the main content of the dance and the vehicle for spectacle.

Mechanisms of Meaning

The structure of this dance reveals the spectacle of a woman lost in a rising tide of self-pleasure, a goddess delirious with her own sexuality. It shows a woman renouncing, of her own accord, the powerful pleasure of her own body for a chaste spiritual union with the transcendent. It shows the careful marking out and celebration of each aspect of a woman's physicality, her five senses explored one by one moving in sequence, so that the spectator is drawn into an ever more intimate relationship with her body. This spectacle is displayed in front of a semicircle of male viewers on stage and equally directed outward to the audience.

When it is described in this way, the scopophilic aspects of the piece become apparent. Drawing on psychoanalytic film theories of spectatorship and voyeurism, I maintain that the woman's body is fragmented and fetishized, not only visually but conceptually, into each of the five senses—the woman is the five senses, each displayed separately for investigation by the viewer.[53] The woman, observed "unawares" by the audience in the darkened theater, is caught in a vortex of pleasure. She is further situated as object of the male gaze through the relayed looks of the priests on stage. Their presence also signals the religiosity of the act. (Being priests, they provide no competition for a white heterosexual male viewer in the audience but do provide adequate gender identification.)

At first glance, it appears that any displeasure that may be aroused in a male viewer by the woman's ability to sexually satisfy herself is soon banished by the reassurance that she rejects her own pleasure/power for spiritual fulfilment. The potential terror of female sexuality would thus be constrained by the patriarchal law of the Father in the form of religion, which would demonstrate the control that orientals, women, and all people of color were seen as requiring. However, the dance also unites the goddess/whore duality within the figure of one woman, thus allowing for several possible readings. One reading reassures the male viewer that even "asexual" women are really "women," that is, defined by and reducible to their bodies. Other readings might hold that women themselves are repositories of both relationships to sexuality, indulgence, and control; or that woman's pleasure in her own body is so seductive as to involve a constant struggle between expression and renunciation; or even that the pleasure of the senses is itself a transcendent spiritual experience. That is, the recuperative effect of the religious framing remains ambiguous, allowing for multiple responses.

Scopophilic pleasures of this sort are allowed in high art under certain conditions. St. Denis's contemporary, the Austrian writer Hugo von Hofmannsthal, characterized this requirement when he stated that, although *Radha* "borders on voluptuousness, . . . it is chaste."[54] The mechanism that allows this audience/performer link can be described as what Michel Foucault calls the "confessional" mode.

The Pleasures of the Confessional Mode

One way of looking at the dynamics of meaning in *Radha*, with its religious discourse, is in the form of a Christian confessional. The confessional structure is a ritual expression, a truthful telling of forbidden behaviour, especially—as Foucault emphasizes in *The History of Sexuality*—sexual behaviour. It requires a speaker and listener (performer and audience).[55] The act of telling "exonerates, redeems, and purifies" the confessor, and promises him or her salvation.[56] Its redemptive promise simultaneously allows, while disavowing, the illicit pleasures of prurient interest on the part of the audience.

Foucault indicates how the range of the confessional form expanded after the Reformation. By the end of the nineteenth century this range extended into a series of relationships, including those between psychiatrists and patients and delinquents and experts, and it also took several rhetorical forms such as autobiographical narratives and published letters.[57] I would add to this list the relationship between Radha and her audience as it functioned in performance. It was the supposed moral superiority of the viewing audience that was being played to and reinforced in Radha's display and renunciation of the pleasures of her own body. Linda Nochlin has, in her discussion of orientalist painting, called this type of viewing experience a "tongue-clicking and lip-smacking response."[58]

The confessional mode interlocked with St. Denis's own way of conceiving of her work. St. Denis's belief in the Delsartean meaningfulness of movement, and her conviction that her dancing demonstrated the unity of the individual spirit with god (formulated in Christian Science as androgynous, or beyond sexuality), framed her work in moral justification. The confessional mode, as a way of structuring a relationship between performer and spectator, framed sexuality as art and art as moral uplift. Given St. Denis's position as a woman choreographer, then a rarity, I believe that her utilization of these discourses of morality enabled her to subvert the contemporary standards for "respectable" women's display of their own sexuality. In doing so, however, she also reproduced traditional patriarchal designations of that sexuality.

The tensions between the sexuality of the work and its artistic and spiritual framing are reflected in the contemporary critical response. Von Hofmannsthal captured the crux of the dance: "It is consecrated to the senses, but it is higher." Similarly, a British critic called *Radha* athletic in its actuality and ascetic in its refinement. The reviewer for the *Boston Herald* could not help noting that St. Denis's "body is that of a woman divinely planned" but insisted that "there is no atmosphere of sex about her."[59]

Foucault's work can take us farther in a consideration of sexuality and spectatorship. Foucault points out the similarity between two modes of production of truth, the confessional and the scientific discourse.[60] Both were utilized in the expanding nineteenth-century discourses of sexuality, and both implied a will to knowledge that reflected a socially inscribed power to investigate, to judge, and ultimately to reform or punish. In *Radha*, both of these discourses come together. The ethnographic urge to represent the other for the pleasure and uses of the representer[61] combines with the display of sexuality sanctified by the confessional code. The result for the audience is a doubly inscribed "right to look," further enhanced by racial ideologies.[62]

In white Western discourse, both non-whites and non-Westerners are coded as extremely or excessively sexual. The dark (St. Denis used dark body paint in the first versions) goddess from the erotic East, then, implies a surfeit of sexuality. Even when St. Denis switched to a body suit of her own flesh color in later versions, either for reasons of propriety or merely for convenience, she was still perceived as a Hindu goddess, and we know that at that time in North America, Hindus were perceived as black. In one of the first performances, when a Hindu first entered carrying a tray of incense, an audience member jeered in black dialect, "Who wants de Waitah?"[63] The racial implication was so clear that the company did not tour south of the Mason-Dixon line because of the Jim Crow laws.

St. Denis was, of course, known by her audience to be white. Her portrayal of a woman of color had the effect of sexualizing her in the audience's mind. This is similar to the device used in nineteenth-century odalisque paintings where the association of black women with whites served as a clue to the sexual knowledge or availability of the white women.[64] Similarly, while St. Denis is Western, she is here linked to the sensuous, eternal feminine represented by the East.

These several dynamics function to enhance the audience's right to look sexually at the respectable white middle-class woman on the stage.[65] The racial and cultural displacement of *Radha* is precisely what enhances the success of the confessional mode in the context of art. It is this hyperbole of otherness and its reinforcing linkages between ideological notions of race, gender, and non-Westernness that, I suspect, was the key to this dance's popularity.

Conclusions

But if we leave the analysis at that, we fail to consider fully the dynamics of live performance. After all, the representation of Radha is not a story, where the priestess Radha might be imagined, or a painting, where she might be displayed and observed, but a live performance. As I have already mentioned, the middle-class white woman's body is central to the production of pleasure in the relationship of these three markers of otherness as discussed above. But it is also the factor that ultimately confounds binary constructions of meaning. In the ludic or dreamlike space of performance, the performer is both white and non-white, Western and Eastern, and female while usurping the male role of choreographer. (Remember that at that time, although most dancers were female, very few dances were choreographed by women.)

What issues of spectatorship and the production of meaning do these complications raise? At the very least, they unsettle the binarisms of the ideologies that undergird racism, sexism, and orientalism. The element of mastery, however, implied by the right to represent the "other," remains.

But if we look at the choreography, with its combination of skirt-dancing turns, ballet steps, and "Indian" gestures, something else becomes apparent. The dance itself serves as a sign of the cultural process of "othering" through representation—an ongoing process of construction that is always self-reflexive with regard to the culture that produces it. The representative codes of vaudeville skirt-dancing collide with iconic signs of Indianness, mixing with and overlaying one another as a sign of cultural interaction and continually renegotiated meaning.[66]

Although there is no Brechtian self-reflexivity built into the theatrical structure of *Radha*, implicit in every performance is the spectator's awareness of the construction of an illusion."[67] Because of its existence as a temporal art—and a three-dimensional one that is dependent on the physical presence of the performer in the same space as the audience (i.e., not sculpture, not film, not literature)—live performance must produce a convincing linkage of similarity and difference.[68] The performer is both himself or herself and the character who is portrayed. Performance presents this as a dialectical relationship, always in negotiation.

Drawing on psychoanalytic film theories of spectatorship, I could argue that St. Denis as a white Westerner provides an avenue of psychological identification for her white Western audience. Framed by the essentialist, transcendent spirituality of the piece, the audience is brought into ego identification with the white as nonwhite and the Western as Eastern. At the same time, the voyeuristic and fetishistic aspects of the dance (enhanced by its construction as spectacle) objectify it as separate from the observer. A "colored" white woman (since this is not caricature of the minstrel-show variety) also evokes an ambiguous response. While "mixing" sexualizes the white woman, it simultaneously indicates a potential mixing of the races, legally proscribed at the time. If ideologies are based on binary constructions of difference necessary to the maintenance of hegemony, performance thus indicates the ambiguity of such binary constructions and their true dialectical function in the production of meaning.

Certainly St. Denis's rise to fame and her ability to present herself in respectable theaters as a woman alone on the stage is emblematic of the social changes in the women's sphere at the turn of the century. Still, her work remains conservative in its assertion of spirituality as the realm of woman and also in its presentation of woman's body as sexualized. One of St. Denis's achievements was to unite these supposed opposites.

Some critics have begun to pose questions theorizing the body in performance.[69] Questions of the power of representation become more complex when acted out on and through a material body. Is the female appropriation of sexual display in live performance, even within patriarchal norms, an act that in some way threatens the hegemony of patriarchy? That so much of the sexual pleasure in *Radha* is danced as self-pleasure (especially Radha's self-caressing) on the one hand asserts a new self-empowerment for woman and on the other belongs to traditional structures of pornographic viewing.[70]

In any performance, the venue and the particularities of audience are essential to the generation of meaning. Certainly the meanings activated by the first performance, for spectators who had just watched boxing and were soon to see trained monkeys, were somewhat different from those generated by the same piece in a "respectable" theater, framed as "art." Different still is the reception of *Radha* by our students today who dutifully sit through St. Denis films in dance history seminars.

What the investigation of a piece like *Radha* can provide is an example of the necessity of unraveling the multiple strains of ideological meaning that are present in any work of performance and that are variously activated in specific viewing situations. For instance, similar doublings of race, exotica, and sexuality are played out in Josephine Baker's famous "banana dance." As a black woman, however, her construction as "exotic" never played as successfully in North America as in Europe.

As we reconsider the canon of dance history and integrate it with gender studies, it is not enough to ask how St. Denis conceived of her work, or how it relates to the dance history that precedes and follows it. Nor it is enough to ask how St. Denis's work reflected the changing roles of women in her day, or to note stylistic similarities between dance and other types of artistic products in the same historical period. All of these investigations produce valuable information and should not be ignored. But as scholars we must also look more deeply at the mechanisms of meaning on which the performance hinges and investigate the role of live display of the female body in activating those mechanisms, as I have attempted to do in this essay. Only by more fully comprehending the production of ideology in every sphere of social construction, including the female body in performance, can we begin to sever the invisible links that bind racism, sexism, and cultural imperialism so tightly together.

Notes

My thanks to Jennifer Wicke and Virginia Dominguez for commenting on earlier drafts of this article and to Victoria Vandenberg for research assistance.

1. Susan Leigh Foster's excellent *Reading Dancing: Bodies and Subjects in Contemporary American Dance* (Berkeley: University of California Press, 1986) is, as of this writing, the only extended treatment of dance history to draw on theories of semiotics and on the historiographic work of Hayden White to construct a new model for a poetics of dance. This work focuses on developing paradigms for approaching various types of choreography but does not make race, gender, or class central components of its analysis.

2. See Mary Ann Doane, "Film and the Masquerade: Theorizing the Female Spectator," *Screen* 23, nos. 3–4 (September–October 1982): 74–89, for a discussion of related concerns and references to relevant articles.

3. See, e.g., work by Marcia Siegel and Sally Banes such as Sally Banes, *Democracy's Body: Judson Dance Theatre, 1962–1964* (Ann Arbor: UMI Research Press, 1983), and Marcia Siegel, *The Shapes of Change: Images of American Dance* (Berkeley: University of California Press, 1979).

4. In the last few years, some exceptions have begun to appear. See Ann Daly's interesting work on gender and ballet in her "Classical Ballet: A Discourse of Difference," *Women and Performance* 3, no. 2, issue 6 (1987–88): 57–66; and Marianne Goldberg's discussion of gender in Martha Graham's work, "She Who Is Possessed No Longer Exists Outside," *Women and Performance* 3, no. 1, issue 5 (1986): 17–27. Suzanne Shelton's meticulously researched biography of Ruth St. Denis, *Divine Dancer* (New York: Doubleday, 1981), on which I will draw throughout this article, discusses sexuality as a factor in St. Denis's work but does not analyze it in detail. Neither does Foster's consideration of St. Denis, although gender is noted.

5. For the works that discuss *Radha* as part of the general passion for the exotic at the turn of the century, see Elizabeth Kendall, *Where She Danced: The Birth of American Art Dance* (1979; reprint, Berkeley: University of California Press, 1984); Nancy Lee Chalfer Ruyter, *Reformers and Visionaries: The Americanization of the Art of Dance* (New York: Dance Horizons Press, 1979); Christina L. Schlundt, "Into the Mystic and Miss Ruth," *Dance Perspectives*, no. 46 (summer 1971). Foster and Shelton also situate the work in terms of exotica.

6. For a discussion of the relation of narrative and spectacle, see Laura Mulvey's breakthrough article, originally published in 1975, "Visual Pleasure and Narrative Cinema," reprinted in her *Visual and Other Pleasures* (Bloomington: Indiana University Press, 1989), 14–28.

7. Quoted in Shelton, *Divine Dancer*, 54.

8. Ibid., 62.

9. Ibid.

10. I rely on my viewing of a 1941 filmed version of St. Denis performing *Radha*, a print of which is housed in the Dance Collection of the Lincoln Center Library, New York. I draw also on Shelton's verbal reconstruction of the dance, based on her viewing of the same film and supple-

mented by her review of St. Denis's papers housed at Lincoln Center.

11. Kendall, *Where She Danced*, 51.

12. Shelton, *Divine Dancer*, 61.

13. See John Higham, "The Reorientation of American Culture in the 1890's," in his *Writing American History: Essays on Modern Scholarship* (Bloomington: Indiana University Press, 1970), 73–102.

14. Kendall, *Where She Danced*, 22.

15. Ruyter, *Reformers and Visionaries*, 17.

16. Kendall, *Where She Danced*, 24.

17. Ruyter, *Reformers and Visionaries*, 29.

18. Ted Shawn, *Every Little Movement: A Book about François Delsarte* (New York: Dance Horizons Press, 1963), 90.

19. John Kasson, *Amusing the Million: Coney Island at the Turn of the Century* (New York: Hill & Wang, 1978), 17.

20. Ibid., 24.

21. Ibid., 26

22. Mary Baker Eddy, quoted in Shelton, *Divine Dancer*, 47.

23. Margery Fox, "Protest in Piety: Christian Science Revisited," *International Journal of Womens Studies* 1, no. 4 (July–August 1978): 411.

24. Susan Hill Lindley, "The Ambiguous Feminism of Mary Baker Eddy," *Journal of Religion* 64, no. 3 (July 1954): 326.

25. Ibid., 331.

26. St. Denis quoted in Schlundt, "Into the Mystic and Miss Ruth," 24.

27. Ibid., 21.

28. Ibid.

29. Shelton, *Divine Dancer*, 67, 21.

30. Ibid., 46.

31. Vaudeville at this time reflected both its "coarser" origins in variety shows for male audiences and its newer respectability as it targeted a growing middle-class (male and female) audience. St. Denis's work, a respectable presentation of sexuality, fit well with changing codes of performance. Shelton notes: "As ladies began to patronize high-class variety, the atmosphere of the theater became even more self-conscious, with elaborate rationales required to justify the display of female bodies. Scantily clad women appeared as 'living statues' or in tableaux that duplicated famous paintings or biblical episodes" (*Divine Dancer*, 25).

32. Ibid., 54.

33. Ibid., 58.

34. Edward Said, *Orientalism* (New York: Random House 1978), 43.

35. Ibid., 90.

36. Ibid., 5.

37. Ibid., 90.

38. Ibid., 206.

39. Ibid., 208.

40. Ibid., 93.

41. Ibid., 206.

42. Ibid., 40, 206.

43. Ibid., 167.

44. Notions of regeneration were not limited to the West. Said notes that in view of the conditions under colonialism, the Western "Orientalist found it his duty to rescue some portion of a lost, past classical Oriental grandeur" (ibid., 29) in order to ameliorate conditions in the present. In other words, the Westerner could now represent the Orient as it was, is, or should be, not only to himself but also to the Orientals, restoring to them glimpses of their past glories. St. Denis participated in this process when she toured the Orient in 1925–26. Her dances, constructed primarily from library research and from inspiring pictures, were warmly received in India, Japan, and other countries. In India, her respectability may have contributed to a renewal of prestige for traditional classical dancing. However, as one critic noted (see Shelton, *Divine Dancer*, 199), there may have been some irony in the situation for the Indian audiences as they watched a white woman dance a temple dance that was, at the time, usually performed by prostitutes.

45. Said, *Orientalism*, 115.

46. James Clifford, "On Orientalism," in *The Predicament of Culture: Twentieth Century Ethnography, Literature, and Art*, ed. James Clifford (Cambridge, Mass.: Harvard University Press, 1988), 255–276.

47. Said, *Orientalism*, 188.

48. Trinh T. Minh-ha, "Difference: 'A Special Third World Women Issue,'" *Discourse* 8 (fall–winter 1986–87): 30.

49. Said, *Orientalism*, 158.

50. Sander Gilman, "Black Bodies, White Bodies: Toward an Iconography of Female Sexuality in Late Nineteenth-Century Art, Medicine, and Literature," in *"Race," Writing, and Difference*, ed. Henry Louis Gates Jr. (Chicago: University of Chicago Press, 1986), 257.

51. Race theories proposed a division of races into advanced (white) and backward (non-white) categories, just as orientalist thought divided the world into the strong, progressive, advanced West and the weak, primitive, degenerate East. Colonial expansion was seen as proof of the triumph of the fittest.

52. Said, *Orientalism*, 206.

53. Laura Mulvey's article remains a cornerstone for psychoanalytic critical theories of spectatorship in film. She draws on Lacan's extension of Freud's work on ego formation and the construction of sexual subjectivity to develop a theory of visual pleasure based on voyeurism and fetishism. Her work opposes notions of the social construction of the female as spectacle, i.e., "to-be-looked-at," to that of the male as active narrative agent. These ideas have important implications for developing a related theory of spectatorship for live performance. Following Mulvey, I believe that staging *Radha* as a spectacle (see "Spectacle" section under *Radha*, above) enhances the voyeuristic and fetishistic production of pleasure.

54. Quoted in Shelton, *Divine Dancer*, 47.

55. Michel Foucault, *The History of Sexuality*, vol. 1: *An Introduction* (New York: Random House, 1987), 61.

56. Ibid., 62.

57. Ibid., 63.

58. Linda Nochlin, "The Imaginary Orient," *Art in America* 71, no. 5 (May 1983): 125.

59. Quotes from Shelton, *Divine Dancer*, 64. Note also that Shelton, who calls *Radha* a "ritual orgasm," acknowledges the mixed message in the piece and its oriental eroticism. But in her discussion of these qualities she merely states, "This mixed message stemmed from St. Denis's own stage personality and, by extension from the quality of the gestures," which reflected her background as an unassuming New Jersey farm girl (64–65). The intricate dialectic between East and West remains submerged in a discussion of individual artistry.

60. Foucault, *The History of Sexuality*, 64.

61. Houston A. Baker Jr., "Caliban's Triple Play," in Gates, *"Race," Writing, and Difference*, 386.

62. I am using the term "right to look" as it is developed by Jane Gaines in her "White Privilege and Looking Relations: Race and Gender in Feminist Film Theory," *Cultural*

Critique 4 (fall 1986): 59–79. She refers to culturally proscribed economies of vision as they are delineated along lines of race, gender, and class.

63. Quoted in Shelton, *Divine Dancer,* 54.

64. Gilman, "Black Bodies, White Bodies," 240.

65. The class alignment or consignment of successful performers during that time was complex. "Respectable" artists often socialized with the elite, yet remained a class apart, somewhat beyond the pale. In terms of her class origins, St. Denis came from a family relatively poor in economic capital, but rich in educational capital (to use Bourdieu's distinction). Her mother was trained as a doctor, although she did not practice, and her father was an inventor. Certainly, St. Denis's self-presentation in her adult life ("respectably" married to her partner Ted Shawn, for example) indicated an alignment with the middle class.

66. For a consideration of issues of negotiation in colonialism, see Homi Bhabha's "Of Mimicry and Man: The Ambivalence of Colonial Discourse," *October* no. 28 (spring 1984): 125–133.

67. Brecht's theories of theater emphasized the notion of distanciation, or the "alienation effect." By means of such devices as self-reflexivity his plays keep spectators aware that they are participating in the construction of a fiction; thus they avoid the conventions of realism that serve to naturalize ideology. See Bertolt Brecht, *Brecht on Theatre,* ed. and trans. John Willett (New York: Hill & Wang, 1964).

68. The situation is somewhat different with film. While the image composed of reflected light is less material than a play in performance, the evidentiary nature of the photographic image carries with it a strong coding of realism. In some ways, film can allow for a stronger identification (and temporary loss of the sense of self as separate from the fiction) than live performance. The complexities of this relationship between film and live performance will have to be considered as film theory is adapted to performance analysis.

69. For interesting discussions of related concerns, see Elinor Fuchs, "Staging the Obscene," *Drama Review* 33, no. 1 (spring 1989): 33–57; and Jill Dolan, *The Feminist Spectator as Critic* (Ann Arbor: UMI Research Press, 1988).

70. For an analysis of the visual structures of pornographic viewing, see Annette Kuhn, "Lawless Seeing," *The Power of the Image: Essays on Representation and Sexuality* (Boston: Routledge & Kegan Paul, 1985), 19–47.

Two-Stepping to Glory:
Social Dance and the Rhetoric of Social Mobility

JULIE MALNIG

The popularity of classic dancing grows greater every day. It has won its place in American life. Everywhere the dancer is in demand. Startling salaries are paid. And those who can dance for charitable entertainments or for the pleasure of their friends quickly become social favorites.
—SERGEI MARINOFF, "I Can Teach You to Dance Like This,"
Dance Lovers Magazine, November 1922

Dance—particularly social dance—has long had an association with the attainment, or at least the preservation and display, of social status, from the Renaissance court spectacles and balls of Queen Elizabeth, to nineteenth-century New York Cotillions. The editor of *The Director,* a nineteenth-century magazine on "dancing and deportment," describes dance lessons offered at the Knapp Mansion in Brooklyn for children of the middle class where "the absolute necessity of knowing how to dance is, of course, apparent to persons who go much into society."[1] The American debutante ball is a classic example of social dance serving as the gateway for entrance into one's social community.[2] The style and format of nineteenth-century American dance, from which exhibition ballroom dance emerged, carried with it the European tradition of ballroom dance as a symbol of decorum and good social breeding. But how, specifically, did the alignment between dance, social status, and "social mobility" become expressed in the ballroom dances of the early twentieth century? What did the concept of social mobility mean in the early years of the Progressive era when the United States was undergoing significant transformations in its social consciousness? What I show here is

how the concepts of progress and social mobility, social ideals much in the forefront of the minds of Americans, become enmeshed in the very fabric of the ballroom dance practices and contexts themselves. I will explore how both professional and recreational dancers used the dances and their attendant meanings as ways of adjusting to this rapidly changing cultural climate.

The early teens, in particular, presents a fascinating case study for the dance historian examining the relationship between dance and social context. Historians concur that during this time nothing short of a cultural revolution occurred.[3] The country was re-orienting itself to major cultural and technological developments in the wake of industrialization, among them an emerging consumer culture, massive immigration, a burgeoning middle class, and large-scale movements from rural to urban areas. These developments, in turn, led to a wide-ranging re-evaluation of social values and mores including relationships between the sexes, women's role in society, and concepts of morality and sexuality. As the cities became meccas for industry and commerce, a host of new social institutions emerged there, such as cabarets and hotels, dance halls, theatres, movies, and amusement parks. In this publicly oriented culture, mass performances became an important vehicle through which emerging values and ideals were displayed for public consumption.

Ballroom dance of the early twentieth century was one such mass performance form. The cultural and economic "revolution" of these early years rivaled an equally potent "social dance" revolution whose reverberations were felt all across the nation. The social dance phenomenon of the 1910s reflected a profound and changing consciousness regarding the style and manner of dance performed by the public. In terms of both actual movements and rhythms of the dances, as well as the context and manner in which they were performed, early twentieth-century social dances represented a radical departure from previous eras of social dancing. Multiple forces—cultural, economic, and social—converged in these dances to produce a distinctly new aesthetic of social dance, and with it revised codes of social behavior.

While the so-called "modern" ballroom dances breathed fresh life into the social dance arena, they also earned their share of reprobation. During the early teens the country conducted a national referendum on the dances. Newspaper and magazine essays and articles with titles such as "Is Modern Dancing Indecent?" offered soul-searching commentary on the nature and meaning of the dance phenomenon.[4] In 1915 the Pope banned the tango, and at some dance clubs indulging in the current "shoulder-rocking, feet-dragging freak dances" might result in a misdemeanor.[5] A brief look at the contrast between nineteenth- and twentieth-century social dances will help explain this moral outrage. Nineteenth-century balls were typically held either in the drawing rooms of private homes, at clubs, or in large assemblies. A standard program might consist of a mazurka, polka, waltz, and cotillion, performed in that order. Dances were usually listed on dancing cards distributed to the guests.[6] The steps of the dances were performed in a fixed order and were based on the five ballet positions characterized by out-turned feet and pointed toes. The physical stance was prescribed and proper. In the waltz, for instance, considered risqué when first introduced in the eighteenth century, couples were always mindful of keeping the requisite foot-apart distance. In the typical nineteenth-century ball, dancers tended toward group movement. As the dance master called out the steps couples toured the ballroom in small circles attuned to the movements of their fellow dancers. The dances, and the entire circumscribed nature of the dance atmosphere itself, reflected, and also fostered, a restrained sense of cordiality and decorum valued between the sexes.

Musical styles would ultimately influence the changed style of social dance and etiquette of the ballroom of the 1910s. The two-step, a rollicking dance that became popular in the 1890s, was born to the strains of John Philip Sousa's "Washington Post March." In this dance—containing a double-quick march with a light hop or skip in each step—couples adopted a hip-to-hip position with the man's arms around his female partner's waist. The Boston waltz, slower-tempoed than its predecessor, the whirling Viennese waltz, also accounted for a change in style.[7] Here, dancers adopted a forward and backward movement promoting a more natural, walk-like step (a feature of many early twentieth-century dances). It was from the Boston waltz that the Boston Dip emerged—a quick sinking movement made in unison by both partners. As the compositions of well-known black composers, such as James Weldon Johnson and Scott Joplin, filtered through Tin Pan Alley the quick, excited rhythms of syncopation suffused a new era of ballroom dance.

During the years 1906–1908, so-called "rag dances" became wildly popular around the country. With names such as the Grizzly Bear, Turkey Trot, and Chicken Reel, to name a few, these animated dances—performed to syncopated beats—injected into the ballroom a note of irreverence and abandon as couples literally swayed and rocked back and forth with each step. These early dances were essentially fast two-steps or one-steps virtually indistinguishable from one another except for the striking head and arm movements (such as the "pumping" and "flapping" action of the arms in the Turkey Trot) that earned them their "animal" names. Often, in an attempt to promote their compositions, inventive songwriters named their numbers after the colorful body gestures of the dances—and these names then took hold.[8] Ragtime had also invigorated the more traditional waltzes, as well, as in the hesitation waltz where the performer "hesitates" on the second and third counts of a three-step waltz. In terms of the structure of performance of these dances, unlike the conformity of nineteenth-century social dance, where couples stepped and moved in a straight line or a circle around the floor, early twentieth-century social dances allowed couples to improvise steps and become virtually oblivious to the movements of their fellow couples.

What was fascinating and significant about this "social dance revolution" was its simultaneous popularity as both a theatrical genre and a cultural phenomenon. The vogue for this dance form was spurred through the performances of the highly popular exhibition ballroom teams—those professional dancers who created stylish, theatricalized versions of contemporary social dances. The professional teams transformed the earlier rag dances into the sleek fox-trots, Argentine tangos, Brazilian tangos, hesitation waltzes, and one-steps that became the basis for the dances seen at most ballrooms of the teens. Irene and Vernon Castle, Maurice Mouvet and Florence Walton, Mae Murray and Clifton Webb, and Joan Sawyer and Wallace McCutcheon were among some of the most esteemed and widely publicized teams of the day. By the mid-teens most of these major dance couples had numbers created or named for them, such as Joan Sawyer's Aeroplane Waltz (with its distinctive gliding movements) and the Castle Walk, a variation on the one-step inspired by the Castles' composer, the well-known black musician James Reese Europe.[9] Socially, the public copied and transformed these dances for their own recreational purposes in the cabarets and dance halls that by 1915 had sprung up in all the major cities.

At the height of their fame, the exhibition ballroom teams had become national idols, exemplars of current styles of dress, etiquette, physical and emotional ex-

pressiveness, and symbols of emerging values of the 1910s. This evolving ballroom dance style enabled women and men to perceive themselves in different ways. Physically, the teams emphasized a balanced carriage that promoted the smooth and coordinated functioning of two bodies moving in space. More so than in nineteenth-century ballroom dance, these contemporary social dances made greater use of the upper chest and torso. To perform adequately in this physical style, women dancers abandoned the heavy petticoats and tight-laced shoes of the previous era favoring movement-oriented clothing that was loose-fitted at the hips and waist. By 1913 designers were advertising a dress called the "tango-visite," featuring a transparent bodice and mid-calf-length layered skirt—a contrast to the tight-waisted, long flowing Gibson gown fashionable a few years earlier. In the display of this less restrictive clothing, professional dancers "taught" social dancers about the freer and more expressive modes of movement that the dances required. Unhampered by hard corsetting and tightened waists, women could now perfect the goal of rhythmical synchronization with their dance partners, a quality now prized among social dancers since it might make one a more supple, desirable partner.

Irene Castle, a progenitor of the emerging "new woman" of the teens and twenties, served as a potent role model. One of the first of her generation to "bob" her hair, she promoted contemporary styles of dress and movement and appeared in most of the major women's and fashion magazines of the day (figure 26). Her ideas on the virtues of dance as a beautifying agent offered for women, in particular, a refreshing outlook on physical appearance and self concept. Along with the dress reform that the new dancing inspired came a variety of exercise techniques designed to promote women's agility on and off the dance floor. Irene Castle supported this trend. As she said of women and social dance: "It teaches rhythm; it keeps her in tune with life; it gives her a graceful swinging walk; it shows her how to hold her head, and how to use her hands, and, what is more, how to use her feet. Many women are

26. The popular exhibition ballroom dancer Irene Castle displays a typical dance dress of the period, of chiffon material with a layered skirt and loose bodice, for ease and comfort on the dance floor (ca. 1913). Photographer unknown. Reprinted courtesy of the Billy Rose Theatre Collection, The New York Pubic Library for the Performing Arts, Astor, Lenox and Tilden Foundations.

awkward in their ways of moving and standing."[10] Indeed, Irene Castle, with her husband, Vernon, served as a strikingly elegant model for this rhythmical, proportional sense of beauty. Their image as a happily married couple, too, created a potent model for audiences as they suggested a healthy and wholesome sexuality possible between the sexes *through* the joy and spontaneity of social dance. This idea fit in perfectly with expanding Progressive-era notions of marriage as a renewed site of domestic harmony and pleasure.[11]

Clearly, social dancing of the pre-twenties era heralded important social and cultural changes that would have a lasting impact on future generations. Dance historian and theorist Sally Banes, in "Power and the Dancing Body," offers illuminating insights into the relationship of dance and culture that provide a useful methodological frame for this essay and for conceptu-

alizing dance's influence on society generally. As she notes, one view (the more traditional) contends that dance is a mirror or microcosm of culture reflecting cultural ideals and patterns of behavior. As such, dance thus exists side by side with culture. Here the body becomes a mirror where cultural attitudes are "registered from above on passive bodies."[12] Drawing on the ideas of cultural theorists such as John Fiske, Banes notes the alternative view where bodies are "sites of resistance." According to Banes, in this view, "ordinary people . . . become empowered, creating their own social identities by manipulating and reworking the oppressive body images produced by the dominant ideology."[13] In translating this issue into the concerns of this study a relevant question becomes: Are popular dance forms essentially conservative in that they only reproduce the values of the culture—values which may be inherently coercive or pernicious—or do they have liberatory potential?

Urging a middle ground between these positions—in which we are either victimized by or resistant to our culture—Banes argues that we should examine the ways that dance may be viewed as a building block in the development of culture itself. We should look at the ways dance intersects with cultural practices and ideology and, as Banes notes, "actually produces cultural practices outside of the dance world itself."[14] In so doing, we can explain dance's role in culture as one of galvanizing many social forces, and recreating or visualizing those forces in a kinetic language that might serve individuals and help them mediate the demands of their lives. For instance, for the young working girl of 1915, attending the local dance hall, becoming proficient in forms of social dance and its accompanying social rituals might become a way of affirming or expressing her status, and serve as "a channel for etiquette and modes of social behavior, and not the just the repository of etiquette."[15]

The "rhetoric" of social mobility actually refers to an entire system of discourses and rhetorical practices and strategies through which the relationship between social dance and concepts and ideas of progress was expressed. Certainly, the "language" of media and advertising served as a central vehicle, both the literal texts as well as the images and their combined metaphorical ability to represent and express concepts of progress and betterment. The ballroom dance phenomenon, for instance, part of the new wave of mass leisure activities, while not a *product* of early twentieth-century advertising, was certainly aided and enhanced by this system. It was through the new apparatus of advertising that, in large measure, ideas about dance, social mobility, and social values were conveyed. Other "rhetorical" vehicles through which this relationship between dance and mobility was expressed took the form of dance instructional manuals, sheet music, and record catalogues. The events that occurred at institutions such as the cabarets and dance clubs, too, and the ways these events were perceived, generated their own kinds of meanings that got circulated in the culture at large. In exploring these practices in their totality we can begin to determine how an overriding ideology (or ideologies) becomes established in the sense that cultural critics Deborah Rosenfelt and Judith Newton define that term, as a "system of representations, discourses, images and myths, through which we experience ourselves."[16] This strategy enables us to consider those characteristics of the dancers and the entire ballroom dance phenomenon that may have served as potent images and ideals for a culture concerned with moving forward.

For some members of society, certainly, social mobility implied prospering financially in order to move up and into another level of society. Many in this category were the subjects of social theorist Thorstein Veblen's radical critique of the excesses of late-nineteenth-century industrialism, in which one's worth was determined not only by one's acquisition of wealth, but by its ostentatious display.[17] For others, for whom literal upward economic mobility was not possible, it meant the attainment of those behaviors, attitudes, and sensibilities that indicated one's familiarity with the next upper strata of society. Issues of social mobility were not only economic, but socio-cultural, as well. Through attainment of social dance proficiency, for instance, one might become acquainted with the possibility of the idea of social movement, or at least be able to acquire the skills or adopt the values required to circulate properly within another class level. And finally, social mobility to many was connected to the acquisition of the confidence, social poise, and psychological confidence required even before one might hope to "succeed" within or beyond the bounds of one's class.

Social Mobility in the Progressive Era

In the following discussion I locate some of the key concepts and definitions of "progress" during the early years of the Progressive era (1912–1917) that found their way into the rhetoric of the social dance phenomenon.[18] As historian Henry F. May has noted, the idea was not monolithic: "Progress was no longer a universal single movement, but wherever one looked things were getting better."[19] The country as a whole was adjusting physically and psychologically to the major upheaval in the shift from an agrarian to commercial culture, from a world in which the home was the site of production to a land of "consumers." One prevailing notion, certainly, maintained that advances in technology, industry, and commerce inevitably spelled a better way of life for the majority of middle-class Americans, in their ability to purchase goods and services to augment their standard of life, but also in their ability to enjoy their expanded leisure time. Or, as historian John Higham points out—on a less sanguine note—people had digested the credo of the machine age and had come "to comfort themselves with a faith in automatic material progress."[20]

An alternative outlook defined progress less in material terms and more from an activist perspective developed as a reaction to the routine and restriction of the industrial age. The former nineteenth-century exuberance attached to the belief in unbounded materialism became tempered as the reality of "big organizations, the massing of population, and the growing intensity of class conflict" became apparent.[21] Under the influence of Positivist thinkers, such as William James and John Dewey, the idea took hold that individuals had the inherent ability to change the course of their fate and that human will and creative action could result in good works.[22] These ideas of societal betterment accounted, in large part, for the impulse behind the reform movements of Progressivism. What historian Richard Hofstadter has called a widespread cultural tendency toward "self-reformation" led to the creation of settlement houses, protective legislation for workers, immigrant reform, and other forms of social welfare that the country believed might evolve toward a more humane place in which to live.[23] Part of this optimistic sense of progress evolved from the rather nostalgic notion that society could be restored to its former grandeur, before the advent of the machine.

Another type of progress could be measured in psychological and physical terms. Inspired by the popularization of Freudian psychology, social movements such as women's suffrage and the efforts of Progressive reform, writers, commentators, and advertisers preached a new "self help" gospel aligned with social mobility in the sense that attainment of this level of self satisfaction and enjoyment could advance one's life, both materially and spiritually. Cultural historian T. J. Jackson Lears locates this cultural expression within a shift in the early part of the twentieth century from "a Protestant ethos of salvation through self-denial toward a therapeutic ethos stressing self-realization in this world."[24] A symbol of this uplifting spirit was fitness guru and self-improvement specialist Bernarr McFadden, whose popular and widely circulated magazines, such as *Physical Culture* and *True Story*, promoted the virtues of positive thinking and healthy lifestyles. Progress here was measured not only in terms of material acquisitions and wealth, but by the state of one's physical and emotional well-being. In some respects, this ethos represented the popularization of the philosophies of Dewey, James, and others. It was a part of the general revolt against conformity and formality that early twentieth-century social dances expressed.

Mass Leisure and Advertising

It was amidst this evolving consciousness in philosophical outlook that the leisure entertainments flourished. In fact, the mass-entertainment movement was fueled by the expanding consumer economy which created demand for these entertainment forms through advertising and other mass promotion techniques. An improved standard of living meant that Americans could now "choose" to pursue a variety of contemporary leisure activities, "purchasing" them with the same vigor with which they purchased commodities such as furniture or cars. Of course the middle classes typically had more available leisure time and more purchasing power than immigrants or the working classes, but even for the less well off, mass production offered the lure of cheaper goods and amusements.[25] The nickelodeon, for instance, a less expensive form of the movies, and dance halls, scaled-down versions of the higher-priced uptown clubs, offered similar types of entertainment. Various popular entertainment technologies, too, such as the phonograph, brought these leisure activities directly into the home.

The role of ballroom dance as a "disseminator" of some of these modern notions of progress and social mobility was intimately tied to the emerging consumer culture. In what historian William Leach refers to as the "democratization of desire," all consumers are equal in the eyes of advertisers since they all have the same abilities to partake in the fruits of consumerism.[26] During the early years of the century, while there was a great discrepancy in wealth between the richest and the poorest, there was also enormous flux within society.[27] For the large middle class and for working classes and immigrants, there existed the ability to achieve "significant upward occupational mobility, or . . . the possibility of it."[28] Business leaders and others, aware of advertising's potential to manipulate specific audiences, drew on the themes of mobility, success, and the new liberatory morality in relation to dance. As a result of advertising's reach, made possible by means of mass reproduction, these same images and ideas became widely circulated and disseminated among readers of all classes.

But to what extent did advertising subsume these images and messages in consumerist jargon to create "false consciousness"? Assuming, as Leach does, that capitalist consumerism "may have been among the most nonconsensual public culture ever created,"[29] what happens once a message emerges into the public sphere? How does it resist homogenization, and how might ordinary people in their daily lives make sense of these concepts, even *use* them in any other way than to be lured into buying products and services? These questions are relevant to the emergence of leisure activities and to the popularization and role of social dance. It is possible to look to what other and additional kinds of "readings" the performances of the exhibition ballroom teams can withstand, rather than viewing them as simply one more "item" of commodification.

As Fiske points out, relevant to this discussion of social mobility, the ideas and images circulate not only in the realm of the economic, but in the realm of the cultural, and what gets exchanged in the cultural economy "is not wealth but meanings, pleasures and social identities."[30] One can argue that what gets circulated are false dreams and hopes. Fiske, though, suggests the possibility that in the process of commercializing there lies potential for popular entertainments to be put to positive use by users and consumers.

Cultural theorist Raymond Williams, from whom Fiske derives much of his analysis, discusses the complex web of class relationships that comprise corporate culture. He argues that "there is a central system of practices, meanings and values, which we can properly call dominant and effective."[31] Certainly the presumptions and practices of advertising and the mass media can be said to constitute dominant ideologies. But in an industrial culture, with many layers of class stratification and in which mass consumption permeates all classes of society, Williams argues that the ways these values are implemented are not necessarily static or rigidly bound but that "there are always sources of actual human practice which [the dominant mode] excludes."[32] Williams here enables us to consider more fully the range of meanings about social mobility and progress contained within the rhetoric about the dance and dancers and to suggest ways in which "emergent" values may have been expressed. While it is difficult, certainly, to determine with any accuracy how individuals themselves responded to the "rhetoric," or whether as a result of dance proficiency they might have actually moved from one social milieu to another, we can nonetheless examine what the appeals were and what expectations were created.

Mass Media and Ballroom Dance Practice

The rapid spread of the ballroom dance phenomenon became possible as a result of the technology of early twentieth-century industrialism. A vast system of railroad networks, for instance, now made it possible for ballroom dancers to perform on the major vaudeville circuits in cities across the country. Hundreds of small, independent theatres, too, presented variety entertainments featuring exhibition ballroom teams. Many spectators had already been "primed" for these appearances as a result of having read about the teams in mass subscription magazines, or in newspapers, where they were advertised selling products or interviewed for an upcoming engagement. Feature stories appeared not only in middle-class newspapers, but also in newspapers such as the *New York Sun* and the *Journal and Advertiser,* which circulated largely among immigrant and working-class communities. Media exposure such as this also hastened the unique reciprocal process between professionals and social dancers. As the public learned about the dances they, as well as dance teachers, were quick to pick up the numbers and transform them for the ballroom.

In addition, there existed a wealth of other "alternative" sources of mass-media instruction. In addition to published dance manuals written by many of the well-known exhibition ballroom teams (as well as dance teachers), many newspaper articles on the teams contained full-page illustrations and instructions for the dances, functioning essentially as more affordable dance manuals. For instance, to preview the 1916 production of the musical farce *His Bridal Night* starring the Dolly Sisters, the popular single-sex exhibition ballroom team, the *Newark Star Ledger* ran daily articles for an entire week featuring "dance lessons" by the sister duo. Most of the dances featured—such as their Dolly Waltz and Minuet Rag—were based on production numbers from the show although simplified for potential use by social dancers.[33] Sheet music for the popular one-steps, two-steps, fox trots, and other cabaret dances, too, routinely featured dance instructions on the inside or back covers, often with diagrams and foot charts. All of these materials, some of which I will describe, served not only as media publicity for the teams but as successful means of communication of early twentieth-century dance practice and form.

One of the dominant themes for promoting the

teams was their association with high society and their cultivated air of "refinement" and grace. The dancers, however, were almost forced to adopt this persona to dispel the notion that the newer, freer movement-oriented dances were not risqué and to counter the severe criticism leveled at them by moralists. High society leaders themselves also had no choice. To their great moral consternation their own daughters were indulging in the latest rag dances. A headline in the society section of the *New York Sun* noted: "Turkey Trot Seen at Plaza Dance: Southern Society Didn't Want It and Was Somewhat Shocked."[34] Instead of denouncing the dances outright, society matrons actually embraced the teams, presenting them at their balls and social functions, bestowing upon them the title of "society dancers." The "refinement image" appealed to the dancing public who derived pleasure from imagining themselves in this role. As if to remind readers, however, that one need not necessarily be born into this world of privilege and wealth, the press also touted the "success" stories of many of the exhibition ballroom dancers. For instance, acclaimed exhibition ballroom dancer Maurice Mouvet was a working-class youth who reportedly worked his way into the business as a page at the fashionable club Maxim's.[35] For middle- and working-class readers, the inspirational nature of such stories suggested that with ballroom dance proficiency one could be propelled into the ranks of the elite and transcend class barriers.

This phenomenon of dance-linked social mobility bears out Williams's notion of how a "system" of central practices and meanings gets communicated and circulated within a culture. The image of upper-class sensibility served several interests: members of the elite, who needed a way to justify this popular upsurge and assuage their anxieties; dance teachers, who had their own financial interests to protect; the dancers themselves for whom the image bolstered popularity; and advertisers who appropriated the image to win potential customers. As the idea and image of refinement was adopted by advertisers and got circulated in the popular press it became translated by viewers of different classes as a sign of bourgeois respectability. In many advertisements a team's "aura" became "sold" to people of different classes across the country. Maurice Mouvet and Florence Walton, featured in a spread for O'Sullivan's Live Rubber-Soled Shoes—selling for $4.50 a pair—brought home the gospel of American materialism through their "refined" air. As Mouvet noted in a caption: "I would not run my automobile without tires and I don't propose to walk around without O'Sullivan's heels."[36] In their upright, regal bearing Mouvet, dressed elegantly in a tuxedo, and Walton, wearing a fashionably layered, taffeta gown with a wide cape, cut an elegant and persuasive image to which readers, schooled in the latest dances, might respond.

The image of the "modern" dance couple actually became a major selling device for goods and services. A typical sort of advertisement during this period—whether for Pond's Vanishing Cream or Phoenix Silk Hose—featured a classy-looking male and female dance couple, reminiscent of Irene and Vernon Castle, in a contemporary dance pose. Usually the pair was looking at and smiling to readers or gazing at one another, obviously totally absorbed in the moment of dance.[37] Sporting the latest dance dresses, hats, and shoes, the teams lured in readers anxious to learn the proper "look" required on the dance floor. In figure 27, for instance, this sophisticated-looking dance couple demonstrates the body placement and holds characteristic of contemporary social dance with the man's arms gently encasing the woman's back, their bodies engulfed in a unified, carefully synchronized motion. Their graceful demeanor, their wholesome healthiness, and their apparent ease and pleasure together, suggest social dance proficiency as a means to attain those social and physical attributes and traits that afforded one entry into civilized, rational society.

The idea of becoming "educated" in social conventions through dance acquisition was intimately tied to a basic knowledge of current musical styles, therefore popular social dances figured prominently in catalogues and advertisements for the recording industry. In fact, the catalogues accompanying one's purchase of

record albums usually listed the names of social dances in vogue at the cabarets and clubs. The Columbia Records Catalog from 1914 contained the following note: "Practically any of the tangos may be used for dancing the Maxixe [a form of the Brazilian tango] simply by playing the record at a slightly faster tempo than the regular speed used for the tango."[38] From this we can infer how dancers not only *practiced,* but *converted* the dances into those that they could reasonably (physically) perform themselves. Fashioning the dances according to their personal needs and desires led to a certain confidence and poise that might win them popularity, friends, and social invitations. Further supporting Williams's and Fiske's belief that if individuals within communities or groups mold popular culture to forge new social identities, these turn-of-the-century dancers could practice and fashion these dances to their own level of satisfaction, until they were ready to "present" themselves in the ballroom.

Similarly, the ubiquitous Victrola advertisements illustrate the ways that dance and leisure entertainments had become incorporated into the everyday lives of Americans and reveal how the prevailing discourse of social mobility may have been expressed. An advertisement from a 1914 program for a vaudeville ballroom-dance extravaganza, placed by a music distributor, featured two sketches of elegant, spirited couples, one couple swaying to the imagined strains of music from their Victrola, the other from the notes issuing from the player piano. Titled "New Dance Music for Home Parties," the advertisement told readers that "nothing will add to your dancing ability more than practice at home to the music of Victor records, Edison Diamond Disc records, or Rythmodik Player-Piano Rolls."[39] While readers, of course, were exhorted to choose from among their favorite brands, an underlying message was that before venturing out into the socially competitive world of the cabaret or dance club, social dancers could test their dance and social skills in the privacy of their own home. The gaiety of the scene, the couples frolicking amiably, also suggests the social success one might achieve through dance.

At the Dance

WHEN a little Pond's Vanishing Cream has been rubbed in lightly, as a finishing touch, she knows that her skin is wonderfully fresh-looking; that it has the transparency and softness everyone so much admires.

This incomparably smooth cream contains a wonderful skin-softening ingredient which has a *special affinity* for the skin. Vanishing Cream being non-oily may be used *at any time.* It vanishes at once, leaving no trace of greasiness on the skin — only a delicate, elusive odor of Jacqueminot roses.

Send for a large trial tube — a full two weeks' supply — free to readers of The Ladies' Home Journal, provided 4c is enclosed for postage. Or a sample tube will be mailed free on request. Enjoy the admiration a lovely complexion always brings. Address Pond's Extract Co., 129 Hudson Street, New York.

Manufacturers of the famous Pond's Extract, a household necessity for 70 years. Also Talcum, Cold Cream, Tooth Paste and Soap.

POND'S Extract Company's
VANISHING CREAM

27. This advertisement, from the May 1915 issue of the *Ladies Home Journal,* was typical of the way social dancing of the teens became incorporated into the visual iconography of the period. Reprinted courtesy of the General Research Division, The New York Public Library, Astor, Lenox and Tilden Foundations.

The theme of achieving personal salvation and physical liberation through dance as a means of augmenting one's status was communicated frequently in the popular media of the time. The idea of a nostalgic return to nature, to a world untouched by technology, became conflated with the act of dance itself. Actual physical enjoyment of dance, as well as the benefits assumed accrued to one as a result of dance proficiency, was a means to restore this lost eden. Dance, it was believed, promised a type of pure and unmediated pleasure. Much of the advice literature of the day connected these notions of the body, movement, and physical pleasure with psychological and moral growth as a means of succeeding in the business world. Often this idea got conveyed through what William James called "The Gospel of Relaxation," a message preached to business and professional people as well as factory and clerical workers. A chapter in the Castles' *Modern Dancing* (their dance manual and etiquette book), written by Dr. J. Ralph Jacoby, connects social dance ability with the contemporary discourse on the "therapeutic ethos." Jacoby discusses modern ballroom dancing literally as a "system" of re-educating one's muscles to protect oneself against disease. In this example the appeal was to the notion of personal success gained through creative control of the body and mind. Says Jacoby:

> It is known that it is difficult for the man who carries his head erect and throws his shoulders back to be dejected; likewise it is difficult for the stoop-shouldered, frowning, querulous-looking individual to be joyous and exalted. . . . The dancer's main object is to present a good appearance; his muscles are cultivated to give a light and buoyant poise to the body; his facial expression become one of pleasure and laughter. In such a one it is difficult to conceive any mental dejection.[40]

Ballroom dancer Joan Sawyer, an ardent suffragist and one of the first breed of entrepreneurial women to manage her own dance club, appropriated these same concerns in language appealing expressly to young working-women. She told a reporter on one of her cross country promotional tours in support of suffrage: "It seems evident that the spread of the dancing habit has done much for women; not alone in the acquirement of added grace, for dancing is the best form of exercise, both for the body and the mind. . . . It inspires healthy thinking, a sane point of view, and normal poise."[41] Here Sawyer spoke to a generation of women drawing strength from an era infused with new gender consciousness and heightened awareness of women's potential. In linking the rhetoric of physical and psychological progress to dance and to women's new-found freedoms, she offered the possibility that social dance training (along with increased employment and women's right to vote) was yet one more means of aspiring to the values of twentieth-century womanhood.

While it is true that these published statements and appeals got reproduced and churned through the mass consumer and advertising apparatus, they served as more than "hype" for a majority of young middle- and working-class women. Such dance proficiency signified something vital: It was indeed progress to be able to perceive and present one's body in "modern" terms and assert oneself on the dance floor. Here dance could actually become, in Banes's words, the "channel" through which women experienced greater individuality of expression and interaction between the sexes.[42] Through attaining greater command of their physical and psychological selves, women might now possess the skills to prepare themselves for integration into their own class or, perhaps, consider themselves as capable of exceeding their current status.

The Cabaret World

Acculturation in ballroom dance practice and sociality described so far has been of a subtle kind, transmitted through the growing networks and channels of advertising and mass media. But there was another type of social dance "training" that occurred in the cabarets and dance clubs of the teens. In these newly developed cultural institutions the rhetoric of dance as tied to social mobility was most apparent in the relationship between professionals and social dancers and among social dancers themselves. The American cabaret—the precursor of the nightclub that flowered in the thirties and forties—was one of the most frequented leisure venues of the 1910s. Born of the restaurant industry of the late 1900s, it was a wholly American phenomenon that combined dinner, drinks, and floorshow. As a social institution, the cabaret drew together women and men of different economic backgrounds. Moreover, it represented one of the first attempts to take social dancing out of private homes, characteristic of nineteenth-century social dance, into more public settings.

The seeds for the cabaret had been sown around 1900 in the emerging restaurant culture in New York's Times Square area. Fashionable Fifth Avenue hotels, such as the Waldorf-Astoria and others, began catering to the new monied classes who congregated to socialize and conduct business. To maintain their social position, traditionally prominent families—now faced with competition from the emerging industrialists—used these hotels and restaurants, in the words of social historian Lewis Erenberg, as "public stages" to flaunt their social status and "display their monetary power, and hence their industrial might."[43] From about 1900 to 1910, the hotel and restaurant industry mushroomed as a result of the influx of people to the cities and the burgeoning tourist trade for the expanding Broadway theatre. Increasingly, into the teens, the leisure patterns of these wealthier hotels and restaurants filtered down to the middle-class restaurants and hotels along Broadway that created dining rooms with lavish decor, rivaling the opulence of their Fifth Avenue counterparts.[44]

Here was a Veblenesque image of conspicuous leisure at work, a place to demonstrate the ability to participate in leisure activities because of one's material standing. It was in this arena that the exhibition ballroom teams first won such great acclaim. For many spectators and social dancers, enjoyment of the teams, with their aura of glamour and wealth, came to serve as a vicarious means through which they might express their own social aspirations. As the cabaret culture grew, it ultimately came to characterize the behavior of an ever-widening sphere of the middle and even working classes who were now sharing in the values of the upper class. Veblen, no doubt, would have decried these tendencies as so much envy and emulation of the symbolic trappings of wealth. However, there were aspects of the cabaret experience, as I will describe, in which young middle- and working-class women, rather than merely mimicking upper-class values to prove their worth, might assert individuality and aspire toward expanded concepts of self.

Whatever social milieu they catered to, all cabarets had the shared feature of serving as public places for demonstration of contemporary social dances and the physical deportment and conduct those dances inspired. For one, the actual design and interior of the cabaret itself affected the look of modern ballroom dance. The generally small, packed dance floors literally forced dancers to move more naturally and closely (than in nineteenth-century social dancing) if only to keep from bumping into one another. The entire ambiance of the cabaret fostered intimacy and connection with its tightly assembled tables, dimly lit chandeliers, and closely moving bodies. It was in the cabaret that the distinctly reciprocal relationship became established between exhibition ballroom dancers and the audience: after the professional teams performed, the public would rise to the dance floor and "perform" their own versions. For social dancers at the cabaret, the exhibition ballroom teams symbolized and dramatized one of the precepts of early twentieth-century social dance—the notion of a single dance-couple performing apart from the entire group, inventing steps and movements together, independent of direction from a dance master.

Needless to say, the cabaret provoked fears among reformers and conservatives, in large part because of the large number of single, unescorted women who frequented the clubs. The specific source for this apprehension was the "tango teas" (or the dansants, as they were known). Ostensibly an opportunity for young women and men to obtain dance lessons from professional or semi-professional teams, these afternoon soirees, offered by most cabarets and clubs, were places to meet members of the opposite sex. For an entrance fee of one dollar, guests received fifty cents' worth of alcohol—or sometimes tea. The revised rules of social dance, as such, now allowed women to "choose" a male partner for an hour or two, indulging in Grizzly Bear holds or tango dips, then discarding that partner at will. This greater license permitted between couples prompted journalist Ethel Watts Mumford to say of the cabaret environment that "the very air of these places is heavy with unleashed passions."[45] One dance club in particular, the Strand Roof Garden, bears some scrutiny as it was a site of simultaneous freedom and restraint and a breeding ground for indoctrination into middle-class mores.

The Strand was the brainchild of Elizabeth Marbury, a well-known New York City socialite, literary agent, and theatrical manager. Along with her business partner for the venture, Anna Morgan, Marbury opened the dance club in the fall of 1915 designed, in her words, "to provide a wholesome and safe atmosphere for young people."[46] Marbury had long been a champion and supporter of modern ballroom dances; she was the Castles' manager for many years and helped lead them to their cultural pre-eminence. A shrewd businesswoman and publicist, she was quick to see the financial potential of the dance craze. While Marbury generally supported women's full participation in society, in the true reform mentality of her day she believed that young women needed protection from the inherently predatory nature of the male business and entertainment worlds. While she denied that her club was anything like a settlement house, the missionary zeal with which Marbury undertook this project underscored her basic support of Progressive-era morality.

The opening of the Strand Roof garnered much press and fanfare; one reporter called it "that unique institution . . . where lonely souls in the big city may get acquainted and enjoy innocent pastime under proper chaperonage."[47] While the Strand resembled a typical cabaret in most respects, it was specifically intended as a place for young women and men of the working and middle classes to fraternize and learn the latest dances under the watchful eyes of society matrons. Many of those who attended the club were young workers, some without families, grasping for roots in a large industrial metropolis. Part of the Americanization process for young immigrants was participation in local dance halls where youth could escape from the drudgeries of their workaday lives and also assert their new American independence.[48] Marbury's goal was to create a more decent and respectable club than many of the seamy dance halls located in those neighborhoods. Yet she valued the leisure her club afforded: Said Marbury, "All work and no play dulls both Jack and Jill. If young working men and women dance, they fling off morbid introspection; they become alert, alive, full of the zest of life."[49]

Virtually continuous dance activities occurred at the Strand—social dancing as well as dance lessons, contests, and tango teas. A fifty-cent admission fee entitled participants to unlimited numbers of dances for as long as one liked, unlike the upper-middle-class cabarets that charged for each dance. Not surprising, no alcohol was served here—only tea. Although there are few descriptions of the actual dances performed at the Strand, judging from Marbury's general pronouncements about the state of social dance (and her introduction to the Castles' dance manual) we can assume that dancing at her club was of the "refined" variety—no unseemly dips, ungainly hops or trots or Grizzly Bear holds. Certainly no "spieling"—a type of dance often seen at the lower-class dance halls that Marbury decried. At these places young female partners were known to be whirled around at high speeds by their male partners while "the girl's [sic] skirts were blown immodestly high."[50] The one-step that Marbury endorsed, however, "eliminates all hopping, all contortions of the body, all flouncing of the elbows, all twisting of the arms, and above everything else, all fantastic dips."[51]

It was not only in the style of dancing, but the structure of socializing that the Strand provided a seemingly subtle inculcation into middle-class respectability, "gentility," and heterosexual courting practices. The entire decor of the Strand reflected middle-class comfortability with its "dainty decorations in pale green and white . . . silver gray tables and chairs, the green wicker lounges, upholstered in gay colored chintz."[52] Smoking rooms outfitted with the daily newspapers also suggested the atmosphere of a private club. Like other afternoon tea dances, the Strand also offered possibilities for mingling with the opposite sex. Several women chaperones greeted visitors and introduced couples to one another.[53] In some ways these "hostesses" can be viewed as the modern counterpart to the dance master who presided over nineteenth-century balls. While the dance master's role was to instruct in proper steps and dance sequences, Marbury's hostesses insured proper practices of acquaintanceship, sizing up potentially undesirable entrants. Young women, attractively garbed and made up, were literally "taught" how to meet and behave with men. Marbury herself described one young woman who repeatedly rebuffed the dancing requests of an admirer. Although one of the "chaperones" on duty tried to convince her to dance with the young man, she was unrelenting. Days later, the young woman could be found dancing steadily with the same chap, now "cured" it seems of her "opinion of her importance."[54] Young girls take note: if you are too haughty or discriminating you might never find a mate.

Marbury, it can be argued, provided a social milieu that was both patronizing and liberating. Clearly, her watchful guarding of her "girls," while indicative of the protectionist mood of the reform era generally, was probably psychologically and socially stifling to these young people.[55] But certainly for some of her patrons, the club presented a window onto another lifestyle, a dress rehearsal, if you will, for the attainment of middle-class values of leisure, respectability, and romance. While it can't be proven that this dance proficiency along with acquired behaviors and mannerisms might launch any-

one into the middle class, the structure of expectation of assimilation or attainment of middle-class values was literally built into the rhetoric and practices of social dancing of the club. These young people were embodying those values even if for selected periods of time in their weekly schedules.

Beyond parading these middle-class mores there is the alternative possibility that for working-class women adopting styles of dress, behaviors, and movement styles was a way of experimenting with alternative forms of social identity and independence to better oneself within one's *own* community or class, even if not necessarily to move "ahead" or "beyond." Historian Kathy Peiss, discussing immigrant women, has argued that it is "in leisure that women play with identity, trying on new images and roles, appropriating the cultural forms around them [such as] clothing, music, language."[56] (I would argue that the same held true for young working-class men, as well.) Not to be overlooked either is the matter of pleasure acquired in the accomplishment of social dance technique itself, which allowed these identities to be formed. More than simply "borrowing" the modes of dress, hairstyles, or affectations of the consumer representations of exhibition ballroom dance, social dancers might discover and take enjoyment from their own unique ways of inhabiting this cultural role.

Clearly, for some young social dancers who landed on the doorstep of the Strand, greater glory awaited them. At the same time she was providing "wholesome" entertainment for young working people, Marbury used the Strand as a testing ground for dancers for her theatrical productions. A producer of the Princess Theatre musicals, hailed for their intimacy and lack of pretension, she routinely plucked young women from the club and groomed them as exhibition ballroom dancers. In yet another one of her personal and social crusades, Marbury worked to reform working conditions for the exploited chorus girl.[57] Her goal was to find youthful, seemingly guileless young women with a certain charm and verve to inject new life onto the stage. Talent, she believed, could be cultivated.

One such find was Helen Clarke, a young working woman from Washington Heights. Marbury paired her with the British musical theatre actor Quentin Tod in a match that she hoped would rival the success of Irene and Vernon Castle.[58] By the mid-teens, entering the ranks of professional exhibition ballroom dancer had become a sign of success. For young hopefuls, Marbury's Strand Roof Garden cabaret might indeed serve as a serious stepping-stone to a potentially illustrious career.

The entire unfolding of the ballroom dance phenomenon of the early twentieth century represents the powerful way that popular performance can contribute to the shaping of public consciousness. The popularization of the dances and exhibition ballroom teams through the media served to unite people in a mutual and universal desire for social dance, although the phenomenon had diverse consequences. On one hand, the dances became swept up in the entire consumer apparatus. In many ways the desire for ballroom dance, created in part through pervasive advertising, became synonymous with consumer purchasing where, as Raymond Williams has noted, "you buy social respect, discrimination, health, beauty, success, power to control your environment."[59] Yet on the other hand, dance spectators and participants became more than passive consumers of the rhetoric of progress. Despite the implications of Williams's words, they acquired more than illusion. While social dancers had the ability now

to "purchase the look" of ballroom dance, they could also take that image and identity and experiment or "play" with it on the dance floor.

In this time of shifting social, economic, and cultural priorities, as the nation was coming to grips with the effects of urbanization, the rise of a new merchant class, and the influx of a large immigrant population, social dancing provided an arena where people could test their place in society. While social dancers may have enforced certain traditional cultural ideals of progress through dance, it is fair to say that they also participated in re-articulating those goals as they strove towards a new and better future. Depending on one's social class, of course, different issues were at stake. For some pockets of culture, particularly the large and stratified middle class who were experiencing heightened prosperity, attaining economic upward mobility was the desired goal. For those not immediately experiencing improved economic circumstances, the idea of self-betterment and enhancement served as a way to envision oneself in renewed ways that might lead to a better way of life. However social dancers chose to use or interpret the new social dances, there is no question that in their very nature and structure the dances allowed for greater expressiveness and individuality. This was a liberating concept for a nation moving out the confines and strictures of the Victorian era and into the twentieth century.

Notes

1. Melvin Ballou Gilbert, *The Director: Dancing, Deportment, Etiquette, Aesthetics, Physical Training* (Portland, Me.: Melvin Ballou Gilbert, 1897–98), 253 [reissued by Dance Horizons].

2. While the debutante ball is close to defunct, it still exists in the American South. In North Carolina, for instance, the annual debutante ball is a statewide event held at the civic center. Family and friends gather for what is ostensibly the young woman's "entrance" into upper-middle-class society.

3. See the following essays: Lewis Mumford, "From Revolt to Renewal," in *The Arts in Renewal* (New York: A. S. Barnes, 1951); William Leuchtenberg, "The Revolution in Morals," in *The Perils of Prosperity* (Chicago: University of Chicago Press, 1958). See also Henry May's *The End of American Innocence* (New York: Knopf, 1959), and Richard Hofstadter's *The Age of Reform: From Bryan to F.D.R* (New York: Knopf, 1955).

4. William Inglis, "Is Modern Dancing Indecent?" *Harper's Weekly*, May 17, 1913.

5. "Brooklyn in Throes of Turkey Trot Craze," *New York Sun,* January 17, 1914.

6. For information on nineteenth-century social dancing see A. H. Franks, *A Short History of Social Dance* (London: Routledge & Kegan Paul, 1963); Allen Dodworth, *Dancing and Its Relation to Education and Social Life* (New York: Harper & Bros., 1885); Gilbert, ed., *The Director.*

7. Franks, *Social Dance,* 164.

8. The Grizzly Bear then, too, got its name because of the close, tight holds adopted between couples simulating "bear-holds." The origins of the rag dances are obscure. Many of these dances were being performed socially in clubs and dance halls in major cities, such as San Francisco, Chicago, and Memphis, where they were then transformed by professionals as stage dances. Scholars like Marshall and Jean Stearns suggest that many developed in clubs and "honky tonks" in western and southern cities in the early 1900s, and then migrated east onto vaudeville and cabaret stages. While many of the steps and movements of the early rag dances were clearly borrowed from black vernacular dances, they became so "diluted" by 1910 as to be entirely different dances. The popularization of ragtime, particularly in the North, led to the creation of music by both black composers and white songwriters catering specifically to the craze for ballroom dancing. For more information see M. Stearns and J. Stearns, *Jazz Dance: The Story of American Vernacular Dance* (New York: Schirmer Books, 1968), 69.

9. Despite the uphill battle many black composers faced during this time several, such as Ford Dabney and W. C. Handy, were hired by prominent white exhibition ballroom teams and wrote music specifically for the ballroom dance format. The celebrated band leader and composer James Reese Europe worked closely with the team of Irene and Vernon Castle, who billed him in their programs. He composed many pieces for the team. According to the Castles, he introduced them to the fox-trot with "The Memphis Blues," a composition by W. C. Handy.

10. Mr. and Mrs. Castle, *Modern Dancing* (New York: World Syndicate, 1915), 152.

11. For more information on changing concepts of marriage and ideas about domestic union during the teens and twenties, see Elaine Tyler May, "Myths and Realities of the American Family," in *A History of Private Life,* ed. Antoine Prost and Gerard Vincent (Cambridge, Mass.: Harvard University Press, 1987–91), 554. For more on the Castles'

image as "American sweethearts," see Lewis A. Erenberg, "Everybody's Doin' It: The Pre-World War I Dance Craze, the Castles, and the Modern American Girl," *Feminist Studies* (fall 1975).

12. Banes cites the discussion among some cultural theorists about the American pop star Madonna. One side asks if she is an agent of capitalist commodity culture; the other views her as an empowered performer in charge of her sexuality. Sally Banes, *Writing Dancing in the Age of Postmodernism* (Hanover, N.H.: Wesleyan University Press, 1994), 44.

13. Ibid., 46.

14. Ibid., 48.

15. Ibid., 47.

16. Judith Newton and Deborah Rosenfelt, *Feminist Criticism and Social Change: Sex, Class, and Race in Literature and Culture* (New York: Methuen Press, 1985), xix.

17. Thorstein Veblen, *The Theory of the Leisure Class* (1899; reprint, New York: Dover Publications, 1994).

18. The entire Progressive era spanned the time period from approximately 1890 to 1920.

19. Henry May, *The End of American Innocence: A Study of the First Years of Our Time, 1912–1917* (New York: Knopf, 1959), 141.

20. John Higham, "The Reorientation of American Culture in the 1890s," in *The Origins of Modern Consciousness,* ed. John Weiss (Detroit: Wayne State University Press, 1965), 27.

21. Ibid., 37.

22. John Whiteclay Chambers II, *The Tyranny of Change: America in the Progressive Era, 1900–1917* (New York: St. Martin's Press, 1980), 100.

23. Hofstadter, *The Age of Reform,* 5.

24. T. J. Jackson Lears, "From Salvation to Self-Realization: Advertising and the Therapeutic Roots of the Consumer Culture, 1880–1930," in *The Culture of Consumption: Critical Essays in American History, 1880–1980* (New York: Pantheon Books, 1983), 4.

25. Elizabeth Ewen, *Immigrant Women in the Land of Dollars, Life and Culture on the Lower East Side, 1890–1925* (New York: Monthly Review Press, 1985), 24.

26. William Leach, *Land of Desire: Merchants, Power, and the Rise of a New American Culture* (New York: Vintage Books, 1993), 2.

27. Chambers, *The Tyranny of Change,* 79–82.

28. Ibid., 81.

29. William Leach, *Land of Desire: Merchants, Power, and the Rise of a New American Culture* (New York: Vintage Books, 1993), xv.

30. John Fiske, *Television Culture* (London: Routledge, 1987), 311.

31. Raymond Williams, "Base and Structure," in *Problems in Materialism and Culture: Selected Essays* (London: Verso Books, 1980), 38.

32. Ibid., 43.

33. *The Newark Star-Eagle,* a Newark, New Jersey, newspaper, ran this series the week of October 23, 1916. It was titled "How to Do the New Winter Dance Steps as Described by the Dancing Dollies."

34. "Turkey Trot Seen at Plaza Dance: Southern Society Didn't Want It and Was Somewhat Shocked," *New York Sun,* January 14, 1912.

35. "Mons. Maurice Says," *New York Review,* October 31, 1914.

36. This ad was from the *New York Dramatic Mirror* (1914).

37. These ads mentioned appeared in the *Ladies Home Journal* (May 1915).

38. Columbia Recording Corporation, *Columbia Record Catalogues: Columbia Double-Disc Records* (1914), Rodgers and Hammerstein Archives of Recorded Sound, New York Library for the Performing Arts. The "maxixe" (pronounced "max-eesh") was another standard ballroom dance of the day. The maxixe combined steps from the tango and the two-step. For additional information on this dance, and others from the period, see Appendix A in Julie Malnig, *Dancing till Dawn: A Century of Exhibition Ballroom Dance* (New York: New York University Press, 1992).

39. "New Music for Home Parties" advertisement in program, Boston Theatre, May 18, 1914.

40. Castle, *Modern Dancing,* 176.

41. Otheman Stevens, "Healthfully Stimulating, Says She, and Curtails Temptation," *Los Angeles Examiner,* September 11, 1915.

42. Sally Banes, *Writing Dancing in the Age of Postmodernism* (Hanover, N.H.: Wesleyan University Press, 1994), 47.

43. Lewis Erenberg, *Steppin' Out: New York Nightlife and the Transformation of American Culture* (Westport, Conn.: Greenwood Press, 1981), 36, 40.

44. For a full account of cabaret life and nightclub culture, see Erenberg, *Steppin' Out.*

45. Ethel Watts Mumford, "Where Is Your Daughter This Afternoon?" *Harper's Weekly,* January 17, 1914.

46. "What the Stage Owed to Miss Marbury," 1953 magazine article in Elizabeth Marbury Clipping File, Billy Rose Theatre Collection, New York Public Library for the Performing Arts.

47. Helen Clarke, "Helen Clarke Talks of Miss Marbury's Partner," undated newspaper clipping in the Helen Clarke Clipping File, Billy Rose Theatre Collection, New York Public Library for the Performing Arts.

48. Ewen, *Immigrant Women in the Land of Dollars,* 207.

49. Castle, *Modern Dancing,* 22.

50. Rheta Childe Door, *What Eight Million Women Want* (Boston: Small, Maynard, 1910; reprint, New York: Kraus, 1971).

51. Ibid., 20.

52. "The Cleverest Woman in New York" (title obscured), *Journal and Advertiser,* New York, 1915.

53. Ibid.

54. Ibid.

55. "What the Stage Owed to Miss Marbury."

56. Kathy Peiss, *Cheap Amusements: Working Women and Leisure in Turn-of-the-Century New York* (Philadelphia: Temple University Press, 1986), 63.

57. Elizabeth Marbury, "My Girls as I Know Them," *Harper's Bazaar,* August 1917.

58. Clarke, "Helen Clarke Talks of Miss Marbury's Partner."

59. Raymond Williams, "Advertising: The Magic System," in *Problems in Materialism and Culture,* 189.

The Natural Body

ANN DALY

Isadora Duncan's trope of the "Natural" body was forged over a number of years, from a variety of sources. There were, of course, Percy Bysshe Shelley and John Keats. And there were also Walt Whitman, and Ernst Haeckel, and Sandro Botticelli, along with Johann Joachim Winckelmann, Friedrich Nietzsche, and Auguste Rodin. But before the dancer encountered any of them, there was California, whose natural beauty served as its animating identity. At the core of the "California dream," according to Kevin Starr, "was the hope for a special relationship to nature," which was "heroic, eternal, overwhelming," promising "a profusion of gifts: beauty, life, health, abundance, and, perhaps most important of all, a challenging correlative to inner aspiration."[1]

Duncan's deep affection for the Bay Area landscape was surpassed only by her love for dancing and for her children. In Budapest in 1902, when Duncan experienced her first public success and her first adult love affair, she drank in the spring, which flooded her with memories of her beloved California:

> In the world I am a pilgrim; a pilgrim and mendiante—from California I come—there as a child I played in the meadows—California is the land of gold—And [not] the gold which is carried in money but the free glad gold of the oranges and the California poppy—In Spring our fields dazzle the eyes—Dancing in the breeze laughing back its beams to the sun—a host of yellow flowers—

Something of the Golden life of these flowers stole into my heart as a child—and I danced in the Meadows as Their sister—Could I dance as they swayed in the wind.—Could I dance their Golden messages—In the Summer the poppies vanish.—Back to the gold of the Earth they go—Back to the heart of the Sun—They disappear—but still their [sic] is gold in California in the long [illegible] beach strand by the blue Pacific—All during the hot summer the Gold burns As a child I danced on the sea beach by the waves—The hot sand burned my feet—The gold sand burned my eyes—The Sun danced on the waves—The movement of the waves rocked into my soul—Could I dance as they. Their eternal message of rhythm of Harmony?[2]

The gold of the orange groves and poppy fields may have been plentiful, but gold of the monetary sort Duncan never had as a child. The natural wealth of the California landscape provided the precocious young girl with a physical as well as a psychological respite from the less-than-idyllic reality of her fatherless, impoverished, itinerant childhood.

Sometimes, further down the road, when Duncan would tell her life story to the latest in a long line of interviewers, she imaginatively inserted her father into the tale, describing him as an authority on the ancient Greeks. To one reporter she even quoted a line of his poetry: "Greece is living Greece once more." To another she credited her "father's house" with the paintings that had inspired her "Natural" style of dancing:

"I was brought up," she continued,

in San Francisco, where my father's house was plentifully supplied with reproductions of classic art in sculpture and engraving. In this artistic atmosphere I breathed the first years of my childhood. There I became inspired with high artistic ideals, and while a little girl my inborn taste for dancing was developed.

While playing in the garden of my father's house I tried by instinct to impart to my childish dance what I saw exhibited in the models of art. Thus, being deeply imbued with the perfect beauty of the copies of the great masterpieces, enhanced by the simplicity of the dress, from early childhood I have considered the freedom of my body essential to rhythm of movement. For this reason later on, with the development of my inborn disposition, a conscious study of the rhythm was at the same time promoted. Dressed in the beautiful ancient dresses I went on in the mode of dancing which I felt ambitious to render equal in beauty to the Greek dances of the days of old.[3]

One of those classic reproductions—which, at the time, were a popular means of circulating "Culture"—was Botticelli's *Primavera,* which Mrs. Duncan probably took along from her San Francisco home to hang prominently over the bookcase in their subsequent living quarters.[4] Here is the "free glad gold of the oranges," the soft, flowered earth underfoot, and the rhythmic steps of the dance. Duncan saw how the Three Graces' soft, round bodies—selectively revealed and enhanced by transparent drapery—became a part of the natural landscape. And she read the implied movement of the figures—the shifts of weight between their legs, the inflected necks, Venus's mysteriously beckoning gesture. Botticelli's painting made the connections among dance, "Nature," "Culture," and the Greeks. It suggested to Duncan ways of translating the private freedom she felt as a child frolicking au naturel on the beach into a public discourse: Greek gods and goddesses, she discovered, were forces of nature, and depicted as such in painting. Why not do the same in dance?

Flora, or Spring, from Botticelli's painting, was one of the first Greek figures whom Duncan impersonated. She composed several dances on the theme of spring while in New York in the late 1890s, and in London in 1898[5] and again in 1900, variously titled and accompanied. One such paean to the season of birth continued in her repertoire at least until 1909 as *La Primavera,* a painting that had been "done into dance." Duncan enacted a number of the figures in the painting, including Venus's compellingly enigmatic gesture, but it was Flora's costume that she chose to copy. A 1900 photograph shows Duncan in Flora's gauzy ankle-length dress, painted with flowers and ringed with blossoms at the neck and head.[6] "And now with wreathing arms and undulating body and bare, twinkling feet," wrote a Munich correspondent in 1902, "she endeavors to present to us the vibrant atmosphere, the pulsing ecstatic quickening of all life, the langubrous [sic], delicious dolce far niente of this marvelous season as she reads it in Botticelli's masterpiece."[7]

At about the same time that Duncan was composing *La Primavera* in London, she was beginning her "studies" of Greek culture. A professor insisted upon teaching her Greek: she knew "Virtue is the cause of friendship" and "Friendship is the gift of the Gods."[8] A young poet, meanwhile, was entrancing her with the secrets of Apollo. "It was you," she later wrote to the young poet Douglas Ainslie, "who first put me on the way to seek Apollo, and since then how much I have longed for a wee bit [of] wisdom—strength to live that harmony of which you used to talk—beautiful form, color rhythm—."[9] Although Jane Ellen Harrison, the acknowledged leader of the Cambridge ritualists, who pioneered the use of anthropological theories in the study of ancient Greece, was listed as the reader on Duncan's 16 March 1900 program at the New Gallery, I have found no further evidence of a connection between the two women.[10] Duncan, who may or may not have been reading Harrison's *Introductory Studies in*

Greek Art (1892), was indeed reading Winckelmann, the eighteenth-century German art historian and classical archeologist who, like her young poet Ainslie, emphasized the formal purity and passionless perfection of the Greeks—Platonic qualities echoed in the precise draftsmanship and cool balance of Botticelli's *Primavera*. She danced out some Greek friezes with the same halcyon expression, which she described as "impersonal little friezes—of figures that have kept the same attitude for years and years—intent on their own meaning of grass and flowers and earth—with an exquisite aloofness from human things."[11]

But the Elgin marbles, which she undoubtedly encountered in her frequent visits to the British Museum, must have suggested something more to her about the Greeks, something that she later found articulated by Nietzsche. The Phidian sculptures went beyond the delicate, neoclassical tastefulness of Botticelli. They were robust as well as refined, massive as well as buoyant; they were figures of force as well as repose. The reclining and the lunging of several figures on the East Pediment, as well as other Greek temples, soon made their way into Duncan's vocabulary (figure 28a and b).

Nietzsche—whom Duncan discovered, through admirer Karl Federn, in Berlin in 1903—eventually converted Duncan from the Apollonian to the Dionysian. (Nietzsche could not have known the literal truth of what he wrote, that *The Birth of Tragedy*, which Duncan called her "Bible," "had a knack for seeking out fellow-rhapsodizers and for luring them on to new secret paths and dancing places.")[12] She no longer merely contemplated the spirit of the dance, as one who relates the story of something; she threw herself into the spirit of the dance, as one dancing the thing itself. Her pictorial "Done into Dance" aesthetic became less imagistic, less intellectual, less removed. With Dionysus, "Nature" took on a fiercer face, for the dithyramb united with a "Nature" that was sensual and even cruel. As Duncan developed as an artist, "Nature" was no longer just the lovely Flora, heralding the joy of spring; it was also the menacing Furies and the frenzied Bacchantes.

Duncan found early inspiration for this less idyllic side of "Nature" in Rodin's powerful, raw, un-"finished" sculptures, which she had admired since first seeing them in his retrospective exhibition, set up in conjunction with the Exposition Universelle in Paris in 1900. The young dancer, still in search of her aesthetic, must have thrilled to the importance he accorded the form of the body, to the figures' vivid sense of movement, to the pathos embodied in their gestures and postures. Sculptures such as the *Old Helmet Maker's Wife,* with her failing flesh, had helped to redefine the aesthetic concept of "ugly," turning it from a matter of appearance to a matter of Platonic essence. According to Rodin, "Whatever is false, whatever is artificial, whatever seeks to be pretty rather than expressive, whatever is capricious and affected, whatever smiles without motive, bends or struts without cause, is mannered without reason; all that is without soul and without truth; all that is only a *parade* of beauty and grace; all, in short, that lies is *ugliness* in art."[13] Rodin revealed the decrepit and the tortured as simply another side of "Nature." Much later in Duncan's career, when she advanced from her youthful idylls to the darker themes of grief and mortality, she echoed his words: there is nothing "Natural" that is ugly, for the inner "Truth" of "Nature" is always "Beautiful."

As much as Duncan attributed the "Truth" and "Beauty" of the "Natural" body to the ancient Greeks, she founded its divinity in science. In the mid- and late nineteenth century, nature, evolutionary science, and theology went hand in hand.[14] Evolutionists such as Ernst Haeckel, a German, and Herbert Spencer, a Briton whose popularity in America outstripped that of Darwin, extended the paradigm from nature to culture, applying it to social life, art, and even religion.[15] Darwinism, as cultural historian Jacques Barzun has pointed out, "satisfied the first requirement of any religion by subsuming all phenomena under one cause."[16] Spencer generalized the basic premises of evolution, in a more accessible manner than Darwin's scientific rigor, into a totalizing cosmology, seemingly organizing all knowledge into an ultimate, unified reality. The

28a and b. (a) This reclining figure from the East Pediment of the Parthenon, kept by Duncan in her postcard collection, was adapted into her dance vocabulary. (b) Isadora Duncan, photo by Arnold Genthe. Courtesy of the Dance Division of the New York Public Library for the Performing Arts, Astor, Lenox and Tilden Foundations.

novelist Jack London was awed by Spencer's *First Principles,* in which "all the hidden things were laying their secrets bare."[17]

Duncan's generation was enthralled by evolution theory, which they considered an intellectual revolution, either to absorb or to condemn it.[18] It is "hopeless to convey to a younger generation," wrote Edith Wharton about the significance of the theory of evolution, "the first overwhelming sense of cosmic vastnesses which such 'magic casements' let into our little geocentric universe."[19] At the same time that evolution theory opened up the small, geometric world of the nineteenth century into the potential vastness of the twentieth, it also explained the rampant progress of the day not just as a black void of the new but also as a development of the comfortable past. And, in a very important way, that is exactly what Duncan's dancing did—it brought along nineteenth-century transcendentalism into the modern age. In the tradition of Henry David Thoreau and Ralph Waldo Emerson, Duncan believed in an order of "Truth" that transcended the sphere of the external senses, a "Truth" communicated instead through the mediation of "Nature."[20]

Duncan was most influenced by Haeckel, the famous German naturalist and early Darwin supporter, whose *The Evolution of Man* (1874) was subtitled *A Popular Exposition of the Principal Points of Human Ontogeny and Phylogeny,* and whose *The Riddle of the Universe at the Close of the Nineteenth Century* (1899) attempted to tackle metaphysics by means of science.[21] His works, she wrote to him in a 1904 birthday greeting, brought her "religion and understanding, which count for more than life."[22]

Haeckel rejected the tradition of anthropism, which opposes the human organism to the rest of nature and places man at the center of a God-created universe. Merging the theory of evolution with the law of substance, which explained that the universe consists completely of matter and force, Haeckel replaced anthropist dogmas and the duality of orthodox religions with a comprehensive view of the universe. Monism, he asserted, "recognizes one sole substance in the universe, which is at once 'God and nature'; body and spirit (or matter and energy) it holds to be inseparable."[23] The monist position led to a religious pantheism, which replaced a creationist God with the natural forces of evolution. Thus man is not separated from God/"Nature"; rather, man is enmeshed in the divinity of "Nature," which *is* God.

The monist theology revered the trinity of "the True, the Good, and the Beautiful." "Truth" is to be found only in the rational study of "Nature"; "the Good" is found in charity and toleration, compassion and assistance; "the Beautiful" is found not in an afterlife but in this life, in the natural world. "The astonishment with which we gaze upon the starry heavens and the microscopic life in a drop of water," Haeckel wrote, "the awe with which we trace the marvellous working of energy in the motion of matter, the reverence with which we grasp the universal dominance of the law of substance throughout the universe—all these are part of our emotional life, falling under the heading of 'natural religion.'"[24]

This notion of essential unity and orderly design of the cosmos provided the fundamental template of *harmony* for mid- to late nineteenth-century religion, art, and society.[25] "Nature" signified order. "Nature" served as a comforting, orderly matrix for all the fiercely multiplying, often contrary, elements in the universe—a universe whose microscopic and extraterrestrial boundaries were expanding daily, through the rapid-paced discoveries of science. In such an expanding yet enmeshed model of the world, the individual self, though just one link in this cosmic chain, was not diminished but rather ennobled by its connections with the rest of the universe. Thus "Nature" was no longer humbling, as it had been for artists earlier in the nineteenth century, but empowering. "Nature" provided a means for the individual to transcend the self and harness the cosmos.

After reading Haeckel, Duncan came to understand "Nature" not just as seasons or flowers or forces but as a comprehensive system whose inherent harmony she mapped onto her body. "I always put into my movements," she wrote, "a little of that divine continuity which gives to all of Nature its beauty and life."[26] The "Natural" body was one that moved harmoniously, as a single unit whose each minute part functioned interdependently. It embodied the basic wavelike force of movement in "Nature." For Duncan, "Nature" became more than just the worldly pleasure of an orange grove but also the transcendent joy of "the True, the Good, and the Beautiful."

As someone who proudly proclaimed to her young schoolmates that there was no Santa Claus, as someone who invented a father who had really departed in her early infancy, as someone who mastered the process of mythologizing herself, Duncan regarded the search for "Truth" as a complicated concern. And evolutionary science, premised as it was on the knowability of the universe, as revealed through the discoverable laws of nature, was a field of certitude and rationality.[27] This science, rather than myth or religion, was able to assure humankind that there was an ultimate order to existence. Duncan needed that reassurance. Darwin, she wrote to her lover, Gordon Craig, in April 1905, supplied her with

> Divine Philosophy—& if read aright his observations teach the living truth of universal life and Love—And we must have Philosophy—Without that we would die of pain like dumb brutes. When they put on the torture then Philosophy is the thing—or call it what you will. Some people draw it from one source & some from another. A *Van Eyck* before me & a book of Darwin in my hands suits *me*—& Love in and over All—& now and then a Prayer to the Gods. Some people pray one way & some another—sometimes I *dance* mine & sometimes I think them.[28]

Duncan's faith in this "Divine Philosophy" did not endure, perhaps because the unity and order of her universe collapsed so tragically with the deaths of her children Patrick and Deirdre in 1913 and of her newborn in 1914. "What is the truth of a human life, and who can find it?" she wrote in her autobiography. "God Himself would be puzzled."[29] It is one of the few times that she ever wrote of God.

By the teens, Duncan's style of dancing became so popular that dance teachers were compelled to add it to their repertoires. They variously called the style "natural dancing," "classic dancing," or "aesthetic dancing," seeing no dichotomy, as we do today, between what is "natural" and what is "aesthetic." It was the middle term, "classic," that fused these two seemingly opposed ideals: the Greeks had rendered nature into art and, conversely, art into nature. By deploying the Greeks as a strategy to collapse art and "Nature," Duncan posited dance as a part of the cosmic unity and divinity of "Nature" and thus elevated dance into the realm of "high" art. As a result, dance in America, or at least one major strain of dance in America, had become a band of barefoot nymphs in Greek tunics and headbands, each with a knee lifted high and head thrown back, frolicking quite "artfully" 'round a tree or against the skyline. How, in a matter of two decades, had Duncan appropriated the image and idea of the Greeks—as the connecting thread between "Nature" and "Culture"—to legitimize dance as an American "high" art?

By the time that Duncan reappeared in America in 1908, the newspapers had already reported her barefoot-scandal-turned-success, her unconventional costuming, her "reawakening of an art that has slumbered for two thousand years," and her pilgrimage to the heights of the Acropolis. The American press's amused depiction of her as a "Greek" dancer began in reports from Paris salon society in 1901: "Like an Ancient Greek Bas-Relief Come to Life She Astonishes Paris." The article, published with Duncan's byline, was a sensitive account of her ideals and theories. At its end, she made a subtle distinction between reconstruction and interpretation, which all the cable correspondents and metropolitan reporters, whose interest was more in eccentricity than in art, failed to recognize: "I drew my inspiration from Greek sources. Strictly speaking, I do not try to reconstruct Greek dances. This is practically impossible. The inspiration which I draw enables me to interpret what I believe to be not only the idyllic but the ideal dance."[30] Nevertheless, with her first trip to the land of Apollo and Dionysus in 1903, she encouraged the Hellenic link. For example, from an interview published in the *New York Sunday World*:

> My idea of dancing is to leave my body free to the sunshine, to feel my sandaled feet on the earth, to be near and love the olive trees of Greece. These are my present ideas of dancing. Two thousand years ago a people lived here who had perfect sympathy and comprehension of the beautiful in Nature, and this knowledge and sympathy were perfectly expressed in their own forms and movement.
>
> Of all the thousands of figures of Greek sculpture, bas-reliefs, and vases there is not one but is in exquisite bodily proportion and harmony of movement.
>
> This could not be possible unless the artists of that time were accustomed to see always about them beautiful moving human forms. I came to Greece to study these forms of ancient art, but above all, I came to live in the land which produced these wonders, and when I say "to live" I mean to dance.[31]

Greece, she made clear, means "Nature" and "Art." And in connecting dance to Greece, she was also connecting dance to "Nature" and "Art."

Duncan's rhetorical dependence on classical precedents lasted from about 1901 to 1904, when she ended her experiment with a Greek boys' choir singing "authentic" Greek music for her performances.[32] Although she would return to the Greeks later, in the 1910s, for different reasons, during this early period she was stressing the ancients' discovery of beauty in "Nature" and of "Nature" in the human form. The renewal of the Olympic Games in 1896 had sparked interest in the Greek ideal of the body, helping to reinforce Duncan's insistence on its beauty and nobility. Furthermore, the status of dance in Greek culture gave dancing a legitimacy it desperately needed for acceptance by her upper-class audiences. And, not inconsequently,

Duncan's Greek rhetoric ended up functioning as a novelty in an era of novelty-driven theater and journalism. Just as Ruth St. Denis's gimmick was the "exotic" and Loie Fuller's was the "picturesque," so Duncan's was the "classical."

For America in the several decades before and after the turn of the century, "Greece" (conceived more from the likes of Keats's "Ode on a Grecian Urn" than anything archeological) was an idea about cultural legitimacy. An animating cultural fantasy since the Greek Revival in the early 1800s, Hellenist enthusiasm indicated the renewed aspirations of a burgeoning nation, without a pedigreed past equal to that of the great European states, to flourish in all its aspects—scientific, industrial, political, social, and cultural. Greek games flourished at colleges such as Barnard and Berkeley; outdoor Greek theaters, including the one at Berkeley, were built, too. In the wake of the 1893 World's Columbian Exposition, whose organizers purposefully chose a neoclassical architectural style over an incipient American modernism, civic and commercial buildings across the country—the courthouse, the state capitol, the university, the commemorative statue, even the firehouse—were being built in the image of the great Greek temple, its soaring columns and monumentality a visual declaration of collective ambition. In the flush of its imminent world-class status, America—as well as Britain and Germany and France—envisioned itself as the true heir of the great Greek civilization, in all its political, economic, and artistic glory.

So, in preparation for Duncan's August 1908 debut at the Criterion Theatre, producer Charles Frohman's press agents began spreading word of her "celebrated classical dances" before she even reached shore. This idea of translating Greek statuary into dance, however, was hardly new. Back in 1890, for example, at about the same time that "living statues" became a popular pastime for women, the *San Francisco Examiner* ran an article (could Duncan have seen it?) on two rather sophisticated Spanish skirt dancers named Carmencita and Otero, the latter of whom, "in her slow and sinuous movements, seems like a masterpiece of Phidias."[33]

Duncan seemed to make one last effort to qualify the "Greek dance" label before disembarking from London. "While my dancing owes inspiration to the Greeks," she told a reporter, "it is not Greek really, but very modern—my own idea. . . . Please don't say, by the way, that I dress in Greek style." Dutifully, the reporter set the record straight: "Miss Duncan really wears a Parisian Directoire lounging gown,"[34] which was then the most fashionable silhouette in Paris. Such subtleties, however, were the interest of neither press nor management. After several seasons of Indian incantations, Salome dances, and "La Loie" (Fuller) look-alikes, the "Greek" dance was a welcome distraction.

Despite Frohman's efforts to sell her as a Greek dancer, the Criterion audience was not totally responsive to such refined references. As a *Variety* reviewer, clearly more used to vaudeville (which had been showcasing the Brazilian Maxixe, burlesques of *The Merry Widow*, Princess Rajah's snake dance, and, of course, *Salome*),[35] explained:

> To one whose vision is perhaps somewhat warped by too frequent attendance upon vaudeville performances and whose culture in classic Art is rather less than inconsiderable, Isadora Duncan's attempt to monopolize a whole audience—and a $2 audience at that—for an entire evening, has very much the complexion of Paul McAllister's untoward experiment as a condensed "Hamlet" in vaudeville. . . .
>
> Now comes along Miss Duncan with an immense success in Europe as a recommendation and offers Broadway (as distinguished from East 125th Street) an entertainment the lofty pretension to Art of which is in about the same relation to the established standard of entertainment.
>
> . . . It is a fairly safe venture that a goodly percentage of the Criterion's audience who lent their applause to the none too plentiful gaiety of the evening did so because they thought that it was the proper thing to do and not because they found real delight in Miss Duncan's performance.[36]

This audience, which was accustomed to even lighter entertainments than usual during the summer season, was suspicious of anything pretending to "Art." (And yet the *Variety* review makes clear the very real pressure to recognize and acknowledge "Art.") Duncan had better luck with her northeastern out-of-town engagements, but when she returned to New York, she and Frohman canceled their contract. She began, instead, a series of immensely successful engagements with Walter Damrosch's prestigious New York Symphony Orchestra.

Her appearances with Damrosch were in concert halls and opera houses, such as the Metropolitan Opera, with a considerably different audience and set of critics. The audience was privileged, predominantly female,[37] and thirsty for "Art." Duncan performed excerpts from Gluck's *Iphigenia in Aulis* (1905–1915) portraying the Greek maidens as they played ball and knucklebones and spied the Greek fleet in the distance. Then she added *Iphigenia in Tauris* (1914–1915) and *Orpheus* (1900–1915) to her American repertoire, strongly reinforcing her reputation as the "Greek" dancer. The critics flattered Duncan with grand comparisons, however undiscriminating: not only to Greek sculptures and vases, but also to Keats's "Ode on a Grecian Urn" and even to Wedgwood pottery. In order to describe Duncan, the *New York Daily Tribune*'s highly respected music critic, H. E. Krehbiel, invoked the British clergyman/botanist Charles Kingsley's fanciful description of Greek dancing, "in which every motion was a word, and rest as eloquent as motion; in which every attitude was a fresh motion for a sculptor of the purest school, and the highest physical activity was manifested, not, as in coarse pantomime, in fantastic bounds and unnatural distortions, but in perpetual, delicate modulations of a stately and self-sustained grace."[38]

Although Duncan at times denied that she was imitating the ancient Greek dances per se, she did admit to copying Greek clothing, and her audiences immediately recognized the quotation. In the eyes of upper-echelon late Victorians, classical art had made the liberating connection between nudity and nobility that had been impossible within the Puritan tradition. As they saw it, the body, as depicted on the vases and in the statuary, was endowed with an ideal form both moral and beautiful. For women such as Mrs. William K. Kavanaugh of St. Louis, who defended Duncan against a minister who had characterized the dancer as a midway come-on, Duncan was "an exquisite figure on an old vase that we are allowed to admire with all propriety."[39] As Americans constructed it, the unquestioned authority of Greek art *allowed* even a woman to contemplate the naked body with a good conscience and at the same time to congratulate herself on possessing an elevated taste (elevated socially as well as morally).[40]

Despite the identification of the "Natural" body with nudity, Duncan never actually performed nude, just as fifth-century Greek statues were never without some veil or drapery. Her Greek-style costume left her breasts unbound (early versions of the brassiere were not widely marketed as an alternative to the corset until the twenties)[41] but modestly covered her groin, hiding any pubic hair, as was done with the ancient statuary. Duncan's costumes were properly anchored to her body, "fastened on," she said, "with elastics over the shoulders and around the waist."[42] And, if we can extrapolate from what Irma's young American pupils wore to Isadora's own practice, the elastics were further anchored at the shoulders to a leotard-style undergarment made of silk jersey.[43] It is likely, too, that Duncan removed underarm hair, and possibly leg hair.[44] The warm glow of Duncan's stage lighting further softened the reality of bare flesh, as did pancake makeup later in her career.[45] Thus her audiences could accept her chiton as a transparent sign of nudity; moreover, they accepted it as a sign of *classical* nudity, whose claim to the "Natural" guaranteed the moral and the noble.

Besides Duncan's rhetoric, repertoire, and costuming, her movement vocabulary was also identified as classical. She seemed to broadly imitate the leaping, outstretched motions of the Greek vase figures. Sometimes she even appeared to bring a specific one to life: "One of the wildest of her dances she closed with arms outstretched and head thrown back almost out of sight until she resembled the headless Nike of Samthrace [sic]," observed a *New York Times* critic in 1909.[46] Dance critic/historian Deborah Jowitt has compared images of Duncan with photos of Greek sculpture, vase paintings, and bas-reliefs that the dancer likely saw, and demonstrated the close, sometimes exact, duplication of pose. Both sets of images, she found, shared "the resilient yielding to gravity displayed in reclining poses, the lift of the arms with which Duncan ended so many phrases, the head turned away from the direction of forward motion, the strong crossing of the lifted leg in a skip, the arch of the torso."[47]

The aura of Greece—as a symbolic suture between "Nature" and Culture—clung most fiercely to Duncan early in her American career, when her audiences needed to make sense of her unfamiliar style of dancing. After several rounds of tours, when she began dancing to symphonic music, the critics turned their attention to the appropriateness of dancing to concert music. By her next set of tours, in the teens, Duncan rekindled her celebrity through identification with heroic patriotism and maternalism. And by the 1920s, ironically, the same Greek source material that Duncan had appropriated for "Natural" dancing was being reappropriated as a precedent for its very antithesis, the ballet.[48]

Notes

1. Kevin Starr, *Americans and the California Dream, 1850–1915* (New York: Oxford University Press, 1973), 417, 418.

2. Entry dated May 11, 1902, folder 141, Irma Duncan Collection of Isadora Duncan Materials, Dance Collection, New York Public Library for the Performing Arts (hereafter cited as DC).

3. "The California Girl Who Made Athens Gasp by Wearing Classic Grecian Costumes in the Streets and to the Theatres," *San Francisco Chronicle*, November 22, 1903, 8.

4. See Millicent Dillon, *After Egypt: Isadora Duncan and Mary Cassatt* (New York: Dutton, 1990), 162; Duncan, *Art*, 128–129.

5. A program, entitled "The Story of Narcissus: Done into Dance by Isadora Duncan" and performed at Lowther Lodge, London, on July 18, 1898, started with a dance titled *Morgensonne* (Howard Holtzman Documentation of Isadora Duncan).

6. Irma Duncan donated the *Primavera* costume to the DC.

7. Allen Monroe Foster, ". . . Fatherland: Isadora Duncan's Poetic Dances Have Divided Germany into Two Camps," December 1902, Isadora Duncan Clippings, DC.

8. Duncan to Douglas Ainslie, December 22, [1899], Douglas Ainslie Papers, Harry Ransom Humanities Research Center, University of Texas at Austin.

9. Duncan to Ainslie, October 11, 1900, Douglas Ainslie Papers.

10. I have found nothing in the Duncan literature regarding Harrison. Furthermore, according to the archivist in the Newnham College Library at Cambridge, there is nothing connecting Duncan and Harrison in the Jane Ellen Harrison papers (Elisabeth M. C. van Houts, letter to author, September 23, 1993).

11. Duncan to Ainslie, n.d., Douglas Ainslie Papers.

12. Friedrich Nietzsche, "Attempt at a Self-Criticism," in *The Birth of Tragedy; or, Hellenism and Pessimism*, trans. Walter Kaufmann (reprint, rev. ed. 1886 [New York: Vintage Books, 1967], 19. Duncan wrote to Isadora that *The Birth of Tragedy* was her "Bible" (Duncan, *Art*, 108).

13. Paul Gsell and Auguste Rodin, *Rodin on Art*, trans. Mrs. Romilly Fedden (New York: Horizon Press, 1971), 46–47.

14. After initial resistance, the different organized religions in America eventually made their peace with evolutionism in a variety of ways, mostly without disrupting religious convention. Those more on the left wing, such as Lyman Abbott, Minot J. Savage, James T. Bixby, Francis Ellingwood Abbot, and Octavius B. Frothingham, attempted to construct an evolutionary theology which, like Haeckel's monism, posited God as an immanent force rather than as a remote ruler. Cynthia Eagle Russett, *Darwin in America: The Intellectual Response, 1865–1912* (San Francisco: W. H. Freeman, 1976), 25–45.

Robert M. Young argues that Darwinism cannot be thought of as an isolated discourse. It was, rather, part of a wider naturalistic movement in psychology, social theory, science, and religion. "The evolutionary debate," he wrote, "was seen by its participants as occurring within natural theology, with no antitheistic overtones, while those who used evolution for other purposes were themselves devoted believers in the secular religion of Progress, albeit a different religion, but one which has retained its appeal for the faithful" (Robert M. Young, *Darwin's Metaphor: Nature's Place in Victorian Culture* [Cambridge: Cambridge University Press, 1985], 21–22).

15. See Richard Hofstadter, *Social Darwinism in American Thought*, rev. ed. (Boston: Beacon Press, 1955).

16. Jacques Barzun, *Darwin, Marx, Wagner: Critique of a Heritage*, rev. 2d ed. (Garden City, N.Y.: Doubleday Anchor Books, 1958), 65.

17. Jack London, *Martin Eden* (New York: Macmillan, 1908), 108. Quoted in Russett, *Darwin in America*, 16.

18. See Russett, *Darwin in America*.

19. Edith Wharton, *A Backward Glance* (New York: D. Appleton-Century, 1934), 94.

20. See Raymond H. Geselbracht, "Transcendental Renaissance in the Arts, 1890–1920," *New England Quarterly* 48, no. 4 (December 1975): 477.

21. A short essay written by the director of the Haeckel Archives suggests that Duncan read Haeckel's *Natural History of Creation* and probably *The Riddle of the Universe* at the British Museum (folder 34, Allan Ross Macdougall Collection, DC).

At least two dozen English imprints were made of *The Evolution of Man: A Popular Exposition of the Principal Points of Human Ontogeny and Phylogeny*, beginning in 1874. It was originally published as *Anthropogenie oder Entwicklungsgeschichte des Menschen* (Leipzig: W. Engelmann, 1874). *The Riddle of the Universe at the Close of the Nineteenth Century* was first translated into English in 1900, one year after the original German. *Die welträthsel: Gemeinvertändliche Studien über monistische Philosophie* (Bonn: E. Strauss, 1899).

22. From one of two letters quoted in Allan Ross Macdougall, *Isadora: A Revolutionary in Art and Love* (New York: Thomas Nelson & Sons, 1960), 91. According to Duncan biographer Fredrika Blair, the original letters from Duncan to Haeckel are at the Haeckel Archives in Jena, Germany. Fredrika Blair, *Isadora: Portrait of the Artist as a Woman* (New York: William Morrow, 1986), 415. There is

also a letter from Duncan to Haeckel in the Howard Holtz-man Documentation of Isadora Duncan Collection, which went on sale in 1990. Until the collection is open for inspection, it remains to be confirmed whether this is one of the letters quoted by Macdougall or a previously unknown letter.

23. Ernst Haeckel, *The Riddle of the Universe at the Close of the Nineteenth Century,* trans. Joseph McCabe (New York: Harper & Bros., 1901), 20.

24. Ibid., 344.

25. Not all evolutionists interpreted Darwin's theories as positing an inherent design in nature. (Darwin himself was undecided on this issue.) In the philosophical dispute between chance and design, evolutionists such as Thomas Henry Huxley argued against the idea of a grand design by Divine Providence, while Spencer and Haeckel supported the notion of an underlying design and order. See Russett, *Darwin in America,* 32–36. As for these radically contradictory uses for evolution theory, Robert M. Young points out that Darwin's central concept of "natural selection," which "binds all of life together and defines its relations with the rest of nature, was anthropomorphic, deeply ambiguous, and amenable to all sorts of readings and modifications" (Young, *Darwin's Metaphor,* 125).

26. Isadora Duncan, *The Art of the Dance,* ed. Sheldon Cheney (New York: Theatre Arts, 1928), 102–103.

27. See Russett, *Darwin in America.*

28. Francis Steegmuller, ed., *"Your Isadora": The Love Story of Isadora Duncan and Gordon Craig* (New York: Random House & the New York Public Library, 1974), 97.

29. Isadora Duncan, *My Life* (New York: Boni & Liveright, 1927), 344.

30. Isadora Duncan, "Like an Ancient Greek Bas-Relief Come to Life She Astonishes Paris," 1901, Isadora Duncan Clippings, DC.

31. Quoted in Macdougall, *Isadora,* 85.

32. After six months, the boys' voices and behavior were deteriorating. Finally, when Duncan was informed that they were escaping at night and frequenting the cafés, she packed them off back to Athens (Duncan, *My Life,* 138–140).

33. "Wriggling into Wealth. Two Dancing Daughters of Sunny Spain, Carmencita and Otero. The Ballet of the Future Will Have Little Use for Legs. They Are Children of Nature, but Their Mother Seems to Have Taught them How to Dance—They Could Give Delsarte Points on Making Your Body Talk—Poetry of Motion Personified," Performing Arts Library and Museum, San Francisco, California.

34. "Isadora Duncan Raps Maud Allan," *New York Times,* August 9, 1908, 3.3.

35. See Craig Brownell Bowie, "A Survey of Dances and Dancers in Vaudeville" (master's thesis, University of Arizona, 1984).

36. Rush, "Isadora Duncan," *Variety,* August 2, 1908, Isadora Duncan Clippings, DC.

37. "It is doubtful," it was reported in 1909, "if a woman ever appeared on a New York stage with more sincere admirers of her own sex in the audience, than has been the case with Isadora Duncan during her appearance as a Greek dancing girl in her present engagement" (Arthur Mason, "Mistress of the Dance," *Green Book Album* 1 [January 1909]: 139).

38. H. E. Krehbiel, "Miss Duncan's Dancing," *New York Daily Tribune,* November 7, 1908, Isadora Duncan Clippings, DC.

39. "Isadora Duncan's Dance Causes War in St. Louis," *Kansas City Post,* November 5, 1909, Isadora Duncan Clippings, DC.

40. Collections of Greek vases and plaster cast collections of the great statuary circulated in the new urban museums of the late nineteenth century. Even before seeing the British Museum, Duncan herself may have seen San Francisco's brand new collection of Greek vases in the California Midwinter Exposition Memorial Museum, which opened in March 1895. (*See Guide to the Halls and Galleries of the California Midwinter Exposition Memorial Museum,* vol. 1 [San Francisco: H. S. Crocker, 1895].) In New York, she may have seen the plaster casts at the Metropolitan Museum of Art.

41. See Elizabeth Ewing, *Dress and Undress: A History of Women's Underwear* (London: B. T. Batsford, 1978), 114–115.

42. "On with the Dance, Isadora's War Cry" [*New York World,* 1922], Isadora Duncan Clippings, DC.

43. Julia Levien, interview with author, New York City, July 10, 1990. Furthermore, writes Levien: "Those *tea*-dipped undershirts were of silk-jersey (it was *pre*-nylon days). We fashioned them ourselves into a sort of leg-less leotard by just sewing the bottom and cutting the sides high enough not to show. (We also wore briefs underneath this leotard.) The tunic was *pinned* to the shoulders. The complicated elastic harness was also pinned to this, to keep it

from riding around and keeping the drapes in place. We always travelled with bundles of little gold safety pins. . . . However, it is interesting that when we went to have our photos taken by Arnold Genthe (Isadora's favorite photographer) we did not use anything underneath!—He thought the undergarments spoiled the line of the body. This of course added to the legend that we wore nothing under the tunic!" (Julia Levien, letter to author, January 17, 1994).

44. Although the removal of underarm hair did not become popular until the late teens, and the removal of leg hair even later, female performers were removing body hair before 1914. It was the sleeveless dancing dresses of the teens that popularized the removal of underarm hair. See Christine Hope, "Caucasian Female Body Hair and American Culture," *Journal of American Culture 5* (spring 1982): 93–99. I thank Irene Castle's biographer, Susan Cook, for referring me to this source.

45. Levien interview, 1990.

46. "Miss Duncan's Vivid Dances," *New York Times,* November 17, 1909, 11.

47. Deborah Jowitt, "The Impact of Greek Art on the Style and Persona of Isadora Duncan," *Proceedings Society of Dance History Scholars,* comp. Christena L. Schlundt (Riverside, Calif.: Society of Dance History Scholars, 1987), 199.

48. Maurice Emmanuel's *The Antique Greek Dance after Sculptured and Painted Figures,* trans. Harriet Jean Beauley (1895; reprint, London: John Lane, 1916), had been a popular French book at the turn of the century, and by 1916 it had been translated into English. It may well have been one of the dance books that Duncan pored over in the Paris Opera library in 1901. A scholar, Emmanuel embarked on essentially the same project as Duncan: to reconstruct the movement style of the figures on Greek vases. With profuse illustrations and diagrams, he traced the antique images through to contemporary ballet. He argued, at least as convincingly as Duncan, that much, and perhaps most, of the turned-out ballet vocabulary that Duncan labeled artificial was practiced by those Nature-loving Greeks. The Franco-Russian balletomane critic André Levinson seized upon Emmanuel's material as a way to vindicate classical ballet when he insisted that it was "high time that the prejudices which range the antique Hellede upon the side of the Duncans and the Dalcrozes in their combat against the art of the ballet be eliminated, for it is a presumption founded upon a misconception" (André Levinson, "Some Commonplaces on the Dance," *Broom* 4, no. 1 [December 1922]: 17).

Form as the Image of Human Perfectibility and Natural Order

DEBORAH JOWITT

Editor's Note: this address was originally accompanied by a large number of slides showing relevant images from Humphrey's dances and allied designs. Only four could be reproduced here.

In 1954, when I was dancing in Harriette Ann Gray's company, Doris Humphrey (with whom Harriette had danced in the 1930s) invited us to see a run-through of the reconstruction of *With My Red Fires* she had staged with Juilliard students. Karen Kanner was an astounding six-foot-tall Matriarch. I remember sitting in a cramped studio of International House feeling not as if I were watching dance, but as if I were surrounded by forces on the verge of slipping out of control. The following year, *Day on Earth* was presented on one of the mixed bills Bethsabée de Rothschild sponsored at the ANTA theater. (I think I remember *Day on Earth* and Martha Graham's *Cave of the Heart* back to back!) José Limón, Letitia Ide, and Ruth Currier performed, I thought it was the best modern dance I had ever seen (although I hadn't seen much and vastly preferred doing to watching).

Humphrey's *Dawn in New York* in 1956 galvanized me into auditioning for Juilliard Dance Theater—then a semi-professional company under Doris's direction, open to anyone. Accepted, I took Doris's composition course—her last, it would turn out. I had studied Modern Forms with Louis Horst, but I had also been taught to think of composing a dance in terms of locating a great emotional eruption within and running

with it. Harriette Ann Gray had shown me the impulsive, ecstatic side of Humphrey-Weidman dancing and its potential for communicating feeling. Doris's guidelines for composing dances were refreshingly objective. I later came to see a slight rigidity in her viewpoint; much 1960s vanguardism would have fallen beyond her pale. At the time, I found it liberating.

But the experience of being in Humphrey's dances for large groups was the most extraordinary thing of all, even though I didn't fully assimilate it at the time. In the midst of them, you keenly felt not just what you were doing, but the quality of the flow: the stiff, jagged lines of *The Shakers* and the mounting tension as opposing men and women approached the invisible line stretching down the center of the stage that segregated the community by gender. I sensed the contrast between the symmetrical, hivelike structures we built in *Life of the Bee* and the final snaking path of flight; I felt the differences between *Bee*'s straight lines and the irregular scuffle and swoop of us "black doves" in *Dawn,* or the big curves and small curlicues of Humphrey's last work—the first movement of Bach's *Brandenburg Concerto No. 4.*

Even in the rigidly organized society of the bees, the choreography taught me to view myself both as an individual and as part of a community. It's a balance I later learned Doris had had to strive to get right. In the amazing letter she penned to Letitia Ide in 1929, inviting her into the company, she laid out her ecstatic vision of the Group: "I want to visualize with it the visions and dreams that make up the entire impetus and desires of my life";[1] then she added that, of course, "the group depends upon the strength and comprehension and experience of each one." Her dances—particularly those made during the late twenties and early thirties—expressed both that connection and the tensions between individual and group.

In a much-debated sentence in *Feeling and Form,* philosopher Suzanne Langer described the experience of watching a group dance: "One does not see people running around; one sees the dance driving this way, drawn that way, gathering here, spreading there . . . and all motion seems to spring from powers beyond the performers."[2] Humphrey would have argued that one saw both the people running around *and* the created illusion of those forces.

One of the revelations of her composition class was her explanation of how thrilling it could be to cause the spectator's eye to travel certain paths on stage, to make movement (not just the dancers doing it) appear to flow. I finally understood this when I saw *Water Study.* In the opening section, the swell of the ocean tide shapes the rise and fall of each dancer onstage, but the graded levels and canonic timing resolve the entire stage into a wave that rises on the left, crests, tumbles down, and washes up a suddenly created beach, stage right.

Humphrey seems to have interpreted the world in terms of the interplay of dynamic forms and individual wills (or forms that expressed those wills). In *The Art of Making Dances,* she advised the choreographer to note the shapes of the surrounding environment, whatever it might be: "the tangled grotesqueries of water tanks, television wires, ventilators, the 'feel' of congestion, the preponderance of rectilinear lines, and the comedy of the small defiant brownstone squashed between two mammoth chromium and glass monsters." People could either be seen "en masse, as in a street, moving in kaleidoscopic patterns or as individuals, old, middle-aged, young, who are meeting, parting, talking, walking, working."[3]

Early on, such visions separated her from the pictorializations that predominated in ballet and Denishawn, prompting her to write in 1932, "Four abstract themes, all moving equally and harmoniously together like a fugue would convey the significance of democracy far better than would one woman dressed in red, white and blue, with stars in her hair."[4]

Humphrey thought in terms of architecture rather than painting, creating thrusts or arcs of movement that would emphasize the actual three-dimensionality of the stage rather than its apparent flatness. She also emphasized the three-dimensionality of the human body in phrases and groupings more vital than the sculptural plastiques of her early dancing days. The famous Humphrey-Weidman boxes—the cubes and rectilinear forms that could be arranged in a variety of ways—attested to the influence of the powerful stage designs of Adolphe Appia and Gordon Craig; the boxes helped her and her partner Charles Weidman to organize not only the horizontal space of the stage but vertical space as well.

Her vision of how form could express profundities and lift the spirit echoes the Utopian ideas of architects such as Le Corbusier, who wrote in *Towards a New Architecture:* "The Architect, by his arrangement of forms, realizes an order which is a pure creation of his spirit; by forms and shapes he affects our senses to an acute degree and provokes plastic emotions; by the relationships which he creates, he wakes profound echoes in us, he gives us the measure of an order which we feel to be in accordance with that of our world, he determines the various movements of our heart and of our understanding . . ."[5]

Substitute "choreographer" for "architect," change a word here and there, and you understand part of what Humphrey believed fine dance composition could achieve.

Every dance student—or maybe every dance student of a certain age—remembers Doris Humphrey's famous warnings whether they heed them or not ("All dances are too long"[6] certainly hasn't had much influence). "Symmetry is lifeless,"[7] she declared, expanding on that to explain that it was fine for repose, mo-

29. *Dances of Women* (1931). Photo by Soichi Sunami. From the collection of Charles H. Woodford, reprinted with his permission.

ments of calm, resolution, etc., but not to express the passions and disturbances of nature that rock the human being off balance. She was speaking of inkblot symmetry—both on the body and in stage patterns, but there is another sense in which she understood and admired "symmetry" (although she wouldn't have used the word to describe it): symmetry in the Greek sense of due proportion—a principle of nature that governs the relationship of elements of an organism to the whole. Or in art "governs the just balance of variety in unity."[8]

This last phrase is a quote from what she extolled in a letter to her mother as a "new book about dynamic symmetry."[9] The book's premise was the application of the design principles of the Greeks and Egyptians to modern art. After a little sleuthing, I discovered the book to be Jay Hambidge's *The Elements of Dynamic Symmetry.* I can understand why Humphrey found it heavy going—many mathematical equations—and wrote that she'd have to get an architect she knew to explain it to her. But I think Hambidge was one of several writers who struck sparks in her. She might not have immersed herself in his mathematical translation of the spiral into right-angling lines or in the dizzying

30. *Dionysiaques* (1932). Photo by Edward Moeller. Humphrey-Weidman Collection, Courtesy of the Dance Division, The New York Public Library for the Performing Arts, Astor, Lenox and Tilden Foundations.

geometrical shape he termed the "rectangle of the whirling squares."[10] (If, according to a certain formula, you construct within a rectangle ever smaller reciprocal rectangles, you will, as you go, create a series of smaller and smaller squares which appear to coil tighter and tighter.) I do think she was struck by Hambidge's juxtaposition of static symmetry in nature (the snowflake crystal, for example) and dynamic symmetry: the spiralling pattern on a snail shell, the sequence of opposing arcs into which seed pods on a sunflower head fall, the pattern of leaves on a branch. . . . Even in unmoving forms, dynamic symmetry implied motion, leading the eye onward. Doris would have noted the connection to Delsartian Genevieve Stebbins's love of the spi-

ral form because of its upward—therefore aspirational —tendency.

During the late 1920s—when Humphrey made her first independent statements as a choreographer and when she and Charles Weidman founded their company—inkblot symmetry was an important ingredient of ballet, musical comedy, interpretive dance. A "modern" manifestation of this was the ziggurat that gave its form to early skyscrapers: the large base ascending in steps to a small top. Certainly from 1928 on, Humphrey used static symmetry sparingly or tampered with the eye's expectations in subtle ways. The central figure in *Air for the G-String* bends off her vertical axis, and the long trailing curves of the women's gowns make them seem to pour out of the floor like blossoms on a climbing vine, even as you also see them as medieval ladies-in-waiting flanking their mistress. Images from *Dances of Women* (1931), for whose first section Humphrey used growing-plant imagery, *Dionysiaques* (1932), and *New Dance* (1935) tug the eye into subtle asymmetries.

For Humphrey, getting in touch with the modern world did not mean aping the designs of machines in dance—as was popular in Europe. Nor can I remember seeing in a Humphrey dance the images of humanity as a clump of diversity, bristling with gestures (often found in pictures of the Mary Wigman school). It was through the mounting line, the ziggurat made asymmetrical—halved and softened into a fluid staircase—that Humphrey traced in nature and society paths of growth, hope, and disunity becoming unity (an important theme for this most Utopian of choreographers). The spiral that ended *Color Harmony* (1928) suggests dynamic symmetry; dancers representing the various colors (allied with human temperaments) fan out from the white light that contains them all.

She was not alone in her interest in the aspiring line (or its opposite). It seems to have become a design principle in dance beginning in the late twenties. Five women in Elizabeth Selden's *Danse Languide* are pictured in her 1935 book *The Dancer's Quest* ranged in positions from crouching to tiptoe. They're too limp to invoke anything very "dynamic," yet their arrangement does imply a downward motion. You can see similar lines in Laban's movement choirs. You can even note the affinity between one of Selden's drawings[11] and a moment from George Balanchine's 1933 *Serenade* (he also used the staircase pattern in *Apollo* and later in *Concerto Barocco*).

Doris could be pragmatic about design, using it simply as a way to give the spectator's eye rest and variety. I remember her advising José Limón in 1958 to reshape a side-to-side pattern in his *Missa Brevis* by having the dancers execute it along the spokes of a circle. Nor, in her view, were forms immutable. She might use the "whirling star,"[12] as she called it, to express a com-munity with a potential for disequilibrium. In *The Shakers,* the men form one Texas Star, the women another. As the stars, placed symmetrically on either side of the center line, turn, individual men and women of this strictly celibate community stretch their arms spasmodically toward one another as they pass. The gestures could pull the group's equilibrium out of kilter, but the circling progress holds them in check. In *With My Red Fires,* the fierce gestures of the Matriarch/dictator organize the citizens of this strange society into a posse. Shoulder to shoulder in a series of spokes radiating out from her, they run, crouch, stand as if she had them on invisible leashes. The alternation of rapid percussion with sudden silences in Wallingford Riegger's score, her commands, and their responses suggest an immense wheel cranking up speed. Yet in *New Dance,* Humphrey's vision of an ideal community, she used the whirling star in the "Variations and Conclusion" to very different effect. The blocks have been arranged into a pyramid. The dancers prance around them in pairs which become more populous lines, which intermittently become aisles to disgorge soloists at various points around the circle—an image of festivity and courtesy.

I recently re-read Humphrey's notes on *New Dance.* "Since I wished at first to convey a sense of incompletion, I chose the Broken Form, by which I mean unfolding continual change, with contrast but very little repetition."[13] "My main theme was to move from the simple to the complex from an individual integration to a group integration."[14] "It was here I used symmetry for the first time as the best way to express cohesion and completion."[15] "The fugue was eminently suitable to express a harmonious chorus wherein no member was more important than another."[16] Few choreographers think like this anymore. A handful of great ones—Merce Cunningham certainly—have a different world view and construct their forms accordingly. But watching the work of younger, less analytical choreographers, I sometimes think that they wish to affirm a sense of community, but that it never emerges because they've used what Humphrey might have termed the

(Above) 31. *Color Harmony* (1928). Photo by Vandamm Studios. From the collection of Charles H. Woodford, reprinted with his permission.

(Left) 32. Drawings by Elizabeth Selden, from her book, *The Dancer's Quest: Essays on the Aesthetic of the Dance* (1935). Reprinted by permission of The Regents of the University of California.

"Broken Form." Her style, her concerns, her morality arose from the age as she conceived it, her heart as she knew it. However, her sensitivity, her objective vision as to how ideas and feelings might translate into dance constitute a lesson for all choreographers—one that transcends style and fashions and changing times.

Notes

1. Doris Humphrey, draft of a letter to Letitia Ide, 1930, in Doris Humphrey Collection (Folder C280), New York Public Library for the Performing Arts, New York City, New York.

2. Susanne K. Langer, *Feeling and Form: A Theory of Art Developed from "Philosophy in a New Key"* (New York: Charles Scribner's Sons, 1953), 175.

3. Doris Humphrey, *The Art of Making Dances* (New York: Rinehart & Company, 1959), 22.

4. Doris Humphrey, "What Shall We Dance About," *Trend, A Quarterly of the Seven Arts* (June–August 1932), reprinted in Selma Jeanne Cohen, *Doris Humphrey: An Artist First* (Middletown, Conn.: Wesleyan University Press, 1972), 252.

5. Le Corbusier, *Toward a New Architecture,* trans. Frederick Etchells, from the 13th French ed. (New York: Brewer and Warren, 1927), 1.

6. Humphrey, *The Art of Making Dances,* 159.

7. Ibid.

8. Jay Hambidge, *The Elements of Dynamic Symmetry* (1919; reprint, New York: Brentano's, 1926), xiv.

9. Doris Humphrey, letter to her mother, August 30, 1927, in Doris Humphrey Collection (Folder C267), Dance Collection, New York Public Library for the Performing Arts, New York City, New York.

10. Hambidge, *The Elements of Dynamic Symmetry,* 34–36.

11. Elizabeth Selden, *The Dancer's Quest: Essays on the Aesthetics of the Contemporary Dance* (Berkeley: University of California Press, 1935), 70–71.

12. Doris Humphrey, in Doris Humphrey Collection (Folder M25), New York Public Library for the Performing Arts, New York City, New York, reprinted in Cohen, *Doris Humphrey,* 240.

13. Cohen, *Doris Humphrey,* 239.

14. Ibid.

15. Ibid., 240.

16. Ibid.

The Harsh and Splendid Heroines
of Martha Graham

MARCIA B. SIEGEL

Editor's Note: This article was first published in American Poetry Review, *January–February 1975.*

Martha Graham's mind is a transforming mind. She converts literary, historical, and social images into danced reality. Although it's impossible to identify the process of creating a dance with complete accuracy, we know that some choreographers begin with a personal statement or observation and then have to find a theme and a style by which to make it. Some choreographers say they work purely from a movement or a musical impulse—people as diverse as Merce Cunningham and Anna Sokolow, George Balanchine and Twyla Tharp. There are ballets that bring celebrated sculptures to life, and ballets that put stories into motion, and ballets that attempt to suggest a bygone period or a way of living.

Graham seems to start with the world's messages, then she states them in personal terms. I don't know of another choreographer as literary as Graham and at the same time as theatrical, as universal in the themes that inspire her and as personal in the method of translating those themes.

Like Stravinsky's, Martha Graham's range is as important as her endurance. Graham may be the first American dance artist to survive into her own posterity. Other choreographers have lived a long time, but only Graham has created a continuously strong body of work that keeps regenerating itself on new dancers, finding new partisans. The New York spring season at the Mark Hellinger Theater spanned almost thirty-five years of protean work and attracted large, appreciative audiences. Opening night Graham remembered that she'd once told a disapproving friend after an early concert: "I'll keep it up as long as I have an audience." The force of her personality probably won her adherents in those first years when her work was so radical. But behind that presence was and is a marvelously comprehensive intelligence that is evident now in the scope of the repertory.

A Graham dance looks nothing like a ballet or any other Western theater dancing I can think of. It's basically a soloistic form. The action centers on one person at a time, or at the most two. When any more people than that are active on a Graham scene, they usually assume choral patterns, losing their individuality in order to merge with the group. There aren't any real group interactions in Graham, as there are in Antony Tudor, for instance, where you often see several movement ideas or expressions contributing to the progress of a scene.

For a body of work the stature of Graham's, the dances are unexpectedly small. In several of the fourteen works given last spring, the principal dancers outnumber or equal the members of the chorus; some dances have only two, three, or four principal dancers and no chorus; and almost none of them has more than ten dancers in all. This must have come about in part because Graham's company was limited in size—even now she has only twenty-six dancers, about one third of what a major ballet company can get away with. And, of course, until the past decade or so, Graham herself was the central figure in her own work. Even when not choreographing for herself, she made movement that was essentially self-generated and self-directed. The dancer moves to call attention to herself, to define her immediate state or attitude. Graham's choruses, like traditional ballet choruses, are multiples of one, or sometimes multiples of male-female duets. She didn't think of a group as a collection of individuals or interwoven musical motifs as Doris Humphrey did.

Whether the dance is about a Martha-figure and her subordinate characters, or about a small group of related individuals with a unison chorus commenting on their actions, it proceeds in episodic fashion, one self-contained scene after another. The intensity of each episode is kept concentrated. So few characters have to carry the whole import of the dance that each one becomes crucial.

Graham often leaves the dancers onstage when they aren't dancing. There they become frozen observers or efface themselves entirely. The main action gains even more potency because of this constant presence of the other figures in the story. The characters can't escape their past or their community or their fate, whatever those temporarily suspended, brooding presences represent. The typical Graham dance doesn't have the kind of continuity and flow that is created when dancers enter and exit in a freer, more overlapping kind of timing and grouping. It doesn't give you a sense of belonging to any other place, or having any other existence, than the one you see at that moment, in that space.

Within this rather severe and particularized framework, Graham's dances speak of the American temperament; of religion, rite, and atavism; of the anguish of artists and the obligations of kings; and of woman's struggle for dominance without guilt. Graham's dance is above all personal, and because it reflects a far-reaching mind and sensibility most of it traverses the nebulous line between work that is merely insular or eccentric and work of genius.

I think before anything else about Graham's dance crystallized, her movement language did. Within five years after she left Denishawn and began choreographing on her own, she was moving in a way that was unique. The earliest of her dances that could still be seen in recent years—on film or in short-lived revivals—showed her using the body much as she does now, although the style has gradually moderated, softened. Where ballet dancers and "expressive dancers" up to the 1920s had looked for harmony in the body, Graham exposed its discord. Her shapes and pathways were twisted, angular. Instead of concealing the dancer's exertion and trying to make her look serene, Graham made dancers use their tensions, show their power. She kept movement close to the center of the body; the dancer had to do more than move to another spot to change her relationship to others.

As her company grew, as her thematic focus broadened from the concerns of one individual to the transactions of groups and societies, this same way of moving served to define character and situation. Through movement, Graham externalized her own emotional states into something that could stand for much more.

Jason (*Cave of the Heart*) and Agamemnon (*Clytemnestra*) don't walk, they strut. They spread their elbows and clench their fists and their bodies bend only from the tops of the legs. When Graham mocks them, she mocks the arrogance of all kings and the rigidity of kingly succession. Medea's Princess-rival is quick, rounded, playful, but also vain and credulous, while Medea is contorted with jealousy, and shrewd as her obsession can make her. The center of the body, especially in Graham's women, tells you what is going on. They shrink back in fear, narrow themselves in repressed fury, wriggle seductively, flatten out, and expand in their rare moments of calm.

Graham may start out with very specific plots or legends, but there's always more in what the characters do than mere reenactment. *El Penitente* (1940) is a little passion play for three peasants in a flagellant sect in the Southwest. One man plays the role of man the sinner, a woman is Eve and the Marys, and another man a black-robed Christ-figure in a sad mask crowned with thorns. The Christ-figure is very straight up and down, even dancing a lot of the time on the balls of his feet. He towers over the Penitent, chastizes him with a gentle slap, walks spread out like a cruciform, tilting from side to side, as if he were a bit vulnerable or could be swayed. This is not at all the way Christ is pictured in traditional art, but it's one way a naive Indian might imagine a benevolent, paternal deity.

Deaths and Entrances (1943) started out to be a dance about the Brontë sisters—I'm not sure Graham ever considered the black sheep Brontë brother, who also secretly wrote stories all his life. As the dance evolved, though, it lost whatever specific references it ever had to the events at Haworth parsonage; Graham has said the Brontës were only a springboard. What the dance does tell you about is three women trapped by their own indecisiveness and gentility. The women fondle objects that seem to suggest action, but they're unable to act. Characters not definitely real or fictional run in and out, little encounters take place and are broken off, rivalries are intimated but quickly contained.

In one terrible moment at the end, one of the sisters, alone onstage and temporarily free of all the other lives that have been constantly encroaching on her own, gives way to her frustration. She ought to stomp around or smash something, but no, she keeps her rage all inside her body. Shuddering and wrenching, as if she would tear herself to bits from the inside, she hovers over the chess board where the endless familial game is played. She makes little stabbing gestures and steps, pulls back, not daring to breach the boundaries that her mind has constructed. Then it's over, the sisters return, the game begins again. The pattern continues.

It must have been the appalling proprieties of being a minister's daughter in the nineteenth century that drew Graham to the Brontës in the first place. The artist struggling to get liberated from the Puritan's body *is* Graham. Though she no longer practices any religion, she still reveres much that religion represents. She seems, on a more or less visible level in her dances,

always to be grappling with the confinement versus the security imposed by tradition, the disastrous results of trying to conceal one's nonconformity, and the bliss of being able to give in to a higher authority.

When I visited her a few weeks after the spring season, she looked anything but a Puritan, wearing a spectacular emerald green caftan with the kind of confidence in her own glamour that some women possess even if they're not beautiful or young. Graham was in a mood for reminiscing, and she spoke without rancor of her Presbyterian forebears. She told me the Ancestress in her Emily Dickinson dance, *Letter to the World* (1940), had been modeled after her grandmother, a "severe but just" woman who always wore black. "It's a death image, a fear of death," she said. "Children are afraid of people in black. I never touch a child when I'm in my black practice clothes." And she recalled the stern dicta of New England preachers like Jonathan Edwards and Cotton Mather, who promised that man was nothing but "a spider in the hand of God. He's holding you over a flame and he can drop you in if he wants to." Their terrorizing sermons led to the creation of the Revivalist in *Appalachian Spring* (1944). "Fortunately I didn't know many preachers," Graham told me dispassionately.

Graham remembers, as a child, kneeling for morning prayers at home and peeking at her grandmother through the rungs of a chair. She also remembers that "very remote and dignified" lady, in her high-buttoned black dress, sitting right down on the ground in Needles, Arizona, on a very hot day, when the train that was carrying the family across the country broke down. The mixture of intimidating authority and ridiculousness in these images found its way into her dance.

But the dread and the revulsion came out too—in the huge, lurching, monster-strides of the Ancestress, a creature without any resilience in her movement at all, who stifles all chances of escape, breaks apart lovers, presides over funeral processions as if they were orgies. And in the demonic, hellfire frenzy that takes possession of the Revivalist when he's supposed to be preaching a wedding sermon. Yet even in these grisly portraits there is comfort. The Ancestress cradles a momentarily frightened Emily between her knees, and the Revivalist in his stiff, comical way, flirts with four adoring little choir girls.

I was delighted and a little amazed to hear these stories, for I'd always thought Graham's message was so lofty, so cerebral. There does seem to be a breaking point in her total output, when her sources became less personal and more literary. Up to the mid-1940s her dances were drawn from her American heritage, from her political and emotional sympathies, and from real or theatrical characters with whom Graham identified. The scenarios must have developed from her imagination, like *Appalachian Spring,* or been suggested very freely by assorted written texts, like *Letter to the World* and *American Document.*

It would take a critical biographer to investigate thoroughly all the reasons why Graham's approach changed in the forties. But after the small transitional works, *Hérodiade, Dark Meadow,* and *Errand into the Maze,* she stopped doing dances about herself in reference to Mankind, and did dances about Mankind as represented by herself and her company. All her famous Greek pieces were made after 1944, all her dances about Judeo-Christian protagonists—Judith, Saint Joan, Samson Agonistes, and others—and all her big, abstract lyric dances for the group. In these latter works, one feels her intellect at work making connections. The psyche she probes is universal, interpreted by Freud, Jung, and the explicators of myth. The journeys back into her own memory and experience seem fewer and more generalized. Graham was deliberately making her characters larger than life; they didn't merely act out our passions, they symbolized our moral and emotional conflicts.

In *Errand into the Maze* (1947) we can almost see this extrapolation taking place. *Errand* is a duet, a very strange duet. The man doesn't court the woman in any conventional sense, although what she interprets as hostile advances could be his attempts to seduce her. A huge bone or a branch or yoke spans the man's shoulders, and he must keep his arms wrapped around it,

but robbed of his arms and hands he's still a formidable attacker. The woman is alone at the beginning of the dance, and survives alone at the end, having wrestled the man to the ground after a decisive third encounter. Narrow and tentative in her body at first, nervously poking and slithering through space, at the end she swings open her lower body, pelvis and leg, in wide, slow figure eights, as she gazes out of the entrance to the maze.

I've tried to be very factual in my description, to tell nothing but what you see on the stage, but Graham's imagery is so forceful that it can't always be separated from the actuality. There is no real maze; the woman steps along a serpentine path made by a tape laid on the floor. Later she pulls the tape up and slings it back and forth between two branches of a tree-like structure, barring herself inside, or keeping the man out. After vanquishing the man, she undoes the tape and frees herself.

A program note for *Errand into the Maze* tells us that in this dance "the heart" does battle with "the Creature of Fear," without naming or attaching this heart or this Creature to any known persons. But we do know, perhaps from the dance's title, that it's a reference to the Greek legend of Theseus and the Minotaur. In a brilliant stroke, Graham shifted the whole focus of the myth by making the Creature's antagonist a woman. Gone is the standard tale of a hero who saves his people by seeking out an oppressor in its lair. Now it is an investigation of the hero's—heroine's—mind; her inner state of fear and tension, her positive action in going to confront the thing she fears.

Ariadne's thread, which in the myth provided an escape route for the hero, has become a path the woman embarks on to get in touch with danger, a path she no longer needs to retrace after she has arrived at the heart of her fear. We don't know if the dance is "about" making yourself do something you're afraid of doing, or "about" traveling back through your subconscious to encounter the source of your hang-ups. It could be about all these things, or many others.

Above all, what *Errand into the Maze* shows us—

apart from what it suggests and symbolizes—is a woman who thinks, acts, makes more room for herself to operate in. If Martha Graham has one message, that has to be it. She was an early if undeclared feminist, so early that she couldn't entirely shake off society's expectations for her, or the armor of guilt, conflict, repressed violence that society decrees for its female mavericks. Graham's heroines are all nonconformists—artists, doers, women with power beyond their sexuality. And they all suffer for their unorthodoxy.

While I was thinking about this article, I came across the following in Virginia Woolf's diary (August 19, 1918): "The heroic woman is much the same in Greece and England. She is of the type of Emily Brontë. Clytemnestra and Electra are clearly mother and daughter, and therefore should have some sympathy, though perhaps sympathy gone wrong breeds the fiercest hate. . . . Electra lived a far more hedged in life than the women of the mid-Victorian age, but this has no effect upon her, except in making her harsh and splendid." Graham's women are hedged-in, neurotic because they cannot submit to men and tradition, driven to acts of hate and acts of courage, and sometimes, when they give in to their need for masculine domination, reduced to simpering dolls.

Graham not only recognizes her occasional need to be dependent on a man, but apparently feels this need diminishes her. Her two self-satires, *Acrobats of God* and *Every Soul Is a Circus*, both show the heroine as star, but a star who turns all silly when a man cracks his whip. Clytemnestra consciously assumes a kittenish attitude when she's luring Agamemnon to his death. For Graham, a traditional feminine stance can be adopted only as a weapon or a sign of weakness. She seldom found a way for men and women to be equals.

But her view of sexual relationships is not the most important statement she makes as a preeminently gifted feminist. Her dances redo history through a female mind. Almost the entire sum of our intelligence about the world's past has been transmitted to us through the eyes of men, and is pictured with men as the prime movers. I doubt if there's ever been as con-

certed an effort as Martha Graham's to present a more balanced perspective. She didn't set out to make political statements; one way to see her work is as a manipulation of tradition to reflect her personality or provide herself with starring roles. But even if she has been merely making her themes serve her art, she has told the stories another way around. We all know the agony of Oedipus; Graham describes Jocasta's pain. For her "The Oresteia" became *Clytemnestra*.

The extraordinary thing that this refocusing does is to make the women protagonists human, where before they had been the pawns of gods and men. The Joan of Arc story usually comes to us as a tale of a woman's martyrdom. Joan herself is less important than her religious fanaticism and her temerity in playing a man's role in the wars that are the business of kings. It's fascinating, then, to see what elements of the story Graham chose for her version, *Seraphic Dialogue* (1955). The dance is a meditation on three aspects of Joan's life: her youth and early visions, her decision to take up the sword, and her martyrdom. There are no kings or prime ministers in the dance; no peasants or armies or bishops or judges. Joan, played by one dancer, sees her former selves, played by three other dancers, enact her interior struggles, doubts, and spiritual joy. The only other dancers in the work portray Sts. Michael, Catherine, and Margaret.

Once again, the protagonist is a woman who has to make up her mind. Michael helps her, Catherine and Margaret inspire her, but the decision to defy society and realize her calling is hers. The political intrigues that smolder around her might not touch her at all; she has her eye fixed on God. To this Joan it doesn't seem unnatural or disgusting to dress as a man or not have children. Those are minor terms of the pact. What's hard is that she knows the whole venture will be dangerous; every step is a risk and every success will bring her nearer to death. In Graham's universe, Joan wins her own beatification. By the time sainthood is conferred on her—when she's crowned and taken up into Noguchi's stained-glass window set—the glory has already happened.

You could see the same attitude toward sacred figures in Graham's very early masterpiece, *Primitive Mysteries* (1931). A white-clad woman and twelve companions enter and leave very ceremoniously three times. Each of the three dances, Hymn to the Virgin, Crucifixus, Hosanna, suggests the elements of praise, suffering, joy that are part of Christian ritual. But the women experience it, they act out the grief and compassion and exaltation without male intermediaries to do it for them or delineate the forms of their worship.

The dignity and power of Graham's women emanate from her sense that women do have an independent existence, as rich psychically and creatively as that of men. Perhaps nowhere did she explore the variety of that interior existence as deeply as in *Letter to the World* in which Graham was stirred by the New England recluse-poet Emily Dickinson to create a dance that has more changes of mood, more possibility for lyricism in a strong female role, than any other I've seen of hers.

The dance begins with a fast, impulsive solo for Emily (the One Who Dances), in which she mercurially flits from place to place, can't seem to light anywhere before she takes off again. Another Emily, the One Who Speaks, walks sedately behind her, telling of New England ways and weather. She exclaims, "I'm sorry for the dead today!" and suddenly the mood turns black—"Looking at death is dying." The scene is transformed into a "gay, ghastly holiday," Emily stiffened and laid out like a corpse, and handsome young men turned into pall-bearers, and black-veiled women running all bent over with their arms curving down behind them so you can't tell if they're fleeing or hurling themselves into a battle. Finally Emily works up all her courage and spits at the Ancestress: "The Bible is an antique volume, written by faded men at the suggestion of holy spectres!"—and prances off chanting, "In the name of the bee—and the butterfly—and of the breeze, Amen!" (These lines were used as the benediction in a Dickinson poem describing an imaginary funeral for summer.) The dance continues in one unbroken stream of consciousness, bringing alive the childlike, perceptive woman who had to sacrifice love for respectability, but who defied tradition anyway,

by pouring her rebellion and her appetite for life into the secret poems that formed her letter to the world.

When I saw Martha Graham after the season, I asked her how she was able to find the lines of Dickinson that so brilliantly carried the dance from one luminous state of mind to another. She couldn't say, except that she hadn't gone searching for the words; she'd known Emily a long time, lived with her poetry, and when it came time to do the ballet, the words were there.

I've always thought that one of the principal reasons Graham attained her position in the world's esteem is that, although a dancer, she operates so verbally. Her notebooks, published last fall, attest that she is not only a near-poet herself, but an intellectual, a scholar, who reads incessantly and scours literature for choreographic themes. One of her recent works, *Chronique* (1973), was based on a poem by St. John Perse, and had in its first version an actress reciting lines from the poem on stage. Later, the speaker was placed in the orchestra pit, but now Graham says she wants to omit the words altogether. "I'm not pleased with them being spoken as they are. I only use words if they're an intrinsic part of the dance. The words dance their own dance and the dancers dance their own poetry."

I think the physicality of her presence on stage asserted the dance's integrity over its literary sources. The audience could see that mind and mover were one. When she grew less active and finally retired from dancing, her work became diffuse, more literary, less personal. The poem "Chronique" gets its grandeur from its language. "Great age behold us, and take the measure of man's heart." "Divine violence be ours till the last eddy." Graham translated this into a dance of symbolic, anonymous beings—lovers, contestants, seekers—who do beautiful movement that has no core. The words are contemplative, but there's no one in the dance who contemplates; it swirls and ripples across the stage but doesn't ever really come to rest. Graham told me the poem was an affirmation of life and a diatribe against war, but the dance needs a person who affirms.

The same is true with this season's new work, *Holy Jungle*. In a program note, she describes it as "A fantasy of man's sufferings, temptations, strange visions that attack and surround him, on his pilgrimage to the almost forgotten Eden of his dreams," and earlier, in a press conference, she referred to "frescoes in the skull," the memories and legends in man's mind. The figures in the dance are representational. The audience can't connect them with anyone real; they have loaded names like Angel, Celestial Bride, and Lucifer. Graham has a wonderful company of young dancers now, and perhaps she will become interested enough in some of them to make them the motivating characters in future new works, to project onto them the urgency that made her create for herself. At this point her choreography looks imposed from the outside.

I never saw Martha Graham dancing at the height of her powers. All of her pre-1960 works I've seen were performed by other dancers, with the exception of a few on film. So I'm not speaking of some remembered presence shedding invisible wattage on pathetic revivals. Even with other women doing her roles, Graham's theater has magnetism, conviction, consistency.

From the compact, apparently simple but very sophisticated *El Penitente* to the huge, dense, luxurious *Clytemnestra*, her theatrical skill is like one more outlet for the energy that is making the whole dance happen. The props in *El Penitente* belong to the peasant-performers; they might have made them, they're so simple and in the case of the Christ-mask so crudely beautiful. In *Clytemnestra* (1958) the props are immense, like the scale of the dance. Long spears are carried by soldiers and serve at different times as the masts of Agamemnon's ship, the funeral bier for Iphigenia, the sedan-chair on which Agamemnon is borne home. After Clytemnestra has decided to murder her husband, two women come onstage with a contrivance that I'm sure Graham and designer Isamu Noguchi must have invented, a tremendous length of crimson and pink paneled cloth, attached at both ends to curving poles held by the two attendants. The cloth, like a gorgeous river of blood, flows over the stage during the whole murder sequence. Clytemnestra wraps herself in it, winding around her body the awful role she has chosen. It gets stretched across the stage as a kind of welcoming carpet for the king. The attendants stand the poles up in front of the murder-place, pulling them aside just long enough for us to see Clytemnestra striking the fatal blows.

I can't help contrasting this with the way props are used in *Holy Jungle,* where objects stand for life intentions. People play with globes and candy-cane staffs and toy trees. They duel with long, metal rods, touch each other with a paddle sculpted into the form of a hand. The props are used as tools—they substitute for what the dancers haven't actually done. The more striking or strange their design, the more they separate us from the dance idea, rather than enhancing the dance idea.

Graham's is often a theater of polarities, of shocking contrasts or contradictions, but the most telling of these are accomplished by dancers dancing. Oedipus and Jocasta's duet in *Night Journey* (1947) is a series of twinings and inversions in which the dancers lapse from poses of lovemaking into poses of mother and child; one moment he straddles her and the next she's rocking him in her lap.

Images repeat themselves with slight differences, gaining in weight and meaning each time. *Cave of the Heart* (1946) is full of figurehead shapes assumed by Medea and the rival Princess. Each time one of them thrusts her upper body forward and gazes in an arc across the horizon, we are reminded of Jason's journey and the transitoriness of all the events and relationships that are taking place. After poisoning her husband's paramour, Medea actually slips herself inside Noguchi's brass wire branching sculpture and reaches out from the waist in glittering sweeps. Metaphorically she has become a bird, at one with the sky, where her rescuing chariot is to come from. But literally, too, she appends the prop and all its symbolic associations to her own body, not just displaying it, but merging with it.

Graham's theater is priceless because it brings all these things together. It's more than a vehicle for her own performing power and intellect, more than her psychological insights or the particular way she developed nonverbal structures. Now that she is not dancing herself, we can see the totality of its impact better than ever. Throughout her career, Graham worked for the moment, put her energies into the dance that was being made, didn't devote her efforts to preserving or restoring works that had already satisfied their purpose. Now I think that attitude is changing. The audiences at the spring season were very enthusiastic, and Graham was not unaware that there's a revival of interest in her work.

I asked her why she thought her dance appeals to people now. "The audience is much more knowable and aware than we ever had before," she said. "The young people identify with young people—dancers—who are disciplined, because they're not. They've shattered all the idols, now they want something they can idolize. The middle-aged people, well, maybe they studied dance when they were young, and they held those days as an ideal period of charm and emotional strength. People today want something that means something. They get everything else on television. They want something which will quicken and stir them, make them feel more alive."

Then she talked about her company, the excellent young dancers who are so obviously making her feel more alive. And she told me something I never expected to hear from her, something that made me extremely happy. "The dance is a legend, but on the legend the next generation builds. Yes, this season it seems there's more of a chance for the dances to live than I thought."

The Dance Is a Weapon

ELLEN GRAFF

Prologue

When I was cleaning out my mother's apartment I came across a program she had saved from the Inwood chapter of the Peoples Culture Union of America. It was one of my first public appearances. Staged in 1949, just before the full force of McCarthyism compelled all the old-line Communists and fellow travelers to drop out of sight and keep their politics to themselves, this "cooperative" was almost certainly a remnant of the Communist Party's cultural program that had flourished in New York City during the 1930s.

The community of Inwood lies at the northern tip of Manhattan, beyond the Cloisters and the gardens of Fort Tryon Park, in an area bounded by the Harlem River to the north and east and by Dyckman Street on the south. In those days it was a working-class community—half Irish Catholic and half German Jewish immigrants, with the occasional bohemian family thrown in. Mr. and Mrs. Kamarck, who lived just down the street from us, ran the Inwood chapter of the Peoples Culture Union. Mrs. Kamarck was overweight and gave piano lessons in her cramped three-room apartment. On warm spring days she used to take neighborhood children across the street to the park to make crepe-paper flowers. In the wildness of Inwood Hill Park I played make-believe games with her daughter, who was a year or so younger than me. Mr. Kamarck was a printer. He and his wife probably were Communists.

My father was also a printer. He belonged to the International Typographical Union, a militant trade union that was home to many radicals, and he was a member of the Communist-sponsored writers' club Pen and Hammer. Among other memorabilia I encountered as I went through my mother's file cabinet were some articles my father wrote for the *Newspaper* of the Printing Trades Union and for the *New Masses*. A piece he wrote about the International Typographical Union was published under his pseudonym, George Sherman, since the Party wanted to create a cloud of mystery around those involved in its activities. My mother had a pseudonym as well; Virginia Ackerley (her maiden name) became Alice Vaughn when she was taking part in Party activities. I remember seeing copies of the Communist newspaper the *Daily Worker* in our home, and I would not be surprised to learn that my family sold copies.

I do not think that my parents actually joined the Communist Party, although perhaps in the 1950s, when I was growing up, they would not have told me even if they had. Instead, they were fellow travelers, sympathetic to the Party's goals. Looking around the streets of New York in the 1930s, they would have seen breadlines, Hoovervilles, "Hard Luck" towns, and squatters living in Central Park. The Party promised social and economic justice, and the Soviet Union, which they visited in 1930 for their honeymoon, was the bold new state lighting the way. "From each according to his ability, to each according to his needs" was a refrain that echoed throughout my childhood.

Idealism and deeply held convictions animated efforts by my parents and many others, during the turbulent thirties. They wanted to make a better world, and for some years, I think, they felt that they could help bring that about. The choreographic efforts of a group of New York City dancers who shared the same vision are the subject of this essay. While some of them were Communists and some were not, each was driven by a kind of moral fervor to respond to the complex social and political issues surrounding them.

In the midst of the Great Depression the United States underwent a period of economic and political upheaval. President Franklin D. Roosevelt spoke movingly about "the forgotten man" and introduced New Deal legislation to ease economic hardship, while demagogues such as Huey P. Long called for plans to "soak the rich." The Communist Party, USA, enjoyed its most influential decade during the 1930s.

In New York City on March 6, 1930, the Party led a crowd of between 35,000 and 100,000 workers—depending on which press accounts you believed—in a demonstration for "International Unemployment Day."[1] They marched from Union Square to City Hall, and the ensuing confrontation with New York's finest left about a hundred civilians injured. A second demonstration for unemployment relief on October 16, 1930, disrupted the proceedings of the Board of Estimate. It must have been effective, because the next day the board designated $1 million for unemployment relief.[2]

John Reed Clubs, named after the radical American journalist whose body is interred in the Kremlin wall, were organized in 1929 with the goal of creating a proletarian culture; in 1931 a Workers Cultural Federation was formed after a delegation of American artists returned from the Soviet Union with directives for attracting proletarians, intellectuals, and blacks to their ranks, as well as for organizing agitprop theatrical troupes. In New York City 265 delegates, claiming to represent some 20,000 members from 130 different groups, met to endorse the proposition that "culture is a weapon." As the cultural arm of the Communist

Party, the federation was expected to faithfully follow the Party line.[3]

Cultural activities were an important part of many Communist demonstrations. May Day celebrations to honor workers were accompanied by workers' choirs, pageantry, and brass bands. On May Day 1930, for example, a demonstration at Union Square was followed by a celebration at Coney Island, which included performances by several workers' cultural groups. Admission was twenty-five and fifty cents—free to the unemployed.[4] Crowds attending May Day festivities like this one proved an appreciative audience for working-class performing groups.[5]

Meeting places for the union groups taking part in these celebrations were designated in the blocks surrounding Union Square, with the Workers Cultural Federation assigning each group to a different section. A parade route was published. In 1932 demonstrators marched south from Union Square along Fourth Avenue to 14th Street. Turning east on 14th Street to Avenue A, the marchers proceeded south to Houston Street, along Houston to the corner of Ridge and Montgomery Streets, south again to East Broadway, and then west to Rutgers Square, their destination.[6]

Union Square at 14th Street and Fifth Avenue was the hub the of radical activity dominated by the Communist Party during those years. In 1930 CP headquarters overlooked the square. The offices of the *Daily Worker* were located on Union Square East, right next to the Workers Book Shop and above the Cooperative Cafeteria.

Not far away, within easy walking distance, another kind of revolution was brewing. The nascent modern dance movement was making its home in and around Greenwich Village. Martha Graham had a studio, first on West 10th Street, then on East 9th Street, and after 1934 at 66 Fifth Avenue, near 12th Street. Doris Humphrey and Charles Weidman taught classes on West 18th Street. In 1934 Helen Tamiris moved from Lafayette Street to a studio on West 8th Street. A brief walk would take a dancer from a class at one or an-

33. Soloists of the Workers Dance League. Clockwise, starting above: Miriam Blecher in *Woman* (center), Anna Sokolow in *Histrionics;* Jane Dudley in *The Dream Ends;* Lillian Mehlman in *Defiance;* Sophie Maslow in *Themes from a Slavic People;* Sokolow, Maslow, and Mehlman in *Challenge (Death of Tradition);* Nadia Chilkovsky in *Parasite;* and Edith Segal in *Tom Mooney.* Photographs by Nat Messik. Chilkovsky photo by Matyas Caldy. Reproduced from *New Theatre,* January 1935.

other of their studios to the political hurly-burly of Union Square.

This geographic intimacy was convenient for socially conscious dancers, and the collision of the two revolutionary worlds sparked an explosion of choreographic activity. The antiacademy and antielitist basis of modern dance fit nicely within the mission of proletarian culture, just as the proletarian worker proved an eager student and enthusiastic audience for an emergent art. Workers' dance groups sprang up in unions such as the Needle Trades Workers Industrial Union, in recreational clubs such as the German hiking group Nature Friends, and in association with workers' theater groups such as the Theatre Union. A collective known as the New Dance Group delivered affordable dance classes to working-class amateurs.

"Dance Is a Weapon in the Revolutionary Class Struggle" was the slogan of the Workers Dance League, an umbrella organization formed to develop and organize efforts of the various workers' dance groups. The idea for the Workers Dance League seems to have been born at a May Day celebration held at the Bronx Coliseum in 1932 in which eleven of the newly formed workers' dance groups participated. According to the *Daily Worker,* dancers Anna Sokolow, Edith Segal, Miriam Blecher, and Nadia Chilkovsky were responsible for its formation.[7]

The League sponsored concerts and contests among workers' dance groups called Spartakiades and facilitated the exchange of ideas and dance scenarios through *New Theatre,* the workers' theater and dance publication. (*New Theatre* actually replaced an earlier journal called *Workers Theatre,* a collection of mimeographed sheets reporting on issues and events in workers' culture.) Workers reported to the League from Philadelphia, Boston, and Chicago, asking advice and sharing ideas, but New York City was the thriving center of activity. After seeing the First Workers' Dance Spartakiade in 1933, one delegate responded enthusiastically, determined to improve the performance of a group in Boston:

> I want to tell you that I was very inspired and also ashamed after seeing the wonderful work the dance groups are doing in New York. I told as best I could to the group all I learned from watching and listening especially at the council and we have all resolved to work harder and with more purpose hereafter. I feel that my instructing the group will be better because of my trip to New York.[8]

The extent to which social and political ideology could be integrated or could contribute to the aesthetic framework of a dance was debated in periodicals, such as *New Theatre* and in *Dance Observer,* a magazine, founded in 1934 to promote American dance as an art form. While significant subject matter was the primary issue for revolutionary dancers, other articles examined various formal concerns and urged collaborative methods of dance-making in keeping with the communal ideal. In general, dancers such as Martha Graham and Mary Wigman, the leader of the German Ausdruckstanz movement, were criticized by the leftist press for subject matter that was too personal, too mystical, and too divorced from contemporary social issues as well as too abstract and difficult to understand. The revolutionaries, in contrast, were faulted for lack of professionalism and for the simplicity of their message. The agitprop techniques and heavy symbolism they favored were inconsistent with the goals of modernism.

The history of American modern dance blurred distinctions between revolutionary and "bourgeois" dance in interesting ways. In music and in theater, classical and traditional methods of training and composition were labeled "bourgeois" by the leftist press. In dance,

paradoxically, it was the struggling new experiments of people like Martha Graham that came to be considered as the ancien régime. Perhaps if ballet had been an established form in the United States, the new modern dance forms might have been considered revolutionary; they were after all based on an antiacademy and, in that sense, antibourgeois sentiment. Instead, it was the schools of Graham, Humphrey, Tamiris, and the German Hanya Holm (who headed the Wigman School in New York City) that came to be considered as established and traditional training methods, although their techniques predated working-class dance activity by only a few years.

Revolutionary writers and dancers argued over the relative merits of a "revolutionary" technique. Should it be based on communal and folk forms? Or could dancers appropriate "bourgeois" techniques? Grace Wylie, administrator and dancer for the New Dance Group, was one who argued for appropriating technical skills. "[Do] we completely discard their technique and suddenly build our own? We derive whatever is of value to us from the dance as it stands and reject the rest. If the bourgeois dance has anything of value to give us we use it."[9] But Michael Gold, writing in the *Daily Worker,* chastised dancers for being revolutionary in name only. "Do you think you can keep this up forever, this labelling a grey standardized sterile dance by Martha Graham by a hundred different titles—Scottsboro, Anti-fascism, etc., and make us accept the product as revolutionary?"[10]

Other writers argued for an evolutionary approach, suggesting that as revolutionary dancers developed, they would discard the old "bourgeois" technique and create bold new revolutionary forms. They pleaded for critics like Gold to give the dancers a chance.[11]

Debates over technique receded when the Communist Party adopted a new policy called socialist realism, which urged collaboration with bourgeois artists.[12] Dancers in the Workers Dance League were now encouraged to seize bourgeois techniques to make their message more acceptable to audiences. The level of technical expertise may have improved, but the underlying issue—the place of politics in the new art—continued to be controversial.

John Martin of the prestigious *New York Times* set out to define the relationship between art and politics in American modern dance. In October 1933 the nation's first dance critic had gently chided revolutionary dancers by paraphrasing a folk tale about making hare pie—first you had to catch the hare. To the revolutionary dancers he said, "To use art as a weapon, it is essential to see that first of all you have caught your art."[13] In subsequent columns he alternately praised the dancers for making artistic progress and complained that they did not belong on the stage. For example, a solo concert sponsored by the Workers Dance League in 1934 impressed Martin, and he noted the vigor of movement and intensity of feeling that marked the young dancers' efforts.[14] But a program of group dances presented a few weeks later was met with biting criticism—for the manner of presentation as well as for the quality of many of the dances: "Starting half an hour behind schedule, interrupted by two speeches from the stage, badly stage-managed and lacking in general theater discipline, the recital placed itself pretty definitely in the category of the amateur."[15]

By June 1935 Martin launched a full-scale attack on the Workers Dance League, which had recently changed its name to the New Dance League in an attempt to broaden its appeal. Martin could not deny the audience's enthusiasm or the fervency of the dancers' beliefs, but he lashed out at the superficial thinking and danced generalizations that he felt characterized their performances. In what he called an open letter to the group, Martin pulled no punches. He accused it of soapbox electioneering in the middle of a performance and compared the whole thing to a medicine show.[16]

Martin was not exactly a disinterested observer. As one of the earliest advocates of modern dance, he played an important role as a proselytizer and visionary in its development. His writings aimed at educating a new audience as well as educating all dancers to standards of professionalism. In his columns and in the se-ries of lectures that he arranged at the New School for Social Research on West 12th Street in Manhattan, Martin was defining standards for a new American art form, separating the workers' dance movement from what would become the mainstream of modern dance. *The Modern Dance,* four of his New School lectures given in 1931–1932, was published in 1933 and revealed his concerns with form and technique. But content, the hallmark of any revolutionary art, was not discussed. Nadia Chilkovsky and the Workers Dance League were included on the New School series in 1934, but she was dropped the following year despite the fact that an estimated 34,000 people had seen performances by workers' dance groups that season, according to accounts in *New Masses.*[17]

Reports such as these may have been exaggerated. Still, a lot of workers were exposed to new movement ideas during the early 1930s. The audience for American dance was growing, and critics—revolutionary and otherwise—vied for its allegiance. Even balletomane Lincoln Kirstein joined the ideological fray with an article in *New Theatre,* "Revolutionary Ballet Forms." In it, Kirstein lobbied for the European classicist George Balanchine's inclusion in a new socially conscious art form:

> He knows ballet as ballet is dead. . . . Ballet as innocent amusement is far too little to demand of it . . . the greater participation of the audience as a contributory factor in heightening the spectacular tension, the destruction of the proscenium arch as an obstructive fallacy, the use of negros in conjunction with white dancers, the replacement of an audience of snobs by a wide popular support are all a part of Balanchine's articulate program.[18]

When I began researching this article I imagined my subjects as a radical core of propagandists, not to be confused with the creative dancers who were developing what would come to be called modern dance, but which was then known simply as "new" dance. In my thinking, one group, the revolutionary or radical dancers,[19] was clearly dedicated to a socialist vision that could be embodied in staged actions, while the other group, dubbed arty and "bourgeois" by the leftist press, was committed to an aesthetic vision that would be experienced as dance. One was movement, the other art. As I began to write, however, it was clear that distinctions between the two camps were considerably less rigid than I initially thought.

Despite the debate surrounding "bourgeois" dance among leftists, most of the leaders of the revolutionary dance movement continued to study and perform with one or another of the established quartet. The cast for a Workers Dance League solo concert in 1934 included Nadia Chilkovsky and Miriam Blecher, former students of Hanya Holm at the Wigman School, as well as Anna Sokolow, Lily Mehlman, and Sophie Maslow of the Martha Graham company, and Jane Dudley who would join the Graham company the following year. In 1935 Marie Marchowsky from the Graham company and José Limón and Letitia Ide from the Humphrey-Weidman company joined the performers in the League.

The radical propagandists, it seems, willingly made themselves into instruments for the fledgling modern choreographers at the same time that they marched in May Day parades, danced in Communist pageants, and struggled to make a place for themselves as independent choreographers in concerts sponsored by the Workers Dance League. More, the populist audience attending revolutionary dance concerts was introduced to modernist concepts of choreography while they soaked up Marxist ideology. Far from being antagonists, the two movements creatively coexisted, exchanging audiences, bodies, and ideas. It was not a question of dance *or* politics; it was dance *and* politics. The revolutionary fervor of dancing modern—using power and force in a fight for freedom and egalitarianism in movement—was joined with the revolutionary vision promised by the Soviet Union. Throughout a critical period in the development of American dance, writers and dancers were engaged in passionate dialogues concerning the relationship of art and politics.

The terms *revolutionary* and *bourgeois* most accu-rately described ideological divisions existing between American dancers before 1934. Put simply, revolutionary dancers were those responding to Marxist doctrines, while bourgeois dancers were independent of specific political ideology. But while many radical dancers expressed commitment to socialist ideals and sympathy for the new Soviet state, they were not necessarily or always acting on directives issued by the Comintern (the Communist International). They simply set out to change society.

After 1934 the distinction between revolutionary and bourgeois groups became muddy, partly because the Soviet policy of socialist realism influenced revolutionaries to adapt bourgeois techniques and partly because Roosevelt's New Deal and the growth of the Popular Front collapsed some ideological barriers between communism and "Americanism." (Communist leader Earl Browder actually declared in 1935 that communism was twentieth-century Americanism.)[20] Still, performances after that date were clearly influenced by the backgrounds and political commitments that choreographers made earlier. In this respect, the terms remain useful for distinguishing each group's trajectory throughout the 1930s.

In the late 1920s and early 1930s revolutionary dance was characterized by an ideology of participation; workers became actively involved in dancing out their issues. Compositions by choreographers such as Edith Segal, who worked with lay dancers as well as with professionals, enjoyed a ready-made audience generated by the Communist Party. Revolutionary dance was workers' dance—in unions, at summer camps, and on legitimate stages such as the Center Theatre at Rockefeller Center.

While the primarily working-class audience enthusiastically applauded most efforts by revolutionary dance groups, in proscenium theaters critical attention was drawn to the lack of professionalism and technique of some; on the concert stage, reviewed by the mainstream as well as the radical press, many dances and dancers were found aesthetically wanting. "New" dance by this time was gathering its own band of advocates, and only two of the revolutionary groups managed to negotiate the tricky meeting of art and politics. In works produced by the New Dance Group and by Anna Sokolow's Dance Unit, choreographers made dances about working-class causes, but the proletariat was no longer on stage to represent itself.

Beginning in 1936, a populist tradition continued, however, in the work of the Federal Theatre and Federal Dance Projects that employed many revolutionary dancers. Helen Tamiris, always an advocate of dancers' rights and liberal social policies, was the most important figure here, although many other choreographers worked for the project, including Doris Humphrey, Charles Weidman, and Anna Sokolow. The collision with New Deal policies turned the debate from one of workers dancing or dancers dancing about workers into one about dancers working; artists were suddenly actively involved as the issue of collective bargaining in the arts took center stage. This issue was complicated by the dancers' relationship to their employer, the federal government.

The splintering of the leftist movement toward the end of the decade, catalyzed by the Russo-German nonaggression pact, and the disillusionment of some activists with the Communist Party—coupled with the impact of Roosevelt's New Deal, which co-opted some facets of the CP agenda—deflected the early militant thrust of the revolutionary dance movement. Issues of American identity now began to define political activity within the dance world as the looming threat of fascism galvanized artists. Martha Graham made several dances in response to the Spanish Civil War and in support of historical American ideals. The vision of the "people"[21] that Martha Graham put forth in *American Document* (1938) joined workers and bourgeois in a panorama of American history; immigrants and minority populations, the downtrodden and the discriminated against, shared space with the Puritan Fathers on Graham's stage.[22] In the aestheticized folk culture of choreographers Sophie Maslow and Jane Dudley, the ideological construct of the "people" continued throughout the 1940s. Leftist dancers as well as other artists, however, seemed to turn their backs on the gritty world of urban life, appropriating instead songs and dances gathered from rural America; the image of the worker was replaced by an idealized agrarian counterpart, the "folk."

Two things are clear. First, while the revolutionary dance movement united many dancers in a shared goal, each dancer also was different—in physical characteristics, in family background, in educational choices, in religious and political commitments, and in choreographic talents and aspirations. Second, because this art movement was really democratic, because so many participants gave themselves, however briefly, to this ideal, because so little concrete evidence remains of how this vision was embodied, it is not possible to document all of the period's activity. Instead, then, I have sought to understand the ideas and forces that helped shape the era, to identify specific approaches and elements that could be characterized as revolutionary, and, most importantly, to provide a voice for dancers who were part of what is now a forgotten movement.

Notes

1. Harvey Kleht, *The Heyday of American Communism: The Depression Decade* (New York: Basic Books, 1984), 33–34.

2. Ibid., 53.

3. Ibid., 71–74.

4. *Daily Worker*, April 29, 1930.

5. Throughout, *working class* is used to refer to "all those whose primary means of making a living is through the sale of their labor power for wages or salaries and who, as a consequence, exert little or no control over the institutions in which they work." Bruce McConachie and Daniel Friedman, eds., *Theatre for Working-Class Audiences in the United States, 1830–1980* (Westport, Conn.: Greenwood Press, 1985), 4.

6. *Daily Worker*, April 27, 1932.

7. Stacey Prickett in "Dance and the Workers' Struggle" and the *Daily Worker* cite the 1932 date, but an editorial in *New Theatre* placed the date early in 1933. Prickett, *Dance Research* 8, no. 1 (spring 1990): 52; *Daily Worker*, June 8, 1935; *New Theater*, September–October 1933, 20.

8. "From Our Correspondence," *New Theatre*, September–October 1933 (unsigned), 23.

9. Grace Wylie, "A Reply from the New Dance Group," ibid., 22.

10. Michael Gold, "Change the World," *Daily Worker*, June 14, 1934.

11. Edna Ocko, "Reply to Michael Gold," *New Theatre*, July–August 1934, 28. Also Ezra Freeman, "Dance: Which Technique?" *New Theatre*, May 1934, 17–18.

12. Douglas McDermott, "The Workers' Laboratory Theatre," in McConachie and Friedman, *Theatre for Working-Class Audiences*, 124. Significantly, *Workers Theatre* changed its name to *New Theatre* around this time (September 1933).

13. John Martin, "The Dance: The Far East," *New York Times*, October 15, 1933.

14. John Martin, "Success Scored by Dance League," *New York Times*, November 26, 1934, 12.

15. John Martin, "Workers League in Group Dances," *New York Times*, December 24, 1934.

16. John Martin, "The Dance to the NDL," *New York Times*, June 16, 1935, 4.

17. Edna Ocko, "The Revolutionary Dance Movement," *New Masses*, June 12, 1934, 27–28.

18. Lincoln Kirstein, "Revolutionary Ballet Forms," *New Theatre*, October 1934, 14.

19. I have used the descriptive terms *radical* and *revolutionary* interchangeably.

20. Quoted in Klehr, *Heyday of American Consumerism*, 222.

21. Cultural historian Warren I. Susman points to the pervasiveness of the image of the "people" during this decade. See his *Culture as History: The Transformation of American Society in the Twentieth Century* (New York: Pantheon Books, 1984), 172.

22. But as Susan Manning points out in "American Document and American Minstrelsy," Graham staged the white body as the universally American body, a convention common to many choreographers of the 1930s. Manning, *Moving Words: Rewriting Dance,* ed. Gay Morris (London: Routledge, 1996), 183–202.

In His Image: Diaghilev and Lincoln Kirstein

NANCY REYNOLDS

Lincoln Kirstein, American "aristocrat of life and culture," wrote often of "apostolic succession"; indeed, he made the phrase his own. Above all else, in his view, the patient and inevitable rules of such a process gave the world George Balanchine, the inheritor of a grammar of movement and a set of aesthetic beliefs practiced and honed across the centuries. Through devotion, assimilation of what had been learned before, and open-mindedness, Balanchine became an initiate of what Kirstein called a "secret society" or "higher order," an inner circle accessible only to the servants of art.[1]

By those standards of passion and service, which he combined with vision, voracious intellectual activity, and sheer audacity, in his chosen sphere as impresario, patron, and catalyst in the arts, Kirstein can be recognized as Diaghilev's heir in spirit and deed—a successor-initiate himself.

Although Kirstein never met Diaghilev, there is abundant evidence in his writings that Diaghilev's example was the one he wished to emulate. In a letter written to the critic Allen Tate in 1933, he confessed, "I am merely trying to jockey myself into a position where eventually I can act as I like in relation to the employment . . . of the artists of merit in this country. And while I should never attempt to assume the career of a Diaghilev, nevertheless the parallel is useful." Nearly forty years later, in *Movement and Metaphor*, a brilliant, complexly layered work that sums up Kirstein's feelings about dance as history, artistic expression, and politics, he mentions Diaghilev far more than any other figure

from the time of Louis XIV on and concludes: "Of all non-dancers in the history of ballet, Diaghilev is the greatest; he birthed an era more important to us than the *ballet de cour* (1570–1680), *ballet d'action* (1740–80), or *ballet romantique* (1830–70). . . . Diaghilev was a courtier, a gifted musical amateur, a catalyst of genius. His moral energy in bringing his ballet into being and maintaining it in spite of loss of base was heroic. He spans history. He marked the end of one epoch and named another; what he managed remains our model."[2]

As a student abroad in 1929, Kirstein stumbled on Diaghilev's funeral by accident, but it was hardly his first encounter with the great man. Kirstein caught Cocteau's "red and gold disease"—addiction to the theater—at an early age; indeed, he became infected on seeing *The Merry Widow* as a boy of five. "The malady, obsession, advanced state of unease, indeed disease, was compounded of passion for the preposterous, the tease of perfection which was an impersonation of grandeur, or in exalted cases, the superhuman and heroic," he wrote some sixty years later in his typically baroque style. His first "contact" with Diaghilev, albeit at several removes, occurred just a few years later, when his mother decided against taking him to a performance of the Ballets Russes in Boston in 1916. (For years he thought he'd missed Nijinsky, although it is likely that Alexander Gavrilov had danced unannounced in his place.) By the time he saw Pavlova as a teenager, the disease was entrenched: "Whatever it was that lurked as an imaginative need, 'ballet' stuck in my elementary judgment as a luminous magnet. This basic bias soon accumulated conviction, sharp preferences rapidly becoming what counted as 'my taste.' Reputations and fame glowed as a nimbus around the bodies of God-given performers, flaring or withering as I managed to gain first-hand impressions from their galvanic performances."[3]

In the 1920s he began making yearly visits to Europe (often mingling with the Bloomsbury set) and in 1924 saw his first Diaghilev season. He singled out Léonide Massine's *Les Matelots* as "an early statement" of post–World War I modernism. "It satisfied me," he wrote, "more as a declaration of policy than as an independent triumph of dancing, but strengthened my faith in the crusading principles of Diaghilev's policy. . . . *The past was abandoned, rhetoric was left behind, and a new and electric sensibility was available and exploited.* To be a first witness of such dynamism rarely happens in a lifetime."[4] In 1926 Kirstein saw his first Stravinsky ballet, *Firebird*, in which Balanchine appeared in the role of Kostchei, and he continued to follow the company until its collapse in 1929.

Kirstein's diaries of 1933, published forty years later in a putative reconstruction, recount the events of the fateful summer in Europe during which his choice of profession crystallized and the course of ballet in America was forever altered. At this time of attempted self-definition, Kirstein was involved in a tumultuous relationship with Romola Nijinsky, ghostwriting a good part of her book about her husband and gaining entrée into Russian émigré circles. He hoped to become a painter and harbored vague notions about establishing an "American ballet." Among his confidants that summer were the composer Virgil Thomson—who filled him in on ballet styles in Europe and told him that "the main progressive line from Diaghilev is with Balanchine rather than Massine"—and, most important, Monroe Wheeler. Wheeler, Kirstein wrote, "gave me everything I most wanted and needed, and tested my own aims. What did I actually want? What could I actually do? How much money did I actually

have or could I raise[?] . . . Everything cried out for Diaghilev. . . . Could not tell whether he was suggesting I try for this." (As Kirstein later acknowledged, he was.) From Janet Flanner (Genêt of the *New Yorker*) he learned that "ballet activity is greater this year than at any time since Diaghilev's death, but there is no restraining or controlling influence; the dancers (choreographers?) are all too social and uppity; Diaghilev would have permitted none of this nonsense"; from Wheeler, that Boris Kochno, Balanchine's artistic director at the time, "is not powerful enough to last as an impresario."[5]

Finally, there was the meeting with Balanchine in London on 11 July 1933:

> He said one must not revive anything, ever; dancing, a breath, a memory; dancers are butterflies; . . . the idiom of one decade has little to do with the next; must be cleansed repeatedly, like laundry. Conventions and limits of Petipa, intolerable today. Whole academic dance must be restudied from its base. . . . He would like to come to America with twenty girls and five men, in a repertory of classical ballet in his own extended academic "modern" style. . . . Balanchine seemed intense, concentrated, disinterested; not desperate exactly, but without any hope.[6]

After one more meeting, during which Balanchine confessed that America had always been his dream, Kirstein wrote a sixteen-page letter to his friend Everett A. "Chick" Austin Jr., the director of the Wadsworth Atheneum in Hartford, Connecticut. "This will be the most important letter I will ever write you," Kirstein began. "We have a real chance to have an American ballet within 3 yrs. time. When I say ballet, I mean a trained company of young dancers—not Russians—but Americans. . . . We have the future in our hands. For Christ's sweet sake let us honor it."[7]

The medium for this visionary project was to be Balanchine, who, financed by Austin and other friends, duly arrived in the New World on 17 October 1933. By mid-1934 the School of American Ballet had been established, and its students had performed Balanchine's first American ballet, *Serenade*, on an outdoor platform in White Plains, New York. Within a year, Balanchine's American Ballet had become the resident dance troupe of the Metropolitan Opera. In 1946 Ballet Society was founded, and two years later, the New York City Ballet. It was a remarkably direct journey, even if the going was sometimes bumpy. Still, as Kirstein told an interviewer in 1983, "I never doubted the fact that sooner or later, it [the New York City Ballet] would happen."[8]

Diaghilev's collaborative ideal was one that clearly fired Kirstein's imagination and had done so at least since his first visit to Bayreuth and encounter with Gesamtkunstwerk in 1924. As his alter-ego in *Flesh Is Heir* explains, Diaghilev had taken "all the best painters and musicians and dancers. The very best and put them all together and it makes the most perfect thing an artist can do." Kirstein observed this approach at work during the summers he had spent watching the Ballets Russes; he encountered it again in the Blum-Balanchine and de Basil Ballet Russe companies, and in Les Ballets 1933, in which all six of the ballets presented were new. All were choreographed by Balanchine, and most had especially commissioned scores and decors.[9]

Within months of Balanchine's arrival in the United States, Kirstein had put the collaborative idea into practice. The American Ballet, their first, short-lived company, presented several works from the Les Ballets 1933 repertory—*Dreams, Errante,* and *Mozartiana*—as well as a new atmospheric piece called *Transcendence,* which had a libretto by Kirstein on the nature of virtuosity.[10] Gluck's *Orpheus and Eurydice,* staged in 1936 by Balanchine for the Metropolitan Opera, had an extraordinary gauze-and-wire decor and striking lighting effects by Pavel Tchelitchev. Considered one of the most magical works ever designed, it was also highly controversial: with the singers in the pit and the action mimed by dancers, it drew the ire of music critics and opera fans. After only two performances, the production was withdrawn.

Kirstein was able to realize his ideas more fully with Ballet Caravan. Founded in 1936, this chamber-sized summer touring company had a repertory consisting entirely of new works, most with decor and scores commissioned from American artists and many on American subjects. With Balanchine only peripherally involved, Kirstein's principal choreographers were William Dollar, Lew Christensen, and Eugene Loring. The composers and designers included Elliott Carter, Virgil Thomson, Paul Bowles, Robert McBride, Paul Cadmus, Aaron Copland, and Jared French, while the subject matter ranged from Pocahontas to a day in the life of a gas station attendant. Kirstein, who was full of ideas for ballets, contributed seven scenarios, including the perennially successful *Billy the Kid,* the only work produced by the company that significantly outlasted it. In its efforts to employ native talent, to treat everyday subjects unassumingly, to strip away empty glamour, and to appear in large and small towns all over the country, Ballet Caravan was a forerunner of the regional ballet movement.

Never more than a part-time enterprise, Ballet Caravan lasted from 1936 until 1940. World War II surely hastened its death, but there were other problems: the Americana formula was too rigidly followed, often at the expense of theatrical flair, and the low budget and inexperience of the dancers gave an amateurish flavor to the enterprise. As Kirstein wrote, his two-piano arrangements could not compete with ballet orchestras, nor could his earnest young performers erase memories of the likes of Alexandra Danilova, Tamara Toumanova, and Léonide Massine, who could be seen in one-night stands all over America with the various Ballet Russe companies.[11] He had learned something about dance as a spectacular art—that it had, in some measure, to provide the "luminous magnet" that had originally attracted him.

Kirstein's most ambitious attempt to re-create the Diaghilevian synthesis of the arts—and go beyond it—was contained in his plan for Ballet Society, which made its debut in 1946. As he wrote (anonymously) in the prospectus: "Each [new work] will have the planned collaboration of independent easel painters and progressive choreographers and musicians, employing the full use of avant-garde ideas, methods and materials. . . . Emphasis will be on expert musical and dance direction to insure an essential elegance and freshness, rather than on famous stars or the residual prestige of the standard ballet repertory." Unlike Diaghilev, however, who tended to use only one choreographer at a time, Kirstein, while giving Balanchine free rein, sponsored the efforts of several others: John Taras (*The Minotaur*), Todd Bolender (*Zodiac*), William Dollar (*Highland Fling*), Merce Cunningham (*The Seasons*), Lew Christensen (*Blackface*), and Fred Danieli (*Punch and the Child*). John Cage, Elliott Carter, Vittorio Rieti, and Igor Stravinsky were among the commissioned composers; Isamu Noguchi, Estebán Francés, and Horace Armistead among the designers. In its two-year existence, Ballet Society produced sixteen new ballets, including Balanchine's seminal *Four Temperaments, Symphony in C*, and *Orpheus*, and plans were laid for an elaborate two-act Balanchine work—unrealized—on the theme of Beauty and the Beast, with music by Alexei Haieff and decor by Francés. Operas by Gian-Carlo Menotti and dances in idioms other than ballet were also presented. The critics, who had to purchase their own tickets, were generally enthusiastic.

But Kirstein wanted more. He envisioned a select audience that, in addition to "participating" in the creation of new works, would receive monographs, a yearbook ("based on the model of the annuals of the Imperial Russian Theatres"), recorded scores of the ballets, silk-screen prints of stage designs, and invitations to films, poetry readings, exhibitions, and dance demonstrations. In short, Kirstein wanted to offer a complete environment for experiencing dance in all its intellectual, aesthetic, and sensual aspects. Not even Diaghilev had contemplated an enterprise on so vast a scale, nor, even in the best of times, could he afford to ignore the commercial aspect of his ventures as Kirstein, by restricting tickets to Ballet Society members, hoped to do.

But he could not bring it off. The company performed only four programs yearly on unsuitable stages.

Dissolution seemed inevitable when, on the strength of *Orpheus*, Ballet Society's most prestigious collaborative effort (involving Balanchine, Noguchi, and Stravinsky), the group was invited by Morton Baum, chairman of City Center's executive committee, to become a resident constituent of the theater; as the New York City Ballet, it gave its first performance on 11 October 1948. After a fifteen-year struggle, Kirstein and Balanchine had achieved a measure of permanence for their vision.

In the following decade Balanchine produced some of his most felicitous creations: *Firebird, La Valse, Swan Lake* (Act 2), *Scotch Symphony, Western Symphony, Allegro Brillante, Pas de Dix, Agon, Episodes, Tschaikovsky Pas de Deux, Liebeslieder Walzer, A Midsummer Night's Dream*, and *Tarantella*. These ballets, along with such earlier masterpieces as *Concerto Barocco, Apollo, Prodigal Son*, and *Serenade*, established him as the preeminent choreographer of his day (as well as the most prolific), one whose philosophy regarding both theatrical values and dance technique was very much his own. The 1954 *Nutcracker*, a rare mounting of an older work, may be seen as Balanchine and Kirstein's counterpart to Diaghilev's *Sleeping Princess*: a bouquet to the past and box-office security for the present and future. So successful was it as a money maker that it inspired some two hundred imitations throughout the country, starting a new tradition. True to the Kirstein ideal, there were also distinguished and experimental works by Antony Tudor, Frederick Ashton, Martha Graham, and John Cranko, a season of Japanese gagaku, and an entire repertory of original, provocative works by Jerome Robbins, including *The Cage, Afternoon of a Faun, Age of Anxiety, The Concert, The Pied Piper*, and *Fanfare*. In addition to these preeminent figures, there were ballets by Ruthanna Boris, Lew Christensen, Todd Bolender, Francisco Monción, William Dollar, Birgit Cullberg, and John Butler, most of them new, some with new music and interesting decor, almost all with scenarios, themes, or plots.

But with time, Balanchine's vision became the dominant one. Works by outside choreographers of independent reputation were ignored; the occasional new ballet by a Balanchine follower (usually a company member) lasted only a season or two. Commissioned scores became rarer and eventually nonexistent, and decor was downplayed or dispensed with entirely; house designers, not independent artists, dressed the stage. A signal event in this evolutionary process was *Agon* (1957), quite apart from its significance as a work of genius. The last active collaboration between Balanchine and Stravinsky, performed in practice clothes on a bare stage to a twelve-tone score, *Agon* was, unexpectedly, a popular as well as a critical success, meaning that Balanchine's most radical work to date—his most stripped, reductive, and musically uncompromising— had found favor with the general public, not just the cognoscenti. Balanchine had proved he could do it all.[12]

By the 1960s, any pretense of the company's being anything but his personal laboratory had been abandoned, and it must have been apparent that the Diaghilev idea was dead for the New York City Ballet. Somewhere along the way Kirstein had made the decision to suppress his own creative vision in the interests of serving that of Balanchine. Regarding the issues involved in this choice or the precise nature of his relationship with Balanchine, the normally voluble Kirstein provided only the most circumspect observations: "We never had a contract; we never had any kind of legal connection. We never had any disagreements because we never talked about anything. . . . People don't realize the specific way in which George ran the company. . . . There was nothing except what he wished." As if in a footnote, he added, "Generally speaking, he knew what he wanted, but for specifics [in decor and costumes] he needed suggestions, so I could give them to him." The offstage Balanchine who appears in the recollections of his close friend Nathan Milstein, his biographer Bernard Taper, and any number of companions—colorful, passionate, fun-loving, mystical, and deeply religious—is all but absent from Kirstein's writings. Clearly, the two were colleagues, not friends. Kirstein described Balanchine at work as "unassertive, slim, no longer boyish, and,

with his grave, alert mannerliness, the more daunting in his authority, instinctive and absolute"—a brilliant miniature portrait, but one born of closeness without intimacy.[13]

In 1962 the New York City Ballet toured the Soviet Union (Balanchine's first return visit since emigrating); in 1963 it was stabilized by an unprecedented grant of two million dollars (over a ten-year period) from the Ford Foundation; in 1964 after an acrimonious struggle led by Kirstein and Morton Baum against John D. Rockefeller III and the board of Lincoln Center, it became the resident company of the New York State Theater (for which Kirstein had selected the architect); and in 1965 its first subscription drive was undertaken. Clearly, institutional status was at hand. This must have pleased Kirstein, a great believer in order, tradition, and continuity, as his numerous writings on dance (and other subjects) clearly and repeatedly demonstrate.

When Diaghilev died at fifty-seven, his company collapsed. At the same age, Kirstein oversaw the inaugural season of the New York City Ballet at the New York State Theater, a circumstance that he more than anyone else had engineered and an event that heralded a new era of permanence for the company and a new phase in his own career. Driven by a sense of service inherited from his father and honed by his years at Balanchine's side, he continued on as fundraiser, troubleshooter, socialite tamer, and general advocate, supervising the creation of boards of directors for the company and the School of American Ballet and the move of the school to expansive new quarters. He did not formally withdraw from the directorship of either body until 1989, well after Balanchine's death, when at the age of eighty-two he quietly retired.

The irony surrounding Kirstein's accomplishment is that he succeeded to Diaghilev's mantle by abandoning the quest to do so. He gave up much of the creative leadership of the New York City Ballet in order that— unlike the Ballets Russes—the company might survive. But perhaps, despite his years of impassioned rhetoric in favor of the Diaghilev model, this had been in the cards all along. Recalling his second meeting with Balanchine in 1933, in which the choreographer had talked about his problems with Edward James and de Basil, Kirstein wrote: "When he spoke, I began to have a large and growing sympathy for Balanchine himself, not as an historic figure but as an individual, who, like others, depended on factors beyond his own extraordinary capacities, and whom perhaps I might have a real role in supporting. Perhaps it was this personal consideration, up until now quite lacking, that seemed to indicate my ultimate direction."[14]

Kirstein never had a "sole" profession. Had he never met Balanchine, he would have made a name for himself as a cultural critic and historian. After an early apprenticeship as a reviewer of dance and art, he became an outspoken advocate for various overlooked artists. Over the years he rescued or enhanced the reputations of William Rimmer, Elie Nadelman, Gaston Lachaise, and Pavel Tchelitchev and was one of the earliest to argue persuasively for photography as an art form. But he saved his choicest language for the defense of classical ballet, particularly classical ballet in America. During the 1930s his chief targets were modern dance and the expatriate "Russian" troupes that were beginning to tour the country (in the process building new audiences for the ballet, a circumstance Kirstein ignored). His invective on the subject appeared in purest form in his *Blast at Ballet: A Corrective for the American Audience* (1937), in which he attacked not only the "so-called Russian ballet" but also the managers, patrons, critics, and public that supported it, themes reiterated in *Ballet Alphabet: A Primer for Laymen*, published two years later. As his hopes and dreams began to be realized, the tone of his writings grew milder, although at the age of nearly eighty, he could still contribute "The Curse of Isadora" as a lead article to the Sunday *New York Times*.[15]

Kirstein also left a major legacy as a dance historian. While still in his twenties he published *Dance: A Short History of Classic Theatrical Dancing* (1935), the first work in English devoted to the subject. A densely written tour de force, the book covers topics ranging from ritual dances of ancient Egypt to the Renaissance, from Dauberval to Diaghilev; some of the material, such as that on nineteenth-century dance in America, was largely virgin territory. Another work of wide-ranging scholarship and erudition was *Movement and Metaphor: Four Centuries of Ballet* (1970), in which the author examined fifty seminal ballets through the ages in their cultural, political, and technical contexts. As if to dignify the status of his notoriously elusive subject matter and its frequent lightweight treatment in print, he wrote, "The classical dance is a language, and ballets are its constructs, comparable to others formed in other idioms. The battle picture, still life, landscape; the comedy of manners, heroic tragedy; the novel of society or psychological observation create worlds based on tradition, observation, and craft. The universe projected by ballet in its brief temporal duration draws on analogous sources and is capable of maintaining similar metaphors." Reflecting his (then) forty-year association with Balanchine, he also wrote, "if there is a hero, it is choreography."[16] Like *Dance, Movement and Metaphor* is profusely illustrated with remarkable and often little-known images, many from the field of visual arts, attesting to Kirstein's broad interests, knowledge, and continuing love affair with objects in museums.

One of Kirstein's most striking contributions to dance literature was his early recognition of Nijinsky's importance as a choreographer. While other writers were still mesmerized by Nijinsky's sensational and tragic life or waxing idolatrous over his legendary performances, Kirstein was analyzing the radical underpinnings of his choreography. At the time of Diaghilev's death, Nijinsky's work was considered a failure, and, with the exception of *L'Après-midi d'un Faune*, none of his ballets had survived their first season. Nevertheless, in 1935 Kirstein wrote, "Great as he was in the province of the performing dancer, Nijinsky was far greater as a practicing choreographer; in which function he either demonstrated or implied theories as profound as have ever been articulated about the classical theatrical dance." He later elaborated his notion that Nijinsky's ballets "paralleled Freud's chart of man's developing psyche: in *Faune*, adolescent self-discovery and gratification; in *Jeux*, homosexual discovery of another self or selves; in *Le Sacre du Printemps*, fertility and the renewal of the race." Finally, in his handsome monograph *Nijinsky Dancing*, Kirstein wrote boldly: "Launched by sounds without precedent into a style with no history, [Nijinsky] forced himself to find a range of movement, an idiom without a model, which might serve as metaphor for an epoch before remembrance. . . . He put beauty as defined by his epoch mercilessly to the question. . . . Instinctively, or however, Nijinsky . . . for his generation murdered beauty."[17]

In 1940, with some five thousand of his own books, photographs, designs, playbills, manuscripts, and other documents as the centerpiece, Kirstein established the Dance Archives at the Museum of Modern Art, under the curatorship of Paul Magriel—the first such resource in the United States. In conjunction with the opening of the New York State Theater at Lincoln Center in 1964, this material (by now considerably augmented) was transferred to the Dance Collection of the New York Public Library, where Kirstein established a conservation laboratory in 1970. His donations to the Dance Collection continued over the years, and he deeded to this major repository his papers and his copyrights.

In 1942, with the vast material in the Dance Archives as a nucleus for research, Kirstein, Magriel, and Baird Hastings founded the periodical *Dance Index*, an unprecedented undertaking in the then barely defined world of American dance scholarship. Unlike Diaghilev's lavishly produced *Mir iskusstva*, it was modest in format and design. But it was equally adventurous in content. In existence until 1949, *Dance Index* provided a forum for the investigations of George Chaffee (on romantic iconography), Marian Hannah Winter (on preromantic ballet), Lillian Moore (on various subjects, many of them American), and Yuri Slonimsky (on Petipa and Perrot), among others. There were monographs on Duncan, Graham, Balanchine, Nijinsky, and several visual artists, photographers, and critics, in addition to the acclaimed issue "Stravinsky and the Theater," where Balanchine's most famous formulation of his dance philosophy appeared for the first time: "*Apollon* I look back on as the turning point in my life. [The score] seemed to tell me that I could dare not to use everything. . . . I could clarify . . . by reducing what seemed to be multiple possibilities to one that one that is inevitable."[18]

The strength of character that permitted Kirstein to give up artistic domination to Balanchine also produced a constancy that predicated his devotion until the end. His public reputation as someone who was irascible and unpredictable, bore grudges, and cut off friends without explanation notwithstanding, on the big issues there was nothing fickle about Kirstein and his vision. Moreover, the fruits of his mercurial intellect tended to obscure his behind-the-scenes accomplishments as a conciliator and facilitator, of which the fight for control of the New York State Theater is only one example. Although he was "very happy to have been brought up amid the relics and the legacy of the nineteenth century in England," he is the closest thing to a Renaissance man of culture that twentieth-century America has produced. "There can be no second Diaghilev," Kirstein wrote in 1937.[19] A second Kirstein is equally impossible.

Notes

1. In his book of essays on artists, *The Art Presence* (New York: Horizon, 1982), Sanford Schwartz uses "aristocrat of life and culture" as the title for his review of Kirstein's book *Elie Nadelman*. Although he intends the "aristocrat" to refer to the majority of the artists Kirstein champions, Schwartz observes that Kirstein's writings about art are so personal that his characterizations apply as much to himself as to the artists he defends; Lincoln Kirstein, *The New York City Ballet* (New York: Knopf, 1973), 13.

2. His failure to make Diaghilev's acquaintance was the

subject of an entire scene in *Flesh Is Heir*, Kirstein's thinly disguised autobiography written in 1930 and published in 1932 (reprint, Carbondale: Southern Illinois University Press, 1975). First, the young male protagonist explains to his female companion who Diaghilev is: "Some people call him the wickedest man in Europe. . . . He had the imagination to put the ballet across. . . . He never has any money and yet from year to year he goes on and gives the ballet and commissions painters and musicians." She concludes that he is "one of those men who devours people's talent." "Not at all, he makes them use it in the best way" (193–196). Later, following a debate as to whether they should have introduced themselves to Diaghilev earlier in the day, he reproaches her: "I suppose you know you've lost a chance to meet one of the greatest—the greatest men in our century" (202); Kirstein to Tate, May 8, 1933, reprinted in *The Hound and Horn Letters*, ed. Mitzi Berger Hamovitch (Athens: University of Georgia Press, 1982), 185–186; Lincoln Kirstein, *Movement and Metaphor* (New York: Praeger, 1970), 182. In an early draft of the acknowledgments, the author included Diaghilev's "spry ghost" among his inspirations, an indication that the impresario was still a living presence for him.

3. Kirstein, *New York City Ballet*, 13; Kirstein, *Mosaic* (New York: Farrar, Straus & Giroux, 1994), 214.

4. Lincoln Kirstein, *Mosaic*, 214–215 (italics added).

5. Lincoln Kirstein, "For John Martin: Entries from an Early Diary," *Dance Perspectives* 54 (summer 1973): 9 ("the main progressive line") and 24. Wheeler later became publications director of the Museum of Modern Art.

6. Ibid., 43. Much later, Kirstein wrote suggestively, as if continuing the thought: "This remained, even through later years, as my chief impression of him: never wholly discouraged, often depressed, absent as a tangible personality when not in actual labor onstage or in rehearsal" (*Mosaic*, 244).

7. Kirstein to Austin, July 16, 1933, in *I Remember Balanchine*, ed. Francis Mason (New York: Doubleday, 1991), 115, 119. The letter is in the collection of the Wadsworth Atheneum.

8. Lowry, "Conversations," pt. 2, *New Yorker*, December 15, 1986, 58.

9. "Bayreuth, a world wholly, profoundly, dedicated to the realization of the unreal, made a deep and lasting impression, and the seriousness involved in the current festival's operations convinced me that not only was such activity the aim of my life, but that it was also, however remote, a realizable possibility" (Kirstein, *Mosaic*, 65); Kirstein, *Flesh Is Heir*, 193. Les Ballets 1933, the brainchild of Edward James, lasted only a few months, but it provided Balanchine with his first opportunity to create an independent repertory. The six ballets he choreographed were *Mozartiana* (Tchaikovsky/Christian Bérard, designer), *Les Songes* (Darius Milhaud/André Derain), *Les Sept Péchés Capitaux* (also called *Anna, Anna,* or *The Seven Capital Sins*) (Kurt Weill–Berthold Brecht/Caspar Neher), *Fastes* (Henri Sauguet/André Derain), *L'Errante* (Schubert/Pavel Tchelitchev), *Les Valses de Beethoven* (Beethoven/Emilio Terry). In Kirstein's opinion, one program offered "too much Balanchine for one evening, but two out of three knock-outs, not bad." He liked *Mozartiana* and *Les Sept Péchés Capitaux* but was less fond of *Les Songes* ("Entries from an Early Diary," 11).

10. Kirstein commissioned the decors from Franklin Watkins; the music was by Liszt.

11. Lincoln Kirstein, "Ballet: Record and Augury," *Theatre Arts*, September 1940, 650–659. Of his original intentions for Ballet Caravan, Kirstein wrote: "I made Cocteau's philosophy mine: theatrical, indeed all, lyric magic does not derive from the exotic, fantastic, or strange, but from a 'rehabilitation of the commonplace'" (Kirstein, *Thirty Years: The New York City Ballet* [New York: Knopf, 1978], 72). Although the idea may have been provocatively realized in Cocteau's ballet *Parade*, it proved a sterile philosophy for an entire repertory.

12. Kirstein, always a penetrating analyst of Balanchine's work, wrote: "The ballet presents unwinnable games for a dozen dancers and ceremonial competitions between them. . . . Its syntax is the undeformed, uninverted grammar, with shades of courtly behavior and echoes of antique measure. . . . Blocks of units in triads and quartets shift like chess pieces or players in musical chairs. Dancers are manipulated as irreplaceable spare parts, substituting or alternating on strict beats. Here 'production' consists of execution alone. . . . The innovation of *Agon* lay in its naked strength, bare authority, and self-discipline in constructs of stressed extreme movement. Behind its active physical presence there was inherent a philosophy; *Agon* was by no means 'pure' ballet, 'about' dancing only. It was an existential metaphor for tension and anxiety" (*Movement and Metaphor*, 242–243). From 1954 to 1969 Jerome Robbins was busy elsewhere.

13. Lowry, "Conversations," pt. 1, 45; on Balanchine, see, for instance, Nathan Milstein, "My Friend George Balanchine," *Ballet Review* 18, no. 3 (fall 1990): 23–34, and no. 4 (winter 1990): 82–90; Bernard Taper, *Balanchine*, 2d rev. ed. (Berkeley: University of California Press, 1996); and *I Remember Balanchine*. Perhaps the posthumous publication of Kirstein's voluminous diaries and other notes will yield up some of these secrets; Lincoln Kirstein, "A Ballet Master's Belief," in *Portrait of Mr. B* (New York: Ballet Society/Viking, 1984), 15.

14. Kirstein, *Mosaic*, 249.

15. Lincoln Kirstein, "The Curse of Isadora," *New York Times*, November 23, 1986, 2.1 et seq. In this highly polemical piece, Kirstein excoriated "postmodern" and "postpostmodern" dance as an "etiolated exercise." *Lincoln Kirstein: A First Bibliography*, comp. Harvey Simmonds, Louis H. Silverstein, and Nancy LaSalle (New York: Eakins Press, 1978), runs to more than 150 pages, and Kirstein continued to write and publish virtually until his death in 1996. His last two books—*Mosaic* and *Tchelitchev*—both appeared in 1994, when the author was eighty-seven years old. In addition to dance, Kirsten wrote on politics, history, literature, drama, music, film, photography, architecture, sculpture, painting, drawing, and the general cultural scene. A partial list of Kirstein's many other activities would start with his cofounding in 1928 of the Harvard Society for Contemporary Art, and the several exhibitions at the Museum of Modern Art for which he served as curator, cataloguer, and consultant. Over the years, he held positions with the City Center of Music and Drama, WPA Federal Dance Theater, American National Theater and Academy (ANTA), American Shakespeare Festival Theater Academy, and Pro Musica Antiqua, whose twelfth-century *Play of Daniel*, which he produced, became a fixture in the New York cultural landscape for twenty years.

16. Kirstein, *Movement and Metaphor*, 17, v.

17. Lincoln Kirstein, *Dance: A Short History of Classic Theatrical Dancing* (New York, 1935; reprint, New York: Dance Horizons, 1969), 283; Kirstein, *Movement and Metaphor*, 199; Kirstein, *Nijinsky Dancing* (New York: Knopf, 1975), 145 and 42.

18. George Balanchine, "The Dance Element in Stravinsky's Music," *Dance Index* 6 (1947): 254.

19. Lowry; "Conversations," pt. 1, 80; Kirstein, *Blast at Ballet: A Corrective for the American Audience* (1937), reprinted in *Ballet: Bias and Belief*, intro. Nancy Reynolds (New York: Dance Horizons, 1983), 168.

Stripping the Emperor:
The Africanist Presence in American Concert Dance

BRENDA DIXON GOTTSCHILD

Several years ago, a student in my course at Temple University titled "Black Performance from Africa to the Americas" came up to me at the end of the first session and asked, "Should I take this class . . . I mean, as a white person?" The question animated her face with confusion and fear. My response was, "Honey, you're taking it right now; you've been taking it all your life!" As Americans, we are all "enrolled" in this course. Some of us do not know it; some do, but deny it. For Americans, the Africanist legacy is not a choice but an imperative that comes to us through the culture.[1]

Unlike the voluntary taking on of Easternisms in modern and postmodern practice, the Africanist legacy comes to Americans as electricity comes through the wires: we draw from it all the time, but few of us are aware of its sources. To quote Toni Morrison, it is "the ghost in the machine" or "the unspeakable things unspoken."[2] It infuses our daily existence in musical forms such as blues, jazz, spirituals, gospel, soul, rap, funk, rock, and yes, even European orchestral music. It is a considerable force in modern American arts and letters, as has been discussed by Morrison and other literary critics. It permeates American dance forms, from ballroom and nightclub floors to popular and concert stages. Finally, it pervades our everyday lifestyles, in ways of walking, talking, creating hairdos, preparing food, and acting "hip" or "cool."

What Africanisms am I talking about? They emerge from aesthetic principles, or canons, that have been codified and discussed at length by other authors, particularly Robert Farris Thompson, Susan Vogel, Kariamu Welsh Asante, and to a lesser extent, Geneva Gay and Will L. Baber, and Alfred Pasteur and Ivory Toldson.[3] From these sources I have designated five Africanist characteristics that occur in many forms of American concert dance, including ballet. It is important to note that these traits work together and are separated only for the sake of discussion. They indicate processes, tendencies, and attitudes. They are not intended to categorize phenomena. To show their interactive nature, I use the dance routine of Earl "Snake Hips" Tucker to illustrate each canon. An African American novelty dancer who attained enormous popularity in the cabarets of the 1920s, Tucker makes these Africanist principles clearly visible in his work. Ballet, the academic dance of Europe, offers the most dramatic contrast to the Africanist aesthetic. It has been regarded as the repository of European values and is characterized as a reflection of "what is thought most significant in the culture of the West."[4] For these reasons, I use ballet, rather than European vernacular dance, as the European reference point in the five principles that follow.

Embracing the Conflict

In a broad sense, the Africanist aesthetic can be termed an aesthetic of contrariety, while the European perspective seeks to remove conflict through efficient problem solving. The Africanist aesthetic embraces difference and dissonance, rather than erasing or resolving it. Contrariety is expressed in African dilemma stories that pose a question rather than offer a solution; in music or vocal work that sounds cacophonous or grating to the untrained ear; and in dance that seems unsophisticated to eyes trained in a different aesthetic. This principle is reflected in the other four canons and they, in turn, are reflected in it. "Embracing the conflict" is embedded in the final principle, "the aesthetic of the cool," in which "coolness" results from the juxtaposition of detachment and intensity. Those opposites would be difficult to fuse in European academic aesthetics, but there is room for their pairing in Africanist aesthetics. A routine performed by Tucker in such New York clubs as Connie's Inn and Harlem's Cotton Club—as described in Marshall and Jean Stearns's *Jazz Dance*—demonstrates this concept:

> Tucker had at the same time a disengaged and a menacing air, like a sleeping volcano, which seemed to give audiences the feeling that he was a cobra and they were mice. . . .
>
> When Snake Hips slithered on stage, the audience quieted down immediately. Nobody snickered at him, in spite of the mounting tension, no matter how nervous or embarrassed one might be. The glaring eyes burning in the pock-marked face looked directly at and through the audience, with dreamy and impartial hostility. Snake Hips seemed to be coiled, ready to strike.
>
> Tucker's act usually consisted of five parts. He came slipping on with a sliding, forward step and just a hint of hip movement. The combination was part of a routine known in Harlem as Spanking the Baby, and in a strange but logical fashion, established the theme of his dance. Using shock tactics, he then went directly into the basic Snake Hips movements, which he paced superbly, starting out innocently enough, with one knee crossing over be-

hind the other, while the toe of one foot touched the arch of the other. At first, it looked simultaneously pigeon-toed and knock-kneed.[5]

The conflicts are paired contraries: awkward and smooth; detached and threatening; innocent and seductive. But the most significant conflict resides in the routine's deep subtext, in the ironic playing out of power postures by the otherwise disempowered black, male (dancing) body.

Polycentrism/Polyrhythm

From the Africanist standpoint, movement may emanate from any part of the body, and two or more centers may operate simultaneously. Polycentrism diverges from the European academic aesthetic, where the ideal is to initiate movement from one locus: the noble, upper center of the aligned torso, well above the pelvis. Africanist movement is also polyrhythmic. For example, the feet may keep one rhythm while the arms, head, or torso dance to different drums. In this regard, Africanist dance aesthetics represents a democracy of body parts, rather than a monarchy dictated by the straight, centered spine. Again, we turn to "Snake Hips":

> The fact that the pelvis and the whole torso were becoming increasingly involved in the movement was unavoidably clear. As he progressed, Tucker's footwork became flatter, rooted more firmly to the floor, while his hips described wider and wider circles, until he seemed to be throwing his hips alternately out of joint to the melodic accents of the music.[6]

From a "get-down" posture that centered the movement in the legs and feet, Tucker adds the pelvis as another center, illustrating polycentrism. On top of the crossover step, described above, he interpolates a pelvic rhythm, exemplifying the simplest level of polyrhythm. Again, these are interactive principles; embracing opposing rhythms, coupled with a shifting center, demonstrates high-affect juxtaposition.

High-Affect Juxtaposition

Mood, attitude, or movement breaks that omit the transitions and connective links valued in the European academic aesthetic are the keynote of this principle. For example, a forceful, driving mood may overlap and coexist with a light and humorous tone, or imitative and abstract movements may be juxtaposed. The result may be surprise, irony, comedy, innuendo, double-entendre, and finally, exhilaration. All traditions use contrast in the arts, but Africanist high-affect juxtaposition is heightened beyond the contrast that is within the range of accepted standards in the European academic canon. On that scale, it would be considered bad taste, flashy, or loud. "Snake Hips" demonstrates this principle, in part, through his choice of costume—a sequined girdle supporting a seductive tassel:

> Then followed a pantomime to a Charleston
> rhythm: Tucker clapped four times and waved
> twice with each hand in turn, holding the elbow of
> the waving hand and rocking slightly with the beat.
> The over-all effect was suddenly childish, effemi-
> nate, and perhaps tongue-in-cheek. The next move-
> ment was known among dancers as the Belly Roll,
> and consisted of a series of waves rolling from
> pelvis to chest—a standard part of a Shake dancer's
> routine, which Tucker varied by coming to a stop,
> transfixing the audience with a baleful, hypnotic
> stare, and twirling his long tassel in time with the
> music.[7]

Tucker shifts unpredictably from childish and effeminate to challenging and "macho" movements, disregarding European standards for consistency in characterization. In addition, with no preparation or transition, he changes from light, almost cheerleader-like hand and arm gestures to weighted, sensual undulations centered in the lower torso. A third high-affect juxtaposition occurred with the "break," described above. Tucker cut off the movement in the middle of a Belly Roll, came to a break, or full stop, and shifted the mood and rhythm of his intricately structured routine.

Ephebism

Named after the ancient Greek word for youth, ephebism encompasses attributes such as power, vitality, flexibility, drive, and attack. Attack implies speed, sharpness, and force. Intensity is also a characteristic of ephebism, but it is a kinesthetic intensity that recognizes feeling as sensation, rather than emotion. It is "the phrasing of every note and step with consummate vitality," with response to rhythm and a sense of swing as aesthetic values.[8] The torso is flexible and articulate: "The concept of vital aliveness leads to the interpretation of the parts of the body as independent instruments of percussive force."[9] Old people dancing with youthful vitality are valued examples of ephebism in Africanist cultures. Moving with suppleness and flexibility is more important than maintaining torso alignment. Meanwhile, speed, sharpness, force, and attack are comparatively muted concepts in the European ballet tradition. (See descriptions later in this essay by Balanchine dancers, who contrast his sense of speed and timing with that found in traditional ballet.) The percussive force of independent body parts, with rhythm as a principal value, is not a part of the European ballet aesthetic.

> Tucker raised his right arm to his eyes, at first as if
> embarrassed (a feeling that many in the audience
> shared), and then, as if racked with sobs, he went
> into the Tremble, which shook him savagely and
> rapidly from head to foot. As he turned his back to
> the audience to display the overall trembling more
> effectively, Tucker looked like a murderously
> naughty boy.[10]

Tucker's "tremble" is an excellent example of ephebism. This movement articulates the separated segments of the torso, one against the other, in a broken yet continuous movement sequence. It can be accomplished only with a totally flexible torso, which will allow the tremorlike reverberations to ripple nonstop through the body. The movement is also percussive, forceful, and intense in its attack. It racks his

34. Earl "Snake Hips"
Tucker, 1928. Courtesy
Frank Diggs Collection,
Schomburg Center for
Research in Black Cul-
ture, The New York Pub-
lic Library, Astor, Lenox
and Tilden Foundations.

body. An additional fillip of ephebism is demonstrated in Tucker's "naughty boy" self-presentation.

The Aesthetic of the Cool

As Thompson so eloquently explains, the "aesthetic of the cool" is all-embracing. It is an attitude (in the sense that African Americans use that word, "attitude") that combines composure with vitality. Its prime components are visibility—dancing the movements clearly, presenting the self clearly, and aesthetic clarity; luminosity, or brilliance; and facial composure, or the

"mask of the cool." The "cool" embraces all the other principles. Taken together, the sum total of all the principles can be characterized as "soul force." It is seen in the asymmetrical walk of African American males, which shows an attitude of carelessness cultivated with calculated aesthetic clarity. It is in the unemotional, detached, masklike face of the drummer or dancer whose body and energy may be working fast, hard, and hot, but whose face remains cool. The aloofness, sangfroid, and detachment of some styles of European academic dance are completely different from this aesthetic of the cool. The European attitude suggests centeredness, control, linearity, directness; the Africanist mode suggests asymmetricality (that plays with falling off center), looseness (implying flexibility and vitality), and indirectness of approach. "Hot," its opposite, is a necessary component of the Africanist "cool." It is in the embracing of these opposites, and in their high-affect juxtaposition, that the aesthetic of the cool exists.

Throughout Tucker's routine, for example, he strikes a balance between the sexual heat implied in his pelvic movements and the cool attitude of his face. Luminosity and brilliance come through in his direct relationship to the audience and the choreography, and visibility is demonstrated in the fact that he dances not as a character but as himself. These traits are valued in the Africanist aesthetic.

Some people imagine that ballet is about as far away from anything Africanist as black supposedly is from white, but things just are not as defined or clear-cut as that: not even black and white. In spite of our denials, opposites become bound together more often than we admit. Cultures borrow from each other and fusions abound.

The Africanist presence is a defining ingredient that separates American ballet from its European counterpart. Ironically, it was George Balanchine, a Russian immigrant of Georgian ethnicity, who was the principal Americanizer of ballet. Why and how is a story worth telling, even in brief. Balanchine cut his teeth as a choreographer in Europe during the Jazz Age of the 1920s. His early *Apollo* for the Diaghilev Ballets Russes exuded jazz references. After Diaghilev's death, Balanchine worked in major European cities as a ballet master and choreographed revues for the popular stage to earn a living. He also created musical routines for the first feature-length English talking film, *Dark Red Roses*, made in 1929.[11]

The jazz aesthetic was familiar to him before he came to the United States. Once here, he served a long apprenticeship on Broadway which helped him to assimilate popular, social, and vernacular dance influences in the service of a newly defined ballet medium. Beginning in 1936, he choreographed or co-choreo-

graphed a number of musicals, including *The Ziegfeld Follies, On Your Toes, Babes in Arms, I Married an Angel, The Boys from Syracuse*, and, with Katherine Dunham, *Cabin in the Sky*. He worked with the Nicholas Brothers, two extraordinary tap-dancing kids, in *Follies* and *Babes*, and with Josephine Baker in *Follies*. Thus, he had direct contact with African American dancers and choreographers and with genres that were highly influenced by Africanisms.

It is already clear that Balanchine was a ballet choreographer who worked in the ballet medium and subscribed to a ballet aesthetic. What I hope to make equally clear is that, throughout his career, he introduced to the ballet canon Africanist aesthetic principles as well as Africanist-based steps from the so-called jazz dance repertory. He introduced these innovations into the ballet context while maintaining his grounding in the ballet aesthetic. The result was still ballet, but with a new accent. My guiding premises follow:

- Ballet, like all dance, is subject to the influences and presences that are valued in its cultural context. Therefore, it can rightfully be called a form of ethnic dance.
- Influences from past and present cultures are woven into, intermeshed with, and redistributed in any given cultural mode at any given moment in time. (To paraphrase this idea in structuralist terms, every text is an intertext.)
- The Americanization of ballet by a Russian immigrant, George Balanchine, will show both African American and European American influences.
- Looking from an Africanist perspective reveals the Africanist presence in American ballet.

There are many places in Balanchine's ballets where the Africanist legacy comes bursting through, most notably in the new movement vocabulary he introduced to the ballet stage. The displacement of hips or other parts of the torso, instead of vertical alignment; leg kicks, attacking the beat, instead of well-placed extensions; angular arms and flexed wrists, rather than the traditional, rounded *port de bras*—all of these touches usher the viewer into the discovery of the Africanist presence in Balanchine. These elements appear in works throughout his career and are highlighted in ballets such as *Apollo* (1928), *The Four Temperaments* (1946), *Agon* (1957), *Stars and Stripes* (1958), and *Symphony in Three Movements* (1972), among others. If and when they appeared in European ballet, these elements were reserved for lesser, "ignoble" characters and represented that which was comic or rustic, vernacular or exotic. Balanchine wielded these movements in a decidedly nontraditional fashion and assigned them central significance as movements for principals and soloists.

In the first movement of *Symphony*, the corps dancers lunge from side to side, with the straight leg turned in and one arm angularly jutting downward in a style unknown in traditional ballet. Later, a male sextet makes a prancing entrance that only can be described as an updated version of the cakewalk, with the upper torso leaning deeply backward. The second movement opens with torso isolations as a central element in the first duet, the same isolations used more baroquely in *Bugaku* (1963), which, even though it is based on a Japanese wedding ritual, reveals marked Africanist tendencies. This movement vocabulary allows Balanchine to expand the ballet idiom by introducing the articulated torso to its vertical standard.

The second and third duets of *The Four Temperaments*—the allegro tempo second duet and the adagio third—share some of the same Africanist-inflected movements. In both, ballroom dance references are as evident as the traditional *pas de deux* conventions into which they have been inserted. In both duets the male twirl-turns the female on one spot, as social dancers do, except that she is "sitting" in the air in *plié* while on point. The male then pumps his partner's hips forward and back as he grips her waist. He could pull her off the floor with this movement, and they would resemble Lindyhoppers. In the second duet this movement is capped off with jazzy little side lunges, straight, outstretched arms, and flexed wrists, as the two dancers face each other. And they exit with "Egyptian" arms (raised to shoulder height and bent perpendicularly from the elbow). In the third duet the male leads his partner into deep, parallel-legged squats (it would be misleading to call them *pliés*) which she performs while still on point. Then, standing, he offers his back to her. Facing his back, she wraps her arms around his neck, drapes the full length of her body against his, and leans on him. He moves forward for several steps, dragging her along. This looks like a cleaned up, slowed down variation on a typical Lindy exit. (And only in the Lindy have I seen as much female crotch as in these two duets.)

In the first variation of the "Melancholic" section a female quartet enters. Their arms are in second position, not in a traditional *port de bras*, but straight, with flexed wrists. They perform high kicks which are resolved by pushing the pelvis forward on a 1-2, kick-thrust beat, and their legs are parallel as they *bourrée* around the male. The choreography for the male is heavy, low, intense, and marked by deep lunges and acrobatic backbends. He metaphorically follows the music and "gets down"—as if this were a melancholy blues. His ephebism is balanced by the quartet's cool. He exits in a deep, acrobatic, nonacademic backbend, his outstretched arms leading him offstage, his center in his head and arms, not his spine.

There are many instances in the "Sanguinic" variation, especially in the choreography for the female soloist, where the movement is danced from the hips, which are thrust forward. This and the exit in "Melancholic," described above, are examples of the simplest version of polycentrism. Several centers are not occurring simultaneously, but the center has shifted from the vertically aligned spine to other parts of the body. The "Phlegmatic" solo opens and closes as a study in torso isolations and asymmetry. Paul Hindemith's score intimates the chords and intervals associated with blues and jazz.

Why did Balanchine incorporate these Africanist principles in his ballets? Katherine Dunham gives us a clue. "Balanchine liked the rhythm and percussion of our dances," she said, referring to her own African American ensemble. "I think most Georgians have a good sense of rhythm from what I've seen."[12] Balanchine was the perfect catalyst for defining and shaping American ballet. The Georgian rhythmic sense that he culturally inherited was the open door that allowed him to embrace the Africanist rhythmic landscape of his new homeland. With his talent and initiative he was able to merge those two principles, just as he fused ballet's cool aloofness with the Africanist aesthetic of the cool.

The 1928 *Apollo* confirmed that Balanchine was an experimentalist and innovator in the same rank as those in literature, music, and painting who similarly reached out to African, Asian, or Oceanic vocabularies to expand their options. This ballet marked the first of Balanchine's collaborations with Igor Stravinsky who was influenced, in part, by Africanist principles in his radically rhythmic, chromatic scores. Balanchine described this work as a turning point in his career. As the three muses enter together, they perform the same high kicks with pelvis thrusting forward that reappear in *The Four Temperaments* nearly twenty years later. There is a delightful moment when they move by waddling on their heels, their legs straight. On another stage, and in another mood, that would be a tap-dance transition step. And the asymmetrical poses the dancers assume diverge from traditional ballet but are akin to Africanist dance, particularly the moving poses struck in African American stage and social dance styles of the 1920s.

Apollo's first solo is a twisting, lunging affair. He simultaneously jumps, bends his knees so that his heels touch his hips, and twists his hips so that they angle against his torso. His landings dig into the floor as one leg releases and kicks downward on the beat. Indeed, this solo explores the downbeat—the earth, not the air—and the soloist, like a jazz musician, hits the beat on the "one" count, not taking the preparatory "and" count that is traditional in ballet. This passage suggests a fusion between Africanisms and vernacular dance influences from Balanchine's Russian past. Another ex-

ample of Balanchine's nonballetic use of phrasing and timing is recounted by Maria Tallchief, to whom he was married in the late 1940s:

> In a demonstration with Walter Terry and Balanchine, I did an eight-count *développé*, straight up and out with the *port de bras* in the manner in which we most often see it done. Then George turned to me and demanded, "Now out in *one* count and hold the rest." That is an example of the simplicity of his style. [Emphasis Tallchief's.][13]

The nontraditional timing Balanchine introduced into the ballet canon, like his introduction of the articulated torso, stretched the parameters of ballet and revitalized and Americanized the technique.

In his second solo, Apollo does several moves in which he pulls his weight off center as he lunges and stops short in an asymmetrical *plié* on the forced arch. His turns and lunges are grounded and abrupt. He stops them suddenly, as if on a dime. Unlike traditional ballet practice, the turns are not resolved: they simply stop. Both solos manifest ephebism in their speed, attack, and force. Apollo's solos and the "Melancholic" solo from *The Four Temperaments* are dances about weight and groundedness, not defying gravity but meeting it embracing it. The jumps are performed not to highlight the going up, but to punctuate and emphasize the coming down. Ballet's traditional airborne quality is not present here. Instead, we find the connection to the earth characteristic of Africanist dance and American modern dance. In fact, the Africanisms evident here probably came to Balanchine through modern dance as well as social and show dance. This solo is followed by an amusing vaudeville chorus that seems to come out of nowhere. The muses join him and, with no preparation and on an abrupt change in the mood of the score, they all *plié* in an asymmetrical position, settle back into one hip with buttocks jutting out, and bounce in unison to the rhythm. They are setting time for a change in rhythm, and this is their "break." It is a radical juxtaposition, set against the previous mood and movements. It is also a quote from popular dance styles. The work ends as the three muses lean their bodies against Apollo's back, their legs in gradated arabesques, while he poses in a lunge, legs parallel, arms raised, hands flexed.

The Africanist presence in Balanchine's works is a story of particular and specific motifs, of which there are many more examples than the ones given here, from ballets that span the course of his career. In other words, these were not dispensable, decorative touches that marked one or two ballets; rather, they were essential ingredients in his canon. However, the story only begins here. More significant is the underlying speed, vitality, energy, coolness, and athletic intensity that are fundamental to his Americanization of ballet. The tale continues with the radical dynamics, off-center weight shifts, and unexpected mood and attitude changes in Balanchine's work that create a high-affect juxtaposition of elements uncommon in traditional ballet but basic to Africanist dance. Less innovative artists might have held onto the old, but Balanchine could not settle for that. He was enticed by what he saw as American qualities of speed and coolness. Of course, those qualities are predicated as much on the African presence in the Americas as the European. It simply will not suffice to say that jazz dance influenced his work. That term, "jazz," has become another way to misname and silence the Africanist legacy; systematic exclusion of African Americans from American ballet has done the same. Buried under layers of deceit, that legacy in ballet has been overlooked. Some of the hidden story is intimated in Balanchine's original intentions for his new American ballet school, as recounted by Lincoln Kirstein:

> For the first [class] he would take 4 white girls and 4 white boys, about sixteen yrs. old and 8 of the same, *negros* [*sic*]. . . . He thinks the negro part of it would be amazingly supple, the combination of suppleness and sense of time superb. Imagine

them, masked, for example. They have so much abandon—and disciplined they would be *non-pareil*. [Emphasis Kirstein's.][14]

Thus, even before his arrival in the United States, Balanchine was calculating how he could draw upon the energy and phrasing of African Americans. Of course, the primitive trope is at work here, with the concomitant allure of the exotic. Even so, if his dream had been realized, what a different history would have been wrought for American ballet and its relationship to peoples of African lineage. One can only imagine that, innocent and ignorant of American racism, Balanchine understood, once here, that his dream school was unfeasible.

The texts that discuss Balanchine's Broadway musicals praise the ways in which he "improved" on show dancing; none of them acknowledge what he gained from that experience and took with him back to the ballet stage. But Balanchine himself may well have been aware of the two-way exchange. He said in a 1934 interview with Arnold Haskell, soon after his arrival in the United States:

> There are other ways of holding the interest [of the audience], by vivid contrast, for instance. Imagine the effect that would be produced by six Negresses dancing on their pointes and six white girls doing a frenzied jazz![15]

What he suggests, of course, is an example of high-affect juxtaposition. In working on *Concerto Barocco*, described by former New York City Ballet dancer Suki Schorer as a ballet with "a very jazzy feeling," he aimed for clarity in syncopation, timing, and attack, and he characterized a particular step as "like the Charleston."[16] His original intention for this work is expressed by former company member Barbara Walczak in her comparison of two versions of the ballet. Inadvertently, she points out Balanchine's use of the Africanist aesthetic:

The difference between the original and today's *Barocco* is a *timing* difference, an *energy* difference. It was never meant to be lyrical. One difference was that many of the steps were *very off-center*. . . . The energy behind the steps was different. They were *attacked* more than they are now. [Emphasis mine.][17]

Patricia McBride, who danced for Balanchine from 1959 until his death in 1983, says, "Dancing Balanchine is harder—the patterns, the way they change in Balanchine ballets. The ballets are so fast, and they travel much more than a lot of the more classical companies."[18] Speed, timing, and attitude changes are key elements in Balanchine and are key to the Africanist aesthetic. They are not signature components of the ballet from which he emerged. It seems ironic that when Schorer compares the Russian ballet companies with Balanchinian ballet she states that the Russians do not understand "phrasing, counting, the timing within a step. *They've never seen anything.* They only know what they know" [emphasis mine].[19] What they don't know, and what Balanchine was exposed to, is the phrasing, counting, and timing that come from the Africanist influence in American culture, so native to us that we take it for granted. By embracing these elements that he encountered in the United States, Balanchine expanded the definition of ballet. There is no doubt that his redefinition included both Africanist and European elements, fused into a spicy, pungent brew.

Balanchine's legacy, like the Africanist legacy, is a living one, much of which cannot be codified or contained by "the steps." Arthur Mitchell worked well with Balanchine, and Mitchell's cultural background and training helped. His description of *Metastaseis & Pithoprakta* shows Africanisms in Balanchine's way of working through rhythm rather than steps and in requiring the dancing body to be laid back, cool, and free to receive his messages:

Suzanne Farrell and I danced a pas de deux that was one of those eerie things that didn't use steps

per se. He'd say, "I want something like this," and he would start moving. You would just have to be free enough to let your body go and do it. I think one of the things that helped me so much with him was that, *being a tap dancer, I was used to rhythm and speed.* [Emphasis mine.] Many times when he was choreographing he would work rhythmically and then put the step in. If you were looking for a step, it wouldn't be there. But if you got *dah, da-dah-dah-dah*, it would come out. [Emphasis Mitchell's.] The rhythm was always the most important. The choreography was set in time and then space.[20]

According to Mitchell, Balanchine sometimes referred to Dunham in his work with students and sent dancers to study with her. He also regularly called on Mitchell to "come in and show these kids, because they don't know old-fashioned jazz."[21] A final statement from Mitchell is most telling about Balanchine and the Africanist legacy:

There was a fallacy that blacks couldn't do classical ballet—that the bodies were incorrect. But then you talked to Balanchine, who was the greatest master of them all and changed the look of ballet in the world today. He described his ideal ballerina as having a short torso, long arms, long legs, and a small head. If that's ideal, then we [peoples of African lineage] are perfect.[22]

Mitchell's quote acclaims the black dancing body, and the body is the origin and outcome of my thesis. I call this essay "Stripping the Emperor," but what needs stripping is our way of perceiving. Once we dare see the naked truth, as the child in Anderson's tale, we shall see a body, the American dancing body. It is a portrait in black and white.

Notes

Temple University and the Pennsylvania Council on the Arts provided partial support for this ongoing research project.

1. The term "Africanist" is used here to include diasporan concepts, practices, attitudes, or forms which have roots or origins in Africa. ("Diaspora" refers to the dispersion of African peoples from their homeland, beginning in the transatlantic slave trade era.) My precedent for using this term is set in recent scholarship. For example, see Joseph E. Holloway, *Africanisms in American Culture* (Bloomington: Indiana University Press, 1990), and Toni Morrison, *Playing in the Dark: Whiteness and the Literary Imagination* (Cambridge, Mass.: Harvard University Press, 1992).

2. Toni Morrison, "Unspeakable Things Unspoken: The Afro-American Presence in American Literature," *Michigan Quarterly Review* (winter 1989): 11.

3. For a thorough discussion that is applicable to both visual and performing arts, see Robert Farris Thompson, *African Art in Motion* (Los Angeles: University of California Press, 1974). Thompson compiles an Africanist aesthetic paradigm that he terms the "Ten Canons of Fine Form." See also Susan Vogel, *Aesthetics of African Art* (New York: Center for African Art, 1986), and Kariamu Welsh Asante, "Commonalities in African Dance," in *African Culture— The Rhythms of Unity*, ed. Molefi Kete Asante and Kariamu Welsh Asante (Westport: Greenwood Press, 1986), 71–82, for a dance-specific discussion of Africanist aesthetics. For a more generalized discussion of Africanisms in America, see also Geneva Gay and Will L. Baber, eds., *Expressively Black: The Cultivated Basis of Ethnic Identity* (New York: Praeger,

1987), and Alfred Pasteur and Ivory Toldson, *Roots of Soul: The Psychology of Black Expressiveness* (New York: Anchor, 1982).

4. Rayner Heppenstall, quoted in Selma Jeanne Cohen, *Next Week, Swan Lake* (Middletown, Conn.: Wesleyan University Press, 1982), 131.

5. Marshall Stearns and Jean Stearns, *Jazz Dance* (1964; New York: Schirmer Books, 1979), 236.

6. Ibid.

7. Ibid., 236–237.

8. Thompson, *African Art in Motion*, 7.

9. Ibid., 9.

10. Stearns and Stearns, *Jazz Dance,* 237.

11. *Choreography by George Balanchine: A Catalogue of Works* (New York: Viking, 1984), 25.

12. Interview with Dunham in Francis Mason, *I Remember Balanchine* (New York: Doubleday, 1991), 193.

13. Ibid., 239.

14. Letter from Lincoln Kirstein to A. Everett Austin Jr., dated July 16, 1933, reprinted in ibid., 116–117.

15. Haskell, *Balletomania Then and Now* (New York: Knopf, 1977), 98.

16. Mason, *I Remember Balanchine,* 459.

17. Ibid., 259.

18. Ibid., 444.

19. Ibid., 462.

20. Ibid., 395.

21. Ibid., 396.

22. "Talk of the Town," *New Yorker*, December 28, 1987, 36.

Simmering Passivity:
The Black Male Body in Concert Dance

THOMAS DEFRANTZ

Early Concert Dancers

Black men entered the concert dance arena in the late 1920s, and the earliest dances they performed were aligned with modernism in terms of theme, conception, and technique.[1] Hemsley Winfield organized several performance groups between 1925 and 1934, including the Negro Art Theater, and choreographed dances in the manner of Ruth St. Denis and Helen Tamiris.[2] In 1929 he caused a sensation dancing the role of Salome at the Greenwich Village Cherry Lane Theater. Filling in for an absent actress in the all-black cast, Winfield performed "dressed, as it were, in an old bead portiere and nothing else to speak [of]."[3] Drag performance inevitably confronts boundaries of representation; Winfield's successful portrayal, however anomalous, focused attention on issues of masculinity, black men, and the modern.

Among Winfield's numerous concert works, "Life and Death" created for the theatrical pageant *De Promis Lan'* in May, 1930, cast sixteen men as the inexorable force of Death which overcomes the singular being of Life, danced with charismatic vigor by the choreographer himself. A version of this piece became a staple of Winfield's frequent concert presentations until his sudden death in 1933. Reviews and photographs indicate that "Life and Death" bore stylistic resemblances to Ted Shawn's playfully organized movement choirs, but Winfield's dance predated the first concerts of Shawn's all-male company. Modern dance by a large group of men which didn't trade on minstrel stereotypes stood well outside performance norms of the time. Typically, black bodies were essentialized as the material of naive, "primitive" dance.

Winfield premiered his solo, "Bronze Study," at the historic "First Negro Dance Recital in America" co-directed by Winfield and Ruth St. Denis disciple Edna Guy on April 29, 1931. Writing for the *New York Times*, John Martin dismissed the dance as "merely the exhibition of an exemplary physique."[4] For Martin, physique, and its implicit work potential, lingered as the raw material of the dancing black body's value. But surely Winfield's posturing, however prosaic, sought to subvert the critical eye which refused to see beyond race. It is possible that "Bronze Study" replaced the simple marking of an "exemplary black body" with more complex distinctions of muscle tone, flexibility, stillness, cool stance, and most importantly, the public discourse of skin color.

Although the abatement of strict segregation throughout the 1930s allowed some black dancers to perform in integrated groups, their presence triggered deep-set racial biases in audiences and critics. In 1931 Randolph Sawyer danced the Blackamoor in the Gluck-Sandor Dance Center's *Petrouchka*. Reviewing the otherwise all-white production, Martin spoke euphemistically of Sawyer's "native talents" which "equip him to do a type of dance quite out of the range of his colleagues."[5] Audiences still couldn't understand how that "type of dance," implicated by the mere presence of Sawyer's black body, could converse with ballet.

Other artists worked to align the black male body with social reform. Dancer Add Bates solidified his activities with the Communist Party as a member of the Worker's Dance League. Featured in Edith Segal's "Black and White Solidarity Dance," Bates and his partner are pictured on the cover of the March 1933 *Workers Theatre*.[6] Defiantly posed square to the camera, determined and shirtless, Bates raises his thickly muscled arm to the side, with a tightly clenched fist held at eye level. This powerful image of protest aligns the black dancer's body with subversion, tying its weighty volume to the work of social change.

Most pioneer choreographers working to develop an African American audience for modern dance stuck close to mainstream models of male representation. Charles Williams formed the Creative Dance Group at Virginia's Hampton Institute in 1934 as an extension of that school's physical education activities. Hampton had been founded as a Reconstruction-era project of the American Missionary Association to socialize former slaves as they prepared for integrated life. Strong on concepts of work and morality, the school adhered to a conservative doctrine of conduct in which there was little place for the modern performing arts. It took a herculean effort on Williams's part to secure school support for the dance company; not surprisingly, the works he created were muted and discreet. Heavily influenced by Ted Shawn's all-male company, which visited Hampton in 1933, Williams made dances which exploited the physical dynamism of Hampton's male dancers in traditionally masculine settings. *Men of Valor* (1934) featured movements derived from track and field events, and *Dis Ole Hammer* (1935) set a labor dance to traditional work songs. Williams also created African dance suites, in collaboration with African students studying at the school, as well as dances with Afro-American themes, including a 1935 suite of *Negro Spirituals*.[7]

Creative Dance Group, which usually performed for African American audiences, toured the country extensively throughout the 1930s and 1940s in a standard program that progressed from calisthenics and drills to modern dance pieces.[8] The company functioned as a proponent of "official" culture, in this case validated by the missionary administration which founded the college. Williams's dutiful presentation of dance as an extension of physical culture which glorified an idealized black masculinity was certainly not lost on its large African American audience, even if that representation included only athletic, laboring, or pious men. The Hampton group's performing success influenced the formation of a responsive, core African American audience for concert dance and led directly to the founding of concert dance companies at other southern black schools including Fisk, Howard, and Spellman College.[9]

New York performances by Asadata Dafora's African dance company forced issues of authenticity and the native black body for dancers and critics. Dafora staged subtly drawn adaptations of festival dances from his Sierra Leone homeland. *Kykunkor* (1934), the first of several evening-length works mounted by Dafora, drew wide praise for its complex synergy of music and movement. For many critics, the success of Dafora's work hinged upon its use of "authentic" African materials derived from firsthand knowledge of classic West African aesthetics. *Kykunkor* defined successful black concert performance as serious, ritual-based exotica, unimaginably complex and distinct from mainstream modern dance. Though Dafora confirmed the great theatrical potential of West African dance for American audiences and African American dancers, his success set in motion a critical formula which emphasized the exotic novelty of the black body on the concert stage. From this time on, black dancers became increasingly obliged to prove themselves as "Other" to the concert mainstream.

Some dancers resisted the need to demonstrate their "blackness" in easily stereotyped settings. Growing numbers of classically trained dancers, denied participation in white companies, worked for several short-lived, all-black ballet companies. Eugene Von Grona's American Negro Ballet debuted in 1937 at Harlem's Lafayette Theater. The son of a white American mother and a German father, Von Grona formed a company designed to address "the deeper and more intellectual resources of the Negro race."[10] Before starting performances, he spent three years giving his thirty Harlem company members training in ballet and modern dance relaxation techniques. Von Grona choreographed the group's first program to music by Duke Ellington, Igor Stravinsky, W. C. Handy, and J. S. Bach. Lukewarm critical reception and the absence of a committed audience led to the company's demise after only five months. Aubrey Hitchens's Negro Dance Theater, created in 1953, offered the novelty of an all-male repertory company. English-born Hitchens, who "ardently believed in the special dance talents of the Negro race," mixed ballet works set to Bach with dances to generic blues and jazz.[11]

Both of these companies were formed with the express racialist purpose of proving the ability of the black body to inhabit classical ballet technique. The logic that pushed them to capitulate to stereotypical Negro themes in their repertory remains curious. Ballet locates its aesthetic power in the refinement of gesture *away* from everyday bodies and politics; if anything, a proliferation of black *danseurs* might have inspired a *decline* of color fetish among audiences and critics. It is possible that ballet could have *normalized* the black male body to the degree that the idiom *unmarked* the lingering minstrel persona. In giving their audiences familiar black stage types, however, the "get-down" ballets of these early all-black companies obscured issues of the body, black dancers, and western classicism.

Modern dance allowed for more fluid connections between the dancing body, cultural representation, and dance technique, and the post–World War II era saw a number of dancers and choreographers working to redefine the black male presence on the concert stage. West African aesthetic principles, still prominent in

black social dance forms, emerged intact in the concert choreography of Talley Beatty, Louis Johnson, and Donald McKayle, signaling a shift in the political frame surrounding performance. Buoyed by the liberal optimism of the New York dance community of the post-war era, dancers explored ways to self-consciously align power and the black male body onstage.

Alvin Ailey

Alvin Ailey's career in the late 1950s offers a paradigm of contemporary assumptions surrounding the black male body and concert performance. Ailey's choreography formed fires of black machismo in a number of roles he made for himself which literally displayed his body and cast it as the site of desire. Among his earliest works, *Blues Suite* (1958) transferred to the stage traditional assumptions concerning black male sexuality, including overt aggression, insatiability, and an overwhelming despair deflected by the [hetero]sexual act. As a dancer, Ailey created a persona which redefined popular stereotypes of the black male body on the concert stage to include the erotic.

Ailey was born January 5, 1931, into the abject poverty of rural Texas. The only child of working-class parents who separated when he was an infant, Ailey and his mother moved from town to town as she struggled to provide him with basic sustenance. Strictly segregated life in southeast Texas offered a hostile environment for African Americans and nurtured a fear and mistrust of whites which Ailey later recalled: "Having that kind of experience as a child left a feeling of rage in me that I think pervades my work."[12] This background also created a fierce pride in black social institutions, including the church and jook joints which figured prominently in his later work.[13] In 1942 Ailey joined his mother in Los Angeles, where his interest in concert dance was sparked by high school excursions to the ballet and Katherine Dunham's 1945 *Tropical Revue*.

Ailey arrived in California shy, lonely, and particularly sensitive from his itinerant childhood. He found solace in the fantasy world of theater and the movies, and gravitated toward the Hollywood masculinity of dancer Gene Kelly. Kelly's popularity hinged upon his "man's man" persona: "He was a 'man dancer,' one who did not wear tights. Here was a man who wore a shirt, pants, and a tie and danced like a man!"[14] Ailey turned to dance when a high school classmate introduced him to Lester Horton's flamboyantly theatrical Hollywood studio in 1949. Excited by Horton's utopian vision of a multicultural dance melting pot, Ailey poured himself into study and developed a weighty, smoldering performance style that suited both his athletic body and his concern with the representation of masculinity: "I didn't really see myself as a dancer. I mean, what would I dance? It was 1949. A man didn't just become a dancer. Especially a black man."[15]

Ailey may have felt constricted by society at large, but he quickly learned to capitalize on the simmering, hyper-masculine persona he developed at the Horton studio. His appearance in the 1954 Broadway musical *House of Flowers* featured "a very sexy pas de deux" with partner Carmen de Lavallade designed to titillate its mostly white audience.[16] Among the last-gasp attempts at exoticized, "mostly black" Broadway musicals set in foreign locales, *House of Flowers* boasted an extraordinary company of male dancers including Geoffrey Holder, Arthur Mitchell, Louis Johnson, and Walter Nicks. Truman Capote's libretto described two competing West Indian bordellos, and offered African American actresses myriad "hooker" roles. According to Brooks Atkinson's *New York Times* review, the cast exuded a predictable exotic-primitive appeal:

> Every Negro show includes wonderful dancing. *House of Flowers* is no exception in that respect. Tall and short Negroes, adults and youngsters, torrid maidens in flashy costumes and bare-chested bucks break out into a number of wild, grotesque, animalistic dances . . . [which] look and sound alike by the time of the second act.[17]

House of Flowers, a show that embodied the contradictions implicit in racial stereotyping on both sides of the stage lights, introduced Ailey to the New York dance scene as part of the "wildly monotonous" grotesquerie of black bodies performing for white audiences.

Ailey had few African American mentors, and the concert dance techniques he encountered failed to engage him: "I went to watch Martha Graham, and her dance was finicky and strange. I went to Doris Humphrey and José Limón and I just hated it all. I suppose that I was looking for a technique which was similar to Lester's [Horton] and I just did not find it."[18] Between commercial appearances and sporadic dance study, he performed in the one-night seasons of Sophie Maslow, Donald McKayle, and Anna Sokolow. However, Ailey identified more with the theatrical macho of Broadway and Hollywood choreographer Jack Cole: "I was impressed by his style, by the way he danced, by his manner, by the masculinity of his projection, by his fierceness, by his animal-like qualities."[19] While dancing for Cole in the Broadway musical *Jamaica,* Ailey and Ernest Parham gathered a group of dancers to fill an afternoon concert slot at the 92nd Street YM-YWHA on March 30, 1958.

Ailey danced in two of his three world premieres: *Redonda,* a curtain-raiser suite of five dances to a Latin theme, and *Ode and Homage,* a solo dedicated to the memory of Horton. His stage persona in this period, suggested in description, photographs, and films, built upon an impassioned flailing of his body through dance passages steeped in fiery cool. Ailey seemed to enjoy tempting his audiences with an exotic allure delivered from the safe distance of the stage. Critics likened his style to the movements of wild animals: Doris Hering, reviewing for *Dance Magazine,* compared him to "a caged lion full of lashing power that he can contain or release at will" while John Martin noted his "rich, animal quality of movement and innate sense of theatrical projection."[20] Jill Johnston, writing for the *Village Voice,* found Ailey's over-the-top histrionics perplexing: "he moves constantly, in high gear, as though in a panic, and like a synthetic composite figure of a smattering of contemporary influences."[21] Ailey's machismo caused P. W. Manchester to quip that he presented a stage world "in which the men are men and the women are frankly delighted about it."[22]

Blues Suite

Blues Suite, the third Ailey work premiered on the 1958 program, garnered instant popular and critical acclaim. Drawing on fragments of his Texas childhood, Ailey set the dance in and about a "barrelhouse," a backwoods music hall/whorehouse for working-class African Americans. To a musical background of standard twelve-bar blues, ballads, slowdrags, and shams, archetypal Depression-era characters conveyed the fleeting pleasures of dance buried within an evening fraught with fighting, regret, and despair. Costumed with dazzling Broadway-style flair, the suite sizzled with rage and sorrow, at once highly theatrical and pointedly dramatic.

Ailey's original program note aligned his dance with cultural roots: "The musical heritage of the southern Negro remains a profound influence on the music of the world. . . . During the dark days the blues sprang full-born from the docks and the fields, saloons and bawdy houses . . . indeed from the very souls of their creators."[23] The note served to validate the blues milieu for an uninitiated white audience by defining it as both personal (coming from the souls of their creators) and artful (part of a profoundly influential musical heritage). The reference to the dark days (of southern slavery) neatly telescoped cultural history into the premise for the dance: audiences were invited to view the dancing black bodies as authentic bearers of the blues. Blues Suite intended to map this southern musicality onto the concert dance stage.

The bawdy house setting played directly into traditional stereotyping of the black body as at once morally corrupt and titillating. As in House of Flowers, the women in Blues Suite portrayed hookers, and the men, their eager clients. But Ailey managed to locate the gender role-playing within a larger frame of African American pathos. Here, blues dancing stood for the ephemeral release from the overwhelming social in-equities suffered by African Americans. The frame allowed Ailey to foreground harsh political realities in the creation of intensely flamboyant and entertaining blues dance styles.

Blues Suite reached its final form in the fall of 1964. Alternately titled Jazz Piece (1961), Roots of the Blues (1961), and The Blues Roll On (1963) in earlier formats, Ailey's revisions were largely due to shifting company personnel. An overarching narrative suggesting cyclical and inevitable despair remained common to its several versions. The dance became a classic example of the choreographer's early style and remained in the active repertory of the Alvin Ailey American Dance Theater through 1995. The reading of four sections of the dance which follows is based upon filmed performances made in the 1960s and 1970s, and live performances attended in the 1980s and 1990s.

The dance begins with two traditional calls to attention in African American folklore: the train whistle, which suggests movement away from the repressive conditions of the South, and church bells, which toll not only for funeral services, but for the arrival of news worthy of community attention. Fast conga drums beat incessantly as the curtain rises, echoing the talking drum sound which traditionally dispersed information in sub-Saharan cultures. The curtain reveals bodies strewn across the stage in posed attitudes of fitful despair: eyes closed, energy drained. Are the figures asleep or dead? To classic strains that acknowledge the capitulation to oppressive circumstances—"Good Morning Blues, Blues How Do You Do?"—the dancers rise, shake off the inertia which held them, and begin an angry ritual of fighting each other to stake out territory. The atmosphere is heavy with stifled rage and disappointment.

Gradually, the fighting evolves into dance movements. In this casual progression Ailey suggests that his dance occupies a cultural space similar to the blues—as the transformation of social and political rage into art. The lexicon shift—from stasis, through the stylized drama of angry individuals, to a common ground represented in dance—draws the audience into concert dance without removing the markers which distinguish the characters as disenfranchised African Americans. These blues people are black people, and the dance they do is defined by that unique political circumstance, whether it contains elements of social dance, ballet, Graham, or Horton technique.

Although the men in *Blues Suite* are largely defined by their interaction with women, the solo "I Cried" includes a striking demonstration of male public vulnerability. Backed by contrapuntal movements from the group, a single man sits, center stage, his body racked with contractions of pain and anger. As he shakes and trembles in the depths of his anguish, the group extends a hand towards him, bearing witness. He rises towards some offstage goal, his body tensely elongated and brittle. The group reaches after him, offering help; he pushes them away defiantly, wrestling one man to the ground in the process. The group members disperse to strike poses of studied indifference, their faces averted from his dance. As he works out his frustration, the group exits, leaving him alone. As his dance ends the train whistle sounds, stealing his attention, and he exits quickly after it.

The solo is accompanied by the full-throated wailing of singer Brother John Sellars, who has performed this piece with the Ailey company since 1961 both live and on its taped accompaniment. Sellars's wailing has a strident masculine grain rarely heard outside the rural South.[24] His vocal style gives an intensely personal interpretation to what is essentially a common song, without author or copyright. (The lyric, "I cried, tears rolled down my cheek / Thinking about my baby, how sweet the woman used to be" is a simple, bare-bones couplet, practically devoid of character.) Firmly rooted in the Afro-American vernacular, Sellars's aggressive sound masculinizes the connection between the expression of sorrow and the male dancer: it validates concert dance as an "authentic" mode of (heterosexual) male behavior.

The train whistle serves as the bridge to "Mean Ole Frisco," a dance for five men. Entering the space singly, each man looks towards an offstage train, imagined to pass over the audience's head. Watching the train closely, the dancers undulate in seething slow motion, sinking into asymmetrical stances with one hip thrust to the side. A swaying hip movement begins slowly and accelerates, finally matching the fast shuffle tempo of the song. The dance continues with mostly unison phrasing, with some interplay for groups of three against two dancers. The men describe powerful accents at the ends of phrases—shooting an arm into space, stopping the energy with a tightly clenched fist. They dance apart, in wide spatial formation, without ever seeing each other.

Although the dance is about the men's longing for a lover that the train has taken away (the "Frisco" of the blues lyric), sexuality is buried deeply beneath a brawny veneer. Ailey studiously avoided homoeroticism here through blockish phrasing, constant explosive movement, and a fierce abstention from physical or emotional contact by the men. The result is a strangely harsh depiction of black men as unable to relate to each other. The latent homophobia of the staging is made more strange by Ailey's own homosexuality. Ailey performed this dance in the 1960s, his heterosexual stage persona far removed from his offstage reality. In this dance, the desirous black male body is overtly heterosexual, single-mindedly in pursuit of an offstage woman.

"Backwater Blues," the central pas de deux, features a man and woman in a low-down, brutal lovers' battle. Drawn in broad strokes of gender role playing, the dance depicts several stages of a courtship ritual built from boasts, struts, and, Apache-style physical confrontation. The choreography depends heavily upon a realistic acting approach Ailey derived from study at the Stella Adler acting studio.[25] A pervasive use of body language, stance, and gesture fills out details of emotional life between the characters. Formal dance movements function as extensions of the dramatic narrative, making the rare motionless position stand out in sharp relief. In one instance, the woman, precariously balanced on the kneeling man's shoulder, throws back her head to pound her chest in angry defiance.

The image resounds beyond this dance encounter, speaking of the emotional outrage brought about by dysfunctional circumstance—in this case, life in a southern whorehouse.

While trading on the entertainment value of the age-old battle of the sexes, Ailey was able to align black social dance styles with concert performance. Ailey used the dramatic narrative to essentialize black social dance as the site of sexual power negotiation. When markers of black dance appear, in flamboyant percussive breaks at the end of musical phrases, multiple meter elaborated by isolations of body parts, and apart phrasing palpable in layered rhythmic patterns, they are carefully embedded within a theatrically constructed tension between Man and Woman. Here, blues dance is masculinized to the degree it is construed to be (hetero)sexual.

In the brief solos of "In the Evening," which follow the duet, three men prepare for a night at the barrelhouse. Here, Ailey used formal dance vocabulary to describe three distinct personalities in movement terms. Arcing turns, interrupted by slight hesitations; swooping balances cut off by full-bodied contractions; and cool struts, stopped by percussive attacks of static poses, all visualize the music's underlying rhythmic structures in terms of breaks and ruptures. These oppositional contrasts are obvious functions of lingering West African aesthetic principles of compositional balance. Ailey fashioned the phrasing mostly in square blocks of four and eight counts, but sharp accents and strong rhythmic shifts from fast, sixteenth-note foot-tapping accents, to slow, half-note balances separate the dance from the music: the dance is conceived both "to" and "apart from" the steady musical beat.

Conceptually similar to classical ballet variations, these solos oblige the men to demonstrate mastery of dance technique. The difficult rhythmic structures also baldly expose the dancers' musicality and precision. In these pure dance variations, Ailey set a standard of concert dance proficiency accessible to black male bodies. In this case, dance technique is disguised as libidinous male posturing.

The solos end when the women reappear, beginning a long sequence of festive blues dancing by the group and two comic characters constantly out of step. The giddy playfulness of the "Sham" contradicts the anger, despair, and fierce attitude of previous sections, exploring instead the entertainment aspects of blues music. The section ends with tightly focused unison phrases, the dancers' smiling faces turned toward the audience in a gesture of communal celebration. Reminiscent of a scene from a Broadway musical, this false happy ending is followed by the repetition of "Good Morning Blues," signaling the return to the painful everyday life of labor and oppression. Faces are averted and suddenly solemn; bodies carry an intense weightiness: speed and agility are buried within downward directed motions and angry demeanors. In this "real" ending to the piece, the characters are again solitary, sprawled across the stage, separated by forces beyond their control, apprehensive, gloom-ridden, and tormented.

The violent juxtaposition of euphoria and despair which ends *Blues Suite* aptly re/presents the professional experiences of Ailey and other black men through the post-war era of concert dance. Smiling through a fleeting triumph, they were inevitably burdened by political circumstances rife with racism, homophobia, and indifference. Forced to entertain audiences receptive only to broadly stereotyped personae, African American men danced savage, hyper-masculine, aggressively heterosexual, and naive-primitive roles which catered to traditional assumptions about the black male body. Denied the opportunity to perform powerful dance that reflected the realities of their lives outside the theater, African American men simmered passively for decades, awaiting the chance to define themselves in terms of movement.

Notes

1. John Perpener provides an overview of the pioneers and their techniques. See "The Seminal Years of Black Concert Dance" (Ph.D. diss., New York University, 1992).

2. Ibid., 68.

3. Richard Long, *The Black Tradition in American Dance* (New York: Rizzoli Books, 1989), 24.

4. John Martin, "The Dance: A Repertory Movement; Stravinsky's 'Petrouschka' Opens the Dance Center's Season of Experiment—A Novel Theater and Production," *New York Times*, August 30, 1931.

5. Ibid.

6. Long, *The Black Tradition in American Dance*, 23.

7. Perpener, "The Seminal Years of Black Concert Dance," 155–160.

8. Ibid., 159.

9. Lynn Emery, *Black Dance from 1619 to Today*, 2d rev. ed. (Princeton, N.J.: Princeton University Press, 1988), 245.

10. Joan Acocella, "Van Grona and His First American Negro Ballet," *Dance Magazine* 22, no. 4 (March 1982): 30–32.

11. A. Hitchens, "Creating the Negro Dance Theater," *Dance and Dancers* (April 1957): 12.

12. Alvin Ailey, "Alvin Ailey and Company, Ernest Parham and Company," YM-YWHA Program notes (March 30, 1958).

13. J. Latham, "A Biographical Study of the Lives and Contributions of Two Selected Contemporary Black Male Dance Artists—Arthur Mitchell and Alvin Ailey" (Ph.D. diss., Texas Woman's University, 1973), 446.

14. Ibid., 457.

15. John Gruen, "Alvin Ailey," in *The Private World of Ballet* (New York: Penguin Books, 1976), 419.

16. Latham, "A Biographical Study of the Lives and Contributions of Two Selected Contemporary Black Male Dance Artists," 500.

17. B. Atkinson, "Theater: Truman Capote's Musical," *New York Times*, December 31, 1954, 11.

18. Latham, "A Biographical Study of the Lives and Contributions of Two Selected Contemporary Black Male Dance Artists," 582.

19. Alvin Ailey and A. P. Bailey, eds., *Revelations: The Autobiography of Alvin Ailey* (New York: Birch Lane Press, 1995), 80.

20. Doris Hering, "Alvin Ailey and Ernest Parham," *Dance Magazine* (May 1958): 27; John Martin, "The Dance: Review III," *New York Times*, July 6, 1958, 11.

21. Jill Johnston, "Mr. Ailey," *Village Voice*, December 21, 1961, 15.

22. P. Manchester, "The Season in Review," *Dance News* (February 1959): 7.

23. Ailey, "Alvin Ailey and Company, Ernest Parham and Company."

24. A. Murray associates the sound with itinerant folk-style guitar strummers ("Blues Suite," Liner notes to *Revelations* [New York: Dance Theater Foundation Records, 1978]).

25. Carmen de Lavallade, "Alvin Ailey," in Ailey and Bailey, *Revelations*, 165.

Choreographic Methods of the Judson Dance Theater

SALLY BANES

The Judson Dance Theater, the legendary amalgamation of avant-garde choreographers in Greenwich Village in the early 1960s, represents a turning point in dance history for many reasons. Its cooperative nature as an alternative-producing institution was a conscious assault on the hierarchical nature not only of academic ballet but also, more directly, of the American modern dance community as it had evolved by the late 1950s. The youthfulness of Judson's original members signified a changing of the guard in terms of generations and, emblematic of the Kennedy era, a cultural shift in authority from the wisdom and experience of age to the energy and creativity—the modernity—of youth. Aesthetic questions about the nature and meaning of dance and of movement were raised in the workshop and in the concerts, among them—fundamentally— the identity of a dance work, the definition of dance, and the nature of technique. The cooperative workshop was a training ground for most of the key choreographers of the next two decades.[1]

But perhaps the most important legacy the Judson Dance Theater bequeathed to the history of dance was its intensive exploration and expansion of possibilities for choreographic method. In their relentless search for the new, coupled with an intelligently analytic approach to the process of dancemaking, in repudiating their elders' cherished compositional formulae, the members of the Judson Dance Theater experimented with so many different kinds of choreographic structures and devices that for the generations that have followed their message was clear: not only any movement or any body, but also any method is permitted.

Robert Dunn's Choreography Class

The open spirit that animated the group had its roots in the sensibilities of the composition class taught by Robert Dunn out of which the Judson Dance Theater blossomed. Dunn's aspirations as a dance composition teacher were informed by several sources (he himself was, of course, trained as a composer, not as a dancer or choreographer). Most crucially he translated ideas from John Cage's experimental music class, especially chance techniques, into the dance milieu; Cage's class, in which Dunn had been a student, already originated in an expanded view of music that encompassed theater and performance in a more general sense. Not only Cage's methods, but also his attitude that "anything goes," was an inspiration that carried over into Dunn's class. Certainly this permissive atmosphere was reinforced by the inclinations of the students, who were all engaged in various ways and to various degrees in the groundbreaking artistic scene in the Village, from the Living Theater to pop art to happenings to Fluxus, and some of whom studied as well with Ann Halprin, the West Coast experimentalist. But beyond this generative urge toward license, Dunn and his students consciously disavowed the compositional approaches taught in the modern dance "academy." Dunn remembers that he had watched Louis Horst and Doris Humphrey teach their choreography classes and was determined to find another pedagogical method; he found them too rigid and the dances by their students too theatrical.

The original class had started out with only five members—Paulus Berenson, Marni Mahaffay, Simone (Forti) Morris, Steve Paxton, and Yvonne Rainer. By the end of the second year, the participants included Judith Dunn (whose status as student sometimes seemed to blend with that of teacher), Trisha Brown, Ruth Emerson, Alex Hay, Deborah Hay, Fred Herko, Al Kurchin, Dick Levine, Gretchen MacLane, John Herbert McDowell, Joseph Schlichter, Carol Scothorn, and Elaine Summers. Valda Setterfield and David Gordon attended occasionally; Robert Rauschenberg, Jill Johnston, and Gene Friedman were "regular visitors," and Remy Charlip, David Vaughan, Robert Morris, Ray Johnson, and Peter Schumann, among others, came from time to time to observe. The composition of this population alone—it included visual artists, musicians, writers, a theater director, and filmmakers as well as dancers—made for an interdisciplinary brew.

The basis of Dunn's approach at first was to find time structures, taken from musical compositions by contemporary composers (Cage, Stockhausen, Boulez, and others), that dance could share. The principal technique was chance scores, but others included more wide-ranging methods of indeterminacy and various kinds of rules. Students were assigned to use a graphic chance score along the lines of that which Cage had made for his *Fontana Mix*. Another assignment involved using number sequences derived from Satie's *Trois Gymnopédies*. Several students remember dances involving time constraints, for instance, "Make a five-minute dance in half an hour." Trisha Brown recalls distinctly the instruction to make a three-minute dance:

This assignment was totally nonspecific except for duration, and the ambiguity provoked days of sorting through possibilities trying to figure out what time meant, was sixty seconds the only difference between three minutes and four minutes, how do you stop something, why, what relation does time have to movement, and on and on. Dick Levine taught himself to cry and did so for the full time period while I held a stopwatch instructed by him to shout just before the time elapsed, "Stop it! Stop it! Cut it out!" both of us ending at exactly three minutes. (21)

Other assignments involved collaborations in which autonomous personal control had to be relinquished within a "semi-independent" working situation. Others had to do with subject matter, for instance, "Make a dance about nothing special." Still others required the use of written scores or instructions. This had partly to do with Dunn's convictions about "inscrib[ing] dances on the bodies of the dancers . . . on the body of the theater," and the notion of choreography as a kind of physicalized writing. "By planning the dance in a written or drawn manner, you have a very clear view of the dance and its possibilities," Dunn says. "Laban's idea was very secondarily to make a *Tanzschrift* . . . a way to record. Laban's idea was to make a *Schrifttanz*, to use graphic—written—inscriptions and then to generate activities. Graphic notation is a way of inventing the dance" (7).

An interest in Labanotation and the theoretical issues of recording dance was on the rise in the dance community. Dunn's use of scores was certainly also related to the influence of Cage and other contemporary composers who were inventing new methods of scoring music in order to fit their new methods of composition and performance. But the dancers' use of written scores had a practical basis as well. According to Ruth Emerson: "There was no rehearsal space, and Bob understood that. It was well understood by everybody that most people didn't have a studio of their own. But in another week, you were expected to come in with something. [Scores were] the only practical way of conveying information. . . . [They were] expedient" (25–26).

Dunn recalls that his approach developed generally

into supplying a "clearinghouse for structures derived from various sources of contemporary action: dance, music, painting, sculpture, Happenings, literature" (3). (However, because the previous generation of modern choreographers had so tied the meaning of their dances to literary ideas, the verbal arts were the least plumbed.) Beyond the freedom of method and the inspiration by other art forms, a crucial element in Dunn's pedagogy was the discussion of choice patterns as part of the presentation. Through this "post-mortem" verbal analysis, the importance of the dance-making process was underscored. Choreographic method came to be seen as an arena for creativity prior to, sometimes even instead of, movement invention.

Before moving on to the Judson Dance Theater itself, let us examine some of the methods for student works presented either in Dunn's class or at the first end-of-the-year showing for the class, since the students' input, as well as Dunn's, served as a catalyst in that situation, and not all of the students went on to participate in the Concerts at Judson Church.

As I have noted, chance was a favored technique, not surprisingly in light of Merce Cunningham's influence on the group (several danced in his company and several more studied with him, and the class itself was given in his studio). And John Cage's influence was even greater. For Marni Mahaffay, the marvel of chance was that it seemed to create limitless possibilities: "I used the rotation of the moon to make one structure, but it could have been anything—for instance, the routine of getting up in the morning and cooking an egg. The path of the moon indicated where things could happen in space, in the dance" (8).

Chance was compelling, not only for its generative capabilities, but because it performed an important psychological function in forcing the choreographer to give up certain features of control. Mahaffay recalls, "To give up your own clichés, to give up your own movement that you were so attached to, was very exciting. You might only be given enough time to do the beginning of your favorite movement, or to do it much less than you would have preferred to. You ended up

putting movements together in ways that weren't at all obvious or expected" (8). According to Ruth Emerson, chance also seemed an escape route from the domination of hierarchical authority: "For me it was a total change from controlling the process of how you made movement, which was first of all that you were supposed to suffer and . . . struggle with your interior, which I couldn't bear. I hated it. . . . It was such a relief to take a piece of paper and work on it without someone telling me I was making things the wrong way" (25).

Once one accepted all kinds of previously unacceptable formal choices that chance engendered (for example, stillness and repetition), all sorts of other choreographic devices became possible—repetition or stillness or arbitrariness by choice, rather than simply by chance. Despite the calculated formality and fragmentation of these methods, the movements they organized were not always abstract. Rainer wrote, about her movement choices of that period:

I dance about things that affect me in a very immediate way. These things can be as diverse as the mannerisms of a friend, the facial expression of a woman hallucinating on the subway, the pleasure of an aging ballerina as she demonstrates a classical movement, a pose from an Etruscan mural, a hunchbacked man with cancer, images suggested by fairy tales, children's play, and of course my own body impulses generated in different situations—a classroom, my own studio, being drunk at a party. I am also deliberately involved in a search for the incongruous and in using a wide range of individual human and animal actions—speak, shriek, grunt, slump, bark, look, jump, dance. One or many of these things may appear in a single dance—depending on what I read, see, and hear during the period I am working on that dance. It follows, therefore, that no single dance is about any one idea or story, but rather about a variety of things that in performance fuse together and decide the nature of the whole experience. (14)

Here Rainer is laying a groundwork for what would replace chance as the key choreographic structure for postmodern dance: radical juxtaposition. Collage—with roots in dada and Duchamp, but also reflecting the crazy-quilt of the American urban landscape—was a preferred method for many visual artists of the period; the *Village Voice* dance critic, Jill Johnston, likened a 1962 piece by Fred Herko to a Rauschenberg combine. In Rainer's *The Bells* and *Satie for Two* (also of 1962), Johnston finds a precedent for the repetitive choreographic strategy in Gertrude Stein's circular, repetitive writing.

Another choreographic method used in Dunn's class, the stripping down of movement to "one thing," which later would resurface as a stringent asceticism paralleling that of minimalist sculpture, characterized dances by Simone Forti and Steve Paxton. Forti's "dance constructions" from that period dealt in ongoing activity, a continuum of motion rather than phrases or complex movement designs. Even her response to one of Dunn's Satie assignments is telling: rather than ordering her movements to the counts given by the number structures, she used the numbers to cue certain singular actions: "If it was a five she put her head down. If it was a three, she just put her two feet down. It was an exquisite dance," Remy Charlip remembers. Paxton made a dance in which he carried furniture out of the school office a piece at a time, and another in which he sat on a bench and ate a sandwich.

And at least three other devices that would be used in future Judson dances or works by Judson members arose in the Dunn class: rule games, interlocking instructions for a group, and using or "reading" a space (or some other structure not originally made as a score, such as a child's drawing or the activity of other people) as a score.

A Concert of Dance (1)

The second year of Dunn's class culminated in a public showing of work in the sanctuary of the Judson Memorial Church on Washington Square in Greenwich Village.

It was this marathon, hours-long evening, with twenty-three dances by fourteen choreographers, that snowballed into what soon became known as the Judson Dance Theater. As with Dunn's class, the choreographic devices represented on this roster of works were many; since most of the dances had been composed as assignments for the course, the methods reiterate those discussed above, with some additions.

The connection between aleatory techniques and the automatism of surrealism emerged in the first event of the evening, which was not, strictly speaking, a dance, but a chance-edited film by Gene Friedman, John Herbert McDowell, and Elaine Summers. (It was not the last film to be billed as a dance event at a Judson concert.) Ruth Emerson's *Narrative*, the first live event on the program, used a score of interlocking directions involving walking patterns, focus, and tempo, as well as cues for actions based on the other dancers' actions. The "drama" in this "narrative" was physically, rather than psychologically motivated; a change in spatial or temporal relationships between people, no matter how abstractly based, seemed to carry psychological, interpersonal meaning. Emerson's *Timepiece,* based on chance (its very title was a tribute to the stopwatch, the renowned insignia of both John Cage and Robert Dunn), was structured by making a chart that had columns for movement quality (percussive or sustained), timing (on a scale of one to six, ranging from very slow to very fast), time limits (fifteen-second periods, multiplied by factors ranging from one to six), movement material (five possibilities: "red bag, untying; turn, jump, jump; hands, head, plie; walking forward side back side side; heron leg to floor"), space time (10, 20, 30, 40, 50, or stillness), space (five areas of the stage plus offstage), front (direction for the facing of the body, with four square directions, four diagonals, and one wild choice), and levels in space (high, low, or medium). The qualities having to do with movement and timing were put together, along the graph of absolute time, separately from the qualities dealing with space. Thus changes in area, facing, and level in space might occur during a single movement phrase. Given the fact that there were usually six elements in a gamut of choices for a given feature, the choices were probably selected by the roll of a die.

Emerson was a trained mathematician as well as a dancer; chance choreography appealed to her, and her *Timepiece* serves as a paradigm for chance choreography in its categorical exhaustiveness (for this reason, I have described it in detail). Elaine Summers's semiparodic approach to aleatory techniques in her *Instant Chance* signaled a growing impatience with a method that, for many, was becoming unfortunately fetishized. David Gordon complained that in Dunn's class, "Judy and Bob were really very rigid about this chance procedure stuff they were teaching. And I had already been through a lot of this chance stuff with Jimmy [Waring]. I wasn't very religious about it." Rainer wrote, "The emphasis on aleatory composition reached ridiculous proportions sometimes. The element of chance didn't ensure that a work was good or interesting, yet I felt that the tenor of the discussions [in the Dunn course] often supported this notion."[2] In Summers's *Instant Chance*, the "hidden operations" of the chance procedure were made part of the piece when the dancers threw large numbered styrofoam blocks in the air and performed whatever movement sequences were dictated by shape, color, and number of the block.

The use of "one thing" as structure surfaced in two dances that, despite their formal simplicity, were extremely theatrical: David Gordon's *Mannequin Dance*, in which, wearing a blood-stained biology lab coat, he slowly turned and lay down on the floor while singing and wiggling his fingers; and Fred Herko's *Once or Twice a Week I Put on Sneakers to Go Uptown*, which Jill Johnston described as "a barefoot Suzie-Q in a tassel-veil head-dress, moving around the big performing area . . . only the barefoot Suzie-Q with sometimes a lazy arm snaking up and collapsing down. [And] with no alteration of pace or accent" (43). Implicit in these works was the austere, formalist approach that would become rampant in the period I have elsewhere called "analytic postmodern dance" in the seventies,[3] although it had been introduced by Forti at least a year

before, it was not yet a favored method in the "breakaway" years of the early sixties.

Two dances that had been made for a class assignment about "cut-ups" were Carol Scothorn's *Isolations* and Ruth Emerson's *shoulder r*. Scothorn's involved cutting up Labanotation scores and Emerson's included Laban material, among other elements. The cut-up is a subcategory of chance procedures that was favored by the dadaists. Tristan Tzara gives instructions for how to make a dadaist poem based on cutting words out of an article, shaking them up in a bag, and reassembling them. Through Cage, the young New York avant-gardists were familiar with Robert Motherwell's book on *The Dada Painters and Poets*, published in 1951, in which these instructions appear. Perhaps the Tzara manifesto was even the source of this choreography assignment. But, in any case, many of the methods used by the dadaists and surrealists to undercut meaning or to release new meanings—from chance to collage— were consciously explored in the dance arena. That is, through their knowledge of the historical avant-garde, the Judson dancers could find a methodological treasure trove for their own, similar purposes.

The use of instructions is related to chance in that it foregrounds issues of control. Chance undermines the choreographer's control by subverting personal choices. (That, at least, is the theory; ultimately, however, the choreographer's choices are revealed in the original gamuts out of which the chance-decisions are made.) Instruction scores given to the dancer(s) by the choreographer exaggerate control, making palpable and objective the normally implicit, hegemonic position of choreographer over dancer—at least, making it explicit in the choreographic process (since neither chance nor instruction as a generating device is necessarily evident to the spectator). However, depending on how strictly the score codes instructions, such a method can also permit a great deal of freedom of interpretation by the dancer, recasting hegemony into partnership. Steve Paxton's use of a score for *Proxy* grew directly out of thoughts about such issues. He was attempting through the score to make the learning and rehearsal process more objective and impersonal, to get away from the cult of imitation that he felt surrounded modern dance, a cult that began with the direct transmission of movements from teacher to pupil and ended with a hierarchically structured dance company. At the same time, he attempted through the score to go beyond what Cunningham and Cage had done in using chance techniques, for, as he puts it, "My feeling . . . was that one further step was needed, which was to arrive at movement by chance. That final choice, of making movement, always bothered my logic. . . . Why couldn't it be chance all the way?" Paxton's score was made by randomly dropping images and then gluing them in place on a large piece of brown paper: cut-out photographs of people walking and engaged in sports, plus cartoon images (Mutt and Jeff, and one from a travel advertisement). A moveable red dot marked the beginning the dancer had chosen. The score, then, served to mediate between choreographer and dancer, to distance the movements themselves from the choreographer's body and hence his personal style. According to Paxton:

> That was a selection process but one removed
> from actually deciding what to do with the pic-
> tures, because I made the score and then handed it
> over to the performers, and they could take a linear
> or circular path through the score. You could start
> any place you wanted to, but then you went all the
> way through it. You did as many repeats as were in-
> dicated, and you went back and forth as indicated.
> But how long it took and what you did between
> postures was not set at all. It was one big area of
> choice not at all influenced by the choreographer.
> The only thing I did in rehearsing the work was to
> go over it with them and talk about the details of
> the postures. (58)

Summers used a newspaper as a score in *The Daily Wake* for similar reasons. She describes her procedure:

> I took the front page and laid it out on the floor
> and used the words in it to structure the dance, and

used the photographs in it so that they progressed on the surface of the page as if it were a map. If you start analyzing that way, you get deeper and deeper. You get more clues for structure, like how many paragraphs are there? Beginning with *The Daily Wake,* I became very interested in using photos as resource material, and other structures as maps. (53–54)

Another way to distance movement from personal style or personal expression, anathema to this generation precisely because it had become so overblown in the works of "historical" modern dance, was the completion of tasks or the handling of objects. Summers had this in mind in her *Instant Chance*. Robert Morris programmatically developed this method in *Arizona* (to be discussed below).

Yet another term in the debates about choreographic control and the boundaries of chance was the use of indeterminacy, that is, intervention by the performers through limited use of improvisation. This exceeded even Cunningham's relinquishing of control through chance (he was later, in *Story* [1963], perhaps inspired by some of the Judson experiments, to try his hand at indeterminacy, but he was not pleased by the results). Rainer's *Dance for 3 People and 6 Arms*, also performed at Concert 1, was a trio in which the dancers could choose when to perform one of a series of predetermined movement options, most of which, as the title suggests, were concerned with gestures and positions of the arms. Rainer dubbed this method, which combined chance and improvisation, "spontaneous determination." William Davis, one of the dancers, remembers of the first performance (at the Maidman Playhouse in March 1962):

> I think it was the first time dancers were waiting for
> a curtain to go up without having any idea what-
> soever of the shape the dance was going to take.
>   That kind of thing was being done musically [in
> the work of Cage and his colleagues]. What it really
> resembled was jazz musicianship, more than chance

operations, because we were all working for a time when we might, for example, do this, or seeing what someone else is doing, think "Oh yes, I can connect this to that," or "They're doing fine, I'll just let them go at it." It's a sense of shape taking place in three people's minds as the dance is going on. (52)

Without going into detail about the rest of the dances on this historic program, I would like to note several other choreographic devices appearing in this first Judson concert (some of which have already been discussed in the section on Dunn's class or will be discussed further below) that would remain rich lodes for the Judson choreographers to mine: children's and adult's games (Gretchen MacLane's *Quibic*); quoting other artworks, either dance or in other media (Rainer's *Divertissement*, Deborah Hay's *Rain Fur*); the use of popular music and social dancing (Herko's *Once or Twice a Week* . . . , Davis's *Crayon*); collaboration (*Like Most People* by Fred Herko and Cecil Taylor; *Rafladan* by Alex Hay, Deborah Hay, and Charles Rotmil); and the collage, assemblage, or list format (Paxton's *Transit*, Gordon's *Helen's Dance*, Deborah Hay's *Five Things*, Rainer's *Ordinary Dance*, among others).

The Judson Workshop

Shortly after the momentous Concert of Dance in July 1962, Elaine Summers had organized A Concert of Dance 2 in Woodstock, New York, an artists' summer colony (before it became famous for the rock festival held there in 1969). Several dances from the Judson Church concert were shown and some new works by additional choreographers were added.

When in the fall of 1962 Robert Dunn did not continue his choreography class, Rainer and Paxton organized meetings of the group, at first in the studio Rainer shared with James Waring and Aileen Passloff on St. Mark's Place in the East Village, and then, after about a month, at the Judson Church, where they met weekly in the basement gymnasium. The purpose of this workshop was understood to be analytic and critical; new dances were not rehearsed there, but performed for peer scrutiny and feedback. Thus the emphasis in workshop discussions was on compositional method as well as such related issues as performance style.

By January 1963, the Judson weekly workshop had accumulated enough material to organize two concerts. The press release for Concerts 3 and 4 specifically underscored the workshop's emphasis on choreographic method. And, importantly, it pointed out that even though the search was on for new devices, new structures, and new theories, even traditional methods were permitted as but one more possibility in a wide, unrestricted range. "These concerts," it read,

are in the series initiated at the church . . . with the aim of periodically presenting the work of dancers, composers, and various non-dancers working with ideas related to dance. The methods of composition of the works in this series range from the traditional ones which predetermine all elements of a piece to those which establish a situation, environment, or basic set of instructions governing one or more aspects of a work—thus allowing details and continuity to become manifest in a spontaneous or indeterminate manner.

It is hoped that the contents of this series will not so much reflect a single point of view as convey a spirit of inquiry into the nature of new possibilities. (82)

Some of the dances in these two concerts were partly structured by the physical space of the venue: the church gym (for instance a collaboration by Robert Huot and Robert Morris, *War*, which put La Monte Young playing the musical accompaniment in the cage). The constraints of the physical performance space would affect or directly shape the dances in several future Judson concerts, in fact becoming a hallmark of the innovative spirit of the group. One long thread leading from such works was the spate of "environmental" dances in the late sixties and early seventies. But even where such considerations were not explicit in the dances, the space still governed such elements of performance as the intimacy or distance between spectator and performer and the shape and visibility of the "stage." In Concert 5, held in a roller-skating rink in Washington, D.C., Robert Rauschenberg built his entire dance (*Pelican*) on place; in it, Carolyn Brown danced in pointe shoes partnered by two men on roller skates. As well, the enormity of the space led the group to perform in various parts of the rink, making the audience mobile, and sometimes to fill the space (and challenge audience attention) by performing two dances simultaneously in different places. Concerts 9–12, held in the Gramercy Arts Theater—which had a proscenium stage so small one could barely move without moving off it—gave rise to a number of works in which motion was either minimal, very slow, or spilled into the house. These three radical approaches to movement, emerging here out of necessity, would also become approaches of choice, badges of the Judson heritage. Steve Paxton's *Afternoon*, sponsored by the workshop, took place in a forest in New Jersey; for this dance, Paxton was directly concerned with how the natural ground surface and "scenery" would change the movement, which had been constructed in a studio.

Many of the dances for Concert 13 were united both by spatial considerations and by the use of a physical structure (they all happened in, on, or around a sculpture commissioned from Charles Ross) as well as by performance style (the sculpture, evoking a jungle gym, sparked a common spirit of playfulness). Once again, a Judson emblem—dance and art as play—was strikingly condensed in a single event. Finally, a single concert, 14 (one of the last given jointly by the workshop before it disbanded in 1964), was organized around a single choreographic method: improvisation. Although improvisation was not, statistically speaking, a common device for the Judson choreographers, this concert, too, seemed symbolically to lay claim to a new alternative method for making and performing dances.

Some Exemplary Pieces

Nearly two hundred dances were produced by the Judson Dance Theater between July 1962 and October 1964, the time of the last concert officially sponsored by the workshop. After the workshop disbanded, dance performances continued to be produced at the church on an individual basis—the "bus-stop situation," as Judith Dunn later called it. A "second generation" of Judson dancers, including Meredith Monk, Kenneth King, and Phoebe Neville showed work at the church, as did members of James Waring's company (such as Toby Armour, Carol Marcy, and Deborah Lee), Waring himself, Aileen Passloff, and various original members of the Judson Dance Theater workshop. There was even a revival of Judson "hits," presented at the church, as early as 1966.

As I have noted above, many of the seeds of the methodology for the workshop were already planted in the Robert Dunn class; the first concert and those selected concerts discussed in the preceding section represent a sizeable cross-section of the techniques that would continue to provide food for dancing over the next several years, and by the next several cohorts of choreographers. I am concentrating here on the pioneering choreography by the members of the original workshop, but obviously space does not even permit a discussion of every dance performed over the year and a half of the Judson Dance Theater workshop's lifetime (and, of course, since not every dance was the result of an entirely new method, such a review would be tedious). Therefore I would like to devote the next section of the paper to discussing selected dances that not only exemplify the choreographic concerns of the group and of individuals in the group, but that also point in directions that have proved fruitful for the succeeding generations of choreographers in the postmodern mode.

The first full-length evening dance by a single choreographer sponsored by the Judson Dance Theater was Yvonne Rainer's *Terrain*. This dance, in four sections, in retrospect seems a treasure trove of choreographic devices, structures, performance attitudes, and other aspects of style; in it one sees the preoccupations that wend their way in one form or another through the rest of Rainer's oeuvre, reaching their fullest expression in her *The Mind Is a Muscle* and *Continuous Project—Altered Daily*. The title is prophetic, for this dance represents the "terrain" of dance Rainer continued to map out in her choreographic career and even in her film work. The dance used methods culled from child's play and rule games (the sections "Diagonal" and "Play"). It had an entire section based on parody through pastiche ("Duet," in which Rainer performed a ballet adagio and Trisha Brown performed a balletic sequence in the upper body with burlesque bumps and grinds in the lower torso, ending with both assuming "cheesecake" poses, all to a collage of music that included African drumming, American jazz, and fragments of Massenet's opera *Thaïs*). The technique of "spontaneous determination" that had provided the armature for *Dance for 3 People and 6 Arms* also surfaced here, as did elements of repetition and chance, the list as organizational tool, and the generating of movement by turning to another art form—in this case, erotic Hindu temple sculpture. Talking while dancing, a technique by which Rainer had electrified spectators in *Ordinary Dance*, surfaced here in the two sequences from the "Solo" section that used texts by Spencer Holst.

Rainer also used several objects for some of the solos in the "Solo" section of *Terrain*. For the Judson choreographers, as for their contemporaries the pop artists, the ordinary object was particularly resonant. Robert Morris wrote in *The Drama Review* that objects and task behavior were two preferred methods for rinsing the dance of excess expressiveness and to find new ways of moving the body:

From the beginning I wanted to avoid the pulled-up, turned-out, anti-gravitational qualities that not only gave a body definition and role as "dancer" but qualify and delimit the movement available to it. The challenge was to find alternative movement. . . . A fair degree of complexity of . . . rules and

cues effectively blocked the dancer's performing "set" and reduced him to frantically attempting to respond to cues—reduced him from performance to action. (143)

For Morris, objects were superior to tasks as a means to solve problems and thus create a structure for the dance. The manipulation of an object generated movement without becoming more important than the performer or the performance. In *Arizona*, Morris threw a javelin, swung a small light while the stage lights dimmed, and adjusted a T-form; all these objects, he wrote, "held no inherent interest for me but were means for dealing with specific problems," such as setting up relationships among movement, space, and duration, or shifting focus between the "egocentric and the exocentric" in the small light contrasting to the dimming stage lights.

Lucinda Childs in *Carnation* (and in several other works) also built a dance around the cool manipulation of everyday things. Yet here the deadpan attitude itself and the *kinds* of objects used (things associated with women's beauty care or domestic activities such as cleaning and cooking) add up to a seething "hot" significance. (Kenneth King's *cup/saucer/two dancers/radio*, a slightly later dance by a member of the "second generation" of Judson choreographers, radically extends the sense of alienation Childs hints at humorously, partly by equating all the elements listed in the title.) Undoubtedly the fascination with the object—the mute, ordinary, everyday object—reflects a growing consumer society, the burgeoning cornucopia of available goods of the United States during this period.

Yvonne Rainer's *Some Thoughts on Improvisation* (part of Concert 14) is another paradigmatic piece for several reasons: its use of improvisation as a structuring device, its baring of the devices, its analytic reflexivity. This dance, too, like so many others by Rainer during this period, includes a spoken text, but in this case the words are taped, serving as the "musical accompaniment" to the dance—or a sound track, to liken the event to Rainer's later terrain, the cinema. As Rainer improvised the dance, dressed in a black dress and high-heeled shoes (a costume that not only stands for a certain image of femininity, but that also severely limits its movement possibilities), her voice described the improvisatory process, both in general and in this specific case. Her monologue moves from an almost phenomenological description of thoughts and experiences ("So I keep on sizing up the situation, see. And I keep on walking. And I make decisions. He has left the room, I will run; she is standing stockstill, I will bring my head close to hers; that man is moving his arms around, I will do as he does; the wall looms close, I will walk until I bump into it" [196]) to a dissection of the choice-making patterns in improvisation. She lists three aspects of choice: impulses, anti-impulses, ideas. The action, she notes, can come from any of these, including the decision not to follow an impulse. It is, finally, the instinct of the performer, including the assertion of physical and mental control and the mastery of anxiety, that fuels the performance, she concludes. "When it goes forward it moves with an inexorable thrust and exerts a very particular kind of tension: spare, unadorned, highly dramatic, loaded with expectancy—a field for action. What more could one ask for" (197).

Although improvisation is often remembered as one of the most important legacies of the Judson Dance Theater, this particular concert (14), with its eight dances all conjoined by the shared method of improvisation, was not considered successful. Jill Johnston wrote:

> Ironically, one of the concerts on this last series . . . was a great improvisation, with minimal restrictions on freedom, and the most impressive collection of vanguard dancers and artists . . . couldn't get this tacitly accepted Open Sesame (free play) off the ground. Everybody was very polite except for Yvonne Rainer . . . and the response to her nerve should have been pandemonium if anybody had faced the assertion squarely. (198)

Yet it was this improvisatory side of the Judson Dance Theater, signaling freedom, that would later give rise

to, for example, the Grand Union—one of the most brilliant projects of the postmodern dance.

Another key outgrowth of the Judson Dance Theater was the use of multiple media, or intermedia, especially film, in the dance. This seems only fair, since, although many of the dance ideas of the group came from searching for the essence of dance per se, still others came from the inspiration or influence of other media and other art forms, in particular the visual arts, new music, and film. Of course, in the spirit of breaking down the boundaries between the art forms, artists in different fields were making events that so traded in mixing media that it was often difficult to categorize them, except by the author's label. An early mixed-media event at the Judson Dance Theater was Beverly Schmidt's *The Seasons*. It was a vignette from a larger "film-stage" performance, called *Blossoms*, conceived by the choreographer's husband, Roberts Blossom. For *The Seasons*, Schmidt memorized the dance she had improvised for the film shown in the earlier performance, then choreographed a new live solo, which was performed simultaneously with the film projection, sometimes in counterpoint or opposition and sometimes in unison. The dance was in four sections, with live music by Philip Corner and Malcolm Goldstein, and recorded music by Purcell. Each section had a distinctive movement quality, costume, and color—a distinctive mood, which Schmidt made correspond to the four seasons.

The Seasons served as a model for future events in both dance and film. The following year, two evening-length concerts by individual members of the workshop incorporating film into the dancing were sponsored by the Judson Dance Theater—Elaine Summers's *Fantastic Gardens* and Judith Dunn's *Last Point*. Meredith Monk, who arrived on the Judson scene after the end of the workshop, made the fusion of dance and film central to her work from the beginning, in such pieces as *Sixteen Millimeter Earrings* (1966). Reading Johnston's review of Schmidt's dance, one is even reminded of Lucinda Childs's recent collaboration with Sol LeWitt, using film as décor, in *Dance*:

The interplay of images—the soft, majestic volume of the figure on the screen with the diminutive flesh and blood on stage—made a shifting mirror of the kind of dimension that reached far beyond, in the past and future, the moments of reckoning on that small stage. Near the end I had the uncanny feeling of an ancient presence when her head loomed large in an instant of immobilized totemistic grandeur. (159)

The list goes on and on: dances built on parodies of other dances or of performance styles (such as David Gordon's *Random Breakfast*); dances structured like sports events or based on sports movements (for example, Judith Dunn's *Speedlimit*), dances generated out of pure flashes of energy (Carolee Schneemann's *Newspaper Event*, et al.), repetition, tasks, free association, "ritual," unfinished work. As well, choreographers continued to use all the methods and devices I have mentioned above: time structures taken from music, chance, indeterminacy, "spontaneous determination," rules, limits, collaboration, written scores, interlocking instructions for a group, and using or "reading" a space (or some other structure not originally made as a score, such as a child's drawing or the activity of other people) as a score, children's and adult's games, quoting other artworks (both dance and other media), the use of popular music and social dancing, the collage, assemblage, or list format, "a situation, environment, or basic set of instructions governing one or more aspects of a work," automatism, satire, cut-ups, handling objects, responding to physical space, improvisational verbal content, mixing media—and even traditional methods of composition, such as classical musical structures, image construction, and aspiring to values of unity, complexity, and coherence.

I might say a word here about *my* methods. I have tried to get at choreographic structures or devices in a number of ways, not all of which were available for each dance. The dance historian is like an archaeologist, digging up fragments and—depending on the quantity and quality of the shards, their capacity for transmitting various types of information—she puts them together, with a glue partly consisting of informed speculation, to form a picture of the thing as it was. But this picture will almost always still be incomplete.

Using the scores and the oral and written memoirs of the choreographers, on the one hand (which tells us something about sources, intentions, and process), and the descriptions, interpretations, and evaluations of witnesses—colleagues, critics, and spectators—on the other hand (which tells us something about reception and product), I have pieced together the preceding accounts—accounts that, as you have seen, vary in terms of fullness and even in terms of accuracy.

The structures and methods of some Judson Dance Theater works are simply lost and will never be retrieved. (Deborah Hay, for example, destroyed her written records afterwards and does not remember most of her dances of that period.) For other works, we may know about the methods in a general way without gaining any sense of the way the dance looked and felt—its movement details, its performance style. Yet other works are well documented and well remembered enough to live on—some even in live reconstructions (though it is important to realize that reconstructed dances may not necessarily replicate the original exactly).[4]

A ground was cleared at the Judson that created new challenges for the following generation; in the 1970s, an entire wing of analytic, formalist postmodern dancers extended and consolidated that passion for revealing choreographic process, which sprang from the freedom of method (and the concomitant articulation of method) of the 1960s. But, by the 1980s, choreographic process seemed less important than choreographic product—for obvious cultural reasons, but also perhaps because methodological innovation was a frontier so thoroughly explored, to many it seemed no new devices could be discovered. But the 1980s are another story.

Notes

1. The sources for the information in this paper not otherwise footnoted will be found in the text and footnotes of my book *Democracy's Body: Judson Dance Theater, 1962–1964* (Ann Arbor, Mich.: UMI Research Press, 1983). Page numbers from *Democracy's Body* are in parentheses following the quotations.

2. Yvonne Rainer, *Work 1961–73* (Halifax: Press of the Nova Scotia College of Art and Design; New York: New York University Press, 1974), 7.

3. Sally Banes, "Dance," in *The Postmodern Moment:* *A Handbook of Contemporary Innovation in the Arts*, ed. Stanley Trachtenberg (Westport, Conn.: Greenwood Press, 1985), 81–100.

4. A program of Judson reconstructions, curated by Wendy Perron and Cynthia Hedstrom, was produced at St. Mark's Church Danspace in April 1982, as part of the Bennington College Judson Project. The reconstructions were recorded on videotape by the Lincoln Center Library Dance Research Collection and may be viewed there.

Chance Heroes

DEBORAH JOWITT

Editor's Note: In this piece, Deborah Jowitt reviews performances of the Merce Cunningham Dance Company at the Joyce Theater, New York City, September 13 through 18, 1994.

What *is* this world? Its inhabitants are sleek and preternaturally alert. You might think every one of them tall, but that's only because they stand narrow and erect, and because their long, articulate limbs probe the space so extravagantly. Were it not for witty deviations, you'd imagine those legs as calipers marking out recklessly huge orbits. I wouldn't, however, call these people's *behavior* reckless. Gusts of passion don't knock them over or kite them out of control. Calmly they negotiate the most demanding of tasks; calmly they reach out to steady one another. If they appear occasionally fervid, it's because the task of the moment incites heat, the way trying to turn a stiff faucet or dive into a pool gathers our force and heats up even the most serene among us. Simply doing what has to be done with neither too much nor too little intensity gives them the look not only of probity and good breeding, but of channeled passion.

The world, of course, is the one created by Merce Cunningham and by the exceptional dancers he has trained. Like Balanchine—and, to my mind, as protean—Cunningham has liberated his dances from specific narrative, although not from the stories that we may infer. Unlike Balanchine, he doesn't use music as a floor; the musicians' electronically produced or manip-ulated sounds—now soothing, now harsh enough to seem to menace the dancers—surround spectators and performers, as if the street had moved into the theater (the other day I was watching a videotape of some little Balinese girls rehearsing a *legong* in their teacher's kitchen while outside a helicopter clattered and a rooster crowed; John Cage would have loved it). The chance procedures that Cunningham uses to generate choreography and the unforeseen conjunctions of movement, sound, and decor, create situations that, despite the dancers' air of intelligent premeditation, appear fluid and unpredictable.

Cunningham chose to mark the thirtieth anniversary of his first Event by offering only Events—hour-and-a-half collages of excerpts from various works, divorced from their original scores and decor. (He observed in a question-and-answer session that ninety minutes is the length of an average movie, so it ought to feel about right to everyone.) Fittingly, the decor for this series of Events is a vibrant collage of photographs and paint by Robert Rauschenberg, who provided decor for early Events (indeed was part of the decor for the first one). Incorporating previously recorded images and recombining these with other elements, Rauschenberg's collages offer bewitching structural analogies to Events.

Those who see all Cunningham dances simply as swatches of choreography with a frame around them and a title affixed are okay about Events, except maybe they'd rather not sit for so long. Some of those people who honor the form of the original works can't understand why he would deliberately hack them up. *He* likes the riskiness and the gentle slap to the creator's ego.

I like Events too. Especially when I resist the urge to identify the sources of the excerpts. This was particularly difficult during [the company's September 1994 season at the Joyce Theater in New York City] because in addition to inserting parts of his dazzlingly eccentric new computer-aided creations, Cunningham raided works of the 1960s and 1970s that have been out of repertory. ("Isn't this *Locale*?") Or, as Kimberly Bartosik is slowly dragged offstage on a square of cloth in Aaron Copp's darkening light: "*Winterbranch!*" He treated us to moments from *Un Jour ou Deux*, created for the Paris Opera Ballet, and let dancers dash around in curious outfits (a dress and a fencing mask for Jared Phillips), or pass a coiled hose (from the almost uniquely indeterminate *Story* from 1963, a feature of the first Event). If I squelch the historian in me, I can see the stage as an expanse of space and time that defies borders. Of course the proscenium frames the action, and Rauschenberg's background collage might seem to anchor things (except that every time you look at it you see something different); but the dancing gives an illusion of endlessness—happening out of sight in the wings, beginning before we arrive. It was perhaps to relieve us with a semblance of closure that Cunningham chose to end the three programs I saw with a group photo pose or a lineup to bow.

The immense contrasts in speed and density seem especially potent during Events. Trios counterpoint duets; groups drift apart and reassemble. Unison appears out of nowhere and vanishes. Temporary alliances form and dissipate without consequences. Several dancers stand clumped as still as fishing herons. The quiet shatters as they plunge off into disparate actions at high velocity. While Michael Cole thrashes his legs in midair, Banu Ogan stands at the rear, slowly stretching one leg high behind her, arching her back; meanwhile the dials and switches controlled by David Tudor, Takehisa Kosugi, and Ron Kuivila turn Stuart Dempster's trombone notes into soft unearthly wails.

Your eye may be drawn to strangeness (Robert Swinston sternly holding a deliberately awkward balance) or arrested by a thoughtful gesture (Jeannie Steele stirring the air beside her) or dazzled by a virtuosic explosion of steps (Frédéric Gafner buoyantly mastering complexities of elevation in a stunning solo—Cunningham's own solo from *Scramble*, I think). Bartosik lunges deeply in front of Gafner, over and over, as if she were bowing to him, then vaults onto him. You marvel over the odd ways dancers intersect or touch—gently, but often clumsily, as if they still had much to learn about one another.

At a postperformance dialogue, one spectator asked Cunningham what he felt about gender in his dances. With charm and perhaps a trace of disingenuousness, the master pondered, then said, "Well, there are two of them. . . ." In fact, one of the things that gives the people in Cunningham's created world their air of civility is the chivalrous behavior of the men toward the women and the women's acceptance of the men's support. The women—although phenomenally strong and given essentially egalitarian treatment onstage by the choreography—don't lift men and do on occasion arch back to lean on a partner. This somehow "old-fashioned" element in a setting rife with broken conventions and a willingness to unsettle audiences touches me, as does the contrast between Cunningham's insistence on everyday behavior and the virtuosic dancing he makes. Or—and this is even more marked in Events than in repertory dances—the exhilarating tension between the dancers' sane, meditative air and actions that seem to belie cause and effect.

A week of Events—with a new assemblage of material nightly—challenges the dancers' memories as well as their stamina. They may well have been exhausted, frustrated, or despairing; you'd never have known. They danced like gladiators. Like angels. It's all the more amazing when you consider that only four of them—Bartosik, Cole, Swinston, and Jenifer Weaver—were in the company prior to 1990. Thomas Caley joined in August 1993, and he's already giving a beautiful account of a solo hallowed by Cunningham. For better or for worse, they've had to grow into the reper-tory fast. Fluid Lisa Boudreau and tall, sharp-limbed Matthew Mohr joined this summer. I salute them all—those already mentioned and Jean Freebury, China Laudisio, Glen E. Rumsey, and Cheryl Therrien.

Then there's Cunningham himself, every season gradually distancing himself from the others, yet radiantly present. He stumps on for each night's opening one-at-a-time lineup and for the closing. Unlike the others, he's not wearing shiny unitards in dark blue, hot pink, or orange (by Rauschenberg assisted by Suzanne Gallo)—everyone in the same color, different colors for different nights. He's dressed in a long-sleeved polo and trousers, sometimes a jacket too. He has almost no traffic with the others; they clear the stage for his solos like chickadees fluttering off when a blue jay arrives. One night though, Therrien came and sat in a chair he'd been using, and he briefly knelt and laid his head in her lap.

One solo rings changes on a dance he's been doing for some time. His hands twist and twinkle through the air around him. You imagine him twiddling the dials of a fantastic machine. Or, wait, perhaps he's conducting an orchestra. His demeanor encourages you to make up stories like this. He's so alive, so rapt, so clearly seeing and hearing things. He disguises his limp by slinking a bit; seems to forget, then pounce on ideas. On Thursday, he offered an entrancing bit of what might have been self-parody. Sitting on his chair in mid gesture—say a foot held awkwardly up—he'd nod off, then pull himself together with a small start. He also dances with the aid of the portable barre that he uses to demonstrate movements in rehearsal. Edging it offstage, hidden by a moving screen of dancers, he can be glimpsed now and then hoisting himself into a jump, his face a study in pure delight. I think this is not the creator's well-justified pride in his creation, but the spontaneous reaction of a man in love with dancing, one who believes it to be one of the noblest and deepest subjects in the world. That love, monitored by intelligence and daring, brought *his* world into being.

America Dancing: Further Readings

Aldrich, Elizabeth. *From the Ballroom to Hell: Grace and Folly in 19th-Century Dance.* Evanston, Ill.: Northwestern University Press, 1991.

Banes, Sally. "Choreographic Methods of the Judson Dance Theater." In *Writing Dancing in the Age of Postmodernism.* Hanover, N.H.: Wesleyan University Press, 1994.

Barker, Barbara M. "Imre Kiralfy's Patriotic Spectacles: *Columbus, and the Discovery of America* (1892–1893) and *America* (1893)." *Dance Chronicle* 17, no. 2 (1994).

Bean, Annemarie, James V. Hatch, and Brooks McNamara, eds. *Inside the Minstrel Mask: Readings in Nineteenth-Century Blackface Minstrelsy.* Hanover, N.H.: Wesleyan University Press, 1996.

Brooks, Lynn Matluck. "Against Vain Sports and Pastime: The Theatre Dance in Philadelphia, 1724–90." *Dance Chronicle* 12, no. 2 (1989).

———. "Dancing Masters in Eighteenth-Century Philadelphia." *Dance: Current Selected Research,* vol. 2. New York: AMS Press, 1990.

———. "A Decade of Brilliance: Dance Theatre in Late-Eighteenth-Century Philadelphia." *Dance Chronicle* 12, no. 3 (1989).

Buckman, Peter. *Let's Dance: Social, Ballroom, and Folk Dancing.* New York: Paddington Press, 1978.

Calabria, Frank M. *Dance of the Sleepwalkers: The Dance Marathon Fad.* Bowling Green, Ohio: Bowling Green State University Popular Press, 1993.

Cohen, Selma Jeanne, ed. *Dance as a Theatre Art: Source Readings in Dance History from 1581 to the Present.* Princeton, N.J.: Princeton Book Company, 1992.

———. *Doris Humphrey: An Artist First.* Pennington, N.J.: Princeton Book Company, 1995.

———. *The Modern Dance: Seven Statements of Belief.* Middletown, Conn.: Wesleyan University Press, 1966.

Conner, Lynne. *Spreading the Gospel of the Modern Dance: Newspaper Dance Criticism in the United States, 1850–1934.* Pittsburgh: University of Pittsburgh Press, 1997.

Cook, Susan C. "Passionless Dancing and Passionate Reform: Respectability, Modernism, and the Social Dancing of Irene and Vernon Castle." In *The Passion of Music and Dance: Body, Gender and Sexuality,* ed. William Washabaugh. New York: Oxford University Press, 1998.

Croce, Arlene. *Afterimages.* New York: Knopf, 1977.

———. *Going to the Dance.* New York: Knopf, 1982.

Current, Richard Nelson, and Marcia Ewing Current. *Loie Fuller, Goddess of Light.* Boston: Northeastern University Press, 1997.

Dalton, Karen C. C., and Henry Louis Gates Jr. "Josephine Baker and Paul Colin: African American Dance Seen through Parisian Eyes." *Critical Inquiry* 24, no. 4 (summer 1998).

Daly, Ann. *Done into Dance: Isadora Duncan in America.* Bloomington: Indiana University Press, 1995.

DeFrantz, Thomas. "Simmering Passivity: The Black Male Body in Concert Dance." In *Moving Words: Re-Writing Dance,* ed. Gay Morris. New York: Routledge. 1996.

Delamater, J. *Dance in the Hollywood Musical.* Ann Arbor: UMI Research Press, 1981.

Duncan, Isadora. "The Dancer and Nature." In *The Art of the Dance,* ed. Sheldon Cheney. New York: Theatre Arts Books, 1928.

Dunning, Jennifer. *Alvin Ailey: A Life in Dance.* Reading, Mass.: Addison-Wesley, 1996.

Emery, Lynne Fauley, ed. *Black Dance from 1619 to Today*. Princeton, N.J.: Princeton Book Company, 1988.

Erenberg, Lewis A. *Steppin' Out: Night Life and the Transformation of American Culture, 1890–1930*. Chicago: University of Chicago Press, 1981.

Foster, Susan Leigh. "Narrative with a Vengeance: Doris Humphrey's *With My Red Fires*." In *Society of Dance History Scholars Conference Proceedings*. Riverside, Calif. Dance History Scholars, 1999.

Garafola, Lynn, ed. *José Limón: An Unfinished Memoir*. Middletown, Conn.: Wesleyan University Press; Hanover, N.H.: University Press of New England, 1999.

———, ed. *Of, by, and for the People: Dancing on the Left in the 1930s. Studies in Dance History*. Hanover, N.H.: Wesleyan University Press, 1994.

Goldberg, Marianne. "Trisha Brown's *Accumulations*." *Dance Theatre Journal* 9, no. 2 (autumn 1991).

Gottschild, Brenda Dixon. "Stripping the Emperor: The Africanist Presence in American Concert Dance." In *Looking Out: Perspectives on Dance and Criticism in a Multicultural World*. ed. David Gere. New York: Schirmer Books, 1995.

Graff, Ellen. *Stepping Left: Dance and Politics in New York City, 1928–1942*. Durham, N.C.: Duke University Press, 1997.

Graham, Martha. *Blood Memory*. New York: Doubleday, 1991.

Hill, Constance Valis. "Katherine Dunham's *Southland*: Protest in the Face of Repression." *Dance Research Journal* 26, no. 2 (fall 1994).

Johnson, Jill. "The New American Modern Dance." *Salmagundi* 33–34 (spring– summer 1976).

Jowitt, Deborah. "Chance Heroes." *Village Voice*, October 4, 1994.

———. *Dance Beat: Selected Views and Reviews, 1967–1976* . New York: M. Dekker, 1977.

———. "Form as the Image of Human Perfectability and Natural Order." *Dance Research Journal* 28, no. 2 (fall 1996).

———. "Images of Isadora: The Search for Motion." *Dance Research Journal* 17, no 2 / 18, no. 1 (fall 1985 / spring 1986).

———. "The Impact of Greek Art on the Style and Persona of Isadora Duncan." *Society of Dance History Scholars Conference Proceedings*. Riverside, Calif.: Dance History Scholars, 1987.

———. "In Memory: Martha Graham, 1894–1991." *Drama Review* 35, no. 4 (winter 1991).

———. *Time and the Dancing Image*. New York: Morrow, 1988.

Kendall, Elizabeth. *Where She Danced: The Birth of American Art Dance*. Berkeley: University of California Press, 1979.

Kirstein, Lincoln. *Ballet, Bias and Belief: Three Pamphlets Collected and Other Dance Writings of Lincoln Kirstein*. New York: Dance Horizons, 1983.

Lott, Eric. *Love and Theft: Blackface Minstrelsy and the American Working Class*. Oxford: Oxford University Press, 1993.

Magriel, Paul. *Chronicles of American Dance: From the Shakers to Martha Graham*. 1948. Reprint., New York: Da Capo Press, 1978.

Malnig, Julie. *Dancing till Dawn: A Century of Exhibition Ballroom Dancing*. New York: Greenwood Press, 1992.

———. "Two-Stepping to Glory: Social Dance and the Rhetoric of Social Mobility." *Etnofoor: Antropologisch Tijdschrift* 10, no. 1/2 (1997).

Marks, Joseph E. *America Learns to Dance: A Historical Study of Dance Education in America before 1900*. New York: Dance Horizons, 1957.

Martin, Carol. "Dance Marathons: 'For No Good Reason.'" *Drama Review* 31, no. 1 (spring 1987).

Mazo, Joseph H. *Prime Movers: The Makers of Modern Dance in America*. New York: Morrow, 1977.

McDonagh, Don. *Dance Fever*. New York: Random House, 1979.

———. *The Rise and Fall and Rise of Modern Dance*. London: Dance Books, 1990.

Moore, Lillian. *Echos of American Ballet*. Brooklyn, N.Y.: Dance Horizons, 1976.

Odom, Leigh George. "The Black Crook at Niblo's Garden." *Drama Review* 26, no. 1 (spring 1982).

Perron, Wendy, and Daniel Cameron, eds. *Judson Dance Theatre: 1962–1966*. Bennington, Vt..: Bennington College, 1981.

Plett, Nicole, ed. *Eleanor King: Sixty Years in American Dance*. Santa Cruz, N.M.: Moving Press, 1988.

Prevots, Naima. *Dance for Export: Cultural Diplomacy and*

the Cold War: Studies in Dance History. Hanover, N.H.: Wesleyan University Press, 1998.

Rubin, Martin. *Show Stoppers: Busby Berkeley and the Foundation of Spectacle*. New York: Columbia University Press, 1993.

Ruyter, Nancy Lee Chalfa. *Reformers and Visionaries: The Americanization of the Art of Dance*. New York: Dance Horizons, 1979.

Schneider, Gretchen. "Pigeon Wings and Polkas: The Dance of the California Miners." *Dance Perspectives* 39 (winter 1969).

Siegel, Marcia B. *At the Vanishing Point: A Critic Looks at Dance*. New York: Saturday Review Press, 1972.

———. *Days on Earth: The Dance of Doris Humphrey*. New Haven: Yale University Press, 1987.

———. "The Harsh and Splendid Heroines of Martha Graham." In *Watching the Dance Go By*. Boston: Houghton Mifflin, 1977.

———. "José Limón (1908–1972)." *Ballet Review* 4, no. 4 (1973).

———, ed. "Nik, a Documentary." *Dance Perspectives* 48 (winter 1971).

———. *The Shapes of Change: Images of American Dance*. Boston: Houghton Mifflin, 1979.

———. *Watching the Dance Go By*. Boston: Houghton Mifflin, 1977.

Spalding, Susan Eike, and Jane Harris Woodside, eds. *Communities in Motion: Dance, Community, and Tradition in America's Southeast and Beyond*. Westport, Conn.: Greenwood Press, 1995.

Stratyner, Barbara. *Ned Wayburn and the Dance Routine: From Vaudeville to the Ziegfeld Follies. Studies in Dance History*. Hanover, N.H.: Wesleyan University Press, 1996.

Stearns, Marshall and Jean. *Jazz Dance: The Story of American Vernacular Dance*. New York: Macmillan, 1968.

Sweet, Jill Drayson. *Dances of the Tewa Pueblo Indians: Expressions of New Life*. Santa Fe, N.M.: School of American Research Press, 1985.

Tomko, Linda J. *Dancing Class: Gender, Ethnicity, and Social Divides in American Dance, 1890–1920*. Bloomington: Indiana University Press, 1999.

Udall, Sharyn R. "The Irresistible Other: Hopi Ritual Drama and Euro-American Audiences." *Drama Review* 36, no. 2 (summer 1992).

Velenchik, Cathy Leigh. "Dancing Their Way through a War: The Effect of the American War for Independence on Colonial Balls." In *Society of Dance History Scholars Conference Proceedings*. Riverside, Calif.: Dance History Scholars, 1986.

Winter, Marian Hannah. "American Theatrical Dancing from 1750 to 1800." *Musical Quarterly* 24, no. 1 (January 1938).

PART FOUR

Contemporary Dance: Global Contexts

Moving Contexts

For a long time American dance departments contrasted traditional or indigenous forms of dance (seen as the study of dance anthropology) with the study of Western theatrical dance, including key modern and postmodern choreographers (seen as dance history or dance composition). Structured by an ethnocentric mindset that saw creativity as the inspired work of an individual artist (the genius archetype), this way of thinking implicitly set up an evolutionary model of history in which dance developed from communal or tribal dancing to professional and technically virtuosic theatrical performances. This model implicitly suggests that sophistication in dance can be measured by the increasing separation (both physical and psychic) of performer from the audience.

Contemporary dance disrupts this tidy paradigm in a number of ways. Nowadays, not only have many indigenous cultures reclaimed lost traditions by creating professional dance troupes which stage ritual, folk, and court dances as elaborate and colorful spectacles, but many choreographers are searching for ways to connect in an immediate and visceral manner to their audiences. Indeed, a number of contemporary experimental choreographers have been working within intimate and diverse venues, staging dances in warehouses and lofts, on piers, by the sea, in gardens, and on city streets. Once-clear geographic distinctions between East and West, or established cultural differentiations between Asian, European, and African modes of behavior, have frayed in the midst of increasingly rapid human and cultural migrations. The readings in this final part of the book help us to see how contemporary dance is negotiating—at times resisting, and at other times stimulating—an increasingly global world view.

Although some government institutions and private foundations would like to believe that the artistic interface of cultures in contemporary societies is a benign example of neighborly sharing (now that the global has become the local), the current venues for the presentation of different traditions can reproduce a number of complex and discomforting colonial dynamics. Like the global capitalist structures that have generated much of the discourse on multiculturalism over the past decade, these institutional frames can gloss over real political and economic differences. Despite these suspect foundations, however, several international festivals of contemporary dance have staged intriguing intersections of cultural bodies and their movements. To further understand the ethical and creative issues at stake in these interactions, let us look at two international performance festivals that took place during the final decade of the twentieth century.

Inspired by a multicultural evangelistic fervor, Peter Sellars organized the L.A. 1990 Festival under the rubric "Peoples of the Pacific." The festival began with an elaborate opening ceremony, an outdoor event billed as an "international sacred ritual featuring Korean shamans, Hawaiian dancers, Australian Aborigines, Native Americans from the Southwest, Eskimos, and dancers from Wallis and Futuna." These dancers were all dressed in traditional outfits, and the sight of so many world dance forms on the horizon with the Pacific Ocean gleaming in the sun behind them was certainly breathtaking. In addition, audiences could see events such as the Javanese Court Music and Dance Company perform traditional works in a non-traditional setting, a collaborative performance of the *Mahabharata* by both *kathak* and *bharata natyam* dancers (many of whom were trained within Indian American communities in the United States), and John Malpede's L.A.P.D. (Los Angeles Poverty Department, a multiracial theater group of homeless people)—all in the space of one weekend. With the notable exception of the American group L.A.P.D., however, most of the performances were restagings of traditional indigenous dance experiences. The audience was treated to a cross-cultural array of dances without needing to interrogate or see beyond the *National Geographic*–like frames in which the dances were often situated.

Moving through representations faster than either MTV or the fashion industry, the performing bodies at the L.A. Festival piled re-representations on top of representations in a virtual tornado of cultural signification. Clearly, many of the performances were meant to celebrate and give visibility to "ethnic" or "traditional" forms of dance. But unfortunately, the overarching frame of the L.A. Festival tended to reinscribe these terms in such a way as to preserve a static notion of interesting yet exoticized "otherness" which would remain safely marginalized within American culture. Although there were many opportunities for master classes and short workshops in which to share the physical experience of these different forms, the L.A. Festival never found a way to address the more complicated issues of aesthetic values, the politics of differing performance contexts, the questions of reconstruction and revolution within tradition, the differences between ritual, communal, folk, and theatrical forms of performance, and the complexity of audience-performer relationships in cross-cultural exchange. Despite extensive program notes and educational opportunities, there was clearly no way one could possibly pin down an "appropriate"—much less an "authentic"—perspective on these performances. We have to ask if, having traveled across the Pacific to this monster of late capitalist art engineering, these "traditional" forms would ever again carry the same meanings, even in their original contexts.

In this moment of global intersection, cultural contexts are rarely stable or knowable containers, and many contemporary dancers are choosing to play with both the formal, more abstract, elements of choreography and the personal sources of their dance training and heritage. This slippage between the lived body and its cultural representation, between what we might call a somatic identity (the experience of one's physicality) and a cultural one (how one's body—skin, gender, ability, age, etc.—renders meaning in society) is the basis for some of the most interesting explorations of cultural identity in dance. Much contemporary choreography takes up and challenges which cultures belong to which bodies. The fluidity of these exchanges can be either wonderfully liberating, or it can work to reaffirm colonialist dynamics often embedded in first world–third world interactions. Although it is of the body, dance is not just about the body, it is also about subjectivity—about how that body is positioned in the world as well as the ways in which that particular body responds to the world.

Festivals such as the Peoples of the Pacific force us to rethink our notions of context, specifically cultural context. Often we think of cultural context as a sort of nest or a home, all warm and cozy and reassuring, from which one launches oneself, like a fledgling bird, into an existential freefall, hoping some kind of "essential nature" will miraculously kick in to save one's cultural identity at the last minute. Rather than thinking of context as a stable object or static (albeit often romanticized) cultural position, we might reconceive the word in terms of its etymology. *Context* comes from the Latin verb *contexere*, which means to join or weave together. The point of this elaborate textual metaphor is to deconstruct our notion of cultural context as simply a colorful ethnic backdrop against which to look at the movements of a dance, and to take up instead a concept of cultural location as an interactive and constantly changing dynamic.

Because it carries the intriguing possibility of being both very abstract and very literal, dancing can frame the dancer's cultural identity differently. Some contemporary choreography focuses the audience's attention on the highly kinetic physicality of dancing bodies, minimizing the cultural differences between dancers by highlighting their common physical technique and ability to complete the often strenuous movement tasks. Other dances foreground the social markings of identity on the body, using movement and text to comment on (indeed, often subvert) the cultural meanings of those bodily markers. Tracing the layers of kinesthetic, aural, spatial, visual, and symbolic meanings in dance can help us to fathom the complex interconnectedness of personal experience and cultural representation so critical to understanding contemporary dance.

Almost a decade after the Peoples of the Pacific L.A. Festival, the Festival Internationale de Nouvelle Danse (FIND) in Montreal dedicated its biannual event to exploring contemporary African dance. Publicized under the rubric "Afrique, Aller/Retour" (oddly translated into English as "Africa, In and Out"), the festival highlighted several creative collaborations between European choreographers and African dancers, as well as a number of North American premieres by contemporary African choreographers. FIND also sponsored a symposium exploring the theme of cultural hybridity that featured talks by dance critics, cultural theorists, and choreographers. The performances in this festival staged two different perspectives on intercultural exchange. In some pieces there was a desire to explore what we might term a cross-cultural pastiche, where two movement cultures inhabit the same stage environment, and yet the traditions co-exist without merging or changing in any fundamental way. In contrast to this collage paradigm, there were other performances in which the dancing was both culturally grounded and an intriguing hybrid at the same time.

For example, *Antigone*, by Mathilde Monnier, a French choreographer, placed five African dancers on the stage with five European dancers. Monnier had visited Burkina Faso in the early nineties and had been inspired to create a dance based on this myth about grieving and the conflict between individual needs and civic responsibility. Interestingly enough, Monnier found that the African dancers were much more comfortable expressing grief publicly than the European dancers, who tended to see intense grief as a private emotion. The effect of this evening-length movement interface was less one of a meeting and exchange than one of channel flipping. Much of the dancing was performed in small groups of two or three, with some extended solos, and the dancers rarely communicated across their own movement traditions. Indeed, eventually the European dancers seemed almost entrapped by their own abstract, angst-ridden movement for movement's sake, especially given the joy with which some of the African dancers moved.

Ironically, it was a collaboration between two of Monnier's dancers that provided one of the most moving examples of a contemporary hybrid of African and European dancing. *Figninto, ou L'Oeil Troué* was created for three male dancers and two musicians by Seydou Boro and Salia Sanon. The performers' dancing encompassed both African-based movements and the idiosyncratic gestures and stillnesses which punctuate a European postmodern dance aesthetic. There were exceptional moments of choreographic beauty when a barrage of fast, tumbling movements would suddenly arrive at an epic stillness, or when the awesome speed of the dancing would shift into a slower, more timeless quality. During his talk at the symposium, Salia Sanon elaborated on his experience working with Monnier. At first, he reported, he didn't like working in silence, or devising his own gestural sequences. Trained in Africa, he automatically thought of dancing in terms of the music. But, he added, sometimes dancers in Africa can feel as if they are only visual accompaniment to the "real" art of music. Eventually, he found a certain expressive freedom in being able to leave the music and explore the possibility of rhythmic and physical stillness.

This kind of global exposure to many cultural forms

of dance as well as the emerging interconnectedness of hybrid traditions marks much contemporary dance at the beginning of the twenty-first century. The essays in the following section chart only a few of the many interesting pathways taken by choreographers across this ever-changing landscape of global influence. We have tried to select readings that present analyses of dance from both the outside and the inside, from a perspective that charts issues of cultural representation as well as one that takes into account the experience of somatic reverberation within dance.

Perhaps it is the conscious acknowledgment and manipulation of the points of intersection between multiple (and contradictory) cultural influences in butoh that has made this dance form so compelling to American audiences. One of the first butoh groups to be presented in the United States was Akaji Marao's company Dai Rakuda-kan, whose performances at the American Dance Festival in 1982 heralded a new genre of contemporary spectacle. *Sea-Dappled Horse* began in the midst of a dark theater. At first the audience was bombarded with obnoxiously loud static. All of a sudden, there was dead silence and then a flash of bright white lights revealed twelve figures standing, arms spread-eagled, in a semicircle onstage. Naked and arranged in crucifix poses, they were covered from head to toe in a white chalky substance. The men's heads were shaved and the women's long, dark hair was frizzed out in unruly manes that framed their gruesome faces. A rope looped from mouth to mouth, held in place by teeth clenched around red cloth. In another sequence, a man on stilts, wearing a stunning, floor-length, and richly embossed kimono, slowly made his way downstage maintaining a deeply solemn focus, while a live rooster, whose feet were tied to his hat, was frantically beating his wings and calling out in a desperate effort to free himself. Teeming with grotesque sexual temptresses and demented authority figures, this dark world cycled through contradictory moments of hopefulness and hopelessness until suddenly the frenzied action was gone, the stage was bare, and the audience was left in stunned silence.

Influenced by both German expressive modern dance and the traditional Japanese theater arts, butoh appropriates performance techniques from these traditions, but radically alters their theatrical contexts to create a constant sense of cultural fragmentation. Even though the resulting images are often dissonant, grotesque, or even violent, however, the performers maintain a deliberate presence and physical integrity—a bodily commitment to the act of performing which practically borders on the religious. Bonnie Sue Stein's article on butoh traces the legacies of early butoh artists Tatsumi Hijikata and Kazuo Ohno, whose diverse styles influenced many subsequent groups. Because she is aware of both the rigorous physical training as well as the performative excesses in butoh, Stein demonstrates how butoh artists negotiate the minefield of split cultural subjectivities, building their own worlds out of the cultural rubbish of the Eastern and Western superpowers. Predicated on a deep physical engagement with the unknown, butoh carries its own kind of inner logic and offers us a view into the moving reality of cross-cultural survival.

Another article that deals with the reality of surviving within a multicultural, multinational, and multicorporate world is Kathleen Foreman's "Dancing on the Endangered List: Aesthetics and Politics of Indigenous Dance in the Philippines." In her essay, Foreman demonstrates the way that Filipino dancing has become a mode of resistance to the massive ecological destruction of forests and mountainous lands within the Philippines by Western-backed industry. One of the central issues is the disputes over sacred lands and the property rights of indigenous peoples. Coming to Manila in order to lobby for their rights, these tribes gather for a final celebration on an outdoor basketball court within the city to share food, dancing, and political strategies. Yet while their dancing can help galvanize a sense of community and support, there are also government and foreign pressures to stage indigenous dancing for tourists as well. Tracing the development of the Philippine Educational Theatre Association, Foreman details how dance becomes a venue for collective action.

Social activism can take on many different guises within the world of contemporary dance and performance. Understanding the social mores that structure much of the gender politics in India makes Ananya Chatterjea's and Uttara Coorlawala's different responses to Chandralekha's choreographic oeuvre all the more telling. Chandralekha is a radical Indian choreographer whose work draws attention to the oppression of women within India. Creating her own hybrid dance style from the mixture of bharata natyam, yoga, and martial forms such as *chhau* and *kalarippayattu,* Chandralekha choreographs dances in which women both embody and overcome the physical victimization so common for women. Both Chatterjea and Coorlawala agree that Chandralekha's work raises consciousness about women's lives in contemporary India. However, they disagree about how to "read" Chandralekha's relationship to historical texts and Indian nationalism. We have included their separate discussions in order to place their readings in dialogue with one another, recognizing that the complexity of meanings available within any one artist's work will inevitably evoke multiple analyses of its artistic, cultural, and political significance.

The next cluster of readings introduces the historical and cultural contexts in which contact improvisation took root and flourished in North America. Cynthia Jean Cohen Bull's essay "Looking at Movement as Culture" traces the shifting cultural landscape which influenced the development of contact improvisation. She connects the casual, released physicality, the use of touch, and the play with momentum and the physics of weight to a cultural ethos of egalitarianism and new trends in social as well as experimental dance in the early seventies. Peter Ryan's case study of contact improvisation in Canada 1974–95 picks up where Bull leaves off, documenting the evolution of the form and its impact on the development of a distinct style within contemporary Canadian dance companies. He likens contact to the Internet, a vast network of possibilities and uses, always in flux. Steve Paxton's short article, "Improvisation Is a Word for Something That Can't

Keep a Name," provides a meditation (by someone who has been affectionately called the grandfather of contact improvisation) on the physical and psychic space of getting "lost" in order to find alternative ways of sensing and relating to the music, movement, or one's own body. Connecting philosophy with dancing and art history, Paxton provides a master's perspective on improvisation as the act of cultural composting.

As we have seen, history plays an important role in contemporary dance. The next two selections address the work of choreographers Jawole Willa Jo Zollar, Bill T. Jones, and the late Arnie Zane. Susan Leigh Foster's "Simply(?) the Doing of It, Like Two Arms Going Round and Round" analyzes several early collaborations between partners Jones and Zane. She looks at their work in light of Zane's passion for photography and the resultant conscious juxtaposition of bodily images. Placing their work within a lineage of modern African American choreographers, Foster documents how their dancing wove different expressive idioms into a new multidimensional physicality. Interestingly enough, while their joint choreography centered on innovative partnering (clearly influenced by contact improvisation) as well as their cultural legacies as a black man and a Jewish man, it never made their sexuality explicit within their dancing.

Arnie Zane's untimely death in 1988 brought Bill T. Jones into another kind of relationship with his work and his identity. In "Embodying History: Epic Narrative and Cultural Identity in African American Dance," Ann Cooper Albright discusses Jones's 1990 epic work *Last Supper at Uncle Tom's Cabin/The Promised Land* as a reworking of Harriet Beecher Stowe's nineteenth-century novel *Uncle Tom's Cabin.* Developing an idea of history as a dialectic retelling, Albright shows how Jones reiterates racist images from American minstrel traditions in order to assert his own historical agency. She then turns to another contemporary African American epic dance, *Bones and Ash: A Gilda Story,* performed in the mid-nineties by Urban Bush Women. In this piece, choreographer Jawole Willa Jo Zollar and writer Jewelle Gomez construct a mythic retelling of slavery's painful legacies in order to recast its history from a powerful feminist perspective.

The final selections in "Contemporary Dance: Global Contexts" comprise a trio of writings on dance and technology. Lisa Marie Naugle's and Richard Povall's short articles both focus on the creative aspects of working with video, computer image processing, and sound technologies that interact with dancers' moving bodies. Rather than seeing machines as effacing the lived body, these artists see technological advances as interactive tools that allow dancers to see movement in a new light. Ann Dils's essay looks at *Ghostcatching*, a specific collaboration between choreographer Bill T. Jones and designers Paul Kaiser and Shelley Eshkar. Dils analyzes our notions of representational mimesis (what do we want a picture of?) and critiques the nostalgia for the "real" thing implied within the *Ghostcatching* opening exhibit and installation at the Cooper Union Gallery in New York City. She asks whether technologies such as *Ghostcatching* have any responsibility to capture the cultural identity or the material realities of the dancing body, or whether it might be useful to transcend those bodily markers completely, creating a hybrid physicality unbound by historical references.

The contemporary dancing documented here is based on multiple fields of exchange—of both movements and ideas. These articles attempt to map out the importance of dancing that is still vital, that captures the imaginations of bodies training and watching, writing and dancing today. We believe that contemporary dance can both recognize and move across cultural, geographic, and aesthetic boundaries, causing categories such as self/other, nature/culture, body/mind, and personal/political to become more fluid. This interconnectedness of dancing bodies within the world can create a transformative model for living in the twenty-first century. Let's make the most of it.

Butoh: "Twenty Years Ago We Were Crazy, Dirty, and Mad"

BONNIE SUE STEIN

The spotlight settles on a flamboyant figure perched on the edge of an orchestra seat. A seventy-nine-year-old man—face and hands painted white, lips bright red—wears an old-fashioned black velvet dress, a crumpled pink hat, and high-heeled shoes. He adjusts his hat, dabs his face, lowers his eyes, and flutters his eyelids. With mincing arms, he becomes the grotesque shadow of a young co-quette. He drapes himself across the edge of the stage in the serpentine curves of traditional femininity, then kicks his foot high like a carefree young lover. To the slow koto music, he skips, flutters, and poses. Finally he smiles, drops one shoulder and tilts his chin like a scared and puzzled child, curtseys, and tiptoes away.

Pierrot at the big top? An old 42nd Street transvestite? No. To the audience at New York's Joyce Theater he is a revelation. To Japan he is a pioneer of contemporary dance. To the world he is Kazuo Ohno, one of the founders of butoh.

Kazuo Ohno, Sankai Juku, Dai Rakuda-kan, Muteki-sha, Min Tanaka, Tatsumi Hijikata, Yoko Ashikawa, Eiko and Koma, Ariadon, and at least forty other soloists and companies comprise *butoh,* the dance genre that emerged during the late 1950s and early sixties from Japan's contemporary dance scene.

Butoh is:
shocking
provocative
physical
spiritual
erotic
grotesque
violent
cosmic
nihilistic
cathartic
mysterious

In the 1860s, "butoh" was used to define dance in general; later it applied exclusively to "ancient dance." The term was also used to describe Western-style ball-room dancing. Butoh was first used in its current sense in the early sixties by Tatsumi Hijikata to describe his rebellious, syncretic performance style. Hijikata first called the style *ankoku butoh,* or "dance of darkness or gloom."[1] The word "butoh" is comprised of two Japanese characters—"bu," meaning dance, and "to," which literally means step. Today, butoh is used to describe both solo and group dances that seem to be taking very different but parallel directions.

There are many elements of butoh that link it to *noh* and *kabuki,* as well as to the other traditional arts of Japan. Most of these links, however, are superficial. Butoh is an anti-traditional tradition seeking to erase the heavy imprint of Japan's strict society and offering unprecedented freedom of artistic expression. After World War II, Japanese artists turned away from the traditional forms—as well as from the West—and asked, "What is contemporary Japanese dance?" There are some visible similarities to noh and kabuki—the white body paint, also used in kabuki, and the extremely slow noh-like movement. But these traditional forms were viewed as archaic, their codified choreography useless to the early butoh improvisers. Zeami, the great noh master, said that facial expression was cheap. Butoh artists disagreed, emphasizing their faces.

Nakajima said, "We found that we were making the same discoveries as noh actors made, using some of the same terminology, but we had never learned those forms."[2] New York–based dancers Eiko and Koma have said that often they are incorrectly compared to noh and kabuki dancers by Western critics, even though they never studied either form. Their most revered teacher is the German Manja Chmiel, a student of Mary Wigman, who Eiko and Koma studied with in the mid-1970s.

Since Dai Rakuda-kan's 1982 appearance in Durham, N.C., Tanaka's 1981 New York performances and workshops, and the inclusion of Sankai Juku in the 1984 Los Angeles Olympic Arts Festival, butoh has become popular with American art world audiences. Butoh's success can be explained partly by understanding trends in postmodern American dance and by appreciating the general "Asian boom" in the West. Japan has long been a great influence on the experimental dance and theater of the West. From Robert Wilson, Peter Brook, and Mabou Mines to Martha Graham, George Balanchine, Laura Dean, and Lucinda Childs, Japanese elements have been used in sets, mise-en-scenes, staging, movement, and vocalization. In the marketplace, department stores like Bloomingdales build extravagant ad campaigns around their "exotic" imports from the East. In the performing arts, American audiences have begun to show an interest in the Japanese forms of kabuki, noh, *kyogen*, *bugaku*, and now butoh.

There is great variety in the imagery of the butoh dancers, but it is always haunting, and of a lasting impression. One does not generally go away from a butoh performance with an ambiguous feeling—you either love it or hate it. Susan Sontag attended Min Tanaka's

Form of the Sky (1985) at La Mama E.T.C. in December 1985. In Tokyo, she had been very excited about his *Emotion* (1985) but was confused by *Form of the Sky*. According to Tanaka, "she was thinking of my last performance, keeping it in her head. She couldn't throw that one away." Sontag returned to see *Form of the Sky* again. Afterward, she spoke to Tanaka at length. "I think she understands it now," he said. What is this butoh imagery about, and why does it have such an impact on Western audiences of the eighties?

The work of these Japanese artists is so thorough and so "Japanese" that Westerners sense a searing honesty. People rarely question the validity of butoh: they accept both the grotesque and the lyrical images. Because butoh is so obviously demanding, spectators who may not like it—who may even feel uncomfortable confronting such intensity—still respect the experimentation and the performance skills required.

Artists who devote their lives to butoh are not unlike noh performers: their lives are rooted in their art. And it is this passionate, focused attention that Westerners respond to. Audiences are drawn in by the direct and raw emotions. I have seen spectators staring with wide eyes, and I have seen them sleeping—which I consider an escape from the spectacle rather than boredom. In Japan, especially at noh drama, a hypnogogic "dozing" is an acceptable way of taking in the performance. This state is a version of "attention" usually not found in the West.

Awake or not, prior to the Tokyo Butoh Festival of February 1985, relatively few Japanese had seen butoh. In Japan, the form suffers from what is called *gyaku-yunyu*, or "go out and come back." Until an artist gains recognition abroad, s/he is unlikely to win approval in Japan.

Kazuko Kuniyoshi says of the Western reaction to butoh:

Western theater and dance has not reached beyond technique and expression as means of communication. The cosmic elements of butoh, its violence and nonsense, eroticism and metamorphic qualities, are welcomed by Western artists because they are forced to use their imaginations when confronted with mystery. Butoh acts as a kind of code to something deeper, something beyond themselves. What is crucial to this code is its nonverbal nature.[3]

The *New York Times*'s chief dance critic, Anna Kisselgoff, compared American and butoh choreographers:

Whether they acknowledge it or not, American dancers and choreographers are still using Martha Graham, George Balanchine, Merce Cunningham, the Judson Dance Theater of the 1960s and other major figures as reference points. They may extend the ideas or idioms of these choreographers, or rebel against them. But they are still working in their shadow. . . . Movement for movement's sake has been the overriding principle for choreographers seeking new directions. . . . They have increasingly borrowed ideas from the minimalist esthetic in the visual arts and in music. . . . Postmodern dance is actually an extension of a general formalist esthetic. Form was content in American dance.[4]

In contrast, she said butoh uses "natural movement and stylized gestures to convey emotional content or human relationships." In other words, butoh's emphasis is on emotional expression. But a swing toward overt content and representation is in the air and part of the reason is butoh.

In the workshop given by Nakajima at the Asia Society in September 1985, the instructor said that "in America dance became too abstract, so now dancers want to add daily activity. I can understand why. They want to recover what dance is." She felt that most of the dance she had seen in America was mechanical and, therefore, not interesting. Butoh is a "bridge between action and narrative with dance movement or choreography."

Tatsumi Hijikata

Lizzie Slater, a historian who recently lectured in Oxford, England on ankoku butoh, has written:

After Hiroshima the young generation of Japan, mauled by the War and the shattering of the past, needed to shriek out. Okamoto Taro returned from Manchuria and urged his fellow visual artists in 1948 "to destroy everything with monstrous energy like Picasso's in order to reconstruct the Japanese art world" and Okamoto went on to state that art must not be beautiful, technically skillful, or "comfortable." Instead, it should be "disagreeable," disregarding easy beauty and known forms of art. The post-war period in Japan was based on the destruction of old values.[5]

In the art world, the rebellion was made manifest in the work of people like author Yukio Mishima, theatrical experimenters like Shuji Terayama, and dancer/choreographer Tatsumi Hijikata. They explored the dark truths that hid beneath the Japanese social mask. Hijikata wanted to uncover the ignored aspects of Japanese society such as deformity and insanity. These were difficult subjects for performance and led to a great deal of controversy regarding the work he presented:

The aim of Hijikata was a direct assault on the nervous system. The Japanese features in art ceased to be reticent and understated and became arrogant and antagonistic. Hijikata began collaborating with Kazuo Ohno in the mid-50's, but the most significant performance Hijikata staged was *Kinjiki* ("Forbidden Colors," 1959) based on a work by Mishima. This piece was presented as part of a series of performances organized by the All-Japan Art Dance Association in 1959. It was a violent spasm of anti-dance: a young man clutches a live chicken between his thighs, in the midst of a brutalizing act of buggery. In the darkness the audience perceives the advancing footsteps of another man, Hijikata advances on the younger man (Yoshito Ohno, the son of Kazuo). There was no music, the effect was shattering. Several members of the Association were so appalled that they threatened to resign. Instead, Hijikata left, followed by others, including Kazuo Ohno. This represented the break from the modern dance world.[6]

Another famous Hijikata production was the 1968 *Nikutai no Hanran* ("Rebellion of the Flesh"). In this performance Hijikata killed chickens on stage. Dancer Ko Murobushi saw this work and decided at once to join Hijikata's studio.

"I went to the hall alone, in a bit of a rush. I came across a horse in front of the entrance, then a number of objects in the foyer by Takigushi [the surrealist who was a very influential avant-garde figure, organizing many exhibitions at the time], Kano, and by Nakanishi [the primary designer for ankoku butoh in 1965, still an important butoh collaborator]. The performance began with a flying model aircraft which crashed into a huge metal sheet at the back of the stage after circling over the audience, screeching with noise. Hijikata appeared, making slow progress through the audience from the back of the hall, as if he were to be crowned. He was muttering, groaning, singing—in some way dancing. In a later scene, he was suspended from the ceiling like a moth, as if trapped in a spider's web. This was not elegant or aesthetic, but wild, vivid, delicate, the intensity overwhelmed me. No one can show, be NOW, as radically as Hijikata. He became dance itself, the Poet of Darkness."[7]

Mishima is said to have wept at this performance, saying, "It's terrifying, this is time dancing."

Postwar Japan was a time for breeding a new code of ethics. To rebel against a failed society was not surprising. The atmosphere was exciting: very unorganized and messy, the kind of confusion that tends to breed either more confusion or acute creativity. Like

surrealism, early butoh used distortions of nature, and like dada, it used chance as a principle of composition. In another early work which Hijikata called *Dance Experience* (1960), he provoked the audience, often creating a dialog with them, confronting them directly from the stage. Improvisation was used by Hijikata, Ohno, Kasai Akira, and others of this early avant-garde. Chance and improvisation contrasted with Japan's balance and order.

Emotional expressionism entered the dances as well. A people humiliated by losing the war, Japanese artists searched for a way to express themselves. If the rest of life were full of hiding, at least the dance should be free. And so the chaos grew. Every convention was dropped. They danced naked, provoked the audience, played deafeningly loud music. Among others, Takaya Eguchi, Ohno's teacher from 1936 until 1947, had traveled to Germany in 1922 to study with Mary Wigman. He and some of his peers later used elements of this German *neue Tanz* such as loud music and dramatic emotional expressions. Ohno and Hijikata followed suit. Other German dancers such as Harald Kreutzberg had visited Japan around 1939 and left their expressionistic mark. Hijikata integrated eroticism, nudity, provocation, and social criticism with other elements of Japanese culture: classical dance, Japanese body postures, pre-war vulgar entertainment, medieval grotesque paintings. From European culture he took inspiration from the paintings of Bosch, Breugel, and Goya, from surrealism, dada, and later, 1960s pop art.

Most Japanese art forms require a sensitivity to the action continued beyond its limits, to the state of the artist as s/he overcomes self-imposed boundaries. Working beyond one's threshold of endurance increases human potential, thereby increasing emotional and physical strength and reaching *satori*. Studying *kendo* (Japanese fencing) in Japan in 1975–76, I experienced this samurai attitude. In kendo, one is expected to participate in the practice long after the body has tired. To continue means to really "learn" something about kendo. The body and mind are exhausted, self-control is abandoned, and there is nothing to interfere with spontaneous learning. I often felt this happening to me. I would become so involved in the practice that I did not notice my tired body. The room—and time—would disappear. There was a great deal of elation following this feeling, and somehow it seemed the only place for growth. This is a key to butoh: working beyond self-imposed boundaries, passing through the gates of limitation into undiscovered territory. Whether the gestures are slow and deliberate as with Muteki-sha, or wild and self-effacing as with Tanaka, the artists share a common driving dedication to the work. The strength of their commitment is an extension of the samurai/never-give-up spirit that has reasserted itself so powerfully in contemporary Japan, evident in the business world as well as the arts.

Hijikata did not perform in public for at least the last ten years of his life. He choreographed several works for Ohno and Yoko Ashikawa, a woman who is said to have had all her teeth pulled in the early days of butoh in order to create more varied and extreme facial expressions. Koma remembers seeing her dance around 1970. He was so moved by her performance that he decided to quit the university and study with Hijikata. When Hijikata, after years of improvising, began to choreograph for Ashikawa, three principles governed his work.[8] First, in contrast to Western dance, he emphasized discontinuity, imbalance, and entropy instead of rhythm, balance, and the flow of kinetic energy. Second, he used traditional Japanese sources for inspiration. Third, he developed the lower body; Japanese proportions are different from Westerners', and Hijikata wanted to create movement specifically for the Japanese body. This has been extremely liberating for Japanese dancers, whose bodies are not suited to Western modern dance.

In 1984, Hijikata choreographed a dance for Tanaka. Tanaka had always worked independently of both Hijikata and Ohno and, unlike most butoh dancers, had never studied with either of the founding fathers. The success of the collaboration weighed heavily on him. Tanaka and Hijikata worked continuously for two months preparing Tanaka's Tokyo performance. They called the dance *Ren-Ai Butoh-ha* ("Love Butoh Sect," 1984), a name which stood for any work they did together. In the program essay for the December 1985 performance of *Form of the Sky*, Tanaka wrote:

> Since Hijikata stung my eyes, I became his son. . . . Hijikata constantly whispers strategy into my ears, and I would like to introduce him to all of you, hardly standing on enfeebled legs.[9]

Hijikata continued to teach and choreograph in Tokyo until his death in January 1986. [At that time], he was planning his first tour abroad—he had always refused to get a passport because he felt that it was not necessary to leave Japan. He resisted any commercial development of butoh and opened his workshops to the public, training anyone who wanted to learn.

Kazuo Ohno

Ohno lifts his skirts slightly above his shapely calf. He takes a small leap forward and lands in a "new world." Arms outstretched, wrists limp, he tilts his head and pliés like a child in ballet class. Later he returns to the stage in a purple fringed scarf and white bloomers. A Cabbage Patch doll is pinned to the scarf, and a large flower is in his hair. He goes into the audience and offers candy to a man, then tosses candies into the air. He exits, and his son enters, looking like a monk in a long, white high-collared silk robe. In contrast to his father, Yoshito Ohno's movements are extremely slow. I am certain that I saw his ears move as he approached the soft blue light.

Ohno has an immense wardrobe boasting an array of gowns for all occasions. During a recent trip to New York, he purchased an exquisite off-white satin beauty, circa 1890, with puffed sleeves, a high collar, and a four-foot train. At home, he tried on the dress and immediately began to dance. He looked like an old bride whose groom left her waiting at the altar.

Ohno's peers and former students refer to him as a god. He exists for his dance and constant research.

35a and b. Kazuo Ohno, in his tribute to the dancer La Argentina, *Admiring La Argentina* (1977), performed at the Joyce Theatre in November 1985. Photo 35a copyright © Linda Vartoogian; photo 35b copyright © Jack Vartoogian, 1985.

Ohno is a philosopher and loves to talk about dance and his past and to describe his previous performances, both analytically and physically. He writes every day, composing essays with such titles as "What Is a Lesson," "A Rehearsal Scene," "The Encounter with Argentina," and "The Will."

At home, Ohno teaches two days a week in his Yokohama studio. But most of the time he is on tour, dancing and distributing his essays. *Admiring La Argentina* (1977), his most famous work, has been per-

formed in Europe, Israel, North and South America, and Asia. When performing this dance, Ohno feels that he is La Argentina, the famous Spanish dancer he first saw in 1929. In *My Mother* (1981), he becomes his mother, the other great woman who has influenced his work. Other major influences cited by Ohno are his teacher Takaya Eguchi, collaborations with Hijikata, the Japanese avant-garde experimentation of the 1960s, and his deep Christian beliefs.

In *My Mother*, Ohno skips, jumps, lies down. His

metamorphic face and body display a multitude of emotional expressions. There is a lyrical yet pitiful quality to his "mother," as he dances the dance of a tragic clown. Marcia B. Siegel described her reaction to his 1985 appearance at New York's Joyce Theater:

> The 79-year-old performer is waging an intense physical competition, a wrestling match where he gets so intimate with death that he sometimes acquires his adversary's face.[10]

Ohno's performances are structured improvisations. Although he never does exactly the same movements twice, he works from the same inspiration. He does not feel that there is a separation between life and dance. As Eiko said, Ohno "does not commute."

Ohno wrote about improvisation:

> The empty stage, the bare stage you appear on, without any preparation, does not mean that it contains nothing. . . . The vacant space is gradually being filled and in the end, something is realized there. . . . It may be the kind of thing that takes a lifetime to learn—in my case I instantaneously knew the fact that the empty space actually was filled and I danced in joy and excitement.[11]

Ohno feels that he is blessed, fortunate to be able to dance.

The first large butoh festival in Japan was held in February 1985. National Television (NHK) televised the two weeks of sold-out Tokyo performances. Among the performers were Ohno (directed by Hijikata), Kunishi Kamiryo, Tanaka with his group, Maijuku, Dai Rakuda-kan, Dance Love Machine, Teru Goi, and Biyakko-sha.

Hijikata's words of warning to Nakajima prior to her 1984 European tour appeared in her program notes:

> We are surrounded by a mass of tricky symbols and systems. . . . Modern people are aware of the dark uneasiness in front of their eyes . . . but we shake hands with the dead, who send us encouragement from beyond the body. This is the unlimited power of butoh. . . . In our body, history is hidden . . . and will appear in each detail of our expressions. In butoh we can find, touch, our hidden reality—something can be born, can appear, living and dying at the same moment. The character and basis of butoh is a hidden violence. It is a filthy child who has the special ability for butoh—because he knows how to create beautiful patterns. Butoh should be viewed as enigmatic as life itself. I am not sure in the end whether it is a trap or a secret correspondence with something.[12]

Butoh has progressed in a variety of directions since Hijikata and his peers began experimenting in the 1950s. At a September 1985 butoh workshop at the Asia Society, Nakajima said, "Twenty years ago we were described as crazy, dirty, and mad—and now we have a passport."

Tatsumi Hijikata (1929–1986)

On 21 January 1986 Tatsumi Hijikata died of liver cancer in Tokyo. He was fifty-seven years old. A founder of butoh, a term he began to use in 1963, Hijikata touched every butoh dancer/choreographer, in some way. He was the "charismatic center, the artistic force, the inspiration" for butoh, said historian Lizzie Slater.

"A big loss, big loss," said Ellen Stewart, who had planned to bring him to America for his first visit in 1986.

Among the dancers/choreographers who acknowledge Hijikata as Sensei (master/dancer) are Ushio Amagatsu of Sankai Juku, Akaji Maro of Dai Rakuda-kan, Natsu Nakajima of Muteki-sha, Min Tanaka, Yoko Ashikawa, and, although more than twenty years his senior, Kazuo Ohno, who depended on him to refine every work he created.

Hijikata provoked and manipulated his students, pushing them to be individuals and find their own personal expression. Tanaka said, "Kazuo Ohno is a god and Hijikata is the devil."

Notes

1. The source for much of my historical data is Kazuko Kuniyoshi, *An Overview of the Contemporary Japanese Dance Scene,* Orientation Seminars on Japan, no. 19 (Tokyo: Japan Foundation, 1985).

2. All quotes, unless otherwise noted, are from interviews conducted by the author in 1985.

3. Kuniyoshi, *An Overview of the Contemporary Japanese Dance Scene,* 6.

4. Anna Kisselgoff, "Dance That Startles and Challenges Is Coming from Abroad," *New York Times,* October 13, 1985, H14.

5. Lizzie Slater, "Investigations into Ankoku Butoh," unpublished manuscript (1985), 1–2.

6. Ibid., 2.

7. Ibid., 4.

8. Kuniyoshi, *An Overview of the Contemporary Japanese Dance Scene,* 3.

9. Min Tanaka, "I Am an Avant-Garde Who Crawls the Earth: Homage to Tatsumi Hijikata," from the program notes for *Form of the Sky,* trans. Kazue Kobata (1985).

10. Marcia Siegel, "Beating Back the White Noise," *Village Voice,* December 17, 1985, 114.

11. Kazuo Ohno, "A Rehearsal Scene," *Drama Review* 30, no. 2 (T110) (1986): 10.

12. Tatsumi Hijikata, "To My Comrade," from the program notes of *Niwa* by Natsu Nakajima, trans. Natsu Nakajima and Lizzie Slater (1985).

Dancing on the Endangered List: Aesthetics and Politics of Indigenous Dance in the Philippines

KATHLEEN FOREMAN

Circles of dancers wheel, pulse of percussion, chanting voices rise to the sky, tribal finery jingles, rhythm of precise footfalls, uniting with the earth.

For Western Canadians these images may evoke the sights and sounds of summer powwow dances: Traditional, Fancy, Chicken, Round. On recent trips to the Philippines, I was invited to tribal gatherings where indigenous dancing, music and oration are also the catalysts of celebration. Suddenly I saw my prairie experiences within a global context of indigenous dance cultures and their universal struggles.

At one such event, on an outdoor basketball court in Metro Manila, I meet with Jack Yabut, director/choreographer of the Philippine Educational Theatre Association (PETA) dance collective. We arrive early at about 7 P.M. and already the humid night air is velvet thick. Tribal guests gather in groups around the edge of the concrete court, talking and sharing an evening meal, while the urban participants arrive and pitch in to transform the athletic arena into a makeshift performance space. As the organizer, Yabut's duties include fixing the lights, introducing the tribal elders, MC-ing performances by Manila-based singers and musicians and dancing with his company.

On-stage and off, Yabut talks about the marginalized state of tribal peoples, expresses solidarity with their struggles and elaborates on the dance cultures that are so integral to their way of life. He is not a tribal Filipino. Rather, he was born and raised in Ma-

nila, a city of ten million people, its pace far removed from the mountains and tropical forest homes of his tribal guests. He is, however, deeply connected to their fight for survival. As a dancer and cultural researcher, he journeys to remote areas, spends long stretches of time in indigenous communities and learns about their lives and dances.

Comprised of over seven thousand islands, the Philippine archipelago is filled with dance. Including over forty ethnolinguistic groups, the population of the Philippines reflects an eclectic array of cultures. The original tribes of the area were a mix of Indian, Indo-Chinese, Indonesian and Malay peoples. Colonizing influences combined a mix of Spanish, Chinese, Japanese, European and American. First colonized by the Spanish in the 1500s, the aboriginal peoples were introduced to Hispanic folk dance through the spread of Christianity. During community religious celebrations, tribal and folk traditions slowly combined with Hispanic dance forms, a process that took place over several centuries. The colonization of the Philippines was administered through Mexico, and there are similarities between the folkloric dance traditions. Throughout the four hundred years of occupation by Spain, indigenous groups living in the most remote environments managed to retain their religious beliefs and way of life through limited contact with colonists and missionaries.

The Americans first liberated the Philippines in 1899 during the Spanish-American War and then again during World War II from the Japanese. Their extended presence resulted in a political/military occupation and cultural invasion. Dance groups brought over to entertain American troops first left Afrocuban and ballroom dance influences, then later styles associated with rock-and-roll in the fifties. Beginning in the sixties and continuing through to the mid-eighties, the ruling Marcos family, renowned for their love of Western culture, imported ballet and modern dance companies from Europe and America to perform in the newly constructed Cultural Centre of the Philippines. Manila-based dance companies that blended folkloric forms with the imported Western forms produced what came to be known as Filipino Dance Theatre, what one researcher describes as an "infusion of ballet and modern dance with folk themes and styles." During the time of the Marcos administration, remoteness no longer ensured the protection of indigenous peoples. The push to develop the natural resources of the country, heavily backed by Western business interests, placed the remaining tribes on an "endangered peoples" list.

On the basketball court, two dancers from the southern islands step into the light as the gongs settle into a tiered rhythm. The men are barefoot and crouched low, circling to the pulse of the music, machetes held ready. "The image is of the warrior coming to protect a well spring," says Yabut. "Break it down into movement and you can see all the thrusts and blocks and swings. It's a system of fighting but it's a dance with music. The dancers are really in full concentration, trance-like. If they touch each other, the audience laughs—it's a mistake. The skill is to keep on moving and twirling around each other with a shield and sword but not to touch each other."

Yabut describes the Warrior Dance as a form of *Kuntaw,* the Philippine martial art form that is danced to music made by gongs or drums during social gatherings like reunions, weddings or festivals. There are two forms of *Kuntaw—Lanka* and *Bunoan. Lanka,* danced solo, demonstrates versatility and agility; *Bunoan,* meaning to spar or train, is danced in pairs with physical contact and striking and blocking techniques. In the early 1900s, an American army officer described a northern variation of the Warrior Dance as a simulation of fighting: "Everything was light, graceful, agile and quick; leaps forward and back, leaps sideways, the two combatants maneuvering one around the other for position. It was hard to realize that human motions could be so graceful. Then head-knives were drawn, and cuts right and left, cuts at every part of the body, were added to the motion; the man on the defensive making suitable parries with his shield."

Beyond the court, the tropical night air is filled with city sounds. A pool of light and music embraces the circle of dancers, musicians and viewers, seeming to transport us to another time and place. The tribal elders have not gathered in Manila purely for a cultural exchange and celebration. They came to talk to the government, again, about issues that affect their physical and cultural survival. The talks are not as successful as they had hoped. Tonight's festivities, on the eve of their departure, are a chance for both the tribal guests and the Manila support group to come together on a social level. Despite the music, dancing and inspirational oration, there is an ever-present political shadow over the gathering.

"The tribes came together because their lives are endangered," says Yabut. "Whether it's a logging concession, a mining concession, a monocrop plantation, a military base, a subdivision or a fish pond under Philippine constitution, there is no clause that gives recognition to ancestral domain, only for individual ownership of land. For example, the issue of the Mount Apo geothermal plant: for many tribal communities, the mountain is a sacred place so to drill holes there is like drilling a hole in your own cathedral or church.

"Would the Catholics allow that? If we drilled holes into the Vatican? No. It's not a question of development. It's not a question of technology. It's not a question of progress. It is a question of respect. I asked the elders why they chose to do the Warrior Dance. They said, 'So that you can tell other people that there are some things that we will not take lying down. We are ready to fight.'"

The Warrior Dance starts the evening with a show of strength. Then the elders discuss the results of their meetings with the government and I am struck first by similarities to the situation of Native Canadians and secondly by the urgency of the plight of the tribal Filipinos. The Canadian treaty and reserve systems grant some Native peoples a land base but land claims are ongoing. In some cases, like the Oka crisis (1990), the dispute over plans for a golf course on a sacred burial site escalated into an armed standoff. This kind of military intervention is relatively rare in Canada.

In both countries, governments target indigenous lands as prime development areas for mining, hydroelectric or logging projects. In the Philippines, however, any resistance to the government's development initiatives elicits military response to ease the progress of the mining or logging companies. Indigenous communities are under military occupation, which results in the disruption of economic, social and religious practices. Concessions for land use paid to indigenous groups are minimal, local workers are not hired, and the misuse of the land destroys food production and traditional economies.

Aboriginal resistance to development has resulted in the "total war" policies of the Marcos and Aquino governments. Militarization forces these communities to flee their lands in order to save their lives; they are refugees in their own country, unable to return home, make a living, educate their children or practice their lifestyle and spiritual traditions. Physical dislocation, psychological trauma, poverty and disease are the lot of these homeless people, and the threat of ethnocide is a daily reality.

The displacement of tribal groups has had a major impact on their cultural traditions. "These dances are not done as a performance art," says Yabut. "They are done as part of the life cycle of the community: a healing ritual, a death ceremony, a harvest or a celebration. It is a living culture. They are involved in creating new songs, new dances, in response to their actual living conditions. But the situation is no longer their natural situation; they're in a crisis. These dances are endangered because of

invasion from outside. There are some cases where tribal people are told to restage something of their culture because visitors are sponsoring an event. And it's normally not done in that way. [They say] 'OK, we'll do it, just to satisfy them so that there is no trouble.' They don't want trouble. It is being brought to them."

When all the positions have been clearly stated, the gongs start up again and a man and a woman enter the performance space. A small square scarf is draped over their shoulders; their bodies are erect, arms near their sides, wrists turned upward, palms open. They smile at the crowd as they circle each other, dancing on the beat, heels lightly pounding the ground in small mincing steps. In a village setting, the Welcome Dance would gather the community together to greet visitors. The scarf is placed upon your shoulder as an invitation to join along. The more people dance, the more scarves are exchanged until everyone is dancing together. Here, the gongs continue to weave their endless patterns as tribal and urban Filipinos dance together. Alternating performances by both groups, the evening continues with songs, poems and more dancing.

Many of the Manila-based artists performing tonight are associated with PETA, an independent theatre company and school that was founded in 1967. Based in Manila, PETA maintains a network of over four hundred partner groups spread throughout the islands. Struggling to overcome hundreds of years of cultural erosion due to colonization, PETA's primary aim is to develop and promote a national Filipino consciousness and grassroots social change through the arts. Currently, it supports the Kalinangan Ensemble, the dance collective, the children's theatre collective, a television and film production unit and a theatre school.

I ask Yabut about his own dance background and how he became involved with the indigenous peoples and their dances. "My mother is an arts educator," he says. "Every time she would go out on assignments, she would bring something—nose flute or gongs from the provinces—to make us appreciate things that are Filipino. That's part of my influence. I did not want to join formal classes in dance. In Manila, all the classes were ballet or Hawaiian, jazz and folk dances that were kind of Western-looking."

Yabut joined PETA in 1976 as a student and remembers that its approach even back then was interdisciplinary. "It was very integrated: visual arts going into music going into movement. I remember teachers exposing us to Filipino martial arts and creative dance movement. Dance is one of the sources of our culture—taken from north to south, there are thousands of dances. In PETA we believe that the dance collective will enhance the skills of our actors to develop body movement as an additional language and instrument."

In the early 1980s, Yabut was working for PETA in Mindanao, the large island at the southern tip of the archipelago. Creating theatre performances with the urban poor, he was exposed to tribal Filipino cultures and their political situation. Rethinking the focus of his own cultural explorations, he returned to Manila and began to align his work more closely with his heritage. "I had to look back not just in terms of what the Americans and Spaniards taught us but at our culture, traditions, literature, dances and music even before the Spaniards came. I had to look back at least four hundred years."

In 1989, Yabut organized a research project focusing on indigenous dance and music of the southern Philippines. The purpose was not just a gathering of music and steps but rather to investigate the relevance, function and importance of the traditional music and dance within the present situation. "If it is dead, then it is dead," says Yabut. "If it is still alive, fine, then what is alive in it?"

Tribal Filipinos, once among the most studied people in the world on the assumption that their days were numbered, no longer interest academics to the same degree. Increased militarization in the area and eroded traditional lifestyles have slowed the influx of the professionally curious. Because of this history, it took Yabut a long time to gain their trust. Some elders were suspicious of his motives and concerned about his possible political associations. One explained, "Before you, there were in my last count twenty-two re-searchers who came and left and they haven't done anything. How can you say that you are any different?"

Yabut acknowledges this history of cultural abuse. "All these people would tap indigenous sources and then make a book, an exhibit, a production, make money out of it," he says. "Nothing goes back to the community. If there is any chance for a person from the community to see it, it's often transformed beyond recognition, beyond acceptable sensitivities or sensibilities." After a year, tribal elders were convinced that he really was a theatre artist and that his research proposal had some merit. Eventually, he was invited to an internal refugee community where the Native people were living on the sanctuary of church property and could not return to their original lands.

In recounting his experience there, Yabut simultaneously describes and dances to help clarify the intentions and qualities of the movement. "The elders welcomed us into their homes. They played the gong and it was a call to the community to come together, see the visitors and present their hospitality and dance together in a welcoming dance. The gong is much bigger and tied to a rafter of a house. One form of their culture is a vocal tradition, the chant. It is the same melody pattern that was taught to them by their grandparents, but the content is different."

"If you translated their words, they were saying, 'Who are these people? Are they any different from the people that we have run from? Our elders say that we can trust them, we trust our elders, we hope they will not disappoint us.' They would gather people and play the gongs and instruments with us or show us, teach us the dance itself. They also shared what they call social dances. A man and a woman dance a kind of courtship dance, but the code of conduct is that there is no physical contact. They dance close to each other trying to create symmetry. Not to make movements that are identical but to always create different movements and patterns that are interwoven."

Yabut is on his feet, using the square scarf held out in front by two corners. His gaze drops shyly as he sings the gong rhythm softly to himself, his body weaving delicately as his footfalls keep the beat. Demonstrating the male role, he drops into a crouch for an instant, then straightens and tilts his head to illustrate the woman's posture, the transformation complete.

Switching gears, he begins to dance some of the hunter dances of the various tribes. Depending on the home environment, different animals are represented through movement. One moment, he is soaring as an eagle of the northern tribes, body erect, arms outstretched at an angle, fingers lifted as wing tips, head and gaze shifting abruptly, feet smoothing the earth. The next instant he returns to the southern rainforest, drops to the ground in a monkey-like stance, leaping wildly, with great speed, twirling, his facial expressions completing the illusion.

Back on the court, tribal and urban participants mix music and dance with socializing. City time is replaced by the flow of communication unbound by watches or schedules. Yabut circulates to confirm that everyone has shared what they intended, then he rounds up the half-dozen dancers from the PETA collective to present the final performance of the evening. Dressed simply in loose trousers and dance wear, the barefoot dancers line up at one end of the performance area. For the first time that evening, there is no music and, because of the lateness of the hour, the throb of Metro Manila has subsided.

The dancers begin to cross the space, cautiously moving through an imaginary rainforest, watching the canopy above their heads, lifting their feet, single file, machetes clearing a trail. It's a simple story, danced with a blend of interpretive and traditional movements. Suddenly, the roar of bulldozer, chain saw and machine guns disrupts the calm. Terrorized, the dancers flee the intruders. Angular bodies move as if torn in all directions; they are lifted and thrown, in a physical representation of the forest's destruction. Afterwards, people regroup and huddle together; the mood is one of sadness and confusion. As they look out at the forest, a woman rises from the ground and begins to sing a sorrowful lament to the trees. Her song stirs the others to move. I watch as modern dancers articulate ancient movements. For a

moment, they recreate the age-old balance as people and forest become one. As the dance fades to stillness, the circle of observers catches a collective breath in a moment of recognition and despair. Then whistles, cheers and applause charge the night air.

People disperse amid thank-yous and good-byes and Yabut begins to dismantle the temporary dancing arena. As with powwows in Canada, I feel privileged to have witnessed an indigenous celebration. The struggles of the endangered tribal Filipinos now are real to me, and the parallels with the Canadian indigenous situation are unsettling. In his research, Yabut set out to investigate the relevance of traditional dance cultures in the troubled reality of an endangered people. What he found was that, in the extreme situation of the Philippines, dance and politics are inseparable. Dance is the connection to ancient ways of life which define them as a people. They are dancing for their lives.

The music of the gongs echoes through my body; it's very quiet as the last of the equipment is loaded into a van. I ask the exhausted Yabut one last question about the application of his research to the work of the PETA dance collective. "Number one, it's always a source of inspiration," he says. "Secondly, it is a vehicle for the audience to understand what the situation of the tribal peoples is and then see how normal they are: they have their own values, behaviours and set of aesthetics of sound, colour and movement that are different, not backward or primitive. They are not specimens. They are not objects of art. They are not sources of revenue. The commitment that has evolved because of my going there and meeting these people has produced even more responsibilities. Now I am the PETA liaison to the Congress of Tribal Peoples in the Philippines, an inter-tribal organization from the communities nationwide. The work of the dance collective becomes a human experience, not an academic activity or just studio work. There are things that are not seen in the steps but are meant by the history of the steps, by what the dance means as a whole. That is the essence of a dance culture, a celebration that can open the door to the life of a people.

Chandralekha: Negotiating the Female Body and Movement in Cultural/Political Signification

ANANYA CHATTERJEA

The lights coming up from downstage left pick up a group of six women edging their way onto the stage from the diagonally opposite corner, their spines collapsed forward from their pelvises, backs jutting out to emphasize the broken line of the spine, knees flexed low, feet weighted to the ground, arms lying stiff and lifeless at their sides, but their heads still reaching searchingly forward. With their broken backs, they move painstakingly, slowly: the heel of one foot rises almost imperceptibly and drags the foot forward, the sole ever unable to dissociate itself fully from the ground. The weight shifts forward with this arduous endeavor as the body resigns itself onto the forward foot. Now the heel of the other foot rises in a barely visible movement and drags the foot, yet unable to lift itself from the ground, forward. The weight shifts one more time and another step is inched on. And again, the heel of one foot rises almost imperceptibly and drags the foot forward and another step is inched on. Each step speaks of weariness and pain, and a quest in spite of that. One by one, the feet pull themselves forward and haul the body across the stage in this terrifying, weighted effort. Halfway across the stage, the women are halted in this journey as if by some unseen attacker looming large in front of them. Acknowledging their arrested pathway, they begin to retrace their steps. One more time, their backs flexed over, the women drag their broken bodies across to the corner they came from, still searching for their spines, questing for recovery. One more time, the feet disengage themselves from the ground and shuffle back, pulling the body along. This relentlessly repeated walk of silently searching women, inexorably covering the stage from corner to corner, gives the impression of an arduous exodus every step of which must be labored through.

This section from the third part of *Sri*, choreographed by Chandralekha in 1990, where the women move with their backs "broken," creating the image of what happens to women under a patriarchal regime—of how, with their spines broken at base, their voices lost, their bodies weak, and rid of their will to protest, they survive in total submission—lasts only about six minutes. But, in the unremitting cruelty and tension it builds up, it seems interminably long. It is followed by more images of the humiliation and degradation attendant upon women in their contemporary society. As the women are gradually able to raise their backs upright, they continue to move, still huddled together in groups, in defined directions. But, in a unison movement, their heads turn over one shoulder, and they direct the pupils of their eyes back to a certain point in the darkened auditorium. No other feature of the face moves, but the sheer power of that directed look, multiplied manifold by being mirrored in the six pairs of eyes, spells the terror of pursuit and the possibility of assault. It is not safe to speak out yet.

In this essay, I will analyze sections from dance pieces created by Chandralekha, a contemporary choreographer working out of Madras, India, to comment on the unique, embodied sociocultural-political critique in her work. It is as if the body, and particularly the female body, negotiates its way through a complex network of existent values and situations to signify resistance to, and criticism of, hegemonies and oppressions with which life conditions in contemporary India are ridden. I have chosen to focus on the work of Chandralekha not only because of the striking aesthetic that is bodied forth in this critical commentary, or because of the depth of intellectual discourse that is uniquely realized in the materiality of the practice. Chandralekha's work merits special attention also because, while her work critiques existent performance conventions, it is born out of a very re-envisioning of traditions, and because, in this amazing reconceptualization of traditional movement bases which are then used to comment on contemporary life conditions, she gives a new lease on life to the creative development of Indian dance.

It will be helpful, at this point, to specify the context in which Chandralekha works. Originally trained in, and an exponent of, the classical dance style of *bharatanatyam,* Chandralekha is better known today as a contemporary choreographer from India, who works innovatively to rework her classical heritages and to choreograph unique, generally evening-length pieces. Chandralekha is also widely known for her involvement in, and pioneering work with, the women's movement and with other left-wing political movements. At this point of time, she is the artistic director of the Chandralekha Group, a company which, more often than not, is composed of more female than male dancers. The dancers are usually trained in classical Indian dance, particularly bharatanatyam, and in yoga. Chandralekha also works with some dancers who are trained in specific movement forms and performance and martial arts traditions such as *kalarippayattu* and *chhau,* which fall outside of the classification of "classical dance." Chandralekha's audiences are diverse and both national and international, and the company spends a large part of the year touring both within India and outside of it. This is perhaps indicative of the quality of her work and its ability to reach widely different audiences despite its location in a particular Indian/South Asian frame of reference.[1]

The methodology used in this research involves movement analysis based primarily on observations made during live performances and some re-viewings of the same pieces on videotape. I have also observed rehearsals, interviewed Chandralekha, and spoken with several of her dancers, and some of her collaborators, including Sadanand Menon, who is involved with her projects as lighting and/or set designer. Most of my quotations of Chandralekha's words are taken from these interviews with her, which were often continued through letters or phone conversations, and are specified as "personal communication." Other quotations and impressions about her ideas and work are gathered from published interviews or articles written by her. I have tried to intercut this anthropological mode of data collection with a more performance/cultural studies orientation in my analysis and interpretation, so that the performative event is viewed largely in the wider social-cultural-political-economic context, as cultural production. Further, in keeping with Chandralekha's own approach and my own belief in the inseparability of artistic creation and personal politics, my perspective is informed by an inquiry into the politics that inform the artwork. My analysis and interpretation, while informed by Chandralekha's philosophy and ideas and discussed with her, and contextualized by my own familiarity with the sociocultural climate in which she works, are my own.

There is not space here to elaborate on the varied contexts of oppression that are resisted in Chandralekha's work. However, as the analysis of specific movement sections will show, exposing the horror and violence in women's lives is an important motif in her artistic and activist work. For instance, I have referred to the embodiment of the terror and humiliation that dogs the lives of women in *Sri.* However, if anything, the piece rejects a tragic and pathos-laden picture of women's victimization. Within each of these sequences, there is a constantly emphasized pattern of resistance in the midst of utter humiliation. The women fall, but they pick themselves up again and again. Their backs are surely broken, but they reach towards recovery. It is as if Monique Wittig's following thesis about the relationship between the fact of oppression and the recognition of its presence is brilliantly embodied and dramatized. In her essay "One Is Not Born a Woman," Wittig argues that:

> When we discover that women are the objects of oppression and appropriation, at the very moment that we become able to perceive this, we become . . . cognitive subjects, through an operation of abstraction. Consciousness of oppression is not only a reaction to . . . oppression. It is also the whole conceptual reevaluation of the social world, its whole reorganization, with new concepts, from the point of view of oppression . . . call it a subjective, cognitive practice.[2]

Sri is permeated with a similar consciousness. In this piece, Chandralekha reworks the history of the Indian societal structure and the condition of women who live within the system, and casts it in terms of the body and movement. The progression from a social structure where male and female powers are matched and accorded similar respect to a situation of increasing domination over women culminates, however, with a powerful move towards reclaiming of lost strength. In this, the piece looks towards an epistemological overthrow, to a situation where the very structures of knowledge have changed radically. Reminiscent of Homi Bhabha's characterization of "beyondness," a not-here, not-there, but somewhere in a presently unlocated zone, Chandralekha beckons to a space "real-ly" unglimpsed.[3]

Sri, however, is not unique in its deployment of the body in multiple zones of signification—aesthetic, cultural, political: it is typical of Chandralekha's choreography. Later, I will refer to instances from her work to argue that it is in its very location in tradition that the subversive power of her work resides. In fact, it is even through her adherence to the exact dimensions and contexts of Indian classical performance, understood through her own vision, that Chandralekha resignifies herself and the female body again and again against multiple produced narratives, repeatedly blasting the gendered-racialized representations that accrue around the female body.

Indeed, the hallmarks of Chandralekha's choreography are her radical re-envisioning of the classical body of Indian dance and her seamless overlaying of the aesthetic and the political in movement. Disillusioned with the codification of the body in the current forms of classical dance, Chandralekha dissociated herself from the field of dance to work with the women's movement for ten years. When she re-entered the field in 1984, it was as a choreographer-dancer who had fully explored the classical dance idioms that her gurus had made available to her, had relentlessly questioned the meaning of every movement in the contemporary context, had stripped away the adornments and the sentimentality, and had necessarily reconceived the classically trained body in terms of the stark classical delineations of line, space, and time.[4] Moreover, having deconstructed the bharatanatyam idiom to its bases, she worked with those bare classical tenets, combining them with movement forms like yoga and martial art forms like kalarippayattu. Simple movements from our daily repertoire of gestures—the lifting of a hand, the quick turning of a head, the slackening of a tired back—also make their way into the classical base of this idiom as and when Chandralekha needs to expand the movement base to embody experiences unrepresented in the classical movement forms. Thus, in Chandralekha's work, which searches for the forms of the body lurking behind the layers of internalized construction that govern gendered enactment, distant elements of dance idioms are juxtaposed to create a different significance; dance is often dropped away in preference for less stylized versions of movement and martial arts; unhindered by artificial separations of genres, the power of movement is sought to be understood anew. This re-envisioning of idiom, fired with her radical political consciousness, marks the uniqueness of her art. Chandralekha then confronts the bejewelled, smiling, semi-divine *nayika* or heroine of classical Indian dance with a female dancer entirely human, whose body seeks release from the shackles of sociocultural conditioning, whose imbibed inhibitions have been superseded by an understanding of the potential power of the body, and who, resonating with the beauty of her realized strength, sensuality, and spirituality, has discarded the jewels, flowers, and silks. But the minimalist nature of her movement, its rejection of all that is decorative to her, has to be understood as more than a celebration of the ancient concept of *saustabha*—purity of line—and a reconceptualization of bharatanatyam. It is best understood in terms of her exploration of the contextual location of the body and her recasting of its history.

In refiguring a movement base, then, Chandralekha had to work through a complex relationship with tradition. While she rejects the "diabolical smiles" on the vacant faces of today's classical dancers and the pretensions with which the classical dance has become laden, Chandralekha also insists that she is "an uncompromising traditionalist" (Chandralekha, personal communication). Researching little-known texts and prehistoric traditions, she came to her perception that the ancients had always known about the body as the starting point of life. With this understanding, she contests a reading of the Vedic scriptures whereby primacy is placed on the soul, transmitted from body to body through the cycle of rebirths. For her, the body, endowed with multiple energies and powers, stands at the center of the principle of life. This embodied understanding of spirituality is not new to Indian philosophy, or to Indian classical dance, where one of the modes of expressing human love for the divine is through the metaphor of longing for sexual union and erotic fulfillment. However, Chandralekha focusses upon this concept of the non-duality and interdependence of body and soul and explores it as one of the basic aesthetic/philosophical and idiomatic/technical concerns in her work.

The idiomatic refashioning that marks Chandralekha's work is inspired by the mission of renewing the energies inherent in the body, which have been gradually debilitated in the process of socialization. (It is worth mentioning that while Chandralekha is adamant about stating her ideas in terms of "the body," and insists that men suffer similarly shackling conditions under patriarchy, it is my perception that Chandralekha's comments apply more specifically to the bodies of Indian women.) In historicizing the body, and in searching for ancient powers it is imbued with, however, Chandralekha is not locked into a modernist search for origins or for a unitary notion of truth. History is envisioned imaginatively, through an exploration of forms and shapes which are rendered dynamic and three-dimensional, of lines which are charged with energy and mobility, and of the kinesthetic revelation of emotional states. In Chandralekha's conception, the body is an integral part of the cosmos, and the basic position of most styles of Indian classical dance, the *mandala,* is the ultimate realization of this relationship.[5] It is "a holistic concept integrating the human body with itself, the community and the environment . . . a principle of power, balance, stability, of holding the earth . . . of squaring and circularizing the body."[6] In this brilliant conception of the mandala, Chandralekha imbues what has become just a position for many contemporary classical dancers with dynamism and power. With ultimate regard for its classically prescribed dimensions, which provide the starting point for her explorations, Chandralekha proceeds to make it anything but a flat or fixed shape—she upturns it, the feet thrusting up towards the sky; she makes it unstationary, a way of covering space; she takes the principle of opposed but balanced energies, one reaching down through the pelvis, the other reaching up through the spine, and emphasizes it in her versions of the mandala.

It is not only the mandala that is subject to such exploration. Chandralekha had always insisted that the *Natyashastra,* the ancient Hindu scripture of performance, with its conceptualization of the centrality of the body, is "a very modern text."[7] In searching for a movement base she returned to it, and discarding most of the ways in which its precepts have come to be crystallized and treated as lifeless forms, abstracted the principles and ideas, and reinterpreted them in her own terms. In this way, the three basic tenets of classical choreography besides the mandala, the *bhramari* (turns), the *chaari* (walks), and the *utplavana* (jumps) are taken, explored, and reconceived to form Chandralekha's technical base. Bhramaris are aerialized, for instance, chaaris are floored with the body parallel to the ground, floor positions are inserted into utplavanas. Hand gestures, which comprise an entire vocabulary in Indian classical performance, are never used as decorative, but explored more in their capacities to enhance and dynamize forms, to extend the lines of the body, and sometimes, in their classically defined role of signification.[8] In this way, Chandralekha also extracts the principles and technical hallmarks of *abhinaya* (the tradition of dance drama in Indian classical performance)—the use of a detailed repertoire of eye gestures, for instance—but resituates them in an abstract context, not to tell unilinear stories, but to convey ideas.[9]

It is in defamiliarizing and revolutionizing the familiar then, in deconstructing both the classical and the neoclassical modes of Indian dance in spite of its location in tradition, that the subversive power of her work resides. In this, it also implicitly uncovers the power politics of cultural production and reception in national and international arenas. In fact, Chandralekha's work is built out of a core of resistance: resistance to hierarchies of gender, race, caste, class, and state domination, understood in global and local terms. This resistance, which also always reads as a re-creation, marks itself in at least three distinct modes: idiomatically (grounded as it is in the bases of traditional dance and movement forms which are available to her as an Indian woman), choreographically (embodying an exploration of the contemporary relevance of ancient concepts of space, time, and self), and thematically (filtering layers of inherited notions through her painstakingly theorized political consciousness). And in at least these many ways, Chandralekha's work can be understood in terms of a resistive postmodernism which "is concerned with a critical deconstruction of tradition . . . a critique of origins, not a return to them . . . it seeks to question rather than exploit cultural codes, to explore rather than conceal social and political affiliations."[10]

Thus, there is no search for "newness" in her creation of a contemporary Indian dance, but instead a quest for understanding the ancient legacies of the body as they come to be refigured in today's world.[11] Here, where the most radical, the most avant-garde, is based on a recycling and revisioning of roots, past history and present creation coalesce and comment upon each other. Hence, Chandralekha draws on the ancient precept of *Tantra* philosophy and yoga that the spine, along which the *chakras* (energy centers) are located, is the source of the body's strength, to comment on the contemporary degradation of women in Indian society. The comment contains its own looping critique: the image of contemporary women with broken spines in their labored walk challenges the silences of the very past, from which she has drawn, about the suffering women must have endured even then, about the patriarchal hegemonies with which that past is ridden. In the same way, she uses the *sachi* (sideways) look from the classical repertoire of eye gestures to convey a mood unrecognized in the realm of classical dance: women's fear of imminent assault, clearly recognizable in the context of the hideous attacks on the women's movement in contemporary India. The movement sources used by her are thus critiqued, discarded or expanded, and ultimately reborn, in the embodiment of her work.

I will now refer to one of Chandralekha's earlier pieces, *Angika,* to support the above discussion. One of the most important aspects of this work is Chandralekha's effort to recast dance history divorced from the usual sentimentality and religiosity that have come to be regarded as inseparable from it. Thus, while the *Natyashastra*'s delineations of the body and movement were to be valued, Chandralekha insisted on discarding the classical theory of the divine origins of the dance, which shrouded the body in mythology and mystery.

Originating in prehistory, the piece begins with an exploration and expansion of yogic positions, which are practiced not as virtuosic body positions or as demonstrations of remarkable flexibility and balance, but as archetypal and shifting forms which set out the body on an exploration of its own capabilities. This is the beginning of the conscious formalization of movement, the tuning and centering of the body to realize its capacities for line, flow, balance, marking the material origins of the dance. The next sequence, marking the next stage in the history of the performing body as Chandralekha envisions it, explores the principles of the martial arts through movements which integrate the modes of attack and defence, and show the body's progression to develop movements around the concepts of control, balance, coordination, endurance, alertness, lightness, tension, and relaxation. This is followed by a section where the connections between life and work activity and the development of physical artistic traditions become clearer. Drawing one more time on movements from different styles of martial arts and kalarippayattu, the dancers develop walks from their observation of animal movements. These walks are neither realistic imitations, nor are they identical with the more stylized walks later described in the classical scriptures of performance. As they are embodied here, in *Angika,* they are ways of discovering the body and the rudiments of how it operates, of discerning the basic principles of pace, level change, and body attitude, and how they affect movement.

The next sequence moves the piece into the zone of historicity, the Vedic age, when the *Natyashastra* was written. The dancers delineate the development of sophisticated body language, the beginnings of dance, detailed by Bharata, the author of the *Natyashastra.* Chandralekha focusses on the basic elements of the style—she explores Bharata's categorization of movements; his development of repertoires of movements for each body part, all of which can be used to signify variously in different contexts; his refinement of the concepts of body positions, jumps, turns, and gaits into a highly evolved repertoire of dance movements—

all of which define the grammatical base for a classical dance form such as bharatanatyam. Moving on to longer dance units, the dancers perform *adavus,* basic movement phrases of bharatanatyam, with variations of speed, order, and direction. This pure dance *(nritta)* section marks the transition from martial arts and yoga to artistic engagement with the body where aesthetics, not functionality, becomes the prime concern.[12]

It is only fitting that this reference to the development of pure dance should be followed by Chandralekha touching upon the tradition of *nritya* or expressional dance, where dramatic elements (abhinaya) are woven into dance movement. Here, Chandralekha choreographs a scathing comment on the development of the classical dance in a patriarchal society, and the process of commercialization of women's bodies which come to be denuded of the brilliant energies that distinguished the initial development of the dance. Without taking recourse to a simplistic linear narrative, the sequence shows that the energies which celebrated the potential of the body were subverted, fragmented, and ultimately negated, through the socialization of the dance.

> First, the transformation of the body as a vehicle to serve gods, religion, priests. Then, the transformation of the body as a vehicle to serve kings, courtiers, men. The shift of the dance from the temple to the court, of its content from "*bhakti*" (devotion) to "*shringara*" (eroticism), of the focus from the abstract divinity of gods to the concrete divinity of kings. Then the transformation of the body as a vehicle and victim of moralistic society. (Program notes, *Angika*)

The cosmic, martial, and material origins of the dance are thus obscured in the religio-mythical shrouds that are cast over the dance, the art becomes increasingly divorced from real-life concerns and becomes inscribed in a system for the subjugation of women's bodies through the later Vedic ages, the eras of repeated foreign invasions, of colonization, and through the postcolonial era up to contemporary times. In a striking choreographic venture, Chandralekha sets up a stage within the stage, and duplicates the structure of an audience on stage. The two women dance for a double audience: a group of men are seated on either side of the stage, observing the dancers. At one point in the sequence, some of the men turn their focus outward towards the audience, as if to return to them the same scrutinizing and objectifying gaze with which they behold, and have beheld for ages, the performing body of the woman dancer. Chandralekha also improvises on the structure of a *varnam* (traditional abhinaya or dance drama piece in the bharatanatyam repertoire), where the dancer interprets in multiple ways the lyrics of the song that accompanies her, by making the traditionally solo piece a duet danced by two women. More importantly, through an ironic tour de force, she invokes the familiar elements of a classical dance performance such as *pushpanjali* (offering of flowers) and varnam to intervene in and question the institutions surrounding the traditional classical dancer and the systemic support of the appropriation of the dance from her body on the very stage where, and through the very forms through which, she had been appropriated through the colonial and post-colonial years.

The irony is finally heightened in a direct glimpse into the tragic consequences of this history for the dancer herself. The lights focus on the two women who stand huddled together: their bodies are weighted down, held diffidently, shoulders drooping and eyes downcast, bent in gestures of shame. In a vignette that lasts for a few seconds only, we see one woman lowering her head, her neck drooping before herself, while the other woman raises her arms and crosses them to cover her face. Chandralekha's succinct comment points to the violence of a system where, by an unacknowledged slippage, those who are victimized have been persuaded of their own criminality, so that they subsist with complete loss of self-respect, unable to argue for their rights. However, the comment is made in silence and without sentimentality and melodrama: the issues stand out stark and clear for an audience who might prefer to blur them over. The lights black out on this vignette with the dancers still moving.

As if acknowledging the need for resuscitation after this devastating comment, Chandralekha breaks the historical continuum of this piece to recall images from pre-history one more time. This is also the most celebrated sequence from *Angika,* perhaps the most threatening for conservative audiences, choreographed as a collage of images drawn from the ancient pre-Vedic Harappan culture and inspired by Tantric ritual practices. For Chandralekha, these are important sources of inspiration in "reapprising ourselves of the power and potency of the human body—a memory of the past vibrant and alive with images, symbols, cults, rituals" (Program notes, *Angika*). As the lights come up one more time, a man crawls onto stage on all fours. Astride his back, one leg folded in to rest on his back, the other hanging over his shoulder, sits a woman, tall and powerful. This is the *naravahana* image, where the woman rides the man. Though it can be linked to a series of goddess-images in the Hindu tradition where she is portrayed riding on ferocious animals, it remains difficult to read this sequence in religious terms and as a deification of women, particularly because of its positioning in the piece. Also, because of the indigenous traditions from which these images are drawn, where *Shiva* and *Shakti,* the primal male and female energies, are balanced powers, it is difficult to see this as a naive reversal of hegemony. Besides, clearly, the woman is being carried by the man who offers his back as seat of dignity: he is not treated as her victim, nor she as his master.

As she sits atop her human carrier, she uses hand gestures to symbolize the weapons she wields—spear, bow and arrow, sword. She also wields objects more related to cultivation than sophisticated warfare, scythe and chopper. This links her to fertility cults, agricultural traditions, as well as to martial traditions, in which she reclaims her active participation and central role. The remembrance of these images reawakens the originary female energy inherent in women, and we see the coupling of Shiva-Shakti to combat the forces that imperil survival. Importantly, these images are performed without the traditional abhinaya that would accompany the portrayal of any goddess, or without invoking the *veera rasa,* the valorous mood, that might be expected in a classical rendering of a military sequence. This contributes to secularizing the images: the man and woman on stage are just that, and while she is divine-like in her confident power and grace, and reminds us of the goddess-strength in her, her translation from awesome womanhood to goddesshood is difficult.

I would like to conclude with this image where, one more time, Chandralekha celebrates the timeless energies of the woman's body. One more time too, the choreography reveals itself as a celebration of energies which move through and in the body, and as an embodiment of multiple layers of signification. Specifically, this is an image which originates in a reactivation of memory and legacy, working through a performative reimagining of the present, to insist upon a reconfiguration of the political and ideological landscape of the future. Stitching together the prehistoric/past, and the postmodern/future, through the transformative vision inaugurated in the performative now, Chandralekha insists upon an understanding of performance as a space where, and a mode through which, political and personal meanings can be simultaneously resisted and rearticulated.

Notes

I wish to acknowledge the invaluable research of Rustom Barucha on Chandralekha, published in his book, *Chandralekha: Woman, Dance, Resistance* (Delhi: Indus, 1995). While I have not quoted directly from his comments, and while my reading of Chandralekha's work differs substantially from his in some ways, my familiarity with his text may have affected my perspectives and word choices in several places.

1. This is not to effect a slippage between the descriptors "Indian" and "South Asian," but to indicate the commonalities between these identifying categories, especially as they operate in diasporic contexts.

2. Monique Wittig, "One Is Not Born a Woman," *Feminist Issues* 2 (winter 1981): 52.

3. In his introduction to his collection of essays *The Location of Culture* (New York: Routledge, 1994), Homi Bhabha reflects on the peculiar destabilization and shiftiness that characterize the contemporary notion of "post-" or the "beyond": "The 'beyond' is neither a new horizon, nor leaving behind of the past . . . we find ourselves in the moment of transit where space and time cross to produce complex figures of difference and identity, past and present, inside and outside, inclusion and exclusion" (1).

4. Classical delineations of space and time, for instance, are understood in terms of the prescriptions specified in the *Natyashastra,* the ancient Hindu scripture of performance, written between the second and fifth centuries by Bharata Muni. There are, also, very detailed conceptualizations of *angasuddhi* or purity of limb, and *saustabha* or lines of body-in-movement, which govern performance.

5. The mandala is basically defined as a body position. More specifically, it refers to the basic body position from which the dance begins and in which it ends, and in which way of holding the body is encapsulated the aesthetic and idiomatic preferences of that dance form. Compare, for instance, the first position of classical ballet: the mandala in Indian classical dance is defined as strictly, marked by a full turn-out of the hips, a deep flexion of the hips, knees, and ankles, and a fully extended spine above the grounded pelvis. However, each school of classical dance has its own version of the basic mandala which can be regarded as the marker of that style. In bharatanatyam, it is the *araimandi* or *ardhamandala* which is the basic body position. Here, the feet are joined at the heels, though other mandalas where the feet are placed one and a half feet away from each other, or where the feet are placed wide apart, in a stance somewhat wider than the second position of modern dance, are also used. What is typical of the mandala of Indian classical dance, and what makes it different from the plié of classical ballet, is the energy which initiates it: here, the dancer does not go down as a preparation for aerialization, but in order to mark the groundedness that characterizes the dance styles.

6. Chandralekha, "Choreography in the Indian Context," in pamphlet *Indian and World Arts and Crafts* (April 1991): 3.

7. Chandralekha, personal communications with the author 1995–96.

8. *Mudras/hastas* or hand gestures are a vital part of the *angika abhinaya* of Indian classical performance (see below). Each hand gesture has several connotations or *biniyoga,* which are defined according to the context of their use.

9. One of the reigning concepts in Indian classical performance is that of abhinaya—where music, movement, and words are used for the expression of emotions or telling a story. Abhinaya can proceed through several modes: that which uses the limbs *(anga)* is referred to as "angika abhinaya." One of the modes of angika abhinaya is an elaborate repertoire of eye gestures *(drshtiveda)* which can signify variously depending upon the context of their usage.

10. The reference is to Hal Foster's introductory essay in *The Anti-Aesthetic: Essays on Postmodern Culture* (Seattle: Bay Press, 1983), a collection of essays on postmodern culture edited by him. Here, Foster makes a critical distinction between resistive and reactionary postmodernisms: "A postmodernism of resistance, then, arises as a counter-practice not only to the official culture of modernism but also to the 'false normativity' of a reactionary postmodernism." Foster, *The Anti-Aesthetic,* xii. For Foster, then, the primary intent in a postmodernism of reaction is opposition itself, while the intent in a postmodernism of resistance is opposition specifically directed at resisting the status quo and refiguring the concerns.

11. I am referring specifically to the March 1975 edition of *The Drama Review* where Michael Kirby drew attention to the new developments in dance, what he then went on to describe as "The New Dance." While Kirby's is certainly not the definitive view on postmodern dance in America, he is still an influential cultural critic and *TDR* still retains a position of primacy among artistic/cultural journals. Further, Kirby is not isolated in his point of view: this idea of "newness" continues to dominate much popular thinking about "postmodern culture" in America.

12. Classical performance in India can be classified in terms of two broad categories. That part of the repertoire which uses abhinaya is known as *nritya,* which refers to the expressive and dramatic genre of dance and is distinguished from pure dance or *nritta,* which does not have a narrative intent, but is more an exploration and celebration of the aesthetic.

Ananya and Chandralekha—A Response to "Chandralekha: Negotiating the Female Body and Movement in Cultural/Political Signification"

UTTARA COORLAWALA

In her essay on Chandralekha [preceding mine in this volume], Ananya Chatterjea's writing is often brilliant in her ability to identify and summarize key characteristics in Chandralekha's choreographic approach and their complex aesthetic-political signification. In response to her reading of two of Chandralekha's works, *Angika* and *Sri,* dated 1985 and 1992 respectively, I was startled by how glosses and generalized summaries can mislead. When clarified, the same references generate another set of issues that are left out of Ananya's reading (intentionally?), issues which qualitatively change how one might perceive Chandralekha's work.

My response here to Ananya's reading addresses, first, my observations of the actual movement in the described section of *Sri,* and how our differences in observation may result in different significations. Next Ananya's references to ancient Indian texts such as the *Vedas* and *Natyashastra* seem clouded by historical inaccuracies unless she has opted deliberately to re-inscribe a different set of associations upon our gestaltic perceptions of Indian dance. If the latter is the case, then I believe that strategy needs to be acknowledged in the interests of scholarship. Finally, my reading of Chandralekha's departure from standard techniques for expressing devotion differs from Ananya's, for I argue that there are at least two levels of signification in that reading: a monolithic reading where Chandra's work is posited only against the traditional, and an intercultural reading where Chandra's work is

defined against the approach of contemporary Indian dance works and international choreography.

Lest my credentials for intruding on this discourse be questioned, in 1984 when Chandralekha was drawn back to dance to participate in the East West Dance Encounter, I participated in the same event as both dancer-choreographer and artistic consultant in planning the event. I was present in the intimate "Little Theatre" where she spoke of her beliefs and battles and also witnessed the jubilant uproar amid a packed thousand-seat theatre that same evening when we discovered our new choreographer. Indian new dance attracts much larger audiences in India than the classical genres, yet sponsors are far fewer. Since 1984, I have seen all of her major works live, had many discussions with her in private and public forums and followed her career closely. Also, Ancient Indian Culture was my major as an undergraduate at St. Xavier's College, Bombay.

In the opening section (paragraphs 1 and 2), Ananya describes a movement image for the work *Sri,* that the choreographer calls the "drag walk." Ananya's evocative and detailed description refers to images of "total submission," "broken backs," "spines collapsed" and "bodies weak." It is only with this reading of the movement that I differ, and disagree adamantly. In the "drag walk" the back, in fact, is never collapsed. What is "broken" is the line of the vertical body. The back is tautly extended forwards from the hips, and almost parallel to the floor. This near-horizontal line is "broken" by the head which reaches upward, again contra-

36. Drag Walk from *Sri* by Chandralekha. Photo by Dashrath Patel.

dicting the lines of force set up by this agonizing position. The arms are not "lying," they are held close to the torso, and match the intense bound energy of the handicapped but powerful spine.

Maintaining this excruciating position for six minutes is an extreme exercise of strength, flexibility and willpower. It is also an exercise that would be impossible without in some way mobilizing the dynamic energies around the spine. This disturbing vignette cannot be about "weak bodies" or about "total submission." Visually, the position suggests protest and resistance; kinesthetically, it involves dynamic tension and power to such an extent that the strength of the dancers seems awesome.

In 1993, when Chandralekha presented this work in Toronto at the festival "New Directions in Indian Dance," she acknowledged that the choreography had arisen from her own personal body-view of patriarchy. Since Chandra does not conceive of surrender or submission for herself, I posit that my reading that the drag walk is a gesture of resistance rather than of abjection is truer to her intentions. In any case, in my description of the movement, I have focused on actual movement shapes and dynamics and include an illustration.

In discussing Chandralekha's re-envisioning of the body in traditional dance, Ananya states that "she [Chandralekha] contests a reading of the Vedic Scriptures whereby primacy is placed on the soul, transmitted from body to body through the cycle of rebirths." The contents of the *Vedas* (2000–1000 B.C.E.) deal with various aspects of sacrificial ritual, and include hymns that question the human condition and its relation-ship with wondrous natural forces. Unquestionably the meaning of many words in the *Vedas,* particularly the *Rg Veda,* continue to puzzle Indologists and may never be resolved, as these are the earliest Sanskrit texts. It is generally agreed that not until the *Upanishads* and *Brahmanas* (800–500 B.C.E.) does focus shift from questioning immanent experience towards acknowledging and privileging a transmigratory and persistent part of the human being *(atma,* self) over its temporary container, the body.[1] Chandralekha reads Sanskrit, and is familiar with many Sanskrit texts, but as often as I have heard her denounce the neglect of the body in contemporary Indian value systems, I have never heard her associate this with the *Vedas* or "Vedic readings." Further on in the essay, Ananya writes, "The next sequence moves the piece into the zone of historicity, the Vedic age, when the *Natyashastra* was written." Scholars agree that *Natyashastra* was compiled/authored between 200 B.C.E. and 200 A.D.[2] Vatsyayan has noted several references within *Natyashastra,* and in the methodologies it embodies, to Vedic and postvedic Bhramanic and Upanishadic thought.[3] Thus, chronologically speaking, the authorship of the *Natyashastra* cannot be placed within the Vedic period. The claim that is put forward sometimes, that *Natyashastra* is the *Fifth Veda,* is usually said to pertain to its status and is discredited as an indication of the chronological period when it is supposed to have been compiled.[4] Categorizing the *Natyashastra* as *Veda* would place it among the most revered texts/knowledge of ancient times, in the category of revealed wisdom *(Darshana* or *Sruti).* Most *shastra* (manuals, compendiums) are considered part of oral-aural tradition of *smriti,* learned knowledge.

I would also like to point out that, in Ananya's writing, two concepts of time and history are being conflated. One is, of course, the Western concept of the linear progression of time that is documented as a chronology of pre-history and history. The second is the Indian concept of many simultaneous perceptions of time. In addition to linear, cyclic, cosmic structures of time,[5] there is the "Time" beyond time, a primordial, preverbal, pre-"pre" space that is cognized in the mind-heart-body through *pratyaksha,* or direct intimations of its presence. I believe that it is to this that Chandralekha refers when she speaks of reverting to movements and knowledge systems of the body that precede the *Natyashastra.*[6]

Using the historically post-*Natyashastra* language of *tantra,* of physical access points to mystical experience, Chandralekha often speaks of *bindu* as centeredness and as the center of the *mandala*-as-body.[7] She has consistently demonstrated in her performances and lecture-demonstrations that practices generally considered esoteric are not only accessible, but are in fact empowering, especially for women and dancers. This language precedes *Natyashastra* only in the sense that it deals with pre-verbal, pre-conscious processes.

Another point made by Ananya is that "Chandralekha insisted on discarding the classical theory of the divine origins of the dance, which shrouded the body in mythology and mystery." With her own body and perceptions, Chandralekha has creatively explored classical theories of art, the body and human experience. Despite her fiery rhetoric and open criticism of surface and literal interpretations, Chandralekha has not negated the knowledge she received, nor does she discard the traditional. Rather she shifts the focus in her dances to mythic spaces still within traditional thought but outside conventional representation. Instead of narrating the originary myth of the *Natyashastra,* her works explore what the myth actually invokes: macrocosmic activities in the microcosmic human body.

My point here is that Ananya as scholar, and Chandralekha as choreographer, are complicit in what I call the "nationalist agenda." In *Sri,* the choreographer exploits the prehistoric indigenous concept of the body to contest the later concepts of the body that have proved so repressive to sensual experience and to women. By re-envisioning and re-locating the body and the text of the dance in an incontestable indigenous mythic past, both choreographer and scholar can insist that all Chandralekha's concepts of the body are entirely and exclusively Indian, uncontaminated by her knowledge and perceptive appreciation of Western contemporary dance. Writers can then say with dramatic conviction that she resists tradition *exclusively* from within tradition. In doing so, such persons reflect and re-inscribe nationalism with an orientalistic nostalgia for hermetic expressions of isolated Otherness. It goes without saying that, unlike Bharucha, they never allude to Chandralekha's creative collaborations with John Cage and Billy Kluver in 1968.[8] Nor has it been noted that such arguments are invariably put forward in fluent English.[9]

Chandra's use of one historic construct of the body and of being to unseat another construct is undoubtedly subversive and effective. However, it is not uniquely a postmodern process, nor exclusively "Western" nor "Eastern." The dialectical process of revision and re-visions, in Indian cultural history, starts with the *Brahamanas* . . . and goes on and on. . . . In an India that is struggling to grow beyond its colonial structures while still negotiating with Western cultures at large, this claim to source movements from prehistoric indigenous origins bolsters resistance to a long history of not only patriarchy, but also of colonialism as patriarchy, and of interculturalism as a revised form of colonialism.

While I personally have come to share the opinion that this kind of strategy is both necessary and effective in intercultural negotiations, I mark it as a strategy and no more than a strategy. With her recent atomic detonations, India has indicated to the world that she will not tolerate political condescension. This might be a good starting time-place for Indian dancers to consider emerging from their protective armour of nationalistic cultural representation. One would also hope for a reciprocal agreement on the part of Euro-American dance presenters and critics to acknowledge that it is not their right to both demand "Otherness" from the other, and at the same time expect that such representations must transcend cultural differences.

The claim that Chandralekha's work explores concepts prior to the *Natyashastra* resonates with a revivalist fervour not so very different from that of her preceptor, Rukmini Devi Arundale. Rukmini Devi reclaimed a dancing tradition from southeast India, and presented it as the quintessential expression of (pan)Indian culture.[10] Arundale further participated in the discourse that generated the linear mythic construct of the history of Indian dance that is cited by both Chandralekha and Ananya:

> The shift of the dance from the temple to the court, of its content from *"bhakti"* (devotion) to *"shringara"* (eroticism), of the focus from the abstract divinity of gods to the concrete divinity of kings. Then the transformation of the body as a vehicle and victim of moralistic society. (Program notes, *Angika*)

In actuality, that history (of the transformation of *sadir* to bharata natyam) is a complex interweaving of many strands, of levels of performance expertise, of varying degrees of commitment by dancers who located their relationships to dance along a continuum between spiritual self-sacrifice, political or economic negotiations and survival tactics. Chandralekha further shares with her preceptor, Rukmini Devi, her interest in re-presenting empowered female archetypes in her dances and also her use of *Kalaripayattu* (martial movement form from Kerala). However, unlike Rukmini Devi, Chandralekha has consistently denied non-Indian influences in her work.

Even as Chandralekha imaginatively and kinesthetically exploits nationalism in her dances, in her workshops, she vigilantly interrogates patriarchal, national, social and political affiliations. Whereas her successful opposition to hypocrisy and superficial representations is always emphasized,[11] her luminous contribution needs to be placed in a wider perspective. Chandralekha's contribution is far from being a lonely beacon light. Several post-colonial choreographers—Mrinalini Sarabhai, Kumudini Lakhia, Narendra Sharma, Bharat Sharma and Malika Sarabhai, among others—have similarly divorced their dances from Hindu religiosity, while still retaining "Indianness." For many of the Indian choreographers who participated in the watershed 1984 conference, discovering the creative work and existence of others who questioned the classical norms of the day was a powerful affirmation that, indeed, all was not perfect with classical Indian dance. Participants shared similar concerns—speaking the body in movement, the body as friend and teacher, Indian aesthetics, yoga as an empowering practice for performers, investigating early Indian culture, probing the need for and limits of anachronistic performance conventions.

Perhaps Chandralekha differs from her colleagues in her adamant awareness of the political signification of all dance performance and representations of person. In her choreography, she often isolates key movements and concepts from their conventional settings.

She then reframes these images, movements and patterns and repeats each revision relentlessly as if challenging resistant complacent viewers to ignore her statement. She wears her hair long, unbound and snowy white, visually signaling that like the Goddess, as Shakti (power), she cannot be contained by patriarchy or sexuality. She is eloquent, often angry and vehement in espousing her position in all public, national and international forums. Yet, all this has only endeared her to an ever widening group of supporters!

I share Ananya's deeply felt admiration for this artist and especially appreciate how eloquently Ananya has homed in upon the political signification of Chandralekha's choreographic approach. In this response, I only wish to draw attention to historical and descriptive inaccuracies and how they may qualitatively change the readers' experience of the work. I believe it is the writer's responsibility to distinguish between promotional materials and the performed work in its context, no matter how sympathetic the relationship between writer and subject.

Notes

1. I find it difficult to equate *atma* and *soul,* the latter being a term particular to Christianity.

2. G. H. Tarlekar, *Studies in the Natyashastra* (Delhi: Motilal Banarsidass, 1975), 16; P. S. R. Apparao, *On Bharata's Naatya Saastra* (Hyderabad: Naatya Maala Publishers, 1967), 2; Romila Thapar, *A History of India* (1966; reprint, Harmondsworth, England: Penguin Books, 1978), 136.

3. Kapila Vatsyayan, *The Square and the Circle of Indian Arts* (New Delhi: Roli Books International, 1983), 40, 48; Kapila Vatsyayan, "The Indian Arts, Their Ideational Background and Principles of Forms," in *Rasa, the Indian Performing Arts in the Last Twenty-five Years,* vol. 1, edited by Sunil Kothari (Calcutta: Anamika Kala Sangam Trust, 1995), 137–148. See also M. Christopher Byrski, *Concept of Ancient Indian Theatre* (Banaras: Munshiram Manoharlal. 1973). Byrski suggests that, while the Natyotpatti legend in the *Natyashastra* can be dated around 500 B.C.E., its extant literary form "undoubtedly belongs to a much later period" (38).

4. Ibid., 6–11.

5. See Uttara Coorlawala, "Classical and Contemporary Indian Dance: Overview, Criteria and a Choreographic Analysis" (Ph.D. diss., New York University, 1994), 86–121.

6. Rustom Bharucha, "Contextualizing Utopias: Reflections on Remapping the Present," in *Theater: Utopia and Theater* 26, nos. 1 and 2 (New Haven: Yale School of Drama, 1995): 38–40. Bharucha describes it differently, as temporal institutions (memory) mapped/projected onto spatial structures (the body).

7. Chandralekha's lecture-demonstration at the International Dance Festival and Conference in New Delhi, 1990.

8. Personal communications in New York, 1995; and Rustom Bharucha, *Chandralekha: Woman Dance Resistance* (New Delhi: Indus, 1995), 70.

9. Post-colonial Indians educated in and speaking the English language cannot but be influenced by Western thought structures and knowledge systems. Chandralekha has travelled the world and avidly explores the art and ideas of the cultures she visits.

10. For more details on this reconstruction and transformation of a traditional art, see Uttara Coorlawala, "The Birth of Bharata Natyam and the Sanskritized Body," in *Proceedings of the CORD Conference on the Body,* Greensboro, North Carolina, November 1996. Chandralekha's admiration of Rukmini Devi is documented by Bharucha in his biography, *Chandralekha: Woman Dance Resistance.*

11. See Rustom Bharucha, *Chandralekha: Woman Dance Resistance,* and various news articles in Indian papers.

Looking at Movement as Culture: Contact Improvisation to Disco

CYNTHIA JEAN COHEN BULL

In a made-for-television movie shown in Fall 1986, a woman dies . . . or, at least, according to the doctors, she is "body dead." But somehow her brain remains alive, functioning normally. At the same time, a second woman is pronounced "brain dead," but her body continues to breathe and function perfectly. In a miracle operation, doctors place the living brain of the first woman into the living body of the second woman. The ensuing TV drama explores the question of this new person's identity.

The doctors have no problems whatsoever with the woman's identity. Gleeful over their accomplishment, they reassure her that she really is her brain and that her body is essentially irrelevant to who she is. Her husband, however, resists this new body and is disturbed by the fact that the woman looks, moves, and feels totally different; how can she be his wife? His rejection causes her to feel doubt and confusion as to her own identity. Further complications ensue: she is followed around by the husband of the woman whose body her brain now inhabits. She *looks* like his wife; she must *be* his wife, still alive somehow. Eventually, though, the miracle woman and her husband (that is, the husband of the woman whose brain survived) become reconciled to her new body as they both realize that, indeed, she is her brain, and they live, we assume, happily ever after.

This popular consideration of the mind/body split exemplifies some familiar attitudes toward movement. Like the doctors in the television movie, many cultural observers and researchers ignore the body and its actions, seeing them as irrelevant trappings for the mind. They scarcely notice movement and do not consider its role or significance in human events; such omissions are common in accounts of cultural history and anthropology.

If researchers do pay attention to movement and the body, it may be only in order to see the mind which lies behind it. If gestures, for instance, can be translated into verbal messages, then they have been "explained." Cultural observers with this orientation look for the cognitive components of movement systems ("what does the movement stand for?"—a common approach in popular nonverbal communication theory); and/or the social structural implications of the body ("how do concepts of the body duplicate the social order?"—the approach of social theorists such as Mary Douglas). These translations of movement into cognitive systems can be illuminating, but sometimes they subsume the reality of the body, as if people's experiences of themselves moving in the world were not an essential part of their consciousness and of the ways in which they understand and carry out their lives.

On the other hand, researchers who wish to redress the imbalance of mind over body may react by positing the body and movement as the primary reality. Like the husbands in the TV story, they maintain the dichotomy between mind and body by emphasizing the body alone. Some researchers tend to look only "at the movement itself" ("just describe what you see," they say) as if the body, movement, and mind were independent entities, scarcely connected to social and cultural ideas and institutions. Indeed, much writing in dance history tends toward a simplistic, descriptive approach to discussing movement.

The problem here is that the division of mind and body (and the various attitudes toward movement this division suggests) dichotomizes aspects of experience which are not only closely related but which also reflect and refract upon one another. To detach one aspect from another for analytical purposes can contribute valuable insights into the nature of movement, but if one aspect is taken as the whole, distortion results. For, in fact, as sociologist John O'Neill comments, *"Society is never a disembodied spectacle.* We engage in social interaction from the very start on the basis of sensory and aesthetic impressions."[1] The body and movement are social realities interacting with and interpreting other aspects of the culture. Structured movement systems[2] like social dance, theatre dance, sport, and ritual help to articulate and create images of who people are and what their lives are like, encoding and eliciting ideas and values; they are also part of experience, of performances and actions by which people know themselves.

Since movement and the body are often opposed to words and the mind, it is interesting to look at the resemblances between movement systems and language. Both are cultural activities which have biological aspects. Even apparently simple and "natural" actions such as walking or sitting are in part culturally constructed. Also, like language, movement is ubiquitous, a cultural given which people are constantly creating, participating in, interpreting, and reinterpreting on both conscious and unconscious levels.

However, movement is unique. It precedes language in individual development, forming a primary basis for both personal identity and social relationships. It is kinesthetic and visual, rather than aural, and in many instances, movement is less specific (and therefore often more inclusive and ambiguous) than language. But while movement does not usually have structures which are analogous to the grammar that characterizes

every language,[3] it has observable patterns and qualities which can be identified with particular cultures and historical periods. Any traveler knows the reality of these patterns; the "natives" may walk with a different gait, may gesture more or less elaborately, may have a different rhythm and timing. The discomfort of being out of place and recognizable as a foreigner arises in part because of a difference in movement systems.

In order to observe and understand more about movement, one needs to ask what characterizes it in a given setting, how the characteristics form an overall impression, and what kinds of acceptable variations can exist. This requires careful analysis of the movement as it occurs. Understanding movement also involves asking what meanings and associations are embedded in and created by the experience of moving. Looking at movement alone, like examining any "text," can reveal details of the techniques and structures of a movement system; but it cannot tell us how movement is interwoven with other aspects of the culture or what its implications or associations might be in any given circumstance. If we are to read the ambiguity as well as the pattern embedded in movement, we must investigate not only what the movement is like but also what its import might be and how different participants, audiences, and outsiders might understand it. Thus the movement system needs to be viewed as part of the cultural reality. It is patterned, yet it shifts and changes—as does all of culture.

Contact improvisation, an American dance form, provides an example of a structured movement system whose features are part of a shifting cultural landscape.[4] Theatre dancer Steve Paxton and a group of colleagues and students first developed contact improvisation in 1972 by experimenting with partners giving and taking weight improvisationally. The practice of contact improvisation achieved a richly varied, yet defined and identifiable, movement style. It spread to many groups of people in the U.S. (and eventually in Canada and Europe), reaching its peak as a social and performance form in the mid- to late seventies, and is still practiced by hundreds of dancers today.

38. Contact improvisers warming up by engaging in spontaneous, free-flowing movement. Photo by Bill Arnold.

People doing contact improvisation create a dance through collaborative interaction, basing their improvisation on the physical forces of weight and momentum. The dancers are supposed to be absorbed in experiencing the movement and sensing (largely through touch) the experience of their partners; in order to allow momentum to develop, dancers have to keep their energy freely flowing, abandoning self-control in favor of mutual trust and interaction.[5]

Contact improvisation as it emerged in the early seventies was often learned in settings (jams) more akin to social dance situations than to theatre dance classes. Anyone could practice the form and, theoretically at least, perform it publicly. The experience of the movement style and improvisational process itself were thought to teach people how to live (to trust, to be spontaneous and "free," to "center" oneself, and to "go with the flow"), just as the mobile, communal living situations of the young, middle-class participants provided the setting and values which nourished this form. Dancers and audiences saw contact improvisation as, to use Clifford Geertz's phrase, a "model of" and a "model for" an egalitarian, spontaneous way of life.[6]

Contact improvisation has a history of development and change; it also has historical antecedents within both social dance and theatre dance forms. Rock-and-roll dance, a mass cultural form, was characterized by some of the same qualities in movement style and structure as contact improvisation (internal focus, ongoing energy flow, extemporariness) and the same values or concepts with which these qualities were associated (self-expression, freedom, egalitarianism, spontaneity). Theatre dance forms, practiced by relatively small groups of people, shared some of the concerns of contact improvisation, investigating physical forces in dance and "democratic" performance modes. As the contact improvisation movement arose and grew, it existed simultaneously with contrasting movement forms, such as disco dance; eventually, its style changed as technical developments ensued and as the circumstances of its practice and performance were altered.

Shifts and patterns can be perceived by tracing some of this history—noting the presence of some of contact improvisation's movement characteristics and ideas in prior American dance and performance forms, and looking at contact improvisation in conjunction with certain coexisting movement practices. This study illustrates some ways of looking at movement as culture, while at the same time it points to the complexity of the topic. Certain movement qualities appear through time, yet meanings suggested by these qualities subtly shift; contrasting movement styles exist simultaneously, sometimes embodying the same meanings and sometimes opposite meanings. Yet movement, which seems so elusive, can also be very concrete. Evoking the way a group of people move can call up the ambiance of a cultural time and place with clarity and immediacy.

The development of rock-and-roll in the late fifties marked a major, widespread incorporation of dance and music from black communities into the mainstream of American popular dance and music. The powerful influence of black dance and music in shaping American culture has a long history, and the emergence of rock-and-roll dance and music is a key moment in that history.[7] Central to this development were social changes, most notably the civil rights movement, which challenged former boundaries between blacks and whites. Also key, and historically unprecedented, was the postwar media explosion of television, which consolidated rock-and-roll as a mass phenomenon.

The borrowed/incorporated movement qualities and structures from black dance traditions included extensive use of shoulders, head, hips, and knees, often moving independently or in different directions at the same time. Emphasis tended to be on continuity of energy flow and on rhythmic impulses, rather than on the specific positioning of body parts, and on improvisation both by individual dancers and by couples.

By the mid-sixties, people in some communities had carried improvisational flexibility in rock-and-roll dancing to a point at which it was acceptable for dancers to go out onto the dance floor alone or with a group of people rather than a partner, and move in highly individual styles. But although the "steps" were not codified and most people felt they were being "free," the dancing was still typified by certain structural and movement characteristics. Dancers improvised within a specific movement range. They tended to move with a focus inward rather than outward to a partner or to the environment, absorbed by the music and the experience of moving. They frequently danced with a sense of energy freely sent in all directions, creating an impression of abandon and literally giving up control.

These movement qualities were important components of the cultural environment of that time. Engaging in these ways of moving shaped feelings not only about the "right" way to move and to dance, but also about the "right" way to live. The movement style seemed natural, contemporary, free, and not "uptight." Along with the rock music of the period, dancing both reinforced and crystallized an image of the self: independent yet communal, free, sensual, daring. This image of self would be central to contact improvisation.

The movement qualities of rock dancing were also associated with contemporary social movements and practices such as the civil rights movement, youth culture, and drug-taking, and with values such as rebellion, expressiveness, and individualism within a loving community of peers. Dancing encoded these ideas in a flexible and multilayered text, its kinesthetic and structural characteristics laden with social implications and associations. Depending on the circumstances and cultural backgrounds of the participants or observers, different aspects of the dancing would emerge as primary.

For instance, because of its pelvic movements and

open derivation from black culture, the twist (ca. 1961) was at once perceived by segments of the American public as overly sexual, as well as anti-social, because of the separation of one dancer from another. In 1962, one English journalist visiting New York wrote:

> I'm not easily shocked but the Twist shocked me . . . half Negroid, half Manhattan, and when you see it on its native heath, wholly frightening . . . the essence of the Twist, the curious perverted heart of it, is that you dance it alone.[8]

To opponents, the twist was shockingly autoerotic and unwholesome. To those who danced the twist or enjoyed watching it, the movement had similar but more sanguine meanings—it was sexy, exciting, wild. In any given social setting, certain meanings became more prominent than others. For instance, for those who danced it in New York City's Peppermint Lounge, the twist was a symbol of the latest and the newest in hip social circles. But for some teenagers, forbidden to do the dance in schools or community centers, it was an act of rebellion against staid and repressive authority.

Rock dancing throughout the sixties was given significance by dancers engaged in social action. For many members of the counterculture, the free-flowing, internally focused dancing was an integral part of giving up control and losing oneself in the drug experience. For more politically minded people, rock dance was a metaphor for political awareness. The extensive improvisation in rock dance enacted the rejection of explicit structures in New Left and feminist organizations. Being able to "do your own thing" on the dance floor carried out a commitment to individualism and egalitarian ideals frequently voiced in sixties politics. The development of new music and dance forms by black artists was part of an identification with and pride in black culture fostered in the civil rights and black liberation movements. And the lack of differentiation between male and female movement, abhorred by rock's critics, was a positive emblem for some people of a rebellion against American gender roles.

As explicit political phenomena, the student move-ment, the civil rights and the black liberation movements, the antiwar movement, and the women's movement found only tenuous moments of alliance with each other. But dancing, a multivocal and flexible sphere of social activity, could on occasion alleviate and even transcend political differences, emphasizing the shared ethos of these movements for social change.[9]

On the other hand, the experimental dance of the late fifties and the sixties was usually quite different from the social dance of the same time period. An obvious distinction is that rock-and-roll dance and music were large-scale social activities, while theatre dance was confined to a relatively small number of people clustered most noticeably in New York and other metropolitan and university centers. Most theatre dancers participated in social dance, but only a handful of social dancers performed theatre dance.

Movement contrasts were also evident. Rock dance tended to be exuberant and anarchically complex, while theatre dance was often pedestrian and minimal. The familiar joke summarized the situation: in the early sixties, people would go to a dance concert to watch people stand around, and then afterward everyone would go to a party and dance.

At the same time, a fusion of aesthetic and social ideas was occurring. Merce Cunningham's aesthetic dictum that any movement could be considered dance proved a powerful concept for younger dancers engaged by reemerging ideals of social equality and community. Those ideals were embedded in the experience of social dance, which required no formal training and was hence seen as "democratic," but which was also clearly "dancing." According to choreographers Douglas Dunn and Trisha Brown, social dance has played a key role in changing conceptions about movement. In a conversation recorded in the late seventies, Dunn commented, "Before the sixties there was no consciousness of certain things as being dance." Brown added, "I think the 'Twist' helped a lot in the sixties." And Dunn replied, "Rock dancing was a bridge between your daily life which was still unconscious perhaps, and part of your classroom dance life which was not making available that possibility [of all kinds of movement]."[10]

At first, the bridge between daily life and theatre dance was explored by experimental choreographers through the conscious inclusion of "pedestrian" and/or athletic movement. Like Cunningham, experimental choreographers in the sixties were acting in part in opposition to the symbolism and drama of the modern dance tradition: this contributed to the emphasis on the "purely physical"—the austere, the minimal in movement. Yet the ubiquitous rock music and dance, experienced by many young people as the quintessential expression of the times, affected these dancers as well, and the qualities experienced in rock dancing gradually began to appear more and more in theatre dance.

By the early seventies, free-flowing movement, focus on the inner experience of moving, and energy thrown in all directions became prevalent in American theatre dance. They appeared strongly in contact improvisation and in the dance of choreographers such as Trisha Brown, Lucinda Childs, Laura Dean, and Twyla Tharp.

Tharp, for instance, who was consciously influenced by black dance and social dance traditions, developed a style which has been described by movement analyst Billie Frances Lepczyk as freely flowing and internally focused. These qualities, she suggests, are "least pronounced in ballet and in most previous major modern dance styles": they "create a loose, carefree, casual manner which makes the movement appear easy—as if anyone could do it."[11] The movement style of social dance shaped in the sixties and its implications—that it was loose, carefree, casual, easy—continued into the seventies in theatre dance.

Contact improvisers amalgamated the sensual, free-flowing, inwardly experienced movement of sixties rock dance with an "objective" stance toward the physical capacities of the body typical of sixties experimental dance. They borrowed movement exercises from aikido—the Japanese martial art—in order to create dancing that was not based on aesthetic choices. At the same time, a crucial new element was added: touch. If dancers doing the twist never touched, contact improvisers tried to maintain a constant "point of contact" between bodies. The technical investigation of the give and take of weight coincided with the interest in touch so prominent among the therapeutic psychology movements of the early seventies. Although contact improvisers were cautioned not to become involved in "the gland game," as Paxton called it, the sensuality of the form was a major feature for participants and audiences. In this respect contact improvisation can be seen as a culmination of opposition to postwar repression.

Early performances of contact improvisation in the mid-seventies have been described as being like "a hot basketball game," with the audiences gasping, laughing, clapping throughout. After performances, recalls Lisa Nelson, an early contact improviser,

> there would be a lot of dancing in the audience. People would be jumping all over one another. They would stick around and really want to start rolling around and want to jump on you. The feeling was of a real, shared experience among performers and audience, a tremendous feeling of physical accessibility between performers and audience.[12]

The movement in contact improvisation and the social structure of its practice and performance were mutually reinforced. At least through the mid-seventies, many of the participants lived in communal and/or transitory circumstances, organizing their dancing and their lives in the collective styles which had first emerged in the sixties. Participants and fans saw the movement qualities, the improvisational process, and the practice/performance style of contact improvisation as embodying central values arising from the sixties counterculture: egalitarianism, rejection of traditional sex roles, individualism within a group, and an opposition to authority.

However, the social structure of contact improvisation could not be maintained. By 1981, most participants had abandoned countercultural lifestyles and the institutions supporting dance had become less fa-

39. Disco dancers transformed rock dancing's focus on the self as an individual within the group into a display of the self with a partner. Unlike contact improvisers, disco dancers such as these at Studio 54 in the late seventies emphasized female/male pairing. Photo © Jack Vartoogian, 1978.

vorable toward informal performance. Nevertheless, participation in the dancing continued to foster countercultural values. Contact improvisation carried the meaningful aspects of "sixties" social dancing into the late seventies, even after the environment in which the movement originated had changed.

One of the clearest indicators of the changing environment can be seen in a popular dance form coinciding with contact improvisation—disco dance. Whereas contact dancers performed in any combination of male/male, female/male, or female/female, with both people free to give weight or support at any time, disco dancers returned to the traditional form of social dance partnering in which the male led and directed the female. Disco dance was much more controlled than contact improvisation. It emphasized relating to a part-

ner through sight and one-way manipulation, instead of touch and mutual control.

Disco dancers transformed rock dancing's focus on the self as an individual within a group into a display of the self with a partner of the opposite sex. Their movement style was much more outwardly directed and presentational, posed, and controlled. Dancers tended to focus their energy in one direction at a time, often exclusively toward a partner.

The movement in disco dance encoded planning, control, and heterosexual activity to a much greater extent than did either rock dancing or contact improvisation. One has only to think of the dances and story of the film *Saturday Night Fever* for illustration: John Travolta's character uses his showy, aggressive dancing to create a sense of self which is strong, competitive, and sexy. He manipulates his partners physically and emotionally as he dances with them. He matures by realizing that he must exert some of that same control in his everyday life and make something of himself by leaving his working-class neighborhood in Brooklyn for the possibility of upward mobility in Manhattan. Disco dancing becomes a metaphor for life, but at the same time, it is a childish activity, best left behind. The aggressive "macho" image of the dance must be tamed, not so that he can become a liberated man, but so that he can succeed in the real world of money and fame.

Over the past ten years in America, the movement trends evident in disco dancing have become even more prominent. The relaxation prized in the sixties and through the seventies in some communities gave way to "stress management"; and "looseness" gave way to the achievement of "fitness." Dancers participated in and often articulated these changes. Perhaps the most popular "dance form" of the eighties, aerobics, cannot be considered either a social dance form or a theatre form, but a kind of sports training which purports to help a person (usually a woman) gain control over her body and look good. Aerobic dancing focuses on self-control and on the appearance rather than the experience of the body and movement.[13] The ever-growing popularity of sports also seems notable, for the movement qualities and structures utilized in sports activities, although varied from one game to another, inevitably involve control and competitiveness.

Contact improvisation has also changed over time. During the early years of its development, contact improvisation was practiced in slightly different ways by different people: some were more interested in performing, others in simply getting together to dance; some emphasized the aesthetic or athletic aspects of the form, others the therapeutic or interactive elements. In recent years, the unity of theatrical and social impulses embodied in the early years of the form has diminished greatly, a tendency created by changes in the technique of the dancing and, as mentioned earlier, by changes in the lives of the dancers and the circumstances of performing.

As technical skills among contact improvisers increased and the form became more clearly delineated, divisions between skilled and unskilled dancers became more evident. As skilled dancers turned more to performing, difficulties developed over how to maintain a nonpresentational dance style as a theatrical form. This dilemma was both a technical problem—how to structure the dance without destroying its basic conception and ethos—and eventually a practical problem—how to compete in the increasingly competitive business of producing dance.

By 1983, many of the people who originally created and shaped contact improvisation reached a stage in their lives in which marginal living was no longer possible or desirable; as they stopped dancing or moved on to create professional careers, new contact communities could not form in the same way as they had in the early seventies, because economic circumstances were so different.[14] Other professional dancers wishing to add contact improvisation skills to their repertoire of movement could do so more easily, and contact improvisation was treated by many as simply another dance technique.

As a result of all these changes, contact improvisation performances in the past five years have been rare, although the influences of contact improvisation on movement styles and techniques are widespread throughout theatre dance. Those contact improvisation performances I have witnessed have been highly skilled, characterized more by friendly and playful adeptness than by passionate unpredictability. The baseline movement characteristics were the same, but the dancers tended to move with greater control over the movement flow and a greater degree of outward focus. The audiences, while warm, were sedate and reserved, a marked contrast to the audiences twelve years ago.

Other theatre dancers have also articulated changes in recent years, opting in many cases for greater control and flashiness. It is not only younger choreographers like Michael Clark or Molissa Fenley who create these images. Even Martha Graham's company, with its

Halston costumes and attention to body line and arabesques, seems more polished and visually spectacular. This is not to say that dancers conspicuously plan these changes; like all participants in a culture (to paraphrase Marx), they make their own dances, but within a set of rules they do not always personally create.

For example, in 1985, choreographer Bill T. Jones, who practiced contact improvisation early in his career (1974–76), discussed reviving a duet he had made in 1978 called *Shared Distance*. The dance had been created originally with Julie West, who had also trained extensively in contact improvisation and had very little other dance experience.

> Julie and I were both involved in this kind of natural, free-wheeling, raw look when I made the dance. Now I'm working with a different dancer with no contact background and trying to understand how to change or revise the dance. When I push her through space, we [Jones and Arnie Zane] keep saying, "Well, you should keep your legs together." Before, Julie would just come off flying. Why do we suddenly feel that that's not appropriate now, that when I push her away, she should look designed in the air? These things are very real. My past and my future meet in this piece, and I'm trying to understand it. "The messy look," "cleaning up the act"—contact was about messiness.[15]

The sentiments of this choreographer are about very real things. How we move constitutes a part of our past and our future. The "free-wheeling, raw look" is not a fixed definition for the movement characteristics of free flow and multiply-directed energy, but neither is "messiness" (certainly the Polynesians, whose dance contains free flow and multiply-directed energy, do not define the movement in these ways). "Free-wheeling," "raw," and "messy" are meanings which Americans fused with certain movement qualities in particular cultural and historical times. In 1978, Bill T. Jones saw free flow and indirectness as being natural and free-wheeling; in 1985, these same qualities seemed messy.

Structured movement systems can join meaning and movement for many years. But movement systems within any culture are not monolithic and static, nor is their relationship to social contexts always direct. Rock-and-roll dancers in the fifties seem, at least in hindsight, to have anticipated cultural change through movement qualities adapted from black dance traditions. Rock dancers in the sixties epitomized the counterculture and captured a range of social meanings in a variety of settings, while experimental dancers—a much smaller group of people within the same subculture—embodied some of the same social meanings within different movement styles and structures.

Contact improvisers in the early seventies amalgamated movement qualities and social ideas from rock dance and the martial arts with aesthetic conceptions from experimental dance and a fascination with touch among certain educated, middle-class people. Contact improvisers in the late seventies maintained movement qualities and social ideas in small communities after the supporting social bases for those ideas had disappeared, whereas some other theatre dancers adopted their techniques for use in choreography. Disco dance and aerobic dance seem to be more direct expressions of the mainstream social and cultural milieu of the late seventies and eighties, often crossing class boundaries and providing metaphors for the way many American men and women see themselves.

Like other cultural phenomena, establishing laws of cause and effect for movement is neither probable nor advisable. What is of interest in the study of structured movement systems is the description and interpretation of the cultures which they stimulate. By looking at different dance forms, sport, theatre, or everyday movement patterns as cultural realities whose kinesthetic and structural properties have meaning, possibilities emerge for articulating and clarifying our experiences of who we, and others, are.

Notes

1. John O'Neill, *Five Bodies, The Human Shape of Modern Society* (Ithaca, N.Y.: Cornell University Press, 1985), 22.

2. I take the term "structured movement systems" from anthropologist Adrienne L. Kaeppler, who advocates its use as a more inclusive and fruitful way of conceiving of movement when doing cross-cultural studies and comparisons. For a concise statement of her ideas, see Adrienne L. Kaeppler, "Structured Movement Systems in Tonga," in *Society and the Dance*, ed. Paul Spencer (New York: Cambridge University Press, 1985), 92–118.

3. A major exception is American Sign Language, which has a complete grammar. Also, movement systems such as South Indian or Tongan dance contain linguistic structures.

4. A complete ethnographic analysis of contact improvisation is made in *Sharing the Dance* (Cynthia Jean Cohen Bull [Cynthia Novack], [Madison: University of Wisconsin Press, 1990]). The discussion of contact improvisation in this essay focuses on selected aspects of that analysis.

5. My discussion of movement characteristics throughout this article makes use of concepts drawn from Laban Movement Analysis (or Labanalysis) and choreographic techniques and devices.

6. Clifford Geertz, *The Interpretation of Cultures* (New York: Basic Books, 1973), 93–94.

7. Marshall Stearns and Jean Stearns (*Jazz Dance: The Story of American Vernacular Dance* [New York: Macmillan, 1968]) trace the development of black vernacular dance related to jazz music.

8. Beverly Nichols, quoted in Nik Cohn, *Rock from the Beginning* (New York: Hill & Wang, 1969), 105.

9. Dance does not always play a unifying role, of course. It can be used to distinguish one group from another, or to exert control by one group over another. See Paul Spencer, *Society and the Dance* (New York: Cambridge University Press, 1985), for an interesting discussion of this issue.

10. Jean Morrison Brown, ed., *The Vision of Modern Dance* (Princeton: Princeton Book Company, 1979), 170.

11. Billie Frances Lepczyk, "A Contrastive Study of Movement Style in Dance through the Laban Perspective" (Ed.D. diss., Teachers College, Columbia University, 1981), 129–131.

12. Lisa Nelson, interview with author, Middletown, Conn., July 4, 1983.

13. Sally Banes has suggested that the urge for control constitutes the central attitude toward the body in the eighties. (See Sally Banes, "Pointe of Departure," *Boston Review* 2, no. 5 [1986]: 12–13.)

14. Communities that practice contact improvisation exist, but their emphasis lies almost entirely on creating social interaction among members and on dancing as a means for interaction. The theatrical aspects of this form are absent.

15. Bill T. Jones, interview with author, New York, July 15, 1984.

10,000 Jams Later:
Contact Improvisation in Canada, 1974–95

PETER RYAN

In 1974, a group of itinerant dancers initiated forays across Canada's borders to demonstrate contact improvisation, a duet form that eschewed music, choreography, narrative, props, costumes and often the cocoon of the studio. It had an immediate and galvanizing effect on those who sensed its quiet revolutionary potential, its subtle simplicity paired with its spectacular sensual and physical rewards. Those first teachers were Steve Paxton, ex-Cunningham dancer, member of New York's infamous Judson Church Theater and inventor of contact improvisation, and some of his early collaborators: Nancy Stark Smith, Curt Siddall, Nita Little, Lisa Nelson, Danny Lepkoff, John Gamble and Mangrove, a San Francisco improvisational dance company. In subsequent years and various combinations, they shared their work with the first willing Canadians.

Elizabeth Zimmer is now the senior editor of dance at New York's *Village Voice*; in 1974 she was living and writing in Vancouver, where she saw a demonstration of contact improvisation by Steve Paxton and Nancy Stark Smith that, she attests, changed her life. "Contact improvisation hovers somewhere between gymnastics, wrestling and improvisatory dance," Zimmer wrote. "It is unchoreographed, growing in the moment . . . from a point of physical contact between two dancers. [They] work with mass, momentum, gravity; with themselves, each other and the floor. They explore balances, finding new ways to support each other, to free each other to fly. The ideal contacter can walk on hands as well as feet."

The Canadian dancers originally involved were either from an improvisational background, for whom this material was a seamless extension of their own practice, or modern dancers who saw it as a new way to expand their movement vocabularies. Both of these attitudes had the blessing of Paxton; he always felt the improvisation in contact was more interesting than the contact, the latter being "just a way to promote the unpredictable in situations of human interaction, a kind of democratic look at a relationship where both people have equal say all the time throughout the flow of the event." Paxton himself was loathe to define the work too precisely, save for its basic physical parameters. Individual work and initiative were highly valued.

Early on, there was discussion that contact improvisation be organized and teachers certified but the nature of the form and the people involved mitigated against it. Wherever contact spread, people interpreted or modified it to serve their purposes without fear of reprimand because no one policed the form.

Without traditional constraints and within less than a year, Canadians were teaching and performing contact across the country. A social form that people could learn and practise without performance aspirations, it was also a technique whereby a new kind of performance became possible, one that side-stepped spectacle and hierarchy, that glorified the kinetic possibilities of movement and made no assumptions about gender roles or abilities.

In Vancouver, a small group took directly to contact, among them Helen Clarke, Andrew Harwood, Peter Bingham, Michael Linehan and myself, all of whom were part of Linda Rubin's Synergy, a studio dedicated to improvisational dance and influenced by San Francisco–based Anna Halprin. In Toronto, the work began quietly in demonstrations organized by John Faichney, who had participated in Paxton's *Magnesium*, a seminal performance of the elements that became contact improvisation. (*Magnesium* was an all-male ten-minute romp on wrestling mats presented at Oberlin College, Ohio, in 1972.) One of the first to get excited was Toronto musician and improviser John Oswald, who co-founded the Toronto Contact Jam, a weekly dance event currently in its sixteenth year.

In the seventies, Montréal also received its complement of teachers and developed its own community, largely through the efforts of Dena Davida and the contact group Catpoto. Prior to contact's appearance, teacher and performer Vicki Tansey had been leading classes in improvisation; when she left the city, her students gravitated to Davida's classes in contact. On the East coast, Halifax dancers Diane Moore and Sara Shelton established the genre as a presence in Nova Scotia, teaching classes and doing local performances and demonstrations. Across Canada, a contact community was growing, its members touring the country, sharing work, experiences and the strong belief that they were dance pioneers.

Contact improvisation affects people in various ways. Many speak of the sense of freedom inherent in the form. "There's an animalism that isn't inherent in other dance forms," says Allen Kaeja, co-director of Kaeja Dance, whose background includes wrestling and judo. "It allows springing and recovery, the agility and ability to move in any direction at any moment. You trust your body in space to know where it's going, how it's going to get there, how it's going to recover. It offers your brain a lot of freedom."

Dena Davida, who curates the dance program for Montréal's Tangente, recalls that discovering contact made her a fish in water. "It was movement that suited me in every sense," she says. "It was a model for how I wanted to live my life, so much pleasure I couldn't believe it could still be called dance." Louis Guillemette, introduced to contact as Davida's student in Québec City, was fascinated by the physical dialogue and continues to use the form in his improvisational and choreographed performance. "Contact was very concrete," says Guillemette. "If there was no relationship, there was no dance. You had deep physical reactions according to the force, suppleness and imagination, but it was also psychological. Corps esprit confronté avec un autre corps esprit. You couldn't cheat."

Choreographer and improviser Jennifer Mascall at once understood contact in an inverted anthropomorphic sense: "It glorified the physicality of animals that weren't traditionally honoured. Birds evoked lines in space and digital gestures, whereas contact brought in moles, badgers, dolphins and otters. Dancers whose bodies didn't naturally extend into lines in space were almost condemned, yet in contact a whole other body and physicality was glorified."

Peter Bingham, artistic director of Vancouver's Experimental Dance and Music (EDAM), remembers that contact's meditative spirit occupied him for years. "Improvisation was the art form and contact was the practice," says Bingham. "It was about stillness of mind and the openness created by that flow. You got into the flow, practised it, opened your mind and then improvised. It was a totally spiritual practice."

Such reactions highlight the internal and sensory aspects of the form and, for some years, that sufficed for the work to develop and spread. Contact in the studio was a laboratory of the physical, of the nature of the partnering relationship, an open-ended inquiry for student and teacher alike. When dancers took contact on-stage, questions arose about the nature of the work for an uninitiated audience, what it was communicating and whether it was art, spectacle or entertainment.

The answers lay partly in the dancing itself, augmented by the responses of participants and audiences. But in the absence of set rules of appropriate conduct and reaction, dancers and watchers found that they bore mutual responsibility for the nature of the form and the critical and expressive contexts within which it was publicly presented. "I had hoped that it would be plunderable," says Paxton, "that people would find stuff and still remain interested in the idea of composition and the aesthetic choices in space, time and relationships that make it so interesting."

The basic form for contact improvisation outside the classroom and off-stage is the contact jam, an open event to which people come, warm up, and dance, immersed in a casual social ambience. Each jam's participants create their own format, with one or two people taking responsibility for the practicalities. In Toronto, for instance, the duet form is not the sole means of dancing. "There's an easy flow into larger groups, from duets into trios," says Toronto teacher Pam Johnson. Something called art wrestling also emerged at the Toronto jam, a more energetic and forceful style of dancing. With the exception of Toronto, jams were and are cyclic. The same is true of teaching and performance. "We understand the way that it's very hot in London or New York for a three- or four-year period, then everyone will get tired of it, and then it seems to come back," says Paxton. "As soon as it goes away, people realize that it did serve a purpose. After a while people see that it's useful and drop their quibbles about the aesthetics."

Contact has always contained two groups: those who accept it as a performance and teaching medium and those who enjoy it as a recreational dance form. Diane Moore feels that Canadian practitioners have tended more towards the former, although regular contact jams are held in Vancouver, Toronto, Ottawa and Montréal. In the absence of formal teaching situations, the jams are often the sole venue for learning and continuing the practice. Meanwhile, contact affords dancers the choice as to whether it is a central or a peripheral part of their work or life. Either can be satisfying.

For some, the jam format provides an insufficient focus for them to fully develop as contact dancers. Performance is necessary. As a result, several groups formed in Vancouver and Montréal to take their prac-

tice to another level. One of the first was Vancouver's Fulcrum, comprising Peter Brigham, Helen Clarke and Andrew Harwood, a distillation of about a dozen dancers who had immersed themselves in the form, travelling to various schools and intensive workshops in the United States to deepen their training. Fulcrum formed in 1977 and lasted only a year but in that time they performed at the Dance in Canada Conference in Vancouver and toured across the country. At the Toronto Dance Festival, Steven Godfrey described the Fulcrum performance as "one of the best things to happen at the festival, one of the most serene theatrical experiences imaginable." In spite of such praise, the trio soon broke up, although all three continued their work in other combinations.

In the late seventies, Montréal's Catpoto, initially made up of Gurney Bolster, Dena Davida, Evelyn Ginzburg and Carol Harwood, gave performances and demonstrations in cafés and informal studios. Catpoto taught, sponsored workshops and invited other performing groups. They were at the centre of a growing milieu and things looked bright but, according to Louis Guillemette, the dance community "put a stick in their wheels," undermined their efforts and, eventually, they dissolved. Other Montréal groups included Corélieri (Howard Abrams, Louis Guillemette and Louise Parent) and Au-delà . . . danse (Daniel Godbout, Louis Guillemette, Andrew Harwood and Louise Parent), both of which performed and demonstrated contact in Québec during the eighties.

Toronto Independent Dance Enterprises (TIDE) initially used improvisation as part of its compositional palette and contact as one of the primary colours. "Contact opened the door to improvisation as a form and a discipline," says TIDE co-founder Paula Ravitz, with the company from 1978 to 1985. "As we matured and became more skilled we were able to evolve scores and processes that didn't involve pure contact but addressed the elements of movement and movement improvisation. It was a platform from which we moved."

Contact draws upon a realm of deep physical resources and responses that often, even for dancers, remain untapped except in childhood or in some forms of athletic or martial arts training. Many describe it as what they had always expected dance to feel like, implying that other forms didn't provide that satisfaction. "Why is it that dance, at least from the ballet onward, existed in this rarefied atmosphere of the studio," asks Paxton, "with years of rigorous and boring rote training of the body and mind, almost brainwashing the mind, to make it into an instrument, instead of just your body?"

But it was also Paxton who told Bingham that he believed ballet to be one of the most sophisticated movement forms. "I came through contact and improvisation and ended up doing technique and choreography," says Bingham, for whom Paxton's comments were a turning point. "I really understood contact when I started studying ballet, modern and some forms of martial arts. Technique helped me understand why contact was important—not directly but by contrast."

Since the early days, Andrew Harwood danced for Jo Lechay and Marie Chouinard. Today, in his classes in Montréal, he periodically teaches dancers from companies like O Vertigo and Carbone 14. "Perhaps it has to do with the respectability that I gained by performing with Marie," says Harwood, who has parlayed his contact skills into an international reputation. "Or else they came to class and had a great time, getting a really physical workout and pushing their limits as well. They're letting go of their traditional breakfast."

Contact improvisation continues to spread and influence dancers across the country, not via fanfare or marketing but through the direct appeal of the work. Companies such as EDAM have always used contact both in performance and as a primary choreographic tool but Peter Bingham finds that few other companies use it beyond its various physical techniques. "The other dance forms are riddled with it," says Bingham, "but it saddens me because I don't see much understanding of it. I see mimicry, people who know how to move well, who can repeat its shapes. Somehow the

dynamic works but it's not the same as understanding how deep it is."

Yet, recently, the pre-professional students at the National Ballet School received contact training, and the dancers' inherent kinetic knowledge amazed their teachers, Allen Kaeja and Karen Resnick Kaeja. "Their intellectual anatomy was so fine that they picked up things very easily," says the former. "We moved through material quicker with them than with any other group."

Louis Guillemette describes the choreographic process in the early years of La La La Human Steps as collaborative. "I brought contact in because I was doing it when I was warming up, when I was involved in creation and showing large sequences of movement," says Guillemette.

Dena Davida has watched the Montréal scene long enough to accurately identify the roots and branches of current companies. "It's undoubted that the contact you see in La La La came out of the chemistry between Louis Guillemette and Louise Lecavalier," says Davida. "Likewise, Ginette Laurin has seen contact and a lot of what her body loves are contact-like things. The same interests people have in contact she's had as a gymnast. Even Jean-Pierre Perreault, when he does partnering, works with weight, so there's a contact likeness to much of his duet work."

Because contact dancers have an eye for the type of movement that derives from their favourite technique, they tend to see contact's influence in both ballet and modern choreography. "I feel strongly that this work has been fundamental to much of the interactive physical partnering work that we see today, that we now take for granted," says Andrew Harwood. "It's a sensibility that has risen up under the roots of things. Whether people are ready to admit it or not is another thing. It doesn't really matter."

Dance and theatre students are now learning contact in training institutions across the country. "Contact is now the partnering form for modern dance," says Jennifer Mascall, "and it has to be compulsory because how else are they going to learn how to dance together.

This is a provided form." Students graduating with contact as one of their tools can create with it, dance for other choreographers who require such skills and simply be comfortable in the intimate situations that acting often demands. "It does everything from getting people to touch in a nice way to actually strengthening the body to teaching them one kind of technical approach to the whole thing," says Paxton. "It's perfectly useful and that's all it was ever meant to be."

John Oswald, however, still senses resistance to the form even though it seems directly applicable to what many contemporary choreographers need of their dancers. "Dancers ask me how they're going to use this," explains Oswald. "I say, 'Imagine auditioning for Desrosiers. Can you do any of that stuff?' They don't even know how to do front rolls, yet the modern companies in town do material that nobody gets any training for. There's a chasm: everybody wants skills but they don't make the correlation between their eventual performing career and what their training must be to find work."

There truly is something of the chameleon in contact. The look of the work changes as its participants change and teachers from various parts of the country emphasize different aspects, be they overtly physical, sensory or meditative. Some people feel that experience is a major factor, that purity of form and of attitude must imbue the work before anyone can truly understand it. Some believe that a first dance, with a beginner's mind, can teach most of what the form has to offer. The understanding can come in a moment but often only after years of work. "I never understood the effortlessness of dance and how the physicality is eternal until I had an hour-long dance with Steve Paxton in 1985," says Allen Kaeja. "Prior to that dance I was in wrestler mode, and that dance put me into dance mode. He allowed my dance to happen instead of trying to make it happen."

Obviously, contact's reception in Canada has not been all sweetness and light. For example, the policy of the Canada Council has been that contact improvisation does not suffice as a dancer's basic training. Ap-

parently (and partly as a result of inquiries made to the Council during the writing of this article), this situation has changed. Individual contact dancers wishing to expand their horizons into other areas of dance can now do so, yet how many dancers of promise gave up in the face of such non-acceptance? Whether one agrees with the role of Canada Council funding as one of the criteria with which to assess a dancer, the perception exists that if a dance form or technique isn't funded, then it must be second-rate.

Some advocates may have partly brought this situation upon themselves. Contact has a reputation as a sort of lifestyle dance form, without a long tradition of excellence in either teaching or performance. There are, at most, twenty teachers across Canada who could work capably with professionals, and still fewer who could perform publicly and satisfy an audience. The vast majority are not at a high enough level of proficiency or are simply not interested in entering the dance world.

There is most likely no one in Canada who wants to put pure contact on the national stage. Contact as a tool? Yes. Contact mingled with choreography, or choreographed itself? Yes. Contact as part of an improvised performance? Maybe. But contact improvisation performed in its original, minimalist state? Rarely. "We are in a different cultural moment," says Dena Davida. For many, contact performance remains an enigma. "I think it has a very interesting and slightly ambiguous quality in performance," says Paxton. "You don't know what you're going to be seeing, except you know that they're going to be touching, and you don't know what the qualities of good and bad are, what the aesthetic component might be by which you would judge it. Basically you just have to say that you're looking at a natural thing and you have to accept that, the nature of it. When you perform something, there's always been the idea that the thing performed has to be art unless it's mud wrestling or sports of some sort. Since it isn't a sport, nobody wins it and it isn't exactly a spectacle like television wrestling. It isn't about the sheer hormonal content of it either because that content could be about anything. It just has a very ambiguous presence as a spectacle, whether a good one or a bad one."

Contact's influences and later associations, such as massage, meditation, sports, body-mind research and the like, have also imbued it with an aura viewed by many as non-professional. This has changed over the years, but the general antipathy towards a form that demonstrates too much contingency hasn't. A typical attitude might be that life is full of uncertainty, so art should hint at the longer arc of things, for a sense of permanence in a sea of flux. "I don't think the idea of composition has occurred to more than two in a hundred of contacters, or composition in the way that dance as art uses it," says Paxton.

John Faichney also had his problems with the direction that contact took: "My relationship to contact when I came to Toronto was a little bit schizophrenic because I found it wasn't very authorial. I found it hard to develop work that had any choreographic stamp on it and that was the work I was interested in. I went through a period of disenchantment with contact because of this fundamental limitation."

Most contacters have demonstrated little interest in dance's reliance upon choreography. The ones who did encountered problems when they attempted to share their discoveries with the dance community. Resistance was sometimes based on fear or ignorance, sometimes because the form was so new and assumed so much: openness, vulnerability, physical risk in a nebulous context, creativity on a cellular level, the willingness to make and accept mistakes.

Lastly, contact developed as a subform of dance improvisation, and improvisation in this century has always had a rough ride. Its place was maybe in rehearsal or research but no further. "The form has remained marginal," according to John Oswald, "because of its non-spectacle, non-flash aspects, without the big successes of, say La La La, popularizing a certain style of movement on big stages with big production values. In the early seventies we all got involved, but we haven't made big careers out of contact, so we don't provide a huge incentive to go head-over-heels about it."

Canadian dance had nothing like New York's Judson Church Dance Theater as an intermediate step between modern and postmodern. The American dance community, over the better part of a decade, witnessed the evolution (and revolution) that was taking place in that Manhattan church. Still, it is important to realize that the audience for the Judson evenings was not a dance audience but a community one that supported its activities in general. According to Don McDonagh in *The Rise and Fall and Rise of Modern Dance*, "It was an audience that wanted to see movement and presentation in vital and electrifying terms. It was passionate, prejudiced and proud of the artists who presented their works at Judson. It was also friendly."

The participants at Judson and related events in the sixties were what became the cream of New York art and dance in the seventies and eighties: dancers such as Paxton, Yvonne Rainer, Trisha Brown, Deborah Hay, Carolyn Brown, David Gordon and Lucinda Childs collaborated with artists such as Robert Rauschenberg, Jim Dine, Claes Oldenberg, Robert Whitman and Robert Morris, to mention only a few. It was a rich interdisciplinary mix that set the stage for the new dance/theatre/performance/event milieu that was to follow.

In Canada, we have no such tradition; for us it was like a leapfrog from modern to whatever it is we practise today, without the body to jump over. Likewise, we lack the dancers and artists who built upon the Judson experiments to go on to develop bodies of work that legitimized the amorphous yet virtuosic questions of an entire dance generation.

As contact has matured, its apologists have also come of age. Those who began in the seventies have taught and performed for fifteen to twenty years and are now in their forties. Dancers in their forties, no matter what their technique, have more rather than less in common. It has become apparent that contact isn't a flash in the pan: it isn't going away, and those dancers who have endured are capable of full-out dancing with partners twenty years their junior.

Contact improvisation works with lines of force,

both inside and outside the body. It strengthens the body rather than breaking it down, so it enables dancers to move at the limits of their potential. The result is someone who moves in internal and external synchrony, whatever their range, whatever their dynamic. Jennifer Mascall speaks fondly of Paxton's image of the long life of the dancer. "Contact is the only thing that I've discovered that can allow me to have that long life," she says. Peter Bingham feels it has to do with how one begins rather than ends a work session. "Traditionally we think it's how you come out of a class rather than how you go into it that determines how you feel the next day," says Bingham. "There's something about the slow, sensing process of getting warm, as opposed to a repetition of movement, that leaves you undamaged the next time around."

Contact improvisation is now like the Internet: it's a vast community, in a continuous state of flux, with interfaces to suit every need. Its publication, *Contact Quarterly*, currently lists over 250 contact individuals and groups, fourteen of them Canadian. The form is still under no one person's or group's aegis; thus it must monitor itself and rely upon the integrity of its content. The thinking has always been that the cream would rise, that those who taught well, performed well, would continue and those who didn't, wouldn't. With few exceptions, that thinking has been confirmed. Its exponents remain a varied group, some cherishing what they believe to be an original version, others more willing to experiment, still others happy simply enjoying the fruit. Contact improvisation, if anything, is a mirror reflecting individual beliefs, attitudes and aspirations.

Improvisation Is a Word for Something That Can't Keep a Name

STEVE PAXTON

The arts can be related to the senses, roughly speaking—music for the ears, painting for the eyes, dance for the body. But dance suggests an exception, because in the West it has become a spectator art, and it is through the eyes that the audience begins a kinetic response, or a physical empathy with the dancer.

The way the arts relate to the senses gets more and more complicated to describe when we consider the senses as interrelating. We notice that the muscles of the eyes move the visual apparatus to scan and focus. The neck and torso muscles move the head to expedite the eye movement. We move the whole body through space to look at sculpture. And we are able to dance on time to music by virtue of the fact that hearing, which is one of our fastest sensing systems, drives our kinetic response.

In their creation or execution, the arts are deeply connected to specially trained kinetic systems which, in a painting for instance, produce not only images, but characteristic strokes and lines. The "touch" of a musician is as characteristic.

These are ways of regarding the senses which are far from the "five senses" model, which is the way children are taught about the senses and their perceptions of the world. And it seems that little is added to this initial picture in the adult popular mind. I have read newspaper articles about "the five senses and the mysterious sixth sense" just this year. I am not right up to date on the current material analyzing the senses into all their component bits, but they were up to about twenty-five

separate senses (each with identifiable independent nerves) in the late 1970s, which is a much more interesting number. If you are interested in other models, read J. J. Gibson's *The Senses Considered As Perceptual Systems,* read Bonnie Bainbridge Cohen's work on Developmental Movement Systems (in past *CQs*), investigate the premises of yoga, acupuncture, or any of the Oriental physical systems which have been imported into the U.S., and read the provocative and heart-moving *The Man Who Mistook His Wife for a Hat,* by Oliver Sacks. I think we can't have too many models of the senses and their operation when considering a topic like improvisation.

It is a bit self-referential to say that the model I'm working on in this essay is about the effect of models upon the mind, but I can't see any way around it. I should mention in this regard that Buddhist thinking includes the mind as one of the senses. I am fond of that thought for the questions which arise for the analysts (how fast do we sense our thought?). If this is an amusing poser to throw at the sensoral analysts, it is because most of their work on the senses relates to those of the surface, disregarding questions about our sense of gravity, our feeling of the muscles of the body when they are quiet, or the sense of "being," if I may propose such a sense.

Yet the analysts' labor to discover the special nerves for each sensoral aspect is of interest, if only to explain the mechanism which allows us to dance to music, a most popular form of improvisation. If we can bop at a party because our perception of sound is faster by four milliseconds than our perception of our limbs' relative positions, we may surmise something about how the brain interrelates the senses. We could also look at time itself as a thing modified by each of the senses, instead of being an objective measure of duration. In other words, in trying to describe the sensing of time, we must refer to the perception of *times*. These times then must be collated into how long we think an event took, which is a very complex computation involving which of the senses experienced the event.

For instance, if we drop an object from a known height, we have the math to calculate how fast it will be moving when it hits the floor. This formula indicates that, barring air resistance, any object increases its rate of falling constantly. With this mathematical tool, we feel satisfied that we comprehend the event. It is objectively clear.

However, if we drop a soapy dish and before it smashes on the floor, manage to catch it, we can appreciate the sensoral complexity and precision of another point of view—the subjective feeling of gravity's effect on the dish, which enables us to save it. We treasure this facility in sports—eye-hand-body coordination of time, space, and posture getting you there to snag the pop fly.

I was deeply impressed by seeing a blind woman drop and catch a plate she was washing. For once, the eyes didn't have it. It "makes sense," as the phrase goes, that our bodies are completely attuned to the gravitic effect—that the rate a body falls is abundantly obvious to our own bodies; that any discussion of subjective time should mention the gravitic factor in tuning the human time senses.

And we might as well put in right here yet another factor, the state of our endocrine system, which can speed up or retard our experience of these times—just to indicate how extraordinary a job the brain is doing and to get some glimpse of how quickly it does it.

"Quickly," compared to what? Ah, "quickly" compared to how long it would take for the conscious mind to do the job. (This is my conscious mind writing, and I just wish you knew how long it's taking me to describe the little I can deduce about what my unconscious mind is doing.)

Language, a medium in its own right, is deployed to analyze experiences. Language is either written or spoken. It is either for the eye or ear, but finally it is intended to be sensed by portions of the brain which decode sounds or symbols into meanings. We rely extensively upon it to communicate what we feel and think. We use it to qualify, quantify, and confirm and in general to hold our societies together. It is the major medium, I would estimate. Julian Jaynes has speculated (in *The Origin of Consciousness in the Breakdown of the Bicameral Mind*), that consciousness itself arose with the advent of the written word.

The link of language to consciousness suggests many avenues for speculation. (It might explain the relative slowness of conscious thought, for instance.) I think it is well understood that there is much we experience which language cannot touch and should not be used for, but it is such an extraordinary medium that we keep applying it to all sorts of things, in hopes, perhaps, of contriving a successful new formulation; bringing the unconscious, un-"knowable," or unspeakable into literate consciousness.

I would bet that no dancer ever reviewed, however positively, has ever felt their dance captured in print. Yet language, used to describe other arts, forms a very important part of what we think about a work of art. It can certainly influence our point of view and may even suggest what *can* be thought about—that is, limit our perception or experience to the forum encompassed by language. It does seem to me that if we spend much time communicating with others via language about a painting, music, or a dance, we accustom our minds to the language version of the experience.

There are sensible reasons for this. Human societies deeply appreciate evaluations which, like mining for gold, mean eliminating dirt and concentrating on what is considered valuable. Our actual experience of something can include much that is irrelevant to its evaluation. An apt evaluation of a work will likely be repeated by others to their friends. The further it goes from the source of the experience to a verbal or printed version, the less recourse we have to elaborations or answers to our questions. We put such a rendered experience into our own version of a context. It is an idea we flesh out with our own images. As such, it has become a fictionalized picture, it has become un-true, but we do it continually.

Much of what we know about ourselves is described to us via language. The very idea of the "imagination," for instance. How did you learn it existed? In many such respects, we "imagine" ourselves according to categories, descriptions, and names of aspects of whatever we are told (or read) it means to be a human being. I have a soul, in other words, because the Bible tells me so. I have an ego and an id thanks largely to the writings of Freud, and an anima and animus courtesy of Jung. Not to belabor the point, we (think we) are conditioned to a considerable degree by our language.

Not that the particular names, categories and descriptions we apply to ourselves have always been the same nor will they be used always. They reflect a consensus and will change or vanish as that consensus changes. Jaynes is fascinating as he tries to describe the state of the human mind prior to consciousness. But we don't have to reach into the past to grasp some idea of how arbitrary our notions about ourselves are, we can examine ideas of cultures paralleling our own and feel the disconcerting void of (our own) recognizable terms of existence.

Language is not only prominent, but it can be coercive. We may opt to disregard experiences which don't work in language.

Tom Wolfe wrote a scathing article called "The Painted Word," wherein he suggests that painters in the New York school of abstract expressionism were in fact led by the writings of a few prominent critics to paint as they did. He seemed to feel that this was a degenerate situation which devalued the art produced.

It could be said however that this was an exceptional case of painters and writers developing the ideas of a movement in concert—exceptional in that it was a very intimate scene with a mix of artists, musicians, dancers, and critics in close communication, and with regular forums for discussion. Language could then be developed to account for the paintings at the moment of their creation. What Wolfe and the rest of us are accustomed to is a five-to-ten-year lag, to give time for critical language to be invented to describe the work. When this has been accomplished it has the effect Wolfe was describing: people learn to imagine in and with the new concepts, and artists and student artists elsewhere paint in the described manner.

One medium may support another, rather like the sensoral model: one sense may support another. However, I have begun to think that one medium cannot accurately describe another. We are used to the attempt to make films of novels, and then read critiques in which, to no one's surprise, the film is found a more or (usually) less successful "adaptation." Films are now "novelized" to similar effect. Critiques do not adequately portray the art, either: it all seems to boil down to "you had to be there." There is nothing like the real things, whatever version of "real" we happen to start with.

Analysis of perceptions shows us the realms of "reality" we are able to tap with the senses. Seeing, hearing, touching, smelling, imagining are, to me, each so very different from each other, seen subjectively, that I am apt to think of them as sensoral dimensions. Again, we adapt one dimension to another; "loud" colors, for instance, is an "auralization" of a sight. But the point here is to notice how the sensoral dimensions are *different*, since we are so used to confirmations of events through their blending. Watch a carpenter drive nails at close range—eyes see and ears hear the hammer. Then, move into the distance—eyes see first . . . then ears hear. What we originally felt as one experience has been divided between the two senses. We are mildly bemused by the organic "analysis" we experience.

In the 1960s there arose an artistic movement called "mixed media" in which one saw dances, films, language, etc., used in the same work. Now that I understand the senses and the mind as "mixed media," I am very surprised that the movement got this name. It seems to me that what was really going on was "un-mixed media," since the words usually did not relate to the dance or film which did not relate to each other in familiar ways. The audience was challenged with an event occurring in several sensoral dimensions, and the effect was similar to that of the lag between the visual and aural hammer-at-a-distance. The mind's habit of synthesizing perceptions was confounded. This was for me an agreeable aesthetic experience, because it illuminated ordinary perceptions a bit. It served to train the mind to examine different modes of sensing, and created in the midst of life a new game to play.

As I recall, during that time no one mentioned that the theater, opera, and dance were already "mixed." No one noticed that film had been mixed. Perhaps that was because people were excited over the possibilities for further mixes. Sounds emanated from sculptures. Words emanated from dancers. New mixes occurred even within the same media: for instance, Bach and rock together within a dance performance. Paintings became three-dimensional, sculptures were made with new materials such as cloth or compressed cars. Painters made happenings which were a kind of theater loaded with colors and shapes and textures and people and costumes and props; in fact, they were paintings moving freely into the third and fourth dimensions, using "in reality" what before would have been the models for two-dimensional works.

It was a period of radical interface. We were confronted with unaccustomed juxtapositions, and of course came to see things that way.

It was rather different than our former way of seeing and from this contrast came little sparks of information. That is how I evaluate it anyway; or value it. When we have two things to contrast, it seems to cause one to notice, and to learn. It was difficult to appreciate exactly *what* we learned in the complex midst of a happening; I suppose it all got synthesized in the mind, and one began to notice things that had escaped notice previously. It led me to consider the process of learning, and I came to regard the overall experience as a rather powerful conceptual tool with which one could cause change in experienced reality.

The question arises, why did we not notice media mixed before? That is what is so interesting. John Cage had been doing it for decades, and Duchamp's work suggested it decades before that. The surrealists seemed to be concocting mixed media images, and Picabia and Picasso began to collage—to contrast painted images and real objects, to sculpt images from found materials.

Perhaps the answer lies in language. Most folk couldn't "get it" because they were still quite busy trying to "get" what had happened in impressionism and pointilism. Cubism caused folk further consternation. And who could include melting clocks or a urinal or a prepared piano or a bus ticket in the same conceptual frame? The critical thought and conceptual tools of the day were already busily employed elsewhere, and the media did not dispense images or rationales as quickly as they do now. The arts, in those days, had begun to change far more rapidly than our language could accommodate.

During this century it became clear that changes were occurring on every level more rapidly than before. But this experience needed time to be finally understood, and those early examples, such as the more radical examples of Duchamp, were put aside to accumulate a kind of critical mass. By 1960, with enough hindsight, the times' changing had provided us with the model for the mix, and many artists were at once ignited. By then the popular media and critical establishment were ready, and the mixed medium event was considered seriously and widely announced, after more than a half-century gestation period.

Apparently an object doesn't have a life of its own, an objective meaning, but is imbued with values by the way we, with our changing minds, evaluate it. For many people, an object such as Duchamp's birdcage filled with small white cubes of marble was not illuminating, but only absurd. The mix can appear quite empty and gratuitous unless the mind has some context in which to work with it. So during the 1960s when so many artists began to mix images, terms were arrived at to convey the impressions. Then the Duchamp objects were re-evaluated and it was possible to see them, not as obscure Dada jokes, but as objects with a particular luminosity, which operate in some other dimensions of the mind than the linguistic one. They resolutely resist meaning anything; and as it turned out, this quality became highly prized in that period of intense critical and artistic interchange. The laughter changed from dismissal to delight, and the last laugh was probably Duchamp's.

The special gift of the mixed media was to provide a contrast to our conventional use of media and the senses. We had to admit that we did use conventions to convey our thoughts and feelings, and to run our society at large. The new mixes indicated that, once in place, conventions can dictate what the mind will allow itself to think. It seems to be the nature of the mind, the senses, the body, and of the society made up of these, to fall into habits, which are necessary for continuity, aids to individual survival and collective civilization. Individual habits and collective conventions prod us to adapt what we perceive into the most convenient shareable mental construct.

From the music we are accustomed to hearing, we form an idea of the intervals between notes. As our ears become more educated, we can become quite accurate in reproducing these intervals. Confronted with music in a different scale than usual, however, this aural education works against accurate reproduction. The unfamiliar intervals will be "adapted" to the nearest known intervals. This adjustment is so automatic and unconscious that the person attempting to reproduce the new intervals will probably not even realize their mistake.

Given another level of training in the logic of different musical scales, reproduction becomes possible, if difficult. For those who don't have such training, being confronted with an unfamiliar system can lead to confusion. Indian music, for instance, may remain opaque and possibly even disturbing; the intervals will seem wrong compared to the scale we are familiar with. In addition, it will be very difficult for the person to say why it seems wrong. The result may be a kind of unease and possible retreat from the unfamiliar system, a sensation of being lost. Not just lost, but without knowledge of *how* we are lost, for there are many dimensions in music where it is possible to go astray. Under these conditions, a little information about the nature of the systems is very useful for re-orientation.

However a very different sort of aid is an appreciation of the feeling of being lost.

Getting lost is possibly the first step toward finding new systems. Finding parts of new systems can be one of the rewards for getting lost. With a few new systems, we discover we are oriented again, and can begin to use the cross pollination of one system with another to construct ways to move on.

Getting lost is proceeding into the unknown. To reject the familiar, so rooted in our nervous system and minds, requires discipline. The difficulty is that we have to know so much to understand what it is we do and why we do it, in order to know what to avoid. We are not attempting to simply eliminate the known systems, but also to realize how we have adapted to those systems. It is the habits of adaptation which will keep us reproducing the system. The system itself is not the problem, but rather this human capacity to imprint unconsciously a new system upon our old system—or to embody the maps of our acquaintance, however tenuous.

We are close to improvisation here. When lost, we will have to relate appropriately to unknown and changing conditions. The dictionary explains that improvisation means "extemporare," or "out of the time." I suggest that we interpret "out of the time" in two contradictory ways. I suggest we discard all notions of clocks, and the half-life of cesium, or celestial mechanics, none of which are capable of improvisation, and equate time with human experience of duration, which is to say the experiences accumulated in life, so that "the time" will mean who we have become. "Out of the time" will mean that, out of experience (conscious or not), there is material for making something.

Simultaneously, "out of" should be construed as "aside from." We have to use what we have become in such a way as to not be so controlled by it that it is automatically reproduced.

Improvisation is a word for something which can't keep a name; if it does stick around long enough to acquire a name, it has begun to move toward fixity. Improvisation tends in that direction.

Dance is the art of taking place. Improvisational dance finds the places.

—to be continually continued.

Simply(?) the Doing of It,
Like Two Arms Going Round and Round

SUSAN LEIGH FOSTER

Here they are: two arms going round and round. What does their motion mean? And how do they mean what they do? Does it matter that one arm is white, the other black? that both are male? that one appears much shorter than the other? Does it matter where they are performing their circular motions? or what has come just prior to this action? or what might follow it? How might we examine their significance as both motion and meaning? What difference does it make that a choreographer has chosen this action over others? This essay endeavors to answer these questions through reference to the early work of Arnie Zane and Bill T. Jones. It addresses the ways in which Zane and Jones constructed identities for themselves in dance by analyzing the choreographic decisions that they made repeatedly in their early dances. It also connects these decisions to heritages of choreographic endeavor with which they were in dialogue during this formative period of their artistic investigation.

Between 1980 and 1984, Zane and Jones made six works for which video documentation exists: three co-choreographed duets, *Valley Cottage* (1980–81), *Blauvelt Mountain* (1980), and *Rotary Action* (1982); a co-choreographed work for six dancers, *Freedom of Information* (1984); Zane's solo version of a duet with Jones from 1974 entitled *Continuous Replay* (1982); and Jones's group work *Social Intercourse* (1982). None of these works is discussed here in detail, yet all of them contributed to this assessment of Zane/Jones's choreographic strategies. Aggressively casual, critically reflex-ive, abundant with sheer physical vitality and monu-mental energy expenditure, these dances embarked on an exuberant and exhaustive investigation of move-ment's possibilities. They also dramatized how the act of choreography is a theorization of identity, corporeal, individual, and social.

Every Little Movement

Both Zane and Jones came into dance at a moment when its parameters were at their most expansive for considering what dance is and what the dancing body might look like. Afro-American choreographers, ex-panding on Katherine Dunham's inquiries into African diasporic dance forms, cultivated connections between contemporary modern dance and a rich African aes-thetic legacy. White choreographers challenged as-sumptions about the vocabulary, construction, and location of dance, opening up dance to include pedes-trian and task-oriented activities, unorthodox and hap-penstance structuring principles, and even the possibil-ity that dance might occur without the knowledge of the dancers who performed it or the viewers who wit-nessed it. Contact improvisation continued this exper-imental and open-ended investigation of human movement by charting a course between art, sport, and life. Challenging gendered assumptions about who could lift whom and hierarchical assumptions about who could dance with whom, it defied standard no-tions of virtuosity. It eschewed the formality and spectacularity of proscenium performances, preferring instead the theatre-in-the-round of the dance studio and the spontaneity of undetermined beginnings and endings. And it connected its radical investigation of human contact to a vision of social change, one in which the choreographic values of sensitivity, egalitarian sharing of space and weight might form a foundation for all social interaction.

Together these distinctive explorations of a danced aesthetics challenged the prevailing assumptions of earlier generations of American modern dance choreographers about the dancing body, its function and its significance. Where choreographers from the thirties, forties, and fifties had worked to integrate all parts of the body into a single expressive whole, the training and dance-making initiatives in which Zane/Jones participated labored to dis-integrate the body. Where Martha Graham, Helen Tamiris, and Doris Humphrey presumed a functionally distinctive expressive role for each region of the body, Zane/Jones aspired to construct for each bodily segment the same range of possibilities for expressiveness.

Ted Shawn, one of the first and most prominent male choreographers in modern dance, exemplified the earlier integrative aesthetic in both his choreography and his writings about dance. Influenced by the American reception of nineteenth-century French movement theorist François Delsarte, Shawn catalogued the codes for all body parts and their associated expressive functions in his primer *Every Little Movement*. Like Delsartians Genevieve Stebbins and Steele McKaye, Shawn classified body parts into one of three types: intellectual, emotional, or physical.[1] The most obvious division of the body—into head, torso, and pelvis—corresponded to these functions, but also the periphery of the body aligned with the intellectual, whereas elbows and knees were associated with the emotional, and the shoulders and hip joints were construed as physical. This classification system was replicated at ever greater levels of detail such that each finger, for example, contained its own intellectual (the tip), emotional (the joints), and physical (the knuckle) areas.

Integrating all these distinctive regions were the wave-like motions of movement across the body.[2] A gesture of welcome might originate in the shoulder, travel through the elbow, and end in the extending of the hand, in which case physical, emotional, and intellectual centers of experience participated genuinely in the greeting. Alternatively, the impulse might begin in the hand, traveling back up the arm to the shoulder. Such a "false succession" belied the forced propriety of the gesture and the underlying unwillingness to interact with the other person.

For Shawn, the identification of corporeal codes such as these marked the uncovering of a universal system of bodily meaning, one that choreographers instinctively implemented when crafting movement for their dances. They might utilize a wave-like path for movement in order to involve multiple regions in a single statement, or they could eliminate the use of some part of the body in order to convey a different message. The head, for example, might flow in sequence with the rest of the body through a series of whip-like turns, or it could remain frozen, torqued off its spinal axis as the rest of the body convulsed. In each case the intellectual center of the person would be contributing a different kind of statement. This is not to say that choreographers studied the system of expressive possibilities and carefully calculated how their specific intent might best be conveyed. Rather, Shawn's interest in the Delsarte system provides insight into the presumption of a functionally integrative bodily system that underlay choreographic inquiry.

The Delsarte-based system continued to guide choreographic production until experimentation in the 1960s began to probe its limits, exposing its interpretation of the body as a set of culturally specific representational conventions. Percival Borde, teaching his own and his wife Pearl Primus's Afro-American technique, as well as Alvin Ailey, provided one kind of critique by introducing movement that referenced a non-European cultural legacy.[3] His dances unsettled the presumption of a universal meaning associated with Delsarte's Euro-American system of bodily codes.

Merce Cunningham conducted an alternative critique by cultivating a random and non-hierarchical structuring of physicality. For Cunningham, each region or part of the body boasted a certain autonomy with its own set of movement options that could be collated with those of other parts to create movement phrases.[4] Judson Church choreographers mounted yet a third critique through their incorporation of pedestrian tasks and their nonsensical sequencing of mundane actions.[5] They contended that movements such as running or hauling a mattress or rolling one's hair in curlers contained the same expressive potential as more conventional vocabularies of modern dance. Following a decade after these initiatives, contact improvisation explored each part of the body as a potential next site into which the momentum-charged contact between two dancers might travel.

These kinds of choreographic explorations de-stabilized the organic wholeness of the dancing body and challenged the notion of an expressive self that was motivating such a body. Where choreographers such as Shawn had conceptualized the body as the vehicle for an interior subjectivity, subservient to it in the same way that parts of the body served the whole, these choreographic projects imbued the body itself with its own expressive agency. No longer the instrument of the self, the body could now express its physicality, its mobility, and its cultural as well as personal history.

Zane and Jones walked into the middle of this change in paradigms. Their dance training, an amalgam of styles and traditions, focused on constructing the body as a responsive instrument, one minute, and a spontaneous instigator of ideas, the next. From the range of choreographic options available to them, they began to elaborate a dis-integrated physicality, one that would enable the body's parts to tell their own stories. They pursued Cunningham's interest in the spatial, rhythmic, and dynamic potential of all parts of the body, although not his rigorous investigation of indeterminacy. They valued Ailey's affirmation of the Afro-American presence in modern dance and its aesthetic continuity with, if not the specific vocabularies of, African dance forms. They embraced Judson's open-ended and adventurous critique of choreographic conventions if not its rejection of spectacle. And they drew sustenance from contact's polymorphous physicality even as they began to move away from improvising in performance.

Like these other choreographic projects, Zane/Jones's approach unharnessed the body from the disciplining surveillance of the subject, from the domination of the project of expressivity itself. At the same time, it elevated to pre-eminent importance the physical experience of movement. This valuing of physicality presented itself as an extremely attractive choreographic premise to a bi-racial, homosexual couple who loved to dance and make dances.

Posing Choreographic Questions

If there is one choreographic strategy that predominates in Zane/Jones's early work, it is the use of the photograph-like still or pose.[6] Repeatedly, bodies arrest their motion and come into focus as stilled figures. Powerfully motionless for a second or two, these bodies combine physical matter-of-factness with the drama of movement's arrest. Never a harmonious display of bodily geometries, as in the ballet dancer's pose, these bodies' shapes emphasize their non-conformance to harmonious or well-balanced design. The body is not elongated, the arms not perfectly rounded, the feet neither pointed nor flexed. Instead, the poses summon up the off-hand or the torsion-filled, the pragmatic or the dramatic. In these stationary positions, bodies do not display geometric familiarities, nor do they show off their similarities to one another. Instead, each pose shows how different bodies are, one from another. More a design schematics than a mold to which the body must conform, the pose accords each body the idiosyncrasies of its physicality.

The poses never tell a story; they do not depict the narrative of a dialogue between dancers. They sometimes implement the body's conventional codes so as to depict: "I'll give you a hand" or "Are you attracted to me?" or "You surprised me" or "Fuck you." Yet such recognizable gestures do not occur in any logical order, and they are interspersed among other poses that bear no identifiable markers of character or drama. One minute bodies are flirting with or repulsed by one another and the next they are assiduously exploring shape, the mechanics of weight and balance, or the physics of contact.

The poses provide locators from which the body must depart and to which it must arrive. *How* the body accomplishes this passage becomes more visible because of the pose. Although extravagant in its demands for strength, speed, and dexterity, the passage from pose to pose is typically accomplished with task-like neutrality and efficiency. These bodies are solving the problem of getting from here to there. Their approach reveals the facticity of movement; each moved phrase plays a concrete role in conveying the body from one still to the next. At the same time, the poses seem to interrupt the movement, keeping it from achieving an organic flow. As much as the pose functions as the inevitable destination of a movement task, it also abruptly halts the action, startling the viewers' tracking of the body's motion with its unanticipated interruption of the continuity.

The unconventional shapings of the posed bodies become etched in the viewers' memory. Although they never reveal dramatic content, they dramatize the kinetic potential of the body. Having paused here in the middle of so much movement, these bodies exude a powerful, dynamic alertness, a readiness to move. Then, suddenly, they are on the move, in the move. The speed of their passage is competitive; who will finish the complex sequence of actions first? Their arrival in unison is collaborative; how can they sense so closely what the other's body is doing? The unassuming focus of these bodies embroiled in their game-like activity neither downplays nor overplays their differences in body type, size, color, or distinctive capacities for strength and flexibility. The driving forcefulness of these bodies in motion and the delicate simultaneity of their tandemness set the conditions for an endlessly generative choreogra-phy: motion-arrest-movement-pause-action-stillness—it could go on and on. . . .

Even when the pose does not predominate as an organizing device, Zane/Jones approach movement as a series of discrete lexical units. A move happens and then the next move happens, sometimes one per second, sometimes five per second. Because the moves are often non sequiturs—they do not flow logically or lyrically one from another—their discreteness is more pronounced. Most clearly in *Rotary Action,* but also in the other works from this period, signature moves characteristic of a given dance form—hip-hop, ballet, clowning, pantomime, break-dancing, gymnastics, club dancing, or sporting events—suddenly appear alongside other moves with no identifiable origin, incorporated randomly into the longer phrases of movement. These moves stand out, announcing themselves as familiar even as they are executed with the same commitment and neutrality as all other movement.

Having the move be semi-independent invites the onrush of energy that moves through the move. Both the move and the energy that activates the move become more visible. The drive to dance, to exert physical vitality is tempered by the edges of each move. The move's specificity bends the energy to its clearly shaped purposes. As a result, bodies appear to engage in a kind of physical labor. They do not move through or past the moves; rather, they work to accomplish movement. Never do they yearn to transcend their spatial and temporal specificity, to chart a transformation from flesh into spirit. Always they glow with intricate, zestful physical articulation. When we view this dancing on video, we apprehend only the faintest trace of the energized exertion displayed during live performance. The image may be there on tape, but the effort is not.

Complex and innovative partnering also highlights the separateness of the moves and the exertion needed to display them. As bodies make contact with one another, they seem to inventory answers to the following questions: how many spaces adjacent to itself can a body create where another body might locate itself? how many places on the body can bear another body's weight? how many places can a body grasp, interlock, or lodge itself so as to lift another body? how many positions can a body hold while being moved through space by another body? into how many segments, each with its own abbreviated stop-action, can a transfer of weight into or out of a carry be broken? Bodies offer up an inexhaustible wellspring of possibilities, augmented still further by the use of the floor as yet another partner: how many different bodily surfaces can make contact with the floor? how many different and isolated parts of the body can support one's own weight? how many ways can two bodies make contact with the floor so as to support their mutual weight?

Typically, the choreography presents twenty or thirty different answers at a time to these questions, usually over the space of fifteen to thirty seconds. Sometimes the interactions are even more prolonged, the solutions ever varied; other times they endure for only a brief interval as bodies transit past each other. None of the moves that transports the body from one point of contact to the next is immense or effort-filled. Even the most spectacular lifts, inversions, or catches are accomplished with the same incremental use of force as the smallest shifts of posture. (And this is how they achieve their spectacularity.) The next move, never beyond the body's reaches, features a novel bodily articulation: did you ever balance on the side of your waist? or on your heel and elbow? walk across someone's sternum? crouch on their shoulder? share weight through the tops of your heads? And each of these instances where weight merges occurs before and after other such innovative investigations of bodily options.

During sections of partnering and also alone, bodies often break the seeming flow of a motion into measured units. This is yet a third way in which moves attain discreteness from one another. A body may launch into a whirling turn or a suspenseful fall, but quickly arrest the ongoing impulse so as to punctuate the motion with brief halts. Through these halts, the choreography conducts an anatomical investigation, not of the body, but of its movement. What was previously conceptualized as whole and continuous is now displayed in pieces. In order to accomplish this parsing of motion, bodies utilize a regulated economy of energy expenditure. They do not indulge in the fall or rebound, the surging momentum, promised by certain actions. Instead, they relentlessly pursue one move and then the next.

This economy of motion and execution emphasizes the thingness of movement, the ability to manipulate and play with action. It thereby separates the moves themselves from their performance, asking viewers to look at both simultaneously. In more classical dance traditions, ballet or even modern dance, motion and execution typically meld into a single expressive gesture. In contrast, Zane/Jones's dances tease apart choreography from enactment so that execution can be seen alongside the pattern as an influence upon it. Each body's performance inflects the movement phrases with distinct elements while at the same time letting the choreography stand on its own.

Unison among dancers highlights the separateness of choreography from performance. In both their duets and group dances, each body's different approach to performance matters. Unison in either modern dance or ballet usually represents the similarities between bodies and uses the effect of similarity to create a sculptural mass, or an anonymous community, or a harmonious agreement between bodies. Within these configurations individual bodies are stripped of their differences, divested of their distinctiveness. Male/female duets may use unison to point up subtle variations in execution by male and female dancers, confirming gender differences at the same time that they show how much range the two genders share. In same-sex unison bodies most often strive to approximate one another so as to display how individual uniqueness can be transcended by the sharing of the same action. Zane and Jones, however, capitalized on the differences in their physiques and performance styles in their early duets. Their unison celebrates the discrepancies in their height, mass, and style of motion; it revels in the distinctiveness of their stilled shapes, their attack, and the accommodations of one body to the other.

Sometimes, because they perform so distinctively, it takes a few moves to register that the two bodies have locked into unison. One minute they are maneuvering, gallivanting, gesticulating as wildly independent bodies, and the next they are dancing alongside each other in tandem. The sudden in-tuneness of the two bodies is nothing short of thrilling; the breaking away from that unison to plot individual trajectories is equally dramatic. Moving in and out of synch, the dancers intimate the existence of a larger pattern of which each individual is aware. These bodies playfully engage a communality and then strike out on their own, yet tacitly, they seem aware of the other's whereabouts and the ways in which they are mutually engaged. The dancers' focus reinforces this sense of a simultaneous attention to individual and communal patternings: they are casual, neutral, yet their eyes engage peripheral space as part of the sensing of the other's body. Then, occasionally, they break their absorption in the task at hand to smile or look at one another. When they acknowledge one another directly, their bodies momentarily consolidate as personalities—this is Bill smiling wryly at Arnie. The rest of the time, their bodies, rather than their personalities, do the looking. Their bodies focus with absolute dedication on the movement being performed, yet always they assess the progress of the other's body as they go. They know how to catch, duck, lean, or careen, because they are tracking their own and the other body's fulfillment of the movement score they have devised.

We could call this score in which the dancers are engaged the choreography. The choreography is, after all, the plan of the dance that each body helps to fulfill. Yet in Zane/Jones's dances the organization of bodily action seems to symbolize an even grander plan. Not cosmic or divine, the choreography nonetheless projects an expanded relationship between body and performance. Because the choreography exists apart from any given enactment of it, it takes on a life of its own. Life is not a dance, but the dance is making itself with help from the dancers. As a result, dancers articulate a different sense of agency: each body is unique and makes distinctive choices, but always in relation to a larger sociability, the features of which are unfolding through and alongside all individual actions.

In *Continuous Replay* this vision of the dance making itself is commemorated in the very premise of the piece: a single, accumulating phrase is set in motion; it continues to return to its beginning and to accumulate new moves throughout the course of the dance. The phrase provides a template taken up by an unspecified number of dancers at any given time. As the phrase continues to develop, dancers break out of it to perform alternative movement sequences at various moments, only to take up the phrase again, not where they left off, but in its current elaboration. Even if all the dancers simultaneously diverged from the phrase to perform their own movement, they would necessarily track the phrase as it continued to develop virtually, so that they could rejoin it in the appropriate place.

In *Blauvelt Mountain* the choreography asserts itself through patterns of re-combined, reordered, and reiterated sections of movement. The dance is composed from a dozen or more distinctive sections, each of which embroil bodies in very different projects. In one section, for example, Zane and Jones create a complicated series of poses on the floor that circle around each other; in another one sits at the side while the other solos; and in a third, they tour the stage space casually discussing the choreography and their performance of it. Over the course of the dance each of these sections is brought back numerous times, most often in a different sequence with other sections. This recombinative ordering of sections allows each to comment on those adjacent to it, highlighting new connections among movement material that, in turn, reconfigure the identities of the dancers. The viewer learns more and more about who these two men are from watching the cycling of projects in which they engage.

As much as the dancers enact the choreography, it displays the kinds of energy needed for its enactment. The choreography, casually disparate and then strikingly ordered demands an economical and measured execution alternating with a pell-mell bursting/busting through movement. Underlying this alternation of energies, a relentless commitment to physicality drives the action forward. Through motion to arrest, from efficient to over-abundant energy, alternately casual and demanding—the choreography revels in these energies, using them to move the dance.

Black Arm, White Arm

Jones reminisces about a street performer he saw one day bringing traffic to a halt in downtown Manhattan:

> He oozed across the blistering crosswalk like King Lear. There was something in what he said and how he moved that makes me remember him burning. At this time, performing for a congregation of strangers, I beg him to come into my body. Percy Borde used to tell us of the supplicants in Haiti who would dance for hours until the spirit of Dhambala shot through their spines, causing them to undulate in spasm like a cobra about to strike. At this time I am turning and others are moving 'round me, sometimes real and sometimes imagined.[7]

Here, Jones aligns his performance with that of Haitian Voudun practitioners. In so doing, he tacitly references the Afro-American dance lineage of artists who, beginning with Katherine Dunham and Beryl McBurnie, have investigated the African diasporic legacy. Dunham, founding her own school in New York City, and McBurnie, teaching at the New Dance Group, influenced subsequent generations of Afro-American choreographers including Pearl Primus, Talley Beatty, Donald McKayle, and Louis Johnson. Jones needs these figures backing him up as he makes his way through the predominantly white, avant-garde dance scene. And they populate the dances, handing him some very cool moves; moves that reference black street dance, social dance, African dance, black sports idols, and the very "coolness" that marks an Africanist aesthetic. Yet these references, fleeting and juxtaposed with countless other vocabularies, do not enunciate a

clearly bounded ethnic or racial identity such as that elaborated by neo-African choreographers Rod Rodgers or Charles Moore. Jones's blackness and Zane's whiteness articulate a new kind of relationship with their bodies, and their identities. How?

Thus far, this essay, like Zane/Jones's early choreography, has circumvented the obvious about their dances: Zane is white and Jones is black; Zane is Jewish and Jones is Afro-American. AND THEY ARE DANCING TOGETHER, INTIMATELY. This difference, the first thing one sees when the lights illuminate the stage, is understated by the choreography. But how can it be ignored? When in the history of modern dance has this ever happened, a white man and a black man dancing intimately together?

In 1930 the Communist choreographer Edith Segal created a duet for two women, one white and one black, entitled *Black and White Workers Solidarity*. Using as slogan for the dance "Black and white, Unite and fight," she and her partner, Allison Burroughs, performed the piece on several occasions for workers' sponsored events. Appearing on make-shift stages in a variety of locales, the dancers

> depicted the history of exploitation that each race suffered and proposed a solution along Party lines. The victims (because each suffered under the capitalist system) found that by supporting each other they could overcome the forces that oppressed them. Composed of literal gestures based on work motifs and tending toward static poses, the dance ended with the black figure and the white figure helping each other rise from the ground, symbolizing the power that each could provide to the other.[8]

After several successful performances, two male dancers, Afro-American Add Bates and Jewish Irving Lansky, took over the duet and presented it with Afro-American, Communist activist Angelo Herndon on tours throughout the U.S.

Dance historian Ellen Graff reconstructs Segal's choreography as exemplary of Communist and leftist artists' initiatives from the early 1930s. Guided by a

Marxist critique of working-class oppression, choreographers staged many different versions of workers struggling against, and sometimes prevailing over, their capitalist bosses. One of the few choreographers who addressed racism, Segal saw the potential of the workers' struggle to bridge the black-white divide, and she succeeded in presenting an integrated cast on stage. Still, her dance subordinated racism to class-based forms of oppression. In so doing, it did little to challenge the whiteness of the leftist modern dance movement or the presumed universality of the white body characteristic of the modern dance tradition since its inception.

Founders of modern dance such as Isadora Duncan and Ted Shawn deployed racist arguments to distinguish their new genre of theatrical dance from other forms of entertainment. Both alluded to the prurient potential of the dancing body as exemplified in African dance and its descendant jazz, and they worked to define their new modern dance initiatives in opposition to Afro-American dance forms.[9] Although the 1930s witnessed a number of radical choreographic statements that condemned racial prejudice, such as Segal's dance or Charles Weidman's *Lynchtown* (1934), they were insufficient to redress the racism already inscribed within the tradition and society at large. White choreographers unabashedly appropriated Afro-American music and dance forms to enliven their dances, never questioning their own entitlement to represent all bodies regardless of color or history. Although, as Graff has shown, color lines retained some flexibility throughout the 1930s, with white dancers traveling uptown to Harlem to learn the latest social dance innovations. Afro-American dancers and choreographers, dismissively treated by producers and critics, largely pursued the separatist development of an Afro-American modern dance tradition.

Focusing on the production of danced spirituals by both white and black choreographers, dance historian Susan Manning argues that the universal subjectivity of the white dancing body prevails until the 1940s.[10] After World War II modern dance choreographers integrate their companies, allowing both white and black bodies to represent the concerns of the dance. At the same time, a number of Afro-American choreographers come to prominence, yet they are burdened in their fame by the presumption that they will undertake choreographic projects that specifically address Afro-American themes and values. Pearl Primus's *Strange Fruit,* Alvin Ailey's *Revelations,* and Donald McKayle's *Rainbow Round My Shoulder,* canonical works in the Afro-American dance tradition, all portray life in the South and provide vivid images of Afro-American community.

Given the prominence of these Afro-American artists, the white dancing body could no longer presume to portray all racial and ethnic subjects, yet it sustained its universalist position, particularly through appeal to experimentation. Merce Cunningham, contesting the model of dance as an expression of psychological dilemmas and dynamics, claimed a new focus for choreography on the spatial and temporal elocutions of the body. In so doing, he exposed the way in which subjectivity had expanded within the expressionist model to encompass pan-human feelings. Working to construct a more modest role for the choreography, he eschewed all attempts, such as those made by Tamiris or Graham, to represent the feelings of all races or ethnicities. But he did not interrogate the division of labor that enabled white choreographers to experiment with "value-free" compositional methods such as chance procedures, while asking black choreographers to purvey colorful, ethnically specific images of Afro-American culture.

Similarly, Judson and other experimental choreographers from the 1960s opened dance up to the pedestrian world of movement and to multi-media collage, thereby expanding dance to embrace unskilled performers, talking and dancing, and the uncanny juxtaposition of bodies, props, and actions. Yet it is striking how white both the artists and audiences were for these events. As Brenda Dixon Gottschild has observed, powerful similarities between Judson's experimentation and a range of Africanisms such as the use of juxtaposition, double-entendre, and dead-pan, demonstrate the embeddedness of African and African diaspora aesthetics within this white dance initiative, yet these experimental choreographers aligned themselves exclusively with European and white American avant-garde histories.[11] Even contact improvisation, as it held out the promise to treat all bodies equivalently, nonetheless attracted a predominantly white and middle-class group of dancers and dance viewers. It never extended its own politics of inclusivity to include contemporaneous forms of improvisation such as break-dancing.

Jones is one of the first black performers to enter the post-Judson alternative dance scene. In Binghamton, Brockport, San Francisco, and Amsterdam, Jones and Zane's early haunts, the generic modern dance class and the contact jams are all largely white events, with only Percival Borde's Afro-Haitian class sustaining a black dance tradition. But how are racial politics playing out in dance, and how does one perform Afro-American identity in the late 1970s and early 1980s?

In 1983 the Brooklyn Academy of Music hosts the first comprehensive Dance Black America, presenting a large number of Afro-American dance companies with a range of aesthetic interests. Yet renowned black dancer and choreographer Gus Solomons is not invited to participate and writes to the organizers in protest:

> I have spent twenty years making dances that stem from my honest experience and my perception of dance as an expression of energy-as-motion, not as a vehicle for the expression of racial anger or social oppression, which, fortunately, do not happen to be part of my personal background. It saddens me to realize, if indeed it is the case, that my work is apparently being ignored by my Black colleagues because it refuses ethno-cultural categorizing.[12]

Solomons's protest raises the questions that the festival and any emerging black artist from the period were struggling to answer: What is "Black" dance? Is it the product of an Afro-American choreographer? an Afro-American dance company? a set of references (how many, which ones) to an African aesthetic repertoire?

to Afro-American community or life experience? to the experience of racism in the U.S.? How can a black artist be a part of that tradition and, at the same time, not be constrained by it (and by the white establishment against which it is necessarily defining itself) to conduct a specific kind of choreographic inquiry?

Jones and Zane navigate their way through these questions by focusing intently on what the physical body can do. They build a representation of a bi-racial relationship between a black man and white man, an Afro-American man and a Jewish man out of physical endeavors, task-like feats of physical accomplishment. This relationship privileges team-work, trust, and a deep knowledge of the other's body, its size, weight, flexibility. Their black and white bodies seldom reference the stereotypic vocabularies associated with Black or Jewish ethnic communities. Instead, they engage an eclectic vocabulary that demands intense physical exertion and coordination. Their bodies resist speculation about their symbolic significance because the practical matters at hand consistently claim their own and the viewers' attention.

Through this focus on physical articulation, the racial identity of the dancers forms a part side by side with, but neither interior or exterior to, all that they are.[13] Their bodies' color never vanishes, and occasionally, it intensifies as when the choreography inserts specifically black vernacular movement. Yet their color is never construed as the origin or cause of this movement, as was demanded of the Afro-American choreographers of the 1950s and 1960s. Nor is color conceptualized as entirely protean, something a body could take up or put down at will. Instead, it is there, integral, yet in motion, working with the body to produce an exceptional physicality, full of alacrity, quick-wittedness, and bold strength. Is this not the promise and hope proclaimed by their dances, that a white man and a black man really could partner one another in this way?

Does sexuality in Zane and Jones's dances operate in the same way as their representation of race, announcing itself visibly and partnering their bodies' endeavors? When they took their bows, as they left the stage,

Arnie and Bill touched one another with such intimate familiarity. Sometimes one kissed the other, or they hugged snugly, or they exited sauntering arm in arm. How many people in the early eighties knew? suspected? cared? that they were lovers, and what difference did it make to the way their work was viewed?

Although their early dances displayed an enormous knowledge of one another's bodies, it refrained from any identifiable gestures towards desire or sexuality. Following the polymorphous sensuality of contact improvisation, the choreography elaborates a carefully non-sexualized physicality. All areas of the body are treated equally and with an emphasis on their physical potential for movement rather than their capacity to arouse sexual desire. Thus the dancers never sidle up to one another, stroke one another, or embrace in a way that intimates sexual knowledge. Even when their explorations of pose and passage place buttocks next to head, or genitals next to genitals, these regions are treated as merely another set of adjacencies, physical proximities among the endless number of possibilities. In *Valley Cottage,* for example, Arnie dives onto Bill as he lies on the floor, and together the two bodies roll across the floor. Yet Arnie's head remains determinedly aloof from their fierce embrace, as if to indicate the pure formality of their momentary proximity. Only a second and a half in length, this encounter, like many similar moments in their performances, works to preserve the chastity of their relationship.

Not only do they de-erogenize the body, but they resist any divisions of labor that could project a sexual partnership. Each lifts the other; each leads and follows; each exerts equally a range between passive and active effort. Each is manly. In the reminiscences, anecdotes, questions and answers that they deliver while dancing, they reference an intimate knowledge of the other's personal history, yet they refrain from any phrasing that alludes to sexuality or sexual practices. Like Cage and Cunningham, their primary relationship appears to be that of artistic collaborators, yet unlike Cage and Cunningham, they sweat together, grasp one another, catch and are caught by one another.

Off stage Zane and Jones were leading the post-Stonewall, pre-AIDS gay life. Unlike the quiet, matter-of-fact domesticity of Cage and Cunningham, Zane and Jones inhabited the bars, partook of the scene in Amsterdam, San Francisco, and New York City. Onstage there is no residue of this lifestyle. The workmanly environment of the dance expels all forms of cruising—flirtatious glances, innuendoes, dalliances, masquerades. Even the rare pose that passes as a come-on loses its allure through its placement within the formalist confines of the dance's syntax. Like the brief references to black vernacular dance, the sparsely placed innuendoes are contained and isolated from one another, unable to muster any coherence. Unlike the black dance motifs that build upon the color difference of the dancing bodies so as to assert the presence of a discourse on race, the occasional pass is drained of its desire by the anti-narrative thrust of the choreography.

Could viewers find in the proximity and knowledgeability of their physicality evidence of homoerotic desire? Surely. Could they project a gay relationship onto the couple? Undoubtedly. Could the possibility of the couple's homosexuality never occur to them? Why would it? The dance's sexual orientation depended upon the viewer's desire to find or deny a homosexual relationship between the dancers. In presenting viewers with this opportunity, however, it did not cover anything up for them to uncover.

"It's simply the doing of it, like two arms going round and round"[14]

Zane and Jones introduce speaking as part of the performance in several of their early dances. *Valley Cottage, Blauvelt Mountain,* and *Rotary Action* all contain sections where the dancers talk while they dance. The speaking is pragmatic in quality, delivered in an everyday, conversational tone, and with the same neutral efficiency as the movement is performed. The dancers are never "acting" when they talk, or rather, they are representing their everyday selves, conferring, observing, reminiscing while they dance. Sometimes they make observations about the action, current or preceding. Other times, they ramble on about unrelated, mundane topics, creating absurd non-connections with the movement. Although the talking never sustains an interactive dialogue with the movement, speech and movement sometimes stop or start at the same moment, as if to indicate that they have been partnering each other all along.

Appearing randomly and with little connection to the movement, speech is constructed within the dance as a separate discourse that occurs alongside, as one of, the performed activities. One minute the dancers are moving, pedal to the metal, thoroughly engrossed in the action at hand; the next they are sustaining that commitment to action while at the same time conversing about unrelated events. The talking enhances the workmanly environment of the dance, eradicating any potential for the body to portray a transcendental authenticity. These bodies are what they are doing and nothing more or less. At the same time, the talking adds to the choreography's capacity for meta-commentary. The choreography is abundant with strategies that call attention to its making of the dance: the eclectic mixture of vocabularies, the differently sized bodies, the sudden smile or laugh, the unpredictable switching between formal and informal energy, the use of the pose to reference and analyze motion. The talking, another of these strategies, fuels the dance's critical reflexiveness. It asserts the potential for re-viewing the dance from a more distant place.

At the same time (have I ever used this phrase so often in describing a dance?), the talking secures the relentless intensity of the action. The talking configures the performers as neutral and detached commentators, whereas the dancing, although it alternates between calm and exertion-filled action, always commands the dancers' full attention. The fact that the dancers engage in verbal reminiscence or reflection only enhances the dance's driving energy. Compounding the contrasts—between motion and arrest, casual and virtuoso, economy and exuberance—upon which the dances are built, the talk-

ing boosts the body's tenacious hold on the movement over the top. These dancers are running from/running to. They are hunted/haunted. They cannot stay in any one place. The only antidote to the immobilizing categories that are circumscribing their choreographic efforts—interracial couple, gay couple, male couple (in dance), each of which is spilling over into the next—is to keep on the move, to out-distance, to out-endure, to persevere in the endlessly generative. There's always another pose, always another move.

But is the move simply the doing of it? Yes and (at the same time) no. For those who choreograph and perform, dance's muteness can serve as refuge from and resource against multiple forms of marginalization. Any attempts to describe, categorize, and interpret dance must inevitably fail to represent all that it is, and by extension, the full identities of its practitioners. Yet even as dancing protects its participants from the full certainty that rationalizes prejudices of all sorts, it brings into play the representational conventions through which identity is constructed. Zane and Jones may insist on being viewed as two bodies in motion, yet they are also a black and white body, two male bodies, and a host of other defining attributes that become increasingly evident during their performance.

Earlier in this century dancers exercised dance's indescribability through references to an unspeakable spiritual or psychological transcendence achieved through dancing. Since Cunningham, dancers have often insisted instead on the power of movement, not to transport the psyche, but to articulate itself. Simply doing the moves achieves all the significance there needs to be. Zane and Jones reinvigorate this assertion by charging it with the enormity of everything else that the moves can mean while also meaning themselves. They mobilize motion and meaning, crafting a duet between these two choreographic elements that resembles their duo dances. Meaning itself is running from/running to, underlying, overarching, embracing the doing of it . . . just like two arms going round and round.

Notes

1. Nancy Lee Chalfa Ruyter provides an excellent analysis of the use of Delsarte's theory in the U.S. physical culture movement and its influence on the first generation of modern dance choreographers in *Reformers and Visionaries: The Americanization of the Art of Dance* (New York: Dance Horizons, 1979).

2. Ted Shawn, *Every Little Movement: A Book about François Delsarte* (Pittsfield, Mass.: Eagle Printing, 1954), 35.

3. For a good overview of Ailey's career and choreographic accomplishments, see Thomas DeFrantz, "Revelations: The Choreographies of Alvin Ailey" (Ph.D. diss., New York University, 1997).

4. Cunningham's conceptualization of body parts and actions is vividly depicted in his own summary of his early choreographic production *Changes: Notes on Choreography* (New York: Something Else Press, 1968). For comprehensive documentation of his career, see David Vaughn, *Merce Cunningham* (New York: Aperture, 1997).

5. For a detailed description of these choreographers' performances, see Sally Banes, *Democracy's Body: Judson Dance Theatre, 1962–64* (Ann Arbor, Mich.: UMI Research Press, 1983).

6. Zane studied photography prior to and during the first years of his involvement with dance. The original version of this essay appeared as part of a catalogue celebrating his photographic achievements. I am deeply indebted to Jonathan Green and Bill Bissell for their roles in making the photo exhibit and related activities happen.

7. Bill T. Jones in Elizabeth Zimmer and Susan Quasha, eds., *Body against Body: The Dance and Other Collaborations of Bill T. Jones and Arnie Zane* (Barrytown, N.Y.: Station Hill Press, 1989), 38.

8. Ellen Graff, *Stepping Left: Dancing and Politics in New York City, 1928–1942* (Durham, N.C.: Duke University Press, 1997), 37–38.

9. Ann Daly discusses Duncan's treatment of jazz in *Done into Dance* (Bloomington: Indiana University Press, 1995), 215–220; Ted Shawn's references to Negro dance may be found in *The American Ballet* (New York: Henry Holt, 1926).

10. Susan Manning, "Danced Spirituals: The Performance of Race, Gender, and Sexuality in American Modern Dance 1930–1960," in *Moving Ideologies*, ed. Andre Lepecki (Middletown, Conn.: Wesleyan University Press, forthcoming).

11. Brenda Dixon Gottschild, *Digging the Africanist Presence in American Performance* (Westport, Conn.: Greenwood Press, 1996), 47–58.

12. Richard A. Long, *The Black Tradition in American Dance* (New York: Rizzoli, 1989), 142.

13. I believe that this theorization of race also informs later works such as *Last Supper at Uncle Tom's Cabin/The Promised Land* (1990) where the history of racial oppression is explicitly addressed.

14. Jones speaking in the dialogue between Zane and Jones in *Rotary Action*. The dialogue for *Rotary Action* is printed in Zimmer and Quasha, *Body against Body*, 70.

Embodying History: Epic Narrative and Cultural Identity in African American Dance

ANN COOPER ALBRIGHT

What would it mean to reinscribe history through one's body? What would it mean to recreate the story of a life and the history of a people? How does one rewrite the history of slavery, the history of faith, the history of a past, in order to project the story of our future? How can we reenvision the historical legacies of our time through the eyes of hope and human survival instead of rage and cynicism?

These questions guide my reflections on a genre of contemporary performance that I call the New Epic Dance. Over the past decade, I have witnessed full evening-length dance/drama as by choreographers as diverse as Garth Fagan, David Rousseve, Jawole Willa Jo Zollar, and Bill T. Jones. These works explore various facets of African American cultural heritages, refiguring written history in order to embody a tale of the choreographer's own making.[1] I am particularly interested in how these theatrical dances both enact and rework mythic and historical images of slavery, colonial power, and religious faith within a contemporary parable that allows individual dancers to infuse the story with their own histories and physicalities. Using dance as a metaphor for the physical desire to survive and the metaphysical need to fill that survival with hope, these choreographers have, with the help of their collaborators and companies, created theatrical spectacles that evoke the elegiac as well as the celebratory spirit of a people wedged in between two worlds. In many ways, these epic works remind me of the term that Audre Lorde used to describe her autobiographical work "Zami: A New Spelling of My Name." Grounded in, but not limited to, the historical facts of a people's existence, these epic dance narratives weave what Lorde calls a "biomythography," elaborating visionary sagas of social and personal survival.

The creation of an individual life narrative, or an (auto)biography is expanded in the New Epic Dance to include expressions of cultural identity that call upon mythic and archetypal, as well as historical, images of African Americans. Works such as Garth Fagan's *Griot New York,* David Rousseve's *Urban Scenes/Creole Dreams,* Urban Bush Women's *Bones and Ash: A Gilda Story,* and Bill T. Jones's *Last Supper at Uncle Tom's Cabin/The Promised Land* focus on the collective survival stories of African peoples in America. Because of their narrative scope, which is to say their desire not only to remember the past and document the present but also to narrate future possibilities, as well as their ambitious integration of dance, song, and theatrical text within a full evening-length performance, these works are clearly epic in scale. There is, of course, a crucial distinction between the traditional Western Homeric epic and these late twentieth-century revisitations of that densely layered form of narrative. Traditional epics tend, generally, to celebrate conquest and the lives of warrior statesmen. By contrast, these contemporary African American epics celebrate and honor the legacy of a people who have survived conquest; heroism is located not in the defeater, but rather in the spirit of those who have refused to be defeated.

In order to be effectively and potently embodied in performance, history has to be recast, so to speak— situated in a different light and taken up by different bodies. The importance of history here is not the importance of historical fact or artifact; such documents, authorized in the service of white dominance, are rightfully suspect. Rather, history for so many African Americans is located in the story—in the telling again and again. This retelling of ancestral blood memories is the compelling force behind much of the New Epic Dance. For stories to be historically meaningful, however, they need two things: a sense of truth (which, while it does not need to be static, must be galvanizing); and a sense of community between speakers and listeners, a realization of what is at stake in this exchange of the word.

The genre of contemporary African American performance that I am defining as the New Epic Dance is staged in Jones's and Zollar's work as a collective biomythography. These dance/dramas combine music, dance, and text to present a revised history that plays with the tropes of ironic repetition, reenactment, and reinterpretation. While all the works I have mentioned deserve in-depth discussion, the limitations of time and space, as well as my desire not to treat these important works in a cursory fashion, have prompted me to confine my extended analysis to two works: Bill T. Jones and Arnie Zane Dance Company's *Last Supper at Uncle Tom's Cabin/The Promised Land* (1990), and Urban Bush Women's *Bones and Ash: A Gilda Story* (1995–1996). I have chosen these two performative epics to compare because they provide a very different kind of theatrical experience for the audience, foregrounding the representation of race, memory, and historical experience in ways that ask their viewers to engage with their own historical memories. Although these two works look and feel very different from one another, they are both animated by a visionary sensibility that seeks to reform the legendary evils of greed and the lust for power in order to create a new infrastructure of social interaction. Both works refuse our contemporary cynicism, meeting a fin-de-siècle hopelessness with a conviction that humanity can be reborn. And both works are, I believe, deeply feminist in spirit, if not always in detail. The complex interweaving of oral, danced, and theatrical texts in *Last Supper* and *Bones and Ash* documents our national legacy of interracial hate and gendered and ethnic inequalities. Yet this very bleak history is enriched by personal narratives of love, religious faith, and spiritual transcendence. By reinterpreting classic stories and cultural stereotypes through contemporary dancing bodies, both Jones and Zollar refuse the static doneness of historical documentation, lifting the black and white printing off the page and imbuing it with the ability to move, shift, and, finally, to transform itself.

> In this chain and continuum, I am but one link. The story is me, neither me nor mine. It does not really belong to me, and while I feel greatly responsible for it, I also enjoy the irresponsibility of the pleasure obtained through the process of transferring. Pleasure in the copy, pleasure in the reproduction. No repetition can ever be identical, but my story carries with it their stories, their history, and our story repeats itself endlessly despite our persistence in denying it.[2]

These words by Trinh T. Minh-ha begin the story of my telling, my witnessing. For in the context of this writing, I am the conduit—the speaker who translates —these epic performances for a reading public. The dances I have seen have influenced how I think, how I see. Taken in and witnessed through my body, they come alive through my language and my ideas. Unfortunately, most people will not have had the opportunity to see these works for themselves and so my writing may be the only exposure they have to these epic dances. This is, indeed, a great responsibility. Thus I want to be clear about how I, a white, feminist dancer and writer, negotiate the position of witness and critic here. My experiences with these works may well be different from other dance writers, particularly African American dance critics. Yet while I acknowledge the potency of experiences of racism and my privilege in this regard, I do not believe that this difference invalidates my perception, nor do I believe that I can't write about African American performance in a way that is both cognizant of this difference and informed by a knowledge of that cultural perspective. In other words, while I would never pretend to have an "insider's" viewpoint, neither will I be satisfied with claiming my outside status as a way of refusing responsibility for representing this very important work. Being white is no excuse for not making the effort to learn about and come to understand the complexities and multiple layers of meaning in contemporary African American epic dance.[3]

In his inspiring book *Negotiating Difference: Race, Gender and the Politics of Positionality*, Michael Awkward takes up the negotiations of power that are inherent in white critics' writing about black texts. Awkward is a professor of English and so his examples come mostly from literature, yet his careful delineation of a critical position that could both register the racial privilege inherent in white criticism and also recognize what he calls the possibility of "interpretive crossing-over" can provide an important example of conscious criticism for cultural critics involved with any form of cultural production. In his chapter "Negotiations of Power: White Critics, Black Texts, and the Self-Referential Impulse," Awkward analyzes various interpretive positions across the continuum of white criticism of African American literature. While many white critics still approach African American literature in purely formal Euro-aesthetic terms, as (to use Houston Baker's term) "super-ordinate authorities," Awkward argues for the possibility of other kinds of readings. "I want to emphasize my belief that neither a view of all essential incompatibility between black literature and white critics nor of whites as always already dismissive and unsophisticated in their analyses of the products of the Afro-American imagination is still tenable."[4] Awkward later uses Larry Neal's discussions of white critical practices to suggest the possibility of a "thick" reading

that reflects "some understanding of [black] cultural source."[5] For Awkward, race is as much a political ideology and commitment as it is an essential or biological fact.

For Neal, critical competence with respect to Afro-American expressivity is determined not by tribal connections into which one is born; rather, it is gained by academic activity—"by studying"—in the same way that one achieves comprehension of the cultural matrices that inform the work of writers like Joyce, Yeats, and e.e. cummings. Demystifying the process of acquiring an informed knowledge of Afro-American expressivity, Neal insists that the means of access for all critics, regardless of race, is an energetic investigation of the cultural situation and the emerging critical tradition.[6]

My essay on African American epic performance is compelled by the conviction that this work is too important not to deal with, even if that means taking a risk by putting myself in a less comfortable critical position. Because I am a dancer and a theorist who is concerned about the fate of material bodies at the end of the twentieth century, I want to expand Neal's notion of "studying" to include not only book work, but also the physical situatedness of a culture—that is to say, investigating the ways African American bodies live, move, perform, tell stories, walk, etc. Although issues of racial difference have greatly influenced academic discourse over the past two decades, too often these discussions of "race" or "difference" remain purely abstract, content to stay in the comfort of armchairs and ivory towers. I believe, however, that there is a crucial difference between merely talking about "attention to diversity" and actually committing oneself to a critical and personal engagement that recognizes and connects with the power and variety of African American expressivity. I quoted Minh-ha earlier because I felt that her elaboration of the continuum and transmission of culture at once recognizes the differences between "I" and "they" ("No repetition can ever be identical") and sees the interconnectedness, the "our" ("but my story carries with it their stories, their history, and our story repeats itself"). It is with a recognition of this difference, in tandem with the belief that this difference can produce a viable critical engagement, that I continue.

*Re*writing, *re*inscribing, *re*creating, *re*envisioning, *re*figuring, *re*framing, *re*incorporating, *re*interpreting, *re*presenting—the reader will no doubt have noticed the frequency with which I have used the prefix *re* so far. This is not merely a poststructuralist tic of mine. The act of going back to take up again—returning, reclaiming, repossessing—this is a strategy that is central to contemporary African American performance. Adrienne Rich once described this process as "re-vision—the act of looking back, of seeing with fresh eyes, of entering an old text from a new critical direction."[7] Nowhere is this device more provocatively explored than in the first section of Jones's *Last Supper at Uncle Tom's Cabin/ The Promised Land*. Here, Jones both reenacts the sentimentalized Christian ethos of salvation embedded in Harriet Beecher Stowe's 1852 novel *Uncle Tom's Cabin*, and deconstructs the racist stereotypes connected to the popularized minstrel versions of that abolitionist story. At once fragmenting and reinventing the tropes of blackface, the family, religious faith, womanhood, slavery, and "Uncle Toms," Jones outlines the ambivalent relationship his dancers have with those historical characters. Employing theatrical devices to foreground the performance of racial and gendered stereotypes, Jones indicates the contradictory closeness and distance—the similarities and the differences—between then and now.

Given the cultural baggage that "Uncle Tom" has acquired over the past 145 years, it seems reasonable to ask why an African American male choreographer would want to recreate Stowe's narrative onstage. Is it in order to lend a more authentic voice to the story? Is it in order to rewrite the ending of Tom's life, to reject his Christian martyrdom in favor of a more strident rebellion? Or perhaps to reanimate a figure who, although written into existence by a white northern woman, has been repeatedly restaged by both black

and white bodies throughout the histories of minstrelsy, regional theater, and Hollywood cinema? Fortunately, Bill T. Jones has been—not uncharacteristically—quite verbal and forthcoming about his artistic process. But the journey from a 1989 entry in his recently published autobiography, *Last Night on Earth*— "I read Uncle Tom's Cabin. I find it to be hokum, misinformation. I find it moving, infuriating, beautiful, embarrassing, and important"[8]—to the description one page later of *Last Supper at Uncle Tom's Cabin/The Promised Land*—"It would speak about being human. About how we are the places we have been, the people we have slept with. How we are what we have lost and what we dream for"[9]—requires more than a fleeting summary of Jones's artistic intentions; it requires a close analysis of the complex cycle of referentiality that gives his work such resonance for a contemporary audience.

The first section of Jones's *Last Supper* is staged as a frame within a frame. This scene is played within a two-dimensional backdrop created by hanging a checkered gingham patchwork quilt that opens like a makeshift curtain to reveal a small stage. This "cabin" set simultaneously evokes both the influences of early Americana and the stylized replication of that period as "folk" art. It is on this stage-within-a-stage that we witness a much abbreviated version of Stowe's novel. Like many nineteenth-century theatrical renditions of *Uncle Tom's Cabin*, Jones's take is a series of allegorical vignettes and tableaux that punctuate Tom's narrative of redemptive faith with the equally uplifting and equally melodramatic stories of Eliza and Eva. With the notable exceptions of the narrator (played by Justice Allen), the authoress Stowe (played by Sage Cowles), and the character of Uncle Tom (played by Andrea Smith), most of the other dancers have on masks with highly exaggerated and often grotesque features. For example, the slave trader Haley's mask looks almost comically evil, a cross between a skeleton and a German Expressionist painting. The blackface masks are also cartoonish, especially the figure of "black Sam." However, to simply label these figures stereotypical caricatures, as many reviews of the *Last Supper* have done, is to misrepresent the ironic repetition in Jones's staging. For Jones's reenactment of the iconographic features of the minstrel tradition doesn't simply repeat the racist stereotypes that underlie Stowe's novel and run rampant throughout most of the minstrel versions of Uncle Tom's story. Rather, Jones ironically reframes these caricatures in order to create a perspective that at once distances and embraces this legacy of cultural reproductions.

Jones's work reflects the proliferation of meanings implicit in any reclaiming, reinscribing, or rewriting of one's history. In *Love and Theft*, Eric Lott describes the strategy of reclamation in Martin Delany's black nationalist novel *Blake* in terms that also reflect what I think Jones is doing in his version of Uncle Tom's Cabin. "*Blake* writes black agency back into history through blackface songs taken 'back' from those who had plundered black cultural practices. Rather than reject the cultural territory whites had occupied by way of minstrelsy, Delany recognizes that occupation as fact and occupies in turn."[10] Throughout his epic narrative of struggle and faith, Jones is employing repetition—but repetition with a crucial difference. Like Lott's description of Delany's work, Jones's redeployment of the minstrel tradition reflects that tradition's hybrid nature while also claiming it as a vehicle through which to reassert his own historical voice.

For instance, the masks—literally a face on top of a face—foreground the performative nature of stereotypes, forcing the audience to recognize the clichéd sentimentality of those images. And yet these two-faced characters operate in a very postmodern fashion, for they split the actor and the character, refusing any essentialist notions about who should play whom. Indeed, Jones's use of masks allows him to cast across the performer's own racial, gender, or age groups. Aunt Chloe is played by a white man, Larry Goldhuber, while Simon Legree, the monstrous slave owner described in the text as a mean man who prides himself on having a "fist of iron for hittin' niggers," is portrayed by a black man, Justice Allen.

This kind of reframing, refiguring, and cross-referencing is most striking in the very first dance sequence when Harry, "a beautiful quadroon boy," is asked to entertain the slave trader by doing the "Jim Crow." Now the "Jim Crow" has a highly complicated history. The term first entered the national discourse in the 1820s with the arrival of T. D. "Daddy" Rice, a white northern performer who popularized a parody of the "dancing darkie" by "blacking up" and performing a syncopated jig. To "jump Jim Crow" quickly became a main attraction in the minstrel shows, and even as African American performers entered that tradition after the Civil War, the caricature remained a staple of minstrelsy. Played ironically by black performers in blackface, the "Jim Crow" is a dance that simultaneously lampoons the white master and caricatures the black slave, at once portraying and ironically displacing racist notions of African Americans' inherent musicality and natural dance ability.[11]

Although the "Jim Crow" first became known through white performances of black dancing on the minstrel stage, Harriet Beecher Stowe naturalizes this racist portrayal of the black body by placing it on the plantation. In Stowe's novel, the "Jim Crow" dance, performed by the young (and desirable) quadroon boy Harry, actually sets the dramatic action in play. The book begins with a conversation between the "kindly" (and paternalistic) slave owner Mr. Shelby, who owes money to the not so kindly slave trader Mr. Haley. Their discussion is interrupted by Harry, who enters the scene and is requested by Shelby to entertain Haley by doing the "Jim Crow." Stowe's description of the boy's dance reveals the racist views concerning the dancing black body so prevalent even among the abolitionists of her time. "The boy commenced one of those wild, grotesque songs common among the negroes, in a rich, clear voice, accompanying his singing with many comic evolutions of the hands, feet, and whole body, all in perfect time to the music."[12] It is after seeing Harry dance that Haley wants to buy him, underlining the connection between the performing body's public visibility (that it is always available for the spectator's gaze) and the slave's body's inevitable purchasability (that it is always for sale).

In the "Cabin" section of Jones's *Last Supper* the "Jim Crow" is performed by Sean Curran, a wonderfully accomplished white dancer whose roots in Irish step dancing give him the necessary skills to execute a very good "Jim Crow." Despite its entertaining rhythms and virtuosic footwork, it is difficult to watch this divertissement without confronting the colonialist legacy of this dance. As Jacqueline Shea Murphy makes clear in her essay on Jones's epic, "Unrest and Uncle Tom": "The term 'Jim Crow' itself provides a clear instance of how tightly intertwined African American performance and violent oppression have been in this country. 'Jim Crow' originally named a minstrel song-and-dance act that today one understands to have stereotyped, parodied, and degraded African Americans; the term became synonymous, late in this century, with a system of (sometimes violently enforced) racial segregation."[13] The effect of this contemporary cross-racing of an historically racist image is both curiously disturbing and sensational. Jones's restaging of the "Jim Crow" takes place within Stowe's narrative, but the spectacular element of the scene is emphasized such that he provokes a double critique. In this scene, the audience witnesses the ambiguity of simultaneous entertainment and political confrontation. We see Curran, in blackface mask, aping a minstrel portrayal of "Jim Crow" and yet we also see him doing a very virtuosic solo that demands respect in its own right. By way of his directorial choices, Jones seems to be suggesting that there is absolutely nothing essential about the connection between the sign of "Jim Crow" and its referent in the black body, a move that allows Jones both to criticize the historically racist portrayals of "Jim Crow" and to elaborate on the performative nature of any identity category.

The postmodern flickering in and out of history, race, and identity at play in much of this first section of *Last Supper* is grounded by the powerfully realistic representations of Eliza and Uncle Tom. The Eliza character, for example, is portrayed by a tall, lean,

young African American woman, Andrea Woods. Although the figure of the heroically maternal Eliza is masked in the "Cabin" section, her brief appearance in this section must be realistic enough to foreshadow her magnificent solo in the next scene of the dance. "Eliza on the Ice" is a complex theatrical meditation on the very brief but important moment in Stowe's book where Eliza escapes to freedom with her son by jumping on moving blocks of ice to cross the Ohio River. In his staging of this scene, Jones elaborates on the existential meanings implicit in Eliza's state of liminality—of literally being suspended between two shores—by creating multiple Elizas, variations on a central theme. This section is a good example of how Jones negotiates between deconstructing deterministic essentialist or racist notions about the inextricability of color and identity, and recognizing the historical legacies of such constructions. Jones knows that in order for history to be refigured, it must first be figured in such a way that powerfully evokes the real bodies at stake within the representation.

The "Eliza" section begins in darkness. As the lights rise slowly, they reveal a line of five different Elizas standing one behind the other. The first woman, Andrea Woods, holds the Eliza mask she wore in the first section of the dance. She removes the mask and turns to hand it to the woman behind her, who in turn hands it to the woman behind her. The mask passes through the hands of the four women until it ends up with the Stowe character. As she begins to recite Sojourner Truth's famous "Ain't I a Woman?" speech, the first Eliza (whom Jones has dubbed "the historical Eliza") begins to dance. To the stirring words of Truth's rhetorical questioning ("I have ploughed and planted and gathered into barns and no man could head me! And ain't I a woman?"), Woods delivers a physical evocation of generations of black woman working, rejoicing, and confronting the world. Her movement is wide and strong as her torso loops down to the ground and then arches up to the sky, catapulting her long legs out into the space around her. Her arms can be powerfully direct, as in the moment when she shoves her arm straight to the audience in a defiant gesture, or wonderfully generous, as when she reaches out to embrace the possibilities of the world around her. Suddenly, the slow, punctuated rhythm underlining Truth's speech switches gears and becomes upbeat and bouncy. Woods responds in kind until the final moment, which ends with a rolling strut offstage to Truth's declaration "And now I am here."

The next Eliza is a contemporary portrayal by Heidi Latsky, a short Jewish woman whose fierce dancing provides a tangible accompaniment to the story of abuse and betrayal she recites. In this section, we move from the archetypal figure of Eliza as an African American woman struggling with crossing over from slavery to freedom to a contemporary portrait of Eliza as a survivor. Her text (which she speaks into a microphone held by the Stowe character as she moves across the stage) is potently embodied in Latsky's movement eruptions. "I believe . . . My father told me turn the other cheek . . . My mother told me not to expect much," contextualizes her dancing, which is marked by the contrast between clenching her body to herself and striking out at the forces around her. Pulling at her own body, Latsky seems, at times, to want to tear off her own skin. The lyrical movement of the historical Eliza changes here into the tight, explosive movement of a woman who desperately wants to resist society's admonishments to "be good." This Eliza is also caught between the shores of expectation and freedom, but the terms of her struggle have changed.

The next two Elizas similarly embody archetypal situations for women, but because their solos have no direct textual accompaniment, they are much less specific in narrative detail. The third Eliza is danced by Betsy McCracken, a tall, white dancer whose legs shoot out with military precision as she wields her staff around the stage. Her character is like a powerful Greek goddess, perhaps Athena, who directs the male corps de ballet into parade-like formations. Jones speaks of this Eliza as the one "who commands men—part Joan of Arc, part dominatrix, and part martial arts master."[14] This power is, of course, extremely tenuous,

and it is exhausting to watch McCracken always on her guard, never able to release the tension in her body. Eventually she decides that this power isn't worth the stakes involved and, throwing her staff away, she runs offstage—free at last.

The fourth Eliza is Maya Saffrin, whom Jones describes in his autobiography as "exotically pretty," and whose dance is a metaphoric struggle between the various men who lift and pass her among themselves and the first Eliza, who tries to rescue her from their control. This Eliza is clearly the most disempowered. Almost zombie-like, her passive physical presence makes it seem as if she has no will of her own. Even when she dances a duet with the first Eliza, she is dancing her partner's movement, always looking at her friend for guidance. Although she is not floppy like a rag doll (which in some ways would be a sort of resistance, making it hard for anyone to lift or carry her), her energy is so contained that one wonders whether this Eliza would even have left the first shore, let alone have the strength of purpose actually to make it across to the promised land.

As this fourth Eliza exits, a fifth and final Eliza—one the audience has not previously seen—enters. This Eliza is danced by a very tall African American man, Gregg Hubbard. He is wearing only a bright white miniskirt and white pumps. Perhaps the most contemporary of all, this Eliza is figured as a gay man in drag. Standing awkwardly on these heels, his almost naked body giving him a childlike innocence, he executes a series of gestural movements very much like Jones's signature gestures where the arms continually circle the upper body to form an elaborate frame. Tracing his hands over his head and down the front of his body, Hubbard stops to grab his crotch in a sudden gesture. Is he meant to surprise us or reassure himself? This brief moment of doubt changes into a "work it" attitude as he turns and walks off the stage with a body wave slyly snaking from his head down to his toes.

In the *Alive from off Center* television special focusing on the making of *Last Supper* (aired in 1992), Jones details the process of creating these various Elizas. He speaks eloquently about the importance of the dancers involved in the making of these solos, especially with regard to the first two Elizas, whose own personas were so deeply embedded in their characters. Then Jones shifts to a discussion of the final Eliza and talks about this figure's own struggles between a different kind of slavery and freedom. Speaking as a gay man about this final Eliza, Jones declares: "Our sexuality exists on neither shore, that of femininity and that of masculinity. It is its own thing, but because of the strictures of our society, we are left suspended, doubtful, fearful even, of where we belong."

Jones clearly identifies the "Eliza on the Ice" section of his epic undertaking as feminist statement of sorts. Certainly the progression from the historical Eliza to Hubbard's gay Eliza thoroughly deconstructs the static concept of woman so embedded in Western representation. Woman as a universal term actually meaning "white," "feminine," defined by her relationships to men, or even as suggesting a biological femaleness, is fractured by the different and contradictory embodiments of Eliza. Although Jones is playing here with the historical/fictionalized character of Eliza, he is also intent on underlining the universal dimensions of a liminal state, the way in which many people find themselves existentially "between two shores." The final Eliza could be problematic for feminists who are hesitant to fully deconstruct the category of woman altogether (for as Hubbard's crotch-grabbing gesture makes clear, a man in a skirt really hasn't given up his social power, it is merely hidden, available to be reerected, so to speak, at a moment's notice). Yet, for me, the crucial question is whether "her" appearance actually adds another dimension to this investigation of gender in our culture, or whether it serves to dismiss the earlier images of women's struggles. I believe that Jones consciously left Hubbard's Eliza out of the original lineup in order to give these female Elizas their own voices. Indeed, the autobiographical as well as historical character of their stories allows Jones to make the ideological connection—that gay men's sexualities are also suspended between two shores—without usurping

the material and political realities of women's lives. Jones thus problematizes, even deconstructs, gender without rendering it a completely vacant category. This balance of realism and performative spectacle is absolutely critical to the genre of epic dance. The potency of the form lies precisely in its witnessing of people's stories as well as its reconstructing of their historical legacies. And too, there is the issue of merged identities here, for Jones has often declared the powerful influence that black women have had in his life, most notably his mother (who appears onstage in this piece) and his sisters. If we take the Hubbard character as Jones himself, one might argue that he is, in fact, trying to bring out the female embedded in the male persona.[15]

Nonetheless, Hubbard's appearance at the end of the Eliza section serves to return the focus of the narrative back to men. For, as with the majority of Jones's work, most of *Last Supper* concentrates on the telling of his/story. This story starts with that of Uncle Tom and is told and retold in various forms throughout the dance. This is the story of black men in a white man's world—the history of racism and tales of its (and their) survival. This authorial voice is evident from the beginning of the "Cabin" section, embodied in the onstage figure of the narrator by Justice Allen. Much like a master of ceremonies, Allen welcomes the audience to Uncle Tom's Cabin and introduces the figure of Harriet Beecher Stowe, played by Sage Cowles. Allen and Cowles take turns telling the story of *Uncle Tom's Cabin* until the figure of Uncle Tom is introduced into the scenario. Uncle Tom is played by Andrea Smith, a strapping young man who infuses this character with a riveting stage presence. His powerful voice is first heard in sermon. The moment is striking because he is the first character within the staged drama to speak. Up to this point all the other characters' thoughts, feelings, and actions have been either mimed or narrated by someone else. The fact that Uncle Tom controls his own voice gives him an immediate dignity within this minstrel setting. In *Last Night on Earth*, Jones mentions the combination of optimism, gentleness, and sensuality that he thought Smith could embody in his portrayal of Uncle Tom. "Andrea was young in many senses of the word, and the openness and curiosity implied by his youth were necessary in recreating such a worn, misunderstood icon as Uncle Tom."[16]

Recreated by Jones's directorial vision, this Uncle Tom is vulnerable yet strong, young yet wise. Interestingly enough, Smith's presence onstage immediately stands out in contrast to the minstrel icons surrounding him. Whereas their movements are often puppet-like, repetitious, and spatially truncated, his physical presence is grounded but graceful, with his arms arching to the heavens. Working in union with his voice, his movement commands attention. While preaching, he stands above the others like a magnificent old tree whose branches dance in the wind, all the while being rooted deeply to the earth. Uncle Tom's spiritual and inspirational leadership is foreground by Jones's use of theatrical retrograde. After Uncle Tom is killed by Simon Legree and ascends to heaven, Stowe asks what is there for those who are left behind. The cast faces out and together shouts "Freedom!" Refusing closure in order to rewrite the possibilities of another kind of resistance back into the story, Jones stops the play and all the characters backtrack through their movements until the scene where Legree tries to "break Tom's spirit." Here, Jones reproduces, with a crucial difference, the stylized whipping of slaves by Legree. Instead of one or two characters, the whole cast comes back out without masks and one by one lines up to confront Legree. Shaking their heads "No!" and circling their arms in front of their bodies in a defiantly martial gesture, these people—black, white, young, old, male, female—refuse Legree's domination, even as he whips them. They line up again and again such that Legree has a constant group of protesters in his face. Their perseverance and their refusal to become submissive (like Tom's refusal to be beaten down even as he was beaten up) make Legree's relentless whipping gesture look increasingly ridiculous.

In this section, Jones sets up a narrative logic that he will pursue throughout *Last Supper at Uncle Tom's Cabin/The Promised Land*. In scene after scene, Jones highlights the importance of African American men's experience and then connects that experience to issues of power, exclusion, pain, and survival that affect us all. Allen, Smith, Hubbard, and Arthur Aviles are spotlighted as the central figures, as various embodiments of Christ in the Last Supper. In the documentary on the making of this dance, Jones tells us that "this dance is a dance about differences—race, sexual, class. About how we can work through those differences and move to another place." The desire to balance a sense of specific history with a sense of global harmony serves as the impetus for the following sections of the dance ("The Supper" and "The Promised Land") in which Uncle Tom becomes Bill T. Jones becomes Justice Allen becomes Christ becomes naked becomes us all.

Resurrection in the sense of rebirth—even in the more literal sense of arising from the dead with a new knowledge—is one of the central themes in Urban Bush Women's *Bones and Ash: A Gilda Story*. In this epic her/story, choreographer Jawole Willa Jo Zollar and her company are joined by the writer Jewelle Gomez, the composer Toshi Reagon, and co-director Steven Kent in a dance/theater collaboration that recreates another nineteenth-century literary genre—that of the vampire story. Jewelle Gomez's lesbian vampire novel, *The Gilda Stories*, serves as the textual basis for *Bones and Ash*, although some features of the novel were dropped and others were added to make this story into a performance. In this retelling of a European genre, however, the self-indulgent, obsessive vampire figure is transformed into a caring, maternal angel-cum-lover, who is a spiritual guide for humanity. In the context of an African American tradition, sharing blood is less an aspect of sadistic seduction than of a mutual exchange, marking a respect for balance based on African ideologies of ritual sacrifice. Gomez's work is much more surreal than Stowe's domestic novel, for it chronicles the evolution of the Girl character from her rescue as a runaway slave in 1850 and her conversion into a vampire called Gilda (what is called, somewhat euphemistically, the "long life") through the twentieth century right into the future in a chapter entitled "Land of Enchantment 2050." Although the need for theatrical coherence has limited the time frames of *Bones and Ash*, the performance still highlights a sense of history as a continuum of people—a literal bloodline that, interestingly enough, has little to do with biological family and more to do with emotional families. Epic in scale and mythic in genre, *Bones and Ash* traces historical change through the life of one body—one body, that is, that will live for hundreds of years.

Like Gomez's novel, *Bones and Ash* has two central vampire characters: Gilda (played by Deborah Thomas in the 1995 version I first saw, and more recently played by Pat Hall-Smith) and Bird (played by Emerald Trinket Monsod, a guest artist). These two women's historical knowledge gives them both the wisdom and the responsibility to guide their surrogate daughter, a runaway slave, called Girl (played by company member Christine King). Gilda, who lived in Brazil several hundred years ago, runs a bordello with her lover, Bird, a Filipino woman who lived with the Lakota tribe before starting this life. It is the coming of yet another war, the Civil War, that compels Gilda to give up her eternal life. But before Gilda can cross over into the promised land, she and Bird must teach Girl how to understand her terrifying nightly dreams, which mix disturbing images of past fears and present realities. In effect, they must teach her how to understand her history fully so that she can begin to envision her future. These lessons take the form of a dancing apprenticeship in which Bird helps the Girl to literally re-member her own body by leading her through a series of martial dance forms that gives the Girl a renewed sense of agency and pride. It is only once she is physically present that the Girl can begin to remember and embrace her own history. "Of her home their mother spoke about, the Girl was less certain. It was always a dream place—distant, unreal. Except the talk of dancing. . . . Talking of it now, her body rocked slightly as if she had been rewoven into that old circle of dancers. She poured out the images and names, proud of her own ability to weave a story. Bird smiled at her pupil who claimed her past, reassuring her silently."[17]

Once the girl has reclaimed her past—found the voice with which she can tell her own history—Gilda can move on, bequeathing her spirit and her name to the Girl. Because Gilda is a vampire, her "gift of long life" takes place as an "exchange of blood," where the two individuals involved in the exchange suck blood (not from the neck, as one might expect, but from a space just below the breast). This motif of exchange—of blood, life, and body—reverberates throughout the individual biomythography of Jewelle Gomez. In her collection of writings, *43 Septembers*, Gomez has a piece entitled "Transubstantiation: This is my body, this is my blood." She begins this essay with a very simple summation of the contradictions that defined her childhood religious experience: "I was raised a Black Catholic in a white Catholic town."[18] Although Gomez has since revised her spirituality to accommodate more fully her life choices, the passion and the physical vitality of that early training have never really left her. Thus, the blood of communion becomes the blood of social action and a belief in the interconnectedness of people and their histories.

> The key is in the sea change: the place where the small incident is transformed into the belief, the daily wine into the blood. In that change I am learning to treasure the things of my past without being limited by them. . . . To make the past a dimension of my life, but not the only perspective from which I view it. In that way my youth is not more important than my middle years; . . . my knowledge is not better or truer than anyone else's, its value comes when it is made useful to others."[19]

For Gomez, blood becomes the bond becomes the body that can change, through the redemptive power of love, the ordinary into the spiritual, life into history, and words into a dance.

In *Bones and Ash*, however, the exchange of blood is not the central event that it is in Gomez's novel. Rather it is the exchange of movement, of energy, of dancing among the company that signals the physical and spiritual interconnectedness of the women onstage. This is most striking in the dancing sections, which serve as metaphoric frames to the narrative action of the first act. The opening scene of *Bones and Ash* is a prologue spoken from the present about the past. The light comes up slowly to reveal a lone figure, moving through the shadows of the stage's dim lighting. An offstage voice is heard speaking memories about a life that has lasted many centuries. The woman onstage begins a solo that will parallel many of the emotional states called forth by the poetic prose. At times she lifts her arms slowly, fluidly, stretching her body luxuriously. Other times she skips lightheartedly, and yet other times she seems agitated. Although she is silent, it is clear that we are hearing her memories, her thoughts, her story. Images of cotton and blood are woven into a tapestry of reflection that speaks of slavery and a historical memory that is an ongoing puzzle. For the past, like the vampires at the center of this story, refuses to "lie down and die."

> The shape of my life is motion through fields, through time, through blood. Each decade is woven into the next, embroidered centuries draped across my shoulders, a rainbow of lives, every one my own. Behind me—one hundred and fifty years of those I've loved, those I've lost. All taking or giving blood. Dangerous, Reviving, Vital. The thin red line I follow down one row, up the next. A rhythmic dance draws the attention of the gods— Yemeya, Yellow Woman and many others. I am enamoured of motion.
>
> Someone said to me once: It must be hard in this world being black, descended from slaves, 'buked and scorned, benign neglect. I said no . . . actually it's being two hundred years old that pulls my patience. To live forever is a puzzle. Each piece snapping into place beside the next, but the picture is never fully seen.[20]

This sense of life and history as movement is triply reflected in the figures of the Irissas who soon enter up-

stage. In the program for *Bones and Ash*, the characters of the Irissas are described as the oldest teachers, the wise elders who guide their vampire family through the ages.[21] Danced by Gacirah Diagne, Beverley Prentice, and Christine Wright, these dancing sages often appear behind the scrim or sheer curtains, as if they are protecting, by the mere fact of their presence and attention, those onstage. In the prologue, they haunt the upstage space, emerging from the shadows to follow the Girl's journey across the space. Quick and light-footed, breathy yet grounded and forceful, their dancing can shift unexpectedly from a slow, steady bowing and rising motion to a whirling dervish–like spinning that sweeps across the stage, sending energy out in every direction. Their breathing is often audible and sometimes they whisper or sing advice to the central characters. Half Greek chorus, half African shaman, the Irissas embody archetypal spirits whose presence underlines life's continuity.[22]

The Irissas' presence in *Bones and Ash* provides a historical metanarrative to the specific action going on downstage, for they embody the past as well as the future. In many ways, their otherworldly presence has an angel-like quality. The main characters may sense the Irissas as they move with or surround them, but they never seem to see these dancing spirits. Like the vampires in Gomez's novel, the Irissas can hear other people's thoughts and, entering their minds, change those thoughts into more positive ones. They remind me of the trenchcoated angel figures in Wim Wenders's film *Wings of Desire*, whose very presence next to someone on a subway can alter the most cynical and disheartened thoughts, bestowing the gift of hope. In the middle of the first act, the Irissas chant the mantra of life-enriching vampires: "We take blood not life. Leave something in exchange." Indeed the difference between good vampires, embodied by Gilda and Bird, and bad ones, embodied in the figure of Fox, is clearly demonstrated in the first act. When Gilda and Bird come upon a distressed figure who is flailing around the stage, obviously confused, they surround him with sympathy, embracing him more as sisters than vampires, even as they take the blood they need. When they leave him, his sense of purpose is restored. In contrast, Fox seduces a woman with a courtly dance, and then leaves her dead.

In her study of vampires in nineteenth- and twentieth-century literature wittily entitled *Our Vampires, Ourselves*, Nina Auerbach expresses her frustration with what she calls the "anestheticizing virtue" of these good fairy vampires in Gomez's novel.

> Instead of killing mortals, Gilda and her friends bestow on them edifying dreams after taking fortifying sips of blood. Vampirism is not bloodsucking or feeding or the dark gift; it becomes "the exchange," an act of empathy, not power, whose first principle is, "feel what they are needing, not what you are hungering for" (p. 50). Like the construction of lesbianism *The Gilda Stories* celebrates, vampirism is purged of aggression.[23]

Although they do not fit into Auerbach's own definition of power as domination, the vampires in both *The Gilda Stories* and *Bones and Ash* provide what I consider a radical new vision of humanity. It is certainly true that these vampires don't excite that frisson of dangerous seductivity that seems a mainstay of traditional vampire novels. Yet their commitment to a sense of common bond with others, even those very different from themselves (i.e., mortals), presents an intriguing reconfiguration of identity, desire, and love within this gothic genre. The vampire figure rewritten as storyteller, as griotte, as spiritual guide, is a compelling example of how *Bones and Ash* weaves an Afrocentric belief in the interconnectedness of the world into a Eurocentric literary genre. Drawing on performative traditions that include ritual possession as well as West African and diasporan dance cultures, Urban Bush Women's collaborative epic builds on these influences to create the climactic ending of act 1, where Gilda "crosses over" to her final death. Once Gilda has decided to leave this world, she first initiates the Girl into the vampire life. At this moment, the theatrical action or "plot" is temporarily suspended as Gilda and the

Girl are joined by the Irissas in a ritual exchange of identity.

As Gilda's farewell letter is read by an offstage voice, Gilda begins her journey back to the earth. Alone onstage, Gilda emerges from the shadows with movements that suggest she is struggling to find the right pathway back. Her dancing becomes more convulsive as she continues, flinging her head first in one direction and then in another. Turning here and then there, bending down and arching up, twisting one way and then another, she seems to be fighting with her own choice, dissatisfied with every available position. Slowly the background fills with the rest of the company, newly dressed in African robes. They line up at the back of the stage as if they are protecting her from what lies beyond. Drawn to their presence, Gilda moves back and forth across their space, trying to find the right fit—the right rhythm, the right pathway, the right expression for her death. A drummer enters the space, intermittently accompanying her movement with ambient sound. Soon, however, the company's breaths take on a rhythm of their own as they first speak and then sing to Gilda. The drummer joins their rhythm and then starts to intensify it as Gilda works herself into a state of divine possession. Suddenly, this energy quiets down as she opens her body to the voyage over. Two women help her to disrobe, and a priestess figure (played by Valerie Winborne) begins to sing "Coming Home through the Morning Light," metaphorically washing Gilda down with her powerful voice. A slide of a river delta, then a closeup of the river are projected on the back scrim as Gilda opens the curtains and disappears into the water.

The exchange of energy between the company and Gilda in this last scene is paradigmatic of much of Urban Bush Women's work in which an individual transformation is assisted by the energy of the group. This sense of inter-connectedness between self and community is reflective of both the present moment and a historical continuity—defining who your community is at present and who your community was several hundred years ago. As their name suggests, Urban

40. Urban Bush Women in *Bones and Ash: A Gilda Story*. Photo by Tom Brazil, copyright © Tom Brazil.

Bush Women bring their ancestral roots into the twentieth century. In commenting on the diversity of African American women within the company, Veta Goler describes what she calls the "stunning mosaic of black womanhood." Despite the clear celebration of individuality, Urban Bush Women's work usually focuses on the sense of community between women. Goler describes this legacy of collective experience:

> Historically, black women have always established ways of coming together for mutual benefit. From the female networks in the family compounds of traditional African societies to the club movement and extended families of the New World, black women have supported and affirmed each other. Urban Bush Women's name evokes images of women assisting each other in

maneuvering for their survival within challenging environments.[24]

Most of Zollar's choreography for Urban Bush Women centers on the cultural experiences of African American women, creating what Goler calls a "cultural autobiography."

In many ways, the trope of the vampire allows Zollar literally to trace that cultural autobiography through different bodies. In this vein, vampires can help us to create a new sense of family, subverting the notion of bloodlines to fit different styles of familiar relationships. This is clearly a theme within Gomez's novel, which focuses on the vampire as lesbian more than *Bones and Ash* does. The lesbian perspective of Gomez's novel (which has several very steamy passages) is replaced by a less sexual and more womanist perspective in Zollar's choreography. What gets exchanged through the dancing in *Bones and Ash* is not so much desire, but memory and history. Urban Bush Women is the only professional African American women's dance company, and Zollar and the company members are committed to making manifest that legacy of challenge, survival, and hope. In an essay entitled "The New Moderns: The Paradox of Eclecticism and Singularity," Halifu Osumare describes Zollar in terms that echo her sense of legacy: "In Jawole Willa Jo Zollar one sees Katherine Dunham's and Pearl Primus's fierce passion for roots, their bold adventurousness in walking the urban back alleys and the rural dirt villages to research their subject matter, and their ingenious artistic transformation of cultural information."[25]

Given her very conscious representations of African American women's cultural experiences in her choreography, I was surprised to find out that Zollar doesn't see herself as directly addressing issues of race or gender in her work. This is not to say that Zollar is not acutely aware of racism or misogyny within representations of African American women. Anyone who was present at her plenary talk at the 1990 Dance Critics Association conference in Los Angeles cannot doubt her commitment to these issues.[26] However, she doesn't foreground the categories of race and gender in quite the way that Jones does. Instead, she builds on a specific cultural experience right from the start, never framing race as a topic within the performance, but rather speaking right away in an Afrocentric idiom. This strategy allows Zollar to claim a black female voice while also refusing the problematic assumption that, by claiming that culturally rooted voice, you are speaking only to people with knowledge of that specific experience. Rather, Zollar believes, as does Jones, that ultimately, many experiences of exclusion and oppression, as well as inclusion and community, are shared across cultural differences.

Although Jones's epic originates in the historical perspective of an African American gay man, his work continually interrogates these identities, even while claiming them. In "The Cabin" and "Eliza on the Ice" sections of his dance, which I discussed earlier in this essay, Jones questions the constructions of race and gender. In almost every scene, the audience is confronted with the issues surrounding how we come to see "blackness," "maleness," and "femaleness." But what is also clear is that we are never allowed to see these performers, even when they are in blackface or drag, as statically defined objects of our gaze. In this work, performers claim and embody identities in ways that resist pat or simplistic constructions of race, gender, or sexuality. Thus, for example, when Justice Allen tells his life story, he fulfills a stereotype of the black criminal on drugs but at the same time refuses its deterministic rigor mortis by also claiming an identity as a writer and performer who is "rockin' 'round the world with Bill T. Jones."

Jones is a deconstructionist at heart and rarely gives his audience any answers to the questions he insistently asks. What he does give us is a consistent strand of spectacular dancing. This is undeniably the role that Arthur Aviles (a self-described New York-rican, who is one of the company's most virtuosic dancers) takes on throughout *Last Supper*. Although Aviles doesn't have a speaking role and is never placed in a specific identity (such as Gregg Hubbard's drag scene at the end of "Eliza on the Ice"), his dancing serves as a sort of physical antidote to the existential quandaries implied by the text. This is true of the scene in which he is dancing downstage while "Uncle Tom" and Allen are speaking on the table. It is also Aviles's dancing that precipitates the final section of the dance, "The Promised Land," in which the stage is flooded with fifty-two naked people of all sizes and shapes who stand and face the audience.

I see Aviles's dancing as the physical metaphor for faith, the other focus of Jones's epic dance. Even as Jones doggedly deconstructs our assumptions about race, gender, life choices, family, and much more, he relies on a leap of faith to take his audience to the promised land. His improvisational questioning (maybe grilling is a more apt word) of a member of the clergy chosen from whichever community he is performing in is quite relentless. On the video of the premiere at the Brooklyn Academy of Music he is talking with Paul Abel, a gay minister. After asking him a series of questions including "What is faith? Is Christianity a slave religion? What is evil? Is AIDS punishment from God?" Jones probes Abel's feelings about serving a religion that doesn't recognize his own life choices. Yet this insistent line of questioning takes place after two scenes in which faith is reclaimed; Jones's improvising to his mother's praying, and his dancing to the story of Job as narrated by the clergy. In both instances, Jones's dancing, like Aviles's, fills an existential void with a very potent physical reality. Even though Jones questions faith in the midst of loss, he can still choreograph dances in which being present in the world with others takes on a healing spirituality. This is certainly the message of the final scene. In his autobiography, Jones sums it up this way:

> The Promised Land, with its hordes of naked flesh coming wave after wave into the footlights, pubic patches, pert breasts, sagging breasts, wrinkled knees, blissful eyes, furtive expressions of shame, is a visual manifestation of my profound sense of belonging. This was my portrait of us. All of us. And this is who I am too. One of us. It was my battle to disavow any identity as a dying outcast and to affirm our commonality. In it, some one thousand people from thirty cities stood naked, took a bow, and said, "We are not afraid."[27]

This mass of naked humanity is meant to place the very real bodily differences of race, age, ability, and gender in the midst of a symbolic embodiment of vulnerability and sameness. One wonders, however, how different things really are once the euphoric final moments have subsided and everyone is clothed again. Although he began *Uncle Tom's Cabin/The Promised Land* with a searing critique of race, mimesis, and representation, Jones ends this epic dance rather blandly, bringing his audience through a potentially uncomfortable confrontation with histories of dominations and survival to a present-day communitas. Is community really that easy? Didn't the 1960s teach us that politics are harder to change than one's clothes?

Like Jones's piece, *Bones and Ash* draws on African American memory and spirituality to stage the history of black women's bodies. Registering both the abuse and resistance of these women's lives, *Bones and Ash* celebrates a spirituality based on the interconnectedness of past, present, and future. In Gomez's and Urban Bush Women's vision, the exchange of self and other is considered an intersubjective act, not one of domination and subordination. This exchange of life force that does not destroy one partner (be it another person or the environment), but rather creates a mutual energy, is, of course, a wonderful model of performer/audience interaction—a model of responsiveness that is also grounded in African aesthetics and spirituality. Watching this piece, I came to appreciate the interconnectedness among the women onstage without feeling a need to identify their experience as my own. Unlike the final scenes in "The Promised Land" where difference is multiplied to the point of losing its meaning in a mass of humanity, *Bones and Ash* holds onto its own cultural moorings. I don't think that this differentiation is necessarily a problem. Indeed, it might be a very healthy distinction, one that recognizes the interconnectedness of our histories without erasing the importance of difference in choreographing the body's identity.

Notes

1. Although these days most editors do not hyphenate *African American*, I still think it is valuable to recall Trinh T. Minh-ha's concept of the hyphenated realities of underrepresented peoples. I rather like the inseparability of *African-American*, suggesting that this is an identity that, while contradictory, is a whole, not the sum of two parts.

2. Trinh T. Minh-ha, *Woman, Native, Other: Writing Postcoloniality and Feminism* (Bloomington: Indiana University Press, 1989), 121.

3. This is the excuse that Sue-Ellen Case uses in her simultaneous recognition and dismissal of theater by women of color at the end of her book *Feminism and Theater* (New York: Methuen, 1988). For an interesting analysis of her critical position see Michael Awkward's book *Negotiating Difference: Race, Gender, and the Politics of Positionality* (Chicago: University of Chicago Press, 1995), 87–90.

4. Awkward, *Negotiating Difference*, 60.

5. Ibid., 60.

6. Ibid., 61.

7. Rich, quoted in Awkward, *Negotiating Difference*, 41.

8. Bill T. Jones, *Last Night on Earth* (New York: Pantheon Books, 1995), 205.

9. Ibid., 206.

10. Eric Lott, *Love and Theft: Blackface Minstrelsy and the American Working Class* (Oxford: Oxford University Press, 1993), 236.

11. In *Love and Theft*, Lott elaborates the multiple and complex layers of meaning and subversion in the American minstrel tradition, complicating the analysis of blackface that serves only to reveal its racist stereotypes by asking what kinds of unconscious desires and conscious class connections are also negotiated in blacking up.

12. Harriet Beecher Stowe, *Uncle Tom's Cabin or, Life among the Lowly* (New York: Penguin, 1987), 44.

13. Jacqueline Shea Murphy, "Unrest and Uncle Tom: Bill T. Jones/Arnie Zane Dance Company's *Last Supper at Uncle Tom's Cabin/The Promised Land*," in *Bodies of the Text: Dance as Theory, Literature as Dance*, ed. Ellen W. Goellner and Jacqueline Shea Murphy (New Brunswick: Rutgers University Press, 1995), 82.

14. Jones, *Last Night on Earth*, 207.

15. I thank Caroline Jackson-Smith for pointing out this reading to me.

16. Ibid., 207.

17. Jewelle Gomez, *The Gilda Stories* (Ithaca, N.Y.: Firebrand Books, 1991), 39.

18. Jewelle Gomez, *43 Septembers* (Ithaca, N.Y.: Firebrand Books, 1993), 69.

19. Ibid., 78–79.

20. This quotation is a transcription of the narrator's voice-over during this section of the piece.

21. I saw a performance of *Bones and Ash* in Columbus, Ohio, on September 23, 1995, and another one in New York City in November 1996. I am grateful to the company for providing me with an early video of their performance in Iowa City (September 15, 1995). These are the sources for my movement descriptions of the piece. As with any performance work, the dancing and even the text can go through various and multiple revisions. Recently, Pat Hall-Smith has replaced Deborah Thomas as Gilda in the first act.

22. Although the Irissas are not featured in Gomez's *The Gilda Stories* per se, there are teacher characters like them in the novel, particularly Sorel and Anthony.

23. Nina Auerbach, *Our Vampires, Ourselves* (Chicago: University of Chicago Press, 1995), 185.

24. Veta Goler, "Dancing Herself: Choreography, Autobiography, and the Expression of the Black Woman Self in the Work of Dianne McIntyre, Blondell Cummings and Jawole Willa Jo Zollar" (Ph.D. diss., Emory University, 1994), 167.

25. Halifu Osumare, "The New Moderns: The Paradox of Eclecticism and Singularity," in *African American Genius in Modern Dance*, ed. Gerald E. Myers (Durham, N.C.: American Dance Festival, 1993).

26. See the printed version of Zollar's talk in *Looking Out: Perspectives on Dance and Criticism in a Multicultural World*, ed. David Gere (New York: Schirmer Books, 1995).

27. Jones, *Last Night on Earth*, 223.

A Little Technology Is a Dangerous Thing

RICHARD POVALL

Technology is with us—it's a part of our daily life and culture, and while some fear and decry the technocrats, we also consciously or otherwise revel in their works and indulge their perceived control over us. Computers have made life simpler and better for all of us, whether we are performing artists, academics, theorists or historians. Artists have used technology for centuries, for millennia, even. Artists, in fact, have often been creators of new technologies, refusing to be satisfied by currently available tools. There is a received wisdom amongst the dance community, however, that technology is a dangerous thing—that to use technology as an integral element in a work is to detract from the body, from the choreography and design, from the core of what is dance. It is a thing to be feared. We don't discuss the dangers of using increasingly high-tech lighting systems; we don't question that computers can at some level be used to help choreographers make work; we don't doubt that computers can help us refine and develop notation systems and that video cameras are at least partially successful in their ability to capture work for later retrieval and analysis (that the video camera has become, in fact, an invisible yet essential day-to-day tool for many choreographers).

But what I want to talk about is the use of technology as a creative partner—the use of interactive technologies as an integral part of performance. In the context of my own work, to use interactive technology is to use tools for making performance environments in which the motion of the performer can directly influence the sonic or visual environment in the moment. I use the word "environment" here because, well, there really is no more appropriate word. These environments live only when a body is moving within them—without movement they are silent and dark and lifeless. Similarly, the performance itself cannot happen without the environment. The environment *is* the stage, as well as the instrument upon which the performer is playing. So in an attempt to define our terms, perhaps we can say that *interactive technology* or *performance* is that which exists only in an integral (symbiotic?) relationship with the performer, and with all the other elements that go into making a performance.

I'm a composer, trained as a classical musician, with about as much bodily sense as the keyboard I'm using to write this essay. I've used technology in my artmaking for twenty years. I don't question its validity, I don't doubt its efficacy; I do constantly question its appropriateness and value with every piece I make. I've worked with dancers and choreographers for many years, and with interactive technologies for most of this decade—but more importantly I've now worked with the same primary collaborator for five years, which builds an entirely different relationship than the kind that happens in the context of making a single piece. My use of technology, and the art I make, is entirely influenced and af-fected by the input I receive from my choreographer/writer/collaborator, Jools Gilson-Ellis. I'm not very good anymore at creating work without a computer. I can't really sit down in front of a piece of manuscript paper and "write" a piece a music. The muses just don't speak to me in those terms anymore. Is this a loss? Of course. My long relationship with fickle and ever-changing tools, however, has been rewarding, albeit not without pain. So, given that I cannot question the place of technology within performance making, I will attempt to talk about what I see to be the positive and negative aspects of using these technologies, and how our relationship to them might change as they, and we, mature.

There are still only a handful of artists in the world successfully using dance technologies (see my definition above: I will henceforth use this term generically to mean the use of interactive motion-sensing technologies to control sound, video projections, lights, and all manner of other things). This is true largely for two reasons: the amount of time involved in getting to know the tools, and the amount of time necessary to develop work with all participants present.

These are possibly the two most significant barriers in a time of economic restraint in which fiscal support of the arts is often seen as a low priority (or, in the United States, possibly not a priority at all). These kinds of pieces are by definition expensive to make, not because of the technology cost, but because of the time required. By example, look at the work of the Frankfurt Ballet, with choreographer William Forsythe. It is not atypical for the company to spend almost a full year in developing a new work, during which time they do not perform. There is likely to be a full-time dramaturg and a full-time composer, and a host of other support staff to help the company develop improvisatory structures, experiment with a variety of technologies, and develop the content of the work in harness with the technology it utilizes. There are a minuscule number of companies who can afford to work in this way. As a result, how often do we see work with new technologies that is remarkably superficial or unsuccessful? How often do we see work in which the technology is dominant, in which the choreography and the performer have been completely subsumed by the technology? Is it any wonder that dance technology is viewed skeptically by practitioners and audiences alike? What's remarkable to me is that audiences have not reached the stage where they *expect* this work to fail, but instead our ever-optimistic view of the technological world keeps audiences coming back for more, however disappointing their previous experiences.

Another barrier to creating work using these kinds of technologies is the fundamental shift in process their use demands. Composer and choreographer must give up a huge amount of control; the performer or performers must be given much more control; work must often be devised with at least some degree of collaboration with the performers, with all the technology in place; time must be spent simply learning a new performance environment—usually at the same time that environment is being created; all involved must be willing to experiment, and be willing to cooperate in the making of a performance environment that is also the performance (and be willing to accept that quintessential paradox). So, if you're working with techno-virgins, on their first trip into Interactive Land, you are in one fell swoop asking performers to be: choreographers, improvisers, actors (in our work, anyway), composers, and listeners. This is often too much, and the amount of time required to acquire so many skills within so many challenging performance modalities is inordinate, even when you are working with the most accomplished and experienced professionals.

Above all, there must always be an awareness that the technology has to be made subservient to the ideas the piece is trying to work with, and a willingness to fail, or to confront at least partial failure. This sounds like the easy part, but in fact remains particularly difficult and challenging. How many times have you seen people looking at a video screen (television) just because it's *on* and for no other reason. Technological devices are bullies.

Dance technologies demand an experimental approach to building performance environments which creates a fundamentally different paradigm of collaboration between the makers and the performers. The finished piece, even its final form, cannot be realized until all the elements are in place, working in harmony. This makes it difficult or impossible to develop work in isolation—the conventional working paradigm in which the individual creators (choreographer, composer, lighting designer, etc.) bring their separate, pre-designed parts to the table, ready to be knitted together into the glorious whole). The making of an interactive performance environment makes significant demands on the creative process. The nineteenth-century notion that the composer's scratches on paper are set in stone as though they represent some kind of prophetic gift from the deity, never to be blasphemed by alteration or mistake, never to be molded to the environment in which they are played, is still remarkably pervasive (postmodernity is as elusive as ever, it seems), as is the notion of music and everything else being subservient to the choreography. Choreographers, while never quite so remote from their performers or quite so didactic in their approach as composers, nevertheless tend to demand ultimate control over movement choices. Of course, there have been many challenges to these paradigms, but as conservatism returned in the late 1970s and 1980s, the unassailed leadership role of the maker returned with it. In music, to use the form with which I am most familiar, the experimentalism (sometimes described as the dying gasp of the modernists) that began at the turn of the twentieth century and continued through the 1960s and early 1970s, was replaced by such movements as minimalism (highly rigorous and exacting, despite its apparently meditative outer shell); the new complexity school (the post-serialist composers of England); and all kinds of "neo" movements that attempted to revive the romanticism of the nineteenth century and the formalist classicism of the seventeenth and eighteenth centuries. Creating music in which not only final control, but even final form are at least to some degree unknown is fundamentally challenging to the maker/performer paradigm—an interactive technology system creates a framework that demands radical ways of thinking and

creating. The end results, however, are (or should be) remarkably holistic. Challenging the maker/performer paradigm in this way can be said to be a political act—but the outcome should not be overtly political or dominated by a new politics of creation. The work, if it is successful, ought to be as seamless, as dominated by the performer(s) as any other work.

The audience should be absorbed in the *performance*, not in the technology or the tricks, or the gee-whiz effects that so much high-tech performance work relies on. If the technology is not almost entirely transparent, or at least, entirely seamless and integrated into a performance, the work has failed. If the audience is more concerned with the *how* than the *what*, then the piece has failed. If the makers are more concerned with the tools than with the content, then the piece should, and probably will fail.

But what of access? There is certainly a whiff of elitism in this discourse, a sense of I-have-you-don't-never-will superiority and smugness. The practitioners of technology within the dance performance world have been able to rest on their newness, on their novelty, for too long. If the use of technology is taken for granted, rather than being perceived as a challenge or a threat, then almost by definition there must be better work—work in which the central concern is the content, and not the tools. Many of us have witnessed the monstrous apparatus devised by scientists and technicians intended to capture movement—the body suits that look like spacesuits, and allow about as much movement; the infrared or ultrasonic systems that surround the performer with a scaffold of wires and objects, only to result in a few silly plinks and plonks of sound as the "dancer" moves within his or her scaffold prison. It's generally the artists, those who constantly work with the tools within a performance environment, who have made successful leaps in the technology itself. Mark Coniglio and Dawn Stopiello's *Midi-Dancer* is one of the best examples of this. What started out as a suit that looked good on the body and allowed reasonable freedom of movement, but which tethered the dancer to the computerized nervous system by a thick loom of wires has turned into an elegant, wireless suit in which the technology is almost invisible to the viewer. Why? because Coniglio, who builds the suits and writes the software, and Stopiello, who moves and devises the movement, are a creative team who have consistently made work for their technology as it evolved, and whose work as a result has achieved a remarkable level of sophistication and understanding of the essential issues. But we can't all be engineers or programmers—nor should we have to be. The sign of a mature technology is ease of use, and a new generation of software environments are available that require little or no programming skills, and only moderate computer skills. The performance software coming out of STEIM (Amsterdam) exemplifies this level of simplicity and sophistication. STEIM, an organization that for thirty years has specialized in designing and building performance instruments, has recently begun building software-for-the-rest-of-us— interactive tools that are relatively simple to use and cheap to buy. BigEye, their motion-sensing software (available from their Web site at <http://www.steim. nl>) is simple and remarkably effective. I have taught workshops in which totally inexperienced users are making interesting and engaging environments by the end of a weekend's work—environments which are often concerned less with the technology itself than with an idea that drives the piece, but is able to take advantage of the technology.

So please, let's once and for all discard the notion that advanced technologies and dance are incompatible. Let's by all means question their use, their appropriateness to a particular piece, their dominance and overbearing nature. Let's demand that the technologies be sensitive to and understanding of the body (rather than the other way round). But let us also consider these technologies as the mature tools that they are beginning to be—simply part of a technical and artistic panoply that might be used in the making of any performance.

Technique/Technology/Technique

LISA MARIE NAUGLE

For the past seven years, I have been using interactive technology in performance and in education. During the past two years, my experience has primarily been with distance learning and performance utilizing various kinds of networked computer systems in collaboration with dancers and musicians.

As dance performers and dance educators, we sometimes feel uncertain about our role in the rapidly changing field of computer technology. As we examine the increasing and widespread use of computers in performance, workshops, installations and education, questions still arise concerning the value of dance that is represented as data through a machine. Artistic and educational forums involving technology illuminate recent developments in computer-based systems and have profound social implications. In these forums, I see structures and procedures for integrating dance behavior with digital technologies while considering aesthetic and educational issues.

If face-to-face interactions are increasingly mediated, and in some cases replaced by a computer, and if the essence of experience lives in the body, what are the pedagogical implications of technology for dance?

By nature, the use of computers consists of an intervention that helps us with the processes of communication, expression, discovery, monitoring, visualization, analysis and creativity. Effective computer-mediated communication requires that we receive it as it currently exists and at the same time develop an appreciation for emerging resources and possibilities. We are dealing with our own vulnerability as bodily limitations and technological capabilities are revealed.

For those of us claiming to be responsible dance artists, dismissing the evolving efforts going on in the use of technology may be incongruent with claims that we contribute to social improvement. Since what we do has a presence and consequences in the cultural domain, thinking in terms of what any computer technology is going to do for us is important. There is no reason to create anything if aspects of our own intelligence are not brought forth into space and time. Instead of information being passively imposed upon us, we can be active users of technology as a means of enabling us greater expressive potential and opportunities.

Technologies such as video, film, computer image processing, sound recording, printing, the pointe shoe, the tap shoe and lighting have had widespread influence on the refinement of dance quality and on dance variety. Dance technique is also a technology—a skill, a tool, a means of expression, an embodiment. As a tool, dance technique is developed, in part, to serve in specific kinds of actions, performances, and relationships. Metaphorically, bodies are "wired" and "connected," amplifying inner knowledge into movement that is constructed through various social processes. The computer is a repository for material created by living, conscious human beings.

In an effort to understand computers we employ metaphors, cultural concepts, graphic icons and behavioral rules for interaction. Computers respond, in both synchronous and asynchronous time, to stimulation from the outside, while translating and reconstructing our experiences. Human-computer interaction can be characterized as non-linear, abstract, multiple and contradictory.

Both the presence and absence of technique and technology shape expression. Technology affords multiple ways of establishing a critical stance on political, cultural and aesthetic grounds. Yet, no single body of knowledge defines the dance-technology continuum. Indeed, does a dance-technology continuum actually exist?

Theories of cyborgology maintain that we live in a society where machines are intimately interfaced with humans on almost every level of existence. Such ideas may be helpful in understanding the relationship between dance and technology. When we think about inorganic or material forces on the act of dancing, should we not remember the achievements of Loie Fuller, Hanya Holm, Martha Graham, Alwin Nikolais, Merce Cunningham, Trisha Brown, Elizabeth Streb and others? Who does not use technology?

Technology can help build bridges between art forms, and it offers artists and educators expanded options for expressing ideas. In dance education, technology can be a powerful medium for exchange of knowledge and beliefs by people of different cultures. Through the use of the Internet we have a chance to communicate with people all over the world. The question is, toward what kind of interactions are we working?

If embodiment is mainly about how we perceive, grasp and use experience in our bodies, then the limits of embodiment must be our ability to sense and act in the world. Do we embody technology? Yes, in one way or another, since we utilize technique or skill in our interactions all the time, with varying degrees. If we view the relationship between dance and technology as a kind of foreign exchange, possibly it is because there is difficulty in recognizing the "essence" of technology. The essence has not changed since people first started using hunting and gathering methods. Through time,

the process by which people adapt to technology appears to be similar.

Why then do computers seem somehow extraordinary in the development of technology? Perhaps one reason is that computers seem to threaten us with disembodiment—seemingly dangerous ground for a dancer. But do we become disembodied when using computers? No, because we still hold custody of our bodies and respond with our senses as a way of orienting our presence. Networked communication can provide us with many new opportunities to remain within reach of our distant collaborators while constructing a new landscape for dance. Thinking about and responding to technology are necessary components of what we teach and what we do. As dancers, choreographers and educators, creating and recreating from the vantage point of the body, we can see how extending what we know is facilitated, in part, through the use of computers. The building of equitable relationships, especially over great distances where contact would otherwise be difficult or unlikely, is one of the strengths of teaching and learning about dance through computer-mediated communication. Peer support can be recognized as both a process and an objective.

Interaction between people and computers consists of both human experience and mechanical functioning. In becoming further and further involved with technology in our daily pursuits, we are flooded with choices for adopting unfamiliar, yet potentially significant, computerized tools into our dance experience. Exploring the ways in which we interact and invent becomes the material of which dances are made. If there is an offensive or daunting aspect of the technological, perhaps it reflects a confrontation with ourselves about what is in our control and what is not. Again, we have circled back to the issue of technique.

We all have some experiences of, or ideas about, what a technique class is. But what about a technique class that incorporates an interactive system? Such a system could capture movement by video camera and movement processor connected to a music synthesizer while displaying images of the dancers. Furthermore, what if such a class were synchronously linked with a dance class at a remote location with the same equipment installed? A dance studio that utilizes an expanding array of technologies in an effort to deliver dance technique classes may eventually affect the conceptual framework of the art form.

When we teach or learn on the Internet, there is a tremendous potential to grasp knowledge and ideas about the world. Using collaborative online methods, learners respond to ideas and communicate in fundamental ways: sensing and feeling through words, images and actions sent by others, we begin to understand how dance relates to other cultural elements both locally and globally.

In my effort to understand the kind of cohesion and transparency necessary to use computer technology more effectively, I favor exploration and discourse. Indeed, my relationship with computer-mediated communication is a gateway to creative work, a process countering the notion that technology is a force for disembodiment.

Absent/Presence

ANN DILS

Think of every man sitting down in the sun and leaving his facsimile in all its full completion of outline and shadow, stedfast on a plate, at the end of a minute and a half. . . . I long to have such a memorial of every being dear to me in the world. . . . It is not merely the likeness which is precious in such cases—but the association and the sense of nearness involved in the thing . . . the fact of the very shadow of the person lying there fixed forever! [original spelling preserved][1]

Motion capture is the latest in a long line of technological advances that allow us to, as Elizabeth Barrett suggests of the daguerreotype, fix our shadows forever. Motion capture technology has been used most often to record the generic actions of generic movers as part of the process of animating characters for video games and movies. In the new media video *Ghostcatching*, Paul Kaiser and Shelley Eshkar of the multimedia studio Riverbed use the recorded actions of a pointedly non-generic mover, dancer and choreographer Bill T. Jones, to animate abstract virtual dancers in an eight-and-a-half-minute virtual dance. Should I see Bill T. Jones's involvement in *Ghostcatching* as I would any other movers' participation in an animation project, as providing a movement base for figures with little relationship to their progenitor? If so, is *Ghostcatching* an abstract dance made spectacular through Jones's movement and the skills of new media artists? Or does Jones's involvement in *Ghostcatching* signal something more?

In this essay, I argue that *Ghostcatching* is both an abstract dance and a movement portrait of Jones. The former interpretation is based on writings found in the exhibition catalog, especially Paul Kaiser's article "Steps," and repeated viewings of the work as displayed at Cooper Union in January 1999 and of Quicktime video clips available on the Riverbed Web site.[2] By "abstract dance," I mean that I rely on elements such as line, shape, and color that imply Western aesthetic discourses in understanding the work, more so than its relationships with the outside world.

Two additional resources inform my discussion of *Ghostcatching* as a movement portrait. First is an examination of an explanatory exhibit accompanying the work at Cooper Union, as that provides a valuable frame for connecting the "ghosts" of the work to Bill T. Jones. (While I refer to the animated figures of *Ghostcatching* throughout my essay as ghosts, I don't think of them as disembodied spirits. What remains of Jones are movement patterns that suggest spirit or personality. But his animus—his animating spirit or will—and material body are both missing. The figures are, perhaps, movement phantoms, embodiments of Jones's movement.) Second, I compare *Ghostcatching* to Jones's 1994 large group work, *Still/Here,* a two-part dance about devastating illness and the acceptance of death.[3] *Ghostcatching* might be fruitfully compared to several Jones works, especially in exploring the questions of identity posed by the skinless, faceless dancing ghosts. But I find comparison to *Still/Here* especially helpful.

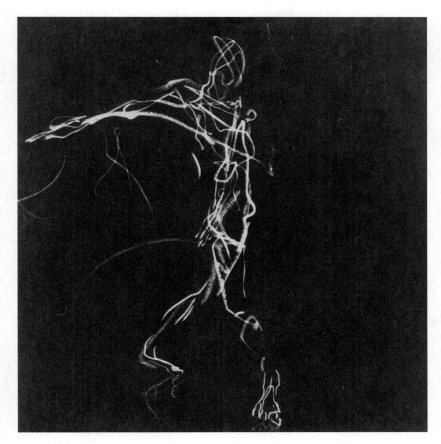

41. Still from *Ghost-catching,* a virtual dance installation by Bill T. Jones, Paul Kaiser, Shelley Eshkar. Copyright © 1999 by Bill T. Jones, Paul Kaiser, and Shelley Eshkar.

I argue that in both works, meaning is derived from portraits of specific people done in still images, videotape, and sound. Some may see these portraits as satisfyingly full, as Elizabeth Barrett enjoyed the "full completion of outline and shadow" of the daguerreotype. Motion capture does offer a three-dimensional depiction of movement, a change from the two-dimensional images of videotape. But I see the partial, *only* outline and shadow, nature of the portraits in both works as important. In these portraits, artists capture something essential about their subjects, paring down their representations to give telling, rather than detailed impressions. The partiality of the portraits prompts me to expand upon the images with the stuff at the back of my brain, sense perceptions of remembered movement, flashes of dance photographs and moments from live dances, and personal stories, especially the sagas of illnesses. This process is affecting. Barrett describes a similar experience of the daguerreotype as "the precious[ness] of . . . the association and the sense of nearness involved in the thing . . . the fact of the very shadow of the person lying there fixed forever!" Since I don't know the people in the portraits, my associations are broader. The images prompt an assessment of my connections to other people, my experiences of loss, and my appreciation of our frail human physicality.

Ghostcatching is valuable as an opportunity to think about dance in the virtual world. We've seen dance on film and video for decades now, and are used to seeing the physical possibilities of movement altered through those mediums, as timings are condensed or expanded and different spaces spliced together, for example. *Ghostcatching* takes this a step further by letting us see human movement on other-than-human bodies. By comparing dancing in the virtual world to real-world dance experiences—a process that seems part of watching all virtual dance, albeit with varied outcomes—we understand more about how both kinds of bodies produce meaning and the implications of transferring human activity to virtual space. One simple difference between virtual and real dancers is that virtual dancers are often transparent. I can see through their bodies and appreciate the three-dimensional look at their movement, but I catch myself musing about the gutless, heartless appearance. What does movement mean for us if there's nothing internal driving the motion? If the thinking of the movement comes from outside the body? Aspects of dance that may seem fundamental become "ghosts in the machine" in this and other virtual dance works, lost in the motion capture and animation processes.[4]

If the *Ghostcatching* dancers are disconnected from Jones's living body, the work is abstract, lines moving beautifully through space. This vision of *Ghostcatching* is clear from the QuickTime video clips Kaiser and Eshkar make available at the company Web site <http://www.riverbed.com>. In the first clip, an elegant figure made of swirling light blue and white lines leaps away from the rectangular box that houses another figure. As the figure leaps, echoes the leap with a lilting arm gesture, and performs a final plié, he leaves vapor trails against the black void of his virtual stage, fluid lines that make the spatial patterns of arms and legs more lasting and apparent. In another, the "camera" pans through a maze of multicolored vapor trails to catch a nervous figure made of terse white lines in a headlong leap onto all fours. On the virtual stage of *Ghostcatching*, the rules of gravity are suspended so a dancer can swing from an invisible overhead bar. An everyday sense of matter is denied as bodies become transparent, appear and disappear, and leave traces long after they've passed from view.

One way of appreciating an abstract *Ghostcatching* is as an exposition of drawing set in motion. Instead of making figures that look like Bill T. Jones, Kaiser wanted to "get away from photorealism, which everyone in 3-D is into . . . " and make the ghosts 3-D drawings.[5] In an essay written for the exhibition catalog,

Kaiser describes his interest in the performative aspects of drawing and the idea of mental space, illustrating these through his own experiences. Drawing, as an accumulation of light and bold actions, becomes physical and, as the artist creates and modifies the elements of a still image, becomes theater. The mental space of the artist or the theatrical space of the drawing might be entered with the help of animation.[6]

In *Ghostcatching*, I enter the minds of Paul Kaiser and Shelley Eshkar as they re-present Bill T. Jones's movement embodied in drawings. What is especially apparent is the way the artists preserve and represent movement quality through their use of color and line. It's important that the nervous figure is white and the lines that make up that figure are jagged and that smoother movement is done by blue figures made of more fluid lines. They add shadows or reflections to some figures to give them more weight and vapor trails to other figures to lend a sense that the figure is cutting through space.

Seen as a chance to enter an artistic mental world, *Ghostcatching* is very like Kaiser and Eshkar's collaboration with Merce Cunningham, *Hand-drawn Spaces*, a work that affords a look at Cunningham's movement imagination. Life-sized, sexless, virtual dancers inhabit this work. Formed by tapering colored lines with an occasional suggestion of a ribcage or shoulders, they are fantasy versions of the long-limbed, balletic-looking dancers Cunningham has long prized. Their movement is generic Cunningham dance. Although the motion capture work was done with specific dancers, Cunningham dancers Jeannie Steele and Jared Philips, their individual motions have been overlapped and blended together and assigned to many virtual bodies.

In *Hand-drawn Spaces,* the dancers traverse three black screens. Sound helps the viewer trace the dancers' paths through limitless space. As they recede into, emerge from, and cross over the void, their footsteps and breathing grow softer, get louder, or seem to streak past. Occasionally, Cunningham can be heard quietly counting. Figures appear and disappear, accompanied by the sounds of drawing and erasure.[7]

RoseLee Goldberg proposes another way of viewing *Ghostcatching* as abstraction in her "Catching Jones." She discusses the virtual dance in relation to Jones's 1997 full-evening length *We Set Out Early, Visibility Was Poor,* as both began with the same "disciplined choreographic premise: strip the body of connotations—political, psychological, racial, even sexual— and concentrate on pure movement as the sole design for dance." Later, she equates watching *Ghostcatching* with watching a dance company:

> Transformed technologically, from solid self to cipher, it fascinated Jones that the computer could reproduce bodies that moved exactly like his own, just as he had attempted to do in *We Set Out Early.* . . . Dance, as Jones points out, is a teacher-to-student art form. "One human being teaches another human being what the form is, and the other human being has to fill it with his or her essence." For Jones, and for us, *Ghostcatching* is an absorbing virtual stage where that transmission process can be examined in all its complexity.[8]

While I appreciate Goldberg's idea that animation can confound (although not deny) our habit of viewing bodily identity cues, her description of the dance learning process as a "transmission" of movement is troublesome. Dancers not only must inhabit motion with their "essence," they must also translate and adapt it to their bodies and movement talents. We don't see this process of adaptation happening in *Ghostcatching.* What we do see is what happens when human movement is transferred to a non-human body digitally created to suit that movement.

Kaiser and Eshkar nudge the viewer toward considering *Ghostcatching* abstract dance by creating non-life-like dancers and a richly designed visual world. These showcase their understanding of movement quality and ability to translate motion into color and line. Is it important that we understand that movement as specific to Bill T. Jones? Kaiser and Eshkar reinforce associations with Jones in several ways. These make

Ghostcatching a portrait and were probably quite deliberate. Kaiser remembers that,

> [Merce Cunningham] had no qualms about motion capture or computer composition or hand-drawn rending, all seen as different means to the same end he'd been pursuing for the past fifty years. Not so Bill T. Jones. . . . "I do not want to be a disembodied, denatured, de-gendered series of lines moving in a void," he said.[9]

While not everyone will experience *Ghostcatching* in the same way, the initial exhibition of the piece at Cooper Union during January 1999 underscored the connection between Jones and the ghosts of his movement. In six giant images positioned outside the gallery where the digital projection was shown, Jones moved from flesh and blood to cartograph. First was an image of Jones improvising at Cooper Union. Next were images of the motion capture and animation processes that showed Jones transforming from self, to dots that represent movement patterns, to a biped figure that provides the scaffolding for the animated figure, and eventually to the animated ghost. A video of Jones improvising in the Cooper Union gallery and huge stills of *Ghostcatching* figures completed the exhibition, dramatizing and connecting the beginning and end points of the process. While the ghosts didn't look like Bill T. Jones, the exhibit was convincing; I was able to see Jones in these figures. The nature of *Ghostcatching* will change for audiences without this rich source of comparison.

Jones's movement might have been made to inhabit very different kinds of bodies, like those of *Hand-drawn Spaces,* or bodies that are like his own dancers, slight bodies, stout bodies, or womanly bodies. (The "Dancing Baby" figure of prime-time television and the Internet, an infant doing an adult dance, was created this way.)[10] But none of this occurs. The ghosts don't look like Jones, but they look male. They all have broad shoulders and are rendered to emphasize muscle. The figures are just solid enough to encase the movement and to suggest muscle and skeleton, but not so solid as to seem like separate beings. As we hope to see the parent in the child or the theme in the variation, we look to see Jones in the images. The differences between the ghosts seem like changes in mood or character, in the way that individuals transform with time and experience or that dancers transform themselves on stage. In his article for the *Ghostcatching* catalog, Paul Kaiser remarks that he and Eshkar saw Jones creating characters through his improvisations—a sculptor, a dog, an athlete—and that Jones picked up on these observations and used them to push the dancing they recorded.[11] While I didn't particularly see these characters in *Ghostcatching*, they gave each Jones incarnation a different edge.

Associations with Jones are also reinforced in the choreography of *Ghostcatching*. From the beginning, the ghosts are envisioned as growing out of each other, rather than being unrelated beings that happen to occupy the same space. As the projection begins, a light blue figure made of straight lines stands encased in a rectangular blue box. The figure moves through an alphabet of postures—a lunge forward, a lean to the side with arm raised—while reciting corresponding letters, A through F. Paul Kaiser calls this straight blue man an "ancestral figure," some basic self who spawns all the other figures.[12] An elegant figure made of swirling light blue and white lines emerges from the blue one and mirrors his progenitor, then leaps away. More figures appear, orange, red, blue, yellow, and purple men made from lines that are brief or languid, straight or spiraling. While they sometimes share the space, making the virtual atmosphere dense with boomeranging energy, there is a sense of meeting and parting, or recognition and relationship between the figures. Sound keeps Jones present. He hums, breathes, and delivers snatches of monologue, "I want you to look here in the trunk. I've got cornbread in here. . . ." The sound of footsteps keeps him present and adds weight, force, and a sense of direction to the movement. In the end, seven versions of the ancestral figure, linked together with straight lines, endlessly push and pull at each other as they open and close their own limbs.

Ghostcatching may be a story about a man who ends up being yoked to his offspring or who is a composite of many selves. It may be a story about history—dance history—where founding figures inspire new generations of movers, who in turn, become founding figures. But the piece is most convincingly a moving portrait of Jones. I see him in the fluid transformations of his movement life and, stimulated by the visual and aural elements of the piece, exercise my own powers of association and memory. I see him as a red figure performs a proud walk, imperiously adjusting his head and shoulders as he surveys his domain and as an athletic ghost supports weight on his arms.

This process of comparison, shuttling back and forth between virtual and more true-to-life representations and my own memories of Jones, creates a sympathetic response that I experience as a sense of intimacy and a sense of loss. These feelings are common to *Ghostcatching* and Jones's *Still/Here* and are made possible by the mildness of both works. *Still/Here* and *Ghostcatching* are surprisingly gentle and visually pleasing. Jones is known for getting audiences to think by confronting them with self-confession, nudity, and explicit language. But in these works, Jones's approach is mild, getting at our sentiments and memories, avoiding any shock and indignation. Considering what *might* have happened in these dances—the possibility of showing human wasting in *Still/Here* and the bodily transformation possible with animation in *Ghostcatching*—the works are restrained and polite.[13]

In preparation for *Still/Here*, Jones organized a series of workshops with seriously ill people. Jones includes video portraits of some of the workshop participants in the dance, especially near the middle of the work, just before the break between *Still* (a confrontation with illness) and *Here* (an acceptance of illness and death through individual strength and group support). These individuals are smiling or look dignified and thoughtful. A few are creased and careworn or bald, but a few of the dancers are bald as well. Some of the people in the video portraits speak, but Jones doesn't have them convey their pain or the stories of their illnesses directly. We must understand these things by sifting through other information in the work, creating our own links between faces, taped conversations, snatches of words sung as part of the sound score, and motion. The bulk of the work is dancing, solos and duets with large ensemble work. Woven into the dancing are the kicks and spins of a martial artist, the dancing and running of a young girl, the embraces of lovers and family members, and the embarrassed, uncertain gestures of women whose illnesses leave them doubting, longing for, their sexual selves. At the same time, the movement is spectacular, full of difficult leg extensions, tricky partnering, athletic jumps, and running. Emotional discomfort—anguish, sadness, and anger—are evident in the dancing, but the only hint of physical pain is in the medical slides that flash during the central section of the piece and in Odetta's singing. The audience reads between the lines, using their memories to piece together the stories of the individuals in the video portraits, supplying information about similar pain in their own lives.

In *Ghostcatching*, Jones's portrait is established in fragments, through snatches of words, movements, and sound that have to be integrated and enlarged by the viewer. This process occurs within the work and in thinking between the work and the exhibit. Like *Still/ Here,* this portrait might have been much more directly drawn. One of the curiosities of *Ghostcatching* is not part of the video, but a lobby image of Jones preparing for the motion capture process. Jones is pictured naked with motion capture sensors taped to his body—the exhibition catalog says there were twenty-four sensors taped to Jones's body—including his penis. *Ghostcatching* began as a project that involved animating some 1983 images of Jones, naked and body-painted by Keith Haring, by Tseng Kwong Chi, hence his nakedness in the motion capture studio.[14] Prompted by an article in the *Village Voice* in which Austin Bunn quips that the marker is on Jones's penis to " keep at least the gender . . . er . . . straight," I went back through every image I could find of *Ghostcatching* to see if the marked penis was ever apparent.[15] One or two images include what might

be a penis, but is probably a vapor trail left by an arm gesture. As the project became disentangled from the earlier photographs, Kaiser, Eshkar, and Jones may have struggled with what to do with that part of the movement information available for their piece. Appropriate? Inappropriate? This part of the captured motion is clearly not a feature of the finished work, but the lobby image suggests that *Ghostcatching* might have been a much less subtle work.

The oblique approach of these works allows for a sense of intimacy. A connecting up between the dance and the viewers' internal storehouse of images, movement, and personal experience always happens in watching dance, but in these works you connect, seemingly, with real-life people, rather than people as theatrical entities. In *Still/Here*, strangers participate in the emotional pain of illness, something usually reserved for loved ones and caregivers. In *Ghostcatching*, intimacy is created because Jones is identified primarily through movement rather than through his public persona, his well-known face and the cultural moorings of race and sexuality that mix into his public image. Seeing *Ghostcatching* is a bit like being invited into the home of a very formal colleague, the outward manifestations of the person's identity fall away and something less public, more vulnerable, and closer to personality than identity becomes apparent. This is not to say that the movement patterns of *Ghostcatching* are devoid of traces of aspects of Jones's identity and training. Motion-captured movement may, in the twenty-first century, be what handwritten signatures were to people in the nineteenth century, "indicative of the movements of the mind as well as the movements of the pen . . . clues to the decipherment of character."[16]

Absence is important to both dances. *Still/Here* is haunting because although the piece presents people who are very much alive, fighting, and hopeful, some of these very alive people may have already passed away while others face painful futures. By the end of *Still/ Here,* Jones asks his audience, as he asked the workshop participants, if we can mentally walk through our lives, picturing even our deaths. And we realize that the workshop participants have been absent from the final section of the work, with only some reverberations of their movement remaining.

In *Ghostcatching*, I miss the activity of Jones's dancing, including aspects of his motion and his animus. Not only are the ghosts weightless and gutless, but they're missing movement information not recorded in the motion capture process. As explained through the *Ghostcatching* exhibit, motion capture occurs in a special studio where Ping-Pong ball–sized sensors are attached to the body along articulations in the spine and at the joints. As the dancer moves, special cameras track the relational disposition of the sensors, recording movement as changing coordinate points on a three-dimensional graph. (Paul Kaiser mentions that Jones's body directly eluded capture during this step. As he sweated in the motion capture studio, the sensors attached to his naked body kept popping off.)[17] In a related process, dancers are tracked as they move wearing reflective tape. All this information is brought into a central computer and combined to give a digital picture of the movement.

Motion capture records movement in space and time, but doesn't directly record changes in weight (our relationship with gravity) and flow (the relative tension or relaxation of muscles). Too, the sensors record the motion of a finite number of points, not really the whole body, so some of the pliancy of the body is lost. The result is movement that's a little pale, a little less than full. Kaiser and Eshkar fill in some of the missing movement through their skills as media artists and the viewer infers other aspects of movement. When a figure is supported on all fours, for example, I infer tension in the upper body. When a figure is in a low crouch, legs bent, pelvis slightly rocked under, I infer the drop in weight and the thousands of accommodations in the stomach and back that accompany that action in real life.

The sense of Jones as a mover with animating purpose is missing. In sorting through the layers of information I get when I look at a dancer—cultural imprints and performances, technical facility, the role portrayed or choreography to be fulfilled—I realize that I see the individual most when I am surprised, when dancers take control of the performance. This occurs often when Jones improvises, when he does something that exceeds or varies from what I know of his dancing or of bodily capability. Although I know the movement in *Ghostcatching* is based on improvisation, it remains the same with every viewing of the film. While the outlines of Jones's movement present in *Ghostcatching* suggest his movement character, the movement is no longer developing, emerging. The sense of human possibility that inhabits motion is gone.

Kaiser and Eshkar provide the essential intelligence that inhabits *Ghostcatching*. They are also the most active performers of the work. Jones's movement intelligence is represented, but not active. As *Ghostcatching* unfolds, I appreciate Kaiser and Eshkar's changing, nuanced interpretations of the body in motion, as seen in their renderings of Jones's ghosts. I felt my own role as spectator was unusually active with *Ghostcatching*. I watched it numerous times, standing, sitting, and pacing in a gallery, rather than sitting in a comfortable seat. While spectators always complete the meaning of a work, *Ghostcatching* is, perhaps, unusually variable in meaning. I would have seen the work much differently had I not seen the accompanying exhibit at the Cooper Union, if I had never seen Bill T. Jones dance, or if my interests were in new media rather than in dance.

Ghostcatching is particularly interesting because it may influence dance documentation. *Ghostcatching* is related to an effort to preserve the work of dancers and choreographers who are HIV-positive or lost to AIDS. Jones, Eshkar, and Kaiser will use Jones's movement as part of a pilot dance preservation project, the Dance Motion Capture Program, sponsored by The Estate Project, a group that preserves and digitally presents the work of visual artists with AIDS. Motion capture will combine with a new brand of digital dance analysis that can highlight the pattern of footfalls (changes of weight, as in walking or running) and the trajectory of movement through space.[18] It's unclear whether these digital records will be virtual portraits and analyses of dances or if they will serve as blueprints for dance reconstruction. The virtual dance portrait is especially compelling when dancers' lives may be cut short. Not only would their dances be preserved, but we would also have, in some sense, their dancing. Potentially, their motion-captured movement might allow designers to create more virtual dance from their movement, a virtual dance life after death.[19] Despite the allure of magical technology, we need to be cautious about expecting any one medium to capture dancing. We need all the translations of performance possible—autobiographies, biographies, interviews, reviews, still photographs, videotapes, and notated scores—as each captures motion differently and each feeds our storehouses of image and association.

In Jones's new evening-length solo dance *The Breathing Show*, he includes an improvisational section entitled "The Ghost in the Machine." In excerpts from Jones's diary included in the Sunday, February 13, 2000, *New York Times* Arts and Leisure section, he also calls this section "Ghostcatching." Jones says he uses improvisation because

> it catches me at my most animal, most un-self-conscious and most bold. There are difficult and peculiar coordinations I pull off because they are spontaneous and free of concern for effect or technique. These are the most inventive and the most difficult to recapture. Here is my truest contribution to contemporary dance.[20]

Are the ghosts in this dance the live manifestations of the movements of *Ghostcatching*? Or is Jones telling us that he—his living, improvisational, sweating, responsive self—is the ghost of *Ghostcatching*? Perhaps those fleeting moments when all of us, not just improvising master dancers, are most alive, self-revealing, and engaged become our ghosts. Some of these inhabit *Still/Here*. They can be glimpsed in the generous revelations captured on video and in the memories of peo-

ple we've known in similar straits that appear in our heads prompted by Jones's dance. Perhaps the ghosts that should appear in our heads during *Ghostcatching* are our own moments of engaged physicality.

A final connection between *Still/Here* and *Ghostcatching* is a call for personal responsibility. In *Still*, Jones is careful to show each individual alone on video, although it's clear that he's often present. I think Jones suggests that while others can help us, we ultimately must face our dark hours alone. In the second section, *Here*, illness is transcended through partnering, community support, and individual acts of faith and hope. The company is intertwined, supporting each other in complicated weight-sharing configurations, or they partner, carrying, tossing up and catching, or supporting each other in ways tender and spectacular. This section is calmer. While the accompanying projections sometimes suggest a body shattering into abstract shapes, the anger is gone. Jones returns to the individual in the final moments of the work. Although his voice is heard often throughout *Still/Here*, Jones doesn't dance, but appears only at the end on videotape, suggesting that this work has also revealed a personal story. Jones's face, then a blur of images can be seen on two television screens wheeled around the space. In the final moments of the work, Jones asks, "Can you picture your death? Can you picture it? Own it? Be responsible for it? And now that that part's over, what happens next?"

Behind *Ghostcatching* is the implicit question of dancers' involvements in the virtual world: What happens after we enter the virtual world? Can we picture it? Own it? Be responsible for it? On the one hand, virtual dance opens the possibilities of the dance field to new kinds of collaborations and new ways to envision dance. All dances will not become virtual dance, we're only increasing the opportunities for dance, translating dance into new mediums, and allowing dance to register the impact of our online lives. On the other hand, we buy into a world where dance will have an uncomfortable home. If *Ghostcatching* is any example, we enter a world where we are liberated from some of the restrictions of race, sex, and physical condition, but lose the richness of physical difference as well. While dance training in the real world is often a privilege of class, dancing in the virtual world increases our need for education, connection, and money. In the virtual world, our abilities to express ourselves lie not in our bodies but in our access to and facility with technology. In the virtual world, kinesthetic feeling is less important than visual impact. As we fix our shadows and make them digitally available, we leave our most animate selves behind.

Notes

1. Betty Miller, ed., *Elizabeth Barrett to Miss Mitford* (London: John Murray, 1954), 208–209, quoted in Hillel Schwartz, *The Culture of the Copy* (New York: Zone Books, 1996), 93–94.

2. *Ghostcatching* [exhibition and digital video], Cooper Union School of Art, Arthur A. Houghton Jr. Gallery, New York City, January 6–February 13, 1999. I attended the exhibit twice on January 30, 1999, watching *Ghostcatching* several times. *Ghostcatching* was partially sponsored by Cooper Union and its production and surrounding events were important to the school's curriculum during the 1998–1999 school year. *Ghostcatching* images are available at <http://www.riverbed.com> (February 14, 2000) and <http://www.cooper.edu/art/ghostcatching/> (February 14, 2000).

3. *Still/Here* [videorecording], 1994 Next Wave Festival, Brooklyn Academy of Music in association with the Foundation for Dance Promotion; conceived, choreographed, and directed by Bill T. Jones, 1994. Dance Collection, New York Public Library and Museum of the Performing Arts at Lincoln Center. I also saw this work at the Next Wave Festival, Brooklyn Academy of Music, New York City and the television version of *Still/Here*, by Bill T. Jones and Gretchen Bender, for Alive TV. Available at <http://www.pbs.org/ktca/alive/stillhere.html> (February 14, 2000).

4. Toni Morrison uses the phrase "ghost in the machine" to describe aspects of African culture that are important to American culture, yet go unexamined and uncelebrated, in her *Playing in the Dark: Whiteness and the Literary Imagination* (Cambridge, Mass.: Harvard University Press, 1992). Brenda Dixon-Gottschild, in her article in this volume, uses the same phrase to discuss Africanisms in American dance. I use the phrase here with an altered meaning, as I believe Bill T. Jones does when he uses the phrase as the title for an improvisational section of his 2000 evening-length solo work, *The Breathing Show*.

While I emphasize *Ghostcatching*'s value in helping us debate perceptions of virtual dance, *Still/Here* has also been important to conversations about "victim art." Arlene Croce refused to see *Still/Here* in 1994, believing that Jones's inclusion of seriously ill people in the work precluded a critical response to the formal properties—what she sees as the artistic content—of the work. Her article in the *New Yorker*, "A Critic at Bay: Discussing the Undiscussable" (December 26, 1994–January 2, 1995), 54–56, 58–60, opened up a national debate about art, political correctness, and critical responsibility.

5. Paul Kaiser interview, quoted in Zoe Ingalls, "Using New Technology to Create 'Virtual Dance,'" *Chronicle of Higher Education* 14, no. 21 (January 29, 1999), A30.

The look of the ghosts may also skirt current technical limitations of animation. Schwartz, in *Culture of the Copy*, 110, states that it's extremely difficult to model skin, especially the skin as it responds to the movement of joints or the changing features of the face. The modeling of contact between two bodies is also difficult, so animated bodies often seem to overlap, rather than accommodate or respond to another form.

6. Paul Kaiser, "Steps," *Ghostcatching* [exhibition catalog], ed. Ann Holcomb (New York: Cooper Union School of Art, 1999), 21–27.

7. Paul Kaiser and Shelly Eshkar, "Hand-drawn Spaces," <http://www.riverbed.com/duoframe/duohand.htm> (February 14, 2000).

8. All quotes in the paragraph are from RoseLee Goldberg, "Catching Jones," *Ghostcatching*, 20.

9. Kaiser, "Steps," 39.

10. There are many sites that feature various "dancing babies." A particularly accessible site is <http://dancingbaby.net/Baby/BabyMus1.htm> (February 14, 2000).

11. Kaiser, "Steps," 45–46.

12. Ibid., 47.

13. Marcia Siegel discusses the mild nature of *Still/Here* in Marcia B. Siegel, "Virtual Criticism and the Dance of Death," *Drama Review* 40, no. 2 (T150) (summer 1996): 60–70.

14. Kaiser, "Steps," 39–40.

15. Austin Bunn, "Machine Age" *Village Voice* 44, no. 1 (January 12, 1999) (reprint).

16. Dawson Turner, *Turner's Guide toward the Verification of Manuscripts, by Reference to Engraved Facsimiles of Hand-writing* (1848), quoted in Schwartz, *The Culture of the Copy*, 219.

17. Kaiser, "Steps," 39–40.

18. "The Estate Project's Dance Motion Capture Program," unpublished document received from Patrick Moore, Director, Estate Project, 4. Available at <http://www.artistswithaids.org/director/news.html> (February 14, 2000).

19. If the intent of the Dance Motion Capture Program is to produce blueprints for dance reconstruction, their appeal is less apparent. It's unclear how movement qualities beyond changes in space and time will be indicated. I also wonder if these blueprints will present dance as a stream of ongoing action, rather than an analysis of choreography that clearly lays out relationships between parts of the dance that can be stopped and contemplated, as in a Labanotation score.

20. Bill T. Jones. "Hopes and Doubts during the Gestation of a Dance," *New York Times*, February 13, 2000, 1, 32.

Contemporary Dance: Further Readings

Acocella, Joan. *Mark Morris*. New York: Farrar Straus Giroux, 1993.

Adair, Christy. *Women and Dance: Sylphs and Sirens*. New York: New York University Press, 1992.

Albright, Ann Cooper. *Choreographing Difference: The Body and Identity in Contemporary Dance*. Hanover, N.H.: Wesleyan University Press, 1997.

Alexander, Elena. *Footnotes: Six Choreographers Inscribe the Page*. Amsterdam: G+B Arts International, 1998.

Banes, Sally. *Democracy's Body: Judson Dance Theatre 1962–1964*. Ann Arbor, Mich.: UMI Research Press, 1983.

———. *Terpsichore in Sneakers: Post-modern Dance*. Boston: Houghton Mifflin, 1980.

———. *Writing Dancing in the Age of Postmodernism*. Hanover, N.H.: Wesleyan University Press, 1994.

Benjamin, Adam. "In Search of Integrity." *Dance Theatre Journal* 10, no. 4 (autumn 1993).

Bharucha, Rustom. *Chandralekha: Woman, Dance, Resistance*. New Delhi: Harper Collins, 1995.

Bordo, Susan. "Reading the Slender Body." *Body/Politics*. New York: Routledge, 1990.

Bull, Cynthia Jean Cohen. *Sharing the Dance: Contact Improvisation and American Culture*. Madison: University of Wisconsin Press, 1990.

Burns, Judy. "Wild Bodies/Wilder Minds: Streb/Ringside and Spectacle." *Women and Performance* 7, no. 1 (1994).

Croce, Arlene. *Sight Lines*. New York: Knopf, 1987.

"Dancing with Different Populations." *Contact Quarterly* 17, no. 1 (winter 1992).

Dempster, Elizabeth. "Women Writing the Body: Let's Watch a Little How She Dances," In *Grafts*, ed. Susan Sheridan. London: Verso Press, 1988.

Desmond, Jane C., ed. *Meaning in Motion: New Cultural Studies of Dance*. Durham, N.C.: Duke University Press, 1997.

Foster, Susan. *Reading Dancing: Bodies and Subjects in Contemporary American Dance*. Berkeley and Los Angeles: University of California Press, 1986.

Gallotta, Jean-Claude. *Groupe Emile DuBois*. Paris: Editions Dis Voir, 1988.

Goler, Veta. "Dancing Herself: Choreography, Autobiography, and the Expression of the Black Woman Self in the Work of Dianne McIntyre, Blondell Cummings and Jawole Willa Jo Zolar." Ph.D. dissertation, Emory University, 1994.

Gottschild, Brenda Dixon. *Digging the Africanist Presence in American Performance: Dance and Other Contexts*. Westport, Conn.: Greenwood Press, 1996.

Hay, Deborah. *Lamb at the Altar: The Story of a Dance*. Durham, N.C.: Duke University Press, 1994.

Johnston, Jill. *Marmalade Me*. Middletown, Conn.: Wesleyan University Press; Hanover, N.H.: University Press of New England, 1998.

Jones, Bill T. *Last Night on Earth*. New York: Pantheon Books, 1995.

Jones, Bill T., and Arnie Zane. *Body against Body*. Barrytown, N.Y.: Station Hill Press, 1989.

Jowitt, Deborah. *The Dance in Mind: Profiles and Reviews 1976–83*. Boston: Godine, 1985.

———, ed. *Meredith Monk*. Baltimore: Johns Hopkins University Press, 1997.

Klosty, James. *Merce Cunningham*. New York: Saturday Review Press, 1975.

Kostelanetz, Richard, ed. *Merce Cunningham: Dancing in Space and Time*. Pennington, N.J.: A Capella Books, 1992.

Livet, Anne. *Contemporary Dance*. New York: Abbeville Press, 1978.

Malone, Jaqui. *Steppin' on the Blues: The Visible Rhythms of African Dance*. Urbana: University of Illinois Press, 1996.

Morris, Gay, ed. *Moving Words: Rewriting Dance.* New York: Routledge, 1996.

Myers, Gerald E., ed. *African American Genius in American Dance.* Durham, N.C.: American Dance Festival, 1993.

Paxton, Steve. "Three Days." *Contact Quarterly* 17, no. 1 (winter 1992).

Rainer, Yvonne. *Work 1961–1973.* Halifax: Press of the Nova Scotia College of Art and Design; New York: New York University Press, 1974.

Ramsay, Margaret Hupp. *The Grand Union (1970–1976): An Improvisational Performance Group.* New York: Peter Lang, 1991.

Servos, Norbert. *Pina Bausch-Wuppertal Dance Theater.* Hamburg: Ballett-Buhnen-Verlag Koln, 1984.

Siegel, Marcia B. "Bridging the Critical Distance." In *Routledge Dance Studies Reader*, ed. Alexandra Carter. London: Routledge, 1998.

———. "Multicult—The Show." *Hudson Review* 49, no. 3 (autumn 1996).

———. *The Tail of the Dragon: New Dance, 1976–1982.* Durham, N.C.: Duke University Press, 1991.

Smith, Amanda. "Autobiography and the Avant-Garde." *Dance Magazine* 59, no. 1 (January 1985).

———. "Making the Personal Political." *Village Voice*, April 24, 1984.

Vaughan, David. *Merce Cunningham: Fifty Years.* New York: Aperture, 1997.

Viala, Jean, and Nourit Masson-Sekine. *Butoh: Shades of Darkness.* Tokyo: Shufunotomo, 1988.

about the contributors

Joan Acocella is a staff writer for *The New Yorker*. She is the author of *Mark Morris* (1993), *Creating Hysteria: Women and Multiple Personality Disorder* (1999), and *Willa Cather and the Politics of Criticism* (2000). In addition, she has edited *The Diary of Vaslav Nijinsky* (1999) and coedited *André Levinson on Dance* (1991). She was a Guggenheim fellow in 1993 and is a fellow of the New York Institute for the Humanities.

A performer, choreographer and feminist scholar, **Ann Cooper Albright** is an associate professor in the dance and theater program at Oberlin College. Her book, *Choreographing Difference: the Body and Identity in Contemporary Dance*, was launched at the 1997 International Festival of New Dance and has since garnered several awards. Combining her interests in dancing and cultural theory, she is involved in teaching a variety of dance, performance studies, and gender studies courses, which seek to engage students in both practices and theories of the body. Most recently, Ann has been performing a series of dances that reembody some of the intellectual issues she raises in her scholarly writings. She has also been trying to get other academics to realize that they too have bodies with her "Engaging Bodies: The Politics and Poetics of Corporeality" workshops, which she has presented on campuses in the United States. She recently completed an American Council of Learned Societies Contemplative Practice Fellowship.

Kariamu Welsh Asante is a professor of African and African American dance and aesthetics in the School of Music and Department of Dance at Temple University. She has edited *The African Aesthetic: Keeper of the Traditions* (1992) and *African Dance: Artistry and History* (1994) and is the author of *Zimbabwe Dance* and *The Umfundalai Technique: The Shape of Rhythm* (both 1999). Dr. Welsh Asante has received several fellowships, including three Fulbright awards, the Pew Charitable Trusts Fund fellowship in the Arts, and a Simon Guggenheim fellowship. She serves on the editorial board of the *Journal of Black Studies* and the Commonwealth of Pennsylvania State Council of the Arts dance panel, edits the *International Journal of African Dance,* and is the director of the Institute for African Dance, Research and Performance at Temple University.

Sally Banes is the Marian Hannah Winter Professor of Theatre History and Dance Studies at the University of Wisconsin at Madison. Her books include *Terpsichore in Sneakers: Post-Modern Dance, Democracy's Body: Judson Dance Theater, 1962–64, Writing Dancing in the Age of Postmodernism, Dancing Women: Female Bodies on Stage,* and *Subversive Expectations: Performance Art and Paratheater in New York, 1976–85,* and she is the director and producer of the documentary video *The Last Conversation: Eisenstein's Carmen Ballet.* She is a past president of the Society of Dance History Scholars and the Dance Critics Association.

Melissa Benson is an independent curator in New York City.

Erika Bourguignon, a cultural anthropologist, is professor emerita and former chairperson of the Department of Anthropology at the Ohio State University. Her writings include *A World of Women: Anthropological Studies of Women in the Societies of the World* with other contributors (1980), *Possession* (1976), and *Diversity and Homogeneity in World Societies* with Lenora S. Greenbaum (1973).

Barbara Browning is an associate professor of performance studies at New York University. She is author of *Samba: Resistance in Motion* (Indiana University Press, 1995) and *Infectious Rhythm: Metaphors of Contagion and the Spread of African Culture* (Routledge, 1998).

Cynthia Jean Cohen Bull (Cynthia Novack) pioneered the study of dance as a cultural practice with her book *Sharing the Dance: Contact Improvisation and American Culture* (1990), now in its second printing. A choreographer and a dancer as well as a scholar, Bull performed improvised choreography with the Richard Bull Dance Theater for more than twenty years. She taught cultural and historical studies of dance, dance composition, improvisation, and technique at SUNY Brockport, Barnard College, and Wesleyan University. At the time of her death in 1996, she was collaborating with Richard Bull and others on a book about improvisation.

Ramsay Burt is a senior research fellow in the Department of Dance at De Montfort University, Leicester, United Kingdom. His Ph.D. thesis on representations of masculinity in British new dance formed the basis for his first book, *The Male Dancer* (Routledge, 1995); his book *Alien Bodies: Representations of Modernity, "Race" and Nation in Early Modern Dance* was published in 1998 by Routledge.

Ananya Chatterjea is a dancer, choreographer, dance scholar, and educator who was trained in Indian classical and folk dance forms, and who has worked with "different" dance styles in her attempts to understand how variously the body can be conceived and performed. She is now an assistant professor in the Department of Theatre Arts and Dance at the University of Minnesota at Minneapolis. Dr. Chatterjea has won the Society of Dance History Scholars's Gertrude Lippencott Award and is the artistic director of Women in Motion, a company of South Asian women doing political theater.

Uttara Asha Coorlawala, born in Hyderabad, India, teaches dance technique, world dance history, and issues in intercultural dance at Long Island University's C. W. Post Campus and at Barnard College. She edits the newsletter of the *Congress of Research in Dance* and is a member of the Editorial Board for *Dance Research Journal*. Her articles have been published in *Dance Chronicle, Dance Research Journal*, and *Sangeet Natak Akademi Journal* and included in anthologies on Indian and intercultural dance, and she is a regular correspondent for *Sruti* (India's leading magazine for music and dance). She has danced throughout India, Europe, and the United States and as a designated cultural representative of India.

Ann Daly is an associate professor of dance history and criticism at the University of Texas at Austin who has written on dance and culture for many publications. Former president of the Dance Critics Association, she is a contributor to the *New York Times* Arts and Leisure section and contributing editor to *TDR: A Journal of Performance Studies*. Her book, *Done into Dance: Isadora Duncan in America*, was awarded the 1996 Congress on Research in Dance Award for Outstanding Publication. Her book-in-progress is entitled *When Writing Becomes Gesture*.

Thomas DeFrantz is an assistant professor of theater arts at the Massachusetts Institute of Technology. He is the editor of the forthcoming anthology *Dancing Many Drums: Excavations in African American Dance*.

Formerly a professional dancer and choreographer, **Jane Desmond** is currently an associate professor of American studies and women's studies at the University of Iowa, where she also co-directs the International Forum for U.S. Studies, which she co-founded in 1995. She is the editor of *Meaning in Motion: New Cultural Studies of Dance* (1997), author of *Staging Tourism: Bodies on Display from Waikiki to Sea World* (1999), and editor of *Dancing Desires* (forthcoming, University of Wisconsin Press).

Ann Dils is an assistant professor in the Department of Dance at the University of North Carolina at Greensboro. She has recently published writing in *Performing Arts Journal*, the *Korean Journal for Dance Studies,* and *Dance Research Journal*. Dils is a past president and past endowment chair of the Congress on Research in Dance.

Lisa Doolittle founded the experimental dance collective Co-Motion in 1977 and co-founded the internationally distributed *Dance Connection* magazine. As an associate professor in the Division of Theatre Arts at the University of Lethbridge since 1989, she has established a strong movement and dance program and has developed numerous projects in interactive theater for social change. Her publications focus on Canadian dance and cultural history and interactive theater.

Heather Elton is a writer and editor in London, England. She was the publisher and editor of *Dance Connection*, Canada's magazine for contemporary dance, and *Last Issue*, an interdisciplinary arts magazine. She has written extensively about dance performance, and has served as editor of the Banff Centre Press. She is co-director of Vanguard Arts Association, a U.K. organization dedicated to performance and training in movement disciplines.

Kathleen Foreman is a performing artist and teacher specializing in actor training, improvisation, mask creation, and performance and educational drama. She is currently an associate professor in the Department of Drama at the University of Calgary in Alberta, Canada.

Susan Leigh Foster, choreographer, dancer, and scholar, is a professor of dance at the University of California campuses of Riverside and Davis. She is the author of *Reading Dancing: Bodies and Subjects in Contemporary American Dance* and *Choreography and Narrative: Ballet's Staging of Story and Desire* and the editor of *Choreographing History* and *Corporealities*.

Mark Franko is a professor of dance and performance studies at the University of California at Santa Cruz and co-director of the university's graduate program in visual and performative studies; he also directs the company NovAntiqua. He is the author of *Dance as Labor: Performing Work in the 1930s* (forthcoming from Wesleyan University Press), *Dancing Modernism/Performing Politics, Dance as Text: Ideologies of the Baroque Body,* and *The Dancing Body in Renaissance Choreography* and co-editor of *Acting on the Past: Historical Performance Across the Disciplines.* His research has been supported by the Getty Research Center, the American Philosophical Society, and the American Council of Learned Societies.

Lynn Garafola is the author of *Diaghilev's Ballets Russes* and editor of *Rethinking the Sylph: New Perspectives on the Romantic Ballet, Dance for a City: Fifty Years of the New York City Ballet,* and *The Ballets Russes and Its World.*

Brenda Dixon Gottschild, former professor of dance studies at Temple University, is a critic and feature writer for *Dance Magazine* and the author of numerous scholarly essays and articles. Her books include *Digging the Africanist Presence in American Performance: Dance and Other Contexts* (1998) and *Waltzing in the Dark: African American Vaudeville and Race Politics in the Swing Era* (2000).

Ellen Graff is an associate professor of dance at California State University at Long Beach. She is a former member of the Martha Graham Dance Company and has a Ph.D. in performance studies from New York University. Her book *Stepping Left: Dance and Politics in New York City, 1928–1942* was awarded a special citation by the de la Torre Bueno Prize Committee in 1997.

Shawna Helland is a teacher of French, dance, and yoga at the high school and junior high school levels. Her fascination with dance, music, and language has taken her on extensive journeys around the world to study various cultures. She has directed and produced educational videos on ethnocultural dance and has written French curricula for the Alberta Department of Education.

Millicent Hodson is an American choreographer and dance historian who, with her husband, Kenneth Archer, has created six original ballets and reconstructed lost works by Vaslav Nijinsky and George Balanchine. Hodson has received the Nijinsky Medal from Poland, choreographic grants from the U.S. National Endowment for the Arts, and a Radcliffe Fellowship in Dance. Her production sketches are often exhibited, and her score of dance drawings, *Nijinsky's Crime against Grace,* was published in 1996.

Deborah Jowitt has written a dance column for the *Village Voice* since 1967 and has published two collections, *Dance Beat* (1977) and *The Dance in Mind* (1985). Her *Time and the Dancing Image* won the de la Torre Bueno Prize in 1989. In 1997 she edited *Meridith Monk* (Johns Hopkins University Press). She teaches in the dance department of New York University's Tisch School of the Arts.

Joann W. Kealiinohomoku is an anthropologist of the performing arts with a special focus on the cultural dynamics of dance. Dr. Kealiinohomoku is co-founder of Cross-Cultural Dance Resources in Flagstaff, Arizona, where she conducts research and is director of collections. The CCDR mission is to promote a holistic appreciation and understanding of dance and related arts in cultures, locally and throughout the world, in order to promote world peace.

Lee Kyong-hee is editor-in-chief of the *Korea Herald*. She is the author of *Korean Culture: Legacies and Lore* and *World Heritage in Korea*.

Julie Malnig is an associate professor in the Gallatin School of Individualized Study at New York University, where she teaches courses in dance and theater performance, arts and culture of the early twentieth century, and gender and performance. She is the author of *Dancing till Dawn: A Century of Exhibition Ballroom Dance* (1995) and is the current editor of *Dance Research Journal*. Professor Malnig is a former senior editor of *Women & Performance Journal*, a member of the board of directors of the Congress on Research in Dance, and the associate chair of the Gallatin Interdisciplinary Arts Program at NYU.

Susan Manning is an associate professor of English, theater, and dance and an affiliate of the doctoral program in arts and culture at Northwestern University. Her first book, *Ecstasy and the Demon: Feminism and Nationalism in the Dances of Mary Wigman*, won the 1994 de la Torre Bueno Prize. She is completing a second book, titled *Making an American Dance: Black, White, and Queer*.

Avanthi Meduri is a visiting assistant professor in the Department of Performance Studies at Northwestern University, a visiting fellow in the Art and Aesthetics Department at Jawaharlal Nehru University, New Delhi, and the academic and artistic director of the Institute for Contemporary Culture, Performance, and Media, New Delhi. Her doctoral dissertation has been adapted into a postcolonial theater script and theatrical performance entitled *God Has Changed His Name*. Both the play and her book, *Alien Eyes and Bejeweled Bodies: Sexuality, Translation, and Performance in South India*, are forthcoming.

Lisa Naugle is an assistant professor of dance at the University of California at Irvine, where she teaches courses in modern dance technique, improvisation, composition, and digital dance. Lisa has been exploring the artistic uses of Lifeforms 3-D Choreographic Software for stage and education since 1989 and is on the Advisory Board for the development of a new interface between Lifeforms and Labanwriter software. She is coauthor of "Dancing in Cyberspace: Creating with the Virtual Body," an online choreography course; her most recent works, *The Cassandra Project* and *Janus/Ghost Stories,* are Internet-based performances integrating dance, music, and theater.

Sally Ann Ness is an associate professor at the University of California at Riverside in the Departments of Dance and Anthropology. She is the author of *Body, Movement, and Culture: Kinesthetic and Visual Symbolism in a Philippine Community*, winner of the de la Torre Bueno Book Award from *Dance Perspectives* in 1993 and the CORD Outstanding Publication Award in 1995. Ness holds a Ph.D. in anthropology from the University of Washington and a Certified Movement Analyst degree from the Laban Institute of Movement Studies.

Steve Paxton has been busy dancing, performing, and choreographing for forty years, focused on improvisation since 1970. He is a contributing editor for *Contact Quarterly*.

Richard Povall is a multidisciplinary composer, researcher, and educator who has been involved with experimental electronic media for almost twenty years. His longtime collaborator is writer and performer Jools Gilson-Ellis, and together they form the company *half/angel*. He is also codirector of Aune Head Arts, and a senior fellow at the Centre for Research into Creation in the Performing Arts (Rescen) based at Middlesex University and London's South Bank Centre. He has served as director of the Division of Contemporary Music and associate professor of computer music and new media at the Oberlin College Conservatory of Music; as a research fellow and senior lecturer in new performance media at Dartington College of Arts; and was involved in the creation of the pioneering interdisciplinary MFA program at Rensselaer Polytechnic Institute's iEAR Studios.

A former dancer with the New York City Ballet, **Nancy Reynolds** is now an editor and author. Her publications include *Repertory in Review: Forty Years of the New York City Ballet*, which won the de la Torre Bueno Prize, *Dance Classics* (co-authored with Susan Reimer-Torn), *The Dance Catalog*, and *Choreography by George Balanchine: A Catalogue of Works*, for which she was research director. She is an editor of the multivolume *International Encyclopedia of Dance* (1998) and is writing a history of theatrical dance in the twentieth century, to be published by Yale University Press. Since becoming director of research for the George Balanchine Foundation in 1994, Ms. Reynolds has initiated archival videotape projects with Dame Alicia Markova, Maria Tallchief, Patricia Wilde, Marie-Jeanne, Frederic Franklin, Todd Bolender, Allegra Kent, and Melissa Hayden, among others.

Peter Ryan has been involved in theater and dance as a teacher, performer, and writer since 1975. He has taught and performed across North America and was a founding member of EDAM, Vancouver's innovative dance and music collective. He teaches both professionals and students in theater, dance, and physical education, and is writing a book on physical training for actors.

Marcia B. Siegel is an internationally known dance critic, historian, and teacher. She is the author of *The Shapes of Change: Images of American Dance* and *Days on Earth*, a biography of Doris Humphrey, and has published three collections of reviews and commentary, the most recent of which is *The Tail of the Dragon: New Dance, 1976–1982*. From 1983 to 1999 she was a member of the resident faculty of the Department of Performance Studies at the Tisch School of the Arts, New York University, where she taught graduate courses in dance and cultural history, movement analysis, and writing. She is now a regular critic and contributing writer for the *Boston Phoenix*.

Deidre Sklar, assistant professor of dance at the University of California at Irvine, is an interdisciplinary scholar with a performance and directing background in corporeal mime and ensemble theater. She has been recognized for her work in somatic approaches to performance, and her articles have appeared in the *Journal of American Folklore*, *The Drama Review*, *Dance Research Journal*, and *Body/Language*. Dr. Sklar's book, *Dancing with the Virgin: Body and Faith in the Fiesta of Tortugas, New Mexico*, was published by the University of California Press in 2001.

Bonnie Sue Stein, has been executive director of GOH Productions since 1988. Prior to that she was the program associate of performing arts at the Asia Society and worked as an independent director, choreographer, and writer in New York, Japan, and Eastern Europe. In New York, Ms. Stein has hosted numerous independent artists and groups from Eastern Europe and Asia in projects produced under the auspices of GOH Productions. Ms. Stein contributes articles on the performing arts to *Dance Magazine*, the *Village Voice*, the *Drama Review*, and program notes for various performing arts venues. She has written an article on Japanese butoh pioneer Kazuo Ohno for the 1999 book *Fifty Contemporary Choreographers*, and has lectured on the performing arts of Japan in universities and art centers in the United States and Europe.

Z. S. Strother is the author of *Inventing Masks: Agency and History in the Art of the Central Pende*. She is an associate professor in the Department of Art History at the University of California, Los Angeles.

Choreographer **Catherine Turocy** is artistic director and co-founder of the New York Baroque Dance Company. In 1995, she and her husband, conductor James Richman, were knighted by the French government for their contributions to the fields of dance and music. Ms. Turocy's ballets have been commissioned by the Kennedy Center, the Lincoln Center, L'Opéra de Lyon, Teatro San Carlo in Lisbon, Théâtre du Châtelet in Paris, and Festival d'Aix-en-Provence.

Sharyn R. Udall is an art historian and curator with a special interest in interdisciplinary approaches to the arts. She resides and teaches in Santa Fe, New Mexico.

Karin van Nieuwkerk is a lecturer in anthropology in Nijmegen University's Department of Languages and Cultures of the Middle East. Van Nieuwkerk has published several articles on women in the Middle East, particularly in Egypt, and the book *A Trade Like Any Other: Female Singers* *and Dancers in Egypt* (1995). She is currently involved in a research project on religion, gender, and identity in a multicultural society, focusing on Dutch women's conversion to Islam.

Judy Van Zile is a professor of dance at the University of Hawaii at Manoa. She first studied Korean dance in Hawaii in the early 1970s with Halla Pai Huhm and her assistant Kim Chung-won, and subsequently in Korea during four residencies, from 1979 to 1990. She has presented materials on Korean dance at national and international conferences, and has published on various aspects of Korean dance in journals and book chapters.

Marian Hannah Winter is the author of *The Pre-Romantic Ballet* (Dance Horizons, 1975), *The Theatre of Marvels* (B. Blom, 1964), and many articles on eighteenth- and nineteenth-century theatrical dance.

permissions

mission. / **Mark Franko**, "Writing Dancing," reprinted courtesy of Mark Franko. / **Lynn Garafola**, "The Travesty Dancer in Nineteenth-Century Ballet" reprinted by permission of the author. / **Brenda Dixon Gottschild**, "Stripping the Emperor: The Africanist Presence in American Concert Dance," excerpted from *Looking Out . . .* , ed. D. Gere et al. The complete essay is chapter 5 of Dixon Gottschild's *Digging the Africanist Presence in American Performance* (Greenwood, 1998). Reprinted by permission. / **Ellen Graff**, "The Dance Is a Weapon," from *Stepping Left: Dance and Politics in New York City, 1928–1942,* copyright © 1997, Duke University Press. All rights reserved. Reprinted with permission. / **Shawna Helland**, "The Belly Dance: Ancient Ritual to Cabaret Performance," reprinted from *Dance Connection, Canada's Magazine for Contemporary Dance* 6, no. 6 (January/February 1989): 26–35. Reprinted by permission. Chronology excerpted from *Earth Dancing* by Daniela Gioseffi (Stackpole Books, 1980). / **Millicent Hodson**, "Searching for Nijinsky's *Sacre*," first published in *Dance Magazine* (June 1980). Reprinted by permission. / **Deborah Jowitt**, "Writing beneath the Surface," first presented at the conference "Perspectives on Movement: Interpretations of Dance through Writing," City University of New York, March 1995, published in *Writings on Dance* 16 (winter 1997). Reprinted by permission. / **Deborah Jowitt**, "Form as the Image of Human Perfectability and Natural Order," presented at the conference "Doris Humphrey: A Centennial Celebration Celebrating the Past, Envisioning the Future," Teachers College, Columbia University, New York City, October 1995. Published in *Dance Research Journal* 28, no. 2 (fall 1996). Reprinted by permission. / **Deborah Jowitt**, "Chance Heroes: Merce Cunningham," first published in *Village Voice*, October 4, 1994. Reprinted by permission. / **Joann Kealiinohomoku**, "An Anthropologist Looks at Ballet as a Form of Ethnic Dance," first published in *Impulse Magazine* (1969–1970). Reprinted by permission of author. / **Lee Kyong-hee**, "Epitome of Korean Folk Dance," from *Korean Herald* (1993): 109–13. Reprinted by permission. / **Julie Malnig**, "Two-Stepping to Glory," first published in *ETNOFOOR* 10, nos. 1/2 (1997). Reprinted by permission. / **Susan Allene Manning** and **Melissa Benson**, "Interrupted Continuities: Modern Dance in Germany," first published in *TDR/The Drama Review* 30, no. 2 (T110, summer 1986): 30–45. Rights reverted to authors, Susan

Manning and Melissa Benson. Reprinted by permission. / **Avanthi Meduri**, "Bharatha Natyam—What Are You?" first published in *Asian Theatre Journal* 5, no.1 (spring 1988): 1–22. Reprinted by permission. / **Lisa Marie Naugle**, "Technique/Technology/Technique," originally published in *Dance Research Journal* 30, no. 1 (spring 1998). Reprinted by permission. / **Sally Ann Ness**, "Dancing in the Field: Notes from Memory," reprinted from *Corporealities*, ed. Susan Foster (London: Routledge, 1996). Reprinted by permission. / **Karin van Nieuwkerk**, "Changing Images and Shifting Identities: Female Performers in Egypt," in *Images of Enchantment: Visual and Performing Arts in the Middle East,* ed. Sharifa Zufar (Cairo: American University in Cairo Press, 1998), published by permission of the American University in Cairo Press. / **Cynthia Jean Cohen Bull** (Cynthia Novak), "Looking at Movement as Culture: Contact Improvisation to Disco," first published in *TDR/The Drama Review* 32, no. 4 (T120, winter 1988): 120–134. Rights reverted to author. Reprinted by permission. / **Steve Paxton**, "Improvisation Is a Word for Something That Can't Keep a Name," first published by *Contact Quarterly Dance and Movement Journal* (spring/summer 1987): 15–19. Reprinted by permission. / **Richard Povall**, "A Little Technology Is a Dangerous Thing," first published in *Dance Research Journal* 30, no. 1 (spring 1998). Reprinted by permission. / **Nancy Reynolds**, "In His Image: Diaghilev and Lincoln Kirstein," is excerpted from a more comprehensive piece by the same name, and was first published in *The Ballet Russes and Its World*, ed. Lynn Garafola and Nancy Van Norman Baer (New Haven: Yale University Press, 1999). Reprinted by permission. / **Peter Ryan**, "10,000 Jams Later: Contact Improvisation in Canada, 1974–1995," reprinted from *Dance Connection: Canada's Magazine for Contemporary Dance* 13, no. 3 (September/October 1995): 16–24. Reprinted by permission. / **Marcia B. Siegel**, "The Harsh and Splendid Heroines of Martha Graham," first published in *American Poetry Review* (January–February 1975), reprinted in *Watching the Dance Go By*, by Marcia B. Siegel. Reprinted by pemission. / **Deidre Sklar**, "Five Premises for a Culturally Sensitive Approach to Dance," first published in *Dance Critics Association News* (summer 1991). Reprinted by permission. / **Bonnie Sue Stein**, "Butoh: 'Twenty Years Ago We Were Crazy, Dirty, and Mad.'" *TDR/The Drama Review* 30, no. 2 (T110) (summer 1986):

index

as, 401; Korean dance as, 181; Native American dance as, 115, 234
popular culture, 162; and African art, 159–160; and German modern dance, 219
postmodernism: and butoh, 378; and European dance, 372; and Judson Dance Theater, 350–361
Povall, Richard, 375
Prentice, Beverly, 449
Primus, Pearl, 144, 428, 433, 452. Dance: *Strange Fruit*, 434

racial issues: in American dance, 234–235, 433–435, 440–453; in *Bones and Ash*, 374–375, 440, 448–453; in capoeira, 165–172; in Chandralekha's work, 393; in *Last Supper at Uncle Tom's Cabin*, 374, 440–447, 452–453; in St. Denis's work, 256–267; in Zane and Jones's work, 433, 435–437
Rainer, Yvonne, 351–355, 419. Dances: *The Bells*, 353; *Continuous Project—Altered Daily*, 358; *Dance for 3 People and 6 Arms*, 355; *Divertissement*, 356; *The Mind Is a Muscle*, 358; *Ordinary Dance*, 356, 358; *Satie for Two*, 353; *Some Thoughts on Improvisation*, 358–359; *Terrain*, 357; *Trio A*, 13, 236
Rambert, Marie, 19, 21, 22
Rameau, Jean Philippe, *Hippolyte et Aricie*, 202, 204
Ranum, Patricia, 207
Rauschenberg, Robert, 351, 353, 419. Dance: *Pelican*, 357
Ravitz, Paula, 416
Reagon, Toshi, 447
Redfield, Robert, 39
Reed, David, 252
religions and dance: Buddhism, 174–176, 182–186, 421; Christianity, 30, 31, 36, 381, 384, 442, 447, 453; Confucianism, 95, 180, 182; Hinduism, 105, 401; Islam, 129, 141
Renaissance, ballet in the, 191–200
representation. *See* African American dance; cultural studies; disability;

gender and gender representation; Indian dance
Reynolds, Nancy, 234
Rice, T. D. "Daddy," 251, 443
Rich, Adrienne, 442
Robbins, Jerome, 326
Robeson, Paul, 250
Robinson, Bill "Bojangles," 149, 250
rock-and-roll dancing, 385, 406–412
Rodgers, Rod, 433
Rodin, Auguste, 290
Roerich, Nicholas, 18, 24, 25
Rogers, Ginger, 14
Roosevelt, Franklin D., 316, 320
Roosevelt, Theodore, 247
Rosenfelt, Deborah, 275
Russo, Mary, 59
Ryan, Peter, 374

Sacharoff, Alexander, 219
Sachs, Curt, 37, 39, 128–129, 134
Saffron, Maya, 445
Said, Edward, 262–264
St. Denis, Ruth, 2, 130–131, 135, 218, 259–262. Dances: *Egypta*, 262; *Radha*, 235–236; 256–267; *White Jade*, 261
Saint-Leon, Arthur, 212, 217. Dance: *Coppélia*, 50, 211, 214
Salimpour, Jamila, 135
Sallé, Marie, 204, 208
Salome, 135
salp'uri. *See* Korea
Salsbury, Nate, 254
samba, 92, 144, 149, 167, 169, 172
Samea, 132–134
Sanon, Salia. Dances: *Fignito, ou L'Oeil Troué*, 372
Sawyer, Joan, 281
Sawyer, Randolph, 237, 342
Schlemmer, Oskar, 221
Schmidt, Beverly. Dance: *The Seasons*, 359
Schneemann, Carolee. Dance: *Newspaper Event*, 360
Scothorn, Carol, 351. Dance: *Isolations*, 354
Sedgwick, Eve Kosofsky, 49, 51, 52
Segal, Edith, 237, 317, 320, 343. Dance:

Black and White Workers Solidarity, 433–434
Seldon, Elizabeth, 304, 305
Sellars, Brother John, 347
sexuality: in ballet, 51–53; in *Bones and Ash*, 451–452; and men dancers, 44–46, 48–49, 52–53, 436; in St. Denis's work, 263–267; in Zane and Jones's work, 435–436
Shapiro, Laura, 10
Shawn, Ted: and Delsartian theories, 205, 209, 260, 428, 429; and homosexuality, 45, 52; and Jacob's Pillow, 232; and men dancers 342, 343; and modern dance history, 237; and racism, 434; and Ruth St. Denis, 257
Shelton, Sara, 415
Shelton, Suzanne, 258
Siddall, Curt, 62, 414
Siegel, Marcia B., xv, 10, 235, 382
Sitting Bull, 116–117
Sitting Eagle, Gerald, 124–125
Sklar, Deidre, 4, 93
Slater, Lizzie, 378, 382
slavery: and capoeira, 167–168; and dance as resistance, 95; and Juba, 250
Sloan, John, 244
Slonimsky, Yuri, 329
Smith, Andrea, 442, 446–447
Smith, Nancy Stark, 414
social class, dance as expression of, 271–285, 412
social dance, 97, 115, 178, 235, 272–273, 404, 407–412; in America, 235, 251, 254, 272–289; at court, 191–192; and culture, 405; in Zane and Jones's work, 436
social identity. *See* African American dance; cultural identity; disability; gender and gender representation
Sokolow, Anna, 8, 237, 317, 320, 321
Solomons, Gus, 59, 60, 435
Song-Jun, Han, 174, 185
Sontag, Susan, 8, 9, 247, 377
Sorell, Walter, 34–39, 41
Spencer, Herbert, 290
Speyer, Louis, 25